GREAT EVENTS FROM HISTORY
NORTH AMERICAN SERIES

GREAT EVENTS FROM HISTORY
NORTH AMERICAN SERIES

Revised Edition

Volume 3
1895 – 1955

Edited by
FRANK N. MAGILL

Associate Editor
JOHN L. LOOS

Managing Editor, Revised Edition
CHRISTINA J. MOOSE

Salem Press, Inc.
Pasadena, California   Englewood Cliffs, N.J.

Editor in Chief:	Dawn P. Dawson
Managing Editor:	Christina J. Moose
Acquisitions Editor:	Mark Rehn
Manuscript Editor:	Irene Struthers
Research Supervisor:	Jeffry Jensen
Research Assistant:	Irene McDermott
Photograph Editor:	Valerie Krein
Proofreading Supervisor:	Yasmine A. Cordoba
Map Design and Page Layout:	James Hutson
Data Entry:	William Zimmerman

Library of Congress Cataloging-in-Publication Data

Great events from history : North American series / edited by Frank N. Magill ; associate editor, John L. Loos.
— Rev. ed.
    p. cm.
Includes bibliographical references (p.   ) and index.
ISBN 0-89356-429-X (set). — ISBN 0-89356-432-X (vol. 3)
  1. North America—History. 2. United States—History. I. Magill, Frank Northen, 1907-   . II. Loos, John L.
E45.G74   1997
970—dc21   96-39165
                                                                                                                    CIP

First Printing

PRINTED IN THE UNITED STATES OF AMERICA

CONTENTS

LIST OF MAPS

GREAT EVENTS FROM HISTORY
NORTH AMERICAN SERIES

1895 ■ BOOKER T. WASHINGTON'S ATLANTA EXPOSITION ADDRESS: *controversial advocacy of accommodationism has a major influence on African American political and economic strategies*

DATE: September 18, 1895
LOCALE: Atlanta, Georgia
CATEGORIES: African American history; Civil rights; Cultural and intellectual history
KEY FIGURE:
Booker T. Washington (1856-1915), prominent African American educator

SUMMARY OF EVENT. Booker T. Washington was born a slave on a small Virginia plantation and gained his freedom at the end of the Civil War. After emancipation, Washington worked in a salt furnace and coal mine, and he learned to read by studying spelling books and occasionally attending a school established for African American children. In 1872, Washington enrolled at Hampton Institute in Virginia, a technical and agricultural school established for emancipated slaves. After graduation, he taught in Malden, West Virginia. He later returned to Hampton Institute to serve as a dormitory moderator to a group of newly admitted Native American students and to administer Hampton's night school.

In May, 1881, Washington received an invitation to join a group of educators from Tuskegee, Alabama, to help establish a technical and agricultural college for African American students. Tuskegee Institute opened on July 4, 1881, with Washington as its principal.

Tuskegee's first academic building was a dilapidated church, and its first dormitories were shacks and cabins, but Washington raised funds, acquired land, supervised the construction of buildings, and recruited talented faculty members. In a decade, the school had gained a national reputation for providing outstanding technical and occupational training for African American students. Washington toured the country, soliciting donors, recruiting students, and making speeches that extolled the value of the occupational training being delivered at Tuskegee Institute.

In the spring of 1895, Washington was invited to join a planning committee for the forthcoming Atlanta Cotton States and International Exposition, which would be held in September. The exposition would highlight the South's most recent developments in agricultural technology. Washington was asked to deliver one of the key addresses during the exposition's opening ceremonies, a speech that would focus on the role of African Americans in the South's agricultural economy. Washington saw the address as an opportunity to discuss the achievements that African Americans had made in the South since emancipation and to stress the need for further advancements.

Washington delivered his Atlanta Exposition Address on September 18, 1895, to an audience of several thousand listeners. He opened by thanking the directors of the Atlanta Exposition for including African Americans in the event and expressing his hope that the exposition would do more to "cement the friendship of the two races than any occurrence since the dawn of our freedom."

Washington went on to predict that the exposition would awaken among both white and black Southerners "a new era of industrial progress." He illustrated his point by telling a parable of a ship lost at sea whose crew members were desperate for fresh water. The captain of another ship, hearing the pleas for water by the captain of the distressed vessel, urged the lost sailors, "Cast down your bucket where you are." When the captain of the lost ship followed that advice, his crew members brought aboard sparkling fresh water from the Amazon River.

Washington then urged his African American listeners to cast down their buckets "in agriculture, mechanics, in commerce, in domestic service, and in the professions." He said that African Americans would prosper "in proportion as we learn to dignify and glorify common labour and put brains and skill into the common occupations of life. . . ." He added that "no race can prosper till it learns that there is as much dignity in tilling a field as in writing a poem."

Washington also told his white listeners to cast down their buckets among the South's African Americans, "who have, without strikes and labour wars, tilled your fields, cleared your forests, builded your railroads and cities, and brought forth treasures from the bowels of the earth, and helped make possible this magnificent representation of the progress of the South." He encouraged white Southerners to educate African Americans in "head, heart, and hand" so that they would remain "the most patient, faithful, law-abiding, and unresentful people that the world has seen." He asserted that in "all things purely social we can be as separate as the fingers, yet one as the hand in all things essential to mutual progress."

Washington concluded his speech by expressing his belief that the "wisest among my race understand that the agitation of questions of social equality is the extremest folly, and that progress in the enjoyment of all the privileges that will come to use must be the result of severe and constant struggle rather than of artificial forcing." He emphasized that African Americans must achieve economic self-reliance before they received "all the privileges of the law," that the "opportunity to earn a dollar in a factory just now is worth infinitely more than the opportunity to spend a dollar in an opera-house." Before surrendering the podium, Washington pledged to his audience his untiring effort to solve the racial animosities in the South and thereby bring to the region "a new heaven and a new earth."

Washington's address was enthusiastically received. Governor Rufus Bullock grasped Washington's hand and offered his congratulations. Others rushed to shake Washington's hand. Over the next few days, newspapers in the North and South praised the speech in editorials. President Grover Cleveland wrote a congratulatory note. Washington received dozens of

Booker T. Washington, educator, author, and first head of Tuskegee Institute. His Atlanta Exposition Address espoused education and gradual advancement for African Americans. (Library of Congress)

invitations to speak around the country and deliver his pragmatic message of economic self-reliance and political accommodationism.

Nevertheless, critics of Washington's philosophy soon surfaced, accusing Washington of making an unsatisfactory compromise by accepting an inferior social and political position for African Americans in exchange for economic opportunities. These critics argued that the tools for economic independence alone would not lead African Americans toward full citizenship and that the widespread segregation of and discrimination against African Americans in the United States,

especially in the South, was proof of the flaws of Washington's reasoning.

Perhaps the most eloquent critic of Washington's message was W. E. B. Du Bois. In *The Souls of Black Folk* (1903), Du Bois, who would later found the National Association for the Advancement of Colored People (NAACP), asserted that Washington "represents in Negro thought the old attitude of adjustment and submission," that the ideas expressed in what he called Washington's "Atlanta Compromise" were merely "a gospel of Work and Money" that prompted African Americans to surrender political power, civil rights, and opportunities for higher education. In contrast to Washington, Du Bois advocated that African Americans receive the right to vote; civic equality; and opportunities for higher academic education, as opposed to the kind of occupational training offered at Tuskegee Institute.

Despite this criticism, Washington remained an important African American spokesman. In 1901, he published *Up from Slavery*, an autobiography that chronicled his rise from slavery to national prominence. This rags-to-riches story was translated into several languages, giving Washington an international reputation. That same year, Washington founded the National Negro Business League. He wrote several other books on the African American experience, including *Frederick Douglass* (1907) and *The Story of the Negro* (1909). He died at Tuskegee Institute in 1915.

The issues that Washington articulated in his Atlanta Exposition Address continued to influence African American dialogue throughout the twentieth century. Although Du Bois was proven correct in his belief that economic advancements for African Americans would not be forthcoming until they achieved political rights and social equality, Washington's message—that African Americans must be allowed to enjoy the fruits of America's economic prosperity—has been repeated by African American civil rights leaders throughout the twentieth century. —*James Tackach*

ADDITIONAL READING:

Bontemps, Arna. *Young Booker: Booker T. Washington's Early Days.* New York: Dodd, Mead, 1972. Bontemps, an African American poet and critic, traces Washington's life from its beginnings through the Atlanta address.

Du Bois, W. E. B. *The Souls of Black Folk.* 1903. Reprint. New York: Penguin Books, 1989. In chapter 3 of his study of African American life, Du Bois critiques the ideas expressed in Washington's Atlanta Exposition Address.

Franklin, John Hope, and Alfred A. Moss, Jr. *From Slavery to Freedom: A History of African Americans.* 7th ed. New York: McGraw-Hill, 1994. An extensive history of African Americans. Chapter 14 discusses Washington's philosophy and its critics.

Harlan, Louis R. *Booker T. Washington: The Making of a Black Leader, 1856-1901.* New York: Oxford University Press, 1972. This text, the first of a two-volume biography of Washington, contains a detailed discussion of the Atlanta address.

Smock, Raymond W., ed. *Booker T. Washington in Perspective: Essays of Louis R. Harlan.* Jackson: University Press of Mississippi, 1988. Contains twelve essays on Washington by his biographer, Louis R. Harlan.

Washington, Booker T. *Up from Slavery.* 1901. Reprint. New York: Bantam Books, 1970. In chapters 13 and 14, Washington describes the events leading to the Atlanta Exposition Address, records the entire address, and discusses reactions to it.

SEE ALSO: 1905, Niagara Movement; 1909, National Association for the Advancement of Colored People Is Founded; 1917, Universal Negro Improvement Association Is Established.

1896 ■ PLESSY V. FERGUSON: *American apartheid is upheld as constitutional if public facilities are "separate but equal"*

DATE: May 18, 1896
LOCALE: Washington, D.C.
CATEGORIES: African American history; Civil rights; Court cases
KEY FIGURES:
Henry Billings Brown (1836-1913), associate justice in the Supreme Court
Charles E. Fenner (1834-1911), associate justice in the Louisiana Supreme Court
John H. Ferguson, judge of the Criminal District Court for Orleans Parish
John Marshall Harlan (1833-1911), associate justice in the Supreme Court
Louis A. Martinet (died 1917), black New Orleans resident who led the organization challenging the separate but equal law
Homer Adolph Plessy (died 1925), the litigant, a New Orleans resident of one-eighth African ancestry
Albion Winegar Tourgée (1838-1905), chief attorney for Plessy

SUMMARY OF EVENT. On July 10, 1890, the Louisiana General Assembly, over the objection of its eighteen African American members, enacted a law which read, in part:

> . . . all railway companies carrying passengers in their coaches in this state shall provide equal but separate accommodations for the white and colored races, by providing two or more passenger coaches for each passenger train, or by dividing the passenger coaches by a partition so as to secure separate accommodations.

The law empowered train officials to assign passengers to cars; passengers insisting on going into a car set aside for the other race were liable to a twenty-five-dollar fine and twenty days' imprisonment. In addition, the company could refuse to carry an obstreperous passenger and, if it were sued for doing so, was immune from damages in state courts. A third section outlined the penalties for noncomplying railroads and provided that "nothing in this act shall be construed as applying to nurses attending children of the other race."

At first the Separate Car Bill was stymied by the black legislators and by railroad officials who were as anxious to avoid the economic burden of providing separate facilities as they were to avoid a boycott of irate black passengers. Once the black legislators had helped to override the veto of a major lottery bill, however, the legislature revived the Separate Car Bill and enacted it by a safe margin.

After its enactment, some of the railroad companies were inclined to disregard the law, and they apparently collaborated with blacks testing its validity. In 1890, the railroads had unsuccessfully challenged a Mississippi "separate but equal" law; the Supreme Court of the United States had held that such a law, when applied solely to travel within the state, did not encroach upon interstate commerce (see *Louisville, New Orleans and Texas Railway Co. v. Mississippi*, 133 U.S. 587 in 1890).

The prominent black community of New Orleans organized to mount a legal attack upon the new law. A group calling itself the Citizens' Committee to Test the Constitutionality of the Separate Car Law, led by Louis Martinet and Alexander A. Mary, organized to handle the litigation and enlisted the services of Albion W. Tourgée. Tourgée was to serve as chief counsel and devote his considerable talents to rallying public opposition to the Jim Crow system typified by the Louisiana law. The new counsel had served as a classical carpetbagger in North Carolina during Reconstruction and, among other accomplishments, had published a number of novels about the Reconstruction era, among them *Fools Errand*, *An Appeal to Caesar*, and *Bricks Without Straw*. Martinet engaged James Walker to assist in handling the Louisiana phase of the controversy. Before the first test of the Louisiana law (also featuring an African American who could "pass for white") could be settled, the Louisiana Supreme Court decided that the 1890 law could not be applied to interstate travelers since it was an unconstitutional regulation of interstate commerce (*State ex rel. Abbot v. Hicks*, 11 So. 74 in 1892). The Plessy case, then, relitigated the question raised in the 1890 Mississippi railroad case, but as a problem in the constitutional law of civil liberties rather than one of interstate commerce.

The person recruited to test the segregation law was Homer Adolph Plessy, a person of seven-eighths Caucasian and one-eighth African ancestry, in whom "the mixture of colored blood was not discernible." On June 7, 1892, holding a first-class ticket entitling him to travel on the East Louisiana Railway from New Orleans to Covington, Louisiana, Plessy took a seat in the car reserved for whites. The conductor, assisted by a policeman, forcibly removed Plessy and, charging him with violating the segregation law, placed him in the parish jail. The state prosecuted Plessy in the Orleans Parish criminal district court before Judge John H. Ferguson. Plessy's plea that the law was unconstitutional was overruled by Ferguson, who directed the defense to address itself to the questions of fact. Having no defense in the facts, Tourgée and Walker appealed Ferguson's ruling on the law's constitutionality to the Louisiana Supreme Court by asking that court to issue a writ of prohibition which in effect would have directed Ferguson to reverse his ruling on the constitutional question.

On December 19, 1892, Associate Judge Charles E. Fenner of the Louisiana Supreme Court ruled the law constitutional in an opinion which served as a model for that written later by Justice Henry Billings Brown of the United States Supreme Court. After a delay of almost four years—a delay that Tourgée encouraged on the grounds that it gave the opponents of segregation needed time—the United States Supreme Court heard the arguments in Plessy's case on April 13, 1896. On May 18, 1896 (163 U.S. 537), Justice Brown handed down the majority opinion, supported by six other justices (Justice David Brewer did not participate, and Justice John Marshall Harlan dissented).

Justice Brown first disposed of Tourgée's argument that the segregation law was a "badge of servitude," a vestige of slavery prohibited by the Thirteenth Amendment (1865). Decisions in 1873 (*Slaughter-House* cases, 16 Wall. 36) and 1883 (*Civil Rights* cases, 109 U.S. 3), wrote Brown, indicated that it was because the Thirteenth Amendment barred only outright slavery and not laws merely imposing "onerous disabilities and burdens" that the movement for the Fourteenth Amendment was successful. Later in his opinion Brown blended the "badge of servitude" argument of the Thirteenth Amendment with his treatment of the equal protection question:

> We consider the underlying fallacy of the plaintiff's argument to consist in the assumption that the enforced separation of the two races stamps the colored race with a badge of inferiority. If this be so, it is not by reason of anything found in the act, but solely because the colored race chooses to put that construction upon it.

If Plessy was to gain any relief, it had to be from the Fourteenth Amendment, but that amendment, according to Brown

> merely . . . enforced the absolute equality of the two races before the law, but in the nature of things it could not have been intended to abolish distinctions based upon color, or to enforce social, as distinguished from political, equality, or a commingling of the two races upon terms unsatisfactory to either.

To support his point, Brown cited state school segregation and antimiscegenation laws and federal laws prescribing segregated schools for the District of Columbia. Special stress was placed on the 1849 decision of *Roberts v. Boston* (5 Cushing 198, 59 Mass. 198), in which Chief Justice Lemuel Shaw of the Massachusetts Supreme Judicial Court had upheld the constitutionality of separate but equal schools for Boston. Brown did not mention that the Massachusetts legislature had repudiated Shaw's doctrine in 1855.

To the plaintiff's argument that the principle of segregation could be used by the state to enforce extreme and arbitrary forms of racial discrimination, Brown responded that every exercise of state power must be "reasonable, and extend only to such laws as are enacted in good faith for the promotion of the public good, and not for the annoyance or oppression of a particular class." There was nothing unreasonable about the Louisiana law according to the Court; in determining what is reasonable, state legislators could "act with reference to the established usages, customs, and traditions of the people, with a view to the promotion of their comfort, and the preservation of the public peace and good order." Finally, Brown in his opinion delivered a famous statement on the relationship between law, prejudice, and equality:

> The [plaintiff's] argument also assumes that social prejudice may be overcome by legislation, and that equal rights cannot be secured to the negro except by an enforced commingling of the

two races. We cannot accept this proposition. If the two races are to meet on terms of social equality, it must be the result of natural affinities, a mutual appreciation of each other's merits and a voluntary consent of individuals.

The law in question, of course, specifically interfered with the "voluntary consent of individuals."

Tourgée's fears were realized: The Court had sanctioned Jim Crowism. What comfort blacks derived from the case had to be found in the strong dissenting opinion of Justice Harlan, who once again proved himself to be a staunch champion of a broad interpretation of the Reconstruction amendments. Harlan construed the ban on slavery to cover segregation laws; he insisted on Tourgée's thesis that a railroad was a public highway and that under the Fourteenth Amendment government could make no racial distinctions whether one considered the case under the privileges and immunities, due process, or equal protection clauses of that amendment. Harlan attacked the Court's reliance on pre-Fourteenth Amendment precedents; his most memorable language appeared in connection with his charge that the majority usurped constitutional power by assuming authority to decide on the "reasonableness" of state social legislation:

The white race deems itself to be the dominant race in this country. And so it is, in prestige, in achievements, in education, in wealth, and in power. So, I doubt not that it will continue to be for all time, if it remains true to its great heritage and holds fast to the principles of constitutional liberty. But in view of the Constitution, in the eye of the law, there is in this country no superior, dominant, ruling class of citizens. There is no caste here. Our Constitution is color-blind, and neither knows nor tolerates classes among citizens. In respect of civil rights, all citizens are equal before the law.

Harlan turned out to be a competent soothsayer:

The destinies of the two races in this country are indissolubly linked together, and the interests of both require that the common government of all shall not permit the seeds of race hate to be planted under the sanction of law.

It would, however, take the general public and the justices of the Supreme Court decades to adopt Harlan's views and interpretation of the Constitution. *Plessy*'s strong sanction of segregation in transportation lasted formally until 1950 (*Henderson v. United States*, 339 U.S. 816) and in education until 1954 (*Brown v. Board of Education of Topeka, Kansas*, 347 U.S. 483). Antimiscegenation laws were not outlawed until 1967 (*Loving v. Virginia*, 388 U.S. 1).

—*James J. Bolner, updated by Brian L. Fife*

ADDITIONAL READING:

Kauper, Paul G. "Segregation in Public Education: The Decline of *Plessy v. Ferguson*." *Michigan Law Review* 52 (1954): 1137-1158. Kauper contends that the Court did not deal definitively with the validity of segregation legislation, relying instead on its view of "reasonableness."

Lofgren, Charles A. *The Plessy Case: A Legal-Historical*

Interpretation. New York: Oxford University Press, 1987. In tracing the history of transportation law, Lofgren concludes that *Plessy* did not cause Jim Crow but instead confirmed the American racism of its era.

Mueller, Jean West, and Wynell Burroughs Schamel. "*Plessy v. Ferguson* Mandate." *Social Education* 53 (1989): 120-122. Traces the historical events leading to the Court's ruling, as well as teaching strategies for instructors.

Roche, John P. "*Plessy v. Ferguson:* Requiescat in Pace?" *University of Pennsylvania Law Review* 103 (1954): 44-58. Roche believes that the *Plessy* decision reflected the political climate of its time and was a judicial attempt to deal with a social and political problem.

Woodward, C. Vann. *American Counterpoint: Slavery and Racism in the North-South Dialogue.* Boston: Little, Brown, 1971. Woodward discusses the irony of Justice Brown's and Harlan's positions, in light of the origins of the two men.

SEE ALSO: 1865, New Black Codes; 1865, Thirteenth Amendment; 1866, Rise of the Ku Klux Klan; 1866, Race Riots in the South; 1868, Fourteenth Amendment; 1883, Civil Rights Cases; 1890, Mississippi Disfranchisement Laws; 1954, *Brown v. Board of Education*.

1896 ■ KLONDIKE GOLD RUSH: *gold fever sparks a new wave of settlers in the northern territory*

DATE: August 17, 1896
LOCALE: The Klondike, Yukon, Canada
CATEGORIES: Canadian history; Expansion and land acquisition
KEY FIGURES:

George Washington "Siwash" Carmack (1869-1922), first prospector to stake a claim on Bonanza Creek, beginning the Klondike gold rush

Kate Mason Carmack, George's wife, who some say was the first to find gold in Bonanza Creek

Robert Henderson, first prospector to strike gold in the Klondike, but not the first to stake a claim

Jack London, (1876-1916), prospector in the Klondike gold rush, who later wrote about his adventures

"Skookum" Jim Mason, a Tagish Indian and brother-in-law and mining partner of George Carmack

SUMMARY OF EVENT. In August of 1896, a whoop and holler shattered the silence of the Klondike Valley. "Gold!" shouted George "Siwash" Carmack, his wife, Kate Mason Carmack, and his two Indian companions, Tagish Charlie and "Skookum" Jim Mason. Their exclamations echoed through the Yukon, into Alaska, and rippled eventually down into the lower forty-eight states by way of Seattle, where a ship delivered the largest shipment of gold dust ever handled at that port. Soon, the whole world was listening, captivated by the promise of riches and adventure found in Bonanza Creek.

Three weeks before Carmack and his partners were able to get downstream to the mining settlement of Forty Mile to register their claim, they held a meeting on the hill overlooking Rabbit Creek. During this meeting, they decided to change the name of the creek. The miners in the north were mostly veterans of former gold rushes. They had a habit of changing the names of gold-bearing creeks to traditional mining names, such as "Bonanza," thus removing the strangeness from a strange country. Thus it was that Rabbit Creek became a name on old maps and Bonanza became the name that lured thousands north for the world's last great gold rush.

There was a time when it was not so well known. Over the hill from Bonanza Creek, a prospector named Robert Henderson was seeking that elusive strike. It was Henderson who suggested that Carmack try his luck on Rabbit Creek. It was Henderson who continued to prospect just a stone's-toss away from the wealth of Rabbit Creek, while hearing of a creek called "Bonanza" where nuggets lay in the ground for the picking. It was not until two years later, when it was too late to stake a claim, that Henderson discovered that the two creeks were one and the same.

On August 17, 1896, after Carmack had panned out enough gold dust for a "grub stake," he made his way to Forty Mile, where he announced his discovery. The stampede did not begin immediately. Miners at Forty Mile were skeptical. Carmack was married to an Indian, Kate Mason Carmack, and consequently did not enjoy a good reputation. Carmack had never been a zealous prospector; the Indian life of fishing and hunting had appealed to him more than the grind of gold mining. Still, miners could not ignore such an electrifying report, especially after Carmack had shown them a shotgun shell filled with coarse gold. Soon, men traveled upriver from Forty Mile to have a look, and by the time winter came, the reports of other miners confirmed the strike.

By early winter, most of the men of Forty Mile had rushed to the new ground and staked claims. It was said that butchers dropped their aprons on the spot, druggists ground up their last prescriptions, and clerks tallied up their final bill of sale, all with the urge to head north to the Klondike. The Klondike was a magnet that drew miners and nonminers from everywhere.

Victims of the Klondike fever numbered in the tens of thousands—casual laborers, farmers, students, bankers, and miners. Some, such as George Pilcher and Wyatt Earp, preferred to go on their own. Others, such as Will Ballou and John Hewitt, formed joint companies with like-minded neighbors who were willing to pool their resources. Many were backed by investors who wanted a share in the northern enterprise. Guidebooks soon were published, advising readers on transportation routes. There was an all-water route to the gold fields from the West Coast; there was a steerage passage from Seattle to Skagway, Alaska; and there was a trail one could hike into the interior over the Chilkoot Pass and White Pass.

Most of the 1897-1898 argonauts chose Seattle as their port of embarkation to the north. Among the sixty thousand stampeders was Jack London. He and his partners were among the thirty to forty thousand argonauts to choose one of the passes from the head of Lynn Canal as their route to the Klondike. From the coast to the city of Dawson was six hundred miles, but it was the first eighteen miles, from Dyea to the summit, that caused the most anxiety to travelers.

The trails, especially the Chilkoot Trail, had always been difficult to travel. At the base of the mountains, eight miles from the coast, the slope ascended sharply for ten miles to the summit, an elevation of thirty-five hundred feet. Crossing the pass under ideal weather conditions on the hard-packed snow of early spring was difficult, but undertaking it during a winter blizzard through deep, soft snow was extremely treacherous. What made the Chilkoot Trail a cruel punishment for most stampeders was the necessity of tackling it time after time, weighed down by heavy backpacks. Most brought one thousand to two thousand pounds of supplies, which meant that twenty or more crossings had to be made after one's base depot was made at camp. Pack animals could not make it over the Chilkoot; the White Pass Trail proved a death trap for horses and mules. Hundreds fell from the twisting, narrow trail into the valley below; others foundered in deep snow or mud, or broke their legs fording the rocky streams, leaving a trail lined with rotting carcasses.

Two thundering avalanches of snow and ice killed many prospectors. In September, 1897, fierce winds forced loose the glacier's edge, releasing a lake that heavy rains built up on the glacier. More than a score of men were struck down with typhoid fever in 1898. Drowning on the upper Yukon accounted for many other deaths. Still other menaces were spinal meningitis, starvation, frostbite, claim jumping, and robbery. The next stage of the journey called for boat building. Men sweated through the arduous winter work of building boats without benefit of sawmills. This work strained many men beyond endurance; it ended partnerships and dissolved families.

All was not grimness on the Klondike Trail. Gamblers ran their games wherever a number of people gathered. All the entrepreneurs along the trail contributed to a carnival mood. Many argonauts seemed more interested in fun than in gold.

Within two years, thirty to forty thousand persons were added to Alaska's population, with a corresponding increase in its commerce and material prosperity. In 1897 alone, $22 million was taken from the Klondike field. The discovery of gold prompted people to start spending money around the globe, ending the economic depression that had made life difficult in the latter part of the 1800's. The irresistible pull of the Klondike gold exerted its influence on men and women of all ranks and stations of life throughout North America and beyond.

—*Susan M. Taylor*

ADDITIONAL READING:

Adney, Tappan. *The Klondike Stampede*. Vancouver: University of British Columbia Press, 1994. A factual story of the adventurous people who brought the Alaskan Yukon to the nation's attention.

Berton, Pierre. *The Promised Land: Settling the West 1896-1914*. Toronto, Ont.: McClelland & Stewart, 1984. The final volume in the author's tetralogy of the national dream, the Klondike gold rush.

Hunt, William R. *North of 53°: The Wild Days of the Alaskan-Yukon Mining Frontier, 1870-1914*. New York: Macmillan, 1974. A rigorous social document supported by the records and diaries of the people who built Alaska.

Mathews, Richard. *The Yukon*. New York: Holt, Rinehart and Winston, 1968. An intriguing history of the Yukon as a study of contrasts in people, wealth, and culture.

Mayer, Melanie J. *Klondike Women: True Tales of the 1897-98 Gold Rush*. Athens: Swallow Press/Ohio University Press, 1989. Firsthand accounts of the adventures, challenges, and disappointments of women on the trails to the Klondike.

Schell, Karen. *Westward Expansion II*. 9 vols. Farmingdale, N.Y.: Cobblestone, 1993. Gives a rich, complex image of the people, time, and places of the Klondike gold rush.

SEE ALSO: 1848, California Gold Rush; 1858, Fraser River Gold Rush.

1896 ■ McKINLEY IS ELECTED PRESIDENT:
Republican victories mark the beginning of the party's thirty-six-year domination of Congress

DATE: November 3, 1896
LOCALE: United States
CATEGORY: Government and politics
KEY FIGURES:
William Jennings Bryan (1860-1925), Democratic
    presidential candidate
Stephen Grover Cleveland (1837-1908), twenty-second
    (1885-1889) and twenty-fourth (1893-1897) president of
    the United States
Marcus "Mark" Alonzo Hanna (1837-1904), Republican
    campaign manager
Garret Augustus Hobart (1844-1899), Republican vice
    presidential candidate
William McKinley (1843-1901), Republican presidential
    candidate
Arthur Sewall (1835-1900), Democratic vice presidential
    candidate
Thomas Edward Watson (1856-1922), Populist vice
    presidential candidate

SUMMARY OF EVENT. The Republicans approached the elections in 1896 confident that they would regain the presidency that they had relinquished only twice since the Civil War (both times to Grover Cleveland, in 1884 and 1892). The failure of the Cleveland Administration to deal effectively with the severe economic depression that followed the Panic of 1893 had led to significant losses for the Democrats in the 1894 elections. Republicans gained more than one hundred seats in the

William McKinley, twenty-fifth president of the United States. The campaign between McKinley and the Democrats' William Jennings Bryan hinged on the issue of free silver—a looser money supply that would enable easier payment of debts but might threaten inflation. McKinley's victory marked the beginning of a Republican stronghold on federal government for the next generation. (Library of Congress)

House of Representatives, the largest transfer of congressional strength in U.S. history up to that time. The Democratic Party was dangerously split over the issue of silver, and President Cleveland had been repudiated by many in his own party. The Republicans, controlling the House of Representatives and seeing the continuing difficulties of the opposing parties, were certain that they could defeat the Democrats and the Populists in the presidential race.

The leading candidate for the Republicans was William McKinley, the former governor of Ohio, who had the nomination assured by the time that the Republican National Convention assembled in St. Louis on June 16, 1896. As the most popular figure in his party, McKinley defeated his disorganized rivals and won the nomination easily on the first ballot. He selected Garret Hobart of New Jersey as his running mate. Their platform promised to preserve the existing gold standard but to seek a wider use of silver through international agreements. The East liked the pledge for gold; the West admired the bow toward silver. McKinley expected to base his campaign on the gold standard and the protective tariff. The Republicans did not anticipate a serious challenge from the eventual Democratic nominee.

The Democrats were hopelessly divided about silver and its inflationary implications. Cleveland and his allies favored the gold standard. Party members in the South and West wanted "free silver," the rapid expansion of the money supply, to raise agricultural prices and make debts easier to pay. The pro-silver forces controlled the platform at the national convention that met in Chicago in July. No clear front-runner for the nomination had emerged, but a young Nebraskan named William Jennings Bryan hoped to sway the delegates when he spoke for silver during the debate on the platform. Bryan's "Cross of Gold" speech became an eloquent statement of the free-silver cause, and his oratory captivated the audience. The next day, the thirty-six-year-old Bryan was nominated on the fifth ballot. To balance the ticket, the convention chose Arthur Sewall, a Maine banker who favored free silver, as Bryan's running mate. Some Democrats who advocated remaining on the gold standard bolted the party and formed the Gold Democrats.

The nomination of Bryan and the adoption of a free-silver plank in the Democratic platform placed the Populists, whose national convention gathered on July 22 in St. Louis, in a dilemma. If they nominated Bryan and "fused" with the Democrats, they would advance the cause of free silver but render their party irrelevant. Nominating a separate ticket could guarantee the victory for McKinley and the Republicans. The delegates decided to endorse Bryan for president and select their own vice presidential candidate. They chose Thomas Watson of Georgia, a longtime Populist leader. As a result, there were two Bryan tickets in the field, with different vice presidential candidates. Bryan never accepted Watson as an official candidate, but the result was a good deal of confusion on many state ballots.

Free silver became the dominant issue of the election. Debtors and those who mined silver believed that silver in unlimited quantities should be minted at the fixed ratio of sixteen-to-one with gold. They argued that increasing the money supply would raise prices for agricultural products and make debts easier to pay. Supporters of the gold standard countered that inflation would penalize those with savings or on a fixed income. Silver supporters in the Republican ranks held a national convention and supported Bryan and Sewall. The Gold Democrats nominated John M. Palmer of Illinois as their presidential candidate. Prohibitionist and Socialist-Labor Party candidates were also on the ballot in many states.

Bryan waged a vigorous personal campaign. He traveled eighteen thousand miles, made more than six hundred speeches, and was heard by an estimated five hundred thousand people. Crowds cheered the Boy Orator of the Platte, as Bryan was known. The Democrats' main asset was Bryan himself. Otherwise, the party had little money or effective campaign resources. In the East, conservative Democrats supported McKinley or the Gold Democrats. The major battleground of the election became the Midwest.

Knowing that he could not match Bryan's skills as a speaker, McKinley conducted a "front-porch" campaign from his home in Canton, Ohio. Republican groups came to meet with him and hear the short, effective speeches that McKinley gave about the dangers of free silver and the virtues of the protective tariff. The candidate warned workers that inflation would erode the value of their paychecks. Under the leadership of campaign manager Mark Hanna, the Republican raised four million dollars from large contributors and corporations. Hanna used the money on a campaign of education that saw 250 million pamphlets of Republican literature distributed to the voters. Speakers for McKinley crisscrossed the North in a well-organized drive to arouse Republican voters.

At the outset of the campaign, a wave of enthusiasm swept the country for Bryan. Some conservatives warned that the nation stood on the brink of social revolution. It proved difficult, however, for Bryan to sustain his one-issue campaign throughout the entire presidential contest. By the middle of the fall, some of the luster of the silver issue had dulled and the Republicans surged ahead in the key states. McKinley's pluralistic and inclusive style attracted voters, particularly in the industrial states, to his message. Meanwhile, the divided and underfinanced Democrats could not overcome the obstacles that the Cleveland Administration had imposed upon them.

The excitement and controversy of the 1896 campaign produced a large voter turnout in percentage terms. Women and minorities were still barred from voting, but more than 75 percent of the eligible male electorate went to the polls in the North. Two million more people voted than in the previous presidential contest. McKinley captured 271 electoral votes, and Bryan had 176 (including 27 Bryan-Watson electors). Bryan's strength lay in the Plains and Southern states; McKinley ran well in the industrial Midwest. The popular vote totals were 7,104,779 for McKinley to Bryan's 6,502,925. Bryan and the Democrats alleged that corporations supporting McKinley and Hanna had coerced workers into voting Republican, but Bryan's inflationary ideas were a better explanation of why so many industrial employees voted Republican. The outcome of the election completed the electoral upheaval of the 1890's and made the Republicans the majority party for a generation. McKinley interpreted his victory as a victory for the gold standard and the concomitant interests of big-business industrialism over agrarian Populism. Passage of the Dingley Tariff Act in 1897 and the Gold Standard Act in 1900 attest that victory.

—*Lewis L. Gould, based on the original entry*
by Mark A. Plummer

ADDITIONAL READING:

Gould, Lewis L. *The Presidency of William McKinley*. Lawrence: University Press of Kansas, 1980. The first chapter looks at the 1896 election and McKinley's rise to national prominence. The book stresses McKinley's skill as a politician.

Gould, Lewis L., and Craig H. Roell, eds. *William McKinley: A Bibliography*. Westport, Conn.: Meckler, 1988. Contains a thorough listing of articles and books on the election that were published before 1988.

Jones, Stanley L. *The Presidential Election of 1896*. Madison: University of Wisconsin Press, 1964. Contains a wealth of information about the activities of all the major participants in the 1896 contest. A balanced, fair treatment of the election.

McGerr, Michael. *The Decline of Popular Politics: The American North, 1865-1928*. New York: Oxford University Press, 1986. A review of campaign styles, useful for placing the partisan techniques in 1896 within a historical context.

Morgan, H. Wayne. *From Hayes to McKinley: National Party Politics, 1877-1896*. Syracuse, N.Y.: Syracuse University Press, 1969. A well-written narrative history of U.S. politics during the late nineteenth century. Argues that the outcome in 1896 was the culmination of Republican policies of nationalism and economic development.

Williams, R. Hal. *Years of Decision: American Politics in the 1890's*. Prospect Heights, Ill.: Waveland Books, 1993. Excellent narrative. Includes information on the election of 1896 and its significance. Good discussion on the emotions the election aroused.

SEE ALSO: 1863, National Bank Acts; 1869, Scandals of the Grant Administration; 1873, "Crime of 1873"; 1892, Birth of the People's Party; 1913, Federal Reserve Act.

1897 ■ LAURIER ERA IN CANADA: *a dynamic, bilingual prime minister leads Canada into a new century*

DATE: 1897-September 21, 1911
LOCALE: Ottawa
CATEGORIES: Canadian history; Government and politics
KEY FIGURES:
Robert Laird Borden (1854-1937), Laurier's Tory opponent and successor
Henri Bourassa (1868-1952), French nationalist who opposed Laurier
Wilfrid Laurier (1841-1919), prime minister of Canada, 1897-1911
Oliver Mowat (1820-1903), Ontario Liberal who opposed free trade with the United States
Clifford Sifton (1861-1929), minister who encouraged immigration
SUMMARY OF EVENT. The Liberal government headed by Sir Wilfrid Laurier ushered Canada into the twentieth century. At the end of Laurier's decade-and-a-half tenure, Canada was recognizably different from the country it had been at its beginning.

Laurier was a French Catholic from Quebec, but he also was a fervent admirer of British literature and culture. He especially esteemed the British tradition of moderate political liberalism. Thus he was acceptable to both of Canada's two founding peoples, the English and the French. The Laurier government was immediately confronted with a divisive cultural and linguistic issue. Catholics living in Manitoba, most of whom spoke French, wanted their children to go to separate Catholic, French-speaking schools, and they wanted these schools to be supported by public tax money. Drawing on the advantages he possessed by virtue of his Francophone background, Laurier resolved the situation by permitting a religious element to be attached to the school curriculum after formal instruction had ceased for the day. This achievement won for Laurier a reputation as a leader who could bring Canadians together.

Laurier next was confronted with problems in foreign relations. The Laurier era saw, for the first time, foreign relations becoming important in Canadian politics and Canada becoming a significant factor in world affairs. Canada still possessed many symbolic and constitutional ties to Great Britain, including the same head of state. Yet despite Canada's close association with the mother country, Canada was in effect self-governing. Moreover, Canada's three-thousand-mile-long border with the United States made that country at least as important for Canada as faraway Britain. Laurier had to contend with divisions in his own party as he attempted to navigate these difficult issues. Himself a supporter of free trade (also known as "unrestricted reciprocity") with the United States, Laurier had to mollify a substantial degree of dissent among Liberals. Such dissent was personified by Sir Oliver Mowat, the Liberal premier of Ontario, who under no circumstances wanted free trade with the colossus to Canada's south.

More popular was the idea of the imperial preference in trade. Under this scheme, Canada would give preference in trade to Great Britain and to other British dominions, such as Australia, thereby cementing ties between the various parts of the British Empire, so that the former colonies would no longer be the object of neglect and contempt on the part of Great Britain. Imperial preference was a popular idea in the Laurier era, because of the growing self-confidence and pride of the British Empire, and also the growing awareness of the military threat posed by Germany. The greatest manifestation of imperial solidarity in the Laurier era was Canadian participation on the British side in the Boer War in South Africa, beginning in 1899. For the most part, this cause was enthusiastically supported by the Canadian populace. Yet Laurier always held back from proposed schemes of imperial federation, under which Canada would grow closer politically to the other countries related to Great Britain. Laurier recognized that the process was running the other way, toward greater Canadian independence and national self-reliance. The rise of a robust

Canadian spirit was seen not only in politics but also in culture and the arts. In literature, Canadian writers, such as novelist Sara Jeannette Duncan and poet Charles G. D. Roberts, made Canadians realize that they did not have to import their culture wholly from Great Britain. In art, Canadian painters began representing the landscape as they perceived it to be, not necessarily constrained by European models. Canada began to gain a cultural cohesion equal to or greater than its political unity.

The greatest threat to Canadian national cohesion was, then as throughout the twentieth century, the problem of French-speaking Quebec. Although Laurier was French-speaking and Catholic in background, he was mistrusted by many French-speaking leaders, especially the energetic Quebec journalist and politician Henri Bourassa. Bourassa was a thorn in Laurier's side throughout his government. Bourassa was especially vigorous in his opposition to any form of closer ties between Canada and Great Britain, claiming that the mother country simply wished to have Canadians fight in British wars. Laurier found himself caught in the middle, frowned upon by imperial federationists for being too nationalistic and excoriated by Francophones who thought he was too adapted to British culture and manners.

That these tensions between the peoples of Canada did not explode into serious difficulty in the Laurier years can be attributed to the wave of prosperity that swept over Canada in this period. The Laurier era was, almost without doubt, the most prosperous in Canadian history. Spurred by the growth of new manufacturing enterprises in the cities, millions of Canadians left their parents' farms and homesteads to seek employment in the cities. Canadian corporations became large and influential, investing in foreign countries as well as within the nation itself. Canada shifted from being primarily a rural, agricultural economy to becoming urban and industrialized.

Canada's vast reserves of natural resources became of substantial value in the world economy. Canadian wheat, produce, minerals, and precious metals (evidenced by the gold rush in the Yukon) brought an increasing inflow of wealth and investment into the country, especially into the western provinces. In the United States, 1890 usually is perceived as the year of the closing of the frontier. In Canada, the frontier era lasted until about 1910, and the Laurier years saw phenomenal expansion in the prairie provinces of Manitoba, Saskatchewan, and Alberta, the last two of which joined the confederation under Laurier's government. Although market forces were responsible for much of this expansion, the Laurier government crucially assisted it by promoting the construction of a transcontinental railroad. The railroad provided the crucial transportation backbone to the prairie economy.

The settlement and prosperity of the Canadian West was important for the country because it made Canada a transcontinental power in the manner of the United States. Not only did Canadian territory reach from the Atlantic to the Pacific, but Canadian population and settlement did as well, making it far less likely that Canada would ever be annexed by the United States. The axis of Canadian politics also moved away from the long-standing rivalry between English-speaking Ontario and French-speaking Quebec—although the new provinces were overwhelmingly English-speaking, and thus the sense of alienation on the part of the Francophone population began to increase.

English and French were not the only languages heard in the Canada of this era. For the first time in its history, Canada encouraged large-scale immigration from non-English-speaking countries, especially from eastern and southern Europe. The pioneer of this policy was Clifford Sifton, minister of the interior in the Laurier cabinet. Sifton extolled the virtues of the hardworking new Canadians, and he saw them as making valuable contributions to the fabric of Canadian national identity. The immigrants tended to settle largely in the booming western provinces, and they contributed substantially to the fundamental identity of the prairie region. Canada was on its way to becoming a truly multicultural nation.

The Laurier regime thereby took initiatives designed to please a substantial majority of Canadian society and bring Canada with confidence into a new century. Inevitably, though, some element of Laurier's grand coalition had to cause a rupture, and the rupture occurred in 1910 over relations with the United States. Laurier wanted Parliament to approve a reciprocity treaty with the United States, guaranteeing unrestrained trade. Canadian manufacturers protested the agreement, although Laurier had gained very advantageous terms in negotiations with the United States. The final blow to the agreement's chances was struck when Sifton, the champion of the new West, opposed the accord on the grounds that it would cripple the Canadian produce industry. Laurier took his case to the people, but the vehemence of the opposition by Canadian mercantile interests swayed a majority of the electorate. With the defeat of the Liberals in national parliamentary elections on September 21, 1911, the Laurier era ended, and Robert Laird Borden, Laurier's Tory opponent, became prime minister of Canada.

—*Nicholas Birns*

ADDITIONAL READING:

Brown, R. Craig, and Ramsay Cook. *Canada, 1896-1921: A Nation Transformed.* Toronto: McClelland and Stewart, 1974. Focuses on the nation's metamorphosis during the Laurier era.

Clippingdale, Richard. *Laurier: His Life and World.* Toronto: McGraw-Hill Ryerson, 1979. A general introduction, with photographs.

Dafoe, John W. *Laurier: A Study in Canadian Politics.* Toronto: McClelland and Stewart, 1963. A sharply critical study of Laurier.

Neatby, H. Blair. *Laurier and a Liberal Quebec: A Study in Political Management.* Toronto: McClelland and Stewart, 1973. Discusses Laurier's relationship with his fellow Francophones.

Schull, Joseph. *Laurier: The First Canadian.* Toronto: Macmillan of Canada, 1965. An admiring and comprehensive biography of Laurier.

1897 ■ DINGLEY TARIFF: *successful protective tariff policies of the late 1890's become the focus of criticism after 1900*

DATE: July 24, 1897

LOCALE: Washington, D.C.

CATEGORIES: Business and labor; Economics; Laws and acts

KEY FIGURES:

Nelson Wilmarth Aldrich (1841-1915), chair of the Senate Finance Committee

Stephen Grover Cleveland (1837-1908), twenty-second (1885-1889) and twenty-fourth (1893-1897) president of the United States

Nelson Dingley (1832-1899), chair of the House Ways and Means Committee

William McKinley (1843-1901), twenty-fifth president of the United States, 1897-1901

Thomas Brackett Reed (1839-1902), Speaker of the House of Representatives

SUMMARY OF EVENT. One of the most controversial political issues of the late nineteenth century was the protective tariff. Republicans argued that high customs duties on imports to the United States protected U.S. businesses from foreign competition and provided jobs to farmers and workers. Democrats countered that the policy raised prices to consumers and favored some businesses at the expense of others. The tariff became a key issue dividing the two major parties, with the Republicans united behind protection and most Democrats advocating lower tariffs. In the presidential elections of 1888 and 1892, the two parties offered very different approaches to trade policy. The Republicans received support for protectionism in 1888; the Democrats elected Grover Cleveland in part on the promise of lower tariffs in 1892.

Republicans enacted the protective McKinley Tariff in 1890 and saw their control of the House of Representatives vanish as voters rejected the higher prices associated with the law. When the Democrats regained the White House in 1893 under President Cleveland, they endeavored to pass a law to lower the tariff. Divisions within the party over other issues and the onset of the economic depression of the 1890's made it difficult for the Democrats to agree on a reform law. The result was the Wilson-Gorman Tariff of 1894, which lowered rates somewhat but also made concessions to protectionist sentiment within the Democratic Party in order to get a bill through Congress. Cleveland let the bill become law without his signature, and the Republicans hammered away at the measure in the congressional elections of 1894. When the Republicans regained the House of Representatives in that year, they promised that if a Republican president were elected in 1896, the tariff would be revised upward.

The Republican nominee in 1896 was William McKinley, who had long been associated with the protective tariff in the House of Representatives. By this time, however, McKinley

had decided that it would be wise to include a policy of reciprocal trade whereby the United States would moderate its tariff rates in return for concessions from other trading partners. The new president was not a free-trader. Reciprocity would occur within the protective system, but he envisioned an expansion of trade with this approach.

After he defeated William Jennings Bryan in 1896, McKinley urged Congress to move ahead quickly on a tariff law. He summoned the lawmakers into session in March, 1897. Advance planning meant that the House could act quickly on the tariff. The chairman of the House Ways and Means Committee, Nelson Dingley, reported out a new tariff bill, called the Dingley Tariff, on March 18, three days after the session opened. The Speaker of the House, Thomas B. Reed, used the power of the Republican majority to push the bill through within three weeks of the opening of the session.

The situation was more complex in the Senate, where Republican control was less secure. There the Dingley Tariff became entangled with another issue. To achieve a greater use of silver in international trade, the United States had opened negotiations with France about an agreement on a policy known as international bimetallism. The French indicated interest in helping the United States if they could receive some concessions for their products in the new tariff bill. These elements led Nelson Aldrich, chair of the Senate Finance Committee, to produce an initial tariff measure in the Senate that recognized French desires, including lower rates on French luxury products.

As time passed, however, the various interest groups within the Republican coalition increased the pressure for higher tariff rates. The result was a bill that raised duties on such products as wool and woolen clothing, while hiking rates on French items such as silks, gloves, and olive oil. When the bill became more protectionist, Senate supporters of international bimetallism pushed the idea of tariff reciprocity treaties as a way of promising future concessions to France and other nations. The Senate bill, as passed on July 7, included language that allowed the president to negotiate treaties for a reduction of up to 20 percent on the duties in the Dingley bill.

The conference committee of the House and Senate leaned more toward the protectionist side. The final bill retained the raised duties on wool, silk, and other products of concern to France. There was wording that allowed the president to offer countries reductions on specific items and to negotiate reciprocal trade treaties as well. The bill came out of conference on July 19, and both houses approved it by July 24, 1897. Despite not having a dependable majority in the Senate, the Republicans had passed a tariff bill quickly and with little intraparty friction. The French initiative on international bimetallism collapsed later in the summer, for reasons unrelated to the passage of the Dingley Tariff.

Public reaction to the bill was quiet. The returning prosperity of the summer of 1897 made the action of the Republican Congress seem appropriate. Although President McKinley tried to use the reciprocity sections of the law during the remainder of his term, and negotiated agreements with France, Jamaica, Argentina, and other nations, the strength of protectionist sentiment on Capitol Hill limited his accomplishments. In his last public speech, on September 5, 1901, in Buffalo, New York, McKinley argued for reciprocity as a policy of the future and sought to guide public opinion to tolerance of freer trade. The next day he was shot and, with his death on September 14, 1901, reciprocity waned. The new president, Theodore Roosevelt, proved willing to let Congress have its way on the tariff.

Until 1900, the Dingley Tariff enjoyed general political acceptance. As the return of prosperity following the Spanish-American War became more apparent, consumer prices rose and inflation became an issue. The rise of large corporations and public fears about the trusts also were associated with the protective policy. Democrats charged that the tariff law had stimulated the growth of giant corporations and raised prices that average citizens had to pay. Within the ranks of the Republicans, sentiment to reform the tariff law grew, especially in the plains states of the Midwest. Party regulars remained steadfast in support of the law, and an internal dispute about the tariff marked the history of the Republicans during the first decade of the twentieth century.

In the presidential election of 1908, public pressure and the attacks of the Democrats led the Republicans to promise a revision of the tariff following the outcome of the race for the White House. The winner, William Howard Taft, followed through on this commitment and set in motion events that led to the enactment of the Payne-Aldrich Tariff of 1909. The controversy that stemmed from that event led, in turn, to a split in the Republican Party and the election of Democrat Woodrow Wilson in 1912. After Wilson took office, the Democratic Congress passed the Underwood Tariff in 1913, which lowered rates and finally replaced the Dingley Tariff completely.

The Republicans achieved substantial political benefits from the Dingley Tariff during the McKinley Administration. After 1901, it became a source of persistent friction and opposition internally and from the Democrats. In that period, the law gained its enduring historical reputation as the embodiment of the high protective tariff policies associated with the Republican Party during the last twenty-five years of the nineteenth century. *—Lewis L. Gould, based on the original entry by Anne Trotter*

ADDITIONAL READING:

Becker, William H. *The Dynamics of Business-Government Relations: Industry and Exports, 1893-1921.* Chicago: University of Chicago Press, 1982. Considers how U.S. business viewed export policy, and contains useful information on the Dingley Tariff from that perspective.

Gould, Lewis L. "Diplomats in the Lobby: Franco-American Relations and the Dingley Tariff of 1897." *Historian* 39 (August, 1977): 659-680. Uses the French diplomatic archives to trace the relationship between tariff-making and bimetallic diplomacy during the summer of 1897.

———. *The Presidency of William McKinley.* Lawrence: University Press of Kansas, 1980. Considers the enactment of

the Dingley Tariff in the context of the first year of the McKinley Administration and traces the president's use of reciprocity as a bargaining tool in trade relations between 1897 and 1901. Good starting point for research on the Dingley law.

Taussig, Frank W. *The Tariff History of the United States.* New York: Augustus M. Kelley, 1967. In this classic, begun in 1892 and updated yearly with each new tariff act, economics professor and occasional chair of the U.S. Tariff Commission Taussig regards the Dingley Tariff as a transitional measure, reflecting the changing nature of American manufacturing as it faced a new threat of foreign tariff retaliation.

Terrill, Tom E. *The Tariff, Politics, and American Foreign Policy.* Westport, Conn.: Greenwood Press, 1973. Examines the Dingley law from the perspective of whether a search for overseas markets drove U.S. foreign policy during the end of the nineteenth century.

Wolman, Paul. *Most Favored Nation: The Republican Revisionists and U.S. Tariff Policy, 1897-1912.* Chapel Hill: University of North Carolina Press, 1992. The Dingley Tariff forms the starting point for the author's discussion of Republicans who lobbied for downward revision of the tariff after 1897.

SEE ALSO: 1892, Birth of the People's Party; 1896, McKinley Is Elected President; 1909, Republican Congressional Insurgency; 1913, Sixteenth Amendment.

1897 ■ LIBRARY OF CONGRESS BUILDING OPENS: *a new home for the world's largest library becomes an architectural treasure*

DATE: November 1, 1897
LOCALE: Washington, D.C.
CATEGORY: Cultural and intellectual history
KEY FIGURES:
Edward Pearce Casey (1864-1940), the architect who was in charge of construction after 1892
Thomas Lincoln Casey (1831-1896), chief of Army Engineers, who was placed in charge of construction, Edward's father
Bernard R. Green (1843-1914), Casey's assistant
John L. Smithmeyer (1832-1908) and
Paul Johannes Pelz (1841-1918), architects who submitted original plans
Ainsworth Rand Spofford (1825-1908), Librarian of Congress, 1864-1897
John Russell Young (1840-1899), Spofford's successor as librarian

SUMMARY OF EVENT. The origins of the Library of Congress date back to a congressional act passed on April 24, 1800, that appropriated five thousand dollars "for the purchase of such books as may be necessary for the use of Congress" and for housing them "in one suitable apartment in the Capitol." By the time it was destroyed during the War of 1812, it possessed more than three thousand volumes. The library was replaced in January, 1815, with the purchase of Thomas Jefferson's library of six thousand books. A fire in 1851 destroyed thirty-five thousand books of the collection, which had grown by then to fifty-five thousand volumes. Congress immediately voted for funds to expand the holdings of the library and appropriated $72,500 to rebuild its quarters in the Capitol.

During the 1860's, the library was increased by numerous collections that were donated to it. The Smithsonian Institution's library of scientific journals and transactions of learned societies was deposited in 1866, and in the following year, the Peter Force collection of Americana was purchased. The library held only 165,000 books by 1870, when an important development took place. The amended copyright law placed copyrights under the library and provided that two copies of all copyrighted books and publications be placed in the Library of Congress. Within two years, it became obvious to Ainsworth Rand Spofford, Librarian of Congress from 1854 to 1897, and all who used the library that the Capitol quarters were not adequate for its natural growth and development. The library needed its own building.

After years of architectural debate as to the style—with Italian, French, and German Renaissance, and even Gothic styles discussed—the building plans of the firm of Smithmeyer and Pelz were accepted. On April 15, 1886, a congressional act created a commission to direct construction, which was in the hands of John Smithmeyer. As progress was not made and Congress was in doubt as to the exact cost, a second act, on October 2, 1886, repealed the first, and a ceiling of four million dollars was placed on construction costs. General Thomas Lincoln Casey, chief of the Army Engineers, was placed in charge, and he modified the original plans. To the opening session of Congress in December, 1888, he demonstrated that the library would cost six million dollars and would be completed within eight years. With congressional approval, construction resumed under Bernard R. Green, superintendent and engineer appointed by General Casey, aided by Paul Pelz of the original architectural firm.

Work progressed throughout the 1890's, and in the fall of 1893, the octagonal dome, 140 feet in diameter, was completed. In the autumn of 1897, the new Library of Congress, in Italian Renaissance style finished in New Hampshire granite, was completed at a cost of $6.3 million. On Monday, November 1, the library was opened to the public.

The interior decoration was done by leading artists of the day, under the supervision of Edward P. Casey. One newspaper praised the decoration in the following terms: "It is the interior of the building . . . in which it surpasses furthest anything that the United States has done before in the way of public art."

The operation of the library was directed from the rotunda area, which originally handled 260 readers. The stacks that radiated from the rotunda on three sides rose nine stories and could hold four-and-a-half million volumes. It was thought at the time that the library would be adequate for fifty years.

Over the years, the library has greatly expanded its size and services. In 1925, the main building was enlarged; in 1939, a five-story annex, the Adams Building, was completed and nearly doubled the original space. Through congressional appropriations, benefactions of public-spirited citizens, transfers from other agencies, deposit of books for copyright, and the operation of a vast network of international exchanges, the library in the 1990's contained an unrivaled collection of literary, scientific, artistic, and governmental materials.

In addition to its significant size, the Library of Congress is an international repository, having been charged by Congress in the 1960's to gather "all library materials currently published throughout the world which are of value to scholarship." Materials are collected in Asia, Latin America, and Africa, as well as in Europe and North America, and access to these holdings has been automated. Another change in the library is its expansion of mission, from a resource for Congress to a source of information and materials for numerous publics. This increased access is available within the Library of Congress itself or through the outreach programs it sponsors and manages.

The library's panoply of materials requires special care to maintain and to preserve their availability to its diverse publics. To accomplish this, the library has a comprehensive preservation program; the most challenging preservation issue is the high acid content of paper characteristic since the mid-nineteenth century. The library's deacidification program treats, thereby preserving, more than half a million volumes annually. Additionally, digitization of many formats now offers the most secure and effective means of preservation and distribution of the world's scholarly treasures.

Generous bequests, international exchange programs, diversification of formats, and expansion of services to its multiple and dispersed publics made the need for additional space obvious. Construction of the "third annex" was completed in 1980. Named in honor of President James Madison, the James Madison Memorial Building was the largest library building in the world in the 1990's. In appearance, it is simple when compared with the artistic grandeur of the original Jefferson building. It is the home of specific programs of the Library of Congress: processing, copyright, and the Congressional Research Service. The research service, always at the core of the mission of the Library of Congress, is a primary research source for members of Congress.

The Library of Congress' collection of more than one hundred million items in nearly five hundred languages, and its staff of approximately five thousand, honor the goal of its original founders, build on the leadership and diverse vision of its librarians, and equip the Library of Congress to serve both the United States and the world.

—Russell Magnaghi, updated by Ann Thompson

ADDITIONAL READING:

Goodrum, Charles A. *Treasures of the Library of Congress.* New York: Harry N. Abrams, 1980. Heavily illustrated description of the unique and specialized collection of the Library of Congress.

Goodrum, Charles A., and Helen W. Dalrymple. *Guide to the Library of Congress*. Rev. ed. Washington, D.C.: Library of Congress, 1988. A brief treatment of the history, collections, and services of the Library of Congress.

_____. *The Library of Congress*. Boulder, Colo.: Westview Press, 1982. Comprehensive treatment of the history, organization, and functions of the Library of Congress.

Johnston, William D. *History of the Library of Congress*. Washington, D.C.: Government Printing Office, 1904. The first of an unfinished two-volume set that covers the history of the library from 1800 until 1864.

Thorin, Suzanne E., ed. *Automation at the Library of Congress: Inside Views*. Washington, D.C.: Library of Congress Professional Association, 1986. Describes the development of automation within the Library of Congress.

SEE ALSO: 1846, Smithsonian Institution Is Founded.

1898 ■ UNITED STATES V. WONG KIM ARK: the U.S. Supreme Court holds that children born in the United States, even to temporary sojourners, are subject to U.S. jurisdiction regardless of race or nationality

DATE: March 28, 1898

LOCALE: Washington, D.C.

CATEGORIES: Asian American history; Civil rights; Court cases; Immigration

KEY FIGURES:

Melville W. Fuller (1833-1910), chief justice of the United States

Horace Gray (1828-1902), associate justice in the Supreme Court

John Marshall Harlan (1833-1911), associate justice in the Supreme Court

Wong Kim Ark (born 1873), man born in San Francisco of Chinese parents

SUMMARY OF EVENT. After the Civil War, the Constitution of the United States was amended in order to deal with the end of slavery and the legal status of the freed slaves. Under existing law, notably the 1857 *Dred Scott* case (*Dred Scott v. Sandford*), even free African Americans could not become citizens. The Thirteenth Amendment ended slavery. The Fourteenth Amendment, which was drafted to confer citizenship on the newly freed slaves and to protect their rights from infringement by state governments, begins: "All persons born or naturalized in the United States and subject to the jurisdiction thereof, are citizens of the United States and of the State wherein they reside."

The Fourteenth Amendment, of course, ended neither racial prejudice nor various racially based legal discriminations. In 1882, 1884, and 1894, Congress passed a series of laws known as the Chinese Exclusion Acts. These statutes were designed to keep persons of Chinese ancestry out of the United States. They were particularly aimed at the importation of Chinese laborers and at the "coolie" system—a form of indentured labor. The acceptance of low wages by imported Chinese immigrants angered many Americans.

Wong Kim Ark was born in San Francisco in 1873. His parents were Chinese subjects permanently domiciled in the United States. In modern terminology, they would have been called "resident aliens." They had been in business in San Francisco and were neither employees nor diplomatic agents of the government of China. In 1890 they returned to China after many years in the United States. Wong Kim Ark also went to China in 1890, but he returned to the United States the same year and was readmitted to the country on the grounds that he was a U.S. citizen. In 1894 he again went to China for a temporary visit but was denied readmission to the United States on his return in August, 1895. The government's position was that under the Chinese Exclusion Acts, a Chinese born to alien parents who had not renounced his previous nationality was not "born or naturalized in the United States" within the meaning of the citizenship clause of the Fourteenth Amendment. If the government's position was correct, Wong Kim Ark was not a citizen of the United States and was not entitled to readmission to the country. Wong brought a habeas corpus action against the government in the United States District Court for the Northern District of California. That court's judgment in favor of Wong was appealed to the United States Supreme Court by the government.

Justice Horace Gray wrote the Supreme Court's opinion for a 6-to-2 majority. Gray's argument begins with the assumption that the citizenship clause of the Fourteenth Amendment has to be read in the context of preexisting law. The Court's opinion begins with a long review of citizenship practices and legal customs. The U.S. tradition had been to distinguish between "natural-born" and naturalized citizens. This distinction came from English common law. In England, for hundreds of years prior to the American Revolution, all persons born within the king's realms except the children of diplomats and alien enemies were said to have been born under the king's protection and were natural-born subjects. This rule was applied or extended equally to the children of alien parents. Moreover, the same rule was in force in all the English colonies in North America prior to the revolution, and was continued (except with regard to slaves) under the jurisdiction of the United States when it became independent. The first American law concerning naturalization was passed in the First Congress. It, and its successor acts, passed in 1802, assumed the citizenship of all free persons born within the borders of the United States. It was not until the passage of the Chinese Exclusion Acts that any U.S. law had sought to alter the rule regarding natural-born citizens.

On the European continent, however, the law of citizenship was different. Most other European countries had adopted the citizenship rules of ancient Roman law. Under the Roman civil law, a child takes the nationality of his or her parents. Indeed, when *United States v. Wong Kim Ark* reached the Supreme Court, the government argued that the European practice had become the true rule of international law as it was recognized by the great majority of the countries of the world.

This was the historical and legal context for the Fourteenth Amendment's language "All persons *born* or naturalized in the United States. . . ." According to Justice Gray, the purpose of the Fourteenth Amendment was to extend the rule providing citizenship for natural-born persons to the freed slaves and their children. The amendment did not establish a congressional power to alter the constitutional grant of citizenship. Gray's opinion reviews many of the Court's prior opinions upholding the principle. The Chinese Exclusion Acts, passed after the passage of the Fourteenth Amendment, could not affect the amendment's meaning, according to the majority, and therefore did not affect the established rule of natural-born citizenship. The grant of constitutional power to Congress to "establish a uniform rule of naturalization" did not validate the Chinese Exclusion Acts. Wong, as a natural-born citizen, had no need of being naturalized. The Court held that "Every person born in the United States and subject to the jurisdiction thereof, becomes at once a citizen of the United States, and needs no naturalization." Moreover, the majority held that Congress' power of naturalization is "a power to confer citizenship, not to take it away." In other words, Congress had the power to establish uniform rules for naturalization but could not alter the plain-language and common-law meaning of the Fourteenth Amendment's citizenship clause.

The dissenting justices saw the case differently. Chief Justice Melville Fuller wrote an extensive dissent in which Justice John Marshall Harlan joined. In their view, the common-law rule sprang from the feudal relationship between the British crown and children born within the realm. American law was not bound to follow the common-law rule because there were differences between "citizens" and "subjects." In a republic such as the United States, citizenship was a status created by and conferred by the civil law. Because nothing in U.S. law had explicitly endorsed the common-law principle of citizenship, the Fourteenth Amendment did not have to be read so as to include it. Fuller argued that Congress is free to pass statutes that define and interpret the citizenship clause of the Fourteenth Amendment. In the dissenters' view, then, the Chinese Exclusion Acts could constitutionally limit the reach of the phrase "born or naturalized in the United States and subject to the jurisdiction thereof." Under this interpretation, Wong Kim Ark would not have been a citizen and his exclusion would have been constitutional. The Court's decision in this case was important because it stripped the government of the power to deny the citizenship of persons born in the United States of alien parents.

—*Robert Jacobs*

ADDITIONAL READING:

Chan, Sucheng. *Entry Denied: Exclusion and the Chinese Community in America, 1882-1943*. Philadelphia: Temple University Press, 1991. Good discussion of the effects and technical aspects of the Chinese Exclusion Acts.

Corwin, Edward S. *The Constitution of the United States of America: Analysis and Interpretation*. Washington, D.C.: Government Printing Office, 1953. Corwin's monumental compilation of constitutional lore is especially strong on issues such as citizenship, whose fundamental rules date back to the nineteenth century.

Franklin, Frank George. *The Legislative History of Naturalization in the United States: From the Revolutionary War to 1861*. Chicago: University of Chicago Press, 1906. Discussion of naturalization and citizenship precedents of early U.S. history.

McKenzie, Roderick Duncan. *Oriental Exclusion: The Effect of American Immigration Laws, Regulations, and Judicial Decisions upon the Chinese and Japanese on the American Pacific Coast, 1885-1940*. New York: J. S. Ozer, 1971. Discusses the human aspect of the Chinese exclusion laws.

White, Sherwin. *The Roman Citizenship*. London: Oxford University Press, 1973. Complete discussion of the origin of Roman citizenship, the means of acquiring it, and its duties, responsibilities, and privileges.

SEE ALSO: 1857, *Dred Scott v. Sandford*; 1865, Thirteenth Amendment; 1868, Fourteenth Amendment; 1882, Chinese Exclusion Act.

1898 ■ SPANISH-AMERICAN WAR: *the United States begins a colonial empire and becomes an international power*

DATE: April 24-December 10, 1898

LOCALE: Principally Cuba and adjacent waters, and the Philippines

CATEGORIES: Expansion and land acquisitions; Latino American history; Wars, uprisings, and civil unrest

KEY FIGURES:

Pasqual Cervera y Topete (1839-1909), commander of the Spanish fleet sent to the Caribbean

George Dewey (1837-1917), commander of the U.S. Asiatic Squadron

William McKinley (1843-1901), twenty-fifth president of the United States, 1897-1901

Theodore Roosevelt (1858-1919), assistant secretary of the Navy, later a popular war hero

William Thomas Sampson (1840-1902), commander of the U.S. Atlantic Squadron

William Rufus Shafter (1835-1906), commander of the U.S. Expeditionary Force to Cuba

SUMMARY OF EVENT. The United States entered the Spanish-American War to liberate its Cuban neighbors from foreign rule. It emerged from the conflict in possession of a distant Philippine empire whose inhabitants rebelled against U.S. dominance. The war with Spain marked a significant turning point in U.S. history. Acquisition of an overseas empire made

The Rough Riders, a regiment that supplemented the regulars of the U.S. Army during the Spanish-American War, at San Juan Hill. Second-in-command Theodore Roosevelt, the future U.S. president, stands center, hands on hips. (Library of Congress)

the United States a major power on the world stage. Within a few years, however, the people of the United States decided that the expansion achieved during 1898-1899 should not be extended. Disillusionment about the results of imperialism characterized historical memories of the conflict with Spain.

Cuba became an issue for the United States after Cuba's residents staged a revolution against Spain in 1895. The Spanish regarded Cuba as an integral part of their nation. It was "the ever faithful isle," and no Spanish government could long remain in power if it accepted the loss of Cuba without a military struggle. A bitter war ensued, in which the Spanish controlled major cities such as Havana, while the rebels dominated the countryside. In 1896, the Spanish captain general in Cuba, Valeriano Weyler, announced a tough policy of reconcentration. Cuban civilians in certain parts of the island were to be herded into the Spanish-held towns, where they could no longer assist and supply the rebel armies. Thousands of

women and children died of disease or malnutrition in these overcrowded camps. U.S. opinion, already sympathetic to the Cubans, was outraged. Popular newspapers in the United States published sensational stories about Cuban suffering and Spanish brutalities that fed discontent with the rule of Madrid.

President Grover Cleveland, who occupied the White House during the first two years of the Cuban rebellion, took the position that Spain deserved the chance to defeat the rebellion. He resisted pressure from Congress to intervene in the Caribbean. By the time that Cleveland left office in March, 1897, his policy had failed to persuade the Spanish of the need to negotiate with the rebels, and he had lost the trust of the U.S. people over foreign policy.

His successor, William McKinley, came into office with two main reactions to the fighting. First, Spain could try to repress the rebellion, but it had only a limited time to do so. Second, any outcome of the war must be acceptable to the

Cuban rebels. The latter condition ensured eventual fighting between the United States and Spain, because the rebels would accept nothing less than Cuban independence. McKinley played for time, hoping that the Spanish could be persuaded to leave Cuba. The Spanish stalled on their side, expecting U.S. resolve to falter.

Spanish efforts to conciliate the United States included a modification of the reconcentration policy in November, 1897, and limited autonomy for Cuba. Spain retained control over Cuba's international relations. These steps did not resolve the issues between the United States and Spain. Early in 1898, two events pushed the nations toward war. In February, the Cubans published a private letter from the Spanish minister in Washington, Enrique Dupuy de Lôme, in which the diplomat made disparaging remarks about President McKinley; the letter also revealed that the Spanish were using delaying tactics. Dupuy de Lôme resigned in disgrace.

A week later, the United States battleship *Maine* exploded in Havana harbor. Two hundred sixty men of the United States Navy were killed. Modern scientific research has concluded that an internal cause produced the explosion. In 1898, however, many in the United States decided that Spain had either blown up the ship or failed to prevent its destruction. The episode put the two countries on a collision course toward war. As diplomatic negotiations proceeded, it became apparent that Spain would not grant Cuban independence. The most it would concede was to suspend hostilities, a proposal that neither Washington nor the Cuban rebels would accept.

On April 11, McKinley sent a message to Congress asking for the authority to intervene (April 20), and officials informed Spain that failing to grant independence to Cuba would result in the United States' putting the resolutions into effect. Spain broke relations with the United States, a U.S. blockade of Cuba ensued, and Spain declared war on April 24. The president had resisted the popular pressure for war until it became clear that Spain would not yield. After Congress passed resolutions to grant the president the right to intervene, Spain declared war and Congress followed suit. The war came about because both nations saw no way out of the diplomatic impasse other than armed conflict. In the United States, the war was very popular. Volunteers jammed army and navy recruiting offices.

The first U.S. victory came on May 1, 1898, when Commodore George Dewey and the U.S. Asiatic Squadron defeated the Spanish fleet at Manila Bay in the Philippines. The navy attacked the Philippines as part of a long-standing war plan to induce the Spanish to negotiate an end to the war by threatening their possession in Asia. The victory presented Washington with a new challenge of what to do with this unexpected territorial opportunity. The McKinley Administration sent reinforcements to Manila and kept its options open about taking all the islands in a peace settlement.

During June and July, the main focus of military and public attention was on Cuba and the sea and land battles that occurred in the Caribbean. Initial plans for army action in Cuba called for a large-scale landing near Havana during the autumn of 1898. In June, the White House decided to dispatch an expeditionary force of seventeen thousand men to the southeastern Cuban coast. There, in the harbor of the city of Santiago de Cuba, Admiral Pasqual Cervera y Topete's decrepit Spanish fleet had taken refuge. The U.S. Atlantic Squadron, commanded by Admiral William T. Sampson, was stationed outside Santiago ready to do battle if Cervera ventured forth. The revised U.S. strategy called for the capture of Santiago by land invasion, which would force the Spanish fleet to steam out to virtually certain destruction.

Near Tampa Bay in Florida, the bulk of the regular army, under the command of General William R. Shafter, prepared to leave for Cuba. Along with the regulars was the Rough Rider volunteer regiment, of which Lieutenant Colonel Theodore Roosevelt was second in command. Shafter's landing along the coast near Santiago was accomplished late in June. Despite logistical difficulties, the U.S. forces moved forward to engage the Spanish on July 1 near Santiago at the twin battles of El Caney and San Juan Hill. Both battles were U.S. victories. Shafter's troops subsequently occupied the strategic heights above the port city. On July 3, Admiral Cervera, on orders from Madrid, headed out of Santiago harbor and vainly tried to evade the U.S. fleet. By the end of the day, all Spanish ships had been sunk or beached.

Following Cervera's defeat, the end of the war came swiftly. On July 17, after lengthy negotiations, the Spanish soldiers in Santiago surrendered. Puerto Rico was occupied almost without resistance later that month. The Spanish had asked Washington to discuss an end to hostilities during July, which culminated in an armistice on August 12. A peace commission from the United States, led by former Secretary of State William R. Day, met with Spanish envoys in Paris in October to arrange peace terms. The Treaty of Paris, signed on December 10, 1898, recognized Cuban independence and ceded Puerto Rico, Guam, and the Philippines to the United States. By way of partial compensation, the United States paid Spain twenty million dollars.

The war revealed inadequacies in the army's ability to mobilize to meet a foreign policy crisis. The resulting outcry over shortages and inefficiencies focused the blame on Secretary of War Russell A. Alger. President McKinley appointed a commission to probe these problems, and out of these deliberations came later military reforms. For the most part, the armed forces performed well under McKinley's leadership. Following the signing of the peace treaty, a bitter struggle over ratification took place in the United States. McKinley effectively mobilized public opinion to secure approval. The outcome of the war left the United States with an overseas empire and new world responsibilities.   —*Lewis L. Gould, based on the original entry by William I. Hair*

ADDITIONAL READING:

Gould, Lewis L. *The Spanish-American War and President McKinley.* Lawrence: University Press of Kansas, 1982. A brief survey of the major developments of the war that emphasizes the extent to which McKinley's leadership produced victory for the United States.

Morgan, H. Wayne. *America's Road to Empire: The War with Spain and Overseas Expansion*. New York: John Wiley & Sons, 1965. Offers a vigorous defense of McKinley's policies in 1898; provides a clear, concise statement of the origins and consequences of the war.

Offner, John L. *An Unwanted War: The Diplomacy of the United States and Spain over Cuba, 1895-1898*. Chapel Hill: University of North Carolina Press, 1992. Makes effective use of the archives of the United States, Spain, and other nations to provide a thorough analysis of how the war came about.

Smith, Joseph. *The Spanish-American War: Conflict in the Caribbean and the Pacific, 1895-1902*. New York: Longman, 1994. Surveys the background, causes, and events of the war, with an emphasis on the military history of the conflict. Excellent bibliography.

Trask, David F. *The War with Spain in 1898*. New York: Macmillan, 1981. The best one-volume treatment of the war and its military impact.

SEE ALSO: 1895, Hearst-Pulitzer Circulation War; 1899, Philippine Insurrection; 1899, Hay's "Open Door Notes"; 1900, Suppression of Yellow Fever; 1901, Insular Cases; 1901, Theodore Roosevelt Becomes President; 1903, Platt Amendment; 1909, Dollar Diplomacy.

1899 ■ PHILIPPINE INSURRECTION: *early U.S. attempts at colonial administration mark the tenuous beginnings of U.S.-Philippine relations*

DATE: February 4, 1899-July 4, 1902
LOCALE: Philippine Islands
CATEGORIES: Asian American history; Expansion and land acquisition; Wars, uprisings, and civil unrest
KEY FIGURES:
Emilio Aguinaldo (1869-1964), principal leader of the Filipino guerrilla forces
George Dewey (1837-1917), commander of the U.S. Navy's Asiatic Squadron and victor at the Battle of Manila Bay
Frederick Funston (1865-1917), captor of Emilio Aguinaldo
Apolinario Mabini (1864-1903), intellectual leader of the Filipino independence movement
William McKinley (1843-1901), twenty-fifth president of the United States, 1897-1901
William Howard Taft (1857-1930), first civilian governor of the Philippines
SUMMARY OF EVENT. The Philippine Insurrection, known as the War of Independence by Filipinos, is an early example of a country's resisting the United States' rise as an imperial power. It resulted from misunderstanding and indecision on both sides. U.S. and Filipino forces, which had worked together to

end Spanish control of the Philippines, found themselves fighting as enemies in a long, brutal struggle for domination of the Philippine Islands.

United States involvement in the Philippines began during the Spanish-American War of 1898. U.S. naval strategists already had a plan for attacking the Spanish fleet at Manila Bay in the event of war with Spain. As relations between the United States and Spain worsened in 1897, Commodore George Dewey, commander of the United States Navy's Asiatic Squadron, was ordered to move his fleet to Hong Kong, with instructions to attack Manila Bay in case of war. War was declared on April 24, 1898. On the morning of May 1, Dewey's fleet steamed into Manila Bay. By noon, his ships had sunk or disabled every Spanish ship.

Washington was slow to react to the victorious news. The quick defeat of the Spanish fleet was unexpected, and President William McKinley had not planned what to do with the Philippines once the war was ended. McKinley considered either taking the entire archipelago, establishing a naval base, or returning the islands to Spain. Complete independence for the islands was never seriously considered. While McKinley contemplated the fate of the Philippines, relations between the U.S. military occupation force at Manila Bay and the Filipino population deteriorated. At first, the Filipinos welcomed Dewey's forces as liberators. The Filipinos soon realized that the Americans intended to control the islands at least until the end of the war, perhaps longer. In early May, McKinley dispatched an expeditionary force, under the command of General Arthur MacArthur, to Manila Bay. MacArthur arrived just in time to accept the Spanish garrison's surrender at the end of the war, an honor Filipino forces had assumed would be theirs.

Filipino insurgents had been fighting the Spanish since early 1896. Spanish efforts to destroy the infant revolution had failed, as rebel leaders fled to the jungled hills of the islands to hide out and organize bases for guerrilla warfare against the Spanish. In 1897, both sides, weary of the increasingly bloody war, agreed to a cease-fire to discuss peace. The Spanish authorities refused to consider independence, forcing the Filipino insurgents to continue their rebellion. Under the military leadership of Emilio Aguinaldo and the intellectual direction of Apolinario Mabini, rebel leaders established a base of operations at Hong Kong, where they could easily purchase supplies and arms. It was at this time that the Spanish-American War began, bringing an unexpected opportunity for the rebels.

Filipino leaders first believed that the United States would assist them in expelling the Spanish and establishing an independent Philippine state. Aguinaldo accepted anticolonial statements by U.S. consular officers at face value. The Filipinos soon found, however, that Dewey was more cautious, speaking only of military cooperation to defeat Spain and saying nothing of independence. Aguinaldo organized an army of thirty thousand men and won notable victories; nevertheless, the United States held supreme authority, accepting the surrender of Manila Bay and refusing to allow Filipino forces into the city without permission. When the Spanish flag came down, the Stars and Stripes, not the Filipino revolutionary flag, replaced it.

Faced with the realization that the United States was going to annex the islands, Aguinaldo moved to organize a new government. On June 12, 1898, he proclaimed independence for the Philippines. In September, a constituent assembly was convened, and on November 29, a constitution was adopted. The United States largely ignored this move toward independence. The McKinley Administration, mainly because of racial prejudice, arbitrarily decided that the Filipinos were not ready for self-government. In addition, there was a fear that an independent Philippines might fall easy prey to an ambitious European power, such as Germany or Great Britain. Therefore, the United States proceeded to obtain full control by a provision for annexation of the Philippines in the peace treaty ending the war with Spain.

While the United States Senate debated ratification of the peace treaty, a series of clashes between U.S. and Filipino forces beginning on February 4, 1899, soon escalated into large-scale fighting. The Philippine Insurrection against U.S. rule had begun. The United States, because of its decision to assume responsibility for "civilizing" the Filipinos, was forced to wage a bitter war, which would cost much more money and take many more human lives than the war with Spain.

The Philippine Insurrection was, in many ways, a prototype of modern guerrilla warfare. Filipino revolutionary leaders quickly lost the support of conservative Filipinos who accepted U.S. rule. As a result, Aguinaldo and his forces retreated to fight the U.S. troops in the jungles, as they had done earlier against Spanish forces. In early 1899, United States forces moved into central Luzon, where they captured and burned Malolos, the rebel capital. Rebel forces, however, escaped into the hills, where they were supplied by sympathetic villagers until spring rains forced U.S. troops to withdraw.

U.S. troops guard captured Filipino revolutionaries at the "Walled City" in the Philippines c. 1899. After the U.S. victory in the Spanish-American War of 1898, anticolonial forces in the Philippines believed that the United States would help them achieve independence, but instead the United States annexed the islands, sparking clashes between U.S. and Filipino forces. (Library of Congress)

U.S. commanders finally admitted that Aguinaldo had extensive popular support and that total war was necessary to pacify the islands. Washington responded by sending reinforcements, bringing the number of U.S. troops in the Philippines to seventy-four thousand. As the scale of the fighting rose, vicious tactics and brutality on both sides also increased. Both sides committed atrocities involving soldiers and civilians. U.S. forces systematically burned villages and took hostages in an effort to deny popular assistance to rebel forces. Gradually, the overwhelming strength of the United States prevailed, as U.S. forces took rebel strongholds in the hills and rural regions. By 1901, 639 U.S. garrisons dotted the islands, breaking Filipino resistance.

The insurrection finally collapsed with Aguinaldo's capture in March, 1901. He was seized by Colonel Frederick Funston and three other U.S. officers pretending to be the prisoners of a group of Filipino defectors, who led the officers directly to Aguinaldo's headquarters in northeastern Luzon. After his capture, Aguinaldo reluctantly took an oath of allegiance to the United States. By July 4, 1901, civil government, under United States auspices, was instituted everywhere in the Philippines, except in southern Mindanao and the Sulu Islands, where Moro tribesmen continued resistance.

On July 4, 1902, the Philippine Insurrection was formally declared over. The United States issued a proclamation of general peace and amnesty. As a result of the struggle, the United States suffered forty-two hundred dead and twenty-eight hundred wounded. While close to twenty thousand rebels were killed in the war, another two hundred thousand Filipinos died from disease, famine, and other war-related causes.

William Howard Taft served as the first U.S. governor of the Philippines. Taft continued to be heavily involved in the administration of the islands as secretary of war and president of the United States. It was Taft who coined the phrase "little brown brothers," which referred to his hope that the United States could somehow "Americanize" these native peoples. This phrase remained a strong racial force in U.S. relations with the states in the Pacific and Latin America. The Philippine Islands remained under U.S. jurisdiction until 1934, when Congress passed the Tydings-McDuffie Act, granting independence to the Philippines. World War II delayed complete independence for the islands until 1946.

—*Theodore A. Wilson, updated by William Allison*

ADDITIONAL READING:

Brands, H. W. *Bound to Empire: The United States and the Philippines.* New York: Oxford University Press, 1992. This expansive history emphasizes the interaction of cultural forces in United States-Philippine relations and traces the development of the Philippine independence movement.

Dobson, John. *Reticent Expansionism: The Foreign Policy of William McKinley.* Pittsburgh: Duquesne University Press, 1988. One of a few works completely devoted to McKinley's foreign policy, which Dobson characterizes as ambiguous, indecisive, and reactive.

Karnov, Stanley. *In Our Image: America's Empire in the Philippines.* New York: Random House, 1989. Argues that the United States was inept and ineffective in dealing with the Philippine Insurrection and its aftermath.

Miller, Stuart Creighton. *"Benevolent Assimilation": The American Conquest of the Philippines, 1899-1903.* New Haven, Conn.: Yale University Press, 1982. A study of the war in the Philippines and its consequences, including the atrocities committed by the United States Army.

Salamanca, Bonifacio S. *The Filipino Reaction to American Rule, 1901-1913.* Quezon City, Philippines: New Day Publishers, 1984. A Filipino historian's harsh criticism of U.S. policy in the Philippines during the insurrection and the following years of U.S. rule.

SEE ALSO: 1898, Spanish-American War; 1899, Philippine Insurrection; 1899, Hay's "Open Door Notes"; 1901, Insular Cases; 1901, Theodore Roosevelt Becomes President; 1903, Platt Amendment; 1909, Dollar Diplomacy; 1934, Tydings-McDuffie Act.

1899 ■ HAY'S "OPEN DOOR NOTES": *articulation of a policy of free trade between China and all nations, with respect for China's territorial integrity*

DATE: September 6, 1899-January 13, 1905
LOCALE: Washington, D.C.
CATEGORIES: Asian American history; Diplomacy and international relations
KEY FIGURES:
Edwin Hurd Conger (1843-1907), U.S. minister to Peking in 1890
John Milton Hay (1838-1905), secretary of state, 1898-1905
Alfred E. Hippisley, Rockhill's friend, an officer in the Chinese Imperial Maritime Customs Service
William McKinley (1843-1901), twenty-fifth president of the United States, 1897-1901
John Bassett Moore (1860-1947), assistant secretary of state, who urged Hay to dispatch the second of the Open Door Notes
William Woodville Rockhill (1854-1914), Hay's adviser on China, who drafted the first of the Open Door Notes

SUMMARY OF EVENT. John Hay's Open Door Notes are a milestone in the articulation of United States foreign policy in Asia at the turn of the twentieth century. They were circulated to address specific events; however, their cumulative and long-term implications make them critical to understanding the evolution of the United States as a world power.

By 1890, the U.S. frontier had been declared closed, but Americans were still conditioned to expand. Capital needed sources of investment. Industry required markets. The national ego, convinced that the United States had become a world power, sought an arena in which to assert itself. Mission boards were anxious to save new souls. Righteous individuals were eager to shoulder the "white man's burden" and "civilize backward peoples." More reflective persons blamed economic slumps and social ills on overproduction and desired wider markets to solve the problems of overproduction and society at the same time. For these and other reasons, some people in the United States became increasingly interested in China as a possible target for continued expansion.

At the conclusion of the Spanish-American War, a significant expansionist exercise in itself, the McKinley Administration had gained possession of the Pacific islands of Wake, Guam, and the Philippines. The United States began to realize that it not only had a new political interest in Asian developments but also had the requisite coaling stations to give it a commercial interest in the fabled China market.

For some years, Great Britain had dominated the China market, conducting about 80 percent of China's foreign trade. In part because they could afford to do so, the British had pursued a policy of "open door," or free trade, in China. During the 1880's and 1890's, other European nations began to challenge Great Britain's market hegemony and its open door. Germany, France, Japan, and Russia began carving out individual spheres of influence, in which theirs was the only foreign trade permitted. The Chinese people and government remained essentially passive to this exploitation. Great Britain resented it and officially reasserted the open door. Unofficially, the British realized that despite their reassertions, doors were being closed in China.

The British began to seek allies who would be willing to support the open door. In March, 1898, Great Britain's foreign secretary sent a secret message to President William McKinley, asking if the United States were interested in concerted action to support free trade in China. At that time, the United States was occupied in the Spanish-American War, and Secretary of State John Sherman's answer was a firm no. The British continued to pay lip service to the open door in 1898 and 1899 but quietly began to create a sphere of influence of their own. Great Britain leased Kowloon, directly opposite Hong Kong, and eyed the Yangtze Valley as a source of exclusive markets.

At the time of the British overture to the United States concerning the open door in China, John M. Hay was the United States ambassador in London. Hay regretted his government's refusal to support the British. In 1899, Hay, now secretary of state, determined to render at least tardy support to the open door. Hay brought W. W. Rockhill, who was familiar with China, to Washington to advise him, and the two awaited an opportunity to make some U.S. commitment in China. In the summer of 1899, Alfred E. Hippisley—a friend of Rockhill and an official of the Chinese Imperial Maritime Customs Service—visited Washington, D.C. Hippisley resented spheres of influence, especially British activities at Kowloon. Hippisley suggested to Rockhill that a U.S. policy statement on an open door might help. Rockhill had little difficulty convincing Hay, and Hay convinced McKinley.

On September 6, 1899, Hay dispatched a series of notes, drafted by Rockhill, to Great Britain, Germany, and Russia, and shortly thereafter to France, Italy, and Japan. These notes asked the governments of these six nations to agree to three principles: Each nation with a sphere of influence was to respect the rights and privileges of other nations in its sphere; Chinese officials were to continue to collect tariff duties in all spheres; and within its sphere, no nation would discriminate against other nations in levying harbor dues and railroad rates. The responses to Hay's Open Door Notes were qualified and evasive. Nevertheless, the secretary of state announced that the China powers had acceded to the U.S. policy.

This high-level commercial diplomacy presupposed that the Chinese would remain passive, but they did not. In the spring of 1900, China exploded in the Boxer Rebellion against the intrusion of Western "barbarians." The United States joined the European powers in dispatching troops to quell the unrest, and on July 3, 1900, Hay sent his second Open Door Notes. On the advice of Assistant Secretary of State John Bassett Moore, Hay put the United States on record as favoring the maintenance of stability in China, Chinese territorial integrity, and the open door in all parts of China. The second of the notes, actually a diplomatic circular to U.S. diplomats in major foreign capitals, articulated U.S. policy and did not require agreement from the other European nations affected by the action of the Boxers. It was a stronger and more broad-based expression of Hay's position on Chinese territorial integrity and the rule of international law. Hay further confirmed his position during the Boxer attack on foreign legations in Peking, giving explicit instructions to Edwin Conger, his minister in Peking.

People in the United States, then and after, believed that their government had made a stand against the rapacious European powers and Japan in China. Reality was not quite so simple, and was more practical than high-minded. China was not a party to the U.S. action. China never chose the open door. Moreover, indemnities levied by all the powers over the Boxer Rebellion forced China to borrow money from these same powers, further restricting its independence. The Russians used the situation both to withdraw from Peking and to solidify their control over Manchuria. The third of Hay's notes, his final statement on the Open Door Policy of the United States, was sent during the Russo-Japanese War and as a result of a German request that the warring nations respect China's territorial integrity.

The United States, intentionally or otherwise, took advantage of the modified open door to exploit the China market. Later, the United States used Japan as a nominal ally to pursue power diplomacy in China. In a sense, the United States had taken a stand against European colonialism in order to seize a portion of the European market in China.

—*Emory M. Thomas, updated by Ann Thompson*

ADDITIONAL READING:

Clymer, Kenton J. *John Hay: The Gentleman as Diplomat.* Ann Arbor: University of Michigan Press, 1975. Studies Hay's diplomatic thinking. Chapter 4 gives a complete yet succinct description of Hay's views and actions regarding China.

Dennett, Tyler. *John Hay: From Poetry to Politics*. New York: Dodd, Mead, 1934. Awarded the Pulitzer Prize in biography in 1934, this work is still considered the most thorough biography of John Hay. Chapters 24 and 25 discuss the Open Door Notes.

Dobson, John M. *America's Ascent: The United States Becomes a Great Power, 1880-1914*. DeKalb: Northern Illinois University Press, 1978. Places late nineteenth and early twentieth century Far Eastern policy, including the Open Door Notes, in context with other diplomatic actions of the United States.

Esherick, Joseph W. *The Origins of the Boxer Uprising*. Berkeley: University of California Press, 1987. Focuses on internal Chinese affairs and the Chinese government before and during the Boxer Uprising. U.S. policy on the uprising is stated in the second of Hay's notes.

Kennan, George F. *American Diplomacy*. Expanded ed. Chicago: University of Chicago Press, 1984. Contains a section on Alfred E. Hippisley, a major player in the drafting of the first Open Door Notes.

Kushmer, Howard I., and Anne Hummel Sherrill. *John Milton Hay: Union of Poetry and Politics*. Boston: Twayne, 1977. Chapter 6 provides comprehensive discussion of the Open Door Notes in the context of the economic and diplomatic environment within the United States and with other world powers.

Varg, Paul A. *Open Door Diplomat: The Life of W. W. Rockhill*. 1952. Reprint. Westport, Conn.: Greenwood Press, 1974. Covers the role of William Woodville Rockhill in the preparation of the Open Door Notes.

SEE ALSO: 1898, Spanish-American War; 1901, Insular Cases; 1909, Dollar Diplomacy.

1900 ■ SUPPRESSION OF YELLOW FEVER:
discovery that the disease is transmitted by mosquito is the key to sanitation and eradication

DATE: 1900-1904
LOCALE: Cuba and Panama
CATEGORY: Health and medicine
KEY FIGURES:
Carlos Juan Finlay (1833-1915), Cuban physician and biologist
William Crawford Gorgas (1854-1920), surgeon in the U.S. Army Medical Corps
Walter Reed (1851-1902), head of the Yellow Fever Commission

SUMMARY OF EVENT. For more than two hundred years, yellow fever, originating in tropical America, had devastated the Atlantic and Gulf coasts of the United States. In the epidemic of 1878, more than four thousand people died of yellow fever

in New Orleans alone. In 1898, after the Spaniards had lost the Spanish-American War and left Cuba, the United States adopted the objective of eradicating yellow fever from the island. Because physicians in the United States suspected that the fever was caused by unsanitary conditions in Cuba, initial efforts consisted of large-scale cleanup operations.

This task was assigned to Major William Crawford Gorgas, a surgeon attached to the U.S. Army of Occupation. Conditions in Cuba, especially in Havana, the country's largest city, had worsened as a result of the insurrection and the war against the Spaniards. Gorgas, convinced that unsanitary conditions were responsible for the prevalence of yellow fever, set about his work with remarkable energy. By 1899, Havana, he asserted, was probably the cleanest city in the world. The hypothesis that cleanliness would eliminate yellow fever seemed briefly confirmed: During the first six months of the year, only seven deaths in the city were attributed to yellow fever.

In August, 1899, Spanish immigrants arrived in great numbers, and yellow fever again appeared in an epidemic of catastrophic proportions. It became apparent that the low incidence of the disease in the preceding months had not been due to the sanitary conditions introduced by Gorgas but to the lack of nonimmunes (persons who had not developed an immunity to the disease).

By June, 1900, the surgeon general of the United States, George M. Sternberg, appointed a Yellow Fever Commission consisting of four medical doctors: Walter Reed, a major in the United States Army Medical Corps and head of the commission; James Carroll and Jesse W. Lazear of the United States; and Aristides Agramonte of Cuba.

After the commission arrived in Cuba, its members met with Carlos Juan Finlay, a Cuban physician and biologist serving with Major Gorgas on a special commission to diagnose suspected cases of yellow fever. To Finlay, there was no question about the mechanism of contagion of yellow fever. In 1881, he had announced to a medical congress in Washington, D.C., his conviction that the disease was transmitted by a mosquito then called *Stegomyia calopus* and later *Stegomyia fasciata,* now known as *Aedes aegypti.*

Finlay's announcement had been received with skepticism. The concept of an insect serving as a carrier, or vector, of disease was not widely understood, and Finlay had not shown consistent development of yellow fever in volunteers who had been bitten by mosquitoes that had previously bitten victims of yellow fever. Despite years of experimentation, his strongest arguments remained the correlation of yellow fever cases with the range where this mosquito thrived, and certain characteristics of the disease that suggested transmission by injection.

Reed soon became acquainted with Henry Rose Carter, another physician who was studying how yellow fever was spread. In 1898, while an inspector for the Public Health Service, Carter had investigated a yellow fever epidemic in Taylor and Orwood, Mississippi. He had observed that those who visited the house of a person stricken with yellow fever during the first ten to twelve days of the illness seldom contracted the disease, but a large percentage of visitors who came after this period—even if the patient had died and the body had been removed—were stricken.

Carter presented his findings to Reed, who reasoned that this suggested that an insect carried the disease. The health community was just becoming aware of Theobald Smith's discoveries concerning ticks spreading Texas fever and of investigators who had proved that malaria was transmitted by a mosquito species. This gave a new legitimacy to the concept of insect transmission of a disease, and the commission decided to undertake a serious investigation of Finlay's theory.

Stegomyia mosquitoes provided by Finlay were used in the experiments. The mosquitoes were first fed on patients infected with yellow fever and then fed on healthy volunteers taken from among U.S. soldiers and Spanish immigrants. Careful records were kept of the progress of the disease in the

Physician and surgeon Walter Reed headed a commission to determine the cause and mode of transmission of yellow fever. The discovery that it was a mosquito-borne disease paved the way for its suppression by means of insect control. (Library of Congress)

patients and volunteers. After many failures and Lazear's death from the disease, the researchers discovered the disease was infectious only during the first three days of illness. Armed with this information and the knowledge that ten to twelve days must elapse before the disease could be contracted by a second person, the researchers were able to produce yellow fever in nonimmunes at will.

Once it was established that the disease was transmitted by the *Stegomyia* mosquito, the work of eradicating the plague reverted to Gorgas, who eventually decided to do away with the mosquito itself. Gorgas operated under the authority of the U.S. army and had the cooperation of the mayor of Havana, who declared it a crime for persons to allow mosquitoes to breed on their property. The main effort was a vigorous sanitary campaign engineered and supervised by Gorgas.

With military precision and scientific thoroughness, Gorgas devised a plan of attack based on the habits of the *Stegomyia* mosquito: destruction of its breeding grounds (which usually involved house-to-house searches for stagnant water and the imposition of fines on houses in which mosquito larvae were found), fumigations, division of the city into districts under Sanitary Department representatives, and quarantines imposed on the houses of people affected by yellow fever. Crews spread oil on standing water and cisterns to kill the mosquito larvae, inspected land, ordered standing water drained, stocked ponds with fish that ate mosquito larvae, and educated the public about the health hazards. Teams followed up on yellow fever victims, sealing rooms with paper strips, burning pyrethrum powder insecticide to kill the mosquitoes, and attracting mosquitoes to light to be killed directly. Neighbors within range of mosquitoes were watched for symptoms of yellow fever. These techniques were effective, and by the end of 1901, yellow fever ceased to be a serious problem in Cuba.

Gorgas' experience in Havana caused many public health officials in the United States to consider mosquito control not only for the control of yellow fever in the far South, but also for the control of malaria, another mosquito-borne disease. New Orleans, always facing a yellow fever threat, was the first to seize upon mosquito-control measures to curb the disease.

In 1904, Gorgas was ordered to Panama after the United States had acquired the rights to a canal through the isthmus, which officials of the French Panama Company had called "the white man's graveyard." It was yellow fever as much as corruption among the officials of the French-financed project that had thwarted the efforts of the company to build the canal.

In Panama, Gorgas had to battle not only the dreaded mosquito but also the opposition of the authorities in charge of the canal project. It took all Gorgas' persuasive abilities and the specter of an epidemic of catastrophic proportions to convince the canal builders that the eradication of yellow fever depended on the destruction of the *Stegomyia* mosquito. In 1914, the Panama Canal was opened for the first time to commercial transportation. This amazing engineering accomplishment was largely the result of Gorgas' perseverance and insistence on sanitary conditions.

The United States policy of establishing public health services and sanitary conditions in occupied countries continued. During the second occupation of the Dominican Republic, from 1916 to 1922, sanitary regulations were strictly enforced. During the occupation of Haiti in 1915, one of the first measures of the military government was to divide the country into sanitary districts, each in the charge of a public health officer. Such measures instituted in Veracruz in 1914 led to a sharp drop in the mortality rate of the Mexican population, and occupying forces remained free of tropical diseases and pestilences peculiar to the area.

These policies benefited all concerned. Effective pest control and hygienic procedures provided natives with far healthier living conditions and enabled other countries to engage in commercial and military relations within the sanitized areas without risking their own citizens' lives.

—Maurice T. Dominguez, updated by John Richard Schrock

ADDITIONAL READING:

Ellis, John H. *Yellow Fever and Public Health in the New South*. Lexington: University Press of Kentucky, 1992. Vividly describes the impact of yellow fever in the epidemic of 1878, including the formation of sanitary associations in New Orleans and other major Southern cities.

Finlay, Carlos E. *Carlos Finlay and Yellow Fever*. New York: Oxford University Press, 1940. An interesting account of Finlay's life and the development of his theory on the causes and prevention of yellow fever, from records translated by his son. The son's interpretations and the father's papers are interwoven in a harmonizing but distinguishable fashion.

Gibson, John M. *Physician to the World*. Durham, N.C.: Duke University Press, 1950. A useful biography of Major William Crawford Gorgas.

Greene, Emily, ed. *Occupied Haiti*. New York: Writers Publishing Company, 1927. A critical report of the U.S. occupation of Haiti, pointing out that the only aspect of the occupation that the Haitians did not resent was the accomplishment of the Service d'Hygiene.

Hanson, Earl P. *Transformation: The Story of Modern Puerto Rico*. New York: Simon & Schuster, 1955. A highly informative account of U.S. accomplishments in bringing Puerto Rico into the twentieth century, with some references to health and sanitary programs.

Humphreys, Margaret. *Yellow Fever and the South*. New Brunswick, N.J.: Rutgers University Press, 1992. This careful explanation of the history of yellow fever includes original data on the extent of early epidemics, the succession of discoveries, and the campaign waged following the fuller understanding of insect transmission after 1900.

Yellow Fever Studies. Public Health in America. New York: Arno Press, 1977. A collection of critical papers reflecting the major breakthroughs in yellow fever control.

SEE ALSO: 1898, Spanish-American War; 1952, Development of a Polio Vaccine; 1981, First AIDS Cases Are Reported.

1900 ■ TELETYPE IS DEVELOPED:
telegraphic transmission of recorded messages allows speedy communication of news and essential information

DATE: 1900-1925
LOCALE: United States and Europe
CATEGORIES: Canadian history; Communications; Science and technology
KEY FIGURES:
Jean-Maurice-Émile Baudot (1845-1903), French engineer and inventor of the five-pulse letter code
Kent Cooper (1880-1965), traffic manager and later general manager of the Associated Press news agency
Thomas Alva Edison (1847-1931), inventor of numerous devices, including the stock market "ticker," a form of teletype
Edward Ernest Kleinschmidt (1875-1940), developer of the teletype and the high-speed teletypewriter
Howard Lewis Krum (1883-1961), engineer who also was involved in developing the device
Joy Morton (1855-1961), financial backer of the Morkrum Company
Sterling Morton (1885-1961), Joy Morton's son and president of the Teletype Corporation

SUMMARY OF EVENT. The nineteenth century origins of the teletype, also known as the teletypewriter or occasionally the teleprinter, proved to be less important than its twentieth century technical development, which brought it into worldwide use. The device—a form of electric telegraph which it replaced in part—was the outcome of designs and the subject of patent claims on both sides of the Atlantic for many decades. It became identified as an instrument increasingly essential to business, government, and social communication. Although by the late twentieth century the teletype was rapidly being replaced in the newswire services by computerized satellite transmissions that relayed information directly to newsroom computers, the teletype continued to be in demand in areas in which the printed record of a message is also important.

As Samuel F. B. Morse conceived of the telegraph when he developed it in the middle of the nineteenth century, it would be a device that converted electric pulses coming in over the telegraph wire into written dots and dashes that a human operator could translate at leisure to letters and words. However, before the beginning of the twentieth century, the traffic volume of information being conveyed in pursuit of financial, commercial, administrative, governmental, news, social, and business affairs revived the need for both a practical machine to record incoming messages directly in letter form and a transmitting unit that would convert letters to electric pulses to be telegraphed. Although the need was recognized, a general solution was not immediately at hand.

Instead, there were alternative, partial solutions that subsequently would be brought together by 1914 to produce a practical message-sending-and-receiving system using teletypewriters. One of the first of these partial solutions was the duplex technique of transmitting two messages simultaneously, in opposite directions, over the same wire. First put into practice in the United States in 1872, it was followed in 1874 by inventor Thomas Edison's quadruplex system. In that same year in Europe, Jean-Maurice-Émile Baudot devised his five-pulse code, later modified by Donald Murray, which was used by Edison in his famous glass-domed stock market "ticker" that came into use in 1870, reporting stock market quotations in a coded pattern of punched holes in paper tape.

The five-pulse code could be structured into thirty-two different patterns, either by omitting one or more pulses in the sequence of the group of five generated within a fraction of a second or by reversing the polarity of one or more of the pulses. Twenty-six of these patterns were assigned to the alphabet, while the others were used for such functions as introducing spaces between words or conveying numbers, question marks, and other symbols. The pulse patterns were punched into paper tape, where they could either be deciphered by trained eyes or fed into a machine that would respond to the patterns by typing the corresponding letters.

The state of the art of typewriter engineering and design was not, until the turn of the century, sufficiently advanced to provide practical keyboard machines that would utilize the five-pulse code or the later seven-pulse code introduced by Howard L. Krum, which added clarity between transmitter and receiver by using the first and last pulses as "pattern-start" and "pattern-stop" symbols to keep the sender and the receiver synchronized on the same message. Letter-wheel and letter-hammer machines were tried without practical success at first. In 1900, the idea of using a typewriter to send and receive telegraph messages was still a dream of inventors.

Then Joy Morton of the Morton Salt family provided financial backing to Howard Krum, a mechanical engineer who brought his son Charles into the enterprise. The Morkrum Company was organized under Howard Krum's engineering leadership early in the 1900's and produced a number of encouraging teletype designs. At the start, the company used the five-pulse code, a rotating typewheel, and a stationary roller to hold the paper. The success of the Morkrum machines caused the Morkrum Company to combine with the Kleinschmidt Electric Company in 1923 and form the Teletype Corporation, which later was acquired by the American Telephone and Telegraph Company.

In the meantime, the Morkrum teletypewriter was slowly coming into use. Under the impetus of Kent Cooper, at that time traffic manager of the Associated Press newswire service, teletypewritten reports were being transmitted to the press by 1915, and service rates were introduced by the American Telephone and Telegraph Company in 1917. In 1917, the United Press, Associated Press' competitor, signed the first contract for three private-line teletypewriter services. Western Union was also switching to the teletype and by 1927 had more than

six thousand units on line. On the other side of the Atlantic, Britain's nationalized telegraph service began using British-built Creed teleprinters, expanding their use rapidly as part of an effort to counteract the shrinking use of the telegraph as the telephone grew more popular.

The role of the teletype in the communications field in Europe and the United States was influenced by the growing popularity of the telephone and by the economics of the private (in the United States) and the public (in Europe) communications industry. Wire, cable, wireless, and automatic-circuit systems continued to multiply during the second quarter of the twentieth century. During this period, these economic and technical developments extended the teletype's use to major centers of news and of business and government activities worldwide. In 1931, American Telephone and Telegraph Company introduced in the United States the Teletypewriter Exchange Service (TWX), which enabled subscribers to link up their teletypes by telephone lines. In 1932, Western Union introduced a TELEX network utilizing the telegraph lines, and Europe had its own TELEX, which spread worldwide after World War II. By 1940, nearly fifteen thousand U.S. teletype stations were tied together by the TWX network. By 1950, there were more than twenty-eight thousand. During the 1960's, the number passed fifty thousand, and service was extended to Canada. In 1962, TWX converted to automatic dialing, and subsequently, TELEX absorbed TWX to provide a global network.

The service came into widespread use by industry and various governmental agencies. Typically, news reports, administrative messages, and business orders and records were transmitted. The inventors' dream of 1900 had demonstrated its practicality to all doubters before 1925. By mid-century, it was the major vehicle for written-message transmission and was being incorporated into computer-controlled information networks. Speeds that had reached an early plateau of sixty words per minute increased to one hundred words per minute and then moved into the higher magnitudes afforded by computerized operation. Although the teletypewriter had originated as a communications machine in its own right, it became one of the components—along with the telephone, the teletypesetter, the television screen, and the computer—of the numerous and increasingly elaborate worldwide, integrated electronic communications systems during the latter part of the twentieth century.

By the late twentieth century, special lines connecting several teletypewriters on a continuous basis had become commonplace. Although such line costs were high, methods of sending a number of messages over a single line at the same time became widely used. Mechanical methods enabling five or six teletypewriters to share a single wire in the early part of the century were largely replaced by electronic systems that simultaneously sent signals from as many as twenty-four teletypewriters over a single channel of an ordinary telephone network. —*Thomas M. Smith, updated by Peter B. Heller*

ADDITIONAL READING:

Fagen, M. D., ed. *A History of Engineering and Science in the Bell System: The Early Years, 1875-1925.* Murray Hill,

N.J.: Bell Telephone Laboratories, 1975. While the teletype is only one of several nonvoice communications covered in one chapter of this thousand-page survey, the numerous historical tidbits, technical information, and evaluation make it useful even to the lay reader.

Gramling, Oliver. *AP: The Story of News*. New York: Farrar & Rinehart, 1940. The story of the largest U.S. news agency, which was the first enterprise after the stock market to make significant use of the teletype.

Martin, James. *Telecommunications and the Computer*. Englewood Cliffs, N.J.: Prentice-Hall, 1976. Provides technical detail and places the teletype in historical perspective.

Mott, Frank L. *The News in America*. Cambridge, Mass.: Harvard University Press, 1962. Examines the technical, ethical, and professional factors of the mass media facilitated by the use of the teletype and electronics.

United States. Naval Electronic Systems Command. *Principles of Telegraphy, Teletypewriter*. Washington, D.C.: Government Printing Office, 1967. Provides technical details and places the teletype in historical perspective.

SEE ALSO: 1844, First Telegraph Message; 1858, First Transatlantic Cable; 1861, Transcontinental Telegraph Is Completed; 1876, Bell Demonstrates the Telephone; 1879, Edison Demonstrates the Incandescent Lamp.

1901 ■ INSULAR CASES: *the U.S. Supreme Court determines the constitutional status of the United States' overseas possessions*

DATE: May 27, 1901

LOCALE: Washington, D.C.

CATEGORIES: Asian American history; Court cases; Diplomacy and international relations; Expansion and land acquisition

KEY FIGURES:

Henry Billings Brown (1836-1913), associate justice of the United States and author of the key opinions in the Insular Cases

Frédéric René Coudert (1832-1903), chief counsel for the importers in the Insular Cases

Melville Weston Fuller (1833-1910), chief justice of the United States and supporter of the view that "the Constitution follows the flag"

John Marshall Harlan (1833-1911), associate justice of the United States and a supporter of Fuller's views in the Insular Cases

Philander Chase Knox (1853-1921), attorney general and chief counsel for the United States in the Insular Cases

Edward Douglass White (1845-1921), associate justice of the United States and originator of the "incorporation" doctrine

SUMMARY OF EVENT. In 1898, the United States acquired an overseas empire. Hawaii was annexed by joint resolution

of both houses of Congress; and Puerto Rico, Guam, and the Philippine Islands were ceded by Spain under the terms of the Treaty of Paris, which ended the Spanish-American War. In a series of decisions known as the Insular Cases, the Supreme Court was called upon to fashion a constitutional compromise whereby the territorial acquisitions desired by the national political forces were rendered legitimate. The litigation is an excellent example of the flexibility of constitutional and statutory interpretation that the United States Supreme Court enjoys.

The drive to acquire foreign territory was led by Republican chieftains such as Theodore Roosevelt and Senator Henry Cabot Lodge, while opponents of "imperialism" were primarily Democrats. Much of the debate focused on the question of Senate advice and consent to the peace treaty negotiated by President William McKinley with Spain. One of the chief constitutional arguments used by the opponents of expansion was the slogan, "The Constitution follows the flag," designed to dramatize the impractical nature of the annexation of territory that offered no prospect of being organized into states. Such anti-imperialists as Senator George O. Vest of Missouri and George Hoar of Massachusetts argued that the Constitution did not give the federal government the power to acquire territory to be held permanently in subjugation as colonies. The power to acquire territory, they claimed, was inextricably connected with the responsibility to organize territories into prospective states. Moreover, imperialism by its very nature was contrary to the republican form of government established under the Constitution. Anti-imperialists also cited the Declaration of Independence as a general indictment of colonial arrangements. Another constitutional argument against acquisition of colonies was made by Vest when he interpreted the Fourteenth Amendment's declaration that "all persons born or naturalized in the United States, and subject to the jurisdiction thereof, are citizens of the United States. . . ." The advocates of expansion contended that the United States' success in the Spanish-American War destined it for a major role in the world affairs and that it was naïve to postpone the acquisition of colonies. The apologists of acquisition argued that colonies would provide the growing nation with outposts essential to its security, ensure its control of the seas, and underwrite the steady growth of its burgeoning industry.

It is obvious that the accommodation achieved by the Supreme Court was founded fundamentally on considerations of expediency as opposed to legalistic logic. The Court's response prompted the famous satirist Peter Finley Dunne ("Mr. Dooley") to exclaim that "no matter whether the constitution follows th' flag or not, th' Supreme Court follows th' illiction returns."

Arguments in what the Court called the Insular Tariff cases were heard for six days in January, 1901, and the Court's opinions were announced on May 27, 1901. The principles set forth at this time also determined the outcome of the two other cases that had been argued in December, 1899. In

DeLima v. Bidwell, the Court divided five to four on the question of the application of the general tariff laws (the Dingley Tariff) to imports from Puerto Rico following the proclamation of the treaty with Spain. In stating the majority opinion, Justice Henry Billings Brown said, "We are therefore of the opinion that at the time these duties were levied, Puerto Rico was not a foreign country within the meaning of the tariff laws but a territory of the United States, that the duties were illegally exacted, and that the plaintiffs are entitled to recover them back." In a dissenting opinion, Justice Joseph McKenna, supported by Justices George Shiras and Edward White, contended that Puerto Rico's status as a foreign or nonforeign country had nothing to do with whether the tariff laws were applicable. It was clear, argued McKenna, that the island was not a part of the United States and therefore the tariff laws should apply. Justice Horace Gray wrote a separate brief dissent.

The justices who dissented in *DeLima v. Bidwell* were joined by Justice Brown in the companion case of *Downes v. Bidwell* and, as if to dramatize the judicial confusion, Justice Brown again delivered the lead opinion. The question in *Downes v. Bidwell* was the validity of a special tariff law applicable only to Puerto Rico (the Foraker Act). Justice Brown concluded a long opinion surveying the applicable precedents and practices with the declaration that the judiciary must be careful not to impede the development of "the American Empire." The annexation of distant possessions "inhabited by alien races, differing from us in religion, customs, laws, methods of taxation and modes of thought" might some day be desirable. He continued:

> The question at once arises whether large concessions ought not to be made for a time, that, ultimately, our own theories may be carried out, and the blessings of a free government under the Constitution extended to them. We decline to hold that there is anything in the Constitution to forbid such action.

Brown went on to rule that Puerto Rico was a "territory appurtenant and belonging to the United States, but not a part of the United States within the revenue clauses of the Constitution" and that the Foraker Act was, therefore, constitutional.

In a concurring opinion supported by Shiras and McKenna, Justice White introduced his theory of incorporation, which subsequently came to be the prevailing doctrine. According to White, "whilst in an international sense Puerto Rico was not a foreign country, since it was subject to the sovereignty of and was owned by the United States, it was foreign to the United States in a domestic sense, because the island had not been incorporated into the United States, but was merely appurtenant thereto as a possession." It followed from this, said White, that the constitutional requirement that duties be uniform throughout the United States was not applicable to Congress in legislating for the island. Justice Gray solitarily concurred and argued that the law was valid because Puerto Rico was in a transitional stage from conquered territory to statehood.

Chief Justice Melville Fuller's dissenting opinion in *Downes v. Bidwell* was supported by the three justices who, along with Brown, had made up the *DeLima v. Bidwell* majority: John Marshall Harlan, David Josiah Brewer, and Rufus W. Peckham. Fuller urged that the Constitution did indeed follow the flag, that Puerto Rico was not a foreign country, and that Congress had violated the constitutional requirement that all taxes, duties, and imposts be uniform throughout the United States. Justice Harlan wrote a separate dissenting opinion that, among other things, attacked the White theory of incorporation.

Harlan's dissent is considered by many constitutional scholars as one of the great opinions in the history of the Court. Harlan argued that it was not legitimate to argue, as the majority did, that Congress could take away some or any rights from territories of the United States. He held that the Constitution was in force wherever the U.S. flag had been planted. In the case of Puerto Rico and the Philippines, that meant residents of those islands had full constitutional rights and protections from the moment the Senate ratified the treaty making them U.S. possessions. That had been accomplished in 1899, with ratification of the treaty with Spain ending the Spanish-American War. Justice Harlan rejected the racist argument raised by some members of the Court, that the Filipinos and Puerto Ricans were an "alien race" not covered by the Anglo-Saxon-inspired Constitution, in the conclusion of his dissent. He ended with a warning, "The Constitution is not to be obeyed or disobeyed as the circumstances of a particular crisis in our history may suggest. . . . The People have decreed that it shall be the supreme law of the land at all times." Once people become part of the United States, they have all the protections enjoyed by all citizens.

The majority did not accept this view, and residents of the new island territories were denied equal protection of the law, chiefly because they were considered to be racially inferior and unready for most democratic rights. Thus, contrary to what Harlan believed to be the ideas of the Framers of the Constitution, the Court supported a policy that would allow people to be governed without their consent.

In subsequent cases dealing with the question of the Constitution's applicability to territories, the Court was presented with questions having to do with the rights of the criminal defendant within the rights of constitutional guarantees. Justice Brown again employed the extension theory in *Hawaii v. Mankichi* (1903) in finding that Congress had not extended the guarantees of the Bill of Rights to Hawaii. It was permissible, therefore, for Hawaii to try the defendant on the basis of any information instead of a grand jury indictment and to convict him on the strength of only nine guilty votes of a jury of twelve. On the basis of his incorporation theory, Justice White agreed with this opinion, and this time he was joined by Justice McKenna. The next year, in *Dorr v. United States*, White's incorporation theory was adopted by a Court majority; it held that until the Philippines were incorporated into the United States by Congress, the latter could administer the territory under its general power to govern territory and without honoring all of the applicable constitutional guarantees. Subsequently, the Court held that Alaska had been sufficiently incorporated to warrant application of the Fifth, Sixth, and Seventh Amendments; in *Rasmussen v. United States* (1905), the Court reversed a conviction of a defendant found guilty on the basis of a six-person jury. In *Dowdell v. United States* (1911), the Court applied the same logic but reached the conclusion that the Philippines were not incorporated; therefore, it was permissible for territorial authorities to employ juries of fewer than twelve persons. Finally, in *Puerto Rico v. Tapia* (1918), the Court ruled that the congressional grant of citizenship to Puerto Ricans did not necessarily mean that these citizens were protected by the traditional constitutional guarantees.

Alaska and Hawaii, the two territories that were found by the Supreme Court to have been incorporated, became states of the Union on January 3 and August 21, 1959, respectively. The Philippines, Puerto Rico, and the Virgin Islands never were incorporated, although their inhabitants were declared U.S. citizens. Incorporation was never an issue insofar as the other minor possessions were concerned.

—James J. Bolner, updated by Leslie V. Tischauser

ADDITIONAL READING:

Gould, Lewis L. *The Spanish American War and President McKinley*. Lawrence: University Press of Kansas, 1980. Provides useful background material on the acquisition of U.S. colonies. Discusses attitudes of U.S. leaders that led to a denial of equal treatment for Filipinos and Puerto Ricans.

Kerr, James E. *The Insular Cases: The Role of the Judiciary in American Expansionism*. Port Washington, N.Y.: Kennikat Press, 1982. A detailed guide to the intricacies of the Court's decision making. Discusses the attitudes of all nine judges.

LaFeber, Walter. *The New Empire: An Interpretation of American Expansion, 1860-1898*. Ithaca, N.Y.: Cornell University Press, 1963. Describes the attitudes and beliefs of the supporters of expansion. A good summary of events leading to the Insular decisions.

Ringer, Benjamin B. *"We the People" and Others: Duality and America's Treatment of its Racial Minorities*. New York: Tavistock, 1983. A massive book that discusses the constitutional significance of the denial of rights in the Insular decisions. Describes the impact of those decisions on the peoples in the islands.

Thompson, Winfred Lee. *The Introduction of American Law in the Philippines and Puerto Rico, 1898-1905*. Fayetteville: University of Arkansas Press, 1989. The best guide to the various decisions and to the impact of the Court's views on the citizens of the United States' island possessions.

SEE ALSO: 1898, Spanish-American War; 1899, Philippine Insurrection; 1899, Hay's "Open Door Notes"; 1900, Suppression of Yellow Fever; 1901, Theodore Roosevelt Becomes President; 1903, Platt Amendment; 1903, Acquisition of the Panama Canal Zone; 1909, Dollar Diplomacy; 1917, Jones Act.

1901 ■ THEODORE ROOSEVELT BECOMES PRESIDENT: *a presidential assassination requires a young, exuberant vice president to assume the presidency*

DATE: September 14, 1901
LOCALE: Buffalo, New York, and Washington, D.C.
CATEGORY: Government and politics
KEY FIGURES:
Nelson Wilmarth Aldrich (1841-1915), Republican senator who led the majority party in the upper house
William Boyd Allison (1829-1908),
Orville Hitchcock Platt (1827-1905), and
John Coit Spooner (1843-1919), Republican senators aligned with Aldrich
Leon Czolgosz (1873-1901), anarchist who assassinated McKinley
Marcus "Mark" Alonzo Hanna (1837-1904), senator from Ohio and a close ally of McKinley
William McKinley (1843-1901), twenty-fifth president of the United States, 1897-1901
Theodore Roosevelt (1858-1919), vice president under McKinley and twenty-sixth president of the United States, 1901-1909

SUMMARY OF EVENT. Theodore Roosevelt assumed the presidency after the death of the incumbent, William McKinley. At Buffalo, New York, on September 6, 1901. Leon Czolgosz, an anarchist, had shot and seriously wounded the president while McKinley was in a receiving line at the Temple of Music at the Pan-American Exposition. When Vice President Roosevelt rushed to the side of the stricken chief executive, the president's doctors informed him that, despite the severity of the bullet wound to the stomach, McKinley appeared likely to recover. Roosevelt, in a move designed to restore public confidence, left for a mountain-climbing expedition in New York's Adirondacks. McKinley weakened during the next several days, and by September 13, Roosevelt learned from a special messenger that the president was dying. By buckboard and train, Roosevelt rushed back to Buffalo but was unable to reach the city before McKinley's death early on the morning of September 14. That afternoon, Theodore Roosevelt took the oath of office of president of the United States. He promised to carry forward McKinley's policies.

Such a pledge was necessary because suspicions about Roosevelt's reliability as a Republican pervaded the leadership of his party. During his rise to national stature in the 1890's, Roosevelt had often disagreed with the party regulars over issues and tactics, and he had gained a reputation as an impetuous politician. Many party members saw him as too young and untested to succeed McKinley and win the presidency on his own in 1904. His heroism in the Spanish-American War and his record as governor of New York during 1899-1900 had brought him the nomination as vice president in 1900. Party

Theodore Roosevelt, twenty-sixth president of the United States. During his two-tenure administration, progressive advances were made in antitrust legislation, conservation, and social reform. (Library of Congress)

elders had assumed that Roosevelt had been safely sidetracked during a second McKinley Administration. Now he was president of the United States.

In terms of immediate political realities, the new president faced a complex situation. McKinley had been a successful president who had enjoyed good relations with Congress. The nation was at peace and prosperous. Roosevelt could build on these political assets to his own advantage if he made a successful transition to the White House. Elevated to the highest office by tragedy, he needed to establish his capacity to govern effectively. Within the Republican Party, he faced a possible challenge to his leadership from McKinley's close friend, Senator Marcus "Mark" Hanna of Ohio. Hanna disclaimed

any presidential ambitions, but the wary Roosevelt hoped to gain the senator's support for his candidacy in 1904. Roosevelt knew of the power of the Republican senatorial leadership, embodied in "The Four": Nelson Aldrich of Rhode Island, William Allison of Iowa, Orville Platt of Connecticut, and John Spooner of Wisconsin. Roosevelt deferred to these party elders on such issues as the protective tariff and sought to work with Congress during his first years in office.

Roosevelt came to power at a time when issues of political and economic reform were growing more pressing for the United States. The rise of large industrial corporations and urban centers confronted the nation with the question of whether the national government should regulate business to produce a more just and equitable society. On the city and state level, reform mayors and governors were advancing programs to pursue social justice for those whom the new industrial society had left behind. Roosevelt had been a leader in this process as governor of New York. The demand for action by federal authorities gave him an attractive but perilous opportunity for leadership. He identified himself with the reform campaigns that historians have called Progressivism and became the national spokesman for the effort to purify U.S. life of the excesses of industrialization.

The president attacked his problems with skill and energy. He believed that Washington should address economic issues, such as the rise of big business, with national power to demonstrate the authority and supremacy of the federal government. In February, 1902, he ordered his attorney general to file an antitrust suit under the Sherman Antitrust Act against the Northern Securities Company, a giant and unpopular holding company for powerful railroads. The Supreme Court sustained Roosevelt's position in 1904. The initiative established Roosevelt as an opponent of excessive corporate power. Later in 1902, he intervened personally in the Anthracite Coal Strike, a dispute that threatened fuel shortages during the winter, in a way that was evenhanded toward business and labor. He was the first president to recognize organized labor as a legitimate element in making governmental decisions. Roosevelt called this approach the Square Deal. These actions ensured Roosevelt's nomination in 1904 and defused a possible challenge from Senator Hanna. Roosevelt then secured a stunning landslide election victory over his outmatched Democratic opponent, Alton B. Parker of New York, in the 1904 presidential contest. He was, he said at the time, now president in his own right.

Roosevelt also acted forcefully in foreign affairs. To speed the construction of a transoceanic canal, he backed the actions of a revolutionary junta in Panama in 1903 and cleared the way for the construction of the Panama Canal during his second term. In the Roosevelt Corollary to the Monroe Doctrine, announced in 1904, he claimed for the United States the right to intervene elsewhere in Latin America in order to maintain the status quo. Roosevelt also acted as peacemaker during the Russo-Japanese War of 1904-1905, a mediation that succeeded and won for him the Nobel Peace Prize. The president mixed energy with acumen in foreign policy, and achieved a central role on the international stage. He was careful, however, in his use of power and was less warlike than his later reputation suggested. As he put it in a famous phrase, he aimed to speak softly but carry a big stick.

In his second term, Roosevelt carried forward a campaign of strengthening the authority of the national government to regulate business in the public interest. He pushed through legislation to curb the power of the railroads in the Hepburn Act of 1906, to oversee the quality of drugs that consumers purchased in the Pure Food and Drug Act of 1906, and to inspect the meat that they consumed in the Meat Inspection Act of 1906. These policies had brought him into growing conflict with a conservative Congress by the time he left the White House in 1909.

Roosevelt proved to be a charismatic, strong president. He showed how a dynamic leader could use publicity and his personal popularity to deal effectively with Congress, function as a world leader, and persuade the U.S. people of the need at that time for a stronger national government. Perhaps his most visionary accomplishment was the advancement of the conservation movement, which alerted Americans to the need to manage their natural resources with intelligence and foresight. In all these achievements, Roosevelt focused attention on the office and himself, setting an example for future occupants of the presidency in the twentieth century. —*Lewis L. Gould, based on the original entry by Rex O. Mooney*

ADDITIONAL READING:

Blum, John Morton. *The Republican Roosevelt.* Cambridge, Mass.: Harvard University Press, 1954. Good brief introduction to Roosevelt's historical importance. Contains several good chapters on the impact of his presidency.

Cooper, John Milton. *The Warrior and the Priest: Woodrow Wilson and Theodore Roosevelt.* Cambridge, Mass.: The Belknap Press of Harvard University Press, 1983. A comparative study of the two major progressive presidents. Contains insightful comments about the impression Roosevelt made as president.

Gould, Lewis L. *The Presidency of Theodore Roosevelt.* Lawrence: University Press of Kansas, 1991. Looks at the entire scope of Roosevelt's presidential tenure. Extensive coverage of the transition from McKinley to Roosevelt.

Harbaugh, William H. *The Life and Times of Theodore Roosevelt.* New York: Oxford University Press, 1975. Excellent biography. Discusses the impact of his accession to the presidency in 1901.

Morris, Edmund. *The Rise of Theodore Roosevelt.* New York: Coward, McCann & Geoghegan, 1979. A prizewinning account of Roosevelt's early life, which ends with McKinley's death and Roosevelt's taking the oath of office as president.

SEE ALSO: 1823, Monroe Doctrine; 1898, Spanish-American War; 1902, Anthracite Coal Strike; 1903, Platt Amendment; 1903, Acquisition of the Panama Canal Zone; 1906, Pure Food and Drug Act; 1907, Gentlemen's Agreement; 1908, White House Conservation Conference.

1902 ■ ANTHRACITE COAL STRIKE:
presidential intervention to end the strike sets a precedent for future White House involvement in labor disputes

DATE: May 12-October 23, 1902
LOCALE: Pennsylvania, and Washington, D.C.
CATEGORY: Business and labor
KEY FIGURES:

George Frederick Baer (1842-1914), mine operator and an owner of the Reading and Philadelphia Railroad

E. E. Clark (1856-1930), grand chief of the Order of Railway Conductors

Marcus "Mark" Alonzo Hanna (1837-1904), senator from Ohio and a mediator in earlier disputes in the coal industry

John Mitchell (1870-1919), president of the United Mine Workers

John Pierpont Morgan (1837-1913), Wall Street financier and leader of the mine owners

Theodore Roosevelt (1858-1919), twenty-sixth president of the United States, 1901-1909

Elihu Root (1845-1937), secretary of war, who helped to mediate the dispute

William Alexis Stone (1846-1920), governor of Pennsylvania

SUMMARY OF EVENT. On May 12, 1902, 147,000 members of the United Mine Workers, led by their president, John Mitchell, walked out of the anthracite coal mines of Pennsylvania. Their walkout precipitated one of the most important confrontations between labor and capital in U.S. history. Before the strike ended in October, 1902, the nation had reached the verge of panic, the president nearly had ordered federal troops into the coal mines, and influential members of the business community had come to fear widespread social upheaval. The settlement of the strike marked the first time that a president had successfully intervened in a labor dispute as an impartial arbitrator. By his intervention, Theodore Roosevelt increased the power of the U.S. presidency and his chances of being elected as president in his own right in 1904. The episode also marked a significant step in the emergence of organized labor as a force in national politics.

In 1902, the anthracite miners were among the most exploited groups of workers in the nation. With an average wage of about $560 a year, they suffered from irregular employment, dangerous working conditions, and a cruel paternalism that gave life in company towns a feudalistic quality. United Mine Workers' president John Mitchell served as a spokesman for the hard-pressed miners. In 1900, Mitchell had threatened a strike and won a 10 percent increase in wages, largely through the influence of Republican senator Mark Hanna, who persuaded the mine owners that a strike would hurt the reelection chances of President William McKinley. In 1902, despite several attempts at compromise, negotiations broke down and a walkout ensued. The striking miners demanded recognition of their union, a nine-hour day, more accurate weighing of the coal, and a 20 percent increase in pay.

At that time, it was not recognized generally that plentiful bituminous coal could be substituted for anthracite fuel. As winter approached, fear of shortages became widespread among northern urbanites, who dreaded the impending severe weather. In September, the price of anthracite coal, usually five dollars per ton, reached fourteen dollars. The poor, who bought in smaller quantities, paid a penny per pound or twenty dollars per ton. By October, schools began to close, and the meager amount of coal that was available sold for thirty and thirty-five dollars per ton. Mobs in the West began to seize coal cars from passing trains, and mayors from across the nation appealed to the president for help. Republican politicians feared that their party might suffer at the polls in the November congressional elections if the crisis were not resolved quickly. In response to these developments, Roosevelt arranged for an unprecedented conference between labor and management representatives at the White House on October 1, 1902.

George F. Baer, the owner of the Reading and Pennsylvania Railroad, represented the owners of the coal mines, while John Mitchell spoke for the striking miners. Baer already had infuriated much of the country when he had declared that the rights of laborers would be protected best "not by the labor agitators, but by the Christian men to whom God in his infinite wisdom has given the control of the property interests of this country." Baer's imperious demeanor contrasted sharply with the calm and goodwill shown by Mitchell.

The daylong conference between the two antagonists failed to produce a settlement, and a peaceful resolution of the crisis seemed increasingly improbable. The operators claimed that the men wanted to return to the mines but feared union violence. However, when Pennsylvania Governor William A. Stone called out the state militia to protect anyone who wished to work, most of the miners remained on strike. Roosevelt believed that strong presidential action was needed to end the impasse. Rejecting the view that he lacked the power to act, he formulated a scheme that called for federal troops to occupy the mines and operate them in receivership. At the same time, Elihu Root—Roosevelt's secretary of war, a corporate lawyer and a friend of the business community—tried to arrange a negotiated settlement.

On Saturday, October 12, Root met with J. P. Morgan, the powerful New York financier whose railroads crisscrossed the coal fields. Working in tandem, the two men hammered out a possible compromise. On Sunday, George Baer was summoned to New York, where he conferred with Morgan. By Tuesday, an agreement had been ratified by the coal mine operators. The Root-Morgan proposal specified the creation of a five-man independent commission with authority to arbitrate the dispute. The original blueprint did not allow for the appointment of a labor union representative to the arbitration panel. The United Mine Workers insisted on the appointment of a union man and a Roman Catholic priest to the five-man

commission. Once again, a deadlock seemed unavoidable. The operators agreed to the inclusion of a priest, but they adamantly opposed seating a union member.

The creative thinking of President Roosevelt ended the political logjam between owners and workers. He saw that the coal mine owners wanted a face-saving way to have a union man on the commission without granting the union official recognition. Roosevelt named E. E. Clark, grand chief of the Order of Railway Conductors, as a sixth member of the commission. In order to mollify the coal operators, Roosevelt publicly labeled Clark as an eminent sociologist rather than a labor leader. To Roosevelt's amusement, this subterfuge satisfied the owners and allowed the settlement process to go forward. Once established, the commission worked out a compromise solution for the anthracite strike. The United Mine Workers did not achieve recognition of their union, but the commission did award them a nine-hour day and a 10 percent pay raise. The arbitrators settled the weight dispute, and a board of conciliation was created to help resolve future difficulties.

Roosevelt later looked upon the anthracite coal strike settlement as a turning point in his administration. In contrast to the Pullman Strike of 1894, when President Grover Cleveland used his power to break the American Railway Union and end the walkout, Roosevelt acted as an honest mediator between the two sides. The technique embodied what he came to call the Square Deal. The settlement increased his popularity and enhanced his reputation as a spokesperson for the general welfare. At the same time, he showed an appreciation for compromise that allowed his government to function as a successful intermediary between business and labor. Through his handling of the fuel crisis, Roosevelt took a long step toward making the national government and the presidency vital forces in American life.

—*Rex O. Mooney, updated by Lewis L. Gould*

ADDITIONAL READING:

Cornell, Robert J. *The Anthracite Coal Strike of 1902.* Washington, D.C.: Catholic University of America Press, 1957. The best single book-length study to date of the coal strike. Uses the papers of John Mitchell and other primary sources to create a thorough and balanced narrative about the origins, development, and consequences of the coal walkout.

Gould, Lewis L. *The Presidency of Theodore Roosevelt.* Lawrence: University Press of Kansas, 1996. Considers the coal strike in the context of Roosevelt's efforts to enhance the power of his office and to secure election in his own right in 1904.

Phelan, Craig. *The Public and Private Life of Labor Leader John Mitchell.* Albany: State University of New York Press, 1994. Biography of the leader of the United Mine Workers in the 1902 coal strike that brings out the personal and ethical questions that surrounded his tenure as president of the union.

Schaefer, Arthur M. "Theodore Roosevelt's Contribution to the Concept of Presidential Intervention in Labor Disputes: Antecedents and the 1902 Coal Strike." In *Theodore Roosevelt: Many-Sided American*, edited by Natalie Nayor et al. Interlaken, N.Y.: Heart of the Lakes Publishing, 1992. A recent investigation of Roosevelt's role in the strike, which credits him with achieving a major enhancement of presidential power through the settlement.

Wiebe, Robert H. "The Anthracite Coal Strike of 1902: A Record of Confusion." In *Mississippi Valley Historical Review* 48 (September, 1961): 229-251. Argues that the coal strike need not have happened if bituminous coal had been used as a substitute for anthracite. Asserts that Roosevelt's triumph has been overstated and that J. P. Morgan was the real winner in the contest.

See also: 1894, Pullman Strike; 1901, Theodore Roosevelt Becomes President.

1902 ■ Expansion of Direct Democracy: *new measures increase the political tools of direct citizen involvement in government*

Date: June 2, 1902-May 31, 1913
Locale: United States
Categories: Civil rights; Government and politics
Key figures:
Stephen Grover Cleveland (1837-1908), twenty-second (1885-1889) and twenty-fourth (1893-1897) president of the United States
Simon Guggenheim (1867-1941), senator from Colorado
Robert Marion La Follette (1855-1925), reform-minded governor of Wisconsin
William U'Ren (1859-1949), considered the father of direct democracy

Summary of event. Although the Declaration of Independence asserted that all "men" are created equal and, in later years, Abraham Lincoln movingly spoke of government as being "of, by, and for" the people, there was a gap between such sentiments and political realities. Admittedly, by 1890 the franchise included all male citizens. Women, however, were excluded except in a few Western states, and even the enfranchised found their prerogatives circumscribed. They were unable to vote directly for their United States senators and lacked legal methods to force recalcitrant legislatures to take specific action or to rid themselves of unsuitable elected public officials before their terms ended. Clearly something had to be done to make government at all levels more responsive to the will of the people.

The Progressive movement provided the vehicle for change as it initially sought to bring about reforms on the municipal and state levels. Among those responsible for reform were Wisconsin's Robert La Follette and the virtually forgotten William U'Ren of Oregon. They were joined in their attempts to alter state government by hoards of urban reformers who realized that the city was so tied to the state that in order to correct fully the basic problems of the former, the latter had to be changed as well.

In one respect the burden was eased by an earlier reform—the Australian, or secret, ballot—whose ramifications were just beginning to be recognized fully. This new form of voting replaced the older system, under which different colored ballots, printed by the political parties or independent candidates, were distributed to the voters, who then deposited them in the proper box under the watchful eyes of their employers' representatives or the local political boss. Obviously the old system protected those in power. Fraud, bribery, and corruption were rampant. In an attempt to end these evils, Massachusetts adopted the secret ballot in 1888. Through the efforts of such individuals as Grover Cleveland, the system was used nationwide by the election of 1910. Additionally, many Progressive states enacted corrupt-practices laws and limited the amount of money a candidate could spend. Similar federal laws followed.

The early twentieth century also saw the election of the first great reform governor when La Follette bested the ruling Republican machine in Wisconsin. During his years in office, 1901-1906, he transformed that state into a Progressive commonwealth, a "laboratory of democracy." A major accomplishment was to give the voter increased control over the nomination of candidates for public office. On May 23, 1903, Wisconsin held the first statewide primary to select those who would run in the general election. The primary abolished the old boss-dominated party caucus which had previously chosen the candidates.

La Follette's actions seemed to trigger a chain reaction across the West. In 1904 a young reformer, Joseph W. Folk, smashed the unusually corrupt machine running Missouri to become governor. Slowly but surely traditional frontier democracy, lost in the Gilded Age, reasserted itself as some states enfranchised women and almost all enacted fundamental political reforms. Nowhere was this trend more apparent than in Oregon, home of the little-known William U'Ren, who indirectly affected national political life as did few of his more famous contemporaries. U'Ren, a blacksmith turned newspaper editor and lawyer, never held a major political office, yet because of his ability to marshal public opinion was the unofficial fourth branch of Oregon's government. He first became interested in direct democracy in the 1890's, after reading of its use in Switzerland, and spent a large part of his time working to introduce it into Oregon and the rest of the nation. Oregon adopted the initiative and referendum on June 2, 1902, the direct primary in 1904, and the recall in 1910, thereby putting direct democracy into practice. Initiative and referendum made it possible for a majority vote of the electorate to pass laws when the legislature was unable or unwilling to do so, and to veto unpopular legislation. Recall allowed an elected official to be promptly removed if a majority of citizens were displeased with the person's conduct. This device was most often adopted in states west of the Mississippi, where its threat was generally sufficient to bring an official into line. Initiative and referendum, being less tinged with "radicalism" than recall, were usually adopted by the more conservative Eastern states.

Another drive occurring simultaneously was aimed at amending the U.S. Constitution to allow a direct vote for U.S. senators. The Constitution provided for their election by state legislatures as a means of removing the Senate from direct control by the "rabble." By the late nineteenth century, however, the office had become an item to be purchased like a loaf of bread. In 1907 Simon Guggenheim shocked the nation by publicly declaring what he had spent for the office in Colorado. As the stronghold of special privilege, the Senate had opposed and often thwarted Progressive measures such as tariff revision, the abolition of child labor, and revision of the method for selecting U.S. senators. Realizing that an amendment was out of the question, several Western states began holding primary elections to select Senate nominees. In some states the legislature was bound to abide by the decision of the voters. In 1912, with twenty-nine states using this device to circumvent the Constitution and public pressure for change mounting, the Senate reluctantly yielded and submitted an amendment to the states. The Seventeenth Amendment, providing for direct election of senators, was ratified on May 31, 1913.

With this ratification the major political reforms proposed by the Progressives had been accomplished. The responsibilities of the electorate had been dramatically enlarged. Control over the quality of government was now in the hands of the voter. The only question remaining was how the new powers would be exercised.   —Anne Trotter

ADDITIONAL READING:

Cronin, Thomas E. *Direct Democracy: The Politics of Initiative, Referendum, and Recall.* Cambridge, Mass.: Harvard University Press, 1989. The tools of direct democracy are reviewed in this illustrated 289-page book. Bibliography, index.

Goldman, Eric F. *Rendezvous with Destiny.* New York: Alfred A. Knopf, 1952. Highly readable general account of the various reform movements, their goals and accomplishments, from Populism to the New Deal.

Hofstadter, Richard. *The Age of Reform: From Bryan to F. D. R.* New York: Alfred A. Knopf, 1955. Hofstadter's work provides a brilliant analysis of Progressivism and its leaders.

La Follette, Robert M. *Autobiography.* Madison: University of Wisconsin Press, 1911. Introduces the reader to the thoughts and career of one of the earliest and most important political reformers of the period.

Mowry, George E. *The California Progressives.* Berkeley: University of California Press, 1951. Examines the struggles of California Progressives against the Southern Pacific Railroad in their effort to make state government responsive to the will of the majority.

_____. *The Era of Theodore Roosevelt, 1900-1912.* New York: Harper & Row, 1958. Covers the social, economic, and political beginnings of twentieth century American life.

Nye, Russel B. *Midwestern Progressive Politics, 1870-1958.* Ann Arbor: University of Michigan Press, 1959. A well-documented study of reform and Progressivism in eleven Midwestern states. Includes extensive bibliographical information.

Schmidt, David D. *Citizen Lawmakers: The Ballot Initiative Revolution.* Philadelphia: Temple University Press, 1989. A history of the introduction of the ballot initiative. Bibliography, index.

SEE ALSO: 1865, Thirteenth Amendment; 1868, Fourteenth Amendment; 1901, Theodore Roosevelt Becomes President; 1912, Wilson Is Elected President; 1920, U.S. Women Gain the Vote; 1970, U.S. Voting Age Is Lowered to Eighteen.

1903 ■ LONE WOLF V. HITCHCOCK: *the U.S. Supreme Court decides that Congress has plenary power over Native American property and may dispose of it at its discretion*

DATE: January 5, 1903
LOCALE: Washington, D.C.
CATEGORIES: Court cases; Native American history
KEY FIGURES:

Hampton L. Carson (1852-1929), Indian Rights Association lawyer and Springer's co-counsel

Ethan Allen Hitchcock (1835-1909), secretary of the interior

Lone Wolf (c. 1820-c. 1879), Kiowa chief and the principal complainant in the Supreme Court case

William McKendree Springer (1836-1903), Lone Wolf's attorney

Willis Van Devanter (1859-1941), assistant attorney general for the Department of the Interior

Edward Douglass White (1845-1921), associate justice of the Supreme Court who wrote the opinion

SUMMARY OF EVENT. In 1887, after years of agitation and controversy, Congress passed the General Allotment Act (also known as the Dawes Act or Dawes Severalty Act). Under the terms of the legislation, the president was authorized to allot all tribal land in the United States to individual Native Americans. The standard share was 160 acres to each head of a family, with smaller amounts to unmarried men and children. Negotiations were to be carried on with Native American tribes for the sale to the federal government of the land remaining after the allotments were made and for its opening to Euro-American settlement.

The allotment policy, dominating United States-Native American relations for more than fifty years, proved to be disastrous for Native Americans. It transformed Native American landownership from collective to individual holdings, thus severing the Indians' connection with communal tribal organizations, exposed them to wholesale exploitation by land speculators, pushed them onto land that was often arid and unproductive, and led ultimately to a loss of control over two-thirds of their lands. Deceit, duplicity, and coercion undermined the honest, but naïve, objectives of the U.S. reformers who espoused allotment prior to its enactment.

Tribal sovereignty, the allotment policy, and Native American treaty rights came before the United States Supreme Court in *Lone Wolf v. Hitchcock* in 1902. In 1867, the Medicine Lodge Creek Treaty had been signed with the Kiowas and Comanches, whereby the two tribes relinquished claims to 90 million acres in exchange for 2.9-million-acre reservations in Western Oklahoma. A separate treaty placed the plains Apaches on the same reservation. Article XII of the Medicine Lodge Creek Treaty provided that no further cession of any part of the new reservation could be made without the written consent of three-quarters of the adult male members of the three tribes. The commitment to Article XII of the Medicine Lodge treaty lasted twenty-five years. In 1892, the Jerome Commission, composed of a former governor of Michigan and two judges, was able—through fraud and counterfeit signatures—to secure the necessary three-quarters consent to an agreement for the allotment of land to individual tribesmen and for the purchase of 2.15 million acres of what was denominated as surplus land at a price of approximately ninety-three cents per acre.

Almost immediately after the signing of the new agreement, representatives of the Kiowas, Comanches, and plains Apaches claimed that assent had been obtained by fraudulent misrepresentation of its terms by the interpreters, and that three-quarters of the adult males had not consented to the cession. Their argument was ignored by the United States House of Representatives, which voted to execute the agreement, but was more sympathetically received by the Senate, which defeated the bill in January, 1899.

In July, 1900, however, Congress passed an act that allowed the United States to take title to 2,991,933 acres of the Kiowa, Comanche, and plains Apache reservation. After 480,000 acres were set aside as common grazing lands, 445,000 acres allotted to individual members of the three tribes, and 10,000 acres committed to agency, schools, and religious purposes, 2 million acres were left to be purchased by the federal government and opened to white settlement.

Although some Native Americans approved of the act, Lone Wolf, a Kiowa chief, and others were intent upon challenging the act's constitutionality. They retained William McKendree Springer, formerly chief justice of the Court of Appeals for the Indian Territory, to litigate their case before the federal courts.

Springer argued that the congressional act violated the property rights of the three tribes and was, therefore, repugnant to the due process clause of the Fifth Amendment of the Constitution, After losing in the Supreme Court of the District of Columbia and in the Court of Appeals for the district, Springer appealed to the United States Supreme Court.

Lone Wolf v. Hitchcock was argued in the Supreme Court in October, 1901, and reargued the following year. The decision was handed down in January, 1903. In the Court, Springer was joined by Hampton L. Carson, a prominent member of the Indian Rights Association; the Department of the Interior was represented by Willis Van Devanter of Wyoming, who later became a Supreme Court justice.

The unanimous decision of the Supreme Court, written by Associate Justice Edward White of Louisiana, was characterized by a later commentator as the "Indian's *Dred Scott* decision," and January 5, 1903, as "one of the blackest days in the history of the American Indians." Justice White spoke in condescending terms. He called Native Americans an "ignorant and dependent race," "weak and diminishing in number," and "wards of the nation." These contemptuous phrases were not original to White; they were epithets that had long been used in the opinions of Supreme Court justices in relation to Native Americans. More important, White ruled that Congress possessed a paramount authority over Native American property "by reason of its exercise of guardianship over their interests." In exercising such power, Congress could abrogate provisions of a treaty with a Native American tribe.

Justice White then went on to argue that the congressional act of 1900 represented only "a mere change in the form of investment of Indian tribal property from land to money" even though the price paid was below the market value. White held that Congress had made a good-faith effort to compensate the Kiowas for their lands; therefore, there was no violation of the Fifth Amendment. "If injury was occasioned," White concluded, "which we do not wish to be understood to imply by the use made by Congress of its power, relief must be sought by an appeal to that body for redress and not to the courts."

Even before the Supreme Court had ruled in *Lone Wolf v. Hitchcock*, President William McKinley issued a proclamation opening the Kiowa lands to white settlement on August 6, 1901. Lone Wolf watched with chagrin as thousands of potential settlers camped on Kiowa lands near Fort Sill, waiting to register for a lottery; during a two-month period, 11,638 homestead entries were made at the land office.

The importance of the Supreme Court decision in *Lone Wolf* should not be underestimated. Justice White's opinion legitimized the long history of broken promises, of treaties made and treaties ignored, and of Congress' assertion of plenary authority over Indian lands. The opinion justified the alienation, between 1887 and 1934, of eighty-six million acres of Native American property; it also denied to Native Americans recourse to the courts to seek redress for the coerced separation from their lands and its purchase at bargain prices.

In *Lone Wolf*, Justice White told the Kiowas and associated tribes that they would have to seek relief for their alleged injuries in Congress, and the Kiowas had no alternative but to go to the federal legislature to secure redress. It was not until 1955 that the Indian Claims Commission awarded the Kiowas, Comanches, and plains Apaches $2,067,166 in compensation for the lands taken under the congressional act of 1900. It was not until 1980, in *United States v. Sioux Nation of Indians*, that Justice Harry Blackmun, in a majority opinion, held that the *Lone Wolf* doctrine was "discredited" and "had little to commend it as an enduring principle."　　—*David L. Sterling*

ADDITIONAL READING:

Clark, Blue. *"Lone Wolf v. Hitchcock": Treaty Rights and Indian Law at the End of the Nineteenth Century.* Lincoln:

University of Nebraska Press, 1994. A short but comprehensive study of the background and implications of the most significant turn-of-the-century Native American court case.

Hagan, William T. *The Indian Rights Association: The Herbert Welsh Years, 1882-1904*. Tucson: University of Arizona Press, 1985. An account of the organization that participated in the litigation of the *Lone Wolf* case.

Highsaw, Robert B. *Edward Douglass White: Defender of the Conservative Faith*. Baton Rouge: Louisiana State University Press, 1981. An analysis of the judicial record of the writer of the Supreme Court opinion in *Lone Wolf v. Hitchcock*.

Legters, Lyman, and Fremont J. Lyden, eds. *American Indian Policy: Self-Governance and Economic Development*. Westport, Conn.: Greenwood Press, 1994. A series of articles detailing current trends in Native American life and law.

Prucha, Francis Paul. *American Indian Treaties: The History of a Political Anomaly*. Berkeley: University of California Press, 1994. An exhaustive examination of the legal relationship between Native American tribes and the United States, from the American Revolution to the present.

SEE ALSO: 1867, Medicine Lodge Creek Treaty; 1871, Indian Appropriation Act; 1876, Canada's Indian Act; 1887, General Allotment Act; 1924, Indian Citizenship Act; 1934, Indian Reorganization Act; 1953, Termination Resolution.

1903 ■ PLATT AMENDMENT: *the Treaty of Relations underscores Cuba's independence from Spain and secures U.S. influence in Cuba for the next three decades*

DATE: May 22, 1903
LOCALE: Cuba
CATEGORIES: Diplomacy and international relations; Latino American history; Laws and acts
KEY FIGURES:

José Martí (1853-1895), father of the Cuban independence movement

Gerardo Machado y Morales (1871-1939), president of Cuba, 1925-1933

William McKinley (1843-1901), twenty-fifth president of the United States, 1897-1901

Orville H. Platt (1827-1905), Republican senator from Connecticut

Elihu Root (1845-1937), secretary of state under Theodore Roosevelt

SUMMARY OF EVENT. In 1895, Cuban revolutionaries initiated what was ultimately to become a successful revolt against Spanish colonial domination. The break from Spain was brought about by a variety of factors, the two most critical being the repressive nature of the colonial rule of Spain and a change in U.S. tariff policy as a result of the recessions and depressions in the United States during the 1890's. The

Wilson-Gorman Tariff of 1894 imposed a duty on Cuban sugar arriving in the United States, which previously had entered duty-free. With the economy of Cuba reeling from dwindling Cuban-United States trade because of the new tariff, Cuban dissidents, who had been waiting for an opportunity to act, launched a revolution.

Led by José Martí, who had strong ties to the United States, the rebels who called for Cuban independence began a guerrilla war against the Spanish. Even after the death of Martí during the first year of fighting, the ranks of the Cuban rebel forces continued to increase. Spanish authorities responded to the groundswell of domestic support for the rebels by attempting to separate the rebels from their supporters in rural areas. Under a new policy known as reconcentration, more than a quarter-million Cubans were interred in concentration camps guarded by Spanish soldiers. Thousands of Cubans died in the unfit camps, which served as breeding grounds for disease. U.S. sympathy for the Cuban rebels was stimulated by reports of atrocities occurring as a result of the new Spanish policy, and people in the United States began to call for an end to the conflict through reconciliation. The mysterious sinking of the battleship *Maine* in Havana harbor on February 15, 1898, ended all hope of a peaceful resolution to the conflict.

The sinking of the U.S. battleship, which had been ordered to Cuba in an effort to display U.S. concern for events unfolding on the island and to protect U.S. citizens, drew the United States further into the conflict. Naval investigators concluded that a Spanish mine had caused the explosion. U.S. president William McKinley responded to events by demanding that Spain grant Cuban independence. Finding the Spanish response unsatisfactory, McKinley requested on April 11, 1898, that Congress grant him authorization to stop the war in Cuba by force, if necessary. Following some debate, on April 19 Congress declared that Cuba was and should be independent, demanded an immediate withdrawal of Spain from Cuba, authorized the use of force to accomplish that withdrawal, and vowed not to annex the island. Known as the Teller Amendment, the vow not to annex Cuba was perhaps the most controversial of the issues debated.

Despite the Teller Amendment, the entrance of the United States into the conflict initiated the beginning of a exploitive relationship between the United States and Cuba, which was dictated by the former. As the war drew to an end and Spanish withdrawal began to be realized, the United States downplayed the role of the Cuban rebels in the success of the military campaign. The Treaty of Paris, which halted the conflict, required Spain to surrender all claims to Cuba, but the McKinley Administration refused to recognize the former Cuban rebels as a legitimate government or the Cuban people as being capable of self-rule. For two years, the U.S. military performed the functions of government. Although the U.S. military made substantial improvements in the infrastructure of Cuba and generally improved the quality of life on the island, Cubans resented the U.S. occupation. Many Cubans felt that they had traded one colonial master for another.

In 1900, Cubans were allowed to draft a constitution and hold elections. The United States refused to withdraw its troops, however, until provisions were made for the continuation of Cuban-United States relations. Elihu Root, the U.S. secretary of war, proposed such provisions, which ultimately were included in a bill sponsored by Senator Orville H. Platt. Platt, a Republican from Connecticut, attached a rider to the Army Appropriations Bill of 1901 that essentially made Cuba a U.S. protectorate.

The Platt Amendment, as the provisions would come to be known, severely restricted Cuba's ability to make treaties and its right to contract public debt. The United States also declared its right to intervene in Cuban affairs in order to preserve Cuban independence and maintain order. Cuba also was expected to give the United States the right to maintain naval bases and coaling stations on the island. The Cuban government reluctantly appended the provisions of the Platt Amendment to the Cuban constitution. The last U.S. forces finally withdrew from Havana in 1902. The Platt Amendment became a formal part of a U.S.-Cuba treaty on May 22, 1903.

The Platt Amendment formed the basis for United States-Cuban relations for the next sixty years, until Fidel Castro emerged as the leader of Cuba. Forced to submit to the will of the United States, Cuba was soon inundated with U.S. investment. Foreign investors controlled and manipulated Cuban politics and the economy. U.S. troops reoccupied Cuba from 1906 to 1909, under the authority of the Platt Amendment, following an uprising that protested, among other things, U.S. involvement in Cuban affairs.

The election of Franklin Roosevelt as U.S. president in 1933 initially brought little change in U.S.-Cuban relations, despite his "good neighbor policy," which was based on the belief that no state had the right to intervene in Latin America. Roosevelt was forced to deal with a Cuba in turmoil. President Gerardo "the Butcher" Machado y Morales, who had dominated Cuban politics for a decade, was forced to resign in 1933 because of popular opposition and U.S. pressure. His successor, Ramón Grau San Martín, was no more acceptable to the Roosevelt Administration. Viewed as too radical by Roosevelt, the government of Grau was never recognized as legitimate by the U.S. administration.

It was not until Fulgencio Batista y Zaldívar led a coup and installed a government acceptable to the United States that the Roosevelt Administration agreed to discuss revoking the Platt Amendment. The second Treaty of Relations, as it came to be known, eliminated the limitations on Cuban sovereignty imposed by the Platt Amendment. The new treaty did allow the United States to retain its naval base at Guantanamo Bay, which could be revoked only by mutual consent of both states.

Despite the formal end of U.S. involvement in Cuba, the new Cuba, which was controlled by Batista, was no less tied to the United States financially or politically. Batista was viewed by many international observers as a puppet for the U.S. government. Cuba attracted more U.S. investment under Batista than ever before. Many Cubans argued that despite the

end of the Platt Amendment, Cuba was still a U.S. dependency. It was this sense of frustration over their inability to achieve a true sense of sovereignty that served as a catalyst for Fidel Castro's successful coup in 1959. *—Donald C. Simmons, Jr.*

ADDITIONAL READING:

Abel, Christopher, and Nissa Torrents, eds. *José Martí: Revolutionary Democrat*. London: Athlone Press, 1986. A brief but comprehensive account of the life of the father of Cuban independence.

Langley, Lester D. *The Cuban Policy of the United States*. New York: Wiley, 1968. An exceptionally detailed account of the United States' Cuban policy.

Perez, Louis A., Jr. *Cuba: Between Reform and Revolution*. New York: Oxford University Press, 1988. An in-depth look at Cuba's history of economic and political relationships.

_____. *Cuba Under the Platt Amendment: 1902-1934*. Pittsburgh: University of Pittsburgh Press, 1986. A well-written account of Cuba during its early years of independence.

_____. *Intervention, Revolution, and Politics in Cuba, 1913-1921*. Pittsburgh: University of Pittsburgh Press, 1978. A brief account of Cuban domestic and international politics during the period.

Suchlicki, Jaime. *Cuba: From Columbus to Castro*. 3d ed., rev. Washington, D.C.: Brassey's (U.S.), 1990. An excellent history of Cuba.

Thomas, Hugh. *Cuba: Or, The Pursuit of Freedom*. New York: Harper & Row, 1971. Perhaps the most extensive work written about the country.

SEE ALSO: 1898, Spanish-American War; 1901, Insular Cases; 1909, Dollar Diplomacy; 1956, Cuban Revolution.

1903 ■ ACQUISITION OF THE PANAMA CANAL ZONE: *the U.S. agreement to build a transoceanic canal revolutionizes transportation and shipping*

DATE: November 18, 1903
LOCALE: Panama
CATEGORIES: Economics; Expansion and land acquisition; Science and technology; Transportation
KEY FIGURES:
Philippe Jean Bunau-Varilla (1860-1940), French engineer who helped foment the Panamanian revolution
William Nelson Cromwell (1854-1948), lawyer for the New Panama Canal Company
Marcus "Mark" Alonzo Hanna (1837-1904), senator who favored a Panamanian route
John Milton Hay (1838-1905), secretary of state
José Manuel Marroquin (1827-1908), president of Colombia
John T. Morgan (1824-1907), senator who favored a Nicaraguan route
Theodore Roosevelt (1858-1919), twenty-sixth president of the United States, 1901-1909

John Spooner (1843-1919), sponsor of a bill in the Senate recommending the Panamanian route for the canal

SUMMARY OF EVENT. On November 18, 1903, the minister of the new Republic of Panama, Philippe Bunau-Varilla, and the U.S. secretary of state, John Hay, signed the Hay-Bunau-Varilla Treaty. By the terms of the treaty, the United States agreed to pay $10 million cash and an annual rental fee of $250,000 in return for a canal zone ten miles wide that was to grant "to the United States in perpetuity the use, occupation and control." The United States took possession of the canal site on May 4, 1904, and at a cost of $375 million, built the canal that had previously defeated such experienced canal builders as Ferdinand de Lesseps' Suez Canal Company. In the process, Colonel William C. Gorgas of the United States Army Medical Corps perfected techniques—many of which were learned in Cuba during the Spanish-American War—for the prevention of the dreaded yellow fever. The Panama Canal was opened for shipping on August 15, 1914, two weeks after World War I had begun in Europe.

The history of the negotiations for the Canal Zone marks one of the most controversial and colorful episodes in American diplomatic history. The real and perceived participation of the United States in the revolution that brought about the separation of Panama from the sovereign nation of Colombia has been debated since it occurred. Critics of the treaty and of the United States' involvement in the revolution have much ammunition for their argument, and much of their criticism is aimed at President Theodore Roosevelt, who in later years boldly stated, "I took the Canal Zone." In 1921, the United States Senate voted compensation to the government of Colombia in the amount of $25 million in return for Colombian recognition of Panama. This was, in effect, a goodwill indemnity to Colombia for the "big stick" diplomacy of 1903 employed by Roosevelt. The revolution—which was, at the very best, sanctioned by the United States—had deprived Colombia of not only the province of Panama but also a $10 million outright payment for the opportunity to build the canal.

The dream of an isthmian canal can be traced back to the early explorers of the American continent. Even in Christopher Columbus' time, the attractiveness of a Central American shortcut was apparent. The strategic desirability of a canal through Panama became obvious in the Spanish-American War, when the battleship *Oregon* almost missed the war. The major obstacle to the popular goal of an American canal was the Anglo-American Clayton-Bulwer Treaty of 1850, which forbade either nation to build a canal without the participation of the other. Great Britain, eager to maintain its friendship with the United States, agreed to an all-American canal in the first Hay-Pauncefote Treaty in 1900. The United States Senate refused to ratify this agreement because it called for a neutral canal, and demanded the right to defend and fortify it. Great Britain reluctantly agreed to that important amendment, and the second Hay-Pauncefote Treaty, of 1901, was virtually an admission by the British that the United States was the primary power in the Caribbean.

However, the canal battle was just beginning. The major debate concerned the route. Most members of Congress and people in the United States favored a route through Nicaragua, which most believed could be built as a sea-level channel without locks. An Isthmian Canal Commission appointed by President William McKinley supported this view, as did Senator John T. Morgan of the Senate Canals Committee. On January 9, 1902, the House approved the Nicaraguan route, and it seemed certain the Senate would follow.

At this point, two of the most improbable figures in the canal drama appeared upon the scene. One was William Nelson Cromwell, the lawyer for the New Panama Canal Company, which had purchased the assets and rights of the defunct de Lesseps company that had failed to build its proposed canal. The other was Philippe Jean Bunau-Varilla, an engineer with the de Lesseps company, who was hoping to build a canal through Panama in order to vindicate both de Lesseps and French engineering ability. Cromwell offered the rights to the Panama route for $40 million to the United States. Because the Panama route offered many engineering advantages and the proposed route through Nicaragua came uncomfortably close to an erupting volcano, and because Cromwell was an assiduous and effective lobbyist, President Roosevelt, the canal commission, and Congress all reversed themselves. The resultant Spooner Act directed the president to build a canal through Panama if the consent of Colombia, which owned the isthmian site, could be obtained. Otherwise, Congress asked that the Nicaraguan route be taken.

The U.S. government began exerting extreme diplomatic pressure on the Colombian government for a canal treaty. Colombia was torn by internal strife, which had reached almost revolutionary proportions. Colombia was ruled by José Marroquin, officially vice president, who had been elevated to the position of chief executive when a coup deposed the president. The diplomatic correspondence between Bogotá and Washington was affected more by the Colombian political situation than by Hay's insistence upon a treaty. In a tangle of confused instructions and misunderstandings, the Hay-Herrán Treaty was negotiated on January 22, 1903. The treaty called for one payment of $10 million and an annual rent of $250,000, beginning in nine years, for rights to a canal zone six miles wide. Colombia also agreed not to ask for any of the $40 million being paid to the French canal company. The treaty was quickly approved by the U.S. Senate on March 17, 1903, and the U.S. government awaited what it fondly imagined would be automatic approval by the Colombian legislature.

People in the United States, from the president and the State Department on down, failed to comprehend the serious objections that the proud Colombians had to the treaty. The treaty sacrificed Colombian sovereignty at a time when the United States appeared to be in an expansionist mood, it failed to prove enough compensation for a route that had many engineering advantages and a profitable railroad, and it overlooked the fact that the French canal company's rights would expire in

1904. A slight delay would obviate the United States' need to pay $40 million for a defunct company's temporary rights, which contained nothing of substance. The Colombian Senate, with only three dissenting votes, rejected the treaty.

President Roosevelt likened this reasonable exercise of legislative responsibility to a holdup and prepared to proceed in his own way. Roosevelt invoked an 1846 treaty between the United States and Colombia (then New Granada), one reading of which, suggested by the State Department, could be taken to indicate that the United States had the right to guarantee the neutrality of, and free passage through, the Panamanian isthmus. The State Department and President Roosevelt could now point to the Colombian rejection as a denial of free passage. The colony of Panama had long had separatist ambitions; indeed, it had been prevented from revolting on several occasions only by U.S. intervention on behalf of Colombia. The State Department insisted that its intervention had been impartial, but perhaps had benefited Colombia previously. It was a relatively simple matter for Bunau-Varilla to encourage a Panamanian revolution and to inform Roosevelt that a revolt might be likely. It was equally simple for Roosevelt, under the claim that he was guaranteeing the free transit of the isthmus, to ensure Colombia's noninterference by dispatching the cruiser *Nashville* to the scene. Panama City, on the Pacific side of the country, was taken by the revolutionaries on November 2, 1903. The *Nashville* landed U.S. forces at Colón on the Atlantic side to prevent Colombian troops from passing across Panama to crush the rebels. In addition, engines from the Panama Railroad were parked in the jungle between Colón and Panama City, providing no route for Colombian troops to go to the Pacific side, where the revolution was to occur. When Colombia's general allowed Bunau-Varilla to bribe him with money into leaving Colón, the revolution was a success. The revolution was primarily peaceful but, in a feeble attempt to defend Colombian sovereignty, the Colombian gunboat *Bogotá* fired five or six shells into Panama City, killing a Chinese shopkeeper who was asleep and one donkey. The Hay-Bunau-Varilla Treaty and the Panama Canal were a result of the revolution, as were a series of so-called good neighbor policies to assuage Latin American pride at the apparent high-handedness of the entire transaction.

The Hay-Bunau-Varilla Treaty was signed in Washington, D.C., by John Hay, U.S. Secretary of State, and Philippe Bunau-Varilla, the French engineer who had been appointed minister of the Republic of Panama and had been given authority to negotiate until a delegation from Panama could be dispatched to Washington. Not one citizen of Panama was in attendance at the signing. Ironically, a group of Panamanians was en route from New York to Washington and arrived only two hours after the treaty was signed. This fact created considerable embarrassment and anger among the Panamanian diplomats who arrived too late, but in the end nothing was changed. However, the bitterness resulting from the situation would linger for decades.

—Richard H. Collin, updated by Kay Hively

ADDITIONAL READING:

Bunau-Varilla, Philippe. *Panama: The Creation, Destruction, and Resurrection.* London: Constable, 1913. Bunau-Varilla's own memoir and history.

Cooper, John Milton, Jr. *Warrior and the Priest.* Cambridge, Mass.: Harvard University Press, 1985. Explains how understanding the history of the Panama Canal is possible only by understanding Theodore Roosevelt.

Kitchel, Denison. *The Truth About the Panama Canal.* New Rochelle, N.Y.: Arlington House, 1978. A look at the history of the Panama Canal from a conservative view.

Mack, Gerstle. *The Land Divided: A History of the Panama Canal and Other Isthmian Canal Projects.* New York: Alfred A. Knopf, 1944. A wide-ranging look at the history of the Isthmus of Panama, including the canal, the railroad, and other events.

Miner, Dwight C. *The Fight for the Panamanian Route.* New York: Octagon Books, 1940. Examines the controversy surrounding the acquisition of the Canal Zone and Roosevelt's role in it.

Roosevelt, Theodore. *Autobiography.* New York: Macmillan, 1913. Includes Roosevelt's defense of his Panama policy.

SEE ALSO: 1898, Spanish-American War; 1900, Suppression of Yellow Fever; 1912, Intervention in Nicaragua.

1903 ■ WRIGHT BROTHERS' FIRST FLIGHT: *the beginning of a new age of air transportation and technology*

DATE: December 17, 1903
LOCALE: Kitty Hawk, North Carolina
CATEGORIES: Science and technology; Transportation
KEY FIGURES:
Octave Chanute (1832-1910), U.S. flying pioneer and friend of the Wrights
Glenn H. Curtiss (1878-1930), early U.S. flier, airplane designer, and competitor of the Wrights
Samuel P. Langley (1834-1906), secretary of the Smithsonian Institution, scientist, and an early experimenter with flying machines
Otto Lilienthal (1848-1896), German aeronautical engineer and glider pilot
Charles E. Taylor (1868-1956), the Wrights' mechanic, who helped them build the first successful airplane engine
Orville Wright (1871-1948), the younger brother
Wilbur Wright (1867-1912), the elder of the two inventors
SUMMARY OF EVENT. The *Scientific American* editorialized on December 15, 1906: "In all the history of invention, there is probably no parallel to the unostentatious manner in which the Wright brothers of Dayton, Ohio, ushered into the world their epoch-making invention of the first successful aeroplane flying machine." The periodical did not exaggerate. Wilbur and Orville Wright accomplished their first powered flight near Kitty Hawk, North Carolina, on December 17, 1903, in

The first successful powered flight was achieved by the Wright brothers on December 17, 1903, near Kitty Hawk, North Carolina. (Library of Congress)

front of five witnesses. Yet, for three years, few seemed to realize that the dream of flying had been accomplished.

As two of the seven children of Bishop Milton Wright, originally an itinerant minister from a midwestern Protestant sect, and Susan Koerner Wright, Wilbur and Orville were reared modestly. Because the family had moved from Indiana to Dayton, Ohio, neither boy finished high school. In 1892, they opened a bicycle shop in Dayton. They had always been interested in mechanical and scientific matters and were devoted tinkerers. In 1895, the two brothers began to build their own bicycles in a workshop above the store. They also experimented with numerous other inventions. Their interest in flying was aroused by reports of the initial development of the automobile and of Otto Lilienthal's experiments with gliders in Germany in the 1890's.

The Wright brothers started their work as self-made aeronautical engineers by writing to the Smithsonian Institution in Washington, D.C., for suggestions about reading materials in 1899. They discovered that little was known about the subject of flying, despite long interest in it. Octave Chanute and Dr.

Samuel P. Langley, recognized as a foremost scientist, were the leading U.S. experimenters, but the Wrights were especially influenced by aeronautical pioneer Lilienthal. The early experimenters had met a number of setbacks. Lilienthal and Percy Pilcher, a Scottish glider pioneer, were killed in similar accidents. Chanute had given up; Langley was to see his first manned flying machine crash after takeoff.

Unlike their better-educated predecessors, the two bicycle mechanics—with their gift for visualizing abstract principles and then bringing them into operation—discovered the three essential elements of flight that proved to be immutable aerodynamic principles. These involved lift, drag, but especially control for balance and stability in the face of shifting wind patterns and drift. The brothers' use of movable wingtips, a three-axis rudder, and other devices addressed this difficulty, which had caused grief to the other pioneers. After experimenting with kites beginning in 1899, the brothers decided to build a glider and sought a site for test flights. They wrote to the U.S. Weather Bureau, which informed them that Kitty Hawk, North Carolina, on a treeless and isolated barrier beach between the Atlantic Ocean and the coastline and dotted with sandy dunes, had suitable wind currents.

The Wrights transported their glider from Dayton to Kitty Hawk. In 1900, they glided for a few minutes in this first man-carrying device. Then they refined their theoretical aerodynamic calculations, realizing that they had to re-examine every earlier finding. Chanute helped with some advice and money. In 1901, the brothers built their first wind tunnel to test wings, enabling them to draw up accurate tables of air pressures on curved surfaces.

Successful glider experiments in 1901 and 1902 inspired the Wrights to build a powered flying machine, but no one could supply an engine to their specifications. With their indomitable spirit, they decided to build one themselves. In this endeavor, they were greatly and ably assisted by Charles E. Taylor, a mechanic. Except for the crankcase, Taylor machined every component of the engine in the bicycle shop. It was the only aspect of the Wrights' invention that someone else had a significant role in creating. The engine was crude even by the standards of those days—but it worked. The result was a water-cooled, four-cylinder, thirteen-horsepower gasoline engine, weighing less than 180 pounds and providing more power with less weight than any previous model. Its lightness enabled the brothers to keep the total weight of their 1903 Wright Flyer at 625 pounds of wood, fabric, and metal. Most important, the engine and the two chain-driven propellers enabled the craft to move through the air fast enough to generate lift on the wings to keep the machine airborne.

On September 23, 1903, the Wright brothers transported their biplane, unassembled, from Dayton to Kitty Hawk. By December 14, a cold and clear day, the reassembled aircraft was ready to be tested. Wilbur won the toss of the coin to decide who should try first. On leaving the sixty-foot wooden launching rail, the machine climbed a few feet, stalled, and landed after only three and a half seconds. Repairs took until December 17. Orville then made an epochal flight of twelve seconds, covering a distance of 120 feet. Three more tries were made that day. Wilbur flew 195 feet in thirteen seconds. Orville covered 200 feet in fifteen seconds. Finally, shortly after twelve o'clock noon, Wilbur flew 852 feet, lying prone at the controls, as usual, for fifty-nine seconds at thirty-one miles per hour against a twenty-one-mile-per-hour wind. A subsequent gust of wind damaged the plane while it was parked, and no more flying was possible that year.

Only a few newspapers in the country reported the Wrights' feat on the following day. The skepticism could be traced to several facts: Simon Newcomb, a highly respected U.S. scientist, had published "proof" earlier that year that heavier-than-air planes were impossible; Lilienthal's fatal crash in 1896 was still fresh in memory; and Langley's prestigious machine had just failed nine days earlier. Even the brothers underestimated the value of their achievement, which they reported to have cost them more than a thousand dollars. The Smithsonian Institution refused to recognize theirs as the first powered flight, preferring to honor Samuel Langley's attempt. Not until 1942 did the Smithsonian finally publish an unequivocal statement crediting the Wrights with having invented the airplane.

In 1904, the Wrights designed a new aircraft capable of sustained flight and of turning and banking maneuvers. The 1905 Wright Flyer could hold the air for thirty-nine minutes, covering as many kilometers over Huffman Prairie near Dayton, a more convenient test site than Kitty Hawk and one at which the brothers now continued their experiments.

In 1908, the U.S. War Department finally gave the Wrights a contract to build the first military aircraft. By the end of 1909, the brothers had won every flying competition around, and the Wright Company had received enough production orders to make them wealthy and famous men. Parades and medals greeted them everywhere. In 1932, a sixty-foot granite commemorative pylon was erected on the dune near Kill Devil Hills village, from whose slopes the initial flights had been launched.

The Wright brothers' story is one of two high-school dropouts with extensive intellectual curiosity, self-education, a supportive environment, and exceptional intellect who epitomized the American legend of gifted amateurism by conquering the air for humankind.

—Richard H. Collin, updated by Peter B. Heller

ADDITIONAL READING:

Crouch, Tom D. *The Bishop's Boys: A Life of Wilbur and Orville Wright.* New York: W. W. Norton, 1989. Biography showing the effect of the brothers' personalities on their approach to life and work. Distinguishes clearly between their human and inventive qualities.

Hallion, Richard P., ed. *The Wright Brothers: Heirs of Prometheus.* Washington, D.C.: National Air and Space Museum, Smithsonian Institution Press, 1978. The illustrations alone make this volume worthwhile.

Harris, Sherwood. *The First to Fly: Aviation's Pioneer Days.* Blue Ridge Summit, Pa.: TAB-Aero Division of McGraw-Hill, 1991. A simple, chronologically arranged account with excellent photographs.

Jakab, Peter L. *Visions of a Flying Machine: The Wright Brothers and the Process of Invention.* Washington, D.C.: Smithsonian Institution Press, 1990. A historian at the Smithsonian's Department of Aeronautics focuses on the two brothers' thought processes, as well as giving a factual account. Good illustrations and bibliography.

Kelly, Fred C. *The Wright Brothers.* New York: Harcourt Brace, 1943. An early account that was to eventuate as the 1951 epistolary biography *Miracle at Kitty Hawk: The Letters of Wilbur and Orville Wright*, authorized by Orville Wright and published by Farrar, Straus, and Young.

McFarland, Marvin W., ed. *The Papers of Wilbur and Orville Wright.* 2 vols. New York: McGraw-Hill, 1953. One of the most comprehensive collections of the brothers' correspondence, original sketches, diary entries, and other documentation. Exhaustive bibliography.

SEE ALSO: 1926, Launching of the First Liquid-Fueled Rocket; 1927, Lindbergh's Transatlantic Flight; 1961, First American in Space; 1969, Apollo 11 Lands on the Moon.

1905 ■ INDUSTRIAL WORKERS OF THE WORLD IS FOUNDED: *labor joins socialism in a radical workers' organization*

DATE: June 27, 1905
LOCALE: Chicago, Illinois
CATEGORIES: Business and labor; Organizations and institutions
KEY FIGURES:
Eugene Victor Debs (1855-1926), founder of the Socialist Party and a founder of the IWW
Elizabeth Gurley Flynn (1890-1964), founder of the IWW
William Dudley "Big Bill" Haywood (1869-1928), secretary of the Western Federation of Miners and a founder of the IWW
Joe Hill (1879-1915), Swedish-born labor agitator
Mary Harris "Mother" Jones (1830-1930), United Mine Workers organizer and a founder of the IWW

SUMMARY OF EVENT. The years preceding the formation of the Industrial Workers of the World (IWW) were filled with turmoil for workers who attempted to earn a fair wage and to have good working conditions. Influenced by the Populist movement and the Knights of Labor, the Western Federation of Mines (WFM) organized in 1893, with a membership of native white men only. Demanding safety legislation and money instead of scrip, the WFM was associated briefly with the American Federation of Labor (AFL), but split with the AFL when it did not assist in the WFM's 1894 strike at Cripple Creek, Colorado. The strike erupted when miners' wages were cut. Mine owners hired gunmen, and the governor brought in the state militia. After the strike, the WFM began to establish its own mines. Strikes in 1903 and 1904 brought Western miners to the realization that they must combine with workers in the East.

The eastern wing began with Eugene Debs, who had combined railway workers into the American Railway Union (ARU). The ARU was not craft-exclusive but rather open to all who worked for railway companies. With the exception of African American workers, the ARU believed in a brotherhood that included all workers. As head of the Eastern IWW, Debs tried but failed to combine the eastern and western organization in 1902.

On June 27, 1905, in Chicago, the WFM, the ARU, and anti-AFL unionists, socialists, and anarchists joined forces to combine into the IWW. "Big Bill" Haywood chaired the meeting and called for a working-class movement that could control economic powers. Considered to be revolutionary industrial unionism, the IWW combined an ideology of Marxist, Darwinian, and Socialist elements in one large union that would encompass men and women of all races. It was an alternative union to the AFL, whose capitalism and selective membership were opposite of IWW directives.

The IWW was considered to be the most radical movement, one of daring imagination. Members did not want to be a working-class political party but a force that could make economic and political change by revolutionary tactics. Charging low dues, the union committed itself to impoverished workers and operated as thirteen big groups that held sit-ins and street theater to get members and support. The IWW became noted for large numbers of strikes and was not trusted by the general public, who thought the group to be "syndicalists," or people who were capable of overthrowing the government.

One of the IWW's most powerful tactics was the use of direct action, even to the point of violating the law. IWW members believed that such action offered the only way to gain publicity and support. In the West, they held "free speech" fights, which were banned. Members seeking arrest protested and were jailed. Because they had an antireligious approach, they were unable to get permits to hold meetings. Instead, the IWW intruded into meetings of the permit-holding Salvation Army.

Noted for its egalitarian system, the union welcomed women, who were incorporated into male industrial unions except for certain strike meetings. Mary "Mother" Jones, an immigrant dressmaker and organizer of the United Mine Workers, and Elizabeth Gurley Flynn both helped to organize the IWW. Although never top officeholders in the union, women were very active strikers. No other labor union could boast the number of women who were actively speaking or raising funds as could the IWW. Membership included the skilled and unskilled, men and women, African Americans and Mexicans, Chinese and Japanese. The racially and ethnically diverse membership became known as the "Wobblies."

The economic depression of 1907-1908, factionalism, harassment from the government, and the WFM's leaving the union created problems for the fledgling union. Then in 1909, skilled workers joined unskilled immigrant strikers at a Pennsylvania steel car company over an incentive pay system. The plant shut down and when a split occurred between the groups, IWW leaders took charge. The show of force resulted in the owners' breaking down and settling.

In 1912, a hundred women, already on a plant speed-up conducted a massive textile strike in Lawrence, Massachusetts, when their wages were cut. The women were mostly immigrants less than eighteen years of age and suffering from malnutrition. Only two days later, an additional twenty thousand workers of forty different nationalities joined them. IWW leaders, including Flynn, hurried to Massachusetts to help the strikers. Workers were instructed to conduct mass pickets, a method to avoid arrest by forming an unbroken human chain. In Lawrence, the chain consisted of between five and twenty thousand workers walking continuously for twenty-four hours in nonviolent action. The workers were organized according to nationality, and translated literature aided in the continued strike.

When a woman picketer was shot and killed, some union officials were arrested, although they had been miles away at the time. Martial law was declared, meetings were banned, and police were called into action. When a fifteen-year-old Syrian boy was killed by the state militia, strikers sent their children out of Lawrence, which generated much publicity. When companies tried to block the move, the country was outraged and the mill owners were forced to settle the strike, granting the workers raises, overtime pay, and other benefits.

The Lawrence strikes, although successfully joining immigrant workers, did not have the impact of a widespread movement. The wage gains were offset by increased use of mill machinery. Public outcry in Lawrence erupted as the Roman Catholic church campaigned against the Wobblies, and the Citizens Association attacked the IWW as atheistic anarchists. A spy network brought harassment to the victorious workers. A subsequent strike in New Jersey did not meet with success, as laborers fought against one another. The depression of 1913-1914 further hurt the IWW movement.

A revitalization occurred with the initiation of the Agricultural Workers Organization (AWO), a branch of migrant farm laborers who fought for immediate demands. The result was an increase in pay and better working conditions for harvest workers. In 1916, northwestern lumber workers greatly benefited the Wobblies' organization when the strikers tenaciously held out against police brutality and shootings.

In 1914, IWW labor agitator Joe Hill was charged with the murder of two Salt Lake City men. His execution made him a symbolic martyr. Martyrdom could not save the Wobblies, however, as lawmen pursued their members. While gaining worker support, they lost any endorsements to the AFL. Despite an effort to downplay antiwar criticism after World War I began, the IWW's refusal to endorse the fighting brought fierce government attacks, especially when the IWW began to encourage young men not to serve their country. To American nativists, the mainly immigrant members of the IWW made the union appear dangerous. These anti-IWW feelings helped the growth of the AFL. Finally, the Red Scare of 1919-1920 resulted in many Wobblies being put on trial for having communist leanings. Although the organization virtually died, interest in the IWW has peaked and waned over the years. Its membership fluctuated from doing educational work, to renewed radicalism in the 1960's when singer Joan Baez popularized "The Ballad of Joe Hill," to the printing of a newsletter for three thousand in the 1980's, and more recently to a paying membership reduced to mere hundreds.

—*Marilyn Elizabeth Perry*

ADDITIONAL READING:
Bird, Stewart, Dan Georgakas, and Deborah Shaffer, comps. *Solidarity Forever: An Oral History of the IWW.* Chicago: Lake View Press, 1985. A collection of essays and oral histories revealing the dedication of IWW members to its cause.

Conlin, Joseph Robert. *Bread and Roses Too: Studies of the Wobblies.* Westport, Conn.: Greenwood Press, 1969. Six essays analyze the problems encountered by IWW members during their struggles for better working conditions.

Dubofsky, Melvyn. *We Shall Be All: A History of the Industrial Workers of the World.* Chicago: Quadrangle Books, 1969.

A large volume about the IWW, with excellent profiles of union leaders and an absorbing history of the movement.

Foner, Philip S., ed. *Fellow Workers and Friends: I.W.W. Free Speech Fights as Told by Participants.* Westport, Conn.: Greenwood Press, 1981. A collection of personal histories of IWW workers as they relate to their fight for free speech.

Kornbluh, Joyce L., ed. *Rebel Voices: An I.W.W. Anthology.* Ann Arbor: University of Michigan Press, 1964. A chronologically ordered anthology combining Wobbly member narratives, cartoons, songs, and other memorabilia to form a picture of IWW solidarity.

Winters, Donald E., Jr. *The Soul of the Wobblies: The I.W.W., Religion, and American Culture in the Progressive Era, 1905-1917.* Westport, Conn.: Greenwood Press, 1985. A fresh look at the IWW, taking the perspective that its solidarity was comparable to a religious belief.

SEE ALSO: 1882, Standard Oil Trust Is Organized; 1890, Sherman Antitrust Act; 1894, Pullman Strike; 1902, Anthracite Coal Strike; 1919, Red Scare; 1935, National Labor Relations Act; 1935, Congress of Industrial Organizations Is Founded; 1938, Fair Labor Standards Act; 1943, Inflation and Labor Unrest; 1955, AFL and CIO Merge.

1905 ■ NIAGARA MOVEMENT: *a progenitor of the National Association for the Advancement of Colored People lays the groundwork for a new civil rights movement*

DATE: July 11, 1905
LOCALE: Niagara Falls, Ontario, Canada
CATEGORIES: African American History, Canadian history; Civil rights
KEY FIGURES:
W. E. B. Du Bois (1868-1963), African American author and educator, one of the earliest advocates of full, immediate racial equality
Booker T. Washington (1856-1915), African American educator who asserted that blacks would reach social equality only after achieving economic independence
SUMMARY OF EVENT. In the early years of the twentieth century, two major approaches to achieving African American progress were separated by their differing philosophies: Booker T. Washington was a pragmatist who acknowledged current policies toward blacks and wanted to make the lives of African Americans as easy as possible within that framework. Washington held that "it is important and right that all privileges of law be ours, but it is vastly more important that we be prepared for the exercise of those privileges." He assumed that as African Americans became productive workers who were not troublemakers, they would be seen as valuable assets to U.S. society. Then they would slowly but surely move up the economic and political ladder.

The leaders of what came to be known as the Niagara

Movement, by contrast, asserted that Washington's programs would keep African Americans at the bottom of the political, economic, and social ladder. One of the Niagara Movement's major leaders was W. E. B. Du Bois, a professor at Atlanta University at the beginning of the movement. Du Bois maintained that it was important for African Americans to press for the immediate implementation of their civil rights: "We want full manhood suffrage and we want it now. . . . We want the Constitution of the country enforced. . . . We want our children educated. . . . And we shall win!" The leaders of the Niagara Movement were convinced that as long as African Americans were not protected by law, economic and social advances would never come. They believed that the structures of United States society were developed in such a way that, without the force of law, other advances would never occur. These two different views of how to achieve progress for African Americans not only separated Washington and Du Bois throughout their lives but would remain at the heart of discord over how best to achieve freedom and progress for African Americans in the United States.

The Niagara Movement was formed on July 11, 1905, when twenty-nine radical African American intellectuals, headed by Du Bois, met at Niagara Falls, in Ontario, Canada. (Even though some organizational activities were held in Buffalo, New York, on the other side of the U.S.-Canadian border, most meetings were held in Canada because of the difficulty of finding places in the United States that would accommodate African Americans.) On nearly every issue, the Niagara Movement stood in direct contrast to Washington's approach. In sharp language, in a policy statement entitled the Negro Declaration of Independence, movement leaders placed full responsibility for the race problem on whites, denouncing the inequities of segregation and disfranchisement laws; they maintained that economic progress was not possible in a democratic society without the protection afforded by the ballot; and they insisted, above all, that African Americans could gain their rights only by agitation. Members of the Niagara Movement spoke out against an accommodationist approach at a time when almost all white and African American leaders believed that such policies were critical if blacks were to achieve equality in U.S. society and politics.

About five years after it had been established, the Niagara Movement had approximately four hundred members. Most were Northern, urban, upper-class college graduates. The movement never developed the wide following it wanted. Some assert that the movement did not reach a broad enough spectrum in the African American community, let alone create an appeal to the broader society of which it was part. At first women were excluded from the Niagara Movement, both as members and as a focus of emancipation. Some of the movement's organizers reasoned that fighting for women's rights along with rights for African American males would result in defeat of the movement's policies and goals. Du Bois, however, argued that African American civil rights would not be complete without women as well as men tasting the fruits of freedom. He argued that to obtain male suffrage on the backs of women was immoral and not in keeping with the solidarity that African Americans must maintain in the face of the hostility of the dominant white society. Du Bois' position finally prevailed.

During its existence, the Niagara Movement held conferences in 1906, at Harpers Ferry, West Virginia; in 1907, at Boston, Massachusetts; and in 1908, at Oberlin, Ohio. Civil rights protests in cities across the nation were organized by the Niagara Movement, which gained a reputation for demanding recognition of the equality of all human beings through social protest and demonstrations. In the wake of a race riot in Springfield, Illinois, in 1908, the movement began to dissolve as members turned their attention to a new organization. On February 12, 1909, the ideas on which the Niagara Movement was founded were absorbed into the framework of the National Association for the Advancement of Colored People (NAACP), which not only developed a wider following but also addressed the broader issues of equality and civil rights that the Niagara Movement was not able to address effectively. Important members of the Niagara Movement, such as Du Bois, became instrumental in the NAACP as well. Du Bois, however, decided that even the NAACP was not forceful enough in addressing issues such as lynching, rape, and voting rights. He would end his life in exile in Africa.

Although the Niagara Movement survived only five years—formally disbanding in 1910—it had served as the foundation upon which later movements were built. It can be seen as both a negative reaction to Washington's accommodationist approach to African American equality and the progenitor of such later groups as the Student Nonviolent Coordinating Committee (SNCC), the Congress of Racial Equality (CORE), and the Black Panthers.　　*—Paul Barton-Kriese*

ADDITIONAL READING:

Burns, W. Haywood. *The Voices of Negro Protest in America*. New York: Oxford University Press, 1963. Discusses twentieth century protest movements, highlighting the NAACP.

Du Bois, W. E. B. *The Souls of Black Folk*. 1903. Reprint. New York: Vintage Books, 1990. Du Bois' powerful statement about the problem of the twentieth century as the problem of the color line, arguing that black U.S. citizens will progress only via challenge, struggle, and political protest. A direct challenge to Booker T. Washington's program of gradualism.

Hoemann, George H. *What God Hath Wrought: The Embodiment of Freedom in the Thirteenth Amendment*. New York: Garland Press, 1987. A social history of the time in which the amendment that gave African Americans their freedom was written. Also dissects the meanings of words within that amendment.

McKissick, Floyd B. *Three-fifths of a Man*. New York: Macmillan, 1969. An account of the racial basis of the Declaration of Independence, the Constitution, and the Emancipation Proclamation, with an examination of how these documents have influenced race relations.

Nieman, Donald G. *Promises to Keep: African-Americans and the Constitutional Order, 1776 to the Present.* New York: Oxford University Press, 1991. A constitutional history of the United States with special reference to charting the impact of the Constitution on U.S. social history.

Washington, Booker T. *Up from Slavery.* 1901. Reprint. New York: Gramercy Books, 1993. Washington's seminal work, in which he describes his idea of the "talented tenth" and how black citizens of the United States will achieve full equality gradually, through hard work and demonstrating their worthiness. A direct contrast to the more aggressive platform of Du Bois.

SEE ALSO: 1895, Booker T. Washington's Atlanta Exposition Address; 1909, National Association for the Advancement of Colored People Is Founded; 1917, Universal Negro Improvement Association Is Established; 1930, Nation of Islam Is Founded; 1942, Congress of Racial Equality Is Founded; 1957, Southern Christian Leadership Conference Is Founded.

1906 ■ SAN FRANCISCO EARTHQUAKE: *a new era of urban planning and building regulation is spawned by one of the worst natural disasters in history*

DATE: April 18, 1906
LOCALE: San Francisco and vicinity
CATEGORY: Economics
KEY FIGURES:
Frederick Funston (1865-1917), acting commander of the U.S. Army's Pacific Division
Eugene E. Schmitz (1864-1928), mayor of San Francisco
Dennis Sullivan, San Francisco's fire chief
SUMMARY OF EVENT. In 1906, San Francisco's population was an estimated 410,000. The city developed rapidly after the California gold rush of 1849; it prided itself both on its museums and other cultural institutions and on the flamboyant, openly criminal Barbary Coast and Tenderloin districts. Eager for economic growth, developers ignored the San Andreas fault eight miles from the center of San Francisco, although significant quakes had been recorded in 1836, 1857, 1865, and 1868. The city also had suffered major fire damage six times between 1849 and 1851. Despite this history, developers extended the city into the bay, using as filler garbage, junk, rotting wood, and even abandoned ships. By 1906, approximately a quarter of the city's population lived on the filled or "made" land. As early as 1868, experts had warned of the danger of earthquake damage to this land. In 1905, the National Board of Fire Underwriters had warned of major fire hazards; Fire Chief Dennis Sullivan urged repairs of cisterns, development of a saltwater system for fire protection, and training of personnel in the use of explosives to provide firebreaks. These reports were ignored by city officials in a government noted for its corruption.

At 5:12:05 A.M., Wednesday, April 18, 1906, a forty-five-second shock wave was recorded as far away as Tokyo; ten to twelve seconds later, the heaviest jolt was felt. A third severe quake occurred at 8:14, and twenty-four other aftershocks were recorded by 7:00 P.M. The heaviest quake was recorded as a nine on the Rossi-Forel scale of intensity (one through ten) then in use and has been estimated at 8.25 or 8.3 on the modern Richter scale. Every brick building collapsed in Santa Rosa, about twenty miles away; to the south, near San Jose, some hundred residents and employees of Agnew's Asylum for the mentally disturbed were killed. Palo Alto was severely damaged, as were other nearby towns.

In San Francisco, eyewitnesses reported that streets heaved and rocked. Collapsing buildings raised clouds of dust. The largest concentration of dead and injured was in a twelve-by-six-block area south of Market Street near City Hall, an area of cheap frame rooming houses and hotels, stores, and restaurants. According to the 1900 census report, this area was second in population density only to Chinatown. City Hall, then the largest building west of Chicago, had been built on filled land. Portions of the building collapsed. Elsewhere in the area, the collapse of buildings into each other created widespread structural damage. Water conduits, and telephone, telegraph, and fire alarm systems were destroyed, although the Signal Corps reestablished communication lines for the coordination of military efforts. Gas mains were shut off, but gas explosions still occurred. Everywhere, the quakes, fires, and explosions sent crowds massing in the streets, some working with rescuers and some impeding rescue efforts. As fires broke out, many of the injured had to be left to die in the wrecked buildings as rescuers fled the flames.

Fire Chief Sullivan was fatally injured in the first quake. His injuries deprived firefighters of centralized authority; the damage to fire stations had trapped equipment and allowed terrified horses to run away. Although firefighters lacked basic communication systems, they attempted to rescue victims from collapsed buildings and respond to some fifty fires reported within seventeen minutes of the quake. Fires continued to break out. The worst of these, called the "Ham and Eggs" fire, was supposedly started by a woman cooking breakfast in a house with a damaged chimney; the actual cause of the fire was never determined. This Hayes Valley fire rapidly spread toward City Hall and Mechanics Pavilion, where patients from the earthquake-damaged Central Emergency Hospital had been evacuated. The 354 patients at the pavilion again were evacuated. Eyewitnesses reported that stacked bodies were left to the flames.

Mayor Eugene Schmitz and Brigadier General Frederick Funston independently took charge of the city. Both apparently issued unconstitutional orders for the shooting of looters. Many people besides criminals were gunned down, and police and military personnel sometimes joined the looters. After the disaster, residents and businesspersons complained that they had been allowed no chance to protect property or rescue goods; patrols ordered them to evacuate or be killed. In some areas where residents and workers were able to remain, damage from fire was minimal. Six men saved the Long Syrup Warehouse. The U.S. Mint, post office, and courthouse similarly were saved; ten postal employees successfully used dampened mail sacks to beat off the flames in their building. The Ferry Building, vital as an evacuation point, was preserved.

Dynamite blasts set off by untrained personnel caused many of the fires. Funston authorized extensive dynamiting; Schmitz authorized the use of dynamite only when buildings already were about to burn. No coordinated effort was possible. Few of those setting off the blasts were trained in the use of explosives, and buildings were dynamited too soon or too late or too randomly to provide effective firebreaks. The most effective help came from U.S. Navy vessels. Navy personnel, working with California State fireboats, provided hospital assistance and pumps that could draw saltwater from the bay for firefighters on shore and could condense freshwater needed to keep boilers heated on fire department engines. The Navy also removed thirty thousand persons to safety. Together with the 225,000 evacuated by the Southern Pacific Railroad, this constituted the largest peacetime evacuation of any U.S. city.

The last fire ended at 7:00 A.M., Saturday, April 21. Thirty schools, eighty churches and convents, a business section, and a quarter million homes had been lost. Fire had burned 2,831 acres, more than six times that burned by the legendary 1666 fire of London. The best estimate of financial loss was between $350 million and $500 million, about twice the amount spent by the entire federal government that year.

Financial matters dominated the post-disaster period. Estimates of earthquakes and deaths were kept low; government and business interests wanted to encourage new investment and development. Fires, authorities reasoned, could be prevented. Earthquakes could not, and fear of earthquakes might inhibit economic growth. The disaster also was used unsuccessfully as an excuse to relocate Chinatown at Hunter Point and thus remove Chinese from possession of some of the city's most valuable land, while the San Francisco Board of Education planned to rebuild with schools in which Asian students would be segregated. Both plans caused international incidents. Mayor Schmitz and his political patron, Abraham Ruef, were under investigation for bribery and extortion at the time of the earthquake. When President Theodore Roosevelt denounced the proposed segregation, the matter was allowed to die. More lasting controversies were caused by the refusal of many insurance companies to meet claims and by accusations that much of the six million dollars in aid sent to the city had found its way into the hands of corrupt city leaders.

No exact figure can be given for loss of life. Official accounts estimated up to 550 known dead, but many others may have been buried by the quake, burned in the fires, or sickened by the outbreaks of typhoid, smallpox, plague, and meningitis in refugee camps. Fatality figures did not include those who died as a result of lengthy illness and mental trauma. Counting the residents, sometimes illegal, of immigrant sections such as Chinatown, the transient residents of areas of cheap hotels and lodging houses, and the anonymous criminal and prostitute populations of the Tenderloin and Barbary Coast, actual loss of life may have been in the thousands.   —Betty Richardson

ADDITIONAL READING:

Bronson, William. *The Earth Shook, The Sky Burned*. Garden City, N.Y.: Doubleday, 1959. Vivid, easy-to-read, well-illustrated account. Focuses on sequence of events and on individuals caught in the catastrophe.

Ditzel, Paul C. "San Francisco: Leather-Lungs Dougherty." In *Fire Engines, Fire Fighters: The Men, Equipment, and Machines from Colonial Days to the Present*. New York: Crown, 1976. The account of the San Francisco disaster is brief and superficial, but, unlike most other studies, Ditzel's illustrates the machines and other equipment available for firefighting and rescues at the time.

"Earthquake and Flames." In *Great Fires of America*. Waukesha, Wis.: Country Beautiful, 1973. This simple, illustrated summary places the San Francisco disaster within the context of other similar urban catastrophes.

Hansen, Gladys, and Emmet Condon. *Denial of Disaster*. San Francisco: Cameron, 1989. This detailed, profusely illustrated study corrects earlier histories, emphasizes the structural weaknesses and political scandals that led to avoidable damage, and includes an extensive bibliography. Essential reading.

Morris, Charles, ed. *The San Francisco Calamity by Earthquake and Fire: A Complete and Accurate Account of the Fearful Disaster Which Visited the Great City and the Pacific Coast, the Reign of Panic and Lawlessness, the Plight of 300,000 Homeless People and the Worldwide Rush to the Rescue Told by Eye Witnesses*. 1906. Reprint. Secaucus, N.J.: Citadel Press, 1986. A valuable collection, reissued without additions or corrections.

SEE ALSO: 1892, Yellow Peril Campaign; 1911, Triangle Shirtwaist Company Fire.

1906 ■ PURE FOOD AND DRUG ACT:
prohibition of interstate commerce in misbranded and adulterated food is a first step toward consumer protection against unsafe products

DATE: June 30, 1906
LOCALE: Washington, D.C.
CATEGORIES: Business and labor; Laws and acts
KEY FIGURES:
Albert Beveridge (1862-1927), U.S. senator from Indiana
Theodore Roosevelt (1858-1919), twenty-sixth president of the United States, 1901-1909
Upton Sinclair (1878-1968), author of the 1906 novel *The Jungle*
James W. Wadsworth (1846-1926), U.S. representative from New York and chair of the House Committee on Agriculture

Harvey W. Wiley (1844-1930), chief of the U.S. Department
of Agriculture's Bureau of Chemistry

James Wilson (1835-1920), U.S. secretary of agriculture

Summary of event. With the rise of the food processing and
packaging industry at the end of the 1800's, consumers became increasingly concerned about the purity of their food.
Ingredients that had once come from trusted local sources
were now produced by machines and marketed by faceless
corporations unaccountable to the public. In 1883, Harvey
Wiley became head of the U.S. Department of Agriculture's
(USDA) Bureau of Chemistry. Wiley began to investigate and
discover incidents of food adulteration, ranging from the use
of nontoxic extenders and fillers to the presence of poisonous
preservatives. Following the example of Great Britain, which
had passed its first national food and drug act in 1875, Wiley
began to campaign for a pure food law in the United States,
but the powerful food industry lobby branded him a socialist
and blocked his efforts, including an unsuccessful bill in 1889.

Despite Wiley's initial failures, public distrust of the food
supply continued to mount, fomented by the deaths from botu-
lism of U.S. soldiers who had eaten spoiled canned meat in the
Spanish-American War (1898), early exposés of the meatpacking industry by William Randolph Hearst, and various
other muckraking articles and pamphlets. With only scattered
state regulation and none at the federal level, a "buyer beware"
caveat governed food and drug consumption. Some housewives even performed their own chemical tests on their food at
home to determine its makeup and quality.

Food manufacturers countered consumer concerns with advertising designed to emphasize the purity of their products,
promoting them as hygienic and staging pure food fairs
around the country with samples and cooking demonstrations.
While such fairs were very popular and served to introduce
processed food products into U.S. domestic life, consumer
anxiety about manufactured food persisted.

In 1904, socialist journalist Upton Sinclair received a challenge from one of his editors: to investigate and write about
the lives of the industrial working class. Already working on
an article detailing an unsuccessful strike by meat packers in
Chicago, Sinclair chose Packingtown there as his investigative
site and undertook seven weeks of research, disguising himself as a stockyard worker to observe the meatpacking process
at first hand. The result was *The Jungle* (1906), a novel about
a family of Lithuanian immigrants destroyed by the brutality
of stockyard work. The novel's story was tragic, but its true
impact lay in passages graphically depicting unsanitary
slaughtering and processing procedures, exposing the widespread practice of selling to the public products made from
diseased and chemically tainted meats.

The horrors recounted in *The Jungle* included the sale of
spoiled meat whose rot was concealed with chemicals; inclusion of rats' poisoned carcasses and feces in sausages; the
prevalence of tuberculosis among workers handling meat; instances of workers falling into cooking vats, their flesh cooking off into the contents that were subsequently packaged and

sold; the use of tripe, pork fat, and beef suet in potted chicken;
the rechurning of rancid butter; and the treatment of milk
with formaldehyde. In support of his allegations, Sinclair included footnotes quoting from the USDA's meat-inspection
regulations.

Macmillan, the publisher initially contracted to publish *The
Jungle*, declined to do so for fear of libel suits from the food
industry. Sinclair finally found a potential buyer in Doubleday,
Page, and Company, which sent investigators to Packingtown
to confirm Sinclair's allegations. Convinced that the novel's
descriptions could withstand legal challenge and despite pressure from the meat industry, Doubleday agreed to publish *The
Jungle* with one of the first mass publicity campaigns for a book
in U.S. history, ushering in the age of modern mass media.

Doubleday's campaign highlighted the novel's muckraking
exposé and targeted everyone from newspaper editors to President Theodore Roosevelt himself, to whom the publisher sent
an advance proof of the book. *The Jungle* was released in
February, 1906, to an outraged public primed by advance
publicity and became an immediate best-seller.

The economic impact of *The Jungle*'s disturbing descriptions
was dramatic and long-lasting: Domestic meat sales dropped
by more than half and remained depressed for more than two
decades, leading to an industrywide "eat more meat" campaign
in 1928; publication of the book in Great Britain and in seventeen translations created an international scandal and caused
Germany to raise its import duties on U.S. meat. The political
result soon followed: President Roosevelt, after a personal consultation with Sinclair at the White House, wrote to Secretary of
Agriculture James Wilson on March 12, 1906, requesting that
he undertake a secret investigation of the meatpacking industry with Sinclair's collaboration. The resulting Neill-Reynolds
Report gave the president the ammunition he needed to support pure food legislation. Harvey Wiley drafted the law, and
Indiana senator Albert Beveridge, the president's ally and an
architect of Progressive reform, brought it to Congress.

Beveridge's bill passed the Senate on May 26 as an amendment to the Agricultural Appropriations bill, but stalled in the
House at the behest of the chair of the Committee on Agriculture, James W. Wadsworth, who was apparently under pressure
from the meat lobby. Roosevelt responded by releasing the
first part of the Neill-Reynolds report, which confirmed Sinclair's version of meat-processing practices and raised public
outrage to fever pitch. The meat lobby conceded and, after
minor compromises, Congress passed both the Pure Food and
Drug Act (Title 34, Statute 768) and the Meat Inspection Act
on June 30, 1906.

The Pure Food and Drug Act prohibited the interstate transportation and sale of adulterated food, including any product
that is combined or packed with another substance that adversely affects its quality or strength; is substituted in whole or
in part by another substance; has had any essential component
removed; has been blended, coated, colored, or stained to
conceal damage or inferiority; contains poisonous or harmful
additions; is composed of filthy or decomposed animal or

vegetable matter; or is the product of a diseased animal or one that died other than by slaughtering.

Enforcement of the act was consigned to the USDA's Bureau of Chemistry until 1928, when the Food, Drug, and Insecticide Administration (renamed the Food and Drug Administration in 1931) was formed to assume the responsibility. The act was amended in 1911, 1913, and 1919; then, amid charges that the law was laxly enforced and served to benefit the largest food-processing companies, it was superseded by the Food, Drug, and Cosmetic Act of 1938. That act, supplemented by numerous amendments and acts addressing food processing and inspection procedures, fair packaging and labeling, and drug testing and safety, remained the basis of food and drug law in the 1990's. The Food and Drug Administration has remained one of the nation's oldest consumer protection agencies, and its roots clearly extend back to the events of 1906.

Although Upton Sinclair involved himself personally in the passage of the Pure Food and Drug Act, he later stated that the horrific meatpacking procedures he described were but one aspect of what was meant to be a larger condemnation of the evils of industrial capitalism. Still, it was *The Jungle*'s news-breaking story and legislative outcome that earned it a place in literary history and Sinclair his position as one of the nation's preeminent muckrakers. As an inaugural triumph in a U.S. tradition of investigative journalism, the Pure Food and Drug Act stands as a symbol of the public's right to know and the government's obligation to act for its citizens' safety.

—*Elizabeth J. Miles*

ADDITIONAL READING:

Bloodworth, William A., Jr. *Upton Sinclair*. Boston: Twayne, 1977. Biography analyzing Sinclair's work as a muckraker and political figure, including his role in the passage of the Pure Food and Drug Act.

Harris, Leon. *Upton Sinclair: American Rebel*. New York: Thomas Y. Crowell, 1975. Highly personal biography of Sinclair details his relationship with Roosevelt and the congressional machinations surrounding the act.

Root, Waverly, and Richard de Rochemont. *Eating in America: A History*. New York: Ecco Press, 1995. Food historian Root chronicles U.S. eating customs through history, including the advent of the food processing industry and the public outrage that led to the Pure Food and Drug Act.

Shapiro, Laura. *Perfection Salad: Women and Cooking at the Turn of the Century*. New York: Farrar, Straus & Giroux, 1986. This social analysis shows food purity as an important theme of the early twentieth century domestic science movement.

Sinclair, Upton. *The Jungle*. 1906. Reprint. New York: New American Library, 1980. The novel that brought corrupt food industry practices to international attention is one of the first major media exposés in U.S. history.

U.S. Food and Drug Administration. *Milestones in U.S. Food and Drug Law History*. Washington, D.C.: Government Printing Office, 1985. A legislative chronology outlining the development of food and drug law in the United States.

SEE ALSO: 1895, Hearst-Pulitzer Circulation War; 1898, Spanish-American War; 1901, Theodore Roosevelt Becomes President; 1912, U.S. Public Health Service Is Established.

1907 ■ GENTLEMEN'S AGREEMENT:
immigration from Japan to the mainland United States is limited to nonlaborers, laborers already settled in the United States, and their families

DATE: March 14, 1907
LOCALE: United States and Japan
CATEGORIES: Asian American history; Business and labor; Immigration; Treaties and agreements
KEY FIGURES:

Tadasu Hayashi (1850-1913), Japan's foreign minister
Theodore Roosevelt (1858-1919), twenty-sixth president of the United States, 1901-1909
Elihu Root (1845-1937), U.S. secretary of state
Shuzo Aoki (1844-1914), Japanese ambassador to the United States
Luke E. Wright (1846-1922), ambassador to Japan

SUMMARY OF EVENT. From 1638 to 1854, Japan maintained a policy of isolation toward the world, both to preserve peace, which it had not enjoyed for several hundred years, and to protect its cultural values and feudal institutions from foreign influence. This long period of seclusion changed in 1852, when Commodore Matthew Calbraith Perry arrived in Yedo, Japan, to deliver a letter from President Millard Fillmore to the emperor. Diplomatic relations between Japan and the United States began on March 31, 1854, when a treaty was signed opening two Japanese ports to U.S. ships and permitting the United States to receive any future concessions that might be granted to other powers. For the next thirty years, trade flourished between the two countries. A treaty of commerce and navigation in 1884 retained the most-favored-nation clause in all commercial matters.

Until 1868, Japan prohibited all emigration. Without obtaining their government's permission to leave, a group of Japanese laborers, the *gannenmono* ("first-year" people), arrived in Hawaii on May 17, 1868. Japan was in transition during the 1870's and 1880's. During the Meiji Restoration period, following the overthrow of the Tokugawa shogunate (1603-1867), Japan's economy and government had been modernized extensively. However, rapid industrialization in urban areas was not accompanied by similar developments in agricultural areas. By 1884, overpopulation, compounded with high unemployment, conditions of drought, crop failure, and famine, had engendered political upheaval and rioting. These changed circumstances led to the legalization of emigration in 1885.

The first Japanese immigrants who arrived in California in 1871 were mostly middle-class young men seeking opportunities to study or improve their economic status. By 1880, there were 148 resident Japanese. Their numbers increased to 1,360 in 1891, including 281 laborers and 172 farmers. A treaty between the United States and Japan in 1894 ensured mutual free entry although allowing limitations on immigration based on domestic interests. By 1900, the number of Japanese recorded in the U.S. Census had increased to 24,326. They arrived at ports on the Pacific coast and settled primarily in the Pacific states and British Columbia.

An increase in the demand for Hawaiian sugar in turn increased the demand for plantation labor, especially Japanese labor. An era of government-contract labor began in 1884, only ending with the U.S. annexation of Hawaii in 1898. Sixty thousand Japanese in the islands then became eligible to enter the United States without passports. Between 1899 and 1906, it is estimated that between forty thousand and fifty-seven thousand Japanese moved to the United States via Hawaii, Canada, and Mexico.

On the Pacific coast, tensions developed between Asians and other Californians. Although the Japanese immigrant workforce was initially welcomed, antagonism increased as it began to compete with U.S. labor. The emerging trade-union movement advocated a restriction of immigration. An earlier campaign against the Chinese had culminated in the 1882 Chinese Exclusion Act, which suspended immigration of Chinese laborers to the United States for ten years. This act constituted the first U.S. law barring immigration based on race or nationality. A similar campaign was instigated against the Japanese. On March 1, 1905, both houses of the California State legislature voted to urge California's congressional delegation in Washington, D.C., to pursue the limitation of Japanese immigrants. At a meeting in San Francisco on May 7, delegates from sixty-seven organizations launched the Japanese and Korean Exclusion League, known also as the Asiatic Exclusion League.

President Theodore Roosevelt, who was involved in the peace negotiations between Japan and Russia, observed the developing situation in California. George Kennan, who was covering the Russo-Japanese War, wrote to the president:

> It isn't the exclusion of a few emigrants that hurts here . . . it's the putting of Japanese below Hungarians, Italians, Syrians, Polish Jews, and degraded nondescripts from all parts of Europe and Western Asia. No proud, high spirited and victorious people will submit to such a classification as that, especially when it is made with insulting reference to personal character and habits.

Roosevelt agreed, saying he was mortified that people in the United States should insult the Japanese. He continued to play a pivotal role in resolving the Japanese-Russian differences at the Portsmouth Peace Conference.

Anti-Japanese feeling waned until April, 1906. Following the San Francisco earthquake, an outbreak of crime occurred, including many cases of assault against Japanese. There was also an organized boycott of Japanese restaurants. The Japanese viewed these acts as especially reprehensible. Their government and Red Cross had contributed more relief for San Francisco than all other foreign nations combined.

Tension escalated. The Asian Exclusion League, whose membership was estimated to be 78,500 in California, together with San Francisco's mayor, pressured the San Francisco school board to segregate Japanese schoolchildren. On October 11, 1906, the board passed its resolution. A protest filed by the Japanese consul was denied. Japan protested that the act violated most-favored-nation treatment. Ambassador Luke E. Wright, in Tokyo, reported Japan's extremely negative feelings about the matter to Secretary of State Elihu Root. This crisis in Japanese-American relations brought the countries to the brink of war. On October 25, Japan's ambassador, Shuzo Aoki, met with Root to seek a solution. President Roosevelt, who recognized the justification of the Japanese protest based on the 1894 treaty, on October 26 sent his secretary of commerce and labor to San Francisco to investigate the matter.

In his message to Congress on December 4, President Roosevelt paid tribute to Japan and strongly repudiated San Francisco for its anti-Japanese acts. He encouraged Congress to pass an act that would allow naturalization of the Japanese in the United States. Roosevelt's statements and request pleased Japan but aroused further resentment on the Pacific coast. During the previous twelve months, more than seventeen thousand Japanese had entered the mainland United States, two-thirds coming by way of Hawaii. Roosevelt recognized that the basic cause of the unrest in California—the increasing inflow of Japanese laborers—could be resolved only by checking immigration.

Negotiations with Japan to limit the entry of Japanese laborers began in late December, 1906. Three issues were involved: the rescinding of the segregation order by the San Francisco school board, the withholding of passports to the mainland United States by the Japanese government, and the closing of immigration channels through Hawaii, Canada, and Mexico by federal legislation. The Hawaiian issue, which related to an earlier Gentlemen's Agreement of 1900, was the first resolved through the diplomacy of Japan's foreign minister, Tadasu Hayashi, ambassadors Wright and Aoki, and Secretary of State Root.

Before Japan would agree to discuss immigration to the mainland, it was necessary for the segregation order to be withdrawn. In February, 1907, the president invited San Francisco's entire board of education, the mayor, and a city superintendent of schools to Washington, D.C., to confer on the segregation issue and other problems related to Japan. On February 18, a pending immigration bill was amended to prevent Japanese laborers from entering the United States via Hawaii, Mexico, or Canada. Assured that immigration of Japanese laborers would be stopped, the school board rescinded their segregation order on March 13. An executive order issued by the president on March 14 put into effect the restrictions on passports. Subsequently, the Japanese government agreed to conclude the Gentlemen's Agreement. In January, 1908, Foreign Minister Hayashi agreed to the terms of immigration discussed in December, 1907. On March 9, Secretary of State Root instructed Ambassador Wright to thank Japan, thus concluding the negotiations begun in December, 1906.

As reported by the commissioner general of immigration in 1908, the Japanese government would issue passports for travel to the continental United States only to nonlaborers, laborers who were former residents of the United States, parents, wives, or children of residents, and "settled agriculturalists." A final provision prevented secondary immigration into the United States by way of Hawaii, Mexico, or Canada.

When the Gentlemen's Agreement of 1907 cut off new supplies of Japanese labor, Filipinos were recruited to take their place, both in Hawaii and in California, as well as in the Alaskan fishing industry. As U.S. nationals, Filipinos could not be prevented from migrating to the United States.

—*Susan E. Hamilton*

ADDITIONAL READING:

Boddy, E. Manchester. *Japanese in America.* 1921. Reprint. San Francisco: R&E Research Associates, 1970. An account of Japan's emergence from a feudal state. Discusses Japanese immigration and U.S. prejudice toward the Japanese.

Esthus, Raymond A. *Theodore Roosevelt and Japan.* Seattle: University of Washington Press, 1967. An extensive, detailed examination of Roosevelt's relationship with Japan.

Herman, Masako, ed. *The Japanese in America, 1843-1973.* Dobbs Ferry, N.Y.: Oceana, 1974. An extended chronology and collection of documents.

Kikumura, Akemi. *Issei Pioneers: Hawaii and the Mainland, 1885 to 1924.* Los Angeles: Japanese American National Museum, 1992. A brief but well-researched text, with photographs that accompanied the premiere exhibit of the Japanese American National Museum.

United States Department of State. *Report of the Hon. Roland S. Morris on Japanese Immigration and Alleged Discriminatory Legislation Against Japanese Residents in the United States.* 1921. Reprint. New York: Arno Press, 1978. Correspondence regarding the Gentlemen's Agreement.

SEE ALSO: 1854, Perry Opens Trade with Japan; 1892, Yellow Peril Campaign; 1913, Alien Land Laws.

1908 ■ MULLER V. OREGON: *the Supreme Court establishes the validity of "sociological jurisprudence," the principle that economic and social considerations are as significant as legal precedents in deciding the constitutionality of social legislation*

DATE: February 24, 1908
LOCALE: Washington, D.C.
CATEGORIES: Business and labor; Court cases; Women's issues

KEY FIGURES:

Louis Dembitz Brandeis (1856-1941), U.S. jurist who wrote the legal brief setting forth the case for sociological jurisprudence
David Josiah Brewer (1837-1910), Supreme Court justice who wrote the majority opinion in *Muller v. Oregon*
Josephine Goldmark (1877-1950), leader of the National Consumers' league
Florence Kelley (1859-1932), general secretary of the National Consumers' League and a social reformer

SUMMARY OF EVENT. In his famous brief before the Supreme Court in the case of *Muller v. Oregon* in 1908, the United States jurist Louis Dembitz Brandeis of Boston established the validity of "sociological jurisprudence" in determining constitutional questions. According to sociological jurisprudence, economic and social considerations are as significant as legal precedents in deciding the constitutionality of social legislation. Brandeis' brief in *Muller v. Oregon* became a legal model for those lawyers, judges, and social welfare proponents who were determined to humanize industrial working conditions.

Under attack was an Oregon law that limited a workday to ten hours for women workers in an industry. Its critics claimed that it was unconstitutional because it contradicted legal precedent as established by the case *Lochner v. New York* (1905). Because many members of the bar and the judiciary were hostile to social welfare legislation, it was expected that the courts would uphold the claim of unconstitutionality. Many, if not most, lawyers and judges at the turn of the twentieth century believed in natural economic laws and the primacy of property rights over human rights. To attempt publicly to control the use of property, they maintained, was not only unconstitutional but also contrary to the natural order.

Judges in the United States are entitled to review legislation to determine whether it violates state or federal constitutions; as a result, advocates of social welfare legislation viewed the decisions of judges who opposed such legislation as the greatest threat to progress. Federal courts had frequently nullified social welfare legislation enacted by the states. In addition, the Supreme Court had embraced the concept that corporations were persons under the Fourteenth Amendment. No state, it held, could deprive a corporation—in this case, a particular industry—of life, liberty, or property without due process of the law. In social welfare legislation, liberty generally meant the freedom to contract.

In 1905, the Supreme Court had set specific limitations on how far a state could go in legislating hours and other working conditions for its industrial laborers. In *Lochner v. New York*, the Supreme Court ruled that New York laws that limited a baker to working ten hours per day and sixty hours per week were "mere meddlesome interferences with the rights of the individual." A state could not interfere with the freedom of the employer and employee to make a labor contract, unless there were obvious and overriding reasons such as health. The Court asserted that, had the state been able to prove ill health effects on the workers, the Court would have upheld the statute. The stage thus was set for litigation of the Oregon ten-hour law for women. Two social justice reformers, Florence Kelley, chief factory inspector of Illinois and general secretary of the National Consumers' League, and Josephine Goldmark, a leader of the National Consumers' League and Brandeis' sister-in-law, hired Brandeis to defend the law.

Known as "the people's attorney," Brandeis had tried for years to minimize what Thorstein Veblen had called the "discrepancy between law and fact." The law, Brandeis argued, often did not correspond to the new economic and social facts of life in the United States. Lawyers and judges who blindly adhered to legal precedents and natural law actually knew little about twentieth century industrial conditions. These lawyers, blind to economic and social realities, were apt to become "public enemies." In his brief in *Muller v. Oregon*, researched in large part by Kelley and Goldmark, Brandeis sought to make the economic and social reality of the women workers clear.

Brandeis' legal argument took up merely two pages of his brief. He devoted more than one hundred pages to demonstrating that Oregon had adopted its ten-hour law in order to safeguard the public health, safety, and welfare of the women. "Long hours of labor are dangerous for women," Brandeis contended, because of the physiological differences between men and women. "Overwork . . . is more dangerous to the health of women than of men, and entails upon them more lasting injury." Fatigue in working women, Brandeis asserted, often resulted in general deterioration of health, anemia, the destruction of nervous energy, difficulties in childbearing, and industrial accidents. He further asserted that the effect of overwork on morals was closely related to poor health. A breakdown in the health and morals of women, moreover, would inevitably lower the entire community physically, mentally, and morally. The rise of infant mortality was an obvious example. Working hours that did not cause the deterioration of health and morals, on the other hand, actually promoted the good of the entire community. Brandeis marshaled his economic and social data so impressively that the Court was convinced to uphold the Oregon ten-hour law for women. Justice Brewer, who wrote the majority opinion, made reference to the uniqueness and efficacy of the Brandeis brief.

The long-range significance of Brandeis' brief was that it opened the way for the Supreme Court to examine factors other than legal precedents in reaching its decisions. These other factors—social and economic data—were, in Brandeis' words, "what any fool knows," and they became a part of subsequent briefs propounding equitable labor conditions. It was not only in labor cases that sociological jurisprudence became an accepted principle in the law. In 1954, in the landmark case *Brown v. Board of Education*, the Court relied on sociological data in determining that desegregation of the races in education was unconstitutional. Several years after *Muller v. Oregon*, Felix Frankfurter called the case "epochmaking" because of Brandeis' approach. This approach, based on "the logic of facts," has been an intrinsic part of legal and constitutional practice ever since.

—*William M. Tuttle, updated by Jennifer Eastman*

ADDITIONAL READING:

Blumberg, Dorothy R. *Florence Kelley: The Making of a Social Pioneer*. New York: Augustus M. Kelley, 1966. Biography contains little information about *Muller v. Oregon*, but traces the influences that caused Kelley to become a social reformer.

Frankfurter, Felix, ed. *Mr. Justice Brandeis*. New Haven, Conn.: Yale University Press, 1932. Articles by Felix Frankfurter, Max Lerner, Charles Evans Hughes, and Donald R. Richberg; introduction by Chief Justice Oliver Wendell Holmes.

Goldmark, Josephine. *Impatient Crusader: Florence Kelley's Life Story*. Urbana: University of Illinois Press, 1953. A sympathetic study of the militant and socially conscious women reformers who pioneered efforts for the abolition of child labor, and shorter hours and higher pay for women. Little information about *Muller v. Oregon*.

Mason, Alpheus Thomas. *Brandeis: A Free Man's Life*. New York: Viking Press, 1946. An intimate portrait of Brandeis and the four stages of his career. Concise description of his participation in *Muller v. Oregon*.

Paper, Lewis J. *Brandeis*. Englewood Cliffs, N.J.: Prentice-Hall, 1983. A detailed biography with an accurate account of Brandeis' involvement with *Muller v. Oregon*.

Strum, Philippa. *Louis D. Brandeis: Justice for the People*. New York: Schocken Books, 1984. Discusses Brandeis and his importance in the legal world. Contains an in-depth account of *Muller v. Oregon* and the Brandeis Brief.

SEE ALSO: 1868, Fourteenth Amendment; 1911, Triangle Shirtwaist Company Fire; 1954, *Brown v. Board of Education*.

1908 ■ White House Conservation Conference: *a meeting that unites the talented and the powerful displays a national commitment to conserving American natural resources*

DATE: May 13, 1908
LOCALE: Washington, D.C.
CATEGORIES: Economics; Environment
KEY FIGURES:
Frederick Haynes Newell (1862-1932), first head of the Reclamation Service
Francis Griffith Newlands (1848-1917), author of the 1902 Reclamation Act
Gifford Pinchot (1865-1946), chief forester and the innovator behind Roosevelt's conservation policy
Theodore Roosevelt (1858-1919), twenty-sixth president of the United States, 1901-1909

SUMMARY OF EVENT. Few gatherings in the White House had ever been as charged with expectation or as crowded with dignitaries as the White House Conference on Conservation on May 13, 1908, when President Theodore Roosevelt spoke from a temporary platform in the East Room of the White House. The audience included the cabinet, the chief justice and the associate justices of the United States, the leader of the opposition Democratic Party, Andrew Carnegie, the governors of forty-four of the forty-six states, and numerous other distinguished scientists, scholars, and leaders in public affairs. It was one of the most distinguished gatherings that had ever been brought together in U.S. history and would be recognized as the benchmark for similar White House events on other topics. For Roosevelt, the conference was the culmination of seven years of effort on behalf of conservation; for the nation, it marked the beginning of a new climate of opinion that would reverse more than a century of indiscriminate private exploitation of what had once seemed to be an endless public domain. Roosevelt declared in his address to the conference:

> The time has come for a change. As a people we have the right and the duty, second to none other but the right and duty of obeying the moral law, of requiring and doing justice, to protect ourselves and our children against the wasteful development of our natural resources.

The governors agreed with Roosevelt that the time had come to make a stand. In a landmark declaration that was significant not only for conservation but also for a new federal-state relationship, the declaration of the governors, which was passed unanimously, pledged that "the sources of national wealth exist for the benefit of the people, and that monopoly thereof should not be tolerated," and that "in the use of natural resources our independent states are interdependent and bound together by ties of mutual benefits, responsibilities and duties." A month after the conference, Roosevelt established the Federal Commission on the Conservation of Natural Resources, headed by the chief theoretical and administrative influence in Roosevelt's conservation crusade, Gifford Pinchot. Divided into four divisions—water, forest, land, and mineral resources—the federal commission was joined within a year by forty-one state conservation commissions.

Roosevelt was not noted for his modesty, but he admitted that his conservation efforts were not fully his own doing. He had lent the powers of his office and the bully pulpit to the efforts of other persons who had greater scientific knowledge than he. His old friends Gifford Pinchot, Frederick Newel, Francis Newlands, and a few others were the driving force in the conservation movement in Roosevelt's time. The president's greatest contribution was the use of his position and persuasion to gain support for their ideas. Still, Roosevelt, a man of action, did actually participate in conservation work, learning at first hand the joys and problems of the United States' natural resources. In 1937, John T. Ganoe wrote in *Agricultural History*, "More clearly than any other president,

Group portrait of the governors attending the White House Conservation Conference of May, 1908. The meeting marked a new era of national concern for preservation of natural resources and environmental protection. (Library of Congress)

Roosevelt realized the needs of the arid regions. Having gone to Dakota during the boom of the eighties, he knew the needs of the cattle industry from first-hand contact and had witnessed the failure of the more optimistic settlers who tried to farm without irrigation."

When Roosevelt left office in 1909, the federal government lost the greatest single advocate of conservation it had ever had. Pinchot, Roosevelt's able and zealous colleague and friend, carried on the fight, but eventually the crusading chief forester fell victim to a less sympathetic president, as well as to his own crusading zeal. The White House Conference on Conservation was the last grand gesture of Roosevelt's conservation crusade, and it served to keep the idea of conservation alive until Franklin Delano Roosevelt again championed specific legislation to protect the nation's resources. Many years after the conference, Pinchot wrote about it in his autobiography. He declared that it should be regarded as a turning point in human history because it introduced humankind to the newly formulated policy of the conservation of natural resources. He added that the protection, preservation, and wise use of natural resources was not a series of separate and independent tasks, but one single problem.

Roosevelt's commitment to conservation began when he supported the Newlands National Reclamation Act, which firmly established the principle of government participation in reclamation and electric power programs. The act, which Congress passed on June 17, 1902, provided that proceeds from the sale of public lands in the West be used for large-scale irrigation projects; it eventually gave rise to the great dams of the West. Roosevelt created five new national parks, bringing the number to ten. He pressed for the National Monuments Act of 1906 and, with its passage, proclaimed sixteen national monuments from California's Muir Woods to Washington's Mount Olympus. By executive order, he formed fifty-one wildlife refuges. In 1907, Western congressmen sympathetic to lumber interests attached a rider to an appropriations bill, which Roosevelt could not veto, prohibiting the president from setting aside further land for forest services. Before signing the bill, however, Roosevelt withdrew all remaining forests in the public domain, almost 125 million acres, including 4.7 million acres of phosphate beds and 68 million acres of coal lands; in addition, he reserved for public use public power sites, thereby circumventing an attempt to end his effort to conserve what was left of the public domain. He vetoed a bill to permit private use of the power site at Muscle Shoals in Alabama, later to become the nucleus of the Tennessee Valley Authority—an even more revolutionary use of the national domain by the federal government.

Roosevelt realized that for conservation to be effective, responsibility had to pass to local control. As a result, he brought about the climactic Governors' Conference on Conservation in 1907. For the same reason, Roosevelt appointed the Inland Waterways Commission on March 14, 1907, to find ways to prevent the despoilation of the nation's rivers by private exploitation and to help in improving and controlling rivers and streams in matters of flood control, hydroelectric power, irrigation, and navigation. By the time of the White House Conference on Conservation, the public had become aware of the problems of conservation. Congress refused to acquiesce in the recommendations of the conference that the federal government retain ownership of all public lands containing minerals and retain subsoil rights in land that it sold. Nevertheless, newspapers hailed the conference almost unanimously, and for years it served as a reminder of a deep commitment made in the midst of the Progressive reform movement. Later administrations might circumvent Roosevelt's crusade, but none could ignore it. With the White House Conference on Conservation in 1908, the ideals of conservation became implanted firmly in the minds of American citizens, and the dangerous exploitation of irreplaceable natural resources was brought under the control of the people.

—*Richard H. Collin, updated by Kay Hively*

ADDITIONAL READING:

Cutright, Paul R. *Theodore Roosevelt, the Naturalist*. New York: Harper & Row, 1956. Discusses Roosevelt's interest in and study of natural history.

Reisner, Marc. *Cadillac Desert: The American West and Its Disappearing Water*. New York: Viking Press, 1986. A look at how government manipulates natural resources (especially water) in contrast to the philosophies of early conservationists.

Roosevelt, Theodore. *Autobiography*. New York: Macmillan, 1913. Roosevelt's own story, which documents his deeply held beliefs about conservation.

Thayer, William Roscoe. *Theodore Roosevelt: An Intimate Biography*. Boston: Houghton Mifflin, 1919. The story of Roosevelt's personal and public life, told by a friend of forty years.

Turner, Frederick W. *Rediscovering America: John Muir in His Time and Ours*. San Francisco: Sierra Club Books, 1985. A look at the most important conservationist in the West, who greatly influenced Theodore Roosevelt's decision to protect the United States' natural resources.

SEE ALSO: 1916, National Park Service Is Created; 1933, Tennessee Valley Authority Is Established.

1909 ■ DOLLAR DIPLOMACY: *financial intervention in China and the Caribbean begins to characterize U.S. foreign policy*

DATE: 1909-1913
LOCALE: Washington, D.C.
CATEGORIES: Diplomacy and international relations; Economics
KEY FIGURES:
Philander Chase Knox (1835-1921), secretary of state
William Howard Taft (1857-1930), twenty-seventh president of the United States, 1909-1913
SUMMARY OF EVENT. "Dollar Diplomacy," a term first used to characterize the foreign policy of President William Howard

Taft, has since become a favorite expression of those who criticize U.S. foreign policy as being the tool of Wall Street capitalists. Such financiers, critics argue, have manipulated U.S. foreign affairs to assist them in initiating, expanding, and above all protecting their investments abroad, regardless of the impact of such intervention upon the foreign governments and people involved. Although this characterization is partially correct, it does not do justice to the original concept and implementation of Dollar Diplomacy as conceived by its founders.

Taft was unusually well prepared to manage the foreign policy of the United States in the Caribbean and Asian areas when he assumed the presidency in 1909. He had served in key diplomatic positions in these areas from 1901 to 1908. First as chairman of the Philippines Commission, and by 1901, civil governor of the Philippines, he had acquired valuable knowledge of the Asian interests of the United States. When he was appointed secretary of war in 1904, he took on the duties of a roving ambassador. He had primary responsibility for the Isthmian Canal Commission, which dealt with the complex and, for U.S. policy interests, critical implications for the building of the Panama Canal. He had returned to Asia in 1905 and laid the diplomatic foundation for the settlement of the Korean issue with Japan. The year 1906 found him again in the Caribbean, this time Cuba. Following the fall of the regime of Cuba's first elected president, Tomás Estrada Palma, Taft acted as provisional governor of Cuba.

The chief architects of Dollar Diplomacy were President Taft and his secretary of state, Philander C. Knox. Knox was a Pennsylvania lawyer sympathetic to big business but equally concerned with U.S. political and economic interests abroad. Knox and Taft believed that U.S. commerce would best be served in areas where political and economic stability reigned, and the best way to secure both was to employ U.S. capital and financial expertise where instability was the rule. U.S. intervention would be peaceful—dollars instead of bullets—and would bring benefits not only to U.S. business but also to the local population. Taft articulated his position and that of his administration when he stated in 1910,

> There is nothing inconsistent in the promotion of peaceful relations, and the promotion of trade relations, and if the protection which the United States shall assure to her citizens in the assertion of just rights under investments made in foreign countries, shall promote the amount of such trade, it is a result to be commended. To call such diplomacy "dollar diplomacy" . . . is to ignore entirely a most useful office to be performed by a government in its dealings with foreign governments.

Knox echoed the president's views. He declared, "The problem of good government is inextricably interwoven with that of economic prosperity and sound finance; financial stability contributes perhaps more than any other one factor to political stability.

The Taft Administration employed Dollar Diplomacy in two areas, the Caribbean and China. In the Caribbean, Taft and

Knox adopted as their model the program instituted by Theodore Roosevelt's administration in the Dominican Republic. Because of the political disorder of that state and the fear of foreign intervention in its affairs, in 1905 Roosevelt had negotiated an arrangement by which the Dominican government secured a loan from U.S. banks to pay off its outstanding debts. In exchange for the loan, the U.S. president was allowed to appoint the head of the customs service which, as in all Caribbean states, was the chief source of government revenue. This arrangement seemed to work perfectly. After the United States took over the collection of customs revenue, the Dominican Republic enjoyed a period of internal peace and financial solvency that lasted through most of the Taft Administration.

Taking their cue from the success of the Dominican experiment, Taft and Knox applied the same principles to Nicaragua in what is regarded as the best example of Dollar Diplomacy at work. After supporting the overthrow of the powerful dictator José Santos Zelaya in 1909, the administration sent its veteran troubleshooter Thomas C. Dawson to Nicaragua to assist the new government in restoring order. Dawson secured the adoption of a plan to install a U.S. collector of customs and float a loan by New York bankers with the tacit guarantee of the U.S. government. Although the Senate repeatedly refused to ratify this accord, Taft, by executive order, appointed a collector of customs, and the New York bankers made several loans, taking as additional security a controlling interest in the Nicaraguan National Bank and the state railways. Despite these efforts to establish financial stability, however, in 1912, the majority political party of Nicaragua staged a revolt against the U.S.-supported president, Adolfo Díaz, and the Taft Administration reacted by sending warships and marines to keep Díaz in power. Dollars and bullets, rather than dollars only, were needed to assure order in Nicaragua.

The Nicaraguan example showed that, although Taft and Knox had sincerely believed that financial stability would assure political stability in the Caribbean, they oversimplified Latin American political behavior by assuming that ending unrest was merely a matter of retiring debts and balancing budgets. Political rivalry, struggles for prestige and power, social inequality, and resentment of U.S. intervention undermined the administration's policy from the beginning. Even the model, the Dominican Republic, achieved its stability not because of U.S. policy but because of an able president, Roman Cacéras, whose murder unleashed a new wave of unrest that ended only in 1916 with the occupation of the capital city and other centers by United States Marines.

The other area that felt the effects of Dollar Diplomacy was China, but the Chinese situation was quite different from that of the Caribbean. Not only was active competition with other great powers more evident, but also the other foreign powers had far more influence in China than did the United States. In addition, the United States' Far Eastern policy under Roosevelt had depended upon good relations with Japan, whose friendship was regarded as necessary to protect the newly acquired

Philippines as a U.S. possession. Dollar Diplomacy in China constituted reversing this policy by seeking advantages in competition rather than through cooperation with Japan.

The Taft-Knox method of increasing U.S. influence in China focused on pumping U.S. capital into that country. Their tactics never changed. They demanded the admission of U.S. banking groups, on terms of equal participation with other powers, into every foreign loan floated by China; where the demand for funds was lacking, they sought to inspire it artificially. In the case of China, however, the New York financiers upon whom the administration relied for the actual investments lacked both the interest and the accumulation of capital to provide loans of the size the Taft Administration demanded. To raise the money, U.S. banks had to rely on loans they had floated in the money markets of England and France. This practice in many ways defeated the whole purpose of the U.S. investment in China. In fact, Dollar Diplomacy in China did not mean pressure of capitalists upon the government to protect their investments abroad, but pressure of the government upon the capitalists to invest in an area where the administration believed future U.S. political and economic interests would be at stake. Because of the difficulty in securing U.S. funds and the opposition posed by the other major foreign powers, the Taft Administration abandoned its aggressive financial policies in China in 1912 and reverted to the more moderate "Open Door" approach of earlier administrations. Thus, Dollar Diplomacy was by no means as successful or as sinister as some of its critics have portrayed it, but it did much to cast the United States in the role of an imperialistic power in the era prior to World War I.

—Karl A. Roider, updated by Ann Thompson

ADDITIONAL READING:

Anderson, Donald F. *William Howard Taft: A Conservative's Conception of the Presidency.* Ithaca, N.Y.: Cornell University Press, 1973. A valuable addition to earlier works, because the author had access to the Taft papers, which were opened to scholars and the public in 1960.

Coletta, Paolo E. *The Presidency of William Howard Taft.* Lawrence: University Press of Kansas, 1973. Contains an informative chapter on Dollar Diplomacy.

Haley, P. Edward. *Revolution and Intervention: The Diplomacy of Taft and Wilson with Mexico, 1910-1917.* Cambridge, Mass.: MIT Press, 1970. The introduction gives a clear, direct description of the motivation for and scope of Dollar Diplomacy.

Minger, Ralph Eldine. *William Howard Taft and United States Foreign Policy: The Apprenticeship Years, 1900-1908.* Urbana: University of Illinois Press, 1975. Discusses Taft's public service record, especially his diplomatic appointments in Latin America and Asia immediately before he became president.

Munro, Dana G. *Intervention and Dollar Diplomacy in the Caribbean, 1900-1921.* Princeton, N.J.: Princeton University Press, 1964. Considered to be the most complete and comprehensive treatment of Dollar Diplomacy.

Pringle, Henry F. *The Life and Times of William Howard Taft: A Biography.* 2 vols. New York: Farrar and Rinehart, 1939. The definitive biography of Taft. Volume 2, chapter 35, discusses Dollar Diplomacy.

Scholes, Walter V., and Marie V. Scholes. *The Foreign Policies of the Taft Administration.* Columbia: University of Missouri Press, 1970. Provides detail on the policy of Dollar Diplomacy in Asia and the Caribbean.

SEE ALSO: 1895, Hearst-Pulitzer Circulation War; 1898, Spanish-American War; 1899, Philippine Insurrection; 1899, Hay's "Open Door Notes"; 1900, Suppression of Yellow Fever; 1901, Insular Cases; 1901, Theodore Roosevelt Becomes President; 1903, Platt Amendment.

1909 ■ NATIONAL ASSOCIATION FOR THE ADVANCEMENT OF COLORED PEOPLE IS FOUNDED: *creation of a major advocacy group for African Americans in the twentieth century*

DATE: February 12, 1909
LOCALE: New York City
CATEGORIES: African American history; Civil rights; Laws and acts
KEY FIGURES:
Benjamin Franklin Chavis (born 1948), NAACP executive director who resigned in 1994
William Edward Burghardt Du Bois (1868-1936), African American sociologist
Thurgood Marshall (1908-1993), NAACP attorney
Kweisi Mfume (Frizell Gray, born 1948), African American politician who became executive director of the NAACP in 1996
William Monroe Trotter (1872-1934), African American radical leader and journalist
Oswald Garrison Villard (1872-1949),
William English Walling (1877-1936), and
Mary Ovington White (1865-1951), white founders of the NAACP
Booker T. Washington (1856-1915), African American founder of the NAACP and president of Tuskegee Institute

SUMMARY OF EVENT. By the beginning of the twentieth century, many of the civil rights achieved by African Americans during the Reconstruction period were under severe attack. Supported by favorable Supreme Court rulings, such as in *Plessy v. Ferguson* (1896), that affirmed the constitutionality of racial segregation, Southern states enacted laws that effectively disfranchised most African American voters and barred their access to public institutions on an equal basis with whites. In the North, racial discrimination was not sanctioned as openly; nevertheless, it remained an underlying assumption of society. Tension between the two races sometimes flared into violence, taking the form of lynchings or urban riots. In these confrontations, African Americans found little sympathy from the press, the courts, or law enforcement agencies.

Reactions to the deterioration of individual rights varied within the African American community. The most prominent spokesperson for African Americans, educator Booker T. Washington, had adopted a policy of accommodation in the 1890's, urging African Americans to abandon temporarily their drive for civil and political rights and to concentrate instead on acquiring the economic skills that would enable them to find a place in an industrialized United States. Washington believed that if African Americans demonstrated their competence through hard work, American society eventually would grant African Americans the same rights that whites enjoyed. Washington's policies were supported widely by wealthy white philanthropists. His position, which historians call "gradualism," was countered, although ineffectively at first, by W. E. B. Du Bois, a professor at Atlanta University and founder in 1905 of the Niagara Movement, an organization composed of educated African Americans. Du Bois agonized over the steady erosion of African Americans' rights and viewed protest rather than acquiescence as the most appropriate avenue to equality. Black and white support crystallized in 1909 around this second point of view, called "immediatism," to launch an organization dedicated to combating racial discrimination in all areas of American life.

A bloody race riot in Springfield, Illinois, in August, 1908, in which white mobs destroyed much of the black section of Springfield and lynched two African Americans, served as the catalyst that launched the National Association for the Advancement of Colored People (NAACP). The riot left more than fifty African Americans dead or injured, and two thousand African American residents fled the city. The fact that Abraham Lincoln's hometown could be the site of such violence made it clear that racial discrimination and its accompanying violence were not just Southern problems. A group of white liberals began to consider how to rekindle the spirit of moral indignation that had animated the pre-Civil War abolitionists and then channel that indignation into constructive action. William English Walling, a Kentucky journalist and labor organizer, wrote several articles in *The Independent* condemning the Springfield riot and called for a powerful body of citizens to come to African Americans' aid. Early in 1909, Walling met with Mary Ovington White, the socialist descendant of an abolitionist family, and Henry Moskovitz, a New York social worker, to discuss ways of attracting support for his idea. They invited the grandson of William Lloyd Garrison, Oswald Garrison Villard, to join them, and the group was soon expanded to more than fifteen, including two prominent African American clergymen, Bishop Alexander Waters and the Reverend William Henry Brooks.

After initial discussions, this planning committee decided to draw attention to its cause by holding a Conference on the Status of the Negro on May 31 and June 1 in New York City. Sixty prominent African Americans and Euro-Americans signed a "call" to the gathering, pointing to the discrimination and violence that afflicted African Americans and urging Northerners to cast off the "silence that means tacit approval." Three hundred men and women, including many white liberals, attended the two-day meeting, setting up a permanent organization and listening to scientific refutations of arguments that persons of African descent were genetically inferior. The most notable African American in attendance was Du Bois, who suggested in a speech that African Americans' problems were as much political as economic. Booker T. Washington had been invited by Villard to the conference but had been told that the new organization was to be an aggressive one. Under the circumstances, he declined to come.

Washington's absence did not mean that there was complete agreement on the course to be taken. Heated arguments preceded the selection of a Committee of Forty on Permanent Organization and the passage of resolutions demanding equal rights for African Americans and protection against violence. Leading the opposition to Villard's proposals were William Monroe Trotter, editor of the *Boston Guardian*, and J. Milton Waldron, president of the National Negro Political League. Both advocated more radical positions than those favored by the majority. In the end, they were omitted from the Committee of Forty.

Throughout the year that followed, Villard and a handful of committee members struggled to raise funds and plan for a second annual conference. Despite general indifference from the white press and open disputes with Booker T. Washington, the committee succeeded in formulating an organizational framework for presentation to the conference. A National Committee of one hundred members was charged with raising funds and giving prestige to the organization; a smaller Executive Committee, composed primarily of members of the former Committee of Forty, would direct the organization's activities. In an executive session on May 14, 1910, the group, now bearing the name National Association for the Advancement of Colored People, approved this arrangement. The most significant action taken at the Second Annual Conference was the decision to appoint Du Bois as director of publicity and research, thereby underscoring the aggressive direction that the delegates sought to follow. For Du Bois, the post represented an opportunity to redeem his years of frustration with the Niagara Movement. He resigned his faculty position at Atlanta and moved to New York City. Within six months, he had launched the NAACP magazine, *The Crisis: A Record of the Darker Races*, which soon became a major organ for molding opinion on the race issue. The inaugural press run of one thousand copies sold out, and within five years circulation exceeded fifty thousand.

The NAACP continued to grow throughout the twentieth century. NAACP attorneys, such as future Supreme Court justice Thurgood Marshall, mounted numerous legal challenges to the institutional segregation that plagued the United States. Marshall argued thirty-two civil rights cases before the United States Supreme Court on behalf of the NAACP and won twenty-nine. In cases such as *Brown v. Board of Educa-*

tion of Topeka, Kansas (1954), Marshall and other attorneys with the NAACP's Legal Defense Fund worked to demolish inequality in education, employment, and access to public facilities such as restaurants and hotels. These activities continued into the 1990's, as the NAACP helped African American plaintiffs fight racial discrimination on the job and elsewhere. In 1993, the NAACP negotiated an agreement with Flagstar Companies, Inc., a corporation that managed a major U.S. restaurant chain, to eliminate discrimination and to increase management opportunities for African Americans.

The NAACP's successes in fighting racial discrimination occasionally were accompanied by problems within the organization. In the 1930's, a major rift developed between founder W. E. B. Du Bois and newer members, such as Walter White. Internal dissension almost tore the organization apart. Du Bois left, but the organization survived. Similar problems developed in the 1990's. Following the 1993 retirement of Benjamin L. Hooks as executive director of the NAACP, the organization endured two stormy years of controversy and dissension. The new executive director, Benjamin F. Chavis, found himself under attack following the disclosure that he used organization funds to settle a lawsuit brought by a former employee. The organization fired Chavis in 1994. Under the guidance of Board Chairman Myrlie Evers-Williams, the NAACP managed to weather the controversy, although both financial contributions and overall membership declined. In January, 1996, the NAACP announced that Kweisi Mfume, the forty-seven-year-old African American congressman from Baltimore, Maryland, had accepted the position as chief executive officer. With Mfume assuming a leadership role, the NAACP appeared confident that it would continue to fight for racial equality for many years to come.

The founding of the NAACP is significant because it marked the first major attempt since Reconstruction to make African American rights the focus of national reform efforts. The manner of its birth also reveals many of the strengths and weaknesses that characterized it in the immediate years ahead: a substantial proportion of white leadership and dependence on white financial support; a program emphasizing political and civil rights and seeking change through legislation and judicial decisions; and criticism from within the black community on both of these points. In the early years, the protests were loudest from those, such as Washington, who found the new organization too militant; but even at the outset other critics, such as Trotter, felt it did not go far enough. Despite numerous victories, such as *Brown v. Board of Education of Topeka* and *Keyes v. Denver School District No. 1* (1973), those same criticisms continued into the 1990's. Yet despite the competing demands for aggressive action and for moderation, the NAACP managed to move race relations steadily forward for most of the twentieth century.

—*John C. Gardner, updated by Nancy Farm Mannikko*

ADDITIONAL READING:

Finch, Minnie. *The NAACP: Its Fight for Justice*. Metuchen, N.J.: Scarecrow Press, 1981. Provides a general history of the NAACP and its efforts to advance racial equality in the United States.

Kellogg, Charles Flint. *NAACP: A History of the National Association for the Advancement of Colored People*. Baltimore: The Johns Hopkins University Press, 1964. A general history of the NAACP.

Lewis, David Levering. *W. E. B. Du Bois: Biography of a Race, 1868-1919*. New York: Henry Holt, 1993. Fascinating, detailed biography of Du Bois' early life, his interactions with Booker T. Washington, and his evolution into an activist.

Meier, August. *Negro Thought in America, 1880-1915: Racial Ideologies in the Age of Booker T. Washington*. Ann Arbor: University of Michigan Press, 1988. Provides a general context for the debate over accommodation versus aggressive activism.

Zangrando, Robert. *The NAACP Crusade Against Lynching, 1909-1950*. Philadelphia: Temple University Press, 1980. Describes the efforts of the NAACP to eliminate the horrors of lynching from the U.S. South.

SEE ALSO: 1895, Booker T. Washington's Atlanta Exposition Address; 1905, Niagara Movement; 1917, Universal Negro Improvement Association Is Established; 1930, Nation of Islam Is Founded; 1942, Congress of Racial Equality Is Founded; 1957, Southern Christian Leadership Conference Is Founded.

1909 ■ REPUBLICAN CONGRESSIONAL INSURGENCY: *dissent of midwestern Republicans in Congress contributes to tensions that split the party in 1912*

DATE: March, 1909-1912
LOCALE: Washington, D.C.
CATEGORY: Government and politics
KEY FIGURES:

Nelson Wilmarth Aldrich (1841-1915), senator from Rhode Island and leader of the conservatives

Richard Achilles Ballinger (1858-1922), Taft's secretary of the interior

Joseph Gurney Cannon (1836-1926), congressman from Illinois and Speaker of the House

James Rudolph Garfield (1865-1950), Roosevelt's secretary of the interior

Robert Marion La Follette (1855-1925), senator from Wisconsin and leader of the midwestern Progressives

Gifford Pinchot (1865-1946), Roosevelt's chief forester, who precipitated the break with Taft

Theodore Roosevelt (1858-1919), twenty-sixth president of the United States, 1901-1909

William Howard Taft (1857-1930), twenty-seventh president of the United States, 1909-1913

Woodrow Wilson (1856-1924), twenty-eighth president of the United States, 1913-1921

SUMMARY OF EVENT. Early in the twentieth century, two U.S. presidents successfully identified themselves with the cause of reform. Both Theodore Roosevelt and Woodrow Wilson established reputations as spokespersons for Progressive political tendencies at the national level. Still, Progressivism was not entirely dependent upon presidential leadership. During the crucial period from 1909 to 1911, congressional proponents of reform, primarily Republican congressmen and senators from the Midwest, battled President William Howard Taft to determine how the Republican Party would respond to the issues of the tariff, conservation, and corporate regulation.

In March, 1909, Theodore Roosevelt handed over the reins of government to incoming president Taft. The new chief executive believed that his duty was to work with the Republican majority and administer the reform programs of Roosevelt with more effectiveness. Although he entered office as Roosevelt's designated successor, Taft had none of Roosevelt's boundless energy or ability to communicate his ideas to the public. He preferred the company of lawyers to that of reformers, and conservative attorneys soon came to dominate his administration. From the start, Taft moved in directions that foretold trouble with reform-minded members of Congress.

The new president's first difficulties centered on the tariff question. Early in 1909, the House of Representatives approved a downward revision of the existing tariff rates, in compliance with the Republican platform of 1908. Republican senator Nelson W. Aldrich of Rhode Island found that such a strategy did not command the support of a majority of Republican senators. To achieve a viable coalition, he added approximately eight hundred amendments, most of which took tariff rates back toward those of the Dingley Tariff of 1897. For eleven weeks, Senate Progressives such as Robert M. La Follette argued against the Aldrich amendments. Taft stood closer to the Progressives than he did to Aldrich on the issue, and he used his influence to reduce rates on some products. When Congress finally approved the Payne-Aldrich Tariff, which reenacted much of the Dingley law, Taft called the resulting measure the best tariff bill the Republican Party had ever passed. The Midwestern Republican Progressives in Congress were outraged.

Problems involving the conservation of natural resources added to Taft's political burdens. When the new president assumed office, he failed to reappoint James R. Garfield, Roosevelt's secretary of the interior. Instead, he named Richard A. Ballinger, a Seattle lawyer and former commissioner of the General Land Office, to the post. Ballinger soon clashed with Gifford Pinchot, the chief forester of the United States and another Roosevelt intimate. The conflict between the two men reached crisis proportions when Pinchot accused Ballinger of involvement in a plot to defraud the government of coal lands in Alaska. The public accusation led to a congressional investigation that revealed no serious wrongdoing but damaged the prestige of the Taft Administration and further weakened its ties with reform-oriented elements.

A fight over the rules that governed the House of Representatives widened the rift between Taft and Insurgent Republicans in Congress. Many reformers saw Speaker of the House Joseph G. Cannon of Illinois as the main legislative obstacle to enactment of their program. The Insurgents wanted House rules changed to reduce Cannon's power as House Speaker. Taft disliked Cannon, but he knew that the Speaker had the support of the House Republicans on whom the president depended to pass his program. Accordingly, Taft refused to challenge the Speaker's authority. When the Insurgents overthrew the Illinois legislator, Taft again appeared to be at odds with the prevailing spirit of reform. Despite these setbacks, Taft did achieve legislative successes during the 1910 session of Congress, including the Mann-Elkins Act to regulate the railroads.

The congressional elections in 1910 exacerbated the tensions between Taft and the Insurgents. The president worked for the election of conservative Republicans in several states in which the reformers dominated. Roosevelt entered the campaign in an effort to bridge the gap between the chief executive and the Republican Party. Neither Taft nor Roosevelt proved to be a successful strategist. For the first time in sixteen years, the Democrats won control of the House of Representatives. They also gained seats in the Senate, where a small group of Progressives held the balance of power.

The battles fought by the congressional Insurgents sustained the momentum of the reform movement. Despite its conservative leanings, the Taft Administration failed to slow the rate of change. After the 1910 elections, presidential hopefuls, such as Senator Robert M. La Follette, Governor Woodrow Wilson of New Jersey, and Theodore Roosevelt, sought the allegiance of reform-oriented voters. In 1912, the Republican old guard denied Roosevelt a presidential nomination. At the same time, the split in the Republican Party that the Insurgents had initiated assured Wilson's election, and a new, more dynamic phase in the Progressive movement began.

—Rex O. Mooney, updated by Lewis L. Gould

ADDITIONAL READING:

Allen, Howard W. *Poindexter of Washington: A Study in Progressive Politics*. Carbondale: Southern Illinois University Press, 1981. A thorough, informative study of one of the key figures in the Insurgent movement.

Gould, Lewis L. *Reform and Regulation: American Politics from Roosevelt to Wilson*. Prospect Heights, Ill.: Waveland Press, 1996. An analytic survey of U.S. politics between 1900 and 1921 that considers the impact of the Republican Insurgents on party politics.

Holt, James L. *Congressional Insurgents and the Party System, 1909-1916*. Cambridge, Mass.: Harvard University Press, 1968. A New Zealand scholar offers the best modern treatment to date of the Republican rebels against the existing congressional leadership.

Margulies, Herbert F. *Senator Lenroot of Wisconsin: A Political Biography, 1900-1929*. Columbia: University of Missouri Press, 1977. An excellent biographical treatment of a member of the Insurgent bloc from Wisconsin.

Sarasohn, David. *The Party of Reform: Democrats in the Progressive Era*. Jackson: University of Mississippi Press, 1989. Argues that the Democrats were more important in the development of progressive ideas than were the Republican Insurgents.

SEE ALSO: 1897, Dingley Tariff; 1901, Theodore Roosevelt Becomes President; 1912, Wilson Is Elected President.

1909 ■ PEARY AND HENSON REACH THE NORTH POLE: *six North American explorers become the first people to reach the geographic North Pole*

DATE: April 6, 1909
LOCALE: Geographic North Pole
CATEGORY: Exploration and discovery
KEY FIGURES:
Frederick Albert Cook (1865-1940), explorer who claimed to be first to reach the North Pole
Matthew A. Henson (1866-1955), member of Peary's polar expeditions
Robert Edwin Peary (1856-1920), leader of the first expedition to reach the North Pole

SUMMARY OF EVENT. European exploration of the North American Arctic regions began in the late fifteenth century, with the search for a Northwest Passage to Asia as the primary goal. By the nineteenth century, it was clear that an easily navigable northern route to Asia did not exist, and attention gradually shifted toward efforts to reach the North Pole. The race to become the first person to reach the pole was driven more by the challenge involved than by any practical benefits from the accomplishment itself, although many of the expeditions were sent to the Arctic to carry out specific scientific or geographical measurements.

Early American Arctic explorers, including Elisha Kent Kane and Charles Francis Hall, became involved in polar explorations as part of the search for information on the fate of the 1845 British expedition led by Sir John Franklin. The Franklin party, consisting of two ships and 133 men, was the last major effort by the British to find a northern passage through the Canadian Arctic. The last contact with Franklin occurred shortly after he entered Baffin Bay, and it was later discovered that, after terrible hardships, Franklin and all members of his party had perished. The main contribution Kane and Hall made to Arctic exploration was the realization that use of Eskimo clothing and hunting and travel techniques greatly improved the ability of explorers to survive in the harsh Arctic environment.

In 1881, as part of the scientific research program connected with the First International Polar Year, a U.S. Army expedition led by Lieutenant Adolphus Greeley established a camp on Ellesmere Island. The next year, two members of the Greeley party, Lieutenant James Lockwood and Sergeant

David Brainard, along with their Eskimo sled driver, reached 83°24′ north latitude. This set a new record for the closest approach to the North Pole, the first time in three centuries that the record for traveling the farthest north was held by a non-British exploration party. However, the Greeley expedition ended in disaster in 1884, with eighteen of the twenty-four members of the party dying before the rest were rescued.

By this time, several other Americans had become interested in Arctic exploration. Chief among these was Robert E. Peary, who at the time of his first visit to Greenland in 1886 was an engineer in the U.S. Navy. In 1891, Peary returned to Greenland, leading an expedition that included Frederick A. Cook, a doctor from Brooklyn, and Matthew A. Henson, an African American who acted as Peary's servant. Both Cook and Henson would become noted explorers over the next several years. During the second year of his stay, Peary, accompanied by the Norwegian explorer Eivend Astrup, made an eleven-hundred-mile journey across northern Greenland. The journey established Peary as a leader in polar exploration.

After a brief fund-raising visit to the United States, Peary returned to Greenland in 1893 to search for routes to the North Pole. During his three-year stay, Peary, Henson, and Hugh Lee, a third member of his party, retraced Peary's previous path across Greenland. Peary also recovered two of three large meteorites that had served as a source of iron for the Eskimos in the region.

A new Peary expedition returned to the Arctic in 1898 and remained until 1902. Peary's previous exploration of the Greenland ice cap had convinced him that an alternative route to the North Pole was needed, and he therefore spent most of his time on Ellesmere Island. On one early journey, Peary suffered severe frostbite and lost most of the toes on both of his feet. Undaunted, Peary made a four-hundred-mile trip across northern Greenland in 1900, proving that Greenland is an island. In 1902, the last year of the expedition, Peary attempted to reach the North Pole, but was able to travel only to 84°17′ north latitude. This represented Peary's closest approach to the pole up to this time, but fell short of the latitude achieved by Umberto Cagni, an Italian explorer, in 1899.

After three years of preparation, Peary launched a new Arctic expedition in 1906. Winter quarters for the party were established at Cape Sheridan on the northeastern tip of Ellesmere Island. Peary was again accompanied by Matthew Henson. On March 6, 1906, Peary set out on what he believed would be his last attempt to reach the North Pole. Once again, Peary failed to reach his objective, although he did set a new record for farthest north, at 87°06′ north latitude.

Peary returned to the United States, determined to make one final attempt to reach the pole. Financial difficulties delayed him, and it was not until July 6, 1908, that Peary again departed for the Arctic. He again chose Cape Sheridan as the base from which he would launch his journey. During the winter of 1908-1909, Peary and his party moved provisions from Cape Sheridan to Cape Columbia, a more northerly part of Ellesmere Island, from which the trip to the pole would begin. On February 28, 1909, the first supply party set off from Camp Columbia toward the pole. Remaining supply parties, then Peary himself, soon followed. Open water on the polar ice cap delayed their progress, but by April 1, Peary had moved to within 150 miles of the pole. At this point, the last supply party moved south, and Peary began the final part of his journey, accompanied by Matthew Henson and four Eskimos, Egingwah, Ooqueah, Ootah, and Seeglo. Five days later, on April 6, 1909, Peary and his companions reached the North Pole. They set up camp and stayed for thirty hours. After a three-week journey, he returned to Cape Columbia on April 23.

When Peary returned to civilization, he found himself in the midst of controversy. Dr. Frederick Cook, who had been a member of one of Peary's early expeditions to Greenland, claimed that he and two Eskimo traveling companions had reached the North Pole on April 21, 1908, almost a full year before Peary's visit. Cook's claim already had been recognized by the University of Copenhagen, and Cook had received congratulations from a number of other polar explorers, as well as a massive amount of popular support.

For the next several months, the competing claims of Peary and Cook sparked controversy. However, Cook's story gradually fell apart. The Eskimos who accompanied Cook testified that during their journey, their party had never left the sight of land. More damaging, it was found that a previous claim by Cook to have been the first person to climb Mount McKinley was fraudulent. Cook also failed to present convincing proof to support his story. Cook's claim to have reached the pole gradually fell into disfavor, and Cook died a pauper in 1940.

Doubts remain, however, concerning Peary's trip to the North Pole. A committee of the National Geographic Society unanimously confirmed Peary's account of his journey, but the British Royal Geographical Society, which also examined Peary's records, supported his story by a vote of eight to seven, indicating some skepticism. Peary's case was not helped by the fact that several of his previous geographical discoveries, including "Jesup Land" and "Crocker Land," turned out to be in error. Further doubts were raised by discrepancies in Peary's written records of his polar journey. While Peary is generally recognized as having led the first expedition, it is unlikely that it will ever be known for certain whether he was in fact successful in his trip.

—*Jeffrey A. Joens*

ADDITIONAL READING:

Abramson, Howard S. *Hero in Disgrace: The Life of Arctic Explorer Frederick A. Cook*. New York: Paragon House, 1991. A thorough account of Cook's life and explorations, although biased in favor of Cook's claim to have been the first person to reach the North Pole.

Berton, Pierre. *The Arctic Grail: The Quest for the North West Passage and the North Pole, 1818-1909*. New York: Viking Penguin, 1988. An impartial and informative history of nineteenth and early twentieth century Arctic explorations. Chapter 13 examines Peary's and Cook's claims to have reached the North Pole.

Goetzmann, William H. *New Lands, New Men: America and the Second Great Age of Discovery*. New York: Viking Press, 1986. A general history of exploration from the seventeenth to the early twentieth century. Chapter 11 discusses the Cook and Peary polar expeditions.

Henson, Matthew A. *A Black Explorer at the North Pole*. Lincoln: University of Nebraska Press, 1989. A reprint of Henson's 1912 first-person account, *A Negro Explorer at the North Pole*, with added biographical information.

Herbert, Wally. *The Noose of Laurels: Robert E. Peary and the Race to the North Pole*. New York: Atheneum, 1989. A detailed and critical history of the explorations of Peary and Cook by an author with extensive personal experience in the Arctic.

Weems, John Edward. *Peary: The Explorer and the Man*. Boston: Houghton Mifflin, 1967. A well-written but uncritical biography, making extensive use of Peary's personal papers and writings.

SEE ALSO: 1908, White House Conservation Conference.

1910 ■ MEXICAN REVOLUTION: *conflict in Mexico results in a new collectivist constitution and elected governments*

DATE: Mid-October, 1910-December 1, 1920
LOCALE: Mexico
CATEGORIES: Latino American history; Wars, uprisings, and civil unrest
KEY FIGURES:
Plutarco Elías Calles (1877-1945), president of Mexico, 1924-1928
Lázaro Cárdenas (1895-1970), president of Mexico, 1934-1940
Venustiano Carranza (1859-1920), president of Mexico, 1914-1920
Porfirio Díaz (1830-1915), prerevolutionary president of Mexico, 1876-1880 and 1884-1911
Adolfo de la Huerta (1883?-1955), provisional president of Mexico, June-November, 1920
Victoriano Huerta (1854-1916), provisional president of Mexico, 1913-1914
Francisco Indalecio Madero (1873-1913), precipitator of the Mexican Revolution and president of Mexico, 1911-1913
Álvaro Obregón (1880-1928), president of Mexico, 1920-1924
Francisco "Pancho" Villa (Doroteo Arango, 1878-1923), popular revolutionary leader in Chihuahua
Emiliano Zapata (1879-1919), popular revolutionary leader in Morelos

SUMMARY OF EVENT. In 1876 Mexico had come under the governance of Porfirio Díaz, whose motto had been the restoration of constitutional government. There is general agreement that the Mexican government during his reign was autocratic, arbitrary, and repressive. His program might be described as one of "scientific" development of Mexico, and he allowed the suppression of the political rights and the denial of the economic rights of large sections of the Mexican society to meet those goals. To bring about the development of Mexico, Díaz invited the investment of foreign capital under extremely favorable conditions. The economic penetration of foreign investors, especially from the United States, occurred in the areas of railroads, mining, and—more significantly from the perspective of the Mexican Revolution—petroleum and land.

Despite the economic development and its social ramifications, the Mexican Revolution began as a reaction to the suppression of political rights. As such, one could describe the revolution in its initial stage as liberal in character. As the Díaz regime aged, it became subject to much criticism, particularly for its authoritarian political nature, for its exclusion from political office of all except a favored few men, and for its suppression of labor in favor of foreign investors. For public relations purposes Díaz, as the 1910 elections approached, gave an interview to Joel Creelman, an American newspaper reporter, in which he declared that Mexico was ready for a system that included political opposition.

Francisco Madero took the president at his word and declared his candidacy for the presidency of Mexico in 1910. The Madero family was a wealthy landowning, capitalist family from Coahuila that had benefited from and cooperated with the Díaz regime in its early years. Like other prominent families, however, the Madero family and especially Francisco had become disfranchised, dissatisfied, and embittered. Madero was a peculiar man, very intense, almost a mystic, and he obviously took himself seriously. He wanted to be president in order to achieve the reforms that he believed were essential for the progress of Mexico. In 1909, he criticized the Díaz regime and made particular reference to the repeated reelection of the president, a political tenet honored to this day: Presidents cannot succeed themselves and since 1929 have been permitted to serve only once.

Arrested on June 14 for this insubordination, Madero was placed in jail at San Luis Potosí, while Díaz was declared elected. Madero managed to escape in mid-October, issuing his Plan of San Luis Potosí, in which he called for "effective suffrage, no reelection." Madero's challenge to Díaz can be called the beginning of the Mexican Revolution. He called the election fraudulent and revolted under his Plan of San Luis Potosí. Madero claimed that the people sought political freedom and not bread, and he called for armed revolt, which he helped promote with the aid of guerrilla fighters in late 1909 and early 1910. This act opened the gates to a full-scale opposition to Díaz. In 1911, the regime collapsed, and Díaz went into exile.

Madero was elected the new president. His presidency was ineffectual and did not bring peace and stability but rebellions. Both reformers and conservatives fought against the Madero Administration. Finally, reactionary elements, using General Victoriano Huerta, plotted a successful *coup d'état* in February, 1913, in which Madero and his vice president were murdered. General Huerta, in his attempt to reestablish the old regime, caused immediate reaction in several sections of the country. The most significant of these were a revolt in the south led by Emiliano Zapata, an uprising in the north led by Francisco "Pancho" Villa, and the constitutional revolt in the north, which ultimately assumed legitimate power in Mexico.

The armed uprisings against Huerta can only loosely be called coordinated. Zapata, who remains a mythic figure in Mexico, issued his Plan of Ayala, which called for major agrarian reform. This revolt was centered in the southern state of Morelos and was essentially an Indian- and peasant-based action. Villa led his personal revolt from the northern Mexican state of Chihuahua. Venustiano Carranza, who led the third important group, issued the Plan of Guadalupe, which called for the restoration of constitutional government in keeping with Madero's Plan of San Luis Potosí.

Together, these three men reflect the roots of the enormous struggle that today is called the Mexican Revolution: Zapata was of Indian extraction. Villa was of mixed blood and uncertain of his origins; although he is often described as a bandit, his personal magnetism and ambition caused him to join forces with other revolutionists in an attempt to seize political power. Carranza, a man of Spanish extraction from the upper class, was above all else an ardent Mexican nationalist. His followers possessed the most talent and organizational skill of any revolutionary group.

These revolutionary forces worked to overthrow Huerta, and with the aid of the United States they were successful and collectively took control of the government, with Huerta as provisional president. The United States, under the leadership of President Woodrow Wilson, gave assistance to the revolutionary forces in two ways. First, President Wilson opened the borders and permitted aid to flow to the revolutionaries in the north of Mexico. Second, Wilson, in April of 1914, intervened at Veracruz. The U.S. Marines took the city but inflicted casualties numbering in the hundreds, including many civilians of both sexes. A public outcry was raised against the United States, but Huerta was not able to garner additional support. An important effect of the occupation of Veracruz was loss of revenue for the Huerta government, because the customs house at Veracruz was the government's chief source of revenue. In addition, military supplies for the Huerta government came in through the port. Those supplies were now cut off. In July, 1914, Huerta resigned and fled the country, but the leaders of the three forces opposing Huerta began to fight among themselves.

Carranza and the Constitutionalists prevailed for two reasons. One was the extraordinary talent of Carranza's ally Álvaro Obregón. The other was the decision of the Wilson Administration to extend de facto recognition to Carranza's regime in October, 1915 (an action that has been cited as the cause of the Villa raid on Columbus, New Mexico, which led to the Pershing expedition of 1916-1917). It is safe to say that the defeat of Villa at Celaya and the recognition of Carranza by the

Mexican revolutionaries c. 1910. The revolution began as a reaction to the suppression of political rights by the regime of Porfirio Díaz, whose policies had helped industrialize the nation at the expense of labor and the poorer populace. Revolutionaries such as Francisco "Pancho" Villa and Emiliano Zapata would become mythic heroes of the people. (Security Pacific Collection/Los Angeles Public Library)

United States mark the ascendancy of the Constitutionalists and, therefore, the turning point in the Mexican Revolution.

In 1916, Carranza authorized the calling of a constitutional convention that went well beyond the Plan of San Luis Potosí to incorporate some of the more revolutionary ideas, including land reform, labor reform, reform of the extractive industries, anticlerical reform, and nationalistic restrictions on foreigners and foreign capital. The new constitution, which took effect in May of 1917, established the first major modern socioeconomic instrument for the transformation of society. Among the more significant provisions of the Constitution of 1917 are Article XXVII, which dealt with many of the basic socioeconomic demands of the revolution, such as again nationalizing subsoil mineral rights and restoration of the *ejidos*, or communal land of Indian villages, and Article CXXIII, which dealt with the rights of labor. Carranza was not committed to many of the radical goals incorporated into the constitution. He was criticized for not fulfilling many of the promises he had made since 1913; he was also blamed for the lack of stability and order in the country, as civil war, banditry, and corruption continued.

Carranza had other difficulties as well. Villa and Zapata remained armed challengers of his authority, and the president did not continue to have the assistance of Obregón and Plu-

tarco Calles, who had retired to Sonora. In 1919, Carranza "solved" the Zapata problem by permitting the assassination of Zapata. The Villa problem was solved in the next administration first by buying him off and then by assassination.

Carranza also suffered strong opposition from reactionary elements. These elements worked to attempt to overthrow Carranza and reestablish order as known in the period preceding 1910. Carranza selected a surrogate, Ignacio Bonillas, to succeed him on December 1, 1920. The logical candidate for the presidency was Alvaro Obregón, a national hero known in Mexico as a "genius in war and peace." Indeed, Obregón had announced his own candidacy in June, 1919. In an attempt to frustrate that candidacy, Carranza ordered federal troops to move into Sonora, the base of Obregón's power. Within two days a new revolutionary movement emerged. It was led by the socalled Sonora Clique of Obregón, Calles, and Governor Adolfo de la Huerta of Sonora, who wrote the Plan of Agua Prieta attacking Carranza. The Plan of Agua Prieta achieved wide support. Carranza fled the capital and was killed by pursuing forces on May 21, 1920. Adolfo de la Huerta assumed the provisional presidency until November 30, 1920. While in office, he made an accommodation with Villa, which brought an end to the latter's antigovernment activities.

Obregón was elected president of Mexico and assumed

office on December 1, 1920. His election marked the end of the violent stage of the Mexican Revolution. His government brought calm to the country and, although he was a compromiser, compliance to the purposes of the revolution. The tasks of the Obregón Administration were not simple or easy: pacification of the countryside, reform of the society, consolidation of power, and attaining the recognition of his government by the United States. When he left office in 1924, Obregón could claim a considerable success. Although the fundamental reforms had not been fully accomplished, a base had been established from which future administrations could and did take major actions.

Plutarco Calles, who succeeded Obregón in 1924, was considered a radical by landowners, industrialists, and churchmen. Calles continued or initiated programs of land reform, labor reforms, and anticlerical reforms. Between 1926 and 1929, the Cristero War was fought unsuccessfully by the church and its supporters to preserve the wealth and power of the church. Calles had become a repressive dictator by the end of his term in 1928 and continued to exercise political power after he left office. Lázaro Cárdenas was elected president in 1934 and carried the revolution further to the left. He was more deeply committed to social reform than any previous president. Cárdenas redistributed twice as much land as all of his predecessors combined, increased expenditures for education especially in rural areas, reformed labor unions, and nationalized the foreign oil companies. After 1940, the revolution moderated under the leadership of President Avila Camacho.

If the political aspects of the Mexican Revolution can be said to have come to an end in 1920, the socioeconomic aspects took longer to be realize. Indeed there are some in Mexico and elsewhere who claim that the Revolution of 1910 has not yet ended.

—Daniel D. DiPiazza, updated by Robert D. Talbott

ADDITIONAL READING:

Brenner, Anita. *The Wind That Swept Mexico: A History of the Mexican Revolution, 1910-1942.* Austin: University of Texas Press, 1971. Contains an extensive collection of photographs with commentaries telling the story of the Mexican Revolution. The author emphasizes the economic issues and their social effects.

Cumberland, Charles C. *Mexican Revolution: The Constitutional Years.* Austin: University of Texas Press, 1972. Describes the real revolution that occured during the Constitutionalist years, relations with the United States, and the contributions of Obregón.

Hall, Linda B., and Don M. Coerver. *Revolution on the Border: The United States and Mexico, 1910-1920.* Albuquerque: University of New Mexico Press, 1988. The authors describe the impact of the revolution on the border area, the effect of the border area on the revolution, and the relations between Mexico and the United States.

Meyer, Michael C., and William L. Sherman. *The Course of the Mexican History.* 5th ed. New York: Oxford University Press, 1995. Interesting and readable history with three of the ten chapters on the revolution; good coverage of society and culture. Maps and illustrations.

Quirk, Robert E. *An Affair of Honor: Woodrow Wilson and the Occupation of Veracruz.* Lexington: University Press of Kentucky, 1962. The author gives a complete account of U.S. intervention in Veracruz and the long-term ill will created for the United States.

SEE ALSO: 1821, Mexican War of Independence; 1846, Mexican War; 1916, Pershing Expedition.

1910 ■ GREAT NORTHERN MIGRATION: *1.1 million African Americans move from the rural South and Midwest into Northern cities*

DATE: 1910-1930
LOCALE: From Southern and Midwestern to Northern states
CATEGORIES: African American history; Business and labor; Economics
KEY FIGURES:
Robert Sengstacke Abbott (1870-1940), publisher of the *Chicago Defender*
William Edward Burghardt Du Bois (1868-1963), historian, sociologist, and editor
Marcus Mosiah Garvey (1887-1940), founder of the Universal Negro Improvement Association
Langston Hughes (1902-1967), poet, novelist, and playwright

SUMMARY OF EVENT. The Great Northern Migration, a demographic shift of many African Americans from Southern states to both Midwestern and Northeastern states, occurred roughly between 1910 and 1930. Because migration figures are based on the U.S. Census, which is conducted every tenth year, the dating of migration events is imprecise. The data indicate only that this migration took place some time between 1910 and 1930, but other historical evidence suggests that it began some time during World War I (between 1914 and 1918) and ended around the onset of the Great Depression in 1929.

Migration is often measured as net migration, the difference between the number of people moving into a region and the number moving from it during a specific time period. Between 1910 and 1920, approximately 454,400 more African Americans migrated from the South than migrated to it. During the same period, net migration of African Americans to the North was approximately 426,200. Between 1920 and 1930, net migration of African Americans from the South increased to approximately 749,000, while net migration to the North increased to 712,900. In all, net migration of African Americans from the South exceeded 1.1 million during the period of the Great Northern Migration. The total number moving out of the South cannot be accurately estimated, because an unknown number of African Americans moved to the South during the period, offsetting some of the out-migrants, but it has been estimated that two million blacks left the South in that time.

During the Great Northern Migration, the industrial Northern and Midwestern states of New York, Illinois, Pennsylvania, Ohio, and Michigan experienced the greatest positive net migration of African Americans. The greatest net loss of African American population was from the Southern, agricultural states of Georgia, South Carolina, Virginia, Alabama, and Mississippi. As they moved from one region to another, most of the migrants also moved from rural areas to urban areas. Between 1910 and 1920, the African American population of Detroit grew from 5,000 to 40,800; that of Cleveland grew from 8,400 to 34,400; that of Chicago grew from 44,000 to 109,400; and that of New York increased from 91,700 to 152,400. The transition from rural to urban locales was accompanied by a transition from employment in agriculture to employment in industrial or service occupations for increasing numbers of African Americans.

The reasons that African Americans did not leave the South in large numbers until fifty years after the end of the Civil War have been the subject of debate among social scientists and historians. Both social and economic factors were involved. After the Civil War, owners of plantations and farms in the South imposed new ways of controlling labor that were almost as restrictive as slavery had been. As sharecroppers, former slaves and their descendants were allowed to farm land belonging to the property owner in return for part of the harvest.

These arrangements usually left the sharecroppers perpetually indebted to the landowners, so that they were financially obligated to stay on the land although legally they were free to leave. In addition, many African Americans who were born during the period of slavery were accustomed or resigned to their inferior social and economic positions and were reluctant to seek change. According to W. E. B. Du Bois, a leading African American intellectual of the period, African Americans who came of age around 1910 were the first generation for whom slavery was a distant memory. Jim Crow laws that formalized segregation and discrimination and racial violence that included lynchings motivated many in this new generation of African Americans to seek better conditions in the North.

Because the vast majority of African Americans in the South worked in agriculture, particularly in the production of cotton, several bad crop years and a boll weevil infestation in the mid-1910's contributed to the decision on the part of some to migrate when they did. The increase in out-migration was greatest in the areas that experienced the greatest crop failures.

Changing conditions in the North also played an important role in the timing of the Great Northern Migration. Prior to World War I, immigration from Europe had supplied the labor needs of Northern industry, and African Americans in Northern cities usually could find work only as servants, porters, janitors, or waiters. Most industries hired African Americans only during strikes, as a way to exert pressure on Euro-

A rendition of the Great Northern Migration by Jacob Lawrence depicts African Americans traveling northward, migratory birds symbolizing their flight. (Harmon Foundation/National Archives)

American workers. Restrictions imposed during World War I reduced the number of European immigrants entering the United States by more than 90 percent, from 1.2 million in 1914 to 110,000 in 1918. This reduction in the available labor force took place just as the war increased demand for industrial production. Northern factories, mills, and workshops that previously had disdained African American workers were forced actively to recruit them, offering wages that were often twice what African Americans could earn in the South, plus inducements such as free rooms and train fare. Northward migration was encouraged by news of opportunities spread not only by personal letters home from new arrivals but also by advertisements and articles in newspapers such as the *Chicago Defender*, published by Robert Abbott, an African American editor. In some industries, managers attempted to foster racial division among their workers by encouraging segregated labor unions. The strategy was effective, and workplace competition sometimes contributed to antagonism and racial violence.

African Americans in Northern cities established their own communities, including the Manhattan neighborhood of Harlem. Although it was primarily occupied by wealthy European Americans at the beginning of the twentieth century, African Americans had been in Harlem since Dutch colonial times. Philip A. Payton, Jr., was among several African American business people who saw an opportunity when a housing glut in Harlem coincided with an influx of African Americans. He leased apartment buildings and rented the apartments to African American tenants, antagonizing some of the wealthy Euro-American residents. Harlem was soon an almost exclusively African American enclave.

Harlem became not only a home for African American workers, but also a center of intellectual, cultural, and political development. The Harlem Renaissance, fostered by such African American intellectuals as Du Bois and the poet Langston Hughes, was embraced by white liberals as an alternative to bourgeois American culture. Harlem also became known for African American performing arts, which attracted many white visitors seeking entertainment. Jamaican-born Marcus Garvey arrived in 1916 to establish a branch of his newly formed Universal Negro Improvement Association (UNIA), which was intended to unite all the "Negro peoples of the world." The UNIA flourished in New York and other Northern cities during the 1920's. Garvey encouraged African Americans to take pride in their heritage and to establish their own businesses.

The Great Northern Migration ended with the onset of the Great Depression. Because of poverty and the fierce competition with Euro-Americans for scarce jobs, African Americans from the South found the North to be a less desirable destination. During the 1930's, net migration of African Americans from the South was diminished by about one-half, to 347,500. The Great Northern Migration set the stage, however, for subsequent migrations of African Americans that would be even greater in absolute numbers. By the 1940's, the trend had reversed again, with net migration growing to 1,244,700, a level that would be sustained or exceeded during subsequent decades. —*James Hayes-Bohanan*

ADDITIONAL READING:

Hornsby, Alton, Jr. "1918-1932: Between War and Depression." In *Milestones in Twentieth Century African-American History*. Detroit: Visible Ink Press, 1993. Chronicles significant events involving African Americans during a period roughly corresponding to the Great Migration.

Lemann, Nicholas. *The Promised Land: The Great Black Migration and How It Changed America*. New York: Alfred A. Knopf, 1991. Describes the second Great Migration, beginning in the 1940's. Includes biographical sketches of individual migrant families and a comprehensive discussion of political implications.

Long, Richard A. *African Americans: A Portrait*. New York: Crescent Books, 1993. Nineteenth and twentieth century migrations are included in a broad history of African American culture, which also discusses the contributions of prominent African Americans.

Ploski, Harry A., and James Williams, comps. and eds. "Growth and Distribution of the Black Population." In *Reference Library of Black America*. Vol. 2. New York: Gale Research, 1991. Describes demographic changes involving African Americans from colonial times through the 1990 census, including population growth, migration, and urbanization.

Smythe, Mabel M., ed. *The Black American Reference Book*. Englewood Cliffs, N.J.: Prentice-Hall, 1976. Provides demographic details of the Migration; explains demographic concepts such as "net migration" and "natural increase."

Takaki, Ronald. "To the Promised Land: Blacks in the Urban North." In *A Different Mirror: A History of Multicultural America*. Boston: Little, Brown, 1993. Uses primary sources, including music, advertisements, and letters, to detail the impacts of the migration on Northern urban culture and labor relations.

SEE ALSO: 1850, Underground Railroad; 1863, Reconstruction; 1866, Rise of the Ku Klux Klan; 1917, Universal Negro Improvement Association Is Established.

1911 ■ BORDEN GOVERNMENT IN CANADA: *fifteen years of Liberal government under Laurier are followed by Conservative government during the difficult years of World War I*

DATE: 1911-1920
LOCALE: Ottawa, Canada
CATEGORIES: Canadian history; Government and politics
KEY FIGURES:
Herbert Henry Asquith (1852-1928), British prime minister, 1908-1916
Robert Laird Borden (1854-1937), Conservative prime minister of Canada, 1911-1920

William Lyon Mackenzie King (1874-1950), leader of the
Liberal Party, 1919-1921

Wilfrid Laurier (1841-1919), Liberal prime minister of
Canada, 1896-1911, and leader of the Liberal Party,
1911-1919

David Lloyd George (1863-1945), British prime minister,
1916-1922

Arthur Meighen (1874-1960), Conservative solicitor general
in Borden's government

SUMMARY OF EVENT. Under the skillful direction of Prime
Minister Wilfrid Laurier from Quebec, the Liberal Party enjoyed a majority in the Canadian House of Commons from
1896 until 1911. Under the bilingual Laurier, the Liberals
consistently won almost all the seats from Quebec; and with
reasonable support in Ontario and the Maritime Provinces,
they easily maintained their majority in the House of Commons in the general elections of 1900, 1904, and 1908. During
the last ten years of Laurier's service as prime minister, the
leader of the Conservative opposition in the House of Commons was Robert Borden, a bilingual lawyer from Halifax,
Nova Scotia. Although Borden and Laurier had strong political disagreements, they never spoke of each other with bitterness or animosity.

In 1911, Laurier proposed a politically unpopular reciprocity agreement between the United States and Canada, which
would have eliminated many import duties between the two
countries. Borden argued that this agreement would permit
U.S. companies to expand into Canada and to control too
much business in Canada. This argument proved persuasive
with Canadian voters, and in the 1911 general election, the
Conservatives won 134 seats and the Liberals only 87 seats. In
the 1917 parliamentary election, the Conservatives even increased their position in the House of Commons, winning 153
seats to 82 for the Liberals.

Domestic concerns had dominated the 1911 general election, and the Conservative Party even did extremely well in the
Liberal stronghold of Quebec, winning 27 of the 65 seats in that
French-speaking province. Upon assuming power in Ottawa,
Borden expected that he would succeed in unifying the French-
and English-speaking regions of Canada, and that he would
spend almost all of his time improving the Canadian economy
by increasing trade with both the United States and Great
Britain, Canada's major trading partners. Borden had close
contacts in both English-speaking and French-speaking business communities, and his excellent command of French made
him more acceptable to Quebecers than most other English-
speaking politicians of his era.

In 1914, World War I broke out and Canada, as a loyal
member of the British Empire, became involved. Borden's
major concern during these years was ensuring the full participation of Canadian soldiers and sailors in World War I, and he
did not consider the political consequences of the many decisions that he had to make during these years. He firmly believed that Canada's foreign policy should be subservient to
the needs of the British Empire, as interpreted by the British

prime minister. When British prime minister Herbert Asquith
asked Borden in 1914 to send Canadian soldiers and sailors to
fight against Germany, Borden considered it his moral obligation to agree to this request, believing that because Great
Britain had declared war against Germany, Canada therefore
was also at war with Germany.

Between 1914 and 1918, Borden made numerous trips to
England to confer first with Herbert Asquith and then with
David Lloyd George, who succeeded Asquith as prime minister of Britain in 1916. More than 56,000 Canadian soldiers
died in World War I and almost 150,000 soldiers were badly
wounded—large numbers for a country such as Canada, which
had slightly more than seven million citizens, according to the
1911 census. Borden did not find it necessary to argue that
Canadian and not simply British interests required Canadian
participation in this long war. In hindsight, that was a mistake,
because many Quebecers, who felt no sympathy whatsoever
for the German cause, nevertheless could not understand why
it was necessary for so many Canadians to die for Britain.

Unlike many fellow Conservatives, Borden never questioned the loyalty or integrity of Canadians who did not share
his devotion to the British Empire. Laurier and his fellow Liberal members of Parliament were willing to support Canadian
participation in World War I, as long as there was no military
conscription. In 1917, however, Borden became convinced
that too few Canadians were volunteering for military service,
and in May, 1917, he proposed a Military Service Act to the
House of Commons. His actions during the stormy debate in
Parliament revealed his willingness to sacrifice his own political career and the future of his Conservative Party to the need
for political unity during a period of grave crisis. Although his
party held a large majority in Parliament, he offered to share
power and all cabinet positions with the Liberals and even to
resign, if the Liberals would accept military conscription and
join with him in creating a government of national unity.

Laurier appreciated the sincerity of this offer, but he understood that his fellow Quebecers would never forgive the Liberals if they agreed to military conscription, which was loathed
by the vast majority of French-speaking Quebecers. The situation became almost intolerable during the parliamentary debate on the Military Service Act, when Solicitor General Arthur Meighen questioned the patriotism of French-speaking
Canadians, whom he referred to as "a backward people." The
passage of the Military Service Act provoked rioting in Quebec City, which was suppressed by English-speaking police
after Borden's government had suspended habeas corpus.
Calm returned to Quebec only after Laurier and Catholic bish-
ops in Quebec asked their fellow Quebecers to return to their
homes. The Conservatives then alienated Canadians of Austrian and German descent by revoking their right to vote if
they had become Canadian citizens after 1902.

After the end of World War I, French-speaking Canadians
and other non-British Canadians would not forgive the Conservatives for questioning their patriotism and for limiting the
civil rights of Canadians opposed to conscription.

Although Borden was a decent man who thought more of the needs of Canadian soldiers than of his own political career, his insensitivity to the desires and feelings of Canadians of non-British origin created a great deal of resentment in Canada against the Conservatives, who would win only the 1930 general election between 1917 and 1953. Although the Canadian public turned against the Conservative Party after World War I, Borden continued to be admired for his devotion to Canada. After he retired as prime minister in 1920, he lived seventeen more years, and his thoughtful memoirs were published posthumously in 1938. *—Edmund J. Campion*

ADDITIONAL READING:

Borden, Robert Laird. *His Memoirs.* 2 vols. Edited by Henry Borden. New York: Macmillan, 1938. Contains thoughtful insights into Robert Borden's career and family life. Reveals his basic decency in dealing with adversaries such as Laurier, with whom he sharply disagreed in politics.

Bothwell, Robert, Ian Drummond, and John English. *Canada: 1900-1945.* Toronto: University of Toronto Press, 1987. Contains a clear, well-researched history of Borden's domestic and foreign policies during his nine years as prime minister.

Creighton, Donald. *Canada's First Century: 1867-1967.* Toronto: Macmillan of Canada, 1970. Describes objectively the profound distrust that French-speaking Canadians felt toward Borden and other Conservative politicians during and after World War I.

Hutchison, Bruce. *Macdonald to Pearson: The Prime Ministers of Canada.* Don Mills, Ont.: Longmans Canada, 1967. The chapter on Borden explains both his skill in managing the war effort and his inability to understand the feelings of French-speaking Canadians.

Owran, Doug, ed. *Canadian History: A Reader's Guide: Confederation to the Present.* Toronto: Toronto University Press, 1994. Describes the profound political and social changes in Canada during World War I.

Wilson, Harold A. *The Imperial Policy of Sir Robert Borden.* Gainesville: University of Florida Press, 1966. An objective historical analysis of the reasons for Borden's decision to accept British control over Canadian foreign policy during World War I.

SEE ALSO: 1897, Laurier Era in Canada; 1920, Meighen Era in Canada; 1930, Bennett Era in Canada; 1952, Massey Becomes Canada's First Native-Born Governor General.

1911 ■ TRIANGLE SHIRTWAIST COMPANY FIRE: *the deaths of 146 textile workers lead to reforms in building codes, fire laws, labor practices, and the national conscience*

DATE: March 25, 1911
LOCALE: New York City
CATEGORIES: Business and labor; Women's issues

KEY FIGURES:
Joseph J. Asch, owner of the Asch Building
Max Blanck and
Isaac Harris, co-owners of the Triangle Shirtwaist Company
Edward F. Croker (1863?-1951), fire chief of New York City
SUMMARY OF EVENT. The Triangle Shirtwaist Company fire did not just begin with a cigarette tossed into a bin of fabric scraps. It began with a system of clothing manufacture in which the people who made the garments were considered to be as cheap and disposable as that leftover fragment of a cigarette. That small forgotten flame, however, ignited massive social changes that burned their way through decades of industrial indifference.

Before the mid-1800's, all clothing was made one garment at a time and by hand. In 1846, the first U.S. patent for a sewing machine was issued to Elias Howe. The electrification of the sewing machine in the early 1900's, replacing the foot-powered treadle, allowed faster stitching and increased production. Early clothing factories were home-run businesses in which family members worked day and night, paying for their own supplies and equipment in what was called the "sweating system" or sweatshop. Each worker made one entire garment at a time. Garment manufacturers eventually found it more efficient to gather all the workers into one centralized location, divide the garments into individual sections, and have each worker finish only one piece of the garment. This assembly-line technique, also used in the automobile industry, allowed for the production of large quantities of clothing at relatively low prices. The popular shirtwaist blouse of the 1890's, with its high neck, long puffed sleeves, and crisp tucks in thin white cotton, sold for as little as fifty cents each, within the price range of a clothing factory worker, whose wages in 1884 were about seven dollars a week.

When the International Ladies' Garment Workers' Union (ILGWU) was founded in 1900, a sixty-hour workweek was standard; after several strikes, the workweek in 1910 had been reduced to fifty-two hours. If the hours in the factories were oppressive, the working conditions were worse. Poor lighting, inadequate ventilation, and lack of sanitation were uncomfortable, but overcrowding and fire hazards could be lethal. In 1911, one large insurance company in New York City paid out eighty-one claims for shirtwaist factory fires; there had been four previous fires in less than ten years at the Triangle Shirtwaist Company. It was estimated that one death per day occurred in such fires in New York City.

The Triangle factory in 1911 contained a virtual encyclopedia of fire hazards: wooden work tables seventy-five feet long, spaced only feet apart and with access from only one end; wooden chairs and wicker baskets in the aisles between the tables; bundles of flammable fabrics stored in the baskets and two thousand pounds of scraps kept in bins under the tables; machine oil collected in reservoirs under the tables and a barrel of oil stored just yards away from an exit door; exit doors kept locked and fire escapes kept shuttered, with only one narrow exit passage per floor; and a company policy against smoking that was only loosely enforced.

The Asch Building, which housed the Triangle factory, was designed to be fireproof, yet the building itself kept the Triangle workers one floor away from safety in case of fire. The building was ten stories high, one story too short to fall under more stringent building codes requiring metal window frames and stone floors. The Triangle Shirtwaist Company, doing business on floors eight, nine, and ten, was one floor out of reach of fire hoses and ladders, which had a maximum extension of seven floors. The building's single fire escape ended in a glass skylight on the second floor, one level up from safety. Even the placement of the last step in a staircase, inches too close to an exit door, causing it to open inward instead of outward, added to the conspiracy of the building to endanger lives. Yet landlord Joseph J. Asch correctly claimed that his building complied with the letter of the law at the time it was built.

At closing time, 4:45 P.M., on Saturday, March 25, 1911, fire came, and in thirty minutes performed its deadly purge. One hundred forty-six were dead, nearly a third of the workers on duty that day. Death for them came with the terrible choice of plunging one hundred feet to the ground, rupturing fire nets and glass-tiled sidewalks, or being incinerated in the five feet of space in front of their sewing machines. Most of the victims were young female immigrants from Italy and Eastern Europe. The youngest to die were fourteen-year-old girls; they, like their older colleagues, had been supporting families, both in the United States and back in their homelands. The loss of two or even three members of the same family was not unusual.

If the carnage of the flames was appalling, the arithmetic of the disaster made it worse: The insurance settlement to the owners of the Triangle Shirtwaist Company was slightly less than $200,000; to the families of the victims, it totaled just less than $2,000; and the amount of merchandise alleged to have been pilfered by the workers, which had prompted the lethal locking of the exit doors, was just slightly more than $25. The final outrage was the acquittal of the owners of the company, Isaac Harris and Max Blanck, on charges of manslaughter. Harris and Blanck escaped responsibility for the fire as they had escaped the flames from their tenth-floor offices. Within a week of the disaster, they were back in business; within two years, they had been charged four times with additional fire and safety violations, for which they were fined a total of forty dollars.

This, it seemed, was a fire for which no one was responsible. However, the spark of public indignation, like an unseen cigarette butt in a rag bin, ignited a full-scale investigation that lasted four years and yielded three dozen new laws regulating factories and fire hazards, as well as child labor, food processing, night labor, and safe working conditions for female employees. An outspoken advocate for reform was New York City fire chief Edward F. Croker, whose job it had been to remove the bodies of the fire victims, some of which had been burned or battered beyond recognition and were never identified. His plea for fire sprinklers was passed into law, along with mandates for exit doors that opened outward, limits on the number of people who could occupy each floor of a building, and restrictions on workplace smoking.

The fire strengthened the growing ILGWU, boosting membership in it and other unions, and gave grim verification of their warnings about workplace hazards. The disaster was also the first large-scale relief effort for the Red Cross in New York; it distributed more than eighty thousand dollars in aid to those touched by the fire, both in the United States and as far away as Russia.

The commemorative plaque on the New York University building on the corner of Washington Place and Greene Street is not the only residue of the fire. Among the eyewitnesses to the fire was Frances Perkins, who served on the New York State Factory Investigating Commission of 1911, and later as secretary of labor under President Franklin D. Roosevelt. Perkins attributed some New Deal legislation to the lessons learned from the Triangle Shirtwaist Company fire. Among those lessons was that the social conscience of a nation toward its workers could not be ignored or passed off to industry. For those who bore witness to the flames, a sense of outrage was meaningless unless it was turned into a force for reform.

—*Peggy Waltzer Rosefeldt*

ADDITIONAL READING:

Crute, Sheree. "The Insurance Scandal Behind the Triangle Shirtwaist Fire." *Ms.* 11 (April, 1983): 81-83. Discusses the profits made from the fire by the factory owners. Includes an interview with Pauline Newman, a labor union activist who began working at the Triangle Shirtwaist Company when she was ten years of age. Illustrated.

Ley, Sandra. *Fashion for Everyone: The Story of Ready-to-Wear, 1870's-1970's.* New York: Charles Scribner's Sons, 1975. A history of the women's clothing industry in the United States, discussing designers, fashions of the times, labor struggles, and methods of clothing production and distribution. Color illustrations, bibliography, and index.

Mitelman, Bonnie. "Rose Schneiderman and the Triangle Fire." *American History Illustrated* 16, no. 4 (July, 1981): 38-47. A profusely illustrated account of the fire. Includes the text of a speech given days after the disaster by labor union activist Rose Schneiderman, whose impassioned call for action stirred many to demand reform legislation.

Naden, Corinne. *The Triangle Shirtwaist Fire, March 25, 1911.* New York: Franklin Watts, 1971. A brief, simple summary of the fire, its causes, and its aftermath, with detailed maps of each floor of the Triangle Shirtwaist Company on the day of the fire. Written for young readers. Numerous illustrations, bibliography, index.

Stein, Leon. *The Triangle Fire.* 1962. Reprint. New York: Carroll and Graf, 1985. The definitive work on the subject, written on the fiftieth anniversary of the fire. A detailed account drawn from court transcripts, official reports, newspaper articles, and interviews with survivors, which meticulously reconstructs the event through the eyes of the participants. Illustrations, bibliography, and index.

SEE ALSO: 1889, Hull House Opens; 1935, National Labor Relations Act; 1938, Fair Labor Standards Act.

1912 ■ U.S. Public Health Service Is Established: *a federal agency becomes responsible for protecting the health of U.S. citizens*

DATE: 1912
LOCALE: Washington, D.C.
CATEGORIES: Education; Health and medicine
KEY FIGURES:
Alexander Hamilton (1757-1804), secretary of the Treasury, who proposed the establishment of marine hospitals
Joseph J. Kinyoun (1860-1919), physician who began the bacteriological research program
Edward Livingston (1764-1836), congressman from New York who introduced the bill creating the Marine Hospital Service
John M. Woodworth (1837-1879), surgeon who reorganized the Marine Hospital Service

SUMMARY OF EVENT. When, in 1912, the United States Congress passed legislation authorizing the United States Public Health Service to investigate the causes of communicable diseases, lawmakers recognized the evolution of a government agency that had begun many years before. The legislation marked the official transition from the Public Health Service's origins as an agency of government established with a narrow focus—that is, to provide health care for one small segment of the population—into a government agency responsible for overseeing the general health of the entire citizenry of the United States.

The origins of the U.S. Public Health Service can be traced to sixteenth century England. Following the defeat of the Spanish Armada in 1588, the English people established a seaman's hospital in gratitude for the services of their naval personnel. Throughout much of the American colonial period, the British government collected a nominal sum from its sailors, including those from the colonies, to care for the sick and disabled. With the founding of the United States, Alexander Hamilton urged a similar program, on the grounds that an effective merchant marine was essential to U.S. commerce. In 1798, Congressman Edward Livingston of New York pushed through Congress a measure creating the Marine Hospital Service. The law provided that the Treasury Department would collect twenty cents per month from each merchant seaman to support the establishment of hospitals. The following year, Congress amended the act to include personnel in the Navy and Marines. The first temporary United States Marine Hospital was established in Boston in 1799, and the first government-owned hospital was built in Norfolk County, Virginia, shortly thereafter. In 1802, Congress broadened the law to cover crews on boats and rafts sailing down the Mississippi River to New Orleans. As the United States expanded westward, Congress in 1837 provided for additional hospitals in the Mississippi River Valley and the Great Lakes region.

During these years, the Treasury Department only loosely administered the Marine Hospital Service, with financial responsibility resting upon local collectors of customs. Much of the medical care was provided on a contract basis rather than in hospitals owned or staffed by the government. For example, at times both Bellevue Hospital in New York and Charity Hospital in New Orleans treated patients for seventy-five cents per day per patient. Patients in these institutions may have fared better than those treated in private institutions, because the contracts were awarded as a form of political patronage. Still, the caliber of service rendered for the first seventy years varied widely from hospital to hospital.

As the century advanced, the service began to build more hospitals, but political factors often determined their location. In New Orleans, for example, work was started on a Marine hospital in 1837. After lagging for many years, the project was completed in 1851, at a total cost of $123,000, an enormous sum for those days. Despite the obvious mismanagement of this building contract, funds were appropriated for an even larger hospital in 1885. This one was built in a swamp, and one of the walls sank two feet before the structure was completed. The building, which eventually cost half a million dollars, was never used by the Marine Hospital Service.

Complaints about the marine hospitals led Congress to appoint an investigatory commission in 1849. Seven years later, the commission's recommendations for standardizing hospital procedures were put into effect. Although some improvement ensued, political interference and a high degree of decentralization still characterized operations. Critics noted that each hospital operated independently. In 1870, Congress remedied this situation by completely reorganizing the Marine Hospital Service, centralizing control in a bureau of the Treasury Department and placing a supervising surgeon at the head. The first officer to hold this position was Dr. John M. Woodworth, a Civil War veteran and an exceedingly able individual. The same law also increased the hospital tax to forty cents per month. The monthly charge remained the same until 1884, when it was supplanted by a tonnage tax. In 1906, Congress recognized the expanded sphere of duties for the Hospital Service and replaced the tonnage tax with direct congressional appropriations.

Under Woodworth, remarkable gains were made. In 1873, Woodworth introduced a personnel system that was, in effect, a civil service system for all employees. By this and other measures, he gradually raised the caliber of the staff and fostered the development of a strong *esprit de corps*. The next major advance came in 1889, with the creation of a commissioned officer corps, which gave the service a mobile force of highly qualified health experts. Woodworth also provided strong support for the developing public health movement, actively worked for a national quarantine system, and helped draft the first federal quarantine law in 1878. Following the passage of this latter act, the Marine Hospital Service collaborated with state and municipal governments in improving their quarantine agencies. When Congress strengthened the National Quarantine Law in 1893, the Marine Hospital Service began taking over state and local quarantine stations. It completed the work in 1921, when it took over the quarantine facilities of the Port of New York. The Immigration Act of 1891 further broadened the responsibilities of the Marine Hospital Service by requiring its medical officers to examine all immigrants.

Another significant step had been taken in 1887, when Joseph Kinyoun, a physician who had trained in Europe, established a one-room bacteriological laboratory in the Marine Hospital on Staten Island. Four years later, the bacteriological research moved to Washington, D.C., when the Hygienic Laboratory for Bacteriological Research was established there. Reflecting the changing status of the Marine Hospital Service, in 1902, Congress changed its name to the United States Public Health and Marine Hospital Service. In 1912, the name was shortened to the United States Public Health Service.

In the twentieth century, the Public Health Service steadily widened its functions. Its research laboratories have done outstanding work in epidemiology, and the service has played an important role in developing state and local health boards. Under the Social Security Act of 1935, the Public Health Service was given responsibility for distributing eight million dollars annually in grants-in-aid for public health purposes. In succeeding years, both the budget of the Public Health Service and the agency's responsibilities increased dramatically.

By the end of the twentieth century, the Public Health Service had evolved into an agency active in medical research, health education, and disease prevention. As a division of the Department of Health and Human Services headed by the surgeon general, the Public Health Service included the Centers for Disease Control and Prevention, the Health Resources and Services Administration, the Indian Health Service, the National Library of Medicine, the Substance Abuse and Mental Health Services Administration, and the National Institutes of Health. The bacteriological research begun by Kinyoun in the nineteenth century had grown into a medical resource used not only by the United States but also by countries around the world. Researchers at the National Institutes of Health were active in finding the retrovirus associated with acquired immunodeficiency syndrome (AIDS), for example, while researchers at the Centers for Disease Control and Prevention have discovered the causes of infections such as Legionnaires' disease. The Public Health Service is also active in health prevention and education, such as providing educational materials warning young people of the dangers of smoking tobacco or engaging in other risky behaviors.

—*John Duffy, updated by Nancy Farm Mannikko*

ADDITIONAL READING:

Dupree, A. Hunter. *Science in the Federal Government: A History of Policies and Activities.* Baltimore: The Johns Hopkins University Press, 1986. Lucid, comprehensive history of the relationship between science and government in the United States from 1787 to 1940. The chapter on medicine and public health details the evolution of the Marine Hospital Service, its interactions with other government health agencies, and its emergence as a leader in bacteriological research.

Mullan, Fitzhugh. *Plagues and Politics: The Story of the United States Public Health Service.* New York: Basic Books, 1989. A history that focuses specifically on the Public Health Service.

U.S. Department of Health and Human Services. Public Health Service. *For a Healthy Nation: Returns on Investment in Public Health.* Washington, D.C.: Government Printing Office, 1994. Describes the public benefits possible through increased funding for the Public Health Service.

_____. *Healthy People 2000: Public Health Service Action.* Washington, D.C.: Government Printing Office, 1992. A summary of goals for the Public Health Service.

Williams, Ralph C. *The United States Public Health Service, 1798-1950.* Washington, D.C.: Whittet & Shepperson, 1950. Although now dated, this massive tome narrates the rise of the Marine Hospital Service from a single temporary hospital in 1799 to a national health agency. Includes a general history of U.S. public health.

SEE ALSO: 1846, Surgical Anesthesia Is Safely Demonstrated; 1900, Suppression of Yellow Fever; 1906, Pure Food and Drug Act; 1952, Development of a Polio Vaccine; 1819, Adams-Onís Treaty.

1912 ■ INTERVENTION IN NICARAGUA: *after three years of domestic turmoil and civil war, U.S. Marines enter the country to protect a government sympathetic to U.S. interests*

DATE: August 4-November, 1912
LOCALE: Nicaragua
CATEGORIES: Diplomacy and international relations; Latino American history; Wars, uprisings, and civil unrest
KEY FIGURES:
Smedley Butler (1881-1940), U.S. Marine Corps major
Adolfo Díaz (1874-1964), vice president and later president of Nicaragua
Philander C. Knox (1853-1921), U.S. secretary of state
Luís Mena, Nicaraguan secretary of war
George Weitzel, U.S. minister to Nicaragua
Benjamím F. Zeledón (1879-1912), Nicaraguan general who led the Liberal forces in the 1912 rebellion

SUMMARY OF EVENT. In October, 1909, revolution erupted in the Republic of Nicaragua. The rebels, led by Juan Estrada and based in the Atlantic port city of Bluefields, sought to overthrow President José Santos Zelaya, who had ruled Nicaragua since 1893. These anti-Zelayist rebels sought, and would receive, aid from the United States government. The revolt, in its various phases, would continue until U.S. troops intervened in 1912.

The United States had long desired Zelaya's downfall. For years, Zelaya had sought to unite all of Central America under one government—his—and free Central America from foreign control, particularly that of the United States. Such ambitions were increasingly unacceptable to U.S. policymakers. The Venezuelan boundary dispute, the defeat of Spain in the 1898 Spanish-American War, the taking of the Panama Canal zone, and recent economic investments in the Caribbean region indicated the United States' growing commitment to regional hegemony.

By 1909, Zelaya's attempt to interest Great Britain and Japan in a new Nicaraguan canal (rivaling the one being built in Panama), his attempt at a loan of several hundred million pounds from a British syndicate, and his country's invasion of Honduras in 1907 had so challenged the United States' emerging hegemony that U.S. policymakers welcomed any anti-Zelayist initiative. Initially, Estrada's revolt seemed promising. To the confusion of State Department officials, however, the Nicaraguan revolt became a quagmire. From 1909 until 1912, the U.S. government vacillated between promises of financial aid, diplomatic pressure, and the use of U.S. troops in their search for a stable non-Zelaya government.

Estrada's revolt had the backing of the North American business community in the area and the support of the U.S. consul in Bluefields, Thomas Moffat. When the rebels set up a rival government and asked for diplomatic recognition, however, U.S. Secretary of State Philander C. Knox demurred. Yet within two months, the United States had severed diplomatic relations with Zelaya's government, prompting his resignation.

José Madriz, who succeeded Zelaya, was seen merely as a Zelayista puppet and was refused U.S. recognition. The civil war continued, with President Madriz's forces winning. In May and June, 1910, to forestall Estrada's complete collapse, the U.S. government landed troops at Bluefields, saving the revolt. By early August, with his forces now on the offensive and backed by U.S. Marines, Estrada turned the tide. In August, Madriz resigned, realizing that the U.S. government had, with its Marines, given de facto recognition to Estrada's government.

Knox's and the U.S. government's vision of regional hegemony now came into focus. Guided by a special envoy, Thomas Dawson, agreements were signed in 1910 stating that the new Nicaraguan government would name Estrada as president and Adolfo Díaz, a Conservative leader, as vice president; that a mixed claims commission would be created to sort out all unsettled foreign claims against Nicaragua; and that a customs-guaranteed loan from the United States would be arranged. This loan would show Knox's Dollar Diplomacy in action—U.S. dollars would replace bullets to ensure stability, simultaneously undermining European financial influence in the region.

Although supported by the U.S. government, Estrada's grip on power proved tenuous. He was thought to be too dependent on the United States, and his Liberal Party connections an-

tagonized his Conservative cohorts, especially Secretary of War Luís Mena. Amid rumors of revolt, Estrada resigned in May, 1911, replaced by Conservative vice president Díaz.

Díaz proved a more enduring U.S. client than Estrada. By mid-1911, Díaz's government had completed negotiations on the U.S. loan discussed the previous year. The loan treaty was passed by the Nicaraguan Assembly but stalled in the U.S. Senate. Knox, undeterred, arranged for private banking firms in New York City—Speyer and Company, Brown Brothers, and J. and W. Seligman—to go ahead with a new loan. They loaned one million dollars to Nicaragua, with repayment guaranteed through customshouse receipts. This and other loans helped secure, for the U.S. bankers, a 51 percent controlling interest in Nicaragua's new state bank and 51 percent of the state railway. These arrangements, in conjunction with the naming of U.S. colonel Clifford D. Ham as collector of customs in Nicaragua in 1912, committed the United States to Nicaraguan political stability.

Dollar Diplomacy, however, reaped little, if any, such stability. By the spring of 1912, Managua had become embroiled in political intrigue, as Liberal Zelayists, ambitious Conservative leaders, and nationalist politicians plotted insurrection, accusing Díaz of submitting to U.S. interests. General Mena, secretary of war, proved the most determined. In early 1912, Mena, in control of the army and with widespread political support, had himself elected president for the term beginning in January, 1913. Knox declared such action to be in violation of the 1910 Dawson agreements. Mena decided that revolution was his only avenue to the presidency.

In late July, 1912, Mena attempted to replace Managua's garrison, loyal to President Díaz, with 150 of his own troops. When the garrison resisted, Mena's forces attacked them. Mena's forces were driven back, and the U.S. minister, George Weitzel, met Mena and induced him to resign as secretary of war. Mena then fled Managua, set up a rival government, and entered into open rebellion. Zelaya's former minister of war, Benjamín Zeledón, as well as other Liberals, joined in. Within days, the Díaz government tottered.

Following requests for protection from U.S. and other foreign nationals, and upset by Mena's capturing of lake steamers (technically owned by U.S. bankers), Minister Weitzel demanded that Díaz protect U.S. lives and property. He could not. Instead, Díaz requested U.S. intervention.

On the afternoon of August 4, 1912, one hundred bluejackets from the U.S.S. *Annapolis* landed at Corinto and proceeded to Managua, temporarily securing control of the city. This landing constituted the first U.S. military intervention in the region to prevent a revolution from succeeding. Weitzel, understanding that one hundred sailors represented only a stopgap measure, requested additional support. On August 5, the U.S.S. *Tacoma* landed its Marines in Bluefields "to protect the Atlantic coast." On August 14, Major Smedley Butler's battalion of 361 Marines from Panama reached Managua, finding a city reeling from three days of rebel bombardment. By early September, more than one thousand U.S. Marines were committed to Nicaragua. The number would peak at some twenty-seven hundred.

Nicaragua's neighbors, El Salvador and Costa Rica, protested U.S. military intervention, sensing that their own independence was jeopardized. The newly created Central American Court, established with Theodore Roosevelt's support in 1907-1908 in an effort to bring law and order to the region, also condemned U.S. military intervention. The United States ignored its ruling, thus helping to destroy the legal organ it had created.

By early September, 1912, U.S. troops had regained control of the vital railroad link between Corinto on the Pacific Coast and Managua, and had crushed most rebel strongholds. Major Butler remained determined to open the railroad from Managua inland to Granada on Lake Nicaragua and subdue all rebel forces. On September 18, Weitzel announced categorically that the United States would not allow the Díaz government to fall. For many rebels, this meant that their fight was hopeless. General Mena, ailing and beaten, surrendered in late September at his Conservative rebel stronghold in Granada.

The rebels now held only the major cities of Masaya and León. On October 4, Colonel Joseph Pendleton attacked General Zeledón's troops encamped in the hills overlooking Masaya. In the fiercest fighting of the entire campaign, Zeledón's forces were routed and the general was killed. The city of León fell within days, and the civil war ended. Díaz remained in power. By November, all but one hundred U.S. Marines had left Nicaragua. More than one thousand Nicaraguans and more than fifty U.S. citizens died in the 1912 intervention.

The precedent of sending in troops to determine who ruled in the region was set. Once in Nicaragua, U.S. Marines would stay there—except for the period from August, 1925, until January, 1927—until 1933. Knox and several successors learned that bullets as well as dollars were required to maintain U.S. hegemony in the region. Although U.S. policymakers proclaimed a strong desire to bring the United States' democratic ways to the region, military intervention suggested that order and stability were the primary goals. When U.S. troops did leave in 1933, it was not a democratic nation from which they departed, but the emerging dictatorship of Anastasio Somoza.
—Ken Millen-Penn

ADDITIONAL READING:

Berman, Karl. *Under the Big Stick: Nicaragua and the United States Since 1848.* Boston: South End Press, 1986. A general survey of U.S. involvement in Nicaraguan affairs.

LaFeber, Walter. *Inevitable Revolutions: The United States in Central America.* 2d ed. New York: W. W. Norton, 1993. Chapter 1 presents a revisionist account that views U.S. economic imperialism as the major cause behind U.S. intervention.

Langley, Lester D. *The Banana Wars: An Inner History of American Empire, 1900-1934.* Lexington: University of Kentucky Press, 1983. Chapter 6 is a straightforward political and military account of U.S. intervention during the 1909-1912 crisis.

Munro, Dana G. *Intervention and Dollar Diplomacy in the Caribbean, 1900-1921.* Princeton, N.J.: Princeton University Press, 1964. Chapter 5 presents a largely traditional, geopolitical, and sympathetic explanation of the 1912 intervention, which should be read in conjunction with LaFeber.

Musicant, Ivan. *The Banana Wars: A History of United States Military Intervention in Latin America from the Spanish-American War to the Invasion of Panama.* New York: Macmillan, 1990. Written by a former marine, chapter 4 presents an account of the major military campaigns during the 1912 intervention.

SEE ALSO: 1889, First Pan-American Congress; 1898, Spanish-American War; 1903, Acquisition of Panama Canal Zone; 1909, Dollar Diplomacy; 1933, Good Neighbor Policy.

1912 ■ WILSON IS ELECTED PRESIDENT: *a reform-minded Democrat propels the United States in progressive directions domestically and internationally*

DATE: November 5, 1912
LOCALE: United States
CATEGORY: Government and politics
KEY FIGURES:

Louis Dembitz Brandeis (1856-1941), future associate justice in the Supreme Court who helped to formulate the New Freedom

James Beauchamp "Champ" Clark (1850-1921), Speaker of the House of Representatives from Missouri and a candidate for the Democratic presidential nomination

Theodore Roosevelt (1858-1919), twenty-sixth president of the United States, 1901-1909

William Howard Taft (1857-1930), twenty-seventh president of the United States, 1909-1913

Oscar Underwood (1862-1929), influential Alabama congressman and a candidate for the Democratic presidential nomination

Woodrow Wilson (1856-1924), twenty-eighth president of the United States, 1913-1921

SUMMARY OF EVENT. The election of 1912 was one of the most exciting elections in U.S. history. Woodrow Wilson was the victor in the three-way race with Theodore Roosevelt, who had already served almost two full terms as president (1901-1909), and the incumbent, William Howard Taft. Wilson became the first Democrat elected to the presidency since Grover Cleveland and the second since James Buchanan. The campaign broke the normal pattern of U.S. elections, in which issues were usually subordinate to personalities. At stake in 1912 were three competing philosophies: Wilson's New Freedom, Roosevelt's New Nationalism, and Taft's conservative Republicanism.

Debates during the campaign were deep and incisive. The challenge had been building up within a badly divided nation since Theodore Roosevelt had left the presidency in 1909. His handpicked successor, William Howard Taft, was expected to continue Roosevelt's progressive reforms. Roosevelt went off to Africa on a hunting expedition, expecting that Taft's presidency would follow closely his own reforms. Taft, an amiable behemoth of 340 pounds, was physically lazy, temperamentally unsuited to the presidency, and an inept politician. Roosevelt had been able to hold together a tenuous Republican coalition of Old Guard Eastern conservatives and Midwestern and urban Progressives by shrewd political maneuvering and philosophical wavering between liberal and conservative policies. Taft, a conservative at heart, had no taste for political infighting and allowed the party to disintegrate into squabbling and disunity. When Roosevelt returned home in 1910, the party was in a state of great disorder, and the Democrats had scored large gains in the elections that year. It was in 1910

Twenty-eighth president of the United States Woodrow Wilson led the nation through World War I, proposed the League of Nations, and oversaw passage of banking, tariff, antitrust, and social reform measures that would set the tone for Franklin D. Roosevelt's New Deal. (Library of Congress)

that Woodrow Wilson campaigned for and won his first political office, the governorship of New Jersey. As governor, Wilson set in motion basic reforms that transformed New Jersey's government from a corrupt regime dominated by political bosses into the model of a reform state.

By 1912, the Republican schism had become irreparable; when Theodore Roosevelt marched out of the Republican convention in Chicago on June 22, 1912, to form the new Progressive Party, the election of a Democrat to the presidency was virtually assured. When the Democrats assembled in Baltimore on June 24, 1912, the party was at a historic crossroads.

Wilson had enjoyed a distinguished career as a scholar before his entrance into politics. After being graduated from Princeton University in 1879 and attempting a brief, unsuccessful law career, he completed his doctorate in political science and history at The Johns Hopkins University in 1886. His academic career culminated in his election as president of Princeton University in 1902. By that time, Wilson had written three books on the U.S. system of government and was a budding theoretician of U.S. politics. A dispute at Princeton, resulting from long-standing opposition to some of Wilson's educational reforms, coincided with the opportunity for Wilson to enter politics as the Democratic candidate for governor of New Jersey. Wilson accepted the nomination, and his winning campaign, as well as his subsequent reform administration, made him the brightest Democratic political force in the nation and an immediate contender for the presidential nomination in 1912.

Wilson had been the front-runner for the Democratic presidential nomination until the Republican split made the Democratic nomination much more valuable. The new leader for the nomination was James "Champ" Clark, the Speaker of the House, who, like Taft, was temperamentally and intellectually unsuited for the presidency. Clark was an old-line politician who had broadened his political base beyond his native Missouri to attract most of William Jennings Bryan's old Western following. Oscar Underwood of Alabama, another leading candidate, had strong Southern backing. After a bitter convention fight, Wilson finally won the nomination of the Democratic Party on the forty-sixth ballot.

The election turned into a confrontation between two philosophies of Progressivism. Roosevelt's New Nationalism asserted the necessity of a strong Hamiltonian federal government, the retention and regulation of large corporations, and a program of government-supported social welfare. Wilson answered with the New Freedom, which a prominent Massachusetts lawyer, Louis D. Brandeis, had helped to formulate. The New Freedom asserted a Jeffersonian localism, the breaking up of large corporations, and a return to the small entrepreneurial unit. For the first time, the philosophical alternatives of a new industrial age were being debated in a political campaign.

With the Republican vote split between Taft and Roosevelt, the Democratic challenger, Woodrow Wilson, was elected with 6,293,454 votes to 4,119,538 for Roosevelt, 3,484,980 for Taft, and 900,672 for Socialist candidate Eugene V. Debs.

Although he received only 42 percent of the popular vote, Wilson won an overwhelming victory in the electoral college, with 435 votes to Roosevelt's 88 and Taft's 8. As a newcomer in politics, Wilson was not burdened by political debts such as Roosevelt's obligations to Eastern Republican business interests, and he had a sympathetic Congress ready to cooperate in implementing the Progressive reform program.

Wilson strengthened the presidency even further than had Roosevelt. He became the leader of the people as well as the Congress, and he dominated the government in both his terms. He achieved landmark legislative reforms in his first term with vital tariff, banking, and antitrust measures. Later he adopted, in addition to his own ambitious program, almost all the proposals championed by Roosevelt in the great debate of 1912. When World War I engulfed the United States, Wilson became the first of the powerful twentieth century war presidents. The effects of the 1912 campaign and Wilson's election to the presidency have dominated U.S. liberal politics to this day. The New Deal of Franklin D. Roosevelt owed many of its philosophical premises to Wilson's progressivism and much of its implementation to Wilson's expansion of executive power. In international affairs, the spirit of Wilson's Fourteen Points, which promised a "peace without victory," still well expresses one of the idealistic themes in U.S. foreign policy.

—*Richard H. Collin, updated by Michael Witkoski*

ADDITIONAL READING:

Burton, David H. *The Learned Presidency: Theodore Roosevelt, William Howard Taft, Woodrow Wilson.* Rutherford, N.J.: Fairleigh Dickinson University Press, 1988. A comprehensive review of three presidents who were strikingly different, yet similar in significant ways, and who brought a new aura of intellectualism to the nation's highest office.

Cooper, John Milton, Jr. *The Warrior and the Priest: Woodrow Wilson and Theodore Roosevelt.* Cambridge, Mass.: The Belknap Press of Harvard University Press, 1983. An examination of the two highly divergent but equally important political personalities who helped shape modern U.S. political thought. Provides valuable insights into Roosevelt's compulsion to enter the 1912 electoral race, thereby splitting the Republican vote and assuring Wilson's victory.

Heckscher, August. *Woodrow Wilson.* New York: Charles Scribner's Sons, 1991. A full-scale biography of Wilson that places his political career, especially the crucial 1912 election, into long-range perspective. Heckscher, a former president of the Woodrow Wilson Foundation and a member of the editorial committee for the publication of Wilson's papers, offers new and penetrating insights into the public and private career of one of the most important U.S. presidents.

Link, Arthur S. *Wilson.* Princeton, N.J.: Princeton University Press, 1947-1965. 5 vols. This definitive study of Wilson's life and career should be consulted by any serious student of the 1912 election.

Schlesinger, Arthur M., Jr. *1912-1924.* Vol. 6 in *History of American Presidential Elections.* New York: Chelsea House, 1985. Contains the official platforms of the Democratic and Republican parties, as well as speeches and remarks by Wilson, which help give the particular flavor of the times in which the election was held.

SEE ALSO: 1901, Theodore Roosevelt Becomes President; 1909, Republican Congressional Insurgency; 1917, United States Enters World War I.

1913 ■ ARMORY SHOW: *exposure of the U.S. public to revolutionary European art movements encourages the expansion of museums and inspires a generation of American artists*

DATE: February 17, 1913
LOCALE: New York City, New York
CATEGORY: Cultural and intellectual history
KEY FIGURES:
Arthur B. Davies (1862-1928), artist who organized the Armory Show
Mabel Dodge (1879-1962), writer, hostess, and major promoter of the Armory Show
Marcel Duchamp (1887-1968), most popular, but also the most shocking, of the artists who exhibited at the Armory Show
Walter Kuhn (1877-1949), artist who was secretary of the Armory Show
Alfred Stieglitz (1864-1946), photographer who pioneered the display of contemporary art

SUMMARY OF EVENT. On a cold February day in New York in 1913, U.S. art ended its infancy and began its meteoric rise to world recognition in an old, large, drafty armory. The International Exhibition of Modern Art, as the Armory Show was officially called, opened in the Sixty-ninth Regiment Armory at 25th Street and Lexington Avenue in New York City, on February 17, 1913. The exhibition's catalog listed 1,090 works by 306 artists, but as befits a revolutionary event, latecomers were admitted even after the show began, and several hundred more works of art were exhibited before the show ended. It was estimated that seventy-five thousand persons attended the show and saw, for the first time, revolutionary new art from Europe. Figures themselves cannot indicate the enormous influence of the Armory Show upon U.S. art and culture. Probably no single event, either before or after, has ever had such a decisive effect upon the art of the nation.

At the beginning of the twentieth century, U.S. art was provincial and academic, reflecting a prosperous and secure society, a sureness of technique, and a preference for strict representation. Impressionism, which had burst upon Europe in 1870, had been the most recent artistic movement to reach the United States. In the first decade of the twentieth century, revolutionary new techniques in art were introduced in Paris, and the followers of Henri Matisse created the movement called Les Fauves, or "wild beasts," in which nature was reduced to a mere starting point in a picture. In 1905, Paul Cézanne began to show his paintings in Paris; his preoccupation with sculptured form was to mark another great development, which, in turn, would outweigh the new primitivism of Paul Gauguin and the new expressionism of Vincent van Gogh. In 1907, when Pablo Picasso's *Les Demoiselles d'Avignon* was shown in Paris, another important modern movement, cubism, was introduced. All of these movements can best be understood as making up what is still regarded as modernism in art. They all had in common the use of nonrepresentational subjects or unrecognizable objects instead of what had previously been thought the only possible subject of art, the imitation and representation of recognizable objects from nature. Modernism in art actually eliminated the old concept of beauty and substituted aesthetics that were more complex, gave greater range to the imagination, and were completely different from any earlier art form.

It would be a mistake to think that the Parisians took this artistic revolution with equanimity. Conservative critics and the public in general were shocked and repelled. As the new art became familiar, public taste came to accept it, but then began to encounter still more new and revolutionary artistic styles. It is little wonder that the American public reacted with shock, surprise, and puzzlement when the new movements of European art, along with what was new in American art, had to be absorbed in one cataclysmic art exhibit.

The idea of the Armory Show came to a group of young American artists at New York's Madison Gallery in 1911. Walter Kuhn, one of the leading organizers, and several other artists were depressed at the hopelessness of selling original art in the United States. The only way a American artist could show was through museums or artists' associations that were controlled by conservative juries. At the time, the only gallery that consistently exhibited modern art was Alfred Stieglitz's Gallery at 291 Fifth Avenue. Stieglitz had great faith in American artists, but he preferred to concentrate on a few artists. To promote many artists to a broad audience was, however, the chief objective of the Madison Gallery group, and they were resolved to do something about it. By January, 1912, the group had twenty-five members, called the Association of American Painters and Sculptors, who, for the most part, could not be regarded as modernists. What they most sought was independence; freedom from established and conservative museums, patrons, and exhibits; and a chance to show their art without juries or prizes.

It was Arthur B. Davies who transformed the idea of an independent show into an aesthetic revolution and determined to combine the showing of American art with the best art the could be obtained from Europe. Davies' efforts were aided by the work and support of writer and hostess Mabel Dodge. She had an instinct for recognizing talented artists and good art, and promoted both. Dodge became an enthusiastic backer and vice president of the Armory Show.

The show opened to great publicity. On hand was the entire panoply of the new French art, including a fair representation of Cézanne, Gauguin, van Gogh, Picasso, Matisse, Odilon Redon, and the surprise hit and symbol of the show, Marcel Duchamp. Les Fauves and the cubists were the most shocking, but they also drew the most comments; Duchamp's *Nude Descending a Staircase* occasioned some wit, including Theodore Roosevelt's observation that the picture looked like his Navajo bathroom rug, and another description that it was like "an explosion in a shingle factory."

Most American artists were shaken by the new forces in art that they saw for the first time in the Armory Show. Younger artists still relatively uncommitted were affected profoundly, because they did not have to act defensively. Stuart Davies, who was to become a leader in American art in the 1920's, called the show "the greatest single experience . . . in all my work." After showing the new art in New York, the sponsors sent it on a national tour. When it arrived in Chicago, students burned effigies of Henri Matisse and Constantin Brancusi. In Boston, it was snubbed by conservative members of society. Nevertheless, by the end of the tour, the show had been seen by nearly three hundred thousand persons; in a country possessing only a handful of art galleries, such success was little short of spectacular.

As it was intended to do, the Armory Show was also led to a revolution in American art; its emblem was the pine tree—a symbol used by Massachusetts in the American Revolution. Galleries in New York began to multiply, serious collectors began to amass many of the modernistic paintings that hung in American museums in the late twentieth century, a whole new generation of artists received encouragement and inspiration when they most needed it, and art became a familiar topic in the newspapers and periodicals for many who had never before thought of the possibility of looking at pictures.

The Armory Show was a great cultural innovation, but it was more than that. So profound was its effect that the Armory Show can be considered to be the dividing line in the development of American art—to be judged as being either before or after the show. The long-range effects of the Armory Show are primarily twofold: First, the Armory Show gave impetus to the establishment of new museums and the expansion of those that existed. The Museum of Modern Art in New York, for example, can trace its origins to the Armory Show. Second, by making the public aware of modern art, the Armory Show became a powerful force in transforming modern art into big business. In time, works by established artists were looked upon as investments as safe and profitable as, if not more so than, blue-chip securities. Art moved from the studio to the marketplace, not necessarily to its advantage.

—Richard H. Collin, updated by Nis Petersen

ADDITIONAL READING:

Association of American Painters and Sculptors. *The Armory Show*. 3 vols. New York: Arno Press, 1972. Volume 3 is of particular value, because it documents, through original sources such as cartoons and articles, the violent opposition to the Armory Show. Volume 3 also contains Walt Kuhn's pamphlet on the show.

Baur, John I. *Revolution and Tradition in Modern American Art*. Cambridge, Mass.: Harvard University Press, 1951. An interpretation of the main movements and trends in American art that concentrates less on schools of painting and sculpture than on underlying traditions and currents.

Brown, Milton W. *The Story of the Armory Show*. 2d ed. New York: Abbeville Press, 1988. Probably the best all-round account of the Armory Show. Includes diagrams showing how the works were presented and a complete listing of artworks shown and purchased.

Green, Martin. *New York, 1913: The Armory Show and the Paterson Strike Pageant*. New York: Charles Scribner's Sons, 1988. Places the Armory Show in the contemporaneous American social environment, especially as complemented by and contrasted with the Paterson Silk Strike, a pivotal event in U.S. labor history.

Rose, Barbara. *American Art Since 1900*. Rev., expanded ed. New York: Praeger, 1975. The author has revised her original 1967 work after consultation with authorities such as Meyer Shapiro and artists such as Georgia O'Keeffe. Chapters 6 and 7 are especially relevant.

SEE ALSO: 1846, Smithsonian Institution Is Founded; 1893, World's Columbian Exposition.

1913 ■ SIXTEENTH AMENDMENT: *Congress gains the power to levy and collect taxes on personal income, overcoming a Supreme Court decision that held the practice to be unconstitutional*

DATE: February 25, 1913
LOCALE: Washington, D.C
CATEGORIES: Economics; Government and politics
KEY FIGURES:
Nelson Wilmarth Aldrich (1841-1915), senator from Rhode Island
Joseph Bailey (1863-1929), senator from Texas
Albert Cummins (1850-1926), senator from Iowa
Philander Chase Knox (1853-1921), secretary of state in the Taft Administration
William Howard Taft (1857-1930), twenty-seventh president of the United States, 1909-1913
SUMMARY OF EVENT. The Sixteenth Amendment to the Constitution of the United States became law on February 25, 1913, slightly less than four years after it had first been submitted to the states for ratification. This amendment provided that Congress should have the power to levy and collect taxes on incomes, without apportionment among the states and without regard to the U.S. Census. The Constitution originally had stipulated that no direct tax could be levied unless such taxation was in direct proportion to the population of the United States as determined by census. As the result of a Supreme Court ruling in 1895 that categorized the income tax

as a means of direct taxation, the Sixteenth Amendment was drafted explicitly to legalize the levying of an income tax, thus effectively nullifying the problem of whether or not to consider the income tax a direct tax.

The history of the income tax in the United States dates back to the War of 1812, when Secretary of the Treasury Alexander J. Dallas recommended on January 21, 1815, that Congress adopt a tax on incomes to raise funds for prosecution of the war. Although the war had ended with the signing of the Treaty of Ghent on December 24, 1814, this fact was probably not yet known in Washington, D.C., in January, 1815. Later knowledge of the conclusion of the war, however, precluded any action by Congress on Secretary Dallas' request.

The income tax question did not arise again until the Civil War, when the United States' first income tax was levied by the Union government. The Internal Revenue Act of 1862 not only provided for the taxation of incomes but also directed that such taxation would be progressive in character—that is, that the rates would be increasingly higher on higher incomes. For the first time in the history of the U.S. taxation, people were to be taxed according to their ability to pay. This initial measure called for a 3 percent tax on incomes up to ten thousand dollars and a 5 percent tax on incomes greater than ten thousand dollars. The income tax remained in effect, although the rates fluctuated, until 1872, when Congress let the law expire in response to the pressure of numerous business groups.

In the late 1880's, popular agitation for a new income tax began to grow, especially within the populist movement. The national platform of the Populist Party in 1892 contained a demand for a graduated income tax. Two years later, Congress passed the Wilson-Gorman Tariff Act, which contained a provision for an income tax of 2 percent on all incomes greater than four thousand dollars. In 1895, the Supreme Court declared the income tax unconstitutional, ruling in the case of *Pollock v. Farmers' Loan and Trust* that it violated the Constitution's prohibition of direct taxation.

The Democratic Party, whose views on social reform were often akin to those of the Progressives, responded to the Pollock decision by including a call for income tax in its 1896 convention platform. From 1896 to 1909, when William Howard Taft assumed the presidency, political coalitions developed that assured that the idea of an income tax would continue to appear on the political agenda. The protax legislators were generally representatives of the farmer and worker constituencies, while the tax's opponents supported the monied industrialists. Lines also were drawn geographically: the economically powerful East versus Midwestern and Western laborers and ranchers.

As the United States underwent its transition to industrialization and the population grew rapidly, reliance on tariffs for federal support was viewed by the supporters of the income tax as insufficient and unfair. The increasing concentration of wealth in the hands of a few seemed to many people in the United States a direct threat to democracy, and the income tax presented itself as a means of reversing that trend. Its advocates hoped that the income tax would achieve a moderate redistribution of wealth and thus salvage the necessary basis for democracy.

One of the leaders of the struggle was Senator Joseph Bailey, a Democrat from Texas who had favored the income tax since 1897. In April, 1909, Bailey proposed an income tax amendment to the Payne-Aldrich Tariff Bill under consideration at that time by Congress. Bailey's suggestion of a 3 percent tax on all incomes greater than five thousand dollars was soon supplanted by a more radical proposal by Albert Cummins, senator from Iowa, of a graduated income tax ranging from 2 percent on incomes greater than five thousand dollars to 6 percent on incomes greater than one hundred thousand dollars.

Conservative Democrats and Republicans, on the other hand, led by Senator Nelson Aldrich of Rhode Island, opposed the use of taxation for social welfare ends such as the redistribution of wealth. President William Howard Taft held no strong objection to an income tax and spoke in favor of it as early as 1907. The question for Taft was the means, not the end. The role of the Supreme Court was the issue for him. He did not favor a legislative overturn of a Court decision. His solution, contained in his message to Congress on June 16, 1909, called for a constitutional amendment to be achieved by submitting the issue to the states for their decision. Although proponents of the income tax feared that the amendment was merely a conservative ploy to defeat, or at least forestall, enactment of an income tax measure, they finally acquiesced to the idea of a constitutional amendment, and in July, 1909, it was submitted to the states.

The road to ratification was not easy. Conservatives attacked the amendment as the work of demagogues intent on leading the United States down the path to socialism, and throughout 1910 and 1911, conservative Republicans and Democrats bitterly waged war against it. The forces of Progressivism were in the ascendancy in the state governments, however, and in the end, only five states rejected ratification of the amendment. On February 25, 1913, Secretary of State Philander C. Knox certified that the Sixteenth Amendment was officially part of the Constitution.

Shortly after ratification, Congress enacted the first income tax law under the new amendment as part of the Underwood-Simmons Tariff Bill. Although the rate of taxation was low by modern standards, the bill set an important precedent by stipulating a graduated income tax. The Sixteenth Amendment had made no mention of the principle of graduated rates of taxation, but from that time forward, such a principle was accepted. The effect of graduation was to democratize further the tax structure and to shift more of the tax burden to those best able to pay.

The income tax reversed the trend toward concentration of wealth, and after 1913, the poorer classes shouldered a smaller share of taxation in the United States.

—Fredrick J. Dobney, updated by Ann Thompson

ADDITIONAL READING:

Acheson, Sam H. *Joe Bailey, the Last Democrat.* New York: Macmillan, 1932. A biography of the Texas senator who was a leading advocate of income tax legislation.

Anderson, Donald F. *William Howard Taft: A Conservative's Conception of the Presidency.* Ithaca, N.Y.: Cornell University Press, 1973. Provides background to and biographical information about the principal issues and personages involved in the passage of the Sixteenth Amendment.

Coletta, Paolo E. *The Presidency of William Howard Taft.* Lawrence: University Press of Kansas, 1973. Describes the fiscal and judicial positions of Taft before and during his presidency, providing insight into his actions regarding income tax legislation.

Makin, John H., and Norman J. Ornstein. *Debt and Taxes.* New York: Random House, 1994. Provides historical context for the introduction of income tax and describes the tax's evolution to the 1990's.

Ratner, Sidney. *Taxation and Democracy in America.* New York: John Wiley and Sons, 1967. This comprehensive history of taxation policy and legislation in the United States (see especially chapter 14) provides detailed background for the passage of the Sixteenth Amendment.

Stephenson, Nathaniel W. *Nelson W. Aldrich.* New York: Charles Scribner's Sons, 1930. A biography of the coauthor of the Payne-Aldrich Tariff Bill and the Republican leader of opposition to income tax legislation.

Waltman, Jerold L. *Political Origins of the U.S. Income Tax.* Jackson: University Press of Mississippi, 1985. Chapter 1 provides a background and examination of the Sixteenth Amendment. Includes information on followup legislation in 1916, 1917, 1918, and 1921.

SEE ALSO: 1892, Birth of the People's Party; 1896, McKinley Is Elected President; 1897, Dingley Tariff; 1901, Theodore Roosevelt Becomes President; 1909, Republican Congressional Insurgency.

1913 ■ Ford Assembly Line Begins Operation: *mass-production techniques increase availability of automobiles to the middle class and revolutionize industrial manufacturing*

DATE: March 1, 1913
LOCALE: Detroit, Michigan
CATEGORIES: Business and labor; Economics; Science and technology; Transportation
KEY FIGURES:

James Couzens (1872-1936), Ford's vice president, general manager, and treasurer who proposed the minimum wage

Carl Emde, German technician who helped build new equipment for the assembly line

Henry Ford (1863-1947), philanthropist, social reformer, onetime peace activist, and head of the Ford Motor Company

William C. Klann, another technician who contributed to assembly line production

Charles Sorensen (1882-1968), technician who introduced
the concept of the continuous conveyor belt

Frederick W. Taylor (1856-1915), the "father of industrial
management" who advised Ford on the assembly line

SUMMARY OF EVENT. Mass production and the assembly line
are closely associated with Henry Ford, but the ideas did not
originate with him. The three basic ideas of mass production—standardization, simplification, and interchangeabil-
ity—date back to the eighteenth century. Before 1913, numerous industries carried out quantity production of telephone
sets, bicycles, typewriters, and cash registers. Even Henry
Ford had an assembly line system in his original plant which
produced a car every thirteen hours.

After the opening of the Ford Motor Company in 1903,
Ford decided that he would produce only one type of automobile, the Model T. Rival companies which were manufacturing
numerous models saw this move as the beginning of the end of
Ford, who planned to freeze the design of his car and then

spend money, time, and effort on the equipment and machinery to produce it. It was his desire to "build a motor car for the
great multitude," and that could be accomplished only by
producing a single model in volume in order to reduce the
price of the finished product. The Piquette plant had included
a number of assembly line techniques: work was brought to
the men, and the men, machines, and materials were placed in
a sequence of operations. Under these conditions, some twelve
thousand cars were produced in 1909.

In the following year Ford moved to the Highland Park
plant, also in Detroit, which greatly expanded his operation.
Between 1912 and 1913 the continuous assembly line was
developed as a crowning achievement in the creation of mass
production. In this process of mass production, Ford was focusing on principles of precision, economy, organization, continuity, speed, and repetition. He got much assistance from
individuals such as Carl Emde, the German technician who
devised the necessary equipment for the project; William C.

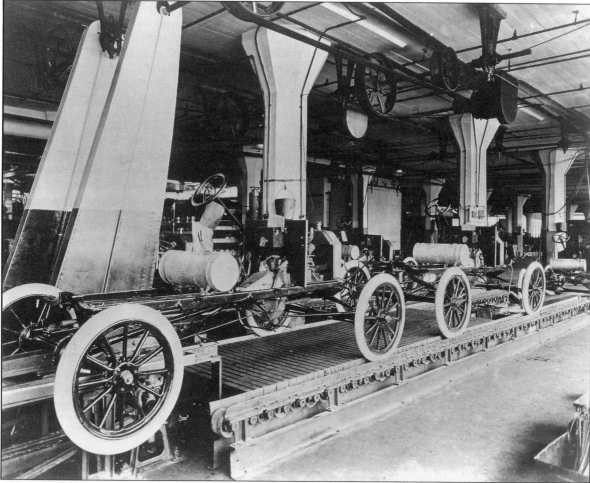

*The Ford Motor Company's Highland Park assembly line made possible the production of thousands of Model T's at an
affordable price, revolutionizing transportation. The company also revolutionized management-labor relations with its five-
dollar-a-day wage and somewhat intrusive incentives for employees to live clean and sober lives. (Library of Congress)*

Klann, who adapted the system to the assembly of engines; and Charles Sorensen, who added the concept of the continuous conveyor belt to the assembly line. Although an exact record of the creation of the continuous assembly line is not available, by March 1, 1913, it was in operation.

The main assembly line involved forty-five operations, and the speed of the process was soon evident. An engine which previously took a worker 600 minutes to assemble could now be put together in 226 minutes. A chassis which had taken a worker twelve hours and twenty-eight minutes to complete could now be assembled in one hour and thirty-three minutes. Annual production figures jumped from 78,440 automobiles in 1911-1912 to 730,041, or some two thousand cars daily, in 1916-1917, testifying to the efficiency of the new techniques.

Accordingly, the Ford Motor Company was on its way to becoming the largest automobile manufacturer in the United States—but at considerable human cost. The mechanization and minute division of labor inspired by industrial engineer Frederick W. Taylor, whose principles of time and motion had won him the title "father of industrial management," demanded little real labor skill except for a few top engineers and managers who designed the product and processes. The stultifying monotony of the endless repetitive work was devastating; the labor turnover rate became alarming.

Technological innovation at Ford, however, was to accompany unprecedented labor policies in large-scale American industry. The workday was reduced to eight hours, the plant increased to three shifts instead of two, and safety measures were improved and extended. Sick leave, better medical care for injured workers, and an improved factory environment were put in place in 1913. Aptitude tests, English-language instruction for immigrant workers, and technical training were added. Special efforts were made to hire workers with physical disabilities and former convicts.

The most spectacular and widely heralded consequences of the introduction of the more efficient assembly line process was the announcement of the five-dollar-per-day minimum wage policy by Henry Ford and James Couzens, business manager at Ford, on January 5, 1914. A number of reasons have been offered to explain this heretofore unheard-of measure: to reduce labor turnover; to counter unionization; to secure a docile labor force that could be exploited through work speedup; and to obtain the pick of Detroit mechanics. Henry Ford observed that his new wage policy was "profit sharing and efficiency engineering." Indeed, some have played up Ford's paternalistic and altruistic motives as underlying his wage innovation, whereas his harsher critics insist on Ford's self-interest and business expediency. Whatever the reason, the new wage scale, involving salary plus bonus, precipitated an onslaught of applicants storming the Ford plant's gates; they were beaten back with fire hoses in freezing weather by security guards.

Not all workers were equally generously treated. To qualify for the five dollars per day—unmatched by competitors—a worker had to meet certain standards. He had to be an individual of sound personal habits with a decent home. He had to give evidence of

being sober, saving, steady, industrious, even churchgoing. To determine whether any particular worker met these standards and to help those who did not, the company created a Sociological Department whose members visited the employees' homes. While the arrangement was criticized for meddling in the private lives of Ford workers, some, especially immigrant laborers, managed to improve their lot substantially and become integrated into the American "melting pot," one of Henry Ford's stated objectives.   —*Russell Magnaghi, updated by Peter B. Heller*

ADDITIONAL READING:

Bryan, Ford R. *The Fords of Dearborn*. Rev. ed. Detroit: Harlo, 1989. While focusing on the genealogy of the Ford family and the role of each in creating the automobile industry, the book adds some useful insights into Henry Ford's persona and motivations.

Lacey, Robert. *Ford: The Men and the Machine*. Boston: Little, Brown, 1986. A masterly work that highlights the human cost of the speedup and monotony that accompanied the introduction of the assembly line and the five-dollar-per-day wage at the Ford plant.

Meyer, Stephen, III. *The Five-Dollar Day: Labor, Management, and Social Control in the Ford Motor Company, 1908-1921*. Albany: State University of New York Press, 1981. Details the crucial events and circumstances that created assembly-line production at Ford as well as the reactions of automobile workers to the new work processes and higher wages. Includes an excellent bibliography.

Nevins, Allan. *Ford: The Times, the Man, the Company*. New York: Charles Scribner's Sons, 1954. An objective view of the controversial persona of Henry Ford based on sources from the Ford Archives and, at times, oral history. The narrative connects the introduction of assembly-line production to the five-dollar-per-day minimum wage. Impressive bibliography.

Rupert, Mark. *Producing Hegemony: The Politics of Mass Production and American Global Power*. Cambridge, Mass.: Cambridge University Press, 1995. Among others, the author, a political scientist, considers the political and ideological struggle in his chapter entitled "Fordism vs. Unionism" flowing from the introduction of assembly line production at the Ford Highland Park plant in Detroit.

SEE ALSO: 1911, Triangle Shirtwaist Company Fire; 1933, National Industrial Recovery Act; 1935, National Labor Relations Act.

1913 ■ ALIEN LAND LAWS: *state measures deprive resident Japanese Americans of property rights*

DATE: Beginning May 20, 1913
LOCALE: California, Arizona, Louisiana, Washington, New Mexico, Idaho, Montana, and Oregon
CATEGORIES: Asian American history; Business and labor; Civil rights; Economics

KEY FIGURES:

William Jennings Bryan (1860-1925), U.S. secretary of state
Viscount Chinda (1856-1929), Japanese ambassador to the
United States
Hiram Warren Johnson (1866-1945), governor of California
Woodrow Wilson (1856-1924), twenty-eighth president of the
United States, 1913-1921

SUMMARY OF EVENT. Immigration from Japan to the United States increased significantly during the final decade of the nineteenth century, with most of the Asian immigrants settling in the Pacific states. In California, the agricultural skills of the Japanese enabled them to transform previously unusable land into fertile soil, in which they were able to grow vegetables and fruit. As the number of Japanese laborers arriving in California increased substantially, however, a strong anti-Japanese sentiment developed: Their success threatened and antagonized the emerging labor unions. The Asian Exclusion League was formed in 1905, and a campaign to bar Japanese immigration was launched. Negotiations begun in 1906 between the United States and Japan resulted in the Gentlemen's Agreement of 1907, which limited immigration from Japan to non-laborers and to families who were joining previously settled laborers. In 1907, an immigration bill was amended to prevent Japanese laborers from entering the United States via Hawaii, Mexico, and Canada.

The California legislature's attempts to pass alien land bills began in 1907. Although President Theodore Roosevelt's personal intervention, in the form of the Gentlemen's Agreement, prevented the enactment of these bills, the California legislature appropriated funds to investigate Japanese agricultural involvement. When the California State Labor Commission submitted a report favorable to the Japanese, the labor commissioner was publicly reprimanded. His report remained unpublished. By 1910, about 70 percent of California's strawberries were produced by the Japanese, and in 1910, twenty-seven anti-Japanese proposals were introduced in the legislature. Enactment of the proposed anti-Japanese legislation was prevented that year by influence from the White House and, in 1911, by President William Howard Taft's direct intervention.

On April 4, 1913, a California bill that would prohibit Japanese and other foreigners ineligible for citizenship from holding or leasing land in California prompted the Japanese ambassador, Viscount Chinda, to make an informal protest to the Department of State, where he spent two hours with Secretary of State William Jennings Bryan. Regarding the incident, *The New York Times* warned that it could "prove to be the beginning of a serious international difficulty rivaling the embarrassing school incident which arose during President Roosevelt's administration." The incident referred to had come dangerously close to producing a serious rift in Japanese-U.S. relations.

The proposed bill in California was modeled on an 1897 federal law barring ownership of land by aliens ineligible for citizenship. The federal law, however, contained a proviso that it would not be applicable where treaty obligations conferred the right to own and hold land. The California bill included a clause prohibiting the leasing of land to Japanese, but the Japanese contended that this right had been conferred previously by the Treaty of 1894 and reenacted in the Treaty of 1911, which provided that citizens of either the United States or Japan would have the right to "own or hire houses . . . and lease land for residential or commercial purposes" in the country of the other.

In Washington, D.C., the introduction of the 1913 California Alien Land bill was viewed seriously. The prevailing opinion was that its effect could be more sweeping than the problems of 1908 and could lead once again to talk of war. When Secretary Bryan and Ambassador Chinda exchanged mutual assurances of continuing friendship between the United States and Japan on April 4, the Department of State expressed confidence that the matter would be resolved amicably. The following day, Secretary Bryan met with the California congressional delegation, which emphasized the necessity of the proposed legislation. Members of the delegation described how, in many parts of California, more than half the farms were operated by Japanese, and neither U.S. nor Chinese workers could compete with Japanese labor. They asserted that despite the Gentlemen's Agreement of 1907, to withhold passports from "coolie laborers," they were arriving continuously. The feeling in California was so strong, they reported, that people who leased land to a Japanese person were ostracized by their neighbors. Members of the delegation intimated that violent protests against the increase in Japanese competition were imminent.

The development of the proposed legislation was largely the result of the influence of labor unions and farmers from districts in which the Japanese had acquired land. The labor unions were reported to hate the Japanese, because their presence reduced the value of adjacent land and because Japanese laborers worked for low wages. It was fear of the labor unions that impelled members of the legislature to vote for the bill; Californians as a whole did not support the legislation.

In Japan, the Tokyo press vehemently opposed the legislation. An editorial in the *Asahi*, a leading independent newspaper, referred to the "hollowness of American advocacy of equality" and stated, "This anti-Japanese agitation will impress us with a keen sense of humiliation, which will require many years to efface." The National Liberal Party urged the governments of Japan and the United States to prevent passage of the bill. The Japanese government filed a formal protest on April 7. President Wilson's position was to remain outside the conflict. He believed that the proposed legislation lay within the rights of a sovereign state. On April 10, it was reported that if no violation of treaty obligations were attempted, the administration would not oppose the bill. President Wilson had concluded that the precise limitations of federal and state jurisdiction in the matter should be determined by the courts.

The final draft of the new law was adopted by the California Senate on April 12. Ambassador Chinda presented his government's formal protest against the bill to the Department of State. Secretary of State Bryan delivered a complete copy of the Alien Land Act to the Japanese ambassador on April 14, after it passed its second reading in the California legislature, thereby rendering it proper for diplomatic consideration. Because of agitation in Tokyo, where the bill was denounced by the press and where demonstrators were calling for war, the California legislature, despite overwhelming margins in both houses, delayed further action until May 20, when the Alien Land Law, known also as the Webb-Henley bill, was signed into law by Governor Hiram Warren Johnson. The statute barred all aliens ineligible for citizenship, or corporations with more than 50 percent ineligible alien ownership, from the legal right to own agricultural land in California, and it limited land-leasing contracts in the state to three years' duration.

Anti-alien agitation began in Michigan following announcements that Japanese laborers from California were going to settle in Alger County, Michigan. During 1917, anti-alien land bills were introduced into the legislatures of Oregon and Idaho but because of the crisis in Europe were subsequently withdrawn. However, an alien land law was enacted in Arizona.

California's 1913 statute was not entirely effective. To prevent the Japanese from circumventing the law, a more restrictive alien land bill was introduced in the California legislature in 1920 to forbid the Issei (first generation Japanese, that is, immigrants to the United States from Japan) from buying land in the name of their U.S.-born children, the Nisei. It also prohibited the transfer of land to noncitizens by sale or lease and established criminal penalties for aliens caught attempting to bypass the 1913 law. In a statewide ballot, California voters passed the 1920 Alien Land Law by a three-to-one margin. A number of cases to test the constitutionality of the new law were instigated by the Japanese. In 1923, the U.S. Supreme Court ruled against the Issei in four of these cases. Further restrictions also were passed in a 1923 amendment, which, together with the 1924 Immigration Act, effectively denied further immigration and determined the status of Japanese immigrants in the United States. The Alien Land Laws in California were not repealed until 1956.

In 1921, Washington, Texas, and Louisiana enacted alien land laws based on the California act, as did New Mexico in 1922, and Oregon, Idaho, and Montana in 1923. They differed from the California statute only in small details. Other states followed: Kansas in 1925; Missouri in 1939; Utah, Arkansas, and Nebraska in 1943; and Minnesota in 1945.

—*Susan E. Hamilton*

ADDITIONAL READING:

Chuman, Frank F. *The Bamboo People: The Law and Japanese-Americans*. Del Mar, Calif.: Publisher's Inc., 1976. Includes good coverage of the alien land laws.

Curry, Charles F. *Alien Land Laws and Alien Rights*. Washington, D.C.: Government Printing Office, 1921. A contemporary account of the alien land laws.

Ichioka, Yuji. *The Issei: The World of the First Generation Japanese Immigrants, 1885-1924*. New York: Free Press, 1988. Includes discussion of the labor-contracting system and

the exclusion movement. Annotated, with a comprehensive bibliography.

McGovney, Dudley. "The Anti-Japanese Land Laws of California and Ten Other States." *California Law Review* 35 (1947): 7-54. A detailed discussion of alien land laws in relation to state, federal, and English common law up the time of publication.

Nomura, Gail M. "Washington's Asian/Pacific American Communities." In *Peoples of Washington: Perspectives on Cultural Diversity*, edited by Sid White and S. E. Solberg. Pullman: Washington State University Press, 1989. Provides specifics of Washington and Texas land laws.

Takaki, Ronald, ed. *Iron Cages: Race and Culture in Nineteenth Century America*. New York: Oxford University Press, 1990. Provides insight into the origin of anti-Asian sentiment and its connection to legislation such as the alien land laws.

SEE ALSO: 1854, Perry Opens Trade with Japan; 1892, Yellow Peril Campaign; 1907, Gentlemen's Agreement.

1913 ■ ANTI-DEFAMATION LEAGUE IS FOUNDED: *creation of a major organization working against anti-Semitism and racial discrimination of all kinds*

DATE: September, 1913
LOCALE: New York City
CATEGORIES: Immigration; Jewish American history; Organizations and institutions
KEY FIGURES:
Leo Frank (1886-1915), Jewish superintendent of an Atlanta pencil factory convicted of the 1913 murder of Mary Phagan
Adolph Kraus (1850-1928), national president of B'nai B'rith at the time of the Anti-Defamation League's founding
Thomas Edward Watson (1856-1922), publisher of an anti-Semitic newspaper and magazine

SUMMARY OF EVENT. The Anti-Defamation League of B'nai B'rith was founded in September, 1913, with the express purpose of disseminating positive messages about Jews and Jewishness; combating negative stereotypes of Jews; and exerting pressure on public libraries, schools, organizations, and companies to improve the image of Jewish people in the United States. The Anti-Defamation League has continued to point out examples of anti-Semitism in the United States and to agitate not only for an end to anti-Jewish propaganda and misinformation but also for a cessation of racism and racist speech everywhere.

The origins of and need for the Anti-Defamation League lie generally in the racist and anti-immigrant feelings prevalent in the United States in the early twentieth century, specifically in the conviction of a Jewish Atlanta businessman, Leo Frank, for the murder of a little girl in August of 1913. The climate of the

United States in the early twentieth century was becoming increasingly unfriendly to new immigrants, for several reasons. First, the new immigrants arriving in the United States after 1880 came from areas of the world that had not traditionally provided large groups of immigrants to the United States: southern and eastern Europe. By the 1890's, 72 percent of new immigrants came from these areas, and Jews fleeing pogroms and other forms of governmental persecution made up more than two million of them. In addition to their sheer numbers, the Jewish immigrants were often derided or feared because few outsiders understood their cultural traditions and beliefs. Finally, labor strife and recurring fears for the stability of U.S. jobs after the depression of the 1880's encouraged the working populace in the United States to fear this highly literate, socially stable, and upwardly mobile group of immigrants.

The government repeatedly took steps to check immigration from southern and eastern Europe, and incidents of persecution, synagogue desecration, and other indignities increasingly were viewed with worry by the Jewish middle class. The final incident leading to the foundation of the Anti-Defamation League was the wrongful conviction of a Jewish man for murder.

Leo Max Frank was born in Texas and raised in Brooklyn, New York, attending Cornell University and graduating with an engineering degree. In 1907, he agreed to go to Atlanta, Georgia, to help his uncle, Moses Frank, run his company, the National Pencil Factory. Married to Lucile Frank in 1911, Leo Frank became prominent in Atlanta Jewish circles and was elected president of the local chapter of the Jewish service fraternity, B'nai B'rith, in 1912. Frank was unknown to the general public until April 27, 1913, when the night watchman at the pencil factory found the dead and mutilated body of thirteen-year-old Mary Phagan in the factory basement. Leo Frank, the superintendent of the factory, had seen Mary Phagan on Saturday, April 26, 1913, when she came to pick up her wages at his office. After two days of investigation, the Atlanta police arrested Leo Frank on April 29 and charged him with Phagan's murder.

Immediately the case became a rallying point for anti-Semitic feeling in Atlanta, throughout Georgia, and around the world. Thomas Watson of Augusta, Georgia, who published a weekly newspaper called *The Jeffersonian* and a monthly magazine called *Watson's Magazine*, immediately seized upon the Frank case and in his opinion columns began calling for Frank's conviction. Circulation greatly increased, so Watson increased his attacks against Frank and Jews in general, which further incited public opinion against Frank.

The investigation procedure used by the Atlanta police was highly suspect from the beginning. The single witness against Frank was Jim Conley, a janitor at the pencil factory who was the only other suspect. Local feelings were further aroused by the fact that workers in Georgia's city factories were among the worst-treated in the country, as well as the lowest-paid. Mary Phagan, originally from the small, outlying town of Marietta, Georgia, became a symbol of the economic exploitation of formerly rural people in the city factories. In such a

climate, the expensive dress and cultured manners of Frank and his family at the trial served only to inflame the passions of the local people against him. Throughout the trial, mobs of people surrounded the Fulton County courthouse and could be heard shouting through the open windows "Hang the Jew!" This atmosphere all but assured that the jury would return a guilty verdict, which was pronounced in August of 1913 after four weeks of trial.

Frank obtained a new lawyer, William M. Howard of Augusta, Georgia, who persuaded the governor, John Slaton, that Frank was innocent of the crime, based on the physical evidence at the scene. The day before his term expired, Governor Slaton commuted Frank's death sentence to life in prison, convinced that eventually a pardon would be issued when all the facts became known. Watson's paper cried for action, and a mob of five thousand people encircled Slaton's house and threatened to kill him; the next day he left the state. On August 15, 1915, a mob of twenty-five men removed Leo Frank from jail and lynched him near Marietta, Georgia, Mary Phagan's hometown. This same group of men later reformed as the modern version of the Ku Klux Klan at Stone Mountain, Georgia.

In September, 1913, four weeks after Frank's trial ended, the Anti-Defamation League was founded. It had been discussed for years among the membership of the B'nai B'rith, the oldest and largest Jewish fraternal organization in the United States, but the Frank case was the immediate and deciding factor. Adolph Kraus, national president of B'nai B'rith at the time, specifically referred to the Frank case and its abuses in the founding statement of the Anti-Defamation League. The aims of the league, according to a 1915 statement of policy, were to encourage libraries to purchase books on Jewish subjects that were factual in nature, enlist prominent public lecturers on Jewish subjects, remove anti-Semitic texts from schoolrooms, stop newspapers from publishing the religious affiliations of known or suspected criminals, demand retractions of scurrilous anti-Jewish articles, monitor plays and movies for unfair and untrue depictions of Jews and Jewishness, and stop hostelries, apartments, and housing developments from discriminating against Jews or advertising that they did so.

Throughout World War I and the interwar period, the Anti-Defamation League achieved many of its stated goals. During World War II, the league was particularly important in responding to Nazi propaganda in both Europe and the United States. In the years since, the Anti-Defamation League has continued to reply to anti-Jewish propaganda with corrective information and has broadened its scope to include condemnations of all forms of racism, including extensive work for the passage of civil rights legislation for African Americans and other underrepresented groups.

In the 1980's, the Anti-Defamation League requested that the Georgia Board of Pardons and Parole issue a posthumous pardon for Leo Frank, based on new data and ample evidence that the initial conviction was prompted largely by a fear of violence from the anti-Jewish mobs outside the courthouse.

Although the board initially turned down the request, on March 11, 1986, the official full pardon was issued at the Georgia State Capitol in Atlanta, close to the courthouse in which Frank was originally tried. The league has continued to work for racial justice and the fulfillment of its stated mission to "strengthen interreligious understanding and cooperation, to improve relations between the races, and above all to protect the status and rights of Jews." —*Vicki A. Sanders*

ADDITIONAL READING:

Dinnerstein, Leonard. *The Leo Frank Case*. New York: Columbia University Press, 1968. An evenhanded, factual overview of the Frank case, including excerpts of testimony, diagrams of the scene, and subsequent information from sources not presented at the trial.

Golden, Harry. *A Little Girl Is Dead*. Cleveland: World Publishing, 1965. The most exhaustive recounting of the Phagan case for the general reader. Describes in simple terms the climate of anti-Semitism in which the trial took place.

Grayzel, Solomon. *A History of the Contemporary Jews from 1900 to the Present*. New York: Meridian Books, 1962. Describes the history of anti-Semitism in the United States, particularly actions against immigrants, which led to the league's founding.

Mendes-Flohr, Paul R., and Jehuda Reinharz, eds. *The Jew in the Modern World: A Documentary History*. New York: Oxford University Press, 1980. Reprints many documents relating to the history of Jewish organizations, including the 1915 mission statement of the Anti-Defamation League.

Woodward, C. Vann. *Tom Watson: Agrarian Rebel*. New York: Oxford University Press, 1970. Provides the best account of Watson's career as a politician and publisher and details his involvement in the Frank case.

SEE ALSO: 1866, Rise of the Ku Klux Klan; 1892, "New" Immigration.

1913 ■ FEDERAL RESERVE ACT: *money and the banking system are placed under control of a central bank, giving the federal government significant economic powers*

DATE: December 23, 1913
LOCALE: Washington, D.C.
CATEGORIES: Economics; Laws and acts
KEY FIGURES:

Nelson Wilmarth Aldrich (1841-1915), Republican senator from Rhode Island who sponsored the Aldrich Plan

William Jennings Bryan (1860-1925), Democratic leader from Nebraska, who influenced the radicals in Congress favoring federal control of the money supply

Carter Glass (1858-1946), conservative Democratic congressman from Virginia and the so-called father of the Federal Reserve Act

William Gibbs McAdoo (1863-1941), secretary of the Treasury under President Woodrow Wilson and advocate of federal control of banking

Robert Latham Owen (1856-1947), Democratic senator from Oklahoma, who worked with the radicals and co-sponsored the Federal Reserve Act

Benjamin Strong (1872-1928), governor of the New York Federal Reserve Bank

Henry Parker Willis (1874-1937), leading bank expert who helped write the Federal Reserve Act

Woodrow Wilson (1856-1924), twenty-eighth president of the United States, 1913-1921, and a leading figure behind the passage of the Federal Reserve Act

SUMMARY OF EVENT. By the beginning of the twentieth century, the U.S. economy was the most powerful in the world, yet its banking system was less than efficient. The United States had two major types of commercial banks: those chartered by the states, and those chartered by the federal government. National banks received their charters through the authority of the National Bank Acts of 1863 and 1864, which required a bank seeking a national charter to purchase government securities and submit to federal regulation. The bank then could issue national bank notes, which became the national currency after greenbacks were withdrawn, beginning in 1865.

Most important, the National Bank Acts either prohibited (in the case of national banks) or did not expressly permit branch banking, particularly interstate branch banking. That had the dual effect of subjecting the individual state systems to the vicissitudes of local or regional economic dislocations, and of producing state-line barriers to rapid transfers of money and capital in the event of such dislocations.

As a result, the nation's banking system operated under two regulatory systems, one for state banks and one for national banks. States had far lower capital requirements for banks, and some states permitted intrastate branch banking, making their systems far more attractive to prospective bankers when they determined to obtain a charter. Thus, after a brief period during which national charters expanded, state-chartered banks soon eclipsed those receiving federal charters. A more significant problem involved the inelasticity of the currency, which meant that the money supply could not expand and contract with the seasonal needs of the economy, particularly in agricultural areas. The system also suffered from flawed redemption mechanisms, making it even more difficult to contract the money supply in bad times than to expand it in prosperous periods.

Interstate branching would have solved many, if not all, of those problems, as would maintenance of the pre-Civil War system of competitive banknote issue, wherein any chartered bank could print its own money. The National Bank and Currency Acts, however, had placed a 10 percent tax on all nonnational bank notes, giving the government a monopoly over currency creation. Thus, the government had the authority, but not the capability, to control the money supply, while private banks had the capability, but not the authority, to do so.

Numerous reform measures were advanced to meet those problems in the latter half of the nineteenth century. The greenback movement of the 1870's and the Populists' agitation in the 1890's for "free silver"—unlimited coinage of silver at fixed (inflated) prices—both sought to address the long-term deflation caused by international economic forces. Both those plans would have required the federal government to inflate the money supply artificially. Other reformers wanted to place more control in the federal government, through creation of a central bank akin to the Bank of England. The United States had not had a central bank since President Andrew Jackson effectively destroyed the Second Bank of the United States by vetoing its recharter in 1832.

Two other factors accelerated the reform agenda. First, the Panic of 1907 persuaded many Americans, including the nation's premier banker J. P. Morgan, that no single private bank or group of banks could rescue the nation from depressions (as Morgan had in the Panic of 1893, when he loaned the government 3.5 million ounces of gold). Many bankers concluded that they needed a lender of last resort to keep banks afloat during periods of financial panic, and that such emergency loans themselves would quell the hysteria and impose financial stability. Second, with the Populists leading the way, Americans grew increasingly alarmed over the concentration of financial power in New York City. Many openly spoke of conspiracies—and especially linked "money power" to Jews, even though the largest New York bankers, like Morgan, were Protestant Christians. As a result, the reform movement focused on creating a lender of last resort, adding elasticity to the system, and reducing the power of New York City.

Following the Panic of 1907, a National Monetary Commission, composed of members of Congress, was created in 1908 to devise a plan for a revision of the banking system. Headed by Senator Nelson W. Aldrich, the commission prepared the so-called Aldrich Plan. That plan called for a voluntary system headed by a central bank, the National Reserve Association, having branch banks that would issue currency and hold the deposits of the federal government, while furnishing reserve credit to member banks. Some large banks supported the Aldrich Plan, but by the time it was submitted to Congress in 1912, it faced strong opposition.

Many Progressives feared that, under the plan, Wall Street would retain control over the nation's financial markets. Unit bankers convinced Congress that interstate banking would permit large New York City banks to extend into middle America, driving the smaller country banks out of business. Woodrow Wilson, elected president in 1912, shared Progressive sentiments. The Democrats controlled the Congress but were divided on the banking issue. Southern and Western radicals followed William Jennings Bryan of Nebraska. Conservatives were headed by Congressman Carter Glass of Virginia, chairman of the House Banking Committee. Bryan, who was joined by William G. McAdoo, soon to be secretary of the Treasury, and Senator Robert L. Owen of Oklahoma, chairman of the Senate Banking Committee, insisted that the govern-ment control any banking system enacted and that it also control the money supply. Glass and his faction opposed any plan for a central bank and favored a loose, disconnected system of regional reserve banks.

In the weeks before Wilson's inaugural, Glass worked with Wilson and H. Parker Willis, a banking expert, on a new banking law to provide a privately controlled system of regional reserve banks, with a general supervisory and coordinating board. The plan developed by Wilson, Glass, and Willis resembled a decentralized version of the Aldrich Plan. After incorporating into it changes demanded by the radical faction, such as a federal guarantee of notes issued by the new system, the plan was submitted to Congress as the Federal Reserve, or Glass-Owen, bill. After further changes, the measure was finally passed in December, 1913, almost a year after its inception.

The Federal Reserve Act had the stated purposes of providing for the establishment of no more than twelve regional Federal Reserve Banks, furnishing an elastic currency, affording means for rediscounting commercial paper, and establishing a more effective supervision of banking in the United States. The twelve "bankers' banks" neither accepted deposits from individuals nor loaned them money, and were controlled by a five-member Board of Governors (later increased to seven members) appointed by the president for ten-year terms. They worked along with the secretary of the Treasury and the comptroller (originally ex officio members) to oversee operation of the system. Member banks elected six of the nine directors of the district Federal Reserve Banks, whose capital was subscribed by the commercial banks that joined the system. Technically, the system was a corporation owned by the member banks, but the "Fed" (as it is called) came to act completely independently of the banks. Although it is directly responsible to Congress, neither Congress nor the president ever successfully exercised control over it. Thus, Fed policies had far-reaching effects on the U.S. economy, yet Fed leadership was virtually unaccountable.

The intent of the Federal Reserve Act was to decentralize power and move it out of New York City; therefore, most of the reserve banks were located in the West and South, with the state of Missouri alone containing two. Yet the New York Fed immediately emerged as the most powerful and quickly dominated the others, thanks to its brilliant governor, Benjamin Strong. Under Strong's leadership, the New York Fed merely took over the role that J. P. Morgan once had held. Strong died in 1928 and was ill before that; his absence left a leadership void in New York as the worldwide economic crises of the 1920's reached their apex.

At that point, another set of factors grounded in the Federal Reserve Act exacerbated economic problems. First, the act essentially had undercut the role of the successful clearinghouse associations that had developed in the absence of interstate branching by the turn of the century. The associations had provided rapid information transmission among members—a task that the Fed assumed for itself. Second, the act had made little mention of the gold standard, assuming that it would continue to function. However, as European nations' economies collapsed in the 1920's, those nations left the gold standard. By the end of the decade, the United States was one of the few countries remaining on the gold standard, which led to a sharp outflow of gold from the United States. Federal Reserve notes were guaranteed by gold, and financial panics started.

The Fed then turned a recession into a disaster by raising interest rates, choking off the money supply at the very time business needed an expanding money supply to sustain growth. In addition, some economists have pointed to the misjudgment of the New York Fed in failing to rescue the Bank of the United States, triggering further runs. The result was the Great Depression, a cyclical downturn exacerbated by, if not caused by, Fed policies.

Congress reformed the banking system yet again during the Great Depression, instituting deposit insurance and separating banking and securities operations. An indirect result of those reforms was the savings and loan crisis of the 1980's, in which the Federal Savings and Loan Insurance Corporation (FSLIC) virtually went bankrupt attempting to support savings and loans that had collapsed due to federal restrictions on their lending. Through the mid-1990's, the Fed has maintained somewhat steady interest rates but has had little success supporting the value of the dollar internationally.

—*Merle O. Davis, updated by Larry Schweikart*

ADDITIONAL READING:

Friedman, Milton, and Anna J. Schwartz. *A Monetary History of the United States, 1867-1960.* Princeton, N.J.: Princeton University Press, 1963. A seminal work that finds Fed policy errors at the root of the Great Depression. Although challenged on some points, the authors' view has remained the accepted interpretation on the role of the Fed in raising interest rates at crucial times and in exacerbating banking panics.

Greider, William. *Secrets of the Temple: How the Federal Reserve Runs the Country.* New York: Simon & Schuster, 1987. A highly political, populist approach to the Fed, contending that the Fed has been too restrictive in its policies and that it should democratize money.

Timberlake, Richard H. "Federal Reserve Act." In *Encyclopedia of American Business History and Biography: Banking and Finance to 1913*, edited by Larry Schweikart. New York: Facts On File, 1990. Interpretive essay focusing on the relationship between the gold standard and the Federal Reserve Act. Argues that the clearinghouse associations had functioned well and needed no further government control.

Wheelock, David. *The Strategy and Consistency of Federal Reserve Monetary Policy, 1924-1933.* New York: Cambridge University Press, 1991. Asserts that the Fed acted consistently with its earlier policies in the late 1920's and did not play the crucial role in causing or prolonging the Great Depression.

White, Eugene Nelson. *The Regulation and Reform of the American Banking System, 1900-1929.* Princeton, N.J.: Princeton University Press, 1983. Points out the weakness of failing to incorporate branching, and notes that during the

reforms of the 1930's, banks that participated in stock market activities were less vulnerable than those that did not.

SEE ALSO: 1863, National Bank Acts; 1873, "Crime of 1873"; 1892, Birth of the People's Party; 1896, McKinley Is Elected President; 1913, Sixteenth Amendment; 1929, Stock Market Crash; 1929, Great Depression.

1915 ■ NATIONAL BIRTH CONTROL LEAGUE FORMS: *one of the earliest attempts to disseminate contraceptive information to women of the United States*

DATE: 1915-1919
LOCALE: New York City, New York
CATEGORIES: Government and politics; Women's issues
KEY FIGURES:
Anthony Comstock (1844-1915), director of the New York Society for the Suppression of Vice, after whom the federal antiobscenity Comstock laws were named
Mary Ware Dennett (1872-1947), first director of the National Birth Control League
Margaret Sanger (1879-1966), best-known agitator for the right to provide birth control information in the early twentieth century
William Sanger (born 1871?), her husband and a supporter of the right to disseminate contraceptive information

SUMMARY OF EVENT. In the early twentieth century, industrial cities in the United States were filled with poor immigrant families. Many lived in squalid conditions, and their children were often sickly and poorly nourished. At the time, rudimentary methods of birth control were known and used by some middle- and upper-class women, but could not be advertised or distributed publicly. Lower-class women were desperately uninformed about reproductive health and personal hygiene, which led to many unwanted pregnancies, sexually transmitted diseases, and illegal or self-induced abortions.

Margaret Sanger, a practicing nurse, had attended to the obstetric care of many such women in New York. Sanger and her husband, William, were active in the radical, intellectual causes of the day. Emma Goldman, another well-known radical, had preached the value of preventing conception for years from a political perspective: that when poor people had large families, they were furthering their own oppression by increasing the size of the labor force and thus driving wages down. Sanger also took a radical political approach to birth control—a term she coined in 1914. In 1912, Sanger had attended to Sadie Sachs, one of many young women who had turned to abortion after her doctor had told her another pregnancy would endanger her health, but gave her no information on preventing pregnancy, beyond the suggestion that she make her husband sleep on the roof. After Sadie's death, Sanger turned her full political energies to attempts to get information about reproduction to women of the working class.

Her first attempt at providing information on sexually transmitted diseases and feminine hygiene to the masses was a series of articles in 1912 for a daily socialist newspaper, the *New York Call*, entitled "What Every Girl Should Know." The Post Office Department refused to deliver the *Call* after learning that the article frankly discussed sexually transmitted diseases. No articles on birth control were written by Sanger at that time, however. In October, 1913, the Sanger family traveled to Paris, where Margaret Sanger was surprised to see that birth control was openly advocated and practiced. She soon returned to the United States with her children and began publishing *The Woman Rebel*, seven issues of which were printed in 1914, until it was suppressed by the Post Office. *The Woman Rebel* focused on the ways in which the capitalist system oppressed women; it also discussed birth control in general terms but did not give specific information. In an early issue of *The Woman Rebel*, Sanger had mentioned a group she was founding, the Birth Control League of America, but before it could become active, Sanger had been charged with nine counts of violating antiobscenity laws. Rather than face trial and likely imprisonment, Sanger left the country alone in October, 1914, and spent the next year in Europe, researching birth control and visiting clinics in Holland, France, and England.

Sanger often exaggerated and dramatized incidents to promote her cause, and herself as its chief spokeswoman. Her proclamation that no information on contraception was available in the United States, requiring her to spend a year in France searching for information—which indeed was more widely available abroad—was inaccurate. An 1898 publication of the U.S. Surgeon General's office had a two-page listing of books and articles on the subject. It was true, however, that such information was not advertised openly, and seldom was available to the lower classes. Among the main barriers to access to contraceptive information were the Comstock laws. A federal law passed in 1872 that prohibited the mailing of obscene material was deemed inadequate by Anthony Comstock, who managed to push a more restrictive law through Congress in 1873. The 1873 law was the first instance in which information regarding the prevention of conception was defined as obscene. Comstock also was appointed by Congress as a special postal agent with the authority to arrest persons who violated the law regarding mailing obscene materials, a job that Comstock embraced with relish.

Before leaving the country, Sanger had written a booklet entitled *Family Limitation*, which dealt with issues of hygiene, explained the contraceptive devices available at the time, and even suggested an abortificant. *Family Limitation* provided specific, accurate contraceptive information, framed in radical socialist terms, advocating that women limit families rather than "supply the market with children to be exploited [and refuse] to populate the earth with slaves." The booklet had to be printed secretly and was distributed primarily through radical labor groups such as the Industrial Workers of the World. While Margaret Sanger was in Europe, her husband was approached by a man who claimed he wanted to obtain a copy of *Family Limitation* in order to translate it into other languages and distribute it to poor families. The man, however, was working for Anthony Comstock, and a month later Comstock himself came to the Sanger home to arrest William Sanger for violation of the Comstock laws. Comstock had set up William Sanger in hopes of flushing his wife out of her exile so that he could personally arrest her. Margaret Sanger did make plans to return to the United States, but Comstock died a few weeks before her return.

William Sanger's trial became a *cause célèbre* not only among advocates of birth control but also as a free-speech issue. Support and donations came in from around the country. At his trial in September, 1915, William Sanger acted as his own attorney, declaring, "The law is on trial here, not I." His thirty-day sentence only added to the general distaste for the Comstock laws. As Margaret Sanger's self-imposed exile had inspired birth control advocates to continue organizing in her absence, her husband's trial spurred greater efforts on the part of radical socialists to preach the gospel of birth control and motivated others to work to overturn the Comstock laws.

While Sanger was out of the country, a group of liberals, including Mary Ware Dennett, Clara Stillman, and Lincoln Steffans, organized the National Birth Control League. The NBCL eschewed the tactics and philosophy of radicals such as Margaret Sanger and Emma Goldman, preferring to cast birth control as a scientific and medical matter, which could not, therefore, be deemed obscene. The secretary of the birth control league set up the previous year by Sanger made Sanger's files and lists of supporters available to organizers of the new group. When Sanger returned from Europe after her husband's arrest, she faced trial on the charges from which she had fled. She appealed to the NBCL for support in her upcoming trial, but the executive committee of the NBCL was unwilling to aid her. The NBCL had been organized to attempt to change the laws restricting information about birth control, and disagreed with Sanger's confrontational tactics and her focus on changing laws through judicial decisions.

By 1919, the National Birth Control League had been replaced by the Voluntary Parenthood League, headed by Mary Ware Dennett and focused on repeal of federal laws prohibiting dissemination of contraceptive information. In 1921, Margaret Sanger formed a short-lived rival group, the American Birth Control League, announced in conjunction with the First American Birth Control Conference in November, 1921, which Sanger also organized.

Doctors began routinely, if discreetly, providing contraceptives and related information, and birth control clinics were established in the United States, largely as a result of Sanger's efforts. It was not until 1970, however, that Congress rewrote the Comstock Act to remove contraceptive information and devices from the obscene list.　　*—Irene Struthers*

ADDITIONAL READING:

Brodie, Janet Farrell. *Contraception and Abortion in Nineteenth Century America*. Ithaca, N.Y.: Cornell University

Press, 1994. Discusses nineteenth century contraceptive methods and the forces that led to their being restricted. Useful background for understanding the birth control struggles of the early twentieth century.

Chandrasekhar, Sripati. *"A Dirty, Filthy Book."* Berkeley: University of California Press, 1981. Discusses the nineteenth century trial of the English publishers of a book on reproduction and contraception. Title comes from the prosecutor's description of the book in court. Includes texts of three famous nineteenth century books on reproduction.

Kennedy, David M. *Birth Control in America: The Career of Margaret Sanger*. New Haven, Conn.: Yale University Press, 1970. Primarily deals with Sanger's public career, with some details of her personal life. Biographical essay, selected bibliography, and extensive index.

Reed, James. *From Private Vice to Public Virtue: The Birth Control Movement and American Society Since 1830*. New York: Basic Books, 1978. Discusses early pioneers of the birth control movement and the social forces against which they struggled. Notes, bibliographic essay, and index.

Sanger, Margaret. *Margaret Sanger: An Autobiography*. 1938. Reprint. New York: Dover, 1971. First-person account is somewhat flawed by exaggeration, as in her taking responsibility for establishing the National Birth Control League, which was founded by others when she was out of the country.

See also: 1857, New York Infirmary for Indigent Women and Children Opens; 1876, Declaration of the Rights of Women; 1889, Hull House Opens; 1912, U.S. Public Health Service Is Established; 1916, National Woman's Party Is Founded; 1923, Proposal of the Equal Rights Amendment; 1960, FDA Approves the Birth Control Pill.

1916 ■ National Woman's Party Is Founded: *the party that brought home the vote to U.S. women also gave birth to the Equal Rights Amendment*

Date: 1916

Locale: Washington, D.C.

Categories: Organizations and institutions; Women's issues

Key figures:

Alva Belmont (1853-1933), philanthropist and founder of the Political Equity League

Harriot Stanton Blatch (1856-1940), daughter of Elizabeth Cady Stanton and leader in the fight for women's economic equality

Lucy Burns (1879-1966), founder of the National Woman's Party

Anne Martin (1875-1951), Nevada historian and first elected chair of the Woman's Party

Alice Paul (1885-1977), founder of the National Woman's Party

Christabel Pankhurst (1880-1958), English suffragist and daughter of Emmeline Pankhurst

Emmeline Goulden Pankhurst (1858-1928), English suffragist and founder of the National Women's Social and Political Union

Summary of event. Alice Paul and Lucy Burns made their entrance onto the stage of U.S. politics at a time when the issue of equal rights for women was at its peak of agitation at the state level. Six states had passed a woman suffrage amendment, accounting for approximately two million women voters. On the national level, however, activity had practically ceased. President Woodrow Wilson offered no active support of women's issues. Paul and Burns became aggressive leaders of the fourth generation of U.S. women to devote themselves to the cause of women's rights.

Alice Paul was born in Mooretown, New Jersey, to Quaker parents and was educated at Swarthmore College, the University of Pennsylvania, and the London School of Economics. In addition to being reared by Quakers, who instilled in her a basic respect for all people, she was descended from a long line of political activists. In 1909, while in London at the university, she became active in the militant suffrage work of mother and daughter Emmeline and Christabel Pankhurst. Paul was arrested and jailed several times for her participation in protests, and during one of these demonstrations she made the acquaintance of another remarkable young American woman, Lucy Burns, from Brooklyn, New York.

Burns was also well educated (Vassar, Yale, University of Berlin) and had intended to pursue a career in academics. A taste of political activity caused her to change her mind, however, and she threw herself wholeheartedly into the fight for women's rights. The meeting between the two women was fortuitous and the partnership that ensued changed the course of history with respect to equality for women in the United States. Both of these courageous women suffered jail sentences and undertook hunger strikes. As leaders they were complementary: Paul was known as the quiet but bold strategist; Burns, as the active, more militant public figure whose fierce leadership was tempered by her Irish sense of humor. Their observations of the Pankhursts readied them to return to the United States and take positions of leadership for their cause. In 1910, when Paul returned to the United States, she joined with Harriet Stanton Blatch to organize suffrage parades in New York.

The next window of opportunity for Paul and Burns was the long-standing Congressional Committee of the National American Woman Suffrage Association (NAWSA), which had become inactive. The original purpose of the committee was to propose an amendment for woman suffrage to the United States Constitution. Under the leadership of Paul and Burns, who served as chair and vice chair respectively, the NAWSA waged a march of five thousand women upon the White House the day before the presidential inauguration of Woodrow Wilson in April, 1913. The idea of holding the party in political power responsible for its actions on important issues was modeled on the work of the Pankhursts in England. Flamboyant publicity, street marches, protests, and demonstrations at federal events became synonymous with the style of Paul and Burns. It was not, however, in keeping with the previous, less aggressive and more educative, style of the NAWSA.

Frustrated by hesitation within the NAWSA to demonstrate actively, Paul and Burns broke away from the association in 1913 to form the Congressional Union (CU). The CU rivaled the NAWSA nationally and had its own newspaper, *The Suffragist*, edited for a time by Burns. The CU sent representatives to campaign against Democratic candidates in states who were not assisting the cause of women's equality under the law.

In 1916, the group formed the Woman's Party. Women voters in the Western states convened in Colorado to make plans to infiltrate the upcoming national election campaigns with women's equality issues. With Anne Martin at its helm, the party worked aggressively to organize voters against the

Democratic national leadership, which had proved weak in its stand on suffrage. Twelve states had allowed women the right to vote, and Paul emphasized the importance of a group of voters, however small, that would not deviate from its mission.

In 1917, under the leadership of Paul and Burns, the CU joined with its Western contingent and became the National Woman's Party (NWP). Paul was elected the first chairperson, with Anne Martin as vice chair. Women from all areas of life—homemakers, union workers, professional women, philanthropists—were represented in the ranks of members. Although the NWP had been effective enough to initiate discussion of the Susan B. Anthony (Suffrage) Amendment on the floor of Congress, women were still not enfranchised in most states. Paul and Burns were recognized for maintaining momentum and imparting a sense to their workers that the fight was in perpetual motion, continually changing and refreshing the party's strategies. Paul's leadership was autocratic; to some

Alice Paul and officers of the National Woman's Party outside the party's Washington, D.C., headquarters. (Library of Congress)

she was the party itself. Nevertheless, she was so selflessly devoted to the single purpose of federal recognition of women's rights that her followers did not object. Her single-issue political strategy did draw fire from other groups, however, when she refused to speak out on issues such as racial discrimination or the Great War, for fear of diluting her effectiveness on the main issue of gender equality. Burns continued her activity as well, traveling often to state functions and inciting groups with her fiery spirit.

The NWP continued to work for suffrage until the ratification of the Nineteenth Amendment in 1920, which finally gave all women in the United States the right to vote. Paul and Burns saw well beyond the suffrage issue, however, and immediately refocused their energies on that of total equality under the law, resulting in the first presentation of the Equal Rights Amendment before Congress on December 10, 1923. The amendment stated simply that "men and women shall have equal rights throughout the United States and in every place subject to its jurisdiction."

Thus began the long history of the campaign to ratify the amendment in all states—an objective that was never accomplished. The amendment that was eventually passed by Congress in 1972, included a requirement that, in order to become law, it must be ratified by three-quarters of the states within seven years. Although Congress extended the deadline by four years, in 1982 only thirty-five of the thirty-eight states required had ratified. —Sandra C. McClain

ADDITIONAL READING:

Cott, Nancy. "Feminist Politics in the 1920's: The National Women's Party." *Journal of American History* 71 (June, 1984): 43-68. Precise, well-referenced article focused specifically on the work of the party and its leaders.

_____. *The Grounding of Modern Feminism.* New Haven, Conn.: Yale University Press, 1987. Provides background and analyzes the effects of the feminist movement on subsequent events. Lengthy bibliographical notes.

Flexnor, Eleanor. *Century of Struggle: The Women's Rights Movement in the United States.* New York: Atheneum, 1972. Good historical overview of the movement, with specific information on forming of the NWP in chapter 21.

Irwin, Inez Haynes. *The Story of the National Women's Party.* New York: Harcourt, Brace, 1921. A thorough account of the founding and early days of the party from the perspective of a contemporary of Burns and Paul. Includes personal reflections from people involved in the suffrage movement.

Kraditor, Aileen. *The Ideas of the Woman Suffrage Movement, 1890-1920.* New York: Columbia University Press, 1965. Clearly outlines differing views of leaders in the feminist movement and presents the two sides of the suffragist argument both before and after the turn of the century.

SEE ALSO: 1869, Rise of Woman Suffrage Associations; 1869, Western States Grant Woman Suffrage; 1872, Susan B. Anthony Is Arrested; 1876, Declaration of the Rights of Women; 1890, Women's Rights Associations Unite; 1920, League of Women Voters Is Founded; 1920, U.S. Women Gain the Vote.

1916 ■ PERSHING EXPEDITION: *U.S. forces enter Mexico in a punitive expedition against Mexican revolutionaries*

DATE: March 15, 1916-February 5, 1917
LOCALE: Mexico
CATEGORIES: Latino American history; Wars, uprisings, and civil unrest
KEY FIGURES:
Venustiano Carranza (1859-1920), provisional president of Mexico
Frederick Funston (1865-1917), commander of the Southern Department and Pershing's immediate superior
Álvaro Obregón (1880-1928), Mexican minister of war and marine, and commander of military forces in Northern Mexico
John J. Pershing (1860-1948), commander of the United States' punitive expedition
Hugh L. Scott (1853-1934), chief of staff of the U.S. Army
Francisco "Pancho" Villa (1877-1923), governor of Chihuahua and Mexican revolutionary
Woodrow Wilson (1856-1924), twenty-eighth president of the United States, 1913-1921

SUMMARY OF EVENT. At 4:15 A.M. on March 9, 1916, a force of about five hundred Mexican revolutionaries commanded by General Francisco "Pancho" Villa attacked the tiny border settlement of Columbus, New Mexico, and the nearby U.S. Army garrison. Less than an hour later, the Mexicans were in full retreat toward their border, closely pursued by a troop of U.S. cavalry. Seventeen persons from the United States were dead, eight of them civilians.

Villa's raid on Columbus was a direct outgrowth of the turbulent and often bloody struggle for the leadership for the Mexican Revolution that had begun with the overthrow of the dictator Porfirio Díaz in 1911. The next president of Mexico, Francisco Madero, had not held office two years before being deposed by one of his own generals, Victoriano Huerta. Although Huerta enjoyed the backing of the Roman Catholic church, the landed interests, and the foreign investors who controlled much of Mexico's natural resources, he had little support from the Mexican people. In addition, one of Huerta's first acts was to arrange for the murder of his predecessor, Madero. The new U.S. president, Woodrow Wilson, horrified by this spectacle of government by assassination, refused to recognize Huerta's government. Wilson gave his support to Huerta's two chief opponents, Venustiano Carranza and Villa, who claimed to be the true heirs of Madero.

In April, 1914, Wilson took advantage of a minor incident at Tampico, Mexico, and ordered the United States Navy to seize the port of Vera Cruz. Wilson hoped to force Huerta's resignation by cutting off both his supply of arms from abroad and a major source of revenue, the Vera Cruz customhouse. A short, bloody battle ensued, during which both the Mexicans and the U.S. troops suffered heavy casualties. Wilson, who had

General Francisco "Pancho" Villa, Mexican revolutionary. Villa represented many Mexicans: He was of mixed Spanish and Indian blood, or mestizo. *Although often described as a bandit, his personal magnetism and ambition raised him to the level of folk hero. Villa's 1916 raid on Columbus, a tiny town on the Mexican border with New Mexico, prompted the punitive Pershing expedition.* (Library of Congress)

not expected the Mexicans to resist, gladly took advantage of an offer of mediation made by Argentina, Brazil, and Chile. Although the mediation was inconclusive, the Vera Cruz incident helped topple Huerta's already shaky government. In August, 1914, Villa and Carranza entered Mexico City, and the civil strife that had plagued Mexico for years seemed to be ending.

Within a few weeks, however, the leaders of the revolution were once more at odds. At one point, it seemed as though Villa would emerge as president of Mexico. His rivals in the revolutionary movement, however, refused to recognize Villa's leadership. Some historians believe conflict between Villa, who favored radical social reform, and Carranza, a political moderate, was inevitable. Frustrated by Carranza's reluctance to institute reforms such as changes in land ownership, Villa attempted a military coup. Under the leadership of General Álvaro Obregón, the regular Mexican Army under Carranza inflicted a series of sharp defeats on Villa's forces, driving Villa back to his home state of Chihuahua. On October 19, 1915, the United States, which had favored Villa, formally recognized Carranza's provisional government as the legitimate government of Mexico.

By early 1916, Villa's army, the remains of his famous División del Norte, had shrunk to a few hundred men hiding from Obregón's troops in the Chihuahua mountains. Villa's motives for attacking Columbus with this small force are not clear. Some historians believe that Villa hoped to provoke an invasion of Mexico by the United States so that he could then emerge as a hero of the people resisting foreign aggressors. If war with the United States was Villa's aim, his raid on Columbus nearly succeeded in provoking it. News of the raid raised a storm of anger throughout the United States. In a rare display of unanimity, citizens of all political persuasions called for Villa's blood. President Wilson announced to the press that troops would be dispatched immediately in pursuit of Villa. Orders were telegraphed to General Frederick Funston in San Antonio to prepare an expeditionary force to pursue and destroy Villa's band. Nothing was said in this order about capturing Villa himself, but the public persisted in the belief that the object of the force was to bring back Villa, dead or alive.

The United States' punitive expedition, comprising some six thousand troops under the command of Brigadier General John J. Pershing, crossed the border into Mexico in the early hours of March 15, 1916. Villa's forces, which numbered some 450 men, continued to move deeper into Mexico. Elements of the Seventh and Tenth Cavalries caught up with them near the town of Guerrero and, in a series of sharp engagements fought between March 28 and April 1, killed or captured most of Villa's men. Villa himself avoided capture and continued south toward the town of Parral in Chihuahua.

The Mexican government, meanwhile, was becoming increasingly concerned at the spectacle of six thousand U.S. troops deployed deep within Mexican territory. President Carranza, who had never formally agreed to allow the U.S. troops to enter Mexico, now addressed a series of notes to Washington, requesting that the expeditionary force be withdrawn on the grounds that it had already accomplished all that could be hoped for, and that Mexican troops were now adequate to police the border. Villa, the self-taught son of a field laborer, enjoyed widespread popular support among the ordinary people of northern Mexico. Carranza knew that the continuing presence of foreign troops on Mexican soil could serve only to weaken his own government and strengthen Villa's guerrilla movement.

While the negotiations over the status of Pershing's forces were being conducted, a mob attacked a detachment from the U.S. Thirteenth Cavalry attempting to purchase supplies in Parral. In the ensuing fight, a large number of Mexicans and two U.S. citizens were killed. In an atmosphere of increasing tension, Carranza agreed to send Obregón, his minister of war and marine, to meet with General Hugh L. Scott, the U.S. Army chief of staff, at El Paso. After much argument, the two generals succeeded in drafting an agreement for the gradual withdrawal of the U.S. expeditionary force. Carranza, however, refused to accept the agreement. It is doubtful whether the U.S. government could have honored it in any case, because on the same day that the agreement was signed, a band of Mexican raiders attacked the towns of Glen Springs and Bougilas in the sparsely populated Big Bend country of Texas, killing three U.S. settlers, one of whom was a nine-year-old boy.

Although the raiders had no connection with Villa, a new wave of anger and exasperation swept the country following this latest demonstration of the defenselessness of the border area. Amid renewed demands for war with Mexico, President Wilson mobilized the national guards of Texas, Arizona, and New Mexico to patrol the border and ordered an additional four thousand regulars to the Southwest.

The Mexicans also were nearing the end of their patience. On June 16, 1916, Carranza warned the U.S. government that if U.S. soldiers in Mexico made further moves in any direction but north, they would be fired upon. Five days later, Captain Charles T. Boyd, commanding a troop of the Tenth Cavalry, attempted to enter the town of Carrizel in disregard of orders from Pershing to avoid places garrisoned by Carrancista troops. The Mexican soldiers in the town opened fire. Twelve U.S. soldiers, including Boyd, were killed, and twenty-three were taken prisoner.

War with Mexico now appeared certain, but President Wilson was determined to avoid it, if at all possible. Carranza, anxious to prevent a U.S. occupation of his country, released the prisoners and offered to enter into direct talks with the United States government to settle the dispute. The long, drawn-out negotiations opened at New London, Connecticut, on September 6, 1916, and ended in a stalemate four months later. They had, however, served to relax tensions and to remove the embarrassing issue of Mexico from the 1916 presidential campaign.

Although the New London talks failed to produce an agreement with Mexico, Wilson and his advisers decided to withdraw the remaining troops. Villa, while still a threat to the Carranza administration in Mexico, was now operating in an area far from the border. In addition, war with Germany was now a distinct possibility, and Pershing's forces might need to be deployed to Europe. On February 5, 1917, the last troops of Pershing's expeditionary force reentered the United States.

Villa continued to plague the Carrancista forces for another four years. In 1920, following the death of Carranza and other changes in the Mexican government, Villa accepted a pardon in exchange for agreeing to leave politics. He retired to a ranch near Parral, where he died in 1923.

—*Ronald N. Spector, updated by Nancy Farm Mannikko*

ADDITIONAL READING:

Alba, Victor. *Pancho Villa y Zapata: Aguila y sol de la Revolución Mexicana*. Barcelona, Spain: Planeta, 1994. A history of the Mexican Revolution that highlights two of the major figures, Emiliano Zapata in the south and Villa in the north. In Spanish.

Goldhurst, Richard. *Pipe Clay and Drill: John J. Pershing, the Classic American Soldier*. New York: Reader's Digest Press, 1977. Biography of Pershing, highly accessible to the general reader.

Harris, Larry A. *Pancho Villa: Strong Man of the Revolution*. Silver City, N.Mex.: High Lonesome Books, 1989. Biography that emphasizes Villa's role as a revolutionary and military leader.

Link, Arthur S. *Wilson: Confusions and Crises, 1915-1916*. Princeton, N.J.: Princeton University Press, 1964. The fourth volume in a definitive study of Woodrow Wilson, on relations with Mexico, shows how close the United States came to war with Mexico because of the Pershing expedition.

Machado, Manuel A. *Centaur of the North: Francisco Villa, the Mexican Revolution and Northern Mexico*. Austin, Tex.: Eakin Press, 1988. Comprehensive biography that provides a social and political context for Villa's activities.

Mason, Herbert Molloy. *The Great Pursuit*. New York: Random House, 1970. Describes the Pershing expedition.

O'Brien, Steven. *Pancho Villa*. New York: Chelsea House, 1994. Biography that highlights Villa's many notable achievements, including his rise from an illiterate orphan to the governorship of Chihuahua and his revolutionary activities.

Rippy, James Fred. *The United States and Mexico*. New York: F. S. Crofts, 1931. For many years the standard work on Mexican-U.S. relations, this book is now somewhat out of date but still contains useful material.

Tompkins, Frank. *Chasing Villa: The Story Behind the Story of Pershing's Expedition into Mexico*. Harrisburg, Pa.: Stackpole Books, 1935. A firsthand account by one of Pershing's commanders who played an important part in the expedition.

SEE ALSO: 1909, Mexican Revolution.

1916 ■ NATIONAL PARK SERVICE IS CREATED: *a new philosophy of natural resource conservation spawns a program of park management*

DATE: August 25, 1916
LOCALE: Washington, D.C.
CATEGORIES: Environment; Organizations and institutions
KEY FIGURES:

Horace M. Albright (1890-1987), second director of the National Park Service

William E. Colby (1875-1964), secretary of the Sierra Club, 1900-1949

William Kent (1864-1928), sponsor of the National Park Service Act in the House

John F. Lacey (1841-1913), author of the Antiquities Act of 1906

Franklin K. Lane (1864-1921), secretary of the interior in the Wilson Administration

J. Horace McFarland (1859-1948), first president of the American Civic Association

Stephen T. Mather (1867-1930), first director of the National Park Service

John Muir (1838-1914), cofounder and first president of the Sierra Club

Frederick Law Olmsted, Jr. (1870-1957), noted landscape architect and conservationist

Gifford Pinchot (1865-1946), first director of the U.S. Forest Service

Reed Smoot (1862-1941), sponsor of the National Park Service Act in the Senate

Woodrow Wilson (1856-1924), twenty-eighth president of the United States, 1913-1921

SUMMARY OF EVENT. Many of the national parks, national monuments, and other areas that eventually would be parts of the national park system predate the creation of the National Park Service. They were created on an ad hoc basis without any clear plan for their management. Yellowstone National Park was created in 1872 because its scenic wonders had impressed those who had visited it, some of those visitors were politically influential and agitated for creation of the park, local officials supported the idea, and the area was considered to have little economic value. Yellowstone was not a part of any state, so if it were to be a park, it would necessarily be a national park. In the years following the Yellowstone Act, Congress reserved other areas of superlative scenery, and—although their legal descriptions differed—the Department of the Interior treated them as national parks. Prominent early parks included Yosemite, Sequoia, and General Grant (now Kings Canyon), 1890; Mount Rainier, 1899; Crater Lake, 1902; Mesa Verde, 1906; Glacier, 1910; Hawaii (now Haleakala and Hawaii Volcanoes) and Lassen Volcanic, 1916. These early parks were created because some individual or organization promoted the idea and because there was no organized opposition.

Other areas that eventually would become national parks were declared to be objects of historic or scientific interest and set aside as national monuments by the president under authority of the 1906 Antiquities Act. Prominent examples were the Petrified Forest, 1906; Grand Canyon, 1908; Mount Olympus (now Olympic) and Mukuntuweap (now Zion), 1909; and Sieur de Monts (now Acadia), 1916. Some national monuments were managed by the Department of the Interior, others by the Department of Agriculture or the War Department.

These parks and monuments enjoyed some legal protection, but practical protection was another matter. Park management was minimal and unsystematic. The Department of the Interior was able to do little to prevent wholesale trespassing and looting; for that reason, between 1883 and 1918 some of the nation's premier parks were administered by the United States Army. Furthermore, even the legal protections proved to be undependable. In 1913, the city of San Francisco received congressional approval to have the Hetch Hetchy Valley of Yosemite National Park dammed for a municipal water supply. Two years later, President Woodrow Wilson cut the size of Mount Olympus National Monument in half to make more lumber available for harvest. Gifford Pinchot, director of the U.S. Forest Service until 1910, had expressed the wish to have the national parks transferred to his agency for management. The precariousness of legal and practical protections enjoyed by the parks convinced many preservationists that the parks needed an organic act providing a firm legal foundation and an agency of the federal government dedicated to their protection and management.

The campaign for a national park service was waged simultaneously inside and outside the government. At the center of the private effort was a coalition of conservationists, headed in the East by J. Horace McFarland, president of the American Civic Association, and in the West by William Colby and John Muir of the Sierra Club. Colby and others organized the Society for the Preservation of National Parks, with John Muir as president and a number of prominent preservationists, including McFarland, on its advisory council. Many of those active in the effort were prolific writers, and their advocacy of the parks appeared frequently in popular magazines, including *Atlantic Monthly, Ladies' Home Journal, National Geographic, Outlook,* and *The Saturday Evening Post.*

Inside the government, the effort was led by Stephen Mather and Horace Albright. Both were recruited to work for Franklin Lane, who had become secretary of the interior in March, 1913. Mather worked tirelessly to make the parks accessible and popular with the traveling public, often using private funds, including his own, when governmental appropriations were insufficient. He forged alliances with interested railroads and worked effectively with the leaders of the American Civic Association, the Sierra Club, and the General Federation of Women's Clubs, all of whom were active in promoting a parks bureau.

In 1910, Congressman John Lacey of Iowa, author of the 1906 Antiquities Act, introduced a bill to create a national park bureau, but it was not acted upon. Thereafter, bills proposing some sort of management agency for the parks were introduced regularly, but there was significant opposition. Much of it came from the Forest Service, which reflected Pinchot's commitment to a multiple-use management philosophy for all the federal lands, and from legislators opposed to bureaucratic growth.

By 1915, McFarland and his associates outside the government were working closely with Mather, Albright, and selected members of Congress. Early in 1916, this informal group drafted a bill that was introduced by William Kent in the House and Reed Smoot in the Senate. Somewhat different bills were passed by the two houses of Congress, and it appeared that the session would end yet again without a park service bill being passed. Albright intervened to facilitate an agreement between the House and Senate committee chairs, and that agreement eventually was ratified by the conference committee. The bill was approved by Congress and signed by President Wilson on August 25, 1916.

The act of August 25 has no formal title, but it is often called the National Park Service Act or, in park circles, the Organic Act. It created the National Park Service in the Department of the Interior and gave it control over all national parks and over those national monuments already administered by the department. In its most important sentence, believed to have been written by Frederick Law Olmsted, Jr., the act charged the National Park Service "to conserve the scenery and the natural and historic objects and the wildlife . . . and to provide for the enjoyment of the same in such manner and by such means as will leave them unimpaired for the enjoyment of future generations."

The creation of a park service did not produce immediate results, but between 1916 and 1933, first Mather and then Albright led the service through an era of growth, consolidation, improved infrastructure, and increasingly professional management.

Since World War II, interest in the parks has grown and visitation has mushroomed. By the mid-1990's, park visits numbered about three hundred million per year, and the Park Service supervised a national park system of eighty million acres, including about fifty national parks and about three hundred other natural, historic, and cultural sites. The National Park Service employed management experts in a variety of fields and was emulated widely by park managers around the world. With increased popularity came a multitude of new problems, however, including crime, overcrowding, inadequate infrastructure, contentious debates pitting preservation against use, and a National Park Service that appeared increasingly influenced by the vagaries of electoral politics.

—Craig W. Allin

ADDITIONAL READING:

Albright, Horace M. *The Birth of the National Park Service: The Founding Years, 1913-33.* Salt Lake City, Utah: Howe Brothers, 1985. The foundation and early years of the National Park Service, as seen through the eyes of one of the most important participants.

Allin, Craig W. *The Politics of Wilderness Preservation.* Westport, Conn.: Greenwood Press, 1982. A political scientist presents the national parks' story as a part of the movement to preserve wilderness in the United States.

Foresta, Ronald A. *America's National Parks and Their Keepers.* Washington, D.C.: Resources for the Future, 1984. Analysis of modern park policies and issues, informed by a sense of history.

Lowry, William R. *The Capacity for Wonder: Preserving National Parks.* Washington, D.C.: Brookings Institution, 1994. Discusses how the political compromises that have shaped the structure of the National Park Service from the beginning have shaped its ability to meet the modern problems of overcrowding, crime, inadequate infrastructure, and environmental pollution.

Rettie, Dwight F. *Our National Park System: Caring for America's Greatest Natural and Historic Treasures.* Urbana: University of Illinois Press, 1995. A tour of the modern national park system and the agency that manages it, from a longtime employee of the National Park Service.

Runte, Alfred. *National Parks: The American Experience.* 2d rev. ed. Lincoln: University of Nebraska Press, 1987. An interpretive history of national parks and what they mean to Americans. Argues that park creation has had more to do with nationalism and commercialism than with environmentalism.

Shankland, Robert. *Steve Mather of the National Parks.* New York: Alfred A. Knopf, 1951. Popular biography of the Park Service's charismatic first director.

SEE ALSO: 1908, White House Conservation Conference.

1917 ■ IMMIGRATION ACT OF 1917:
immigration into the United States is significantly restricted by use of a literacy test, among other measures

DATE: February 5, 1917
LOCALE: Washington, D.C.
CATEGORIES: Asian American history; Immigration
KEY FIGURES:
Grover Cleveland (1837-1908), twenty-second (1885-1889) and twenty-fourth (1893-1897) president of the United States
William Paul Dillingham (1843-1923), senator from Vermont
William Howard Taft (1857-1930), twenty-seventh president of the United States, 1909-1913
Woodrow Wilson (1856-1924), twenty-eighth president of the United States, 1913-1921

SUMMARY OF EVENT. During the early 1600's, the Massachusetts Puritans prohibited newcomers from settling without their permission. As the colonial population grew from

Chinese immigrants on a crowded ship bound for America. A growing tide of anti-immigrant feeling coincided with World War I and such events as the Bolshevik Revolution of 1917, as well as growing fear of Asian and other non-European immigrants already residing within the continental United States. Measures such as the Immigration Act of 1917, with its literacy requirement, were designed to dampen the inflow of non-European foreign nationals. (Asian American Studies Library, University of California at Berkeley)

275,000 in 1700 to 3,929,000 in 1790, each colony made and enforced its own rules: Massachusetts was restrictive; Rhode Island was more lenient; Pennsylvania was a sanctuary from religious persecution. After ratification of the United States Constitution, Congress passed the first Naturalization Act, in March, 1790. The act required two years of residency and limited naturalization to "free white persons." The residency requirement was increased to five years in 1795. The first federal legislation that dealt with the expulsion of aliens from the United States was the Alien Act of June 25, 1798. It allowed the president to deport any alien he considered dangerous, but expired two years after it was enacted.

From 1800 to 1875, no federal legislation restricted the admission into, or allowed deportation from, the United States. Congress enacted other laws related to immigration issues during the period, however. In 1819, concern about

conditions for immigrants on inbound ships prompted the passing of a number of steerage acts to safeguard the passage of people en route to the United States. A limit was placed on the number of passengers that ships of various tonnage could carry, and it was required that sufficient supplies of food and water be taken on board before sailing. Customs officials were authorized to count the number of people debarking from vessels, thus providing a record of arrivals. In 1837, the Supreme Court ruled that individual states could pass their own laws regarding immigrant arrivals.

Throughout the first great wave of immigration, from 1820 to 1880, more than ten million immigrants arrived on American shores. Originating mostly from northwest Europe, they were predominantly Irish and German. As the number of Roman Catholics coming from Ireland and other countries increased, an anti-Catholic sentiment asserted itself through nativist organizations such as the Know-Nothings or American Movement. As members of these organizations were elected to seats in Congress and state legislatures, they called for extensive limitations on immigration, but they were unable to effect a change in national policy. The states passed laws that protected them against the expense of caring for sick, destitute, or otherwise dependent immigrants. In 1848, the Supreme Court ruled against the power of individual states when it found that taxes levied on New York and Massachusetts immigrants were unconstitutional. An outcome of the Supreme Court ruling was that government exercised no control over the movement of immigrants. In response to the Court ruling and the enormous influx of immigrants into the country, in 1875 Congress voted to exclude from entry people who had been convicted of nonpolitical crimes and prostitutes. In 1882, a general immigration act barred the entry of paupers, criminals, the insane, and others likely to become public charges. The Supreme Court also ruled that year that only Congress, not individual states, had the power to make laws restricting immigration (*Henderson v. New York*). All inspection and regulation that previously had been held by the states was restored to the federal authorities by the 1891 immigration act.

The California gold rush in 1848 and 1849 drew settlers not only from the East Coast and Europe but also from South America and China. At first, the Chinese were welcomed, but as their numbers increased and the need for their labor as miners and railroad workers decreased, they became the target of hostility. When the California Assembly concluded that they were a threat to white immigrants, California's governor introduced measures to impede the "tide of Asiatic immigrants." On May 9, 1882, the Chinese Exclusion Act—the first U.S. law prohibiting immigration because of race or nationality—was enacted. It barred the Chinese from naturalization and suspended Chinese immigration into the United States for ten years. The act was extended for ten years in 1892, and on April 17, 1904, it was extended for an indefinite time. This suspension remained in effect until the passage on December 17, 1943, of the Magnuson Act.

From 1880 to 1920, more than 23.5 million people arrived in the United States, mostly from southern and eastern Europe. The Immigration Restriction League was founded in 1894 by a group of New England Brahmins. The league had been pleased with the Forant Act of 1885, which had outlawed European contract labor. This private organization perceived the increasing numbers of immigrants arriving from outside northern Europe as a threat to the United States. The group became a leading advocate of restrictive immigration laws. Laws were passed by Congress in 1903 to exclude from entry polygamists, anarchists, epileptics, and people who had been insane during the previous two years or who had had two or more attacks of insanity at any time previously. Immigration peaked at 1.3 million in 1907. To the prior list of unauthorized aliens were added "feeble minded persons, those with tuberculosis and those whose physical or mental defects hindered their earning a living."

The first Japanese arrived in California in 1871. Rising tensions between Asians and Californians had resulted in a movement to exclude Asians. By 1906, it was apparent to President Theodore Roosevelt that the only way to stem the overt hostility toward the Japanese would be to prohibit the entry of Japanese labor into the country. Negotiations between Japan and the United States began in December, 1906, to redress the situation. The resulting Gentlemen's Agreement of 1907 limited immigration from Japan to nonlaborers and to those laborers already resident in the United States and their families.

The public concern in 1907 over European immigration prompted Congress to establish a Joint Commission on Immigration. The commission comprised three members of the Senate, three members of the House of Representatives, and three others. In 1911, the Dillingham Commission, named after the legislation's author and the commission's chairman, Senator William P. Dillingham of Vermont, issued a forty-two-volume report that advocated the restriction of immigration. It stated that recent immigrants from southern and eastern Europe were more likely to be unskilled, unsettled, and generally less desirable than the northern and western European immigrants who had arrived previously. Experts later disputed these conclusions, but the report was used to justify the new restrictions that Congress continued to write into law in the comprehensive Immigration Act of 1917.

A number of different ways to restrict immigration were suggested by the commission. They included instituting a literacy test, excluding unskilled laborers, increasing the amount of money that immigrants were required to have in their possession, and increasing the head tax. The commission also advocated the principle of racial quotas.

Major attention was directed toward the literacy test. Congress had introduced prior bills requiring literacy tests for immigrants. In 1897, such a bill was vetoed by President Grover Cleveland, who said that immigration restrictions were unnecessary. The House voted to override the president's veto on March 3, 195 to 37. The Senate referred the veto message and bill to the Committee on Immigration. When the bill resurfaced at the Sixty-second Congress, it was the Senate that voted to override President William Howard Taft's veto on February 18, 1913, while the House voted to sustain it on February 19. During the Sixty-third Congress (1914-1917), the House voted to sustain the veto of President Woodrow Wilson.

At the second session of the Sixty-fourth Congress, a bill was introduced "to regulate the immigrating of aliens to, and the residence of aliens in, the United States." Again, Wilson vetoed the bill. On February 1, 1917, the House voted to override the president's veto, 287 to 106, and the Senate voted similarly on February 5, 1917, 62 to 19. The veto was overridden, and the bill became Public Law 301. The act excluded from entry "all aliens over sixteen years of age, physically capable of reading, who can not read the English language, or some other language or dialect, including Hebrew or Yiddish." Other major recommendations made by the Dillingham Commission six years earlier were passed. The head tax was increased, and vagrants, alcoholics, advocates of violent revolutions, and "psychopathic inferiors" all were barred. A further provision created an Asiatic Barred Zone in the southwest Pacific, which succeeded in excluding most Asian immigrants who were not already excluded by the Chinese Exclusion Act and the Gentlemen's Agreement.   —*Susan E. Hamilton*

ADDITIONAL READING:

Bernard, William S., ed. *American Immigration Policy.* Port Washington, N.Y.: Kennikat Press, 1969. Discusses growth and its effect on immigration policy; includes the text of the 1917 Immigration Act.

Cose, Ellis. *A Nation of Strangers.* New York: William Morrow, 1992. Chapters 1 through 4 present an overview of immigration, from colonial settlement to World War I.

Daniels, Roger. *Coming to America: A History of Immigration and Ethnicity in American Life.* New York: HarperCollins, 1990. Part 2 concentrates on immigration from 1820 to 1924.

Harper, Elizabeth J. *Immigration Laws of the United States.* 3d ed. Indianapolis: Bobbs-Merrill, 1975. Includes immigration law terminology; describes classes of inadmissible aliens; discusses immigration history and trends.

Nugent, Walter. *Crossings: The Great Transatlantic Migrations, 1870-1914.* Bloomington: Indiana University Press, 1992. A thorough treatise accompanied by maps, tables, and photographs.

SEE ALSO: 1798, Alien and Sedition Acts; 1840's, "Old" Immigration; 1849, Chinese Immigration; 1882, Chinese Exclusion Act; 1892, "New" Immigration; 1892, Yellow Peril Campaign; 1907, Gentlemen's Agreement; 1913, Alien Land Laws; 1919, Red Scare; 1924, Immigration Act of 1924; 1943, Magnuson Act.

1917 ■ JONES ACT: *the United States forms a unique and permanent relationship with the overseas territory of Puerto Rico*

DATE: March 2, 1917
LOCALE: Washington, D.C.
CATEGORIES: Latino American history; Laws and acts
KEY FIGURES:

Joseph Benson Foraker (1846-1917), chairman of the Senate Committee on Pacific Islands and Puerto Rico

William Atkinson Jones (1849-1918), chairman of the House Committee on Insular Affairs

William McKinley (1843-1901), twenty-fifth president of the United States, 1897-1901

Luís Muñoz Rivera (1859-1916), resident commissioner from Puerto Rico in Washington

Woodrow Wilson (1856-1924), twenty-eighth president of the United States, 1913-1921

SUMMARY OF EVENT. On December 10, 1898, the Treaty of Paris between Spain and the United States ended the Spanish-

American War and set forth terms that became effective April 11, 1900. The agreement transferred the control of Puerto Rico to the United States, thereby legitimizing the occupation of the island and its satellites by U.S. forces. One of the provisions of the Treaty of Paris was as follows: "The civil rights and the political status of the native inhabitants of the territories hereby ceded to the United States shall be determined by the Congress." The natives of Puerto Rico, no longer subjects of the Spanish crown, now found themselves without any citizenship recognized under international law or U.S. domestic law.

The Organic Act of 1900 (known as the Foraker Act, after its sponsor) had established a political entity called the People of Porto Rico (Puerto Rico), but there was no mention of U.S. citizenship for those born on the island, only that they would be "held to be citizens of Porto Rico, and as such entitled to the protection of the United States." Puerto Ricans were now stateless, essentially confined to their island because of the difficulty of traveling without a passport. The U.S. Supreme Court, in cases such as *Downes v. Bidwell* (1901), confirmed that Puerto Rico was merely a possession of the United States, not an incorporated territory, to be disposed of by the U.S. Congress.

The reelection of William McKinley to the U.S. presidency in 1900 favored U.S. imperial expansion. Nevertheless, the debate as to whether racially, culturally, and linguistically distinct peoples brought under U.S. control should be granted U.S. citizenship and, if so, with what rights, continued intermittently between 1900 and 1916. In that year, the Philippines, also seized by the United States from Spain in the war, was promised independence by the Organic Act of the Philippine Islands (also known as the Jones Act). The Organic Act of 1917 (the Jones Act of 1917) did not similarly grant independence to Puerto Rico, but it did confer U.S. citizenship collectively on the natives of the island. Although the Jones Act changed the status of Puerto Ricans from that of U.S. nationals—noncitizens, but owing allegiance to and subject to the protection of the United States—the granting of citizenship did not give the islanders the right to vote in U.S. federal elections because the territory fell short of statehood. In *Balzac v. Porto Rico* (1922), the Supreme Court ruled that as citizens of an unincorporated territory, the islanders enjoyed only fundamental provisions in the Bill of Rights of the U.S. Constitution, not procedural or remedial rights such as the guarantee of trial by jury.

The extent to which Puerto Ricans had participated in the debate relating to their prospective status between 1900 and 1917 remains a matter of conjecture. For one thing, the spokesmen of the Puerto Rican community—such as Resident Commissioner Luís Muñoz Rivera and the Puerto Rican House of Delegates (the local legislature)—were ambivalent and contradictory on the subject. For another, much of the evidence placed before the Congress about the Puerto Ricans' preferences during the drawn-out debate was impressionistic and anecdotal rather than objective.

Accordingly, while some U.S. legislators talked of the yearnings, longings, and aspirations of Puerto Ricans to citizenship, critics claim that citizenship was pressed on the islanders. It is also charged that the expediency of acquiring additional recruits for military service only weeks before President Woodrow Wilson sought a declaration of war on Germany on April 4, 1917, was not absent from congressional thinking. Whatever the truth, making Puerto Ricans native U.S. citizens and the establishment of a seemingly permanent political link between the United States and Puerto Rico by the Jones Act of 1917 contrasted with the creation of an articulately temporary relationship between Washington, D.C., and the Philippines. In fact, the defining of the latter's status under the 1916 Jones Act catalyzed the following year's Jones Act relating to Puerto Rico. The racist comments peppering the congressional debates were infinitely harsher as they related to Filipinos, partly because of their spirited resistance to U.S. occupation, than in regard to Puerto Ricans, who were much more receptive to it. Some legislators even produced statistics to "prove" what a high percentage of the islanders were white in order to justify their being granted U.S. citizenship.

The final version of the Jones bill, introduced in the House on January 20, 1916, was only slightly different from Congressman Jones's earlier versions. The only noteworthy change was that Puerto Ricans residing on the island were allowed one year, instead of six months, to reject U.S. citizenship if they desired. The House passed the bill by voice vote on May 23, 1916; the Senate approved it on February 20, 1917; and the House-Senate Conference Committee followed suit on February 24, 1917. President Wilson, a Democrat, signed it into law on March 2, 1917. Only 288 Puerto Ricans legally declined to accept U.S. citizenship within the statutory period, thereby losing their right to hold or run for any public office on the island. Because the Jones Act had established five different categories in determining the status of different individuals, there was great confusion as to who qualified for citizenship. The U.S. Congress subsequently passed several additional laws in the interest of administrative simplification.

In 1952, the U.S. Territory of Puerto Rico became the Commonwealth of Puerto Rico, known in Spanish as a "free associated state." As such, Puerto Rico elected a nonvoting representative to the U.S. Congress but cast no vote in presidential, congressional, or senatorial elections. While islanders paid no federal taxes, the aid Puerto Rico received from Washington was less than it would have received had it been a state.

On November 14, 1993, a nonbinding referendum, which President Bill Clinton nevertheless pledged to respect, was held regarding the island's future status. Puerto Ricans who opted for continued commonwealth status cast 48.4 percent of the votes; statehood received 46.2 percent; and 4.4 percent of the 2.1 million ballots cast favored independence. The spread between the first two options had narrowed drastically since an earlier referendum in 1967. The issue of Puerto Rico's status—and thus the nature of the citizenship of the islanders—was far from over. It now was up to Puerto Ricans themselves, increasingly aware of their Latino roots, to decide their own political future. —*Peter B. Heller*

ADDITIONAL READING:

Cabranes, Jose A. *Citizenship and the American Empire: Notes on the Legislative History of the United States Citizenship of Puerto Ricans.* New Haven, Conn.: Yale University Press, 1979. A well-annotated, objective account, by a law professor of Puerto Rican extraction, of how Congress decided that the distinct people of a colonial territory should be made U.S. citizens.

De Passalacqua, John L. A. "The Involuntary Loss of United States Citizenship upon Accession to Independence by Puerto Rico." *Denver Journal of International Law and Policy* 19, no. 1 (Fall, 1990): 139-161. A short discussion of the Jones Act of 1917 is included in this article on the effect that independence would have on the legal status of Puerto Ricans.

Gatell, Frank O. "The Art of the Possible: Luís Muñoz Rivera and the Puerto Rico Jones Bill." *The Americas* 17, no. 1 (July, 1960): 1-20. Discusses how the resident commissioner from Puerto Rico in Washington, D.C., fought to liberalize the Jones bill while it was debated in Congress but without his Unionist Party's radical proindependence stand.

Karst, Kenneth L. *Belonging to America: Equal Citizenship and the Constitution.* New Haven, Conn.: Yale University Press, 1989. Argues that equal citizenship for cultural minorities who have experienced exclusion, forced conformity, and subordination under the influence of U.S. nativism has become more topical over the years.

SEE ALSO: 1898, Spanish-American War; 1901, Insular Cases.

1917 ■ UNITED STATES ENTERS WORLD WAR I: *U.S. involvement in the Great War transforms it into a global conflict with worldwide ramifications*

DATE: April 6, 1917
LOCALE: Washington, D.C.
CATEGORY: Wars, uprisings, and civil unrest
KEY FIGURES:
Theobald von Bethmann-Hollweg (1856-1921), chancellor of the German Empire
James Watson Gerard (1867-1951), U.S. ambassador to Germany
Edward Grey (1862-1933), British secretary of state for foreign affairs
Edward M. House (1858-1938), President Wilson's personal representative to European nations
Robert Lansing (1864-1928), U.S. secretary of state
Walter Hines Page (1855-1918), U.S. ambassador to Great Britain
William J. Stone (1848-1918), Democratic senator from Missouri and chairman of the Senate Committee on Foreign Relations
Woodrow Wilson (1856-1924), twenty-eighth president of the United States, 1913-1921

SUMMARY OF EVENT. On April 2, 1917, Woodrow Wilson, president of the United States, stood before the combined members of the House and Senate and asked for a declaration of war against Germany. "It is a fearful thing to lead this great peaceful people into war," he concluded. "But the right is more precious than peace." Four days later, on April 6, the United States was formally at war.

For two and a half years following the outbreak of the war in Europe in August, 1914, the United States had practiced a policy of neutrality. The U.S. government had loaned money and supplies to the Entente Allies—Great Britain and France—but also had attempted to avoid antagonizing the Central Powers—Imperial Germany, Austria-Hungary, and the Ottoman Empire. Neutral U.S. ships carried arms and munitions to the Allies. Because its war effort was being threatened, Germany attempted to restrict this trade by sinking U.S. ships, primarily through the use of submarine warfare. In 1914, 1915, and 1916, Germany announced increases in the kinds of neutral ships that would be subject to submarine attack, only to moderate her demands in the face of strong U.S. threats to break off diplomatic relations. During these years, Wilson tried several times to mediate the European dispute, but his sincere attempts failed.

In early 1917, the German government determined to take a calculated risk. Effective February 1, Germany announced that a policy of unrestricted submarine warfare would begin and that any neutral ship, armed or not, that attempted to bring supplies to the British or French would be attacked. Two days later, Wilson broke off diplomatic relations with Germany. Addressing a joint session of Congress on February 3, he explained that it was the only alternative "consistent with the dignity and honor of the U.S." However, he was not heading toward war, which would come only if Germany indulged in overt acts against the United States.

These acts came in the form of an escalated German submarine campaign, sinking U.S. and Allied vessels and causing massive losses of life. Wilson's response was to call for an armed neutrality, but the subsequent Zimmermann note (an encoded message sent by German foreign secretary Alfred Zimmermann to Mexico's German minister proposing an alliance should war break out) and the threat of Mexican involvement brought the war closer to home. On April 2, 1917, Wilson made it clear before a joint session of Congress that armed neutrality was an insufficient response to German attacks.

Why Wilson went on to ask for a declaration of war two months later has been the subject of intense historical debate. Six major interpretations have been advanced: (1) U.S. bankers and arms manufacturers forced Wilson to declare war because the Allies would not repay their debts if they lost the war; (2) clever British propaganda tricked Americans into believing that moral wrong resided exclusively in Germany; (3) U.S. security would be endangered by a German victory, because Imperial Germany was bent on worldwide aggression; (4) public opinion in the United States demanded war; (5) German submarine warfare forced the United States into the war; or (6) that by

April, 1917, Wilson believed that peace without victory in Europe demanded that U.S. forces be sent overseas, so Wilson personally decided that a declaration of war was necessary.

The first four arguments have their enthusiastic proponents but lack persuasive evidence. Most later historians have emphasized interpretations five and six. German submarine policy determined the course of U.S. neutrality after 1914; the decision to begin unrestricted warfare in February, 1917, was a major reason for the United States' entrance into the war. Not to be discounted was Wilson's personal belief that he could bring about an idealistic peace in Europe only by helping the Allies defeat the Central Powers.

There can be no doubt of Wilson's sincerity in believing that the United States must undertake a moral crusade by fighting a war "to end all wars." In spite of his genuine unwillingness, Wilson opted for war largely through calculations of cost and benefit. His policy of armed neutrality had turned out to be a failure in terms of the losses of lives and property it had entailed and the enemies it had created at home. In addition, it had not been able to release the tensions of war, let alone create the ground for the ideal peace settlement.

For Wilson, the raging war was inglorious, a macabre slaughter of millions of innocent people, a disaster, and a sheer horror. The world needed a new order such as he had outlined in his "peace without victory" address. In the end, the president was left with no choice but to seek that order by entering the war. U.S. intervention would crush the might of Germany and bring Allied victory surely and swiftly. Yet, when the aftermath saw no restoration of international order, critics blamed Wilson's idealism for subsequent problems.

—Burton Kaufman, updated by Sudipta Das

ADDITIONAL READING:

Buehrig, Edward H. *Woodrow Wilson and the Balance of Power.* Bloomington: Indiana University Press, 1955. A pointed analysis of close Anglo-American political, economic, military, and cultural relations, and the corresponding decline in relations with Germany. Explains U.S. entry into the war as shaped by German aggression at sea and the urge to protect British naval superiority.

Ferrell, Robert H. *Woodrow Wilson and World War I, 1917-1921.* New York: Harper & Row, 1985. A superb study covering domestic and foreign developments. Focuses on Wilson as a reluctant and tragic figure amid a national crisis.

Gregory, Ross. *The Origins of American Intervention in the First World War.* New York: W. W. Norton, 1971. Constructs the background to U.S. entry into the war, with focus on Wilson's administration and the domestic forces that shaped its decisions. Deals with outside forces in London, Berlin, and Paris that influenced the course of U.S. policy.

Link, Arthur S. *Woodrow Wilson: Revolution, War and Peace.* Arlington Heights, Ill.: Harlan Davidson, 1979. Wilson's chief biographer and editor of his papers argues that Wilson, imbued with only the highest motives, was influenced by both moral and practical factors. Extensive description of events in belligerent nations and their impact on the United States.

May, Ernest R. *The World War and American Isolation, 1914-1917*. Cambridge, Mass.: Harvard University Press, 1959. Based on multiarchival sources, posits that Wilson, after much soul-searching, could not stay out of war because of U.S. interests and European pressures. Asserts that Wilson's policy was more correct than incorrect.

SEE ALSO: 1912, Wilson Is Elected President; 1917, Propaganda and Civil Liberties in World War I; 1917, Espionage and Sedition Acts; 1917, Mobilization for World War I; 1918, Meuse-Argonne Offensive; 1918, Demobilization After World War I; 1919, Treaty of Versailles; 1919, Red Scare.

1917 ■ PROPAGANDA AND CIVIL LIBERTIES IN WORLD WAR I: *government and public action in wartime curtails civil liberties to ensure national security*

DATE: Beginning April 13, 1917
LOCALE: United States
CATEGORIES: Civil rights; Wars, uprisings, and civil unrest
KEY FIGURES:
George Edward Creel (1876-1953), chairman of the Committee on Public Information
Eugene Victor Debs (1855-1926), leading Socialist who was jailed for his opposition to U.S. participation in the war
William Dudley "Big Bill" Haywood (1869-1928), leader of the Industrial Workers of the World
Woodrow Wilson (1856-1924), twenty-eighth president of the United States, 1913-1921

SUMMARY OF EVENT. On the evening of April 6, 1917, President Woodrow Wilson, in delivering his war message to Congress, said that the United States was to embark upon a crusade to "make the world safe for democracy." Unfortunately for socialists, pacifists, German Americans, and the leadership of the Industrial Workers of the World (popularly known as the Wobblies), who opposed this intervention, the president said nothing about the protection of democracy at home. U.S. participation in World War I gave rise to an alarming attack upon civil liberties, as Congress enacted laws to curtail constitutionally guaranteed freedoms of speech and press. For the first time, the government embarked on a concerted propaganda campaign to "sell" a war to its citizens. As a result, hysteria swept the country. The responsibility for these occurrences rests with Wilson, with George Creel, with Congress, and with thousands of superpatriotic citizens who saw a monumental foreign menace rather than its meager substance.

Two problems faced the government. First, citizens had to be mobilized behind a war that did not involve a direct attack on the United States and that had been entered into slowly and unwillingly. Second, internal security needed to be guaranteed against enemies, real and imagined. On April 13, 1917, Wilson established the Committee on Public Information (CPI), under the leadership of Creel, whose name soon became synony-

mous with the office. The committee was established to convince wavering citizens that the war was a righteous one and to educate them about the government's war aims. Similar offices of war information had been created in Great Britain, Germany, and France.

Propaganda came of age during World War I. Its purposes were multifaceted: to mobilize hatred of the enemy; to preserve friendship among allies; to maintain the friendship of neutrals and, if possible, to gain their cooperation; to demoralize the enemy; to promote the economical use of commodities; to stimulate war production; to encourage the purchase of war bonds; and to alert citizens to the danger of spies and saboteurs. The mobilization of the civilian mind for total war was seen as more important than the preservation of human rights.

George Creel was an excellent choice for chairman of the CPI. A veteran Progressive from Denver and one of Wilson's earliest supporters, Creel had built a reputation as a crusading journalist. Because of his reform record, Creel's appointment was cheered by the press, which had feared repressive censorship. Instead, Creel called for voluntary censorship and usually received cooperation. The committee relied on securing publication of a torrent of government-sponsored reports and stories. During the course of the war, Creel hired 150,000 artists, writers, lecturers, actors, and scholars to sell the war to the public. Colorful posters urged citizens to join the army or navy, buy Liberty Bonds, knit socks for soldiers, and guard against the ever-present danger of spies and saboteurs. Writers turned out hundreds of "true" stories concerning German atrocities and "accounts" of what the Hun planned to do to the United States. Columbia University professor Charles Hazen wrote *The Government of Germany*, a booklet "exposing" the medievalism of a military-dominated Germany. Teams of speakers toured the country delivering anti-German talks. Anti-German motion pictures included *Pershing's Crusaders*, *The Prussian Cur*, and *The Kaiser, the Beast of Berlin*. The public was encouraged to see the Central Powers as constituting a clear and present danger to civilization.

Although the Creel Committee became synonymous in the public mind with censorship, it had no such power. That authority was vested in the Post Office Department and the Department of Justice. Public confusion was understandable. On June 15, 1917, the Espionage Act was passed, after considerable debate and many amendments. This act gave the government authority to limit the rights of speech and the press. Somehow, the public had become convinced that the act conferred enforcement powers upon the CPI, a misconception that Creel never attempted to dispel. This illusion of power was effective in securing public cooperation.

Title I, Section 3, of the Espionage Act made it a crime to make false reports that would aid the enemy, incite rebellion in the armed forces, or obstruct recruitment or the draft. In practice, this section was used to stifle criticism. Those prosecuted included socialists Victor Berger and Eugene V. Debs, and "Big Bill" Haywood, one of the leaders of the Industrial Workers of the World. Socialist and pacifist newspapers were denied use of the mails under Title XII. The editors of *The Messenger*, a New York African American newspaper, were imprisoned for questioning the war. Ricardo Flores Magon, a Mexican American labor organizer, was sentenced to twenty years in prison for his dissent. In October, 1917, another law required foreign-language newspapers to submit translations of all war-related material before distribution to local readers.

The Espionage Act was bolstered in May, 1918, by the Sedition Act, which provided penalties of up to ten thousand dollars and twenty years' imprisonment for the willful writing, utterance, or publication of material abusing the government, showing contempt for the Constitution, for inciting others to resist the government, for supporting the enemy, or for hindering production of war matériel. Under this law, it was unnecessary to prove that the language in question had affected anyone or had produced injurious consequences. The postmaster general was empowered to deny use of the mails to anyone who, in his opinion, used them to violate the act. A total of 2,168 people were prosecuted under the Espionage and Sedition Acts.

The limitations placed on dissent by Congress and the Departments of Justice and the Post Office, together with the Creel Committee's encouragement of pro-Allied sentiment, might have been expected to produce a climate of loyalty in the United States without help from unofficial sources. However, there also appeared a number of superpatriotic volunteer organizations dedicated to spreading propaganda and discovering alleged traitors, saboteurs, and slackers. The most influential of these groups were the National Security League and the National Protective Association. The Boy Spies of America, the Sedition Slammers, and the Terrible Threateners had more picturesque names but were less powerful. These volunteer groups carried patriotism to excess and often were responsible for human rights violations, which the government made no real attempt to discourage. As a result, coercion became the order of the day, and the government never regained control of the explosive situation.

The brunt of government and vigilante activity was borne by the country's largest minority: German Americans. Although German Americans never were interned in camps, their plight during World War I paralleled that of Japanese Americans in World War II: Both were suspected as traitors. Attempts were made to eradicate anything German from American life. Schools and colleges banned the teaching of German, as a "language that disseminates the ideals of autocracy, brutality, and hatred." South Dakota prohibited the use of German on the telephone. Fewer than one hundred of the United States' twelve hundred German-language periodicals survived to 1920. Thousands of Pennsylvania German parents, seventh- and eighth-generation Americans, forbade their children to learn their dialect. Several cities, including Boston, banned the music of Beethoven, Wagner, and other German composers. Pretzels were removed from saloon lunch counters in Cincinnati. German sausages, sauerkraut, German shepherd dogs, German measles, and pinochle were all renamed, as were many towns with names such as Berlin, Frankfurt, and Bis-

marck. Many people hastened to Americanize their German surnames.

The superpatriotic volunteers, encouraged by the Creel Committee's propaganda, produced a wave of hysteria that resulted in bodily or mental harm to thousands of innocent citizens. IWW organizer Frank Little was tortured and lynched in Montana. In April, 1918, a mob in East St. Louis humiliated and hanged a young German American, Robert Prager. Ringleaders were eventually acquitted on the grounds that the murder was patriotic. In Los Angeles, where police ignored the harassment of Mexican Americans—who were all regarded as pro-German— three pacifist clergymen were beaten by a mob and then jailed for expressing "thoughts calculated to cause any American citizen then and there present to assault and batter them."

Once unleashed, antiforeign biases could not be controlled when the war ended. These sentiments eventually backfired on Wilson: His dream of a League of Nations would be rejected by the U.S. public, and one of his own books was banned in Nebraska. Somewhere during the fight to make the world safe for democracy, the United States lost its most democratic ideals: tolerance and compassion. Perhaps the greatest loss, however, was self-confidence. Never again would people in the United States be so certain of their ideas or their ability to absorb peoples with different views and backgrounds. When challenges arose, they would be met with newer, more repressive laws and public hysteria, exemplified in the Red Scare, the race riots of 1919-1920, and other postwar disturbances. It was a high price to have paid for intervention in World War I.

—Anne Trotter, updated by Randall Fegley

ADDITIONAL READING:

Johnson, Donald. *The Challenge to American Freedoms: World War I and the Rise of the American Civil Liberties Union.* Lexington: University Press of Kentucky, 1963. This scholarly monograph examines the attack on civil liberties during the war and the establishment of the American Civil Liberties Union as a watchdog.

Lasswell, Harold. *Propaganda Technique in the World War.* New York: Alfred A. Knopf, 1927. The honesty of Lasswell's general work on World War I propaganda provoked a small furor when published.

Mock, James, and Cedric Larson. *Words That Won the War.* Princeton, N.J.: Princeton University Press, 1939. Ably demonstrates the effectiveness of the Creel Committee.

Parsons, William. *The Pennsylvania Dutch: A Persistent Minority.* Boston: Twayne, 1976. A general history of Pennsylvania Germans, containing an excellent chapter on their wartime situation.

Peterson, H. C., and G. C. Fite. *Opponents of War, 1917-1918.* Madison: University of Wisconsin Press, 1957. Uses a largely biographical approach to provide a broad summary of opposition to the war.

Preston, William, Jr. *Aliens and Dissenters: Federal Suppression of Radicals, 1903-1933.* New York: Harper & Row, 1966. The suppression of civil liberties is put in perspective in this study of early twentieth century U.S. nativism.

Read, James Morgan. *Atrocity Propaganda, 1914-1919*. New Haven, Conn.: Yale University Press, 1941. An excellent summary of the use of atrocity propaganda during World War I.

Thernstrom, Stephan. *A History of the American People: Since 1865*. 2d ed. San Diego: Harcourt Brace Jovanovich, 1989. An excellent overview of the violation of civil liberties during the war.

SEE ALSO: 1913, Anti-Defamation League Is Founded; 1917, Immigration Act of 1917; 1917, United States Enters World War I; 1917, Espionage and Sedition Acts; 1917, Mobilization for World War I; 1918, Meuse-Argonne Offensive; 1918, Demobilization After World War I; 1919, Treaty of Versailles; 1919, Red Scare.

1917 ■ UNIVERSAL NEGRO IMPROVEMENT ASSOCIATION IS ESTABLISHED: *an organization dedicated to advancing African American racial pride and a major step in the growth of black nationalism*

DATE: May, 1917
LOCALE: Harlem, New York City, New York
CATEGORIES: African American history; Organizations and institutions
KEY FIGURES:
Amy Ashwood Garvey (1897-1969), Garvey's secretary and first wife, who helped him to organize the UNIA in Jamaica and New York
Amy Jacques Garvey (1896-1973), Garvey's personal secretary, second wife, and editor of his writings
Marcus Mosiah Garvey (1887-1940), Jamaican founder of the UNIA, self-styled "provisional president" of Africa
SUMMARY OF EVENT. In March, 1916, a young black Jamaican, Marcus Mosiah Garvey, arrived in New York City. He had come to the United States in the hope of securing financial help for the Universal Negro Improvement Association (UNIA), which he had founded in Jamaica two years earlier. After delivering his first public speech in Harlem in May, Garvey began a long speaking tour that took him through thirty-eight states. In May, 1917, he returned to Harlem and—with the help of his secretary and future wife, Amy Ashwood—organized the first American chapter of the UNIA. Though hardly noticed at the time, this infant organization was a significant first step in the growth of black nationalism in the United States. Within a few years, the UNIA would claim millions of members and hundreds of branches throughout the United States, the Caribbean region, and Africa, and Garvey would be one of the most famous black people in the world.

Garvey was born in St. Ann's Bay, Jamaica, in 1887. He claimed to be of pure African descent. His father was a descendant of the maroons, or Jamaican slaves, who successfully revolted against their British masters in 1739. During his early years, Garvey gradually became aware that his color was considered by some in his society to be a badge of inferiority. Jamaica, unlike the United States, placed the mulatto in a higher caste as a buffer against the unlettered black masses. This reality caused a sense of racial isolation and yet pride to grow in the young black man. By his twentieth birthday, Garvey had started a program to change the lives of black Jamaicans. While working as a foreman in a printing shop in 1907, he joined a labor strike as a leader. The strike, quickly broken by the shop owners, caused Garvey to lose faith in reform through labor unions. In 1910, he started publishing a newspaper, *Garvey's Watchman*, and helped form a political organization, the National Club. These efforts, which were not particularly fruitful, gave impetus to Garvey's visit to Central America where he was able to observe the wretched conditions of black people in Costa Rica and Panama.

Garvey's travels as a black Ulysses finally led him to London, the center of the British Empire. There the young man met Dusé Mohamed Ali, an Egyptian scholar, who increased the young Jamaican's knowledge and awareness of Africa. During his stay in England, Garvey also became acquainted with the plight of African Americans through reading Booker T. Washington's *Up from Slavery*. Washington's autobiography raised questions in Garvey's mind: "I asked, where is the black man's Government? Where is his King and his Kingdom? Where is his President, his country and his ambassador, his army, his navy, his men of big affairs? I could not find them, and then I declared, I will help to make them."

Returning to Jamaica in 1914, Garvey created a self-help organization for black people to which he gave the imposing title, the Universal Negro Improvement and Conservation Association and African Communities League. This new organization, renamed the Universal Negro Improvement Association, based its philosophy on the need to unite "all people of Negro or African parentage." The goals of the UNIA were to increase racial pride, to aid black people throughout the world, and "to establish a central nation for the race." Garvey, elected the first president of UNIA, realized that black people would have to achieve these goals without assistance from white people. This self-help concept, similar to the philosophy (but not the practice) of Booker T. Washington, led Garvey to propose a black trade school in Kingston, Jamaica, similar to Washington's Tuskegee Institute. The idea did not attract wide support and Garvey was temporarily frustrated.

In 1915 Garvey decided to come to the United States in order to seek aid for his Jamaica-based organization. Although he had corresponded with Booker T. Washington, Washington had died before Garvey arrived in the United States in 1916. Garvey went directly to Harlem, which in the early twentieth century was becoming a center of black culture

The lives of African Americans were rapidly changing in the first two decades of the twentieth century. Metropolitan areas in the North were experiencing mass migrations of African Americans from the South. In New York City, for example, the black population increased from 91,709 in 1910 to 152,467 in 1920. African Americans were attracted by the promise of jobs and by the possibility of escaping the rigid system of segregation in the South.

African Americans found, however, that they could not escape racism simply by moving. Northern whites also believed in the racial inferiority of African Americans and opposed black competitors for their jobs. The new immigrants, like their foreign-born counterparts, were crowded into the Northern ghettos without proper housing or the possibility of escape. Racial violence broke out in several Northern cities. The North proved not to be a utopia for African Americans.

These harsh realities aided Garvey in establishing the UNIA in New York. The population of Harlem was not attracted to the accommodationist philosophy of Booker T. Washington or the middle-class goals of the National Association for the Advancement of Colored People. Indeed, urban African Americans were wary of all prophets, even Garvey; but the young Jamaican was able to obtain support from the Jamaican immigrants in Harlem, who felt isolated, and he established a branch of UNIA there in 1917. At first, the organization encountered difficulties. Local politicians tried to gain control of it, and Garvey had to fight to save its autonomy. The original branch of the UNIA was dissolved, and a charter was obtained from the state of New York which prevented other groups from using the organization's name. By 1918, under Garvey's exciting leadership, the New York chapter of the UNIA boasted 3,500 members. By 1919, Garvey optimistically claimed two million members for his organization throughout the world and 200,000 subscribers for his weekly newspaper, *The Negro World*.

In an effort to promote the economic welfare of blacks under the auspices of the UNIA, Garvey established in 1919 two joint stock companies—the Black Star Line, an international commercial shipping company, and the Negro Factories Corporation, which was to "build and operate factories . . . to manufacture every marketable commodity." Stock in these companies was sold only to black investors. The Black Star Line was to establish commerce with Africa and transport willing emigrants "back to Africa." Although both companies were financial failures, they gave many black people a feeling of dignity. As a result of his promotional efforts in behalf of the Black Star Line, the federal government, prodded by rival black leaders, had Garvey indicted for fraudulent use of the mails in 1922. He was tried, found guilty, and sent to prison in 1923. Although his second wife, Amy Jacques Garvey, worked to hold the UNIA together it declined rapidly. In 1927, Garvey was released from prison and deported as an undesirable alien. He returned to Jamaica, and then went to London and Paris and tried to resurrect the UNIA, but with little success. He died in poverty in London in 1940. Although a bad businessman, Garvey was a master propagandist and popular leader who made a major contribution toward race consciousness among African Americans.

—John C. Gardner, updated by R. Kent Rasmussen

ADDITIONAL READING:

Cronon, E. David. *Black Moses: The Story of Marcus Garvey and the Universal Negro Improvement Association*. Madison: University of Wisconsin Press, 1955. This first scholarly biography of Garvey remains the best introduction to his life.

Garvey, Amy Jacques. *Garvey and Garveyism*. 1963. Reprint. New York: Collier, 1976. Intimate memoir of Garvey written by his widow two decades after his death.

Garvey, Marcus. *Philosophy and Opinions of Marcus Garvey*. Edited by Amy Jacques-Garvey, with new introduction by Robert A. Hill. New York: Atheneum, 1992. This classic collection of Garvey's speeches and writings was assembled by his wife during the early 1920's, while Garvey was fighting mail-fraud charges. Hill's new introduction places the work in a broad historical perspective.

Hill, Robert A., et al., eds. *The Marcus Garvey and Universal Negro Improvement Association Papers*. 9 vols. Berkeley: University of California Press, 1983-1996. The most extensive collection of original documents by and about Garvey and his movement, this set is the best starting point for all research on the UNIA.

Hill, Robert A., and Barbara Bair, eds. *Marcus Garvey: Life and Lessons*. Berkeley: University of California Press, 1987. Collection of Garvey's most didactic writings, including autobiographical material that he wrote in 1930. A long appendix includes biographies of figures important in his life.

Lewis, Rupert, and Maureen Warner-Lewis, eds. *Garvey: Africa, Europe, the Americas*. Kingston, Jamaica: Institute of Social and Economic Research, University of the West Indies, 1986. Collection of original research papers on international aspects of Garveyism.

SEE ALSO: 1895, Booker T. Washington's Atlanta Exposition Address; 1896, *Plessy v. Ferguson*; 1905, Niagara Movement; 1909, National Association for the Advancement of Colored People Is Founded.

1917 ■ ESPIONAGE AND SEDITION ACTS: *challenges to civil liberties and political reform redefine the Progressive movement*

DATE: June 15, 1917, and May 16, 1918
LOCALE: Washington, D.C.
CATEGORIES: Civil rights; Government and politics; Laws and acts
KEY FIGURES:
Jane Addams (1860-1935), founder of Hull House and leading critic of World War I
Roger Nash Baldwin (1884-1981), creator of the American Civil Liberties Union
Albert Sidney Burleson (1863-1937), postmaster general of the United States
George Creel (1876-1953), head of the Committee on Public Information
Eugene Victor Debs (1855-1926), leader of the Socialist Party of the United States

Learned Hand (1872-1961), federal judge who guarded against government denial of civil liberties

Oliver Wendell Holmes, Jr. (1841-1935), associate justice of the U.S. Supreme Court

Rose Pastor Stokes (1879-1933), Socialist Party antiwar advocate

Woodrow Wilson (1856-1924), twenty-eighth president of the United States, 1913-1921

Summary of event. Enacted by the Congress of the United States on June 15, 1917, the Espionage Act made it illegal to obstruct willfully the recruiting or enlistment of individuals into the armed forces of the United States. The 1918 amendments to this act, known collectively as the Sedition Act, carried the original law even further by making it a crime to voice any criticism about the United States government or government policy with regard to World War I.

Worried about possible opposition to the United States' position in the war, the Wilson Administration called upon Congress to make it illegal to voice opposition to government policy. A nationwide police structure was created to seek out opponents to the war. Raids were carried out by national and local law enforcement units, in many cases without proper warrants, against individuals and groups accused of seditious behavior. Property was confiscated illegally, beatings and worse punishments of those accused became commonplace, and restrictions of civil liberties became the norm.

Official censorship also was common. Postmaster General Albert Burleson denied mailing privileges to any publication officially labeled "radical" on the grounds that it contained treasonable messages. Even if such denial were appealed, the government could take other actions to suppress publications that opposed the war. Such was the case of Burleson's move against the "radical" journal the *Masses*. After federal judge Learned Hand overturned the postmaster's decision to close down the journal, Burleson found another way to force it to cease publication. During the appeal process, the journal had missed an issue. Burleson determined it was no longer a regularly issued publication and therefore was not eligible for second-class postage privileges. The financial burden to the journal was enough to interrupt its regular publication.

Vocal opposition to such government action sprang up immediately. Guarding against objections that might fuel public opinion against the war or government policy in general became the work of the Committee on Public Information. Headed by Denver newspaperman George Creel, the committee sought to manage public opinion. The committee organized efforts to promote draft registration, the purchase of liberty bonds, the conservation of food and fuel, and spying on neighbors who expressed opinions against the war. It employed movie stars, famous writers, and other publicly recognized individuals who supported the United States' entry into the war to encourage a rallying around the flag. Advertisements placed in popular magazines in an attempt to galvanize the population became a weekly event. Factory workers were cajoled by the committee's propaganda into joining loyalty leagues, and citizens were called upon to make personal sacrifices in support of the war effort. Conformity became the message. Under the banner, "one hundred per cent Americanism," the committee sought to unify U.S. expression.

The denial of civil liberties went beyond official action against war opponents. Joining the government action were local vigilante groups and other super-patriotic organizations. The combined forces of patriotism sought out anyone or anything they determined to be radical. Socialists and labor leaders, such as Eugene V. Debs and Rose Pastor Stokes, were arrested. Members of the Industrial Workers of the World, or "Wobblies"—an early labor union that opposed the war—were arrested, beaten, jailed, and even killed. In Canton, Ohio, Debs received national attention when he was prosecuted for giving a speech supporting antiwar protesters. He was sentenced to prison for ten years. After serving thirty-two months, he was pardoned by Wilson's successor, Warren Harding. Stokes received a ten-year sentence for writing a letter to the *Kansas City Star* accusing the federal government of encouraging industrial war profiteering rather than serving the domestic needs of U.S. citizens.

Other antiwar protesters or peace advocates were subjected to social ostracism and acts of violence at the hands of hysterical patriots. In Brisbee, Arizona, the sheriff and two thousand vigilante deputies rounded up twelve hundred workers, herded them into railroad box cars, and shipped them in 120-degree weather to New Mexico. In Montana, six IWW members were lynched because they belonged to an international, not a national, organization. In Chicago, Jane Addams, founder of the Women's International League for Peace and Freedom—who previously had been solicited for her support in the 1916 presidential election by the leaders of the two major political parties—was placed under surveillance by the Department of Justice for speaking out for peace.

The enforcement of these acts also made necessary the increase of national, state, and local police machinery. The Military Intelligence Service grew from a staff of two in 1917 to three hundred in 1918. It was assisted in its domestic spying efforts by a thousand civilians. A newly created Bureau of Investigation, later renamed the Federal Bureau of Investigation (FBI), was charged with crushing all opposition to the war. By war's end, the Department of Justice had prosecuted some twenty-one hundred cases of purported sedition and espionage. Officially sanctioned support groups such as the American Protective League (APL) were organized. The APL mobilized a quarter of a million citizens in more than six hundred U.S. towns and cities who spied on their neighbors and participated in raids on suspected slackers, protesters, and draft resisters.

It was the unofficial machinery that the Espionage and Sedition Acts inspired that most directly challenged U.S. civil liberties. By the end of 1917, newspaper stories told of people harassed by gangs of super-patriots. Explanations for such activity varied: Draft resistance, not displaying the flag, criticizing U.S. war aims, and not contributing financially to the war effort were the most popular. In Nebraska, mechanic

Rudolph Schopke was tarred and feathered for declining to contribute to the Red Cross. Wisconsin farmer John Deml was almost lynched because he could buy no more than $450 in war bonds. Professor J. McKeen, a Columbia University psychologist who was opposed to the war yet still participated on the government committee formed to set guidelines for army aviators, was dismissed from his faculty position. In Tulsa, Oklahoma, S. L. Miller shot and killed a waiter in a restaurant for allegedly making pro-German remarks. He was acquitted after a jury trial.

The Espionage and Sedition Acts were judiciously supported by the courts. The Supreme Court upheld their constitutionality in several cases. In *Schenck v. United States* (1919), the Court unanimously agreed with Justice Holmes's position that Congress could restrict free speech in such circumstances of clear and present danger. In *Abrams v. United States* (1919), the Court upheld the convictions of four Russian immigrants who distributed pamphlets condemning U.S. intervention in the Russian Revolution. In *Debs v. United States* (1919), the Court stated that even though Debs did not specifically urge draft resistance, his speech clearly created a danger for the government.

The raids, arrests, and convictions inspired by the Espionage and Sedition Acts carried over into peacetime. The procedures born out of their creation helped to set the stage for official responses to dissident activity through much of the twentieth century. The anti-radical, anti-trade union, and anti-immigration sentiments that emerged in the 1920's continued the official prosecutions of the war years. The Senate committee investigating German espionage during the war switched to hunting radicals after the war. The roundup of aliens suspected of being radicals became an official activity of the FBI.

The patriotic wartime fever was transformed later into other fears. Stretching beyond the fear of radicalism were fears about trade unionism and the feminist and Civil Rights movements. The social trauma of World War I and the subsequent measure of U.S. identity it inspired produced exaggerated responses to unpopular ideas and speech in the name of national security. The trauma of the war years also produced responses to the denial of civil liberties. Organizations such as the American Civil Liberties Union, Common Cause, and other citizen groups have been founded to check government power and special interests' attempts to define an American identity. —*Thomas J. Edward Walker*

ADDITIONAL READING:

Barnet, Richard J. *The Rockets' Red Glare: When America Goes to War, the Presidents and the People.* New York: Simon & Schuster, 1990. An astute analysis on how the manufacturing of consent influences wartime policy making.

Blum, John Morton. *Woodrow Wilson and the Politics of Morality.* Boston: Little, Brown, 1956. Analyzes Wilson's attempts to define U.S. morality, especially during wartime.

Davis, Allen. *American Heroine: The Life and Legend of Jane Addams.* New York: Oxford University Press, 1973. A penetrating, well-documented biography of the founder of Hull House, which discusses the public role she played in U.S. history.

Preston, William. *Aliens and Dissenters: Federal Suppression of Radicals, 1903-1933.* New York: Harper & Row, 1966. A definitive account of radical activity and government response to it during the early twentieth century.

Walker, Samuel. *In Defense of American Liberties: A History of the ACLU.* New York: Oxford University Press, 1990. A comprehensive examination of the history of the American Civil Liberties Union.

Wilson, Woodrow. *The Papers of Woodrow Wilson.* Edited by Arthur S. Link et al. Princeton, N.J.: Princeton University Press, 1983. A major primary source. Shows how the twenty-eighth president saw the mission of the United States, both at home and abroad, in World War I.

SEE ALSO: 1905, Industrial Workers of the World Is Founded; 1917, Immigration Act of 1917; 1917, United States Enters World War I; 1917, Propaganda and Civil Liberties in World War I; 1917, Mobilization for World War I; 1918, Meuse-Argonne Offensive; 1918, Demobilization After World War I; 1919, Treaty of Versailles; 1919, Red Scare.

1917 ▪ MOBILIZATION FOR WORLD WAR I: *the United States establishes the War Industries Board to manage economic resources for the war effort*

DATE: Beginning July 8, 1917
LOCALE: Washington, D.C.
CATEGORIES: Business and labor; Government and politics; Wars, uprisings, and civil unrest
KEY FIGURES:
Bernard Mannes Baruch (1870-1965), third chairman of the War Industries Board
F. A. Scott (1873-1949), first chairman of the War Industries Board
Daniel Willard (1861-1942), second chairman of the War Industries Board
Woodrow Wilson (1856-1924), twenty-eighth president of the United States, 1913-1921

SUMMARY OF EVENT. The War Industries Board (WIB) was organized on July 8, 1917, to coordinate and control the industrial resources of the United States in its World War I effort against Germany. Establishment of the WIB was the climax of several frustrating months of efforts to mobilize agencies of production and distribution following the nation's entry into the war in April.

Federal coordination of industry had begun in 1915, when Congress authorized the creation of a Committee on Industrial Preparedness to study the supply requirements of the Army and Navy. The committee's work was narrow in scope—its primary accomplishment was the preparation of an inventory of plants able to manufacture munitions. As the war emergency in the United States became more acute, the government extended its power over the nation's industrial life. By the National Defense Act of June, 1916, Congress authorized the president to place orders for war matériel with any source of supply and to commandeer plants when it was in the national interest to do so. Two months later, Congress approved a Military Appropriations Act providing for a Council of National Defense consisting of the secretaries of war, the Navy, the interior, agriculture, commerce, and labor, and an advisory commission comprising civilian representatives from all the major sectors of the nation's economy. The purpose of both committees was to plan for the most efficient use of the country's resources in case of war.

The advisory commission, which served as the executive committee of the Council of National Defense, did most of the work and mapped out extensive preparations to meet wartime needs. Each of the seven members of the commission took charge of a special segment of the economy, such as transportation, engineering and education, munitions and manufacturing, medicine and surgery, raw materials, supplies, and labor. The commission soon became the nucleus of numerous committees and boards that were the forerunners of several wartime agencies, including the WIB. Finally, Bernard Baruch, a Wall Street investor and the commissioner in charge of raw materials, formulated an elaborate plan whereby representatives of various businesses were organized into "committees of the industries" to work with the council in coordinating the country's resources. For their efforts, they received one dollar a year, and thus were known as the "dollar-a-year men."

Because the Council of National Defense had been formed to plan for, rather than direct, industrial mobilization, its powers were only advisory. Moreover, its organization was extremely loose; many of its ablest men served only in a part-time capacity. It was ill-prepared, therefore, to assume the responsibility of directing mobilization, which was forced upon it after the United States' entry into war in 1917. That unpreparedness was readily apparent in the council's attempt to coordinate the purchases of the U.S. Departments of the Navy and War. For that purpose, the advisory commission first established a Munitions Standard Board and then a General Munitions Board, on which members of the commission and representatives from the military purchasing bureaus served. The power and authority of the board were poorly defined, and its machinery nearly broke down under the pressure of the war orders. Within a month after its establishment, it was found that the board merely overlapped in jurisdiction and authority with many of the other committees formed by the Advisory Commission. As a result, it was unable to coordinate the purchases of the military bureaus, which, jealous of their own prerogatives, continued to go their own ways. Realizing that a central coordinating agency was needed, the Council of National Defense, on July 18, 1917, replaced the General Munitions Board with the WIB, comprising five civilians and one representative each from the Army and the Navy.

Before the Civil War, the United States had adopted a policy of procuring many—if not most—wartime goods and weapons from civilian businesses. With the exception of a few shipyards or munitions plants, the government therefore relied primarily on private industry to provide a steady stream of war goods and combat weapons. Coordinating that production and flow was a major problem for a nation that allowed the market to determine the type and number of goods to be supplied. In wartime, the urgency of delivery dictated that coordination of production and delivery systems fall to the government.

While the War Industries Board was given broad responsibilities for the direction of war industry needs, its ability to do effective work suffered from the lack of any executive power. As a result, the government's effort to coordinate the nation's military and industrial efforts continued to flounder for the next eight months. The board's first chairman, F. A. Scott, broke down under the strain of the war; its second, Daniel Willard, resigned because he believed that the board lacked authority.

In the spring of 1918, President Woodrow Wilson reorganized the board and named Bernard Baruch as its chairman. In effect, the president transferred to Baruch the power to coordinate industry that Congress had granted to the president in the National Defense and Military Appropriations Acts of 1916, as well as giving Baruch certain controls over the military that Wilson had in his capacity as commander in chief. Endowed with this authority, Baruch was able to determine priorities, requisition supplies, conserve resources, commandeer plants, and make purchases for the United States and the Allies. The only important control he did not exercise directly was that of fixing prices, which was left to a separate committee within the board.

Despite some sharp criticism later by congressional critics regarding the extent of power that the War Industries Board assumed, the board was highly effective in coordinating the nation's industrial and military effort. The pattern of organization created by the board became the model for the war regulation of industry by the Allies in World War II. Moreover, the introduction of businessmen into government procurement placed professional business managers in close proximity with bureaucrats. This led to an appreciation by business for the role of control and planning, and convinced many in government that business management practices would be effective in improving the government during peacetime. Business already had undergone a managerial revolution that emphasized planning; therefore, the new, centralized control reinforced the notion that stability could be achieved by proper accounting and forecasting. The quintessential proponent of that approach was Herbert Hoover, elected president in 1928, who attempted to apply such nostrums to the Great Depression.

On December 31, 1918, President Wilson directed that the board be dissolved, and it was liquidated on July 22, 1919. Other wartime agencies that were involved in economic mobilization—such as the War Trade Board, which licensed exports and imports and rationed supplies to neutrals, and the United States Railroad Administration, which controlled the nation's railroads—also were dissolved gradually after the war ended.

The friendly relationship between big business and government that emerged from the war cemented an alliance that lasted until the Great Depression. In the short term, business thought that it was the beneficiary of that relationship, receiving government contracts and favorable treatment. Although the boom provided by the Roaring Twenties proved nourishing to many small businesses, as witnessed by the extensive growth of all business during that decade, the special treatment afforded to such new enterprises as airplane and some shipping companies, based on future wartime needs, served to align government with some industries at the expense of others.

More important, however, were the lessons learned by the government during wartime that were inapplicable during peacetime. The government assumed that wartime planning—based on the coercive powers yielded to bureaucrats by citizens facing a national emergency—would provide the same degree of effectiveness in the absence of the emergency. Since the national tendency of government was to increase during emergencies, but never to recede to its original levels, the war intruded federal authority into the lives of millions of people who had never before experienced it. Thus, although the WIB was disbanded after World War I, the notion that government planning and direct management of businesses could keep the economy stable was revived on a larger scale during the Great Depression. —*Burton Kaufman, updated by Larry Schweikart*

ADDITIONAL READING:

Baruch, Bernard. *American Industry in the War*. New York: Prentice-Hall, 1941. A strong defense of the WIB by its third chairman, including the board's official report of March, 1921.

Clarkson, Grosvenor B. *Industrial America in the World War*. Boston: Houghton Mifflin, 1923. A comprehensive history of the War Industries Board that ignores the predecessor Council of National Defense.

Crowell, Benedict, and Robert F. Wilson. *How America Went to War*. New Haven, Conn.: Yale University Press, 1921. An administrative history of the United States during World War I.

Cuff, Robert D. "Bernard Baruch: Symbol and Myth in Industrial Mobilization." *Business History Review* 43 (Summer, 1969): 115-133. Reinterprets the managerial revolution as it affected World War I, emphasizing the role of private suppliers to the government.

Higgs, Robert. *Crisis and Leviathan: Critical Episodes in the Growth of American Government*. New York: Oxford University Press, 1987. Stresses the expansion of the federal government's power during crisis periods, particularly wars. Maintains that the WIB had considerable coercive power.

Schaffer, Ronald. *America in the Great War: The Rise of the War Welfare State*. New York: Oxford University Press, 1991. A similar approach to that of Higgs, but more sympathetic to the rise of government power.

SEE ALSO: 1917, United States Enters World War I; 1917, Propaganda and Civil Liberties in World War I; 1917, Espionage and Sedition Acts; 1918, Meuse-Argonne Offensive; 1918, Demobilization After World War I; 1919, Treaty of Versailles; 1929, Great Depression.

1917 ■ CANADIAN WOMEN GAIN THE VOTE: *a struggle that began in the 1880's succeeds province by province*

DATE: September 20, 1917
LOCALE: Canada
CATEGORIES: Canadian history; Civil rights; Women's issues
KEY FIGURES:
Mrs. Gordon H. Grant (1875-1962), leader of several woman suffrage societies in British Columbia
Emily Howard Stowe (1831-1903), leader and organizer of Ontario's suffrage movement

SUMMARY OF EVENT. The struggle by women to achieve the right to vote in Canada spanned more than fifty years. With the exception of Quebec, the Canadian movement closely paralleled the one in the United States. Woman suffrage in Canada is indebted to the efforts of numerous women. Emily Howard Stowe, Canada's first woman physician, emerged as one of the most active and successful women in the movement, working intensively for the advancement of Canadian women. Stowe and several Toronto women founded the Toronto Women's Literary Club in November, 1876. Apparently, they called the group a literary club because of the negative societal attitudes regarding woman suffrage. One popular argument against women voting was based on protecting women from the contamination of politics. There was also a popular belief that women did not want the vote.

Stowe's efforts are notable for the courage and persistence she showed in working for the enfranchisement of women in the face of society's hostility. In 1882, the Literary Club successfully lobbied the Ontario legislature to pass a law permitting unmarried women with property qualifications to vote on municipal bylaws. In 1883, the club supported the formation of an organization focused completely on woman suffrage. This organization, the Toronto Women's Suffrage Association, went on to serve as a model for other suffrage organizations.

The suffrage movement in Canada had a distinct occupational and economic characteristic. Most suffrage activists came from a narrow spectrum of the female population, characterized by some degree of professionalism, self-employment, or economic independence, or they were the spouses of wealthy men. These characteristics were useful in gaining access to policymakers and withstanding the hostility and resistance to the movement. Unlike the suffrage movement in the United States, the Canadian movement was relatively quiet. Canadian activists were able effectively to employ strategies that relied on persuasion rather than the more militant tactics used in the United States.

The pattern for achieving political equality was initiated at the local level and ended at the national level. For example, by 1900, several provinces permitted women to vote for school trustees and municipal officials; however, as in Ontario, these privileges were likely to be restricted to unmarried women. Around 1900, suffragists began to focus their attention on gaining the provincial and dominion franchises. Between 1916 and 1922, women reached their goal of gaining the vote, except in Quebec. Between 1918 and 1940, Quebec women participated in federal elections, but not in provincial ones.

The first women's organization to support political equality in Canada was the Woman's Christian Temperance Union (WCTU). The WCTU began organizing in Canada on the local level during the 1870's. It used a strategy in which its workers petitioned local, provincial, and federal governments for rights. The most influential and recognized women's organization in Canada was the National Council of Women (NCW), but NCW did not compromise its status quo position during the 1800's by strongly endorsing and supporting women's political rights. It was not until 1904 that NCW established its Standing Committee on Suffrage and Rights of Citizenship, openly acknowledging support for the suffrage movement. At their 1910 Halifax conference, the NCW endorsed woman suffrage. The widespread esteem in which NCW was held made this endorsement extremely important for the movement.

The struggle for suffrage by Canadian women of the prairies was easier than among women from the remainder of Canada, because prairie women had tremendous support from male farmers. The rigors of prairie life required stamina and hard work from women and men, leading men to have fewer illusions regarding the equality of women. Prairie women had support from farmers' associations in Manitoba, Saskatchewan, and Alberta. The women founded associations at which they discussed and organized for woman suffrage. They waged the shortest and easiest fight, becoming the first to achieve woman suffrage in Canada. In Manitoba, success primarily was the result of a well-organized suffrage society, but in Saskatchewan and Alberta, success was mainly a result of influential farmers' organizations and their women's auxiliaries.

In other areas of Canada, women found support from organized labor. For example, in 1912, a labor convention in Kamloops, British Columbia, drafted a resolution that called for woman suffrage. The British Columbia Federation of Labor endorsed this resolution the same year. The Protestant clergy in several English-speaking provinces also came to the support of the suffrage movement. The Roman Catholic church in Quebec, however, consistently rejected woman suffrage. The English-language newspapers gave tacit support to woman suffrage; the French-language press, in contrast, did not hesitate to express their strong opposition to woman suffrage.

The British Columbia equal rights movement began in the mid-1880's. Suffrage activists in British Columbia were primarily isolationist in advancing their cause, unlike the Ontario activists, who were involved in suffrage work in other provinces. One of the most active members and a leader of the British Columbia movement was Mrs. Gordon Grant of Victoria. For more than thirty years, she was active in the WCTU and the Victoria Council of Women. Grant led a delegation to the legislature nearly every year throughout the suffrage movement. During the primary years of the struggle—from 1911 until victory in 1917—Grant and the Political Equality

League (PEL), under her leadership, led suffrage activities in the province. The PEL organized delegations, held public meetings, and brought petitions containing ten thousand signatures to the legislature.

External influences on the Canadian suffrage movement included women's activities in the United States. Canada sent delegates to a women's rights convention in the United States in 1876, which influenced the initiation of suffrage societies in Canada. Canadian groups participated in the 1913 suffrage parade in Washington, D.C., during Woodrow Wilson's presidential inauguration. Suffrage groups arranged for Dr. Anna Howard Shaw and Susan B. Anthony to speak in Toronto in 1889.

On April 12, 1917, the Ontario government yielded to suffragists and approved the right to vote for women. Eventually, all the provinces from the Ottawa River to the Pacific Ocean passed legislation for woman suffrage. In Ottawa, there were long, heated debates before the bill emerged from the upper chamber on September 20, 1917, enacting into law woman's right to vote. More than five hundred thousand Canadian women received the right to vote for the first time. The four eastern provinces granted women the right to vote soon thereafter.

The traditional conservatism of the Maritime Provinces— Nova Scotia, New Brunswick, and Prince Edward Island— held up their struggle for political rights for women. In November, 1917, it was reported that there was little opposition to the demand for woman suffrage, but a tremendous amount of indifference. New Brunswick, however, was very active in the suffrage campaign, mainly due to the presence of an active WCTU. Prince Edward Island was the site of very little activity, attributable to its isolation from the rest of Canada.

Of all the provinces, Quebec put up the greatest and longest resistance. The WCTU, organized in 1883-1884 in Montreal, was the first organization in Quebec to demand woman suffrage. Quebec's legislature refused to acknowledge bills and petitions relating to women's political rights until after World War I. The first bill proposed to grant the provincial franchise to women was introduced into the legislature in 1927. The Montreal Local Council of Women (MLCW), founded in 1893, was active in getting local political victories for women. The MLCW was the main force for women's rights until 1913, when the Montreal Suffrage Association (MSA) became a focal point for Quebec's suffrage activities from 1913 to 1919. The MSA was hindered by its English-speaking orientation and in May, 1919, it disbanded. Montreal was without a suffrage organization until the Provincial Franchise Committee (PFC) was organized on January 16, 1922. The PFC was organized under a dual French and English leadership.

In 1939, suffragists finally had a friendly premier in office and a legislature committed to woman suffrage. For three and a half months between the 1939 election and the opening of the 1940 legislative session, women intensified their campaign. On April 9, Bill Number 18 proposed to give women the dual rights of voting and officeholding in the province. On April 25, the bill passed.   —*Gregory Freeland*

ADDITIONAL READING:

Cleverdon, Catherine. *The Woman Suffrage Movement in Canada*. Toronto: University of Toronto Press, 1950. Excellent critical source on the Canadian woman suffrage movement.

Kealey, Linda, ed. *A Not Unreasonable Claim: Women and Reform in Canada, 1880's-1920's*. Toronto: Women's Press, 1979. Informative, analytical discussion.

Sheehan, Nancy M. "The WCTU on the Prairies, 1886-1930: An Alberta-Saskatchewan Competition." *Prairie Forum* 6 (Spring, 1981): 1-33. A close look at the regional approach to woman suffrage.

Stephenson, Marylee. *Women in Canada*. Don Mills, Ont.: General Publishing, 1977. A good general text on women's history and issues.

SEE ALSO: 1920, U.S. Women Gain the Vote.

1918 ■ MEUSE-ARGONNE OFFENSIVE:
heavy casualties in the final major battle of World War I underscore the necessity of well-trained troops

DATE: September 26-November 11, 1918
LOCALE: Northeastern France
CATEGORY: Wars, uprisings, and civil unrest
KEY FIGURES:
Ferdinand Foch (1851-1929), supreme commander of the Allied Armies
Douglas Haig (1861-1928), commander in chief, British Expeditionary Forces
John J. Pershing (1860-1948), commander, American Expeditionary Forces

SUMMARY OF EVENT. When the United States declared war on Imperial Germany on April 6, 1917, the U.S. Army, consisting of only about 125,000 officers and enlisted men, was not an organized, professional army with modern equipment or training doctrines. The United States found itself embarrassingly short of weapons, uniforms, accoutrements, aircraft, and other critical items. The National Guard, called to the colors by President Woodrow Wilson, numbered only 73,000 to add to the army regulars. The United States did have a huge reservoir of eager recruits, however, and plans were made to raise, via the 1917 Conscription Act, a national army to augment regular and National Guard forces. The commander of the American Expeditionary Forces (AEF), General John J. Pershing, knew that his force was ill-prepared for combat on the Western Front and, after his arrival in France, announced to the Allies that U.S. troops would need to be trained. The ultimate goal of the AEF, however, was to have a strictly American army, with its own sector of the line. Pershing received support in the form of training assistance and facilities from French general Ferdinand Foch and from Field Marshall Sir Douglas Haig, commander of British forces in France and in Flanders. Neither Foch nor Haig, however, was optimistic about an exclusive U.S. zone and the creation of a U.S. army.

Pershing firmly believed in a doctrine of maneuver warfare—getting the troops out of the static trenches, forcing an end to the war by destroying the enemy, and seizing terrain. He argued that trench warfare sapped the aggressive spirit of an army, and he distrusted the morale of both British and French armies after four years of trench fighting. Despite these feelings, Pershing placed the incoming twenty-eight-thousand-soldier infantry divisions under foreign tutelage in training areas and then in the trenches in so-called quiet areas. Pershing, however, stressed maneuver warfare without really knowing the impact of modern artillery, machine guns, aircraft, and chemicals on the battlefield.

By December of 1917, Pershing had four divisions (the First, Second, Twenty-sixth, and Forty-second) in training, but it was not until the German offensives that began on March 21, 1918, that Pershing allowed AEF divisions to see combat. They were then primarily under the operational control of French senior commanders.

One result of the German offensives was the naming of Ferdinand Foch as the Supreme Allied Commander. While Foch was frustrated with Pershing's obstinacy, he understood Pershing's desire to have a U.S. army in the field. In August, Pershing was allowed to form the First U.S. Army, with himself as commander. Pershing divided his army into three corps selecting solid but inexperienced, commanders for the corps. The divisions that would make up those corps were of varying quality. Those divisions that arrived early in France had extensive training and experience, but many of the new divisions did not. Division commanders and staffs had difficulty writing and overseeing the implementation of orders for subordinate brigades and regiments, let alone integrating air assets, tanks, and the like, which were habitually attached to the divisions.

During May and June, four hundred thousand troops made the dangerous ocean crossing. Supplies for this growing force were shipped by rail from the huge Service of Supply (SOS) base in Tours to depots near the Western Front. Yet the SOS remained critically short of heavy-duty trucks, and aircraft, artillery, and heavy weapons had to be begged from the Allies. Despite the shortfall in supply and the tentative training of many AEF divisions, Pershing pushed ahead with plans to reduce the St. Mihiel salient, a large bulge that jutted into the Allied lines. The bulge resembled a triangle, with the town of St. Mihiel at its apex and the city of Metz a few miles from the base.

Setting the attack for dawn on September 12, Pershing moved his most experienced units into line for the attack. The French sent combat divisions and augmented U.S. artillery with a large number of guns. Brigadier General William "Billy" Mitchell assembled more than fourteen hundred aircraft for the attack, and Major General James Harbord's SOS brought up vast quantities of supplies. When the attack began, however, heavy rains made roads impassible for the trucks of the SOS, tanks became bogged down, and aircraft had difficulty flying. Unknown to the AEF, the German High Command had chosen to evacuate the salient, fighting the oncoming U.S. troops with well-placed machine guns and artillery. For four days, U.S. soldiers reduced the St. Mihiel salient, and Pershing firmly believed that maneuver warfare had been proven. He also had promised Foch to have a large U.S. force in place to begin the Meuse-Argonne offensive on September 26.

Pershing hurried forces to staging areas for the offensive. His operational planners, including Colonel George C. Marshall, did not have time to reflect upon reports from the St. Mihiel operation, and a false sense of optimism reigned at the headquarters of the First U.S. Army. Pershing himself wrote that everyone at army headquarters felt alert and confident, but they set impossible objectives, disregarding terrain, the enemy, the climate, and the ability to resupply. Pershing's best and most combat-experienced divisions had yet to leave the St. Mihiel area. The attack would begin with less experienced, less trained combat divisions.

The Meuse-Argonne area resembled a box twenty miles long and about forty miles in depth. There were dense forests such as the Argonne and ranges of rugged, thicketed hills that had been turned into formidable defensive positions by the Germans. There were three solid defensive lines, the strongest being the second line, the *Krimhilde Stellung* (the Hindenburg Line). Unlike at St. Mihiel, the Germans had continually improved their defensive positions with machine guns and more artillery; most important, they had sent first-class infantry to the defense. Against these determined, dug-in defenders, the AEF arrayed divisions with little training or experience. The Thirty-fifth Infantry Division, for example, had had no time to work with its artillery prior to starting the assault against the first defensive line, and by the end of the first day, it was showing signs of confusion.

While Pershing was overly optimistic about the combat capabilities of his troops, his operational instincts were correct. He arrayed from left to right three corps of four divisions each on the start line—the First, Fifth, and Third—which were to advance together. The Meuse-Argonne was not the battle of maneuver that Pershing had preached. It was a head-on, frontal assault that pitted muscle against muscle, and the casualties were appalling. By the end of the operation, 120,000 U.S. troops had been killed or wounded, and the number of stragglers, those who wandered off from their units, numbered near 100,000.

Heavy rains continued, supplies went forward very slowly, and many of the wounded languished in agony for days before they could be removed to combat hospitals. By November, 1918, the AEF was reaching the end of its rope due to combat, fatigue, lack of supplies, climatic conditions, and the German defense.

The attack had begun on September 26 and in four days had ground to a halt. On October 7, Pershing ceased all operations and ordered the Twenty-eighth and Eighty-second Divisions to clear the Argonne Forest of German defenders. This they did, at great cost, for several days, but the *Krimhilde Stellung* had not yet been reached.

In mid-October, the AEF attacked the *Krimhilde Stellung*. Some of the best divisions of the AEF, such as the First and the Forty-second, were used up in the attack. On October 15, a brigade of infantry of the Forty-second Division, under Brigadier General Douglas A. MacArthur, established a foothold on one key position of the line. After another lull, U.S. forces attacked on November 1 with great success. By this time, however, the Germans were in full retreat. Continuing to take casualties against a stiff German rearguard action, the AEF finally reached the Meuse River on November 11, when the armistice was announced. The date would later be dubbed Armistice Day.

The fighting in the Meuse-Argonne came to an end because Germany was at an end. The AEF fought with grim determination, but the army that Pershing commanded was near collapse. Despite the horrendous casualties, Pershing and his many disciples came to believe that the battle had confirmed the correctness of their doctrine: that determined infantry with rifle and bayonet, supported by artillery and machine guns and air, was the decisive factor in war.

Due to strict censorship, few civilians realized the horrendous conditions under which U.S. soldiers fought. For decades, the extent of the slaughter in the Meuse-Argonne remained undiscussed. The Meuse-Argonne offensive, however, showed the fighting spirit of the AEF and fixed the concept that only trained, well-schooled soldiers should be committed to battle. Memories of the early confusion and subsequent combat in the Meuse-Argonne motivated men like General George C. Marshall to train and prepare troops extensively for the next great global conflict. —*James J. Cooke*

ADDITIONAL READING:

Braim, Paul F. *The Test of Battle: The American Expeditionary Forces in the Meuse-Argonne Campaign*. Newark: University of Delaware Press, 1987. A solid overview of the campaign, which examines the weaknesses of the U.S. effort.

Cooke, James J. *The Rainbow Division in the Great War, 1917-1919*. Westport, Conn.: Praeger, 1994. An account of a World War I infantry division, including material on the Meuse-Argonne campaign.

Hallas, James H. *Squandered Victory: The American First Army at St. Mihiel*. Westport, Conn.: Praeger, 1995. An indepth account of U.S. planning for and operations leading up to the Meuse-Argonne.

Pershing, John J. *My Experience in the World War*. 2 vols. New York: Stokes, 1931. Volume 2 contains excellent material on the Meuse-Argonne from the personal viewpoint of the U.S. general.

SEE ALSO: 1917, United States Enters World War I; 1917, Propaganda and Civil Liberties in World War I; 1917, Mobilization for World War I; 1918, Demobilization After World War I; 1919, Treaty of Versailles.

WORLD WAR I: WESTERN FRONT, 1918

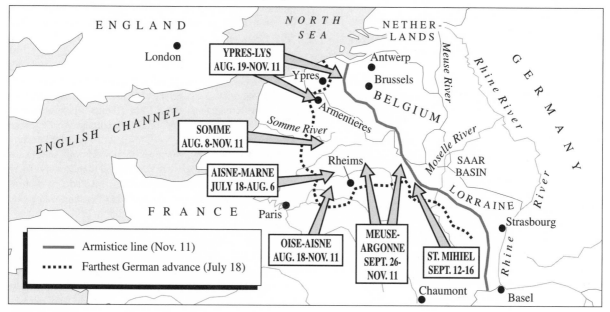

U.S. PARTICIPATION IN WORLD WAR I*

Apr. 6, 1917	United States declares war on Germany. *See* **1917, United States Enters World War I.**
June 14, 1917	General John J. Pershing arrives in Paris.
July-Oct. 1917	U.S. forces mass in eastern France (Toul sector); Pershing establishes headquarters in Chaumont.
Dec. 7, 1917	United States declares war on Austria-Hungary.
Apr. 6, 1918	PICCARDY OFFENSIVE: Germans attack Allied lines near Amiens.
June-July, 1918	THIRD BATTLE OF THE AISNE: U.S. 2d Division recaptures Vaux, Bouresches, and Belleau Wood.
July 18-Aug. 6, 1918	SECOND BATTLE OF THE MARNE: Defense of the area around Rheims ends the German offensive.
Aug. 8-Nov. 11, 1918	SOMME OFFENSIVE: Allied offensive, one of the longest campaigns of the war.
Aug. 18-Nov. 11, 1918	OISE-AISNE OFFENSIVE: Allies advance toward the Belgian frontier.
Aug. 19-Nov. 11, 1918	YPRES-LYS OFFENSIVE: Allied drive east toward Belgium.
Sept. 12-16, 1918	ST. MIHIEL OFFENSIVE: Offensive mounted almost totally by U.S.; ends German threat in the region and demonstrates U.S. military strategy.
Sept. 26-Nov. 11, 1918	MEUSE-ARGONNE OFFENSIVE: U.S. offensive cuts off railroad supplies to Germans, costs 120,000 U.S. dead, ends the war. *See* **1918, Meuse-Argonne Offensive.**
Oct. 24-Nov. 4, 1918	BATTLE OF VITTORIO-VENETO: Allies rout Austrian army.
Nov. 11, 1918	ARMISTICE: Kaiser Wilhelm's flight from Germany leads to proclamation of a German republic; Germans sign armistice halting conflict.
Jan. 18, 1919	PEACE NEGOTIATIONS begin, leading to the Treaty of Versailles. *See* **1919, Treaty of Versailles.**

*Canada automatically entered the war upon Great Britain's declaration of war in 1914, supplying food, munitions, and military personnel. U.S. participation came only after long-standing neutrality.

1918 ■ DEMOBILIZATION AFTER WORLD WAR I: *two million members of the American Expeditionary Force are reintegrated into the U.S. economy*

DATE: November, 1918-June, 1920
LOCALE: United States
CATEGORY: Economics
KEY FIGURES:
Peyton March (1864-1955), chief of staff of the United States Army
John J. Pershing (1860-1948), commander of the American Expeditionary Force
Woodrow Wilson (1856-1924), twenty-eighth president of the United States, 1913-1921

SUMMARY OF EVENT. At 11:00 A.M. Paris time, Thursday, November 11, 1918, World War I, the Great War, ended. News of the German armistice reached the United States at 3:00 A.M. via Associated Press. From the White House that same day, President Woodrow Wilson announced the armistice:

> Everything for which America fought has been accomplished. It will now be our fortunate duty to assist by example, by sober, friendly counsel, and by material aid in the establishment of just democracy throughout the world.

Events of the next two years indicate that Wilson was thinking primarily of his plans for the peace conference soon to open in Paris. The more immediate problems of demobilizing the U.S. armed forces and managing U.S. society itself seems not to have concerned him. By November, 1918, Wilson had planned virtually nothing in the way of a domestic program of postwar reconstruction. Preoccupied with the coming peace conference, he provided no program of his own and encouraged none from his administration.

Even the army seemed surprised when it suddenly faced the problem of disbanding the American Expeditionary Forces. Preparations for military demobilization got under way just before the armistice, when a War Department committee began making tentative plans and was faced with certain immediate problems. Should soldiers be demobilized by military units, and as quickly as possible, without reference to their employment opportunities or the industrial needs of the country? Should the army take the soldiers home before releasing them from service, or would several major mustering-out centers make for a more effective demobilization? In making its plans, the army had no comparable precedent and few European procedures to emulate. With the armistice, massive pressure arose to demobilize quickly. The soldiers' families wanted them home at once, and economic arguments were as strong as family sentiment. On November 11, the war was costing the United States approximately $50 million a day; every day's delay in demobilization added to the burden of taxation required to finance the army's upkeep.

One great problem faced by General John Pershing was timing. Pershing had planned for a massive U.S. offensive in the spring of 1919. Plans had been made for a huge buildup of AEF forces, including the procurement of supplies and the letting of contracts for facilities. After the armistice, all of those plans had to be reversed immediately. On the afternoon of November 11, Pershing received a cable from Washington, D.C., stating that on November 12, all overtime pay and Sunday work would end in the United States. It was clear to Pershing that economy was now all-important. Working with Major General James Harbord, his chief of supply, Pershing quickly identified a large number of contracts with the British and French that would have to be canceled immediately. There were loud protests from both London and Paris, as well as from local contractors and suppliers, but Pershing was bound by his instructions from Washington.

Pershing also ordered that all AEF schools be closed as rapidly as possible. Only those soldiers already in schools and halfway through their course of study would be allowed to complete the training. The massive Air Service training center at Issoudun, which was the largest in the world, would be closed by December, 1918. Several thousand pilot trainees were released from Issoudun by the end of November and ordered to report to processing stations for return to the United States. All over France, the process was repeated, despite the hardships caused to local concerns and protests from the French government.

The AEF at the time had some two million troops, equipped with thousands of horses, trucks, motorcycles, railroad cars, weapons, tanks, and planes. Most of the equipment, animals, vehicles, and weapons remained in France, there to rust, to die, or to be sold in a huge salvage operation. To bring the men home, the army had to find transportation. More than half the AEF had been transported to France in foreign ships, mostly English. At war's end, the British government, wanting to return its people to their countries and also eager to restore its maritime trade, immediately withdrew its ships from use by the United States, as did France and Italy.

The U.S. Army began to convert cargo carriers into troop ships. The U.S. Navy did the same with fourteen battleships and ten cruisers. Several confiscated German ships were added to the demobilization fleet. By June, 1919, that fleet reached its maximum: 174 vessels with one-trip accommodations for 419,000 troops. The fleet could have carried the entire AEF in five trips, with room to spare.

Acting with dispatch, U.S. Army chief of staff Peyton March, on November 16, issued orders for mustering out the first two hundred thousand troops. March expected to release thirty thousand soldiers per day when the process was in full operation. In the months to come, the War Department occasionally tried to demobilize according to a soldier's occupational skill, but such sporadic gestures did not occur until the great machine of military demobilization had begun pouring the AEF back into the United States from stations abroad. For nearly a year thereafter, the homecoming stream continued, reaching a peak in June, 1919, when almost 350,000 troops reached the United States. By September, 1919, only forty thousand U.S. troops remained in Europe, all of them either logistical units or part of the U.S. occupation force in Germany.

At home, demobilization went even more rapidly. In December, 1918, the army discharged more than six hundred thousand of those then stationed in the United States. By April 1, 1920, the U.S. Army contained fewer than one-eighth of 1 percent of those who had enlisted for emergency duty during the war. The U.S. Navy discharged with equal dispatch, releasing four hundred thousand persons within a year after the armistice. The U.S. Marine Corps demobilized fifty thousand in the same period.

Efficient though it was, this massive demobilization suffered delays and frustrations. In France, after the armistice, fifty-one new companies of military police were organized and kept busy as soldiers began to grumble and discipline began to break down. Paris and the French embarkation ports began to collect soldiers who were absent without leave. Barracks graffiti appeared: "Lafayette, we are still here."

Meanwhile, the machinery of demobilization did its job. The U.S. Quartermaster Service chose Brest, Bordeaux, and Saint-Nazaire as French ports of embarkation. Midway between Paris and the Biscay coast of France, at Le Mans, the army built an enormous assembly area for troops bound for the coast. At Le Mans or at the embarkation port itself, the troops received medical examinations, treatment from barbers and dentists, and new or supplementary outfits of clothing. They also went through a delousing center. Coming in from the Western Front with its filth and stench, nine out of ten U.S. service personnel brought with them the infamous louse, or "cootie," parasite of the trenches.

Once they had made the routine voyage across the Atlantic—during which not one life was lost—the troops docked at one of four ports: Boston, New York, Newport News, or Charleston. Each person leaving the army kept a complete outfit of clothing and various items of equipment, such as a safety razor. The enterprising Gillette Razor Company had designed and sold this item to the army, thereby changing the shaving habits of a generation of Americans while making a fortune for itself. The soldiers' duffle bags often bulged with souvenirs. Their eagerness for German Iron Crosses had become so great during and after the war that, according to one report, the Germans began to manufacture the item for the overseas trade.

Once back in the United States, soldiers were rushed through processing stations. Many were told to take all of their military equipment home; the government would send for it later. It never did. Each soldier was to receive sixty dollars in cash to buy a new suit of clothes. The processing was so rapid that a majority of the soldiers did not receive their Victory Medals. When soldiers arrived back home, they found they had no job protection, and many remained unemployed for some time after the war. Recordkeeping tended to be sloppy, given the emphasis on a speedy demobilization, and a large number of soldiers never had wounds or disabilities recorded properly.

While Pershing was under orders to send the troops home as rapidly as possible, he still had to send a sizable military force, eventually numbering thirty divisions, to occupy Germany. This newly created Third Army had to be ready to commence combat operations if the Versailles peace talks failed. The forces sent were the oldest, most experienced combat divisions Pershing had, which caused a good deal of grumbling among those soldiers who had been in combat the longest. U.S. troops were scattered from the port of Antwerp, Belgium, to the west bank of the Rhine River, with army headquarters in Coblenz, Germany. By the spring of 1919, Pershing had begun to send those divisions back to the United States. Many of those returning troops from the occupation suffered the most from the lack of employment.

Until the army of occupation had come home and until the U.S. Army had disposed of its huge properties in Europe, demobilization did not officially end. Portions of the occupation army remained on the Rhine until January, 1923.

Well before that date, the army disposed of its European properties. Pershing had been authorized to sell all surplus property on the spot, and the supply section of the AEF remained busy with contracts. Except for some 850,000 tons of artillery, road-making machinery, and other heavy equipment that it shipped home, the army sold its holdings in Europe or simply allowed them to disintegrate or disappear. The French government agreed to pay four hundred million dollars for some of it. The Czechs bought overcoats; Estonia bought army bacon; the Portuguese bought shoes. At home, the army disposed of much unneeded property through surplus stores. It gave up other items in sundry ways. For example, fourteen National Guard camps, three embarkation camps, sixteen training camps, four flying fields, four hospitals, and various other buildings brought a total return to the government of $4.2 million. One camp in Louisiana, built at a cost of $4.3 million, sold for $43,000 in "salvage recovery."

As army property diminished, so did its regular workforce. As soon as the war ended, debate over the size and function of the peacetime military force began. In June, 1920, through the new National Defense Act, Congress cut the regular army to 280,000 soldiers. It reduced this number still more in the next two years; by 1927, the U.S. Army had been reduced to little more than a token force. The U.S. Navy was reduced in 1921 to fewer than 138,000 men.

When Woodrow Wilson left the White House, the great military force raised to fight the war had been demobilized. Readjustment of those forces to civilian life, the dismantling of war industries, the return of people and of property (such as the railroads) to private industry, and countless other adjustments in United States society after war—all created enormous difficulties, many of which would be felt for another generation. Mustering out its service personnel was, by comparison, a matter of relative ease to the nation. In its broader meaning, demobilization and the consequent adjustment from war to peace would shape the history of the next two decades, until another war brought on an even greater mobilization.

—*Burl L. Noggle, updated by James J. Cooke*

ADDITIONAL READING:

Cooke, James J. *The Rainbow Division in the Great War, 1917-1919*. Westport, Conn.: Praeger, 1994. An account of one of the AEF's oldest combat divisions. Includes much information on the occupation of Germany and demobilization.

Crowell, Benedict, and Robert F. Wilson. *Demobilization*. Vol. 6 in *How America Went to War: An Account from Official Sources of the Nation's War Activities, 1917-1920*. New Haven, Conn.: Yale University Press, 1921. An invaluable work, written by persons who were involved with demobilization.

Hagood, Johnson. *The Services of Supply*. Boston: Houghton Mifflin, 1927. Written by a general in the Service of Supply who had intimate knowledge of the many problems caused by demobilization.

Palmer, Frederick. *Newton D. Baker: America at War*. 2 vols. New York: Dodd, Mead, 1931. Contains a solid chapter on postwar activities.

SEE ALSO: 1917, United States Enters World War I; 1917, Propaganda and Civil Liberties in World War I; 1917, Espionage and Sedition Acts; 1917, Mobilization for World War I; 1918, Meuse-Argonne Offensive; 1919, Treaty of Versailles.

1918 ■ REPUBLICAN RESURGENCE: *the elections of 1918 and 1920 ended an era of progressive reform and returned the United States to Republican dominance until the 1930's*

DATE: November 5, 1918-November 2, 1920
LOCALE: United States
CATEGORIES: Government and politics; Organizations and institutions
KEY FIGURES:
Calvin Coolidge (1872-1933), governor of Massachusetts and Republican vice presidential candidate
James M. Cox (1870-1957), governor of Ohio and Democratic presidential candidate
Harry Micajah Daugherty (1860-1941), Harding's campaign manager and confidant
Eugene Victor Debs (1855-1926), Socialist presidential candidate
Warren Gamaliel Harding (1865-1923), senator from Ohio and president-elect
Henry Cabot Lodge (1850-1924), senator from Massachusetts and chairman of the Republican National Convention
Franklin Delano Roosevelt (1882-1945), assistant secretary of the Navy and Democratic vice presidential candidate
Woodrow Wilson (1856-1924), twenty-eighth president of the United States, 1913-1921

SUMMARY OF EVENT. On November 2, 1920, radio station KDKA made one of the first commercial radio broadcasts in the United States over its facilities at East Pittsburgh, Pennsyl-

vania, and the first commercial broadcast of presidential election coverage. A small scattering of people, straining to hear through the static in their earphones, heard a voice reporting the election returns. The Republican candidate, Warren G. Harding, had won by a landslide over his Democratic opponent, James M. Cox, governor of Ohio, with sixteen million to nine million votes. The U.S. electorate, after eight years of the New Freedom, world war, and postwar tensions, had turned their backs on Woodrow Wilson and the Democratic Party.

The Republican resurgence began in the off-year elections of 1918. The strains of wartime politics and the mistakes of the Wilson Administration had disrupted the Democratic coalition. Midwestern wheat farmers disliked the government's price controls on their crop, liberals resented the suppression of dissent during the war, and business believed that the White House had been too intrusive in regulating their affairs. The Republicans were in an excellent position to gain control of the House of Representatives and a few Senate seats as well. Dislike of Wilson drew such former enemies as William Howard Taft and Theodore Roosevelt together against the common foe.

By the autumn of 1918, with the war obviously won, Wilson was looking ahead to the peace conference at Versailles; he did not want to go to Europe after having been repudiated at home. Worried Democrats pressed Wilson to provide an endorsement of the party's candidates to stave off a Republican victory. Despite the support that many Republicans had given to his foreign policy and to his wartime programs on Capitol Hill, Wilson issued a partisan appeal on October 25 for the return of a Democratic Congress. The Republicans, he charged, had been prowar but antiadministration; peacemaking was no time for divided leadership. The tactic backfired. For Wilson, the election was a stunning upset. On November 5, the Republicans won majorities in both houses of Congress, 49 to 47 in the Senate and 237 to 193 in the House. The Republican Party now had a strong base on which to build a victory in the next presidential election, still two years away. The Democrats found themselves confused and leaderless while Wilson pursued his foreign policy goals at Paris during the first half of 1919.

Between 1918 and 1920, Senator Henry Cabot Lodge of Massachusetts, the new chairman of the Foreign Relations Committee, had the difficult task of maintaining party unity. Senate Republicans were badly divided on the Treaty of Versailles, ranging from a minority of bitter-end isolationists who opposed it in any form to the majority who favored ratification with reservations. The isolationists could defeat the party in 1920 if they decided to bolt on creation of a League of Nations, one of Wilson's Fourteen Points incorporated into the treaty. As Lodge knew, Wilson owed his victory in 1912 to Republican division. If the League of Nations proved successful, that result might offset the domestic problems of the Democratic Party in 1920.

For his part, Wilson had failed to include any prominent Republicans in the American Peace Commission; he now had to accept Republican amendments that would give the League of Nations a bipartisan character, or Lodge would have to defeat it in the Senate. After Wilson suffered a crippling stroke in the autumn of 1919, he resisted all attempts at compromise. Lodge adroitly led his party to victory, defeating the treaty and the League of Nations while keeping together the disparate elements of his party.

Republican delegates were confident when they gathered at Chicago for their national convention. "Any good Republican," said Pennsylvania senator Boies Penrose, "can be nominated for president and defeat any Democrat." At the start of the convention, no clear front-runner had emerged. In the balloting, neither of the two leading candidates, Army chief of staff Leonard Wood and Governor Frank O. Lowden of Illinois, displayed enough strength to secure the nomination. Senator Hiram Johnson of California, another contender, had little support. With the convention deadlocked, the delegates turned to a compromise candidate, Senator Warren G. Harding of Ohio. He was the perfect dark horse. He had made many friends and no enemies in the Senate since his election in 1914. Tall, handsome, with silver hair and a suntan, Harding even looked like a president. He was an acceptable second choice to the delegates, and the next day the convention nominated him. The convention then did the unexpected and named Governor Calvin Coolidge as the vice presidential candidate.

The specter of the stricken Wilson, who had not recovered from his stroke, hung over the Democratic convention at San Francisco. After the Senate failed to ratify the Treaty of Versailles, Wilson sought vindication at the polls. He called for a "solemn referendum" on the League of Nations in the election of 1920. Wilson even hoped to break tradition with a third nomination and to barnstorm the country again on the League of Nations issue. His doctors knew that such an attempt would kill him.

The nomination for which Wilson hoped never came. Three contenders battled one another through four grueling days of roll calls: the former secretary of the Treasury and the son-in-law of the president, William G. McAdoo, perhaps the most able contender; Attorney General A. Mitchell Palmer, most recently noted for his anticommunist crusade during the Red Scare of 1919-1920; and Governor James M. Cox of Ohio. On the forty-fourth ballot, the convention picked Cox as the party's nominee and Franklin D. Roosevelt, the popular assistant secretary of the Navy, as his running mate. Cox, a three-term governor with a progressive record, had the advantage of not being identified with the Wilson Administration and its political failures.

The campaign took place in an atmosphere of postwar upheaval. Since the armistice, a wave of strikes, bombings and attempted bombings, race riots, and lynchings had frayed the country's nerves. The country had tired of Progressivism, bigger government, and higher taxes; it indulged in a period of intolerance and repression of minorities and unpopular ideas. In May, 1920, Harding had accurately captured the mood of the nation. "America's present need," he said, "is not heroics, but healing; not nostrums, but normalcy." Since 1896, the Republican Party had been the majority party, as more voters thought of themselves as Republicans than Democrats.

With his party united behind him, Harding had only to sit back and wait for the most smashing victory up to that time in U.S. presidential politics. Rolling up a 60 percent majority, he carried every state outside the Solid South, and even cracked that region with a victory in Tennessee, leading Cox by 404 to 127 in the electoral college. Socialist candidate Eugene V. Debs, a prisoner in the Atlanta penitentiary, received more than nine hundred thousand votes, about 3 percent of the total. The Republican resurgence took place because of voter disgust with Wilson and the Democrats, and a decade of Republican electoral dominance followed.

—Donald Holley, updated by Lewis L. Gould

ADDITIONAL READING:

Burner, David. *The Politics of Provincialism: The Democratic Party in Transition, 1918-1932.* New York: Alfred A. Knopf, 1968. Takes a close look at why the Democratic Party collapsed during World War I. Notes the impact of such issues as prohibition and woman suffrage on the party's electoral coalition.

Cooper, John Milton. *Pivotal Decades: The United States, 1900-1920.* New York: W. W. Norton, 1990. An overview of the Progressive Era that contains a good analysis of the last two years of Wilson's presidency.

Ferrell, Robert H. *Woodrow Wilson and World War I, 1917-1921.* New York: Harper & Row, 1985. A detailed treatment of Wilson's performance as a war leader, with coverage of key issues leading up to the repudiation of the Democrats in 1918 and 1920.

Gould, Lewis L. *Reform and Regulation: American Politics from Roosevelt to Wilson.* Prospect Heights, Ill.: Waveland Press, 1996. A political history of the period, with a final chapter that considers the Republican victories in the 1918 and 1920 elections.

Livermore, Seward W. *Politics Is Adjourned: Woodrow Wilson and the War Congress, 1916-1918.* Middletown, Conn.: Wesleyan University Press, 1966. A thorough study of the reasons for the Republican success in the 1918 elections, emphasizing the policy mistakes of the Wilson Administration.

SEE ALSO: 1918, Demobilization After World War I; 1919, Treaty of Versailles; 1919, Red Scare; 1920, Commercial Radio Broadcasting Begins.

1919 ■ TREATY OF VERSAILLES:

establishing a fragile basis for European peace, the League of Nations becomes the first global collective security organization, presaging the United Nations

DATE: January 18, 1919-July 2, 1921
LOCALE: Paris, and Washington, D.C.
CATEGORIES: Diplomacy and international relations; Treaties and agreements

KEY FIGURES:

William Edgar Borah (1865-1940), Republican senator from Idaho and leader of the "irreconcilables" in the Senate

Georges Clemenceau (1841-1929), premier of France

David Lloyd George (1863-1945), prime minister of Great Britain

Hiram Warren Johnson (1866-1945), former Republican governor of California and an "irreconcilable" senator

Robert Marion La Follette (1855-1925), Progressive senator from Wisconsin and an "irreconcilable"

Henry Cabot Lodge (1850-1924), Republican senator from Massachusetts and chairman of the Senate Foreign Affairs Committee

Vittorio Emanuele Orlando (1860-1952), premier of Italy

Woodrow Wilson (1856-1924), twenty-eighth president of the United States, 1913-1921

SUMMARY OF EVENT. While World War I had been raging in Europe, President Woodrow Wilson had begun to articulate the hopes of many people in the United States for a liberal peace. He believed that the victors could not indulge themselves in the luxury of vengeance: Only a just and merciful settlement could ensure a lasting peace. In early 1917, three months before the United States entered the conflict, Wilson called for a "peace without victory," with no indemnities and annexations to sow the seeds of future wars. Wilson sought more than a just settlement; he wanted to create a new, rational, international order. On January 8, 1918, addressing a joint session of Congress, he outlined his famous Fourteen Points. The first five applied to all nations: open diplomacy, freedom of the seas, removal of barriers to free trade, arms reductions, and impartial adjustments of colonial claims. The next eight revolved around the principle of national self-determination, listing the French, Belgian, and Russian territory that Germany must evacuate and promising autonomy to the subject nationalities of Eastern Europe. The capstone was Wilson's fourteenth point: the creation of an international League of Nations. Wilson envisioned, above all, the United States playing a permanent role in world affairs through membership in a collective security organization. Great Britain and France had already made secret treaties that violated several of Wilson's points, but on November 11, 1918, representatives of Germany, the United States, and the Allies, meeting in a railroad car in the Compiègne Forest, signed an armistice based substantially on Wilson's program. The Great War was over.

Two months later, on January 18, 1919, the peace conference convened at Paris amid an atmosphere of crisis. The war had left Europe in confusion. Half a dozen small wars still raged. As the Bolsheviks tightened their hold on Russia, communist hysteria swept through Eastern Europe. The conference, although sensing the need for haste, had to consider calmly the fate of much of the world. Thirty-two nations sent delegations, but the actual decision making devolved on the Big Four: Great Britain's David Lloyd George, France's Georges Clemenceau, Italy's Vittorio Orlando, and the United States' Woodrow Wilson.

Clemenceau, the cynical French "Tiger," was suspicious of Wilsonian idealism. "God gave us the Ten Commandments, and we broke them," he said. "Wilson gives us the Fourteen Points. We shall see." The Big Four approved the demilitarization of Germany, Allied occupation of the Rhineland, the return of Alsace-Lorraine to France, and an Anglo-French-U.S. mutual defense pact. These provisions, if maintained, would guarantee French security. Italy received Southern Tyrol, a region populated by some two hundred thousand Austrians. The conference also redrew the map of Eastern Europe. A series of new, independent nations sprang to life: Poland, Czechoslovakia, Yugoslavia, Austria, Hungary, Estonia, Lithuania, and Finland. The boundary areas of Poland and Czechoslovakia included large populations of German-speaking people. In the Far East, Japan took over German economic rights in the Chinese province of Shantun, while Great Britain and France divided up the other German colonies in the Pacific and Africa. The conference forced Germany not only to take full responsibility for causing the war but also to provide a "blank check" for reparations, including damages to civilian properties and future pensions. The Germans signed the treaty on June 28. They would later learn that they owed thirty-three billion dollars.

The Treaty of Versailles hardly lived up to Wilson's ideas of self-determination, although it left a smaller proportion than ever of European people living under foreign governments. Nor was it a peace without victory. Wilson did win acceptance for the League of Nations, however, with the League Covenant being incorporated into the treaty itself. The League, he hoped, would later correct any imperfections in the work of the conference.

When Wilson returned to the United States from Paris, public opinion favored ratification of the treaty and membership in the League of Nations, but the Senate would have the final decision. In March, 1919, Senator Henry Cabot Lodge had ominously secured a "round robin" resolution with the signatures of thirty-seven senators—more than enough to kill the treaty—announcing their opposition to the League Covenant in its current form. Wilson could count on the support of most of the Senate Democrats, but he could not meet the two-thirds majority necessary for ratification without a large block of Republican votes. A dozen or so Republican senators had mild reservations about the League; another group had strong reservations. These latter opposed Article 10 of the League Covenant, a provision binding nations to preserve the territorial integrity and independence of all League members against aggression. Senator William E. Borah was the leader of the "irreconcilables," who unconditionally opposed the treaty with or without reservations.

As chairman of the Senate Foreign Affairs Committee, Lodge played a crucial role in the fight over the League of Nations. Unlike the irreconcilables, he was no isolationist. He claimed to favor the League but with strong reservations. Yet Lodge possessed an intense personal dislike for Wilson and a distrust of his leadership. For two weeks, Lodge stalled for time by reading aloud the text of the treaty, all 268 pages of it. Then he held six weeks of hearings, calling witnesses who opposed ratification. At last, he drew up a list of fourteen reservations, as if to ridicule Wilson's Fourteen Points. Gradually, the mood of the country shifted against the treaty.

Wilson, overworked and ill, decided to go to the people in a whirlwind speaking tour. In three weeks, he traveled eight thousand miles and delivered thirty-six major speeches, typing them out himself on his portable typewriter. On the night of September 25, he fell ill in Pueblo, Colorado. The presidential train rushed him back to Washington. On October 20, in the White House, he collapsed: He had suffered a stroke that paralyzed his left side. For the next six weeks, the country was virtually without a president, and Wilson never fully recovered. When the treaty came to a vote, he passed word for Democrats to vote against the treaty with the Lodge reservations. On November 19, 1919, and in a second vote on March 19, 1920, a coalition of Democrats and irreconcilables sent the treaty to defeat.

The failure of Wilson's efforts to win support for unqualified U.S. participation in the League of Nations ultimately reduced the League's effective operation. As for the peace itself, the U.S. Congress passed a joint resolution formally bringing hostilities to an end on July 2, 1921. Despite the isolationist mood of the country, the United States eventually participated in a number of League activities, although never as a formal member. The absence of the United States from the League Council hampered its peacemaking capacity. More deadly to the League's future, however, were the growing nationalism throughout Europe, the deep resentment among the Germans with regard to what they viewed as unfair Versailles Treaty provisions, and the lack of consensus about how to deal with violations of League Covenant provisions.

Like many of Wilson's idealized Fourteen Points, the League of Nations was a noble experiment that foundered on political realities. The world was not ready for a global collective security organization, but the League's work in a number of economic and humanitarian areas did substantially advance international cooperation. These efforts, coupled with greater realism about power politics and keeping international peace, led to more realistic structures in the League's successor, the United Nations. U.S. policymakers played the lead role in fashioning the new organization, as Wilson had with the League, but they were more careful to build bipartisan domestic support for the United Nations as they seized, rather than spurned, global leadership.

—Donald Holley, updated by Robert F. Gorman

ADDITIONAL READING:

Bennet, A. LeRoy. *International Organizations: Principles and Issues.* 6th ed. Englewood Cliffs, N.J.: Prentice-Hall, 1995. Although focusing more on the United Nations system, this standard text devotes a full chapter to the League of Nations, setting it in historical context and illustrating how the United Nations evolved from it.

Heckscher, August. *Woodrow Wilson.* New York: Charles Scribner's Sons, 1991. In chapters 9 through 11, Heckscher recounts Wilson's role in the formation of the League of Nations and his fight for ratification of the Versailles Treaty.

Levin, N. Gordon. *Woodrow Wilson and World Politics: America's Response to War and Revolution.* New York: Oxford University Press, 1968. This award-winning book explores the social reform components and ideology of Wilson's diplomacy, given the wider dynamics of global politics, communist revolution, and conservative reaction.

Mayer, Arno J. *The Politics and Diplomacy of Peacemaking: Containment and Counterrevolution at Versailles, 1918-1919.* New York: Alfred A. Knopf, 1967. Places the Paris Peace Conference in worldwide perspective and stresses the role of communist hysteria in shaping the settlement.

Northedge, F. S. *The League of Nations: Its Life and Times, 1920-1946.* New York: Holmes and Meier, 1986. A comprehensive history of the League of Nations that critiques the organization and the global political climate that eventually led to its demise.

Stone, Ralph A. *The Irreconcilables: The Fight Against the League of Nations.* Lexington: University Press of Kentucky, 1970. A scholarly study of sixteen senators who fought the treaty.

SEE ALSO: 1917, United States Enters World War I; 1917, Propaganda and Civil Liberties in World War I; 1917, Espionage and Sedition Acts; 1917, Mobilization for World War I; 1918, Meuse-Argonne Offensive; 1918, Demobilization After World War I; 1918, Republican Resurgence; 1945, United Nations Charter Convention.

1919 ■ RED SCARE: *xenophobia and fear of communism reach hysteria in the wake of Russia's Bolshevik Revolution*

DATE: August, 1919-May, 1920
LOCALE: United States
CATEGORIES: Civil rights; Diplomacy and international relations; Government and politics; Immigration
KEY FIGURES:
J. Edgar Hoover (1895-1972), director of the General Intelligence Division, Department of Justice
Alexander Mitchell Palmer (1872-1936), attorney general of the United States
Woodrow Wilson (1856-1924), twenty-eighth president of the United States, 1913-1921

SUMMARY OF EVENT. Late in the afternoon of Friday, January 2, 1920, agents of the Department of Justice, in a concerted raid on reputedly communist headquarters, began arresting thousands of persons in major cities throughout the United States. They poured into private homes, clubs, poolhalls, and coffee shops, seizing citizens and aliens, communists and noncommunists, tearing apart meeting halls, and damaging and destroying property. Agents jailed their victims, held them incommunicado and without counsel, and interrogated them. Prisoners who could demonstrate U.S. citizenship were released, although often into the custody of state officials who hoped to try them under state syndicalist laws. Aliens were released a few days later, unless they were members of the Communist Party or the Communist Labor Party—two factions in the new U.S. communist movement. The Department of Justice hoped to deport these "undesirables." In two days, nearly five thousand persons were arrested; over the next two weeks, some estimates have it, another thousand were seized. The arrests were conducted without regard for due process of law, and the treatment of those who found themselves under arrest was sometimes barbarous. These raids were the climax to a wave of chauvinism, antiradicalism, and anxiety-ridden intolerance known as the Red Scare of 1919-1920.

In 1919, less than half of one percent of adults in the United States belonged to the newly formed communist movement, and even this minute element was ridden with dissension, conflict, and ineffectuality. Although U.S. "Reds" caught the full fury of the raids, it was not merely the communists who had stirred national panic. Emotions that had been building since the turn of the century were brought to the peak of intensity during World War I and required a series of domestic crises after the armistice to burst into overt expressions of xenophobic repression.

When Woodrow Wilson took the steps that led the United States into war in 1917, he dolefully told a friend that war "required illiberalism at home to reinforce the war at the front" and that a "spirit of ruthless brutality would enter into the fiber of American life." Required or not, illiberalism and brutality appeared. Radicals were a prime target, as they had been since at least 1903, when Congress had passed an immigration law discriminating against them, and especially since 1905, when the Industrial Workers of the World (IWW), a socialist labor organization popularly known as the Wobblies, was formed in Chicago. In September, 1917, federal agents raided the headquarters and meetings of the IWW; for two years, Wobblies remained in jail and in the courts, as the government sought their conviction.

The armistice in November, 1918, did not end the ideological war at home. The wartime crusade against anything associated with Germany never slackened but changed direction and surged into the postwar period as a crusade against things un-American—which, in 1919, meant radical or Red. Postmaster General Albert S. Burleson, who during the war had censored mail when, in his view, it obstructed the war effort, now censored mail that espoused radical ideas. Conscientious objectors, who had been imprisoned for their views during the war, remained in jail, because the Wilson Administration refused to grant them amnesty after the war had ended. The American Civil Liberties Union, created in wartime to cope with violations of freedom, now found even more to do. New patriotic societies that advocated "one hundred percent Americanism" abounded and sought to propagandize through schools and fraternal orders. In the summer of 1918, U.S.

troops, along with British, French, and Japanese forces, had entered Russia shortly after that nation's Bolshevik Revolution, ostensibly to renew the war against Germany that the Bolsheviks had abandoned. Whatever Wilson's motives, the presence of U.S. troops on Russian soil served to mark American opposition to the new Bolshevik regime—and, indeed, such opposition was well justified by the Bolsheviks' establishment, in March of 1919, of the Third International, whose avowed purpose was to foment world revolution in service of the new communist world order. Americans, aware of this and postwar atrocities perpetrated by Bolshevik revolutionaries against the old aristocratic classes, were vulnerable to the unreasonable fears that soon would be whipped up by politicians at home.

Amid this residue of wartime fears, a series of events in 1919 brought on a nationwide demand for action to crush what appeared to be a conspiracy to destroy the United States. First came a strike by city police in Boston, which newspapers promptly labeled Bolshevik. Next came a widespread strike in the steel industry, with the United States Steel Corporation playing upon existing anxiety by accusing labor of having Bolshevik affiliations. Labor leaders were trying so desperately to affirm their own "Americanism," that many U.S. communists actually opposed the strike as a futile trade union tactic. Next came a strike in the coal industry. Meanwhile, several public officials had been recipients of crude, homemade bombs that had been sent through the mail or thrown at them.

In early 1919, a congressional investigation into German propaganda activities quickly veered into an anti-Bolshevik investigation. During the summer of 1919, race riots in Washington, D.C., and Chicago, Illinois, seemed to confirm the suspicions of many that not only labor organizations and radical political associations threatened society, but so did African Americans, who were viewed as especially vulnerable to Bolshevik lures because of the economic, social, and political injustice under which they lived. As early as 1918, the Federal Bureau of Investigation had hired its first official black informant, convinced that radicals had already made significant advances in the African American community. Propaganda, often distributed by white supremacists and Ku Klux Klan members, went so far as to suggest that the summer riots were only a prelude to a Red-sponsored race war.

By the fall of 1919, public clamor for some kind of government action was intense. Attorney General Alexander Palmer responded to the swelling chorus that was demanding the arrest and deportation of the alien radicals who supposedly were instigating subversive events. In August, 1919, Palmer had established the antiradical General Intelligence Division in his department. At its head he had placed young J. Edgar Hoover, who promptly began to assemble an elaborate card index of radical organizations, publications, and leaders. On November 7, Hoover's agents raided the headquarters and branches of a labor society known as the Union of Russian Workers. Throughout the country, state and local officials carried out smaller raids on suspected radicals. Congressmen began to introduce deportation bills; one senator even proposed that radical native-born citizens be expelled to a special penal colony on the island of Guam. On December 21, a group of 249 deportees set sail from New York aboard the old army transport ship *Buford*, informally labeled "the Soviet Ark." In January, 1920, came the last and greatest raids, as the Red Scare crested and finally broke.

Although the public's concern over the intentions of the new Soviet regime can be understood, it is difficult, in retrospect, to comprehend the hysteria that engulfed Americans responding to small groups of poorly organized radicals at home. Social psychologists, however, explain the events of 1919-1920 as follows: People who are fearful of losing an established social and economic position in society may become hostile toward or fearful of those whom they see as threatening that equilibrium. They may be willing to launch a purge to seek to be safe from the "intruder" they see as the threat. Rapid changes in American life, brought about first by industrialization and urbanization and then by World War I, may have left many Americans in such a state of disequilibrium that they could not relieve their anxieties and regain their sense of security without taking some sort of action. The postwar drive for "one hundred percent Americanism" may well have been an attempt to reaffirm traditional beliefs and customs and to enforce conformity by eradicating the "alien" who appeared to be wrecking the traditional society. Deportation was literally a purge.

From the perspective of the present day, the actions that took place during the Red Scare may seem despicable. In 1919, however, a few thousand Bolsheviks had suddenly become the masters of more than a hundred million Russians, murdering the czar and his entire family along with thousands of nonconforming Russians. In the light of such an example, many otherwise fair-minded people in the United States were not inclined to allow a few thousand Bolsheviks to repeat the performance in their country.

Whatever the origins of the Red Scare, the raids and deportations sharply diminished after January, 1920. This decline of anxiety is even more difficult to explain than its rise. Perhaps the Red Scare never really ended; amnesty for World War I conscientious objectors and other political prisoners became no easier to obtain under President Warren G. Harding than it had been under Wilson. The U.S. Army conducted antiradical training and seminars during the 1920's. The restrictions on immigration grew tighter: In 1924, the National Origins Act imposed a quota system that drastically checked the flow of aliens into the United States. Throughout the 1920's, neopatriotic organizations appropriated the nationalistic rhetoric of the Red Scare to attempt to deny pacifist associations, such as the Women's International League for Peace and Freedom, legitimacy as foreign policy interest groups. Antipacifists invested words like "patriotism" and "internationalism" with meanings that linked the peace movement to un-American ideas and activities. These attacks often forced pacifists to

moderate their ideas and actions. Other measures, such as loyalty oaths, textbook censorship, and an "American plan" for labor unions, were characteristics of U.S. society in the 1920's.

Nevertheless, the degree of panic after early 1920 was minimal. The very excess of the raids aroused opposition to them and renewed an appreciation for toleration and freedom of expression. Secretary of Labor William B. Wilson, who, in his Immigration Bureau, had never condoned the antiradicals, regained control over them. It is possible that the final withdrawal of U.S. troops from Russia in 1920 and the failure of communist revolutions in Germany and Central Europe brought about a modicum of reassurance. In June, 1920, federal judge George W. Anderson, in the case of *Colver v. Skeffington*, found Justice Department methods to have been brutal and unjust, and its raids sordid and disgraceful. Attorney General Palmer, whose actions had been not entirely unrelated to his thirst for the presidential nomination, failed in his bid at the Democratic National Convention in 1920. Persons of moderation had begun to regain the initiative.

—Burl L. Noggle, updated by Christy Jo Snider

ADDITIONAL READING:

Craig, John M. "Redbaiting, Pacifism, and Free Speech: Lucia Ames Mead and Her 1926 Lecture Tour in Atlanta and the Southeast." *Georgia Historical Quarterly* 71, no. 4 (1987): 601-622. Examines the pervasiveness of Red Scare rhetoric in the attempts of antipacifist, anti-internationalists to discredit women peace activists and deny them legitimacy as a political interest group.

Draper, Theodore. *The Roots of American Communism*. New York: Viking Press, 1957. A detailed examination of the patterns, characteristic themes, and leaders of U.S. Communism in its formative years, during the period from 1919 to 1923.

Kennedy, David M. *Over Here: The First World War and American Society*. New York: Oxford University Press, 1980. This study of the impact of World War I on U.S. society and culture explores topics of race, gender, and radicalism.

Kornweibel, Theodore, Jr. "Black on Black: The FBI's First Negro Informants and Agents and the Investigation of Black Radicalism During the Red Scare." *Criminal Justice History* 8 (1987): 121-136. Discusses the hiring of African American operatives by the Federal Bureau of Investigation during and after World War I to enable the agency more effectively to scrutinize the large number of radical black suspects.

Murray, Robert K. *The Red Scare: A Study in the National Hysteria, 1919-1920*. Minneapolis: University of Minnesota Press, 1955. Analyzes the events, personalities, and fears encompassed by the Red Scare.

Post, Louis F. *The Deportations Delirium of Nineteen-Twenty*. Chicago: Charles H. Kerr, 1923. An account by the assistant secretary of labor in 1920, one of the few men in the Wilson Administration who showed restraint and a concern for due process during the Red Scare.

SEE ALSO: 1905, Industrial Workers of the World Is Founded; 1917, Immigration Act of 1917; 1917, United States Enters World War I; 1917, Propaganda and Civil Liberties in

World War I; 1917, Espionage and Sedition Acts; 1924, Immigration Act of 1924; 1927, Sacco and Vanzetti Are Executed; 1938, HUAC Investigations; 1951, McCarthy Hearings.

1919 ■ BLACK SOX SCANDAL: *fraud besets a beloved institution at the beginning of the era of national spectator sports*

DATE: October 1, 1919
LOCALE: Chicago and Cincinnati
CATEGORIES: Cultural and intellectual history; Organizations and institutions
KEY FIGURES:
Ed Cicotte (1884-1969), pitcher
Charles A. Comiskey (1858-1931), owner of the Chicago White Sox
Oscar "Happy" Felsch (1891-1964), outfielder
Charles Arnold "Chick" Gandil (1888-1970), first baseman
"Shoeless" Joe Jackson (1887-1951), left fielder
Fred McMullin (1891-1952), infielder
Kenesaw Mountain Landis (1866-1944), commissioner of baseball
Charles "Swede" Risberg (1894-1975), shortstop
George Herman "Babe" Ruth (1895-1948), New York Yankees outfielder who restored baseball to popularity with the home run
George "Buck" Weaver (1890-1956), third baseman
Claud "Lefty" Williams (1893-1959), pitcher

SUMMARY OF EVENT. The expectancy that grips the American nation with the beginning of baseball's World Series each year was even more apparent on October 1, 1919, when the great Chicago White Sox, winners of the American League pennant, were to meet the National League winners, the Cincinnati Reds, in the first World Series since World War I had ended. It was to be baseball's longest and darkest moment. So heavily favored were the Chicago White Sox that if a Chicago fan wanted a friendly wager it seemed as if he would be unable to find a bettor. Dramatically and suddenly just before the first game, much of what *The New York Times* called "smart money" began to be bet on the Cincinnati team. Even more surprising was the manner in which Cincinnati's Reds outclassed the White Sox in the first game, winning 9-1 and setting off innumerable rumors. When Cincinnati won the second game 4-2, the murmurs of incredulity became louder. Cincinnati went on to win the World Series by five games to three, but the rumors lingered well into 1920 and 1921, when a Chicago grand jury indicted eight members of the White Sox for conspiring to "throw" the World Series.

The trial was a farce. Evidence disappeared, witnesses failed to appear, three players recanted signed confessions, and the monthlong trial ended as inconclusively as the World Series itself. All eight players were acquitted, although it was clear that Arnold Rothstein and his gambling syndicate were deeply involved in the outcome of the Series. First baseman Chick Gandil was depicted as the initiator of the "fix," whereas third baseman Buck Weaver was banned only because he had advanced information about the conspiracy that he failed to reveal. Shortstop Swede Risberg, infielder Fred McMullin, and outfielder Happy Felsch were alleged to be willing participants, and pitcher Ed Cicotte, left fielder "Shoeless" Joe Jackson, and pitcher Claud "Lefty" Williams provided signed confessions, although the evidence disappeared. Jackson maintained his innocence until his death in 1951, but his confession, which reappeared during the hearing to reinstate his baseball status, is ambiguous. He admitted to receiving five thousand of the twenty thousand dollars promised him for helping to throw the games, but also stated (as reported in *The New York Times* on June 24, 1989, page A43) that he had played to win each game. That confession implicated Gandil and Williams. Chicago owner Comiskey was criticized for paying almost the lowest player salaries, despite the brilliant performance of the team and the highest gate receipts.

The new commissioner of baseball, Judge Kenesaw Mountain Landis, banished the eight White Sox players from the game, insisting that baseball had the right and duty to protect itself and its reputation. In spite of several attempts by the players to be reinstated, Landis upheld his ban, thereby renewing to some extent public confidence in professional baseball—possible in an era when there was less sensitivity to the civil rights of players. Jackson, whose .356 career batting average places him in fourth place in baseball history, would have been chosen for baseball's hall of fame long ago were it not for his alleged participation in this scandal. Baseball, and American sports generally, then entered their golden age. The often-disputed introduction of a livelier ball in 1920 may have radically changed the nature of baseball.

That year the Boston Red Sox traded to the New York Yankees a pitcher-outfielder named George Herman Ruth who was to revolutionize baseball and transform the nature of spectator sports in America during the course of the following three years. With "Babe" Ruth came the spectacular home run. As a result of the huge crowds he drew, the Yankee Stadium, seating more than seventy thousand spectators, was built in 1923 and called "the house that Ruth built." In 1919, the Yankees had drawn a mere 619,614 fans, but with the Babe in the outfield in 1920, the figure doubled to 1,289,422. He became an American folk hero, and crowds followed him wherever he went; with the instincts of a great showman, he rarely failed to give a spectacular performance. In 1921, he hit fifty-four home runs, and the memory of the Black Sox scandal faded amid the glamour and drama of a new era for baseball.

Perhaps the release of so many people from the rigors of war—combined with a new prosperity, shorter working hours, and the shift of the United States from a predominantly agricultural to an industrialized, urban nation—explains the sudden and spectacular increase in sports attendance in the 1920's. Although it was feared that radio broadcasts of baseball games would diminish gate receipts, they actually increased them. In addition to baseball, the forward pass in football had the effect of opening up that game. Crowds flocked to new stadiums throughout the country. Both Yale and the University of California built new sports bowls seating eighty thousand fans, while the University of Illinois, the University of Michigan, and Ohio State University built stadiums each seating seventy thousand people. Every Saturday during the fall season saw these stadiums filled to capacity, and Bowl Games at the end of the year were second only to the annual World Series in national interest.

Boxing also enjoyed popularity for a time as promoter Tex Rickard staged five consecutive million-dollar fights in the 1920's. The million-dollar "gate" in 1926 at the Philadelphia sesquicentennial celebration of the signing of the Declaration of Independence saw Gene Tunney beat the "invincible" Jack Dempsey for the heavyweight championship. Even this achievement was exceeded at the rematch before 145,000 spectators in Chicago's Soldiers Field on September 22, 1927. Enthusiastic fans paid a total of $2,650,000 in admission fees. The first ten rows contained more than two hundred millionaires, and twenty-four special trains brought passengers to the event. Tunney repeated his victory and retained his title; when he retired the following year, he had made more than two million dollars in two years.

Tennis emerged from its elite status, and stars like Bill Tilden and Suzanne Lenglen became public heroes after 1919-1920. Although fan interest in golf was started by Francis Ouimet's triumph over the English competitors in 1913, Walter Hagen and Bobby Jones maintained the public's infatuation with this game in the 1920's. In horse racing, the exploits of "Man of War" excited record crowds. In all major sports, heroes assumed gigantic proportions and performed legendary deeds. Red Grange, a football hero at the University of Illinois in 1925, became the first major college player to continue in professional football when he signed a contract with the Chicago Bears. Professional football, which did not come into its own for two more decades, started at that time. All sports suffered during the Depression and World War II, but the foundations laid during the spectacular 1920's were strong enough to ensure the survival of sports in the public mind. The Black Sox scandal marked the end of an era in American sports, but it also signaled the beginning of the modern epoch of spectator sports on a grand scale and professionalism in the field. —*Richard H. Collin, updated by John D. Windhausen*

ADDITIONAL READING:

Asinof, Eliot. *Eight Men Out: The Black Sox and the 1919 World Series.* New York: Holt, Rinehart & Winston, 1963. The most complete account of the scandal despite the paucity of evidence, much of it lost during the trial. The book became the basis for a motion picture of the same title produced by Orion Pictures in 1988.

James, Bill. *The Bill James Historical Baseball Abstract.* New York: Villard Books, 1988. This remarkable work contains a wealth of statistical and other unusual information not found elsewhere.

Rader, Benjamin G. *American Sports: From the Age of Folk Games to the Age of Televised Sports.* 2d ed. Englewood Cliffs, N.J.: Prentice-Hall, 1990. This standard work features discussion of the expansion of spectator appeal in the 1920's.

Reiss, Steven A. *Touching Base: Professionals Baseball and American Culture in the Progessive Era.* Westport, Conn.: Greenwood Press, 1980. A serious examination of the social effects of baseball on American society in the first part of the twentieth century.

Seymour, Harold. *Baseball: The Early Years.* New York: Oxford University Press, 1960. A scholarly and comprehensive account of the development of baseball from its amateur start to modern baseball, including economic aspects and the relation of the sport to American life.

Voigt, David Quentin. *Baseball: An Illustrated History.* University Park: Pennsylvania State University Press, 1994. Contains a review of the 1919 scandal and the revival of baseball in the 1920's and 1930's, by a recognized scholar of the game.

1920 ■ PROHIBITION: *reform wins a victory, but the attempt to legislate temperance behavior gives a new license to crime*

DATE: January 16, 1920-December 5, 1933
LOCALE: United States and U.S. territories
CATEGORIES: Laws and acts; Social reform
KEY FIGURES:

Alphonse "Scarface" Capone (1899-1947), Chicago mobster who made money bootlegging
Richmond Pearson Hobson (1870-1937), Republican congressman from Alabama
Herbert Clark Hoover (1874-1964), thirty-first president of the United States, 1929-1933
William Squire Kenyon (1869-1933), Republican senator from Iowa
Andrew J. Volstead (1859-1947), Republican congressman from Minnesota
Edwin Yates Webb (1872-1955), Democratic congressman from North Carolina
Wayne Bidwell Wheeler (1869-1927), general counsel of the Anti-Saloon League credited with drafting the Volstead Act
George Woodward Wickersham (1858-1936), former U.S. attorney general who headed the National Commission on Law Enforcement and Observance, 1929-1931
Mabel Walker Willebrandt (1889-1963), former U.S. assistant attorney general in charge of liquor law enforcement, 1921-1929
Woodrow Wilson (1856-1924), twenty-eighth president of the United States, 1913-1921

SUMMARY OF EVENT. National prohibition of the sale of alcohol had its roots in various temperance movements and in local and state laws. As early as 1851, Maine prohibited the sale of liquor, and in 1884 it passed a state constitutional amendment banning alcoholic beverages. Agitation to enact "Maine laws" became strong elsewhere. Thus, by 1917, thirty-six states had already become "dry." National prohibition was not far behind. Also paving the way to prohibition was a belief in human perfectibility, the conviction that drunkenness squan- ders family income and is therefore evil, and a shrewd political campaign spearheaded by the Women's Christian Temperance Union (WCTU) but propagated more effectively (since women did not yet have the vote) by the Anti-Saloon League and the Prohibition Party. The United States' entry into World War I in 1917 made the public more receptive to austerity measures, such as the conservation of grain (used in making alcohol) for the war effort. Federal precedents existed as well. In 1913, the easy passage of the Webb-Kenyon Act over President William Howard Taft's veto had made it a crime to transport alcohol from a wet to a dry state. A coalition of political forces, then—rural, South, Southwest, West, Protestant, and women's groups—combined with a prevailing suspicion of urban, especially Catholic and Jewish immigrant, traditions.

On December 18, 1917, Congress got the necessary two-thirds vote to pass the Eighteenth, or Prohibition, Amendment and submit it to the states for ratification. Section 1 of the amendment read as follows:

> After one year from the ratification of this article the manufacture, sale, or transportation of intoxicating liquors within, the importation thereof into, or the exportation thereof from the United States and all territory subject to the jurisdiction thereof for beverage purposes is hereby prohibited.

The required thirty-sixth state ratified the proposal on January 16, 1919, and the Eighteenth Amendment became law, effective January 16, 1920. It federalized the regulation of liquor previously under mostly state and local control. The enabling National Prohibition Enforcement Act, commonly known as the Volstead Act, was passed on October 28, 1919, overriding President Woodrow Wilson's veto. The Volstead Act incorporated the strictest features of various state laws. Fines would run from one thousand dollars, or six months in jail, for the first offense to ten thousand dollars or five years in prison for the second, while the dispensing store could be closed for a year. The federal government could also impound automobiles or aircraft used in transporting liquor.

The illegal sale of liquor, called bootlegging, became a growth industry, especially in urban areas such as Chicago, Detroit, and New York. Enforcement, despite the dedication of some federal agents, became a futile cause. Some police officers and law enforcement officials were corrupted by the criminal element; mobsters bribed or fought the "feds" as well as one another. Casualties resulted on both sides, but organized crime grew into a vast enterprise nonetheless. Many Americans, moreover, believed that drinking—at least beer and wine, long part of the traditions of even the oldest immigrant groups—was an innocent, even therapeutic, leisure ac-

tivity. The social reform era that had given birth to the temperance movement had given way to the Roaring Twenties, with their revolution in social outlooks, manners, and attitudes; such a time was least propitious for the legislation of morality.

Accordingly, illegal distillation ("stills") and do-it-yourself liquor preparation kits became commonplace. Ironically, the great success of the "drys" in making prohibition so restrictive and total proved to be counterproductive, even an incentive to try the demon drink. Women who had never entered a bar and some whose temperance-minded sisters had tried to smash saloons with hatchets were now "making whopee" in speakeasies, tasting the forbidden fruit.

Soon after taking office in 1929, President Herbert Hoover appointed an eleven-member commission under former U.S. attorney general George W. Wickersham to launch an investigation into law enforcement in general and that concerned with prohibition in particular. While ambiguous enough not to offend President Hoover, the highly divided Wickersham Commission's final report in 1931 seemed to confirm the breakdown in law enforcement and the disrespect for law in general that had grown up around prohibition, arguing for the repeal of the Eighteenth Amendment.

The following year, a Democratic Congress, after mustering the necessary two-thirds vote, mandated that an amendment for repeal be ratified by three-quarters of specially called state conventions rather than the customary state legislatures, to ensure the draft amendment's success. The thirty-six ratifying votes were at hand by December 5, 1933. Section 1 of the resultant Twenty-first Amendment reads, "The eighteenth article of amendment to the Constitution of the United States is hereby repealed." The "noble experiment" was history.

While all the states eventually repealed their own separate prohibition laws—Mississippi not until 1966—most of them returned to the licensing system. Local option laws against liquor remain in effect in many dry towns and counties across the United States. National prohibition nevertheless has left its mark on the American psyche. Its cast of characters included the "good guys" and "bad guys" that have become legendary parts of American popular culture, such as federal agents Eliot Ness and his "Untouchables," "Izzie" Einstein, and "Mo" Smith. Their nemeses included the likes of mobsters Al "Scarface" Capone, Johnnie Torrio, George Remus, George "Bugs" Moran, and Bill McCoy, but even respected middle-class citizens were known to have enriched themselves thanks to national prohibition.

Another legacy concerns the larger issue of the advisability, indeed the practicability, of legislating moral behavior. Not only did prohibition fail; it demonstrably undermined a social contract that resulted in cynicism and disrespect for the law. At the close of the twentieth century, references continued to be made to the prohibition debacle by those debating the pros and cons of legalizing some narcotic drugs. —*Peter B. Heller*

ADDITIONAL READING:

Cashman, Sean D. *Prohibition: The Lie of the Land*. New York: Free Press, 1981. A cultural historian distinguishes between fact and legend as they relate to prohibition and profiles its heroes and villains. Illustrations, bibliography.

Engelmann, Larry. *Intemperance: The Lost War Against Liquor*. New York: Free Press, 1979. Focusing on Michigan, a key location during prohibition because of its proximity to Canada, this work evidences how every community became an embattled testing ground for the "noble experiment" and why Michigan was the first state to ratify its repeal.

Kerr, K. Austin. *Organized for Prohibition: A New History of the Anti-Saloon League*. New Haven, Conn.: Yale University Press, 1985. Using previously unavailable materials, this work traces the history of the pressure group largely responsible for the Eighteenth Amendment but also its decline for both internal and external reasons. Illustrated.

Kyvig, David E., ed. *Law, Alcohol, and Order: Perspectives on National Prohibition*. Westport, Conn.: Greenwood Press, 1985. An excellent collection of essays by contributors examining various aspects of national prohibition, such as its constitutional dimensions, crime, enforcement, and history.

Root, Grace C. *Women and Repeal: The Story of the Women's Organization for National Prohibition Reform*. New York: Harper & Brothers, 1934. Chronicles efforts by the likes of the Women's Christian Temperance Union to continue prohibition.

Rumbarger, John J. *Profits, Power, and Prohibition: Alcohol Reform and the Industrializing of America, 1800-1930*. Albany: State University of New York Press, 1989. A scholarly treatment from a class-oriented perspective, using many original sources.

Sinclair, Andrew. *Era of Excess: A Social History of the Prohibition Movement*. New York: Harper & Row, 1964. A comprehensive, highly annotated history based on primary and secondary sources and describing the evolution of the movement since colonial times.

Spinelli, Lawrence. *Dry Diplomacy: The United States, Great Britain, and Prohibition*. Wilmington, Del.: Scholarly Resources, 1989. This well-documented scholarly study focuses on the impact of national prohibition on foreign, especially Anglo-American, relations in the light of rum-running from the British West Indian colonies to the U.S. coast.

1920 ■ LEAGUE OF WOMEN VOTERS IS FOUNDED: *on the eve of ratification of the Nineteenth Amendment, a new organization marks women's accession to political citizenship*

DATE: February 14, 1920
LOCALE: Chicago, Illinois
CATEGORIES: Organizations and institutions; Women's issues
KEY FIGURES:
Carrie Chapman Catt (1859-1947), founder and honorary president of the League of Women Voters

Marie Stuart Edwards, Indiana suffragist, first treasurer
Edna Fischel Gellhorn (1878-1971), Missouri suffragist, first vice president
Pattie Ruffner Jacobs (1875-1935), Alabama suffragist, first secretary
Maud Wood Park (1871-1935), first president

SUMMARY OF EVENT. The idea for the League of Women Voters was first proposed at the Jubilee Convention of the National American Woman Suffrage Association (NAWSA) held in St. Louis, March 24-29, 1919. The fight for woman suffrage, which had begun in the nineteenth century, was almost over. Nearly thirty states had conceded full or partial voting rights, and women in these states had helped elect increasing numbers of suffrage sympathizers to Congress. Enough pro-suffrage members had been elected in 1918 to guarantee that the Sixty-sixth Congress would pass a federal amendment enfranchising all women in 1919. At the suggestion of NAWSA president Carrie Chapman Catt, the Jubilee Convention voted to create an auxiliary organization, called the League of Women Voters (LWV), to operate in the enfranchised states.

In a dramatic speech, Catt outlined three goals for the LWV: to assist NAWSA in the last stage of the fight for the federal amendment; to press for removal of the remaining legal discriminations against women; and to work for more honest elections and a better-informed electorate. Stressing that ignorance and corruption threatened U.S. democracy itself, Catt proposed pursuing the last goal through a nine-point legislative program that became the mandate of the LWV's first authorized committee, American Citizenship. Its demands included compulsory education laws in every state to wipe out illiteracy and higher qualifications for citizenship and voting to "Americanize" an electorate heavy with immigrants. A second committee, Women in Industry, adopted a legislative program that incorporated demands for protective labor legislation for which women progressives had been working for several decades. Six additional committees—Child Welfare, Social Hygiene, Improvements in Election Laws and Methods, Study of Food Problems, Unification of Laws Concerning Women, and Research—were authorized without formulating legislative agendas.

Initially, the LWV was governed by a council of state presidents chaired by Jane M. Brooks of Kansas. At NAWSA's final Victory Convention, held February 12-18, 1920, in Chicago, the LWV ceased to function as an auxiliary and became a permanent organization with a new structure. The Nineteenth Amendment having passed at last, the suffragists voted to dissolve NAWSA and reconstitute as the National League of Women Voters. It was anticipated that the LWV would preserve NAWSA's organizational momentum for the new challenge of training women to become voters and cast their ballots for constructive social ends. Governance was vested in a ten-member board of directors, with the presidents of the state auxiliaries forming an executive council; headquarters were to be in Washington, D.C.

With ratification of the Nineteenth Amendment, granting woman suffrage, within sight, the National American Woman Suffrage Association reconstituted itself as the League of Women Voters to make the most of women's newfound political power. (Library of Congress)

From the board of directors, the convention elected Maud Wood Park president, Edna F. Gellhorn vice president, Marie S. Edwards treasurer, and Pattie Ruffner Jacobs secretary. Carrie Chapman Catt was made honorary president. The eight standing committees reported legislative agendas numbering more than sixty planks, which the convention endorsed. Resolutions proposed and passed from the floor included support for the League of Nations and defenses of freedom of speech and the press, both of which were under attack as the Red Scare prompted an ongoing government campaign against alleged subversives.

From the legislative program endorsed at the Victory Convention, the LWV chose thirteen planks to present at the Republican and Democratic nominating conventions, hoping for party endorsement. (A fourteenth demand, for the creation of a Woman's Bureau in the Department of Labor, was dropped after Congress passed the necessary legislation in June, 1920.) The first priority was the Sheppard-Towner bill, introduced in Congress the previous year, to provide federal matching funds for state programs to improve maternal and infant health. The women also asked for a constitutional amendment abolishing child labor, increased funding for the Children's Bureau, and new or continued federal aid for three educational objectives: combating illiteracy, improving home economics education, and continuing public education in sex hygiene. Other demands included a federal department of education, a federal-state employment service that would include women's departments, federal regulation of food marketing, and compulsory civics education in the public schools. Three planks dealt specifically with fairness to women: ending sex discrimination in the civil service; independent citizenship for married women, who at that time lost their U.S. citizenship if they married resident aliens; and independent naturalization procedures for foreign-born women, who acquired U.S. citizenship when their husbands did.

The LWV's agenda thus continued the pursuit of social welfare goals via an active, interventionist government that women's voluntary associations had sought during the Progressive Era. The Republicans endorsed five of the planks and the Democrats twelve, but the leadership of both parties united in criticizing the LWV's existence as an attempt to create a separate women's party and divide the electorate along gender lines. Confusion about the LWV's purpose also led some partisan women to denounce the organization, which they feared would duplicate their own efforts in political education and insulate women from political parties.

While Carrie Chapman Catt envisioned the LWV as nonpartisan and all-partisan, she at the same time encouraged members to join political parties as individuals and to run for office; women who held prominent offices in the political parties served on the national and state LWV boards. The dual vision proved difficult to implement, however, and provoked disagreement among the membership as to what the LWV's primary purpose should be. During the 1920 elections, some local leagues mounted well-publicized campaigns to defeat politicians who had opposed suffrage, offending members who interpreted nonpartisanship to mean not simply refusing to endorse candidates but avoiding all kinds of electioneering. Internal dissension combined with hostility from the political parties ultimately led the LWV to embrace strict nonpartisanship and to concentrate its focus on women's political education and studying the issues.

Controversy likewise developed over the LWV program. Some members argued that the League's extensive legislative agenda was too politically controversial, that it duplicated the programs of other women's voluntary organizations, and that it detracted from the goal of pursuing political power. Such criticisms led to the appointment of a Committee on the Simplification of the Program to clarify goals and policies, but the LWV continued to embrace social reform through legislative lobbying. The Victory Convention had directed the LWV to take the lead in bringing together women's organizations to work for legislation of common interest. That autumn, Maud Wood Park issued a call, to which ten organizations responded. On November 22, 1920, they organized the Women's Joint Congressional Committee (WJCC), and Park became its permanent chair. Working in collaboration with the member organizations of WJCC enabled the LWV to realize some of its primary legislative goals: the Sheppard-Towner Act in 1921, the Cable Act guaranteeing women independent citizenship in 1922, and a new child labor law in 1924.

Although the LWV had aimed to preserve NAWSA's membership and momentum, fewer than one hundred thousand of NAWSA's two million members joined the new organization. Carrie Chapman Catt had envisioned state and local suffrage associations dissolving and being reborn as leagues, but only Pennsylvania's actually retained the leaders and membership of its suffrage association. By the end of 1920, the LWV claimed organizations in forty-six states, but seventeen in predominantly rural states were weak and struggling. Local leagues were strongest in large cities where municipal reform movements had flourished during the Progressive Era; state leagues were most vigorous in the more heavily populated states east of the Mississippi River. Active city and state leagues in Connecticut, New Jersey, and New York developed techniques, such as compiling and distributing candidate records and analyzing pending legislation, that served as models for other states.

—*Judith N. McArthur*

ADDITIONAL READING:

Becker, Susan. "International Feminism Between the Wars: The National Woman's Party vs. the League of Woman Voters." In *The Woman's Movement, 1920-1940*, edited by Lois Scharf and Joan Jensen. Westport, Conn.: Greenwood Press, 1983. Describes the LWV's efforts on behalf of protective legislation for women workers.

Gordon, Felice D. *After Winning: The Legacy of the New Jersey Suffragists, 1920-1947*. New Brunswick, N.J.: Rutgers University Press, 1986. Chapter 2 offers an in-depth analysis of a state LWV.

Lemons, Stanley J. *The Woman Citizen: Social Feminism in*

the 1920's. Urbana: University of Illinois Press, 1973. This classic study of women's political activism in the first decade after suffrage is a good brief introduction to the League of Women Voters.

Van Voris, Jacqueline. *Carrie Chapman Catt: A Public Life.* New York: Feminist Press, 1987. Chapter 4 describes the last conventions of the National American Woman Suffrage Association and the beginnings of the League of Women Voters.

Young, Louise M. *In the Public Interest: The League of Women Voters, 1920-1970.* New York: Greenwood Press, 1989. An analytical history based on the organization's records and the papers of its leaders.

SEE ALSO: 1890, Women's Rights Associations Unite; 1916, National Woman's Party Is Founded; 1920, U.S. Women Gain the Vote; 1921, Sheppard-Towner Act; 1922, Cable Act.

1920 ■ MEIGHEN ERA IN CANADA: *the Liberal Party assumes leadership after nine years of Conservative rule*

DATE: July 10, 1920-September, 1926
LOCALE: Ottawa, Canada
CATEGORIES: Canadian history; Government and politics
KEY FIGURES:
Richard Bennett (1870-1947), Conservative prime minister of Canada, 1930-1935
Robert Laird Borden (1854-1937), Conservative prime minister, 1911-1920
William Lyon Mackenzie King (1874-1950), Liberal prime minister, 1921-1930 and 1935-1947
Wilfrid Laurier (1841-1919), Liberal prime minister, 1896-1911, and leader of the Liberal Party, 1911-1919
Arthur Meighen (1874-1960), Conservative prime minister, 1920-1921 and for three days in 1926
SUMMARY OF EVENT. When the respected Canadian prime minister Robert Borden retired in 1920, his successor, Arthur Meighen, thought that, like Borden, he would win general elections and serve as prime minister for many years. In both the 1921 and 1926 national elections, however, Canadian voters expressed their preference for the Liberal leader, William Lyon Mackenzie King, over Meighen. Although Meighen served as prime minister for only seventeen months, he had a long and distinguished career both before and after his service as prime minister. Historians now generally agree that positions taken by Meighen during and just after World War I made him so unacceptable to large segments of Canadian society that his failure in two general elections was almost predictable.

Meighen's background was modest. He was born on an Ontario farm in 1874. His father had emigrated from Ireland to Canada in 1843. Arthur completed his undergraduate studies at the University of Toronto. He then moved to Manitoba, where he studied law and was admitted to the bar in 1902. Thanks to his successful law practice and wise business

investments, he was able to ensure a comfortable life for his wife, Isabel, and their three children. He was elected a Conservative Member of Parliament in 1908. When the Liberal prime minister, Wilfrid Laurier, heard Meighen's maiden speech in the House of Commons in 1908, Laurier recognized Meighen's oratorical skills and perceptively predicted that he soon would become an influential adviser to the Conservative leader, Borden.

When the Conservatives won a majority in the general election of 1911, Borden became prime minister, a post that he held for nine years. Meighen defended the policies of Prime Minister Borden so vigorously and expressed such contempt for those who disagreed with Conservative policies that he created many political enemies, who never forgave him for what they perceived to be his insensitivity and arrogance. When World War I broke out in Europe, Borden and his fellow Conservatives believed that it was the duty of Canada, which still belonged to the British Empire, to fight with Great Britain. Many French Canadians believed strongly that European, not Canadian, interests were involved, and they saw no reason for Canadians to give their lives defending Great Britain. Borden tactfully tried to persuade the Liberal leader, Laurier, who was from Quebec, to support military conscription and to join the Conservatives in a unified government.

Borden understood the importance of not offending French-speaking Canadians. During heated debates in the House of Commons on the conscription bill, Meighen referred to Quebecers as "a backward people" because of their opposition to conscription. He then offended Canadians of German and Austrian descent by questioning their loyalty to Canada. In his position as minister of justice, Meighen argued that it was perfectly legal for the Canadian government to disenfranchise Canadians of German and Austrian birth who had become citizens after 1902. His argument that citizenship did not necessarily grant people the right to vote enraged many ethnic Canadians. In 1919, Meighen angered Canadian union members when he ordered the Royal Canadian Mounted Police to arrest and detain union leaders who had called a legal strike in Winnipeg. Although he admitted that there was no legal justification for these arrests, Meighen had no qualms about abusing his authority in order to end a strike. His actions in the 1910's persuaded Quebecers, union members, and many ethnic Canadians that they should not trust Meighen.

Although Meighen did not realize it when he became prime minister in July, 1920, his defeat in the next general election was almost inevitable. During his short term as prime minister, however, Meighen made a significant contribution to Canadian foreign policy. At the June, 1921, Imperial Conference in London, he informed the British prime minister, David Lloyd George, that henceforth Canada would not necessarily accept British control over Canadian foreign policy. Under Meighen, Canada began to become more independent of Great Britain. On the domestic front, Meighen was less successful. In 1920 and 1921, there was an economic downturn in Canada. Canadian voters decisively rejected the Conservatives in the 1921 election. The Liberals won all 65 seats from Quebec, for a total of 116 seats. The Conservatives won only 50 seats, even fewer than the 65 seats won by the newly created Progressives. The Conservatives went from 153 to 50 seats in the House of Commons. Meighen was defeated for reelection in 1921.

Despite this crushing defeat for his party, Meighen remained the Conservative leader. Four years later, a scandal connected with political appointees in Canadian Customs made King's government somewhat unpopular. No party obtained a majority in the 1925 election, which produced 116 Conservatives, 99 Liberals, 24 Progressives, and 4 independents in the House of Commons. With support from the Progressives, King was temporarily able to govern. When he realized that he was losing the support of the Progressives, King asked Lord Julian Byng, governor general of Canada, to dissolve Parliament. Lord Byng rejected this request and asked Meighen to try to form a parliamentary majority. Meighen accepted this invitation, but his government lasted exactly three days. Canadian law, which has since been changed, at that time required the prime minister and the members of his cabinet to resign from Parliament and then to run for reelection before they could assume their positions. Had they resigned, the Conservatives would not have had enough votes to form a new government.

Meighen came up with a creative solution. He resigned his seat in Parliament, but the members of his cabinet became acting ministers and remained in the House of Commons. King argued in the House of Commons that this was a violation of Canadian law. He accused Lord Byng of violating Canadian sovereignty by refusing to dissolve Parliament, and he further claimed that Meighen's new government was unconstitutional because his ministers had no legal authority. These arguments proved persuasive with enough Progressives, and a vote of no confidence carried by one vote. This time, Lord Byng had no choice but to dissolve Parliament. In the general election of September, 1926, Meighen tried to get Canadian voters to think about the Customs scandal, but King kept speaking about the constitutional crisis created by Lord Byng and Meighen. The Liberals easily won this election.

After his defeat in 1926, Meighen lived for thirty-four more years, but he never again played a leading role in Canadian national politics. He served in the House of Commons until 1930. The Conservative prime minister, Richard Bennett, appointed him to the Canadian Senate in 1932, where Meighen served until 1941. He then resigned from the Senate and once again became the Conservative leader, but he lost his race for a seat in Parliament. Meighen then moved to Toronto, where he became an investment banker. He died in Toronto in 1960 at the age of eighty-six. —Edmund J. Campion

ADDITIONAL READING:

Bothwell, Robert, Ian Drummond, and John English. *Canada: 1900-1945.* Toronto: University of Toronto Press, 1987. Contains a clear description of Meighen's quick rise to political power in the Borden government and explains why he failed to inspire enthusiasm in Canadian voters.

Creighton, Donald. *Canada's First Century.* Toronto: Macmillan of Canada, 1970. Presents a positive image of Meighen's campaigns against King, and many harsh judgments on King's actions.

Graham, Roger. *Arthur Meighen.* 3 vols. Toronto: Clarke Irwin, 1960-1965. This well-documented biography presents a sympathetic view of Meighen's lengthy career in public service and argues that his intense shyness caused many Canadian voters to conclude that he was arrogant.

Hutchison, Bruce. *Macdonald to Pearson: The Prime Ministers of Canada.* Don Mills, Ont.: Longmans Canada, 1967. The two chapters on Meighen describe his lack of accomplishment during his seventeen months as prime minister and his insensitivity to the aspirations of French Canadians.

Owran, Doug, ed. *Confederation to the Present.* Vol. 2 in *Canadian History: A Reader's Guide.* Toronto: University of Toronto Press, 1994. Contains an excellent annotated bibliography of historical studies on Meighen's service as minister of justice and prime minister of Canada.

SEE ALSO: 1911, Borden Government in Canada; 1917, Canadian Women Gain the Vote; 1921, King Era in Canada.

1920 ■ COMMERCIAL RADIO BROADCASTING BEGINS: *the 1920 presidential election returns give occasion to the first major commercial radio broadcast*

DATE: August 20, 1920
LOCALE: Pittsburgh, Pennsylvania
CATEGORIES: Business and labor; Cultural and intellectual history; Science and technology
KEY FIGURES:
Frank Conrad (1874-1941), Westinghouse executive responsible for the KDKA experiment
Harry P. Davis, Westinghouse executive who proposed regular public radio broadcasts
Lee De Forest (1873-1961), American inventor of the Audion tube
Reginald Aubrey Fessenden (1866-1932), Canadian colleague of Thomas Edison
Heinrich Rudolph Hertz (1857-1894), German scientist who first demonstrated radio waves
Guglielmo Marconi (1874-1937), Italian inventor who discovered how to transmit Morse code wirelessly over long distances
David Sarnoff (1891-1952), president of RCA who promoted radio as a commercial venture
SUMMARY OF EVENT. At 8:00 P.M. on November 2, 1920, the airwaves near Pittsburgh, Pennsylvania, crackled with sound as the tiny, newly licensed KDKA radio station broadcast the first scheduled public radio program, the presidential election returns. Using only a 100-watt transmitter, Leo H. Rosenberg of Westinghouse Electric and Manufacturing Company's pub-

licity department, read the returns as they were received by telephone from the offices of the Pittsburgh *Post* newspaper. Westinghouse, owner of the station, had announced the event in advance, and its success set off a boom of enormous proportions for the new radio industry. KDKA's successful transmission into American homes of Warren G. Harding's landslide victory over James M. Cox signaled the beginning of a new era: Republicans were again in control of the White House, Prohibition was in effect, and regularly scheduled broadcasts of radio programs had begun.

The birth of this remarkable cultural innovation was the result of a series of fortuitous circumstances. KDKA's broadcast was really a desperate move by Westinghouse. The company had long been a leader in the large vacuum tube and telegraph industry, but the end of World War I brought cancellation of lucrative war contracts, and the company found itself caught in a corporate squeeze. Its great rival General Electric (GE), along with American Telephone and Telegraph (AT&T) and the newly formed Radio Corporation of America (RCA), controlled the profitable field of international communications, as well as the invaluable vacuum tube—a device that had almost unlimited potential.

Modern radio technology had begun in 1888 when German physicist Heinrich Hertz demonstrated the existence of the electromagnetic waves predicted in 1864 by the Scot James Clerk Maxwell, who had presented a paper entitled "A Dynamical Theory of Electro-Magnetic Field" to the Royal Society. Guglielmo Marconi of Italy built upon Hertz's work and, by 1895, developed the first wireless telegraph designed to send Morse code signals. Great Britain was the first nation to become interested in Marconi's discovery and immediately began to explore its military and industrial applications.

The next major development in radio technology came when Reginald A. Fessenden, a Canadian who had worked with Thomas Edison, discovered that he could transmit not only Morse code but also the human voice and other sounds. By 1906, he and colleague Ernst F. W. Alexanderson had built an alternator at Brant Rock, Massachusetts, from which, on Christmas Eve, he broadcast to ships' wireless operators and amateur radio receivers throughout the world an entire program including violin music and poetry.

In 1907, Lee De Forest patented a modification of the vacuum tube. By adding a third element, called a grid or "audion," he increased the efficiency of the device both as an amplifier and as a detector. Considered a giant leap forward in radio technology, the Audion tube was only one of many contributions De Forest made to the industry. During his lifetime he was granted more than two hundred patents in the field and devoted his career to developing and promoting radio technology.

This flurry of technological activity in the early years of the twentieth century produced a cadre of highly skilled radio technicians. One such was David Sarnoff, an immigrant wireless operator with American Marconi, a company that eventually formed the core of RCA. In 1912 Sarnoff had manned a

wireless set that kept in contact with ships in the vicinity of the *Titanic* as it sank. His dramatic effort captured public attention and generated intense interest in the potential of wireless telephony among the world's giant communications and electrical companies.

Radio's future was still hazy when World War I broke out. The war, however, proved to be a blessing for the radio industry, the promise of which had been dimmed by numerous costly and time-consuming patent disputes. Faced with the emergency of war, the government suspended all such disputes for the duration and pushed forward the full production of vacuum tubes, receivers, transmitters, and a whole range of complex electrical equipment. A giant Alexanderson transmitter at New Brunswick, New Jersey, using the call letters NFF, astounded the world by clearly broadcasting President Woodrow Wilson's Fourteen Points throughout Europe on January 18, 1918. Later in the year, NFF epitomized Wilson's principles of open diplomacy by publicly demanding the overthrow of the kaiser as a prelude to peace.

Many of those involved in radio were aware of the potential of the new electronics. When the war ended and restrictions on electronic equipment were lifted, it was merely a matter of time as to who would first dramatize the possibilities of radio. One who tried was Detroit publisher William E. Scripps, who built a receiver for his son. Using the call letters 8MK, he began broadcasting tests that extended news reports to the airwaves. These tests ended on primary day, August 31, 1920, just months before KDKA made its move.

In Pittsburgh several Westinghouse workers had been experimenting with radio for some time and began to broadcast amateur programs using transmitters built by Frank Conrad, a company executive, in his garage. Harry P. Davis, a Westinghouse vice president, became aware of the commercial possibilities of radio programs when he learned that a local department store was advertising receivers by promoting Conrad's broadcasts. Davis called a conference with other Westinghouse officials and proposed the idea of offering radio broadcasts on a regular basis to the general public. Westinghouse could then manufacture and sell radio sets intended for home use that consumers could use to receive these broadcasts. He proposed trying to have everything in place to broadcast the upcoming election returns. Westinghouse applied to the United States Department of Commerce for a license to begin regular broadcasting and, on October 27, 1920, received notification that the station was to have the call letters KDKA.

Others had tried to make radio a commercial venture. Sarnoff, for example, early grasped the potential of a huge market for radios. As early as 1916, he had declared that radio might become as popular in the home as the phonograph. In January, 1920, he tried to persuade officials of the newly formed RCA to market radio "music boxes" at seventy-five dollars each. He predicted that if they did so, the company would be able to realize an income of seventy-five million dollars in only three years. Unconvinced, the company committed only two thousand dollars to research in radios.

The first station to begin commercial radio broadcasting was actually WWJ in Detroit, on August 20, 1920. After KDKA's groundbreaking broadcast, however, most people in the industry became convinced of radio's commercial possibilities. Westinghouse, whose fortunes were reversed, assumed leadership in the field. Members of the industry at first expected to earn profits primarily through the sale of transmitting and receiving equipment. The early programs, which were usually informal, emphasized entertainment including music and occasionally such dramatic events as the World Series, which was broadcast for the first time in 1921. Broadcasters soon realized, however, that radio could earn profits through the sale of advertising time. The role of radio as an advertising medium began on August 22, 1922, when station WEAF in New York sold a ten-minute "spot" for a commercial message.

As the radio mania swept the country, it became apparent that the industry would have to be regulated. Prior to the first commercial broadcasts, the Radio Law of 1912 had assigned licensing responsibilities to the Department of Commerce. That system proved unwieldy so, in 1927, Congress passed new legislation establishing the Federal Radio Commission, the forerunner of the Federal Communications Commission (FCC). Radio remained the primary vehicle of the electronic mass media until the advent of television. It was and is a crucial part of American life and culture, the roots of which can be traced to that initial commercial broadcast from a garage in Pittsburgh.

—*Richard H. Collin, updated by Jane M. Gilliland*

ADDITIONAL READING:

Barnouw, Erik. *A Tower in Babel: A History of Broadcasting in the United States.* 3 vols. New York: Oxford University Press, 1966. Volume 1 focuses on radio's shift from a largely private industry to a public one. Photographs, bibliography, index.

Douglas, George H. *The Early Days of Radio Broadcasting.* Jefferson, N.C.: McFarland, 1987. Examines radio broadcasting during the 1920's, when the industry "grew from an infant to a giant." Chapter 1 covers KDKA. Illustrations, bibliography, index.

Douglas, Susan J. *Inventing American Broadcasting, 1899-1922.* Baltimore: The Johns Hopkins University Press, 1987. Douglas discusses both the technical development of radio and its social and political implications in the United States. Illustrations, notes, index.

Lewis, Tom. *Empire of the Air: The Men Who Made Radio.* New York: Edward Burlingame, 1991. An overview of the development of commercial radio. Chapter 6 focuses on the quest to broadcast to the general public. Photographs, bibliography, index.

Smulyan, Susan. *Selling Radio: The Commercialization of American Broadcasting, 1920-1934.* Washington, D.C.: Smithsonian Institution Press, 1994. Smulyan details how the American radio business evolved from one that was privately financed to one supported by commercial advertising. Notes, illustrations, index.

SEE ALSO: 1844, First Telegraph Message; 1858, First Transatlantic Cable; 1861, Transcontinental Telegraph Is Completed; 1876, Bell Demonstrates the Telephone; 1879, Edison Demonstrates the Incandescent Lamp; 1900, Teletype Is Developed; 1918, Republican Resurgence; 1939, Debut of Commercial Television.

1920 ■ U.S. WOMEN GAIN THE VOTE:
after more than a century of struggle, the Nineteenth Amendment becomes law

DATE: August 26, 1920
LOCALE: United States
CATEGORIES: Civil rights; Laws and acts; Women's issues
KEY FIGURES:
Susan B. Anthony (1820-1906), founder of the movement pledged to gain the vote for women
Carrie Chapman Catt (1859-1947), suffragist who developed the Winning Plan
Alice Paul (1885-1977), promoter of the drive for a federal woman suffrage amendment
Elizabeth Cady Stanton (1815-1902), founder of the nineteenth century movement for women's rights
Lucy Stone (1818-1893), founder of the American Woman Suffrage Association

SUMMARY OF EVENT. "We hold these truths to be self-evident, that all men and women are created equal. . . ." Written in 1848 at the first Women's Rights Convention, held at Seneca Falls, New York, these words announced the opening of a new movement in which the goal was to establish political, social, and economic equality for men and women. Although the campaign for the vote created the greatest public outcry, suffrage was merely one facet of the larger struggle of women to enter the professions, to own property, and to enjoy the same legal rights as men. By attaining these goals, nineteenth century reformers hoped to see women emerge from second-class citizenship to a status equal to that of their male counterparts.

The 1848 meeting was not an isolated phenomenon; it was part of the general reform spirit of the period. Prosperous middle and upper classes had developed in large urban centers along the Atlantic seaboard. This prosperity had created a new, leisured class of women who could devote at least part of their time to worthy causes. Many chose to support the cause of women's rights in some way. Both men and women worked for social reforms. As each effort was successful, it inevitably led to others, thus creating a climate in which reform prospered. This process could be seen most clearly in the 1830's and 1840's, again in the Reconstruction period, and in the first two decades of the twentieth century. These three periods saw changes in the legal, social, and economic positions of African Americans, women, and labor. As their problems were interrelated, advancement for one group normally brought some gains for the others.

The moving force behind the 1848 meeting and the establishment of an Equal Rights Association was Elizabeth Cady Stanton. Like many other activists for women, Stanton came to the issue from the abolitionist movement. Many of the mid-nineteenth century reformers saw parallels between the position of slaves and the position of all women. Both groups were regarded by society as inherently inferior. Many abolitionists also believed that only when women enjoyed full rights to participate in the political process would they achieve their goal of a more egalitarian society. Thus, from the outset, the idea of women's political rights was regarded by their supporters as both a means and an end in itself. In the early years, Stanton's most important coworkers were Susan B. Anthony and Lucy Stone. Anthony later emerged as the organizing genius of the suffrage drive. Her administrative talents provided a perfect complement to Stanton's gifts as a writer and theoretician.

Although the Equal Rights Association was chronically short of funds, it managed to establish a short-lived newspaper, sponsor hundreds of speeches, and organize women's groups to petition and lobby for the vote in their home states. During the Civil War era, pressure for equal rights was submerged, first by the demand for the abolition of slavery and later by the drive to pass the Fifteenth Amendment. Male abolitionists promised that if women would work to secure suffrage for black men, their turn would come next. Thus the Equal Rights Association was placed in the position of working for a suffrage amendment that did not include women among its beneficiaries.

Anthony and Stanton found such a position intolerable and founded the National Woman Suffrage Association (NWSA) in 1869. Stone, who accepted that women must step aside during "the Negro's hour" of Reconstruction, formed the rival American Woman Suffrage Association (AWSA) that same year. The split in suffrage organizations reflected differences of personality and strategy. The AWSA concentrated on the suffrage as its sole issue and followed a plan to educate citizens to try to achieve votes for women on a state-by-state basis. The NWSA at first allied itself with anyone who supported women's rights, including the self-proclaimed free-love advocate and presidential candidate Victoria Woodhull. After enduring great criticism and financial loss for its endorsement of Woodhull, the NWSA also decided to focus most of its efforts on the suffrage. In 1889, the rival woman suffrage organizations decided to present a united front, and they merged to form the National American Woman Suffrage Association.

The 1890's saw the death or retirement of most of the original suffrage leaders, but fortunately for the movement, the new century brought new leaders, such as Harriot Stanton Blatch, Carrie Chapman Catt, and Alice Paul; new organizations, such as the Boston Equal Suffrage Association for Good Government, the College Equal Suffrage League (1901), and the Congressional Union (1912), later called the Woman's Party; and the adoption of new techniques and ideas. Leaders and participants were better educated and better off financially than before, and in the early twentieth century, the woman suffrage movement joined with other efforts to make the U.S. system more democratic and more just. The crusade for votes for women was an integral part of the Progressive movement and took strength from the widespread support for reform.

Suffragists had learned from the more militant English movement the value of publicity to call attention to themselves. To speeches and petitions, they added mass picketing, demonstrations, and rallies, including a huge suffrage parade in Washington, D.C., in 1913. On that day, when president-elect Woodrow Wilson arrived for his inauguration, he wondered why no crowd met him at the station. People were watching the suffrage parade instead, seeing marchers attacked by boisterous bystanders and rescued by federal troops. The parade drew national attention to the suffrage movement and led to congressional hearings.

Not only did the method of focusing attention on the issue of suffrage change, but also the means for attaining the end. The NAWSA realized that the only way to achieve national woman suffrage was through an amendment to the federal constitution. In 1915, Carrie Chapman Catt became the organization's president. Having helped to orchestrate adoption of woman suffrage in the states of Idaho, Colorado, Washington, California, and Illinois, Catt brought superb organizing skills to the NAWSA. In 1916, she developed her Winning Plan, by which suffragists would move on all fronts. In the states where women could vote, they would pressure their legislatures to urge Congress to pass a federal amendment. The NAWSA set up a Washington, D.C., office with a million-dollar budget to lobby President Wilson and the legislators. Alice Paul and the Woman's Party picketed the White House with banners asking, "Mr. President! How Long Must Women Wait for Liberty?"

Inside and outside Washington, opponents of suffragists also prepared for a struggle. In the conservative South, white supremacists believed that raising the question of votes for women would reopen the question of the black vote. In other states, the traditional friendship between prohibitionists and advocates of women's rights led to liquor interests' financing successful campaigns against woman suffrage. Anti-suffragist groups also drew support from business groups that feared that voting women would eliminate child labor and lead to pressure to improve other working conditions.

Although both political parties included statements endorsing woman suffrage in their 1916 platforms, they failed to translate the words into action after the election, when national attention was focused on European events. The United States' entry into World War I in 1917 led to arguments about the priority of winning the vote versus winning the war. While the more conservative women worked harder for the second goal, others redoubled their efforts for suffrage. How, Paul demanded, could President Wilson talk of fighting for democracy abroad and deny American women the right to vote? The Woman's Party continued picketing the White House, carrying placards addressed to "Kaiser Wilson." Suffragists were denounced as traitors, and many were arrested and sentenced to jail for disturbing the peace. There, the women protested conditions and demanded to be treated as political prisoners. They finally went on a hunger strike. When the public read of the women's miserable imprisonment, including the painful force-feeding of the hunger strikers, popular opinion forced the administration to release the prisoners and drop the charges.

President Wilson endorsed woman suffrage but considered other problems to be more pressing. With his recommendation, the amendment passed the House in 1918 in a dramatic vote, with one member leaving the deathbed of his suffragist wife to cast an affirmative ballot. Although the Senate rejected the amendment in 1918, public opinion was firmly on the side of woman suffrage, and by the following year, passage was inevitable. On June 4, 1919, the proposed amendment passed the Senate and was submitted to the states. On his mother's advice, the youngest member of the Tennessee legislature cast the deciding vote in the decisive state. On August 16, 1920, U.S. women were enfranchised, after seventy-two years and countless hours of work and determination, beginning with the Seneca Falls meeting. Passage of the Nineteenth Amendment opened the door to full citizenship for women in the United States, a necessary step on the road to full equality.

—Anne Trotter, updated by Mary Welek Atwell

ADDITIONAL READING:

Cott, Nancy F. *The Grounding of Modern Feminism.* New Haven, Conn.: Yale University Press, 1987. Views the suffrage movement in the context of a transition from women's rights to feminism.

Evans, Sara M. *Born for Liberty: A History of Women in America.* New York: Free Press, 1989. Discusses diversity, race, and class issues among the advocates of women's rights.

Flexner, Eleanor. *Century of Struggle: The Woman's Rights Movement in the United States.* Rev. ed. Cambridge, Mass.: The Belknap Press of Harvard University Press, 1975. Remains the standard source on the women's movement through the ratification of the Nineteenth Amendment.

Scott, Anne Firor, and Andrew M. Scott. *One Half the People: The Fight for Woman Suffrage.* Philadelphia: J. B. Lippincott, 1975. An exhaustive treatment of the persons and organizations who won women's right to vote.

Woloch, Nancy. *Women and the American Experience.* 2d ed. New York: McGraw-Hill, 1994. Contains a long chapter on the suffrage that examines the movement's meaning to the women who participated in it.

SEE ALSO: 1848, Seneca Falls Convention; 1851, Akron Woman's Rights Convention; 1866, Suffragists Protest the Fourteenth Amendment; 1869, Rise of Woman Suffrage Associations; 1869, Western States Grant Woman Suffrage; 1872, Susan B. Anthony Is Arrested; 1874, *Minor v. Happersett*; 1876, Declaration of the Rights of Women; 1890, Women's Rights Associations Unite; 1916, National Woman's Party Is Founded; 1917, Canadian Women Gain the Vote; 1920, League of Women Voters Is Founded; 1923, Proposal of the Equal Rights Amendment.

1921 ■ SCANDALS OF THE HARDING ADMINISTRATION: *among the worst instances of corruption since Grant's administration and prior to the Watergate affair*

DATE: 1921-1923
LOCALE: Washington, D.C.
CATEGORY: Government and politics
KEY FIGURES:

Calvin Coolidge (1872-1933), Harding's vice president and successor in 1923
Harry Micajah Daugherty (1860-1941), Harding's attorney general
Edward Laurence Doheny (1856-1935), owner of the Pan-American Petroleum Company
Albert Bacon Fall (1861-1944), Harding's secretary of the Interior
Charles R. Forbes (1878?-1952), head of the Veterans' Bureau
Warren Gamaliel Harding (1865-1923), twenty-ninth president of the United States, 1921-1923, a Republican
Harry Ford Sinclair (1876-1956), owner of the Mammoth Oil Company
Harry A. Slattery (1887-1949), veteran conservationist who helped to institute the Teapot Dome hearings
Thomas James Walsh (1859-1933), Democratic senator from Montana

SUMMARY OF EVENT. On August 2, 1923, the twenty-ninth president of the United States, Warren Gamaliel Harding, died in San Francisco. The cause of death was listed as "cerebral embolism," but perhaps William Allen White, his newspaper friend and biographer, was more correct when he asked, "How could the doctors diagnose an illness that was part terror, part shame, and part utter confusion?" Harding had suspected, even before leaving Washington to journey to the West Coast, that there was widespread corruption in his administration, and that this corruption was the work of his cronies. "My God, this is a hell of a job," he told White shortly before embarking on his journey. "I have no trouble with my enemies. . . . But my friends, my God-damn friends, White, they're the ones that keep me walking the floor nights!"

Already, graft in the Veterans' Bureau had come to light. The head of the bureau, Charles R. Forbes, had millions of dollars in contracts and supplies at his disposal, and he proceeded to dispose of them with a callous disregard for the veterans he was supposed to be helping. He made a fortune by declaring vast quantities of hospital supplies worthless and selling them to friends, who in turn resold them to the bureau at staggering prices. For bribes and other favors, Forbes also awarded contracts for hospital sites and construction. In one instance, John W. Thompson of the privately owned Thompson-Black company paid Forbes five thousand dollars for preferential treatment in bidding for government contracts. Upon learning of Forbes's activities, Harding demanded his resignation. Several days later, the legal adviser to the bureau, Charles F. Cramer, committed suicide. After a nine-week trial in 1924, Forbes was found guilty of conspiracy to defraud the federal government, fined ten thousand dollars, and sentenced to two years at Leavenworth penitentiary.

The Veterans' Bureau scandal was merely the beginning. Being an extraordinarily poor judge of men, Harding had surrounded himself with peddlers of corruption. Most of these men were members of the "Ohio Gang"—friends from Marion, Ohio, Harding's home, and from state politics in Columbus. Harding's attorney general was an Ohio friend, Harry M. Daugherty, who, according to one writer, was "a tinhorn gambler and a cheat." Harding appointed the former sheriff of Pickaway County, Ohio, to the directorship of the Mint. His brother-in-law became superintendent of federal prisons. As comptroller of the currency and then governor of the Federal Reserve System, Harding installed a Marion friend whose only experience in banking had been a few months as head of a small bank. Jesse Smith, a friend of Daugherty, was the liaison man between the Justice Department and various lawbreakers who were eager to purchase pardons, paroles, government appointments, liquor withdrawal permits, and immunity from prosecution. "My God, how the money rolls in," Smith used to sing. On May 23, 1923, however, when rumors about Smith's corrupt acts were circulating, he committed suicide in Daugherty's apartment.

Yet it was a non-Ohioan, Secretary of the Interior Albert B. Fall, who provided the most notorious of the Harding scandals. Conservationists were outraged by the appointment of Fall, who had revealed himself to be an enemy of conservation both as a United States senator from New Mexico and as a rancher whose sheep grazed over the range of the Alamo National Forest in violation of the law. Before becoming a member of Harding's cabinet, Fall had been almost bankrupt. Soon afterward, however, he began to build a new ranch house and to stock his herd with blooded cattle. That this sudden wealth did not correspond with his twelve-thousand-dollar yearly salary was obvious. One explanation was uncovered by a subcommittee of the Senate Public Lands Committee chaired by Senator Thomas J. Walsh of Montana. Prodded by Fall, Harding in 1921 had transferred control of the naval oil reserves at Elk Hills, California, and Teapot Dome, Wyoming, from the U.S. Navy to the Department of the Interior. Then Fall had leased Teapot Dome to the Mammoth Oil Company, owned by Harry F. Sinclair, and Elk Hills to the Pan-American Petroleum Company of Edward L. Doheny. The Walsh investigations revealed that Sinclair had given Fall $85,000 in cash, a herd of cattle, and $233,000 in liberty bonds at the time of the secret leasing of Teapot Dome, while Doheny's son had given Fall $100,000 in "a little black bag" for the Elk Hills lease. Although Fall, Sinclair, and Doheny were acquitted of trying to defraud the government, Sinclair later served a jail term for jury-tampering, while Fall, convicted of bribery on October 25, 1929, was fined $100,000 and imprisoned for a year.

Warren G. Harding, twenty-ninth president of the United States. His landslide victory over Democratic opponent James G. Cox—announced to the nation in one of the earliest commercial radio broadcasts—was marred by his poor judgment of character, leading to cronyism and corrupt deals such as the Teapot Dome scandal. (Library of Congress)

Nor was this all. Harding's Alien Property Custodian, Thomas Miller, had received $50,000 for seeing that valuable German chemical patents were sold to private parties. Miller was convicted and imprisoned. Jesse Smith, however, also had received a similar slice of the bribery money. Attorney General Daugherty refused to testify before a Senate committee inquiring into this scandal, contending that he could not do so because of his personal relations with the Hardings. Harding's successor, Calvin Coolidge, then forced Smith to resign. Later, Daugherty was tried and acquitted.

Seldom if ever has the federal government witnessed such corruption. Yet it was ironic that many people were more outraged by the conduct of Senator Walsh and the other men who uncovered the scandals than they were by the conduct of Fall and the "Ohio Gang." For the Democrats, the political fruits to be reaped from the scandals were meager, because Coolidge, the symbol of Puritan virtue, could by no stretch of the imagination be identified with the crimes of the Harding Administration.

—William M. Tuttle, updated by Geralyn Strecker

ADDITIONAL READING:

Bates, J. Leonard. *The Origins of Teapot Dome: Progressives, Parties, and Petroleum, 1909-1921.* Urbana: University of Illinois Press, 1963. A scholarly examination of the years of conflict between conservationists, oil companies, and politicians that led to the leasing of Navy oil reserves during the Harding Administration. Asserts that previously existing conditions, not merely poor judgment on Harding's part, contributed to the Teapot Dome scandal.

Mee, Charles L. *The Ohio Gang: The World of Warren G. Harding.* New York: M. Evans, 1981. An easy-to-read narrative that is sometimes sensationalized but nevertheless informative. Numerous illustrations.

Murray, Robert K. *The Harding Era: Warren G. Harding and His Administration.* Minneapolis: University of Minnesota Press, 1969. Places Harding's administration in a larger perspective in relation to previous and following administrations to show political continuity. Shows that the Harding Administration and its scandals did not occur in isolation, but were, in part, products of their time.

Noggle, Burl. *Teapot Dome: Oil and Politics in the 1920's.* Baton Rouge: Louisiana State University Press, 1962. The first scholarly study to rely primarily upon the involved individuals' papers rather than popular information and media accounts. Asserts that there is insufficient evidence to conclude that Fall was guilty of all of which he was accused.

Russell, Francis. *The Shadow of Blooming Grove: Warren G. Harding in His Times.* New York: McGraw-Hill, 1968. A popular biography, relying heavily on Harding's own papers.

Sinclair, Andrew. *The Available Man: The Life Behind the Masks of Warren Gamaliel Harding.* New York: Macmillan, 1965. One of the first studies to use Harding's papers (made available in 1964) to explore the man behind the mythic construction. Provides evidence that Harding was not merely a puppet president but an active participant in his political career, as both senator and president.

Trani, Eugene P., and David L. Wilson. *The Presidency of Warren G. Harding.* Lawrence: Regents Press of Kansas, 1977. Puts the scandals in context with other events during Harding's administration.

SEE ALSO: 1918, Republican Resurgence; 1924, Coolidge Is Elected President.

1921 ■ KING ERA IN CANADA: *the Liberal administration of King constitutes the longest administration of any Canadian prime minister*

DATE: 1921-1948
LOCALE: Ottawa, Canada
CATEGORIES: Canadian history; Government and politics
KEY FIGURES:
Robert Borden (1854-1937), Conservative prime minister of Canada, 1911-1920
Richard Bennett (1870-1947), Conservative prime minister of Canada, 1930-1935

William Lyon Mackenzie King (1874-1950), Liberal prime minister of Canada, 1921-1930 and 1935-1948
Arthur Meighen (1874-1960), Conservative prime minister of Canada, 1920-1921 and briefly in 1926
Louis St. Laurent (1882-1973), Liberal prime minister of Canada, 1948-1957

SUMMARY OF EVENT. William Lyon Mackenzie King dominated Canadian politics between 1921 and 1948. It is exceedingly unlikely that any Canadian prime minister will ever surpass King's extraordinarily long record of twenty-two years of service as the leader of Canada. Many years after his retirement in 1948 and his death in 1950, historians still find it amazing that King and his Liberal Party managed to remain in power from 1921 until 1957, with only a five-year hiatus, between 1930 and 1935, when the Conservative Richard Bennett served as Canada's prime minister.

King was a skillful politician who managed to hold together for almost three decades a coalition composed of very strong support from Quebec, Ontario, and the Maritime Provinces, and moderate support from the other Canadian provinces. Like earlier successful Canadian prime ministers, including John A. Macdonald and Wilfrid Laurier, King understood clearly that a party could maintain a majority in the House of Commons for extended periods of time only by satisfying the needs and aspirations of both English-speaking and French-speaking Canadians. Until his death in 1941, Ernest Lapointe from Quebec was King's most trusted adviser. Numerous other Quebecers served in important positions in King's governments, which always included a balance of ministers from Quebec and English-speaking provinces. King had an uncanny knack for sensing which policies would be politically acceptable to Canadian voters, and he modified his positions several times during his many years as Canada's prime minister.

Robert Borden, who served as Canada's prime minister from 1911 to 1920, had become exceedingly unpopular in Quebec during World War I when his government imposed conscription. This move was bitterly opposed throughout Quebec. The parliamentary debates on the proposed conscription law were directed by Arthur Meighen, who was then a member of Borden's cabinet and succeeded him as prime minister in 1920. Quebec voters would not forgive Meighen and his Conservatives for what the Quebecers perceived as another attempt by English Canada to mistreat Quebec. In the general election of 1921, the Liberal Party, under King, won all sixty-five seats in Parliament from Quebec; with reasonable support in the other provinces, it was relatively easy for the Liberals to receive a majority in the House of Commons. King also managed to obtain the support of most of the fifty-four members of Parliament from the Progressive Party.

During his first five years as prime minister, King made it clear to the British government that Canada would no longer allow Great Britain to determine Canada's foreign policy. In 1922, he respectfully rejected a request from the British prime minister, David Lloyd George, to send Canadian troops to help British forces then fighting in Turkey. As a further indication of

Canada's growing independence from Great Britain, King sent Ernest Lapointe to Washington, D.C., to sign a fishery treaty with the United States that would come to be known as the Halibut Treaty. Until then, it was generally accepted that Great Britain's overseas dominions would defer to British judgment in matters related to foreign policy. King decided that his government would no longer tolerate such limitations on Canadian independence. In the 1925 general election, neither the Conservatives nor the Liberals obtained a majority in the House of Commons. The twenty-four Progressives and the six independent members of Parliament would determine whether Arthur Meighen or King would become the prime minister of Canada.

Although at first King obtained enough support from the Progressives to form a new government, a scandal in the Canadian customs office caused a decrease in King's support in Parliament. He requested that Governor General Julian Byng dissolve Parliament, but this request was not granted, and Lord Byng asked Meighen to form a new government. Within three days after Meighen's swearing-in as the new Canadian prime minister, King used an extraordinary parliamentary procedure in order to bring about the dissolution of Parliament. Canadian law then required the prime minister and members of his cabinet to resign from the House of Commons. (This law has long since been changed.)

Although Meighen resigned from Parliament, he appointed his cabinet members as acting ministers so that they could keep their seats in Parliament and preserve the narrow majority created with support from some Progressives. King accused Meighen's government of violating Canadian law, and a motion of no confidence was approved by the House of Commons by a vote of 96 to 95. Meighen's second term as prime minister had lasted three days. In the September, 1926, general election, the Liberals won an absolute majority in the House of Commons.

The Liberals probably would have remained in power throughout the 1930's had King not made an incredible blunder in 1930. After the outbreak of the Great Depression in 1929, King was under pressure to do something to relieve the suffering of unemployed Canadians. In his most unjudicious comment, he told Parliament that assistance would not be given to any provincial government ruled by Conservatives. Canadian voters did not forgive him for this insensitive remark, and the Conservatives, under the leadership of Richard Bennett, easily won the general election of 1930. The Canadian economy, however, did not improve during Bennett's five years in office, and the Liberals won 173 of the 244 seats in the House of Commons in the 1935 general election.

Under the leadership of King, the Liberals also won the general elections of 1940 and 1945. During his last thirteen years as prime minister, King was very involved in foreign affairs, especially with organizing Canadian efforts to help the Allies defeat Germany and Japan in World War II. King cooperated fully with the British prime minister, Winston Churchill, and the U.S. president, Franklin D. Roosevelt, throughout the war. British and U.S. forces made extensive use of armaments, airplanes, and boats produced in Canada. The

Royal Canadian Air Force was active throughout the war, and many Canadian pilots flew bombing missions over Germany for the British Royal Air Force. Thousands of Canadian soldiers fought and died with British and U.S. troops during the liberation of France in 1944.

After the Allied victory over the Axis in 1945, King was seventy-one years of age and in poor health. Nevertheless, he was reelected prime minister in 1945 for the fifth time. His government helped Canadian businesses in the transition from a wartime to a peacetime economy. Under his guidance, Canada began to play an increasingly influential role in diplomacy. King and Lester Pearson, who was then the Canadian ambassador to the United States, both participated in the 1945 San Francisco conference that created the United Nations.

Deteriorating health convinced King that he should end his political career. In 1948, he persuaded Louis St. Laurent, his minister of justice from Quebec, to succeed him as leader of the Liberals and as prime minister. King died on July 22, 1950.

—*Edmund J. Campion*

ADDITIONAL READING:

Bothwell, Robert, Ian Drummond, and John English. *Canada: 1900-1945.* Toronto: University of Toronto Press, 1987. Contains an excellent analysis of Canadian political and social history until the end of World War II.

_____. *Canada Since 1945: Power, Politics, and Provincialism.* Toronto: University of Toronto Press, 1989. This useful supplement to the previous book examines economic and political changes in Canada since World War II.

Hutchison, Bruce. *The Prime Ministers of Canada: Macdonald to Pearson.* Don Mills, Ontario: Longmans, 1967. Contains three excellent chapters that deal with King's twenty-two years of service as Canada's prime minister.

McInnnis, Edgar. *Canada: A Political and Social History.* Toronto: Rinehart, 1959. Contains a clear history of Canada from the sixteenth century to the 1950's.

Owram, Doug, ed. *Confederation to the Present.* Vol. 2 in *Canadian History: A Reader's Guide.* Toronto: University of Toronto Press, 1944. Contains a well-annotated bibliography of historical studies on Canadian society and politics since 1867.

SEE ALSO: 1911, Borden Government in Canada; 1917, Canadian Women Gain the Vote; 1920, Meighen Era in Canada; 1924, Halibut Treaty; 1930, Bennett Era in Canada; 1931, Statute of Westminster; 1932, Ottawa Agreements; 1940, Ogdensburg Agreement; 1947, Canada's Citizenship Act; 1948, St. Laurent Succeeds King.

1921 ■ WASHINGTON DISARMAMENT CONFERENCE: *in the aftermath of a naval arms race and World War I, the world's major powers agree to reduce battleships*

DATE: November 12, 1921-February 6, 1922
LOCALE: Washington, D.C.

CATEGORIES: Diplomacy and international relations; Treaties and agreements

KEY FIGURES:

Arthur James Balfour, first earl of Balfour (1848-1930), head of the British delegation

Aristide Briand (1862-1932), prime minister of France, 1921-1922, and chairman of the French delegation

Auckland C. Geddes (1879-1954), British ambassador to the United States and member of the British delegation

Warren Gamaliel Harding (1865-1923), twenty-ninth president of the United States, 1921-1923

Charles Evans Hughes (1862-1948), Harding's secretary of state

Tomosaburo Kato (1859-1923), head of the Japanese delegation

Henry Cabot Lodge (1850-1924), chairman of the Senate Committee on Foreign Affairs and member of the U.S. delegation to the disarmament conference

Elihu Root (1845-1937), former secretary of state, former secretary of war, and member of the U.S. delegation

Kijuro Shidehara (1872-1951), Japanese ambassador to the United States and member of the Japanese delegation

Oscar Underwood (1862-1929), member of the Senate Committee on Foreign Relations and member of the U.S. delegation

René Raphaël Viviani (1863-1925), head of the French delegation after Briand's return to Paris

SUMMARY OF EVENT. Rejection by the United States of membership in the League of Nations did not imply renunciation of U.S. interest in many parts of the world or in certain international problems. U.S. leaders, including those within the Republican administration of President Warren G. Harding, recognized that decisions regarding the limitation of armaments and the critical situation in the Far East must be made, and that the United States must take a leading role in making such decisions. Otherwise, an armaments race between the three great naval powers—the United States, Great Britain, and Japan—was certain. In the tense Far East situation, the United States might be drawn into a disastrous war with Japan and Great Britain because of the 1902 Anglo-Japanese alliance, which had been renewed to run through 1921.

The experience of World War I supported the belief that competition in armaments caused wars. The initiative for an international conference to consider these problems was introduced by Senator William E. Borah, with a resolution in the Senate calling for a three-power disarmament conference even before President Harding and his secretary of state, Charles Evans Hughes, took office in March, 1921. Passed in May, 1921, the Borah Resolution received immediate and overwhelming endorsement from the press and the general public. Harding had to deal with not only agitation by Borah but also difficulties from other former Republican colleagues in the Senate. Harding decided, as part of the party's postwar "return to normalcy," to seize the initiative and propose a conference to limit armaments and forestall renewal of the

alliance between Britain and Japan. He directed Secretary of State Charles Hughes to propose real cuts backed by the industrial power of the United States, and insisted that if diplomacy failed, the United States would be a serious competitor in any ensuing arms race.

The British government had been contemplating a similar conference, but it yielded the honor to the United States and proposed that with the addition of discussions on the Far East, all countries with interests in the Pacific be invited. Accepting the British recommendations, Secretary Hughes on July 8, 1921, dispatched informal inquiries about the idea to interested powers. A suspicion of the motives behind the Western powers' invitation and a dislike for the vague terms of the proposed agenda caused the Japanese to be reluctant to take part in such a meeting. Nevertheless, on August 11, 1921, Hughes issued formal invitations to Japan, Great Britain, France, Italy, Belgium, China, the Netherlands, and Portugal to a conference in Washington the following November.

After a solemn observance of Armistice Day on November 11 by the delegates and the U.S. people, the Washington Disarmament Conference convened. An impressive group of statesmen assembled in Memorial Continental Hall. Secretary Hughes led the distinguished U.S. delegation, which included Republican senator Henry Cabot Lodge, chairman of the Foreign Affairs Committee; Elihu Root, former secretary of state and former secretary of war; and Oscar Underwood, probably the most powerful Democrat on the Foreign Affairs Committee. Former prime minister Arthur Balfour, author of the Balfour Declaration favoring limited Jewish settlement in Palestine, and Ambassador Auckland C. Geddes represented Great Britain. Prime Minister Aristide Briand headed the French delegation, later to be replaced by René Viviani. Baron Tomosaburo Kato and Ambassador Kijuro Shidehara were the principal spokesmen for Japan.

In the first session, Hughes demonstrated the determination of the United States to secure immediate and effective agreement on naval armaments. "The way to disarm is to disarm," Hughes proclaimed, as admirals stiffened with shock. He made two general proposals: a ten-year moratorium on the construction of warships displacing more than ten thousand tons and the scuttling of existing battleships and vessels under construction, so as to reduce United States and British tonnage in capital ships to approximately one-half million tons each, and total Japanese tonnage to three hundred thousand. This proposed ratio of 5:5:3 conformed approximately to existing naval strength.

Over the following four months, representatives struggled to work out agreements on naval armaments and security arrangements in the Pacific that would meet Hughes's stringent demands without upsetting the strategic balance of power. The resulting treaties dealt mostly with the Far East. On December 13, 1921, the United States, Great Britain, France, and Japan signed the Four-Power Treaty, which terminated the Anglo-Japanese Treaty of Alliance that had bound Great Britain legally to come to the aid of Japan in any conflict. Instead, the four powers agreed to respect one another's rights in the Pacific and to refer any future disputes over the area to a joint conference. They also agreed to hold disarmament discussions with one another to decide what measures should be taken if any nation threatened the status quo in the Far East.

The Nine-Power Treaty, signed on February 6, 1922, provided additional guarantees for the status quo. It bound all the members to respect the sovereignty and independence of China, to renounce any desire to exploit the unsettled conditions in China to gain special advantages, and to respect the "Open Door." The United States and Great Britain insisted on this pact; Japan agreed to it only after strong pressure was exerted. Although this treaty was to be the only formal multilateral affirmation of the Open Door ever agreed to, it proved completely ineffectual because the U.S. and British peoples were unwilling to sanction the use of force to aid China.

The major accomplishment of the Washington Disarmament Conference was the Five-Power Treaty, signed by Great Britain, the United States, Japan, Italy, and France on February 6, 1922. This pact called for a ten-year moratorium on the construction of capital ships. It largely confirmed Hughes's proposals for limiting existing battleship tonnages. The ratio for the five leading naval powers was 5 (United States) to 5 (Great Britain) to 3 (Japan) to 1.75 (France) to 1.75 (Italy). Japan was unhappy with the agreement but was somewhat mollified by the promise of the United States and Great Britain not to fortify any of their Pacific possessions. The French delegation, outraged by its relegation to third-class status, finally accepted the agreement on capital ships, and parity with its Mediterranean rival, Italy. No limitations were placed on lesser warships—cruisers, destroyers, and submarines. As a result, international naval competition shifted to cruisers in the 1920's, and that ship type was the subject of the failed Geneva Conference of 1927. It was not until the London Naval Treaty of 1930 that the approximate limits of the Five-Power Treaty were extended to other warship types, although the Japanese pushed for and received a 10:10:7 cruiser ratio.

The United States Senate approved the Washington treaties with only one dissenting vote. The agreements were received with great enthusiasm in the United States but less warmly elsewhere. They did halt a potentially disastrous competition in the construction of battleships, although the United States was allowed to complete three of the superdreadnoughts from its 1916 program, and Britain was allowed to build two new battleships to offset the qualitative superiority of the latest U.S. ships. Total aircraft carrier tonnage was limited (the United States and Great Britain each were allowed 135,000 tons, Japan 81,000 tons, and Italy and France 60,000 tons each); maximum aircraft carrier displacement was restricted to 27,000 tons, but the United States was allowed to convert two unfinished 33,000-ton battle cruisers (the *Lexington* and *Saratoga)* into aircraft carriers. Limits on aviation per se were deemed too complex, given the overlap between civilian and military aviation, and were to be the subject of a future conference, which was never held.

As a result of the Washington Disarmament Conference, the great powers promised to support the maintenance of peace and the status quo in the Far East, an encouraging step at the time, and the conference was regarded by the public as a tremendous accomplishment.

—*Theodore A. Wilson, updated by William M. McBride*

ADDITIONAL READING:

Dingman, Roger. *Power in the Pacific: The Origins of Naval Arms Limitation, 1914-1922*. Chicago: University of Chicago Press, 1976. An extremely competent study of geopolitical relations, naval policy, and the Washington Disarmament Conference.

Glad, Betty. *Charles Evans Hughes and the Illusions of Innocence*. Urbana: University of Illinois Press, 1966. Emphasizes Hughes's agreement with the activist Republican senators and minimizes friction between the Senate and Department of State regarding the Washington Conference.

Hall, Christopher. *Britain, America, and Arms Control, 1921-1937*. New York: St. Martin's Press, 1987. An excellent account of British and U.S. relations and naval arms reductions between the world wars.

O'Connell, Robert. *Sacred Vessels: The Cult of the Battleship and the Rise of the U.S. Navy*. Boulder, Colo.: Westview Press, 1991. A readable, cautionary account of naval strategic weapons, including the Washington Disarmament Conference, and the profession in which these weapons evolved.

Vinson, John Chalmers. *The Parchment Peace: The United States Senate and the Washington Conference, 1921-1922*. Athens: University of Georgia Press, 1955. Argues for a shift in U.S. foreign policy making from the executive to the Senate in the years immediately following World War I.

SEE ALSO: 1899, Hay's "Open Door Notes"; 1912, Wilson Is Elected President; 1919, Treaty of Versailles; 1921, Scandals of the Harding Administration; 1928, Kellogg-Briand Pact; 1932, Hoover-Stimson Doctrine; 1940, United States Builds a Two-Ocean Navy.

1921 ■ SHEPPARD-TOWNER ACT: *the first federal social welfare legislation authorizes matching funds to the states for programs in maternal and child hygiene*

DATE: November 23, 1921-June 30, 1929
LOCALE: Washington, D.C.
CATEGORIES: Health and medicine; Laws and acts; Social reform; Women's issues
KEY FIGURES:
Florence Kelley (1859-1932), executive secretary of the National Consumers' League
Julia Lathrop (1858-1932), U.S. Children's Bureau chief
Jeannette Rankin (1880-1973), Republican representative from Montana and the first woman to serve in Congress

Morris Sheppard (1875-1941), Democratic senator from
   Texas

Horace Towner (1855-1937), Republican representative
   from Iowa

SUMMARY OF EVENT. The Public Protection of Maternity and Infancy Act of 1921, commonly known as the Sheppard-Towner Act, linked a chain of ideas and actions about the proper role of government in the economy and society from the presidency of Theodore Roosevelt to that of Franklin Delano Roosevelt. The link began with the White House Conference on Child Welfare Standards in 1909 and ended with the Social Security Act of 1935. The Sheppard-Towner Act was in many ways the first federal welfare legislation. It authorized matching funds to the states for programs in maternal and child hygiene. The act also broke with the legacy of mothers' aid by providing non-means-tested assistance, although it retained social-control aspects whereby visiting nurses offered advice and help according to the Children's Bureau's norms of good child care (for example, against feeding or cuddling babies on demand), even if these norms went against a client's customs. The Sheppard-Towner Act also represented the first major dividend of women's national enfranchisement.

The U.S. Children's Bureau developed from the White House Conference of 1909, and the Bureau first investigated the causes of infant and maternal mortality. Studies revealed that the United States had high rates, showing, for example, that the nation ranked seventeenth in maternal and eleventh in infant mortality among world nations in 1918. Studies also linked poverty and mortality rates, revealing that 80 percent of America's expectant mothers received no advice or trained care. To remedy this situation, Jeannette Rankin, the first woman to serve in Congress, introduced in 1918 a measure to provide public protection of maternity and infancy. Julia Lathrop, chief of the Children's Bureau, sponsored the measure, and Senator Morris Sheppard of Texas and Representative Horace Towner of Iowa reintroduced the bill in the Sixty-sixth Congress. The bill made little progress until the full enfranchisement of women in 1920.

The League of Women Voters urged the national parties to endorse the maternity bill in their 1920 platforms. The Democratic, Socialist, Prohibition, and Farmer-Labor parties did, while the Republican platform ignored it. President Harding, however, supported the bill in his Social Justice Day speech on October 1, 1920. Sheppard and Towner resubmitted the bill in April, 1921, and it passed the Senate on July 22 by a vote of 63 to 7. Samuel Winslow, chair of the House Committee on Interstate and Foreign Commerce, which oversaw the bill, refused to hold hearings for months. President Warren G. Harding prodded Winslow only after influential women such as Republican National Committee vice chair Harriet Upton warned him that delay alienated many women. The House finally passed the measure by a vote of 279 to 39, while the only woman in Congress, the anti-suffragist Alice Robertson, voted against it. Harding signed the bill on November 23, 1921.

At the time of debate and passage, the inclinations of women voters were an unknown quantity. Suffragists had promised to clean house when they got the vote, and many politicians feared that women voters would vote en bloc or remain aloof from the main parties. Passage of the maternity bill was a goal of newly enfranchised women and took precedence over all other efforts. In 1920, the League of Women Voters helped to create the Women's Joint Congressional Committee (WJCC), which coordinated the lobbying efforts in Washington, D.C., for nearly two dozen women's organizations. Florence Kelley, executive secretary of the National Consumers' League, chaired the WJCC subcommittee responsible for enactment of the measure.

Kelley's successful lobbying efforts overcame powerful opponents who assailed the measure as a threat to the moral foundation of the nation. Such organizations as the National Association Opposed to Woman Suffrage and the Woman Patriots equated feminism and woman suffrage with socialism and communism. Mary Kilbreth, a leading anti-suffragist, wrote Harding that many believed the bill was inspired by communism and backed by American radicals, thereby striking at the heart of American civilization. Organizations such as the Woman's Municipal League of Boston, the American Constitutional League, the Constitutional Liberty League of Massachusetts, and the Massachusetts Public Interest League concurred.

Fearing state medicine, the American Medical Association (AMA) also targeted the Sheppard-Towner Act. State medical societies in Massachusetts, New York, Illinois, Ohio, and Indiana spearheaded the opposition. The *Illinois Medical Journal*, official organ of the Illinois State Medical Society, for example, attacked the act as a product of Bolshevist forces that sought to set up bureaucratic autocracy in the nation's capital. The *Journal of the American Medical Association* campaigned against the Sheppard-Towner Act from February 5, 1921, until its repeal in June of 1929. In 1922, the AMA's house of delegates condemned the legislation as a socialistic machination. Many women physicians, such as Josephine Baker, a constant ally of the National Consumers' League and the League of Women Voters and president of the Medical Woman's National Association in the early 1930's, supported the Sheppard-Towner Act.

The act authorized an appropriation of $1.48 million for fiscal 1921-1922 and $1.24 million for the next five years ending June 30, 1927. Of this sum, $5,000 would go to each state outright; $5,000 more would go to each state if matching funds were provided; and the remainder would be allocated on a population percentage and matching basis. The Children's Bureau would channel the money through state child welfare or health divisions. States retained the right to reject aid. The act provided for instruction in hygiene of maternity and infancy through public health nurses, visiting nurses, consultation centers, child care conferences, and literature distribution. Forty-one states joined the program in 1922, whereas until the act's repeal in 1929, only Connecticut, Illinois, and Massachusetts rejected Sheppard-Towner money.

The attorney general of Massachusetts issued an opinion that the act would misuse the state's tax money and that it was unconstitutional because it violated the rights of the states. Massachusetts filed a suit with the U.S. Supreme Court on behalf of its taxpayers to enjoin the law. Harriet Frothingham, president of the Woman Patriots, filed another suit in the Supreme Court of the District of Columbia in the event that states were deemed ineligible to file a taxpayer's suit. The District of Columbia court dismissed Frothingham's case and the U.S. Court of Appeals concurred. She then appealed to the U.S. Supreme Court. In the interim, U.S. Solicitor General James Beck, who considered the Sheppard-Towner Act to be unconstitutional, encouraged Massachusetts to pursue its case. These suits threatened the range of federal programs which provided either direct aid or matching grants to states. On June 5, 1923, the U.S. Supreme Court dismissed both suits for want of jurisdiction and without ruling on the constitutionality of the act.

Although the Sheppard-Towner Act was considered a permanent law, federal appropriations under the act's provisions were scheduled to cease automatically on June 30, 1927. In 1926, proponents moved to have the authorization extended. The House of Representatives quickly approved a two-year extension by a vote of 218 to 44. The AMA, Woman Patriots, Daughters of the American Revolution, and other opponents, however, mobilized to stop the bill in the Senate. Opponents iterated many of the same themes that had been less persuasive in 1921: primarily that the Sheppard-Towner Act was part of a feminist-socialist-communist plot to sovietize the United States. In the end, proponents accepted a compromise which extended the appropriations for two more years but repealed the law itself automatically on June 30, 1929. Although progressive women still lobbied for the bill, President Herbert Hoover refused to press the matter and allowed the first federal social security law to lapse. The Great Depression precluded any revival of national provisions in the early 1930's, and the loss of federal funds severely restricted many of the forty-five state programs that had continued to provide maternity and infancy aid on their own. Restoration, however, came with the Social Security Act of 1935. Title V of the 1935 act authorized appropriations for the Children's Bureau of $5.82 million for maternity and infancy protection, in addition to $3.87 million for crippled children and $34.75 million for aid to dependent children.   —*Richard K. Caputo*

ADDITIONAL READING:

Bremner, Robert H., ed. *1866-1932*. Vol. 2 in *Children and Youth in America: A Documentary History*. Cambridge, Mass.: Harvard University Press, 1971. Contains excerpts from original source material including provisions of the Sheppard-Towner Act, congressional debates, published opposition, and the 1923 Supreme Court decision upholding the constitutionality of the act. Chronology of significant child-related legislation; topical bibliography; index.

Caputo, Richard K., ed. *Federal Responses to People in Need*. Vol. 1, *Welfare and Freedom American Style I: The Role of the Federal Government, 1900-1940*. Lanham, Md.: Uni-

versity Press of America, 1991. Discusses the legislative history of the Sheppard-Towner Act of 1921 in the context of the federal government's role in promoting social welfare. Notes, bibliography, index.

Gordon, Linda. *Pitied but Not Entitled: Single Mothers and the History of Welfare 1890-1935*. New York: Free Press, 1994. Shows the influence of women on the development of social welfare legislation. Gathered notes, appendix, index.

Lemons, J. Stanley. "The Sheppard-Towner Act: Progressivism in the 1920's." *Journal of American History* 55 (March, 1969): 776-786. A definitive history of the act as seen in the context of the Progressive Era in America. Extensive notes documenting original source material.

SEE ALSO: 1857, New York Infirmary for Indigent Women and Children Opens; 1915, National Birth Control League Forms; 1920, League of Women Voters Is Founded; 1923, Proposal of the Equal Rights Amendment; 1935, Social Security Act.

1922 ■ CABLE ACT: *revocation of the principle that a woman may automatically assume the citizenship of her husband*

DATE: September 22, 1922
LOCALE: Washington, D.C.
CATEGORIES: Civil rights; Immigration; Women's issues
KEY FIGURES:
John Levi Cable (1884-1971), U.S. congressman from Ohio
Warren Gamaliel Harding (1865-1923), twenty-ninth president of the United States, 1921-1923
Maud Wood Park (1871-1955), president of the National League of Women Voters
Lena Lowe Yost (born 1878), president of the West Virginia's Women's Temperance Union

SUMMARY OF EVENT. National laws regulating the acquisition and loss of citizenship fall fully within the sovereign prerogatives of national governments. Certain common rules and procedures have been adopted by various countries, but there remains considerable variation over time and in different countries. This is especially true in regard to the determination of the citizenship status of women who marry foreigners. In many countries, women, upon marriage, automatically lose their original citizenship and assume that of their husband. In other countries, women married to aliens retain their original citizenship unless they specifically renounce it.

The Cable Act of 1922, following closely on the heels of the woman suffrage movement and the passage of the Nineteenth Amendment to the U.S. Constitution, attempted to rectify the negative effects of earlier legislation that had hampered the independence of women in choosing their citizenship status upon marriage to an alien. To understand exactly what the Cable Act did, it is necessary to review briefly the historical setting in which it was promulgated.

Although the Cable Act of 1922 allowed women U.S. citizenship independent of their husbands' status, thereby providing choice to women who married foreign nationals, it also had the effect of hindering Asian women who wished to achieve U.S. citizenship via marriage. (National Archives)

A time-honored tradition of English customary law affirmed the practice of not depriving a female citizen of her citizenship in the event of marriage to a foreigner. This old English practice was followed in U.S. law. This Anglo-American tradition, however, ran counter to the practice of most countries as late as the end of the nineteenth century—that when women married aliens, their citizenship automatically followed that of the husband. Both the United States and Great Britain eventually abandoned the tradition of preserving a woman's citizenship upon marriage to an alien, and by 1908, women marrying

aliens automatically assumed the citizenship of the husband in all the major countries of Europe and Latin America.

In the United States, this shift was gradual. As early as 1855, for example, Congress passed legislation automatically conferring U.S. citizenship on any alien woman who married a U.S. citizen. In the Expatriation Act of 1907, Congress went a step further, providing that "any American woman who marries a foreigner shall take the nationality of her husband." With the passage of this act, the United States fell into line with standard international practice of the time.

Although this new U.S. law was in general accordance with the practice of other countries, it led to illogical domestic consequences. Many American women married to aliens continued to live with their husbands in the United States, but were deprived of their U.S. citizenship while alien women who married American men automatically received U.S. citizenship. The Expatriation Act arbitrarily deprived American women of their citizenship and reduced their independence in choosing their nationality upon marriage. Pressure mounted to rectify the disorderly and arbitrary features of the new legislation. During the political campaign of 1920, both the Republicans and the Democrats incorporated language into their party platforms calling for the independent citizenship of married women. The largest international women's rights organization of the day, the International Council of Women, at its 1920 conference in Copenhagen, Denmark, called upon national legislatures to acknowledge the right of women to choose their nationality upon marriage.

When Representative John L. Cable of Ohio introduced his bill, he noted that "the laws of our country should grant independent citizenship to women." Just prior to the vote in Congress on the Cable Act, a number of prominent women leaders, including Maud Wood Park, president of the National League of Women Voters, and Lena Lowe Yost, president of the West Virginia Women's Temperance Union, called upon Congress to adopt the legislation. The Carnegie Foundation undertook an influential study of judicial opinion on the subject and found that two-thirds of the judges surveyed were in favor of the independence of women in determining citizenship upon marriage. Upon passage of the bill and its imminent signing into law by President Warren G. Harding, Cable spoke even more eloquently to the law's design:

> The purpose of the law is to place citizenship on the highest plane possible. It is a privilege and not a right. It should be acquired upon an independent basis; justice and common sense dictate that the woman should have the same right as the man to choose the country of her allegiance. Participation in our Government and the protection by our country should not be determined solely by wedding ceremonies.

The Cable Act of 1922, which is Chapter 411 of the National Defense Act, in effect amended the 1855 law that automatically granted U.S. citizenship to alien women who married U.S. citizens and the 1907 Expatriation Act, which had deprived U.S. women of their U.S. citizenship when they married foreigners. Although the act reaffirmed the right of any woman to become a naturalized citizen of the United States, without prejudice to her sex or because she was a married woman, it explicitly revoked the notion that a woman would automatically become a U.S. citizen because of marriage to a U.S. citizen or because her husband had been naturalized. Women were to be treated as individuals and, if otherwise eligible for naturalization, could seek U.S. citizenship through regular compliance with naturalization laws. Alien women who married U.S. citizens or whose husbands became naturalized could

choose whether or not to seek U.S. citizenship. The Cable Act did not disturb or invalidate the citizenship of women who had achieved automatic citizenship prior to its passage.

Section 3 of the Cable Act addressed the predicament of American women who married aliens, and who had, under the provisions of the 1907 Expatriation Act, thereby lost their U.S. citizenship. The Cable Act acknowledged that each woman had a right to acquire a new nationality, including that of her husband, and otherwise retain the right to expatriate herself, but that this should be a matter of deliberate choice rather than an automatic effect of the law. The Cable Act states that "a woman citizen of the United States shall not cease to be a citizen of the United States by reason of her marriage after the passage of this Act, unless she makes a formal renunciation of her citizenship before a court having jurisdiction over naturalization of aliens." Although the Cable Act has been criticized by certain advocates of immigrant communities as an attempt to restrict immigration, it actually was adopted for the purpose of increasing the independence of married women. The Cable Act was later amended to streamline naturalization procedures even more.

The Cable Act was an important example of reform in citizenship laws. The new rules it enunciated drew international attention, and in 1926, the League of Nations prepared a new draft convention on the status of married women. This was followed in 1933 by the adoption of the Convention on the Nationality of Women by the Montevideo Conference of American States. However, efforts to internationalize the new U.S. principles for dealing with the nationality of married women did not enjoy immediate or widespread success. The United States and certain Latin American countries ratified it, but most other countries failed to do so. In the 1990's, the determination of laws regarding the nationality of married women remained a matter of national prerogative.   —*Robert F. Gorman*

ADDITIONAL READING:

Kansas, Sidney. *Citizenship of the United States of America*. New York: Washington Publishing, 1936. This dated but useful study contains a copy of the Cable Act, with commentary.

Kettner, James H. *The Development of American Citizenship, 1608-1870*. Chapel Hill: University of North Carolina Press, 1978. Traces the development of the idea of citizenship in the formative stages of the American republic.

The Statutes at Large of the United States of America. Vol. 42 (1922): 1022-1023. Consult this source for a copy of the Cable Act, Chapter 411 of the National Defense Act of September 22, 1922. The Cable Act was passed by Congress as Public Law 346.

United States. Congress. *Congressional Record*. Vol. 62, parts 7, 9, and 12 (1922). Contains verbatim transcripts of the introduction of the Cable Act and subsequent debate on the bill.

Von Glahn, Gerhard. *Law Among Nations: An Introduction to Public International Law*. 6th ed. New York: Macmillan, 1992. This standard text on international law provides a succinct history of the Cable Act.

SEE ALSO: 1917, Immigration Act of 1917; 1920, U.S. Women Gain the Vote; 1945, War Brides Act.

1922 ■ OZAWA V. UNITED STATES: the U.S. Supreme Court rules that Japanese aliens do not qualify as "white" and therefore cannot be naturalized as citizens

DATE: November 13, 1922

LOCALE: Washington, D.C.

CATEGORIES: Asian American history; Court cases; Immigration

KEY FIGURES:

James Montgomery Beck (1861-1936), U.S. attorney general

Takao Ozawa, Japanese immigrant seeking naturalization

George Sutherland (1862-1942), associate justice in the Supreme Court

William Howard Taft (1857-1930), chief justice of the United States

George Woodward Wickersham (1858-1936), Ozawa's attorney

SUMMARY OF EVENT. In the early twentieth century, naturalization was under the effective control of local and state authorities. In California and other Pacific states, fears of the "yellow peril" or "silent invasion" of Asian immigrants were deeply entrenched and politically exploited. In such states, citizenship had been repeatedly denied to both Chinese and more recent Japanese settlers, although there were some rare exceptions. The prevailing belief among the nativist majority was that such settlers should be ineligible for U.S. citizenship.

Partly to test the Alien Land Act—a California law passed in 1913 that barred non-citizens from owning land in that state—Takao Ozawa sought U.S. citizenship in defiance of a 1906 law (U.S. Revised Statute, Section 2169) that limited naturalization to "free white persons," "aliens of African nativity," and "persons of African descent." Although born in Japan, Ozawa had been educated in the United States. He was graduated from high school in Berkeley and for three years attended the University of California. He was aware that some Issei (first-generation Japanese immigrants) had been naturalized, even in California. Specifically, Ozawa may have known of Iwao Yoshikawa, the first Japanese immigrant to be naturalized in California. Yoshikawa had arrived in San Francisco from Japan in 1887. A law clerk in his homeland, in his adopted country he had studied U.S. law and served as a court translator. In 1889 he began the naturalization process, which, presumably, was completed five years later, although there is no extant record of his naturalization. His case was publicized because it broached such issues as mandatory citizenship renunciation and the legality of dual citizenship.

Regardless of Ozawa's knowledge of Yoshikawa, on October 16, 1914, Ozawa applied for U.S. citizenship before the district court for the Territory of Hawaii. He argued that he had resided in the United States and its territory of Hawaii for a total of twenty years, had adopted the culture and language of his host country, had reared his children as Americans in heart

and mind, and was, by character and education, wholly qualified for naturalization.

The district court ruled against Ozawa on the grounds that his Japanese ethnicity denied him access to naturalization. Ozawa then took his case to the Ninth Circuit Court of Appeals, which passed it to the U.S. Supreme Court for instruction. In turn, the Supreme Court upheld the laws that in effect declared Ozawa ineligible for citizenship.

Rather than question the justice of the racial restrictions on naturalization, the opinion limited its focus to clarifying the meaning of the term "white persons" and distinguishing between "Caucasian" and "white person," determining that the latter, while a more inclusive term than the former, is not so inclusive as to include persons of Asian extraction. It concluded that "a person of the Japanese race is not a free white person, within the meaning of U.S. Rev. Stat. § 2169 [the 1906 law], limiting the provisions of the title on naturalization to aliens being free white persons, and to aliens of African nativity, and to persons of African descent, and therefore such Japanese is not eligible to naturalization as a United States citizen. . . ."

In tracing the history of the naturalization laws, the Court attempted to demonstrate that all statutes preceding the 1906 act contested by Ozawa had the same intent: the selective admission to citizenship based on the interpretation of "white," not as a racial appellation but as a reflection of character. It argued that the words "free white persons" did not indicate persons of a particular race or origin, but rather that they describe "personalities" and "persons fit for citizenship and of the kind admitted to citizenship by the policy of the United States." According to that doctrine, any non-African alien, if desired by Congress, might be deemed "white." Thus, the Court reasoned, "when the long-looked-for Martian immigrants reach this part of the earth, and in due course a man from Mars applies to be naturalized, he may be recognized as white within the meaning of the act of Congress, and admitted to citizenship, although he may not be a Caucasian."

Regardless of this race disclaimer, however, the Court, in reasoning through its arguments, distinguished between "whites" (all Europeans, for example) and "non-whites" (such as the Chinese) on ethnic grounds pure and simple. The decision throughout sanctioned racial biases that assumed that an individual's character was in some way delimited by his or her racial heritage. For example, at one point it provided a formulaic approach to determining citizenship eligibility for persons of mixed blood, supporting the idea, widely observed, that in order to be construed as white, a person must be "of more than half white blood." Clearly, the decision upheld the seriously flawed assumption that character and racial heritage were inextricably interrelated.

The Supreme Court's ruling reflected the prevailing nativist bias against Asian immigrants, an attitude that was reflected in both law and policy through the first half of the twentieth century. In fact, no more formidable barriers to citizenship were erected than those facing the Issei (first-generation Japanese), Chinese, and other Asian immigrants. In 1924, an isolationist Congress enacted an immigration act placing numerical restrictions on immigrants allowed into the United States based on national origin. One provision of the Immigration Act of 1924, known as the Johnson Act, excluded immigrants ineligible for naturalization. Its obvious aim—to bar entry of Japanese aliens—quickly led to a deterioration in the diplomatic relations between Japan and the United States.

The plight of Japanese already in the United States also worsened in the anti-Asian climate. In separate rulings, the Supreme Court went so far as to revoke citizenship that had been granted to some Issei. In 1925, it even denied that service in the armed forces made Issei eligible for naturalization, overturning a policy that had previously been in effect. Not only were Issei barred from naturalization; in many states, "alien land laws" prohibited them from owning land and even entering some professions.

That codified prejudice partly accounts for but does not justify the terrible treatment of Japanese Americans during World War II, when 112,00 of them, including 70,000 Nisei (persons of Japanese descent born in the United States), were rounded up and incarcerated in detention centers that bore some grim similarities to the concentration camps of Europe. It was not until the passage of the McCarran-Walter Act in 1952 that the long-standing racial barriers to naturalization finally came down. —*John W. Fiero*

ADDITIONAL READING:

Curran, Thomas J. *Xenophobia and Immigration, 1820-1930.* Boston: Twayne, 1975. Traces the origins of anti-immigrant movements in America, relating the xenophobic tradition to the exclusionist laws and practices of the inclusive period.

Hosokawa, Bill. *Nisei: The Quiet Americans.* New York: William Morrow, 1969. A good general study of Japanese Americans and their struggle against legal and social discrimination. Some photographs; no bibliography or notes.

O'Brien, David J., and Stephen Fugita. *The Japanese American Experience.* Bloomington: Indiana University Press, 1991. Scholarly study with focus on the legal and social problems confronting Japanese Americans before World War II and their rapid acculturation in its wake.

Takaki, Ronald T. *Strangers from a Different Shore: A History of Asian Americans.* Boston: Little, Brown, 1989. An excellent and sensitive overview of Asian American history, with extensive notes and photographs.

Wilson, Robert Arden, and Bill Hosokawa. *East to America: A History of the Japanese in the United States.* New York: William Morrow, 1980. A general history of Japanese migration to North America. Appendices provide census statistics, text of an exclusionist law, and a letter to President Woodrow Wilson pleading the Issei cause.

Yuji, Ichioka. "The Early Japanese Immigrant Quest for Citizenship: The Background of the 1922 Ozawa Case." *Amerasia* 4, no. 2 (1977): 12. Brief account of the reasons for Ozawa's legal action and his desire for citizenship.

SEE ALSO: 1892, Yellow Peril Campaign; 1907, Gentlemen's Agreement; 1913, Alien Land Laws; 1917, Immigration Act of 1917; 1924, Immigration Act of 1924; 1930, Japanese American Citizens League Is Founded; 1943, Magnuson Act; 1952, McCarran-Walter Act.

1923 ■ PROPOSAL OF THE EQUAL RIGHTS AMENDMENT: *an amendment to ensure women's right to equal treatment under the law succeeds suffrage as a goal of the women's movement*

DATE: December 10, 1923
LOCALE: Washington, D.C.
CATEGORIES: Civil rights; Women's issues
KEY FIGURE:
Alice Paul (1885-1977), creator and proposer of the ERA
SUMMARY OF EVENT. After the passage in 1920 of the Nineteenth Amendment to the United States Constitution, which gave women the right to vote, many women who had worked for its ratification disengaged from political activity. However, some realized that although women could vote, there were still many obstacles to real freedom. Among other things, women did not have equal educational opportunities, economic independence, or access to information about family planning.

As people began to address these concerns, issues that had been put aside during the push for suffrage started to come to the surface. Some women, mainly members of the National Woman's Party (NWP), believed in complete equality for women; others, primarily those associated with the National American Woman Suffrage Association (NAWSA), believed that there were some areas in which women needed special protective legislation. In 1908, the Supreme Court had decided:

> The two sexes differ in structure of body, in the functions to be performed by each, in the amount of physical strength, in the capacity for long-continued labour, particularly when done standing. . . . This difference justifies a difference in legislation, and upholds that which is designed to compensate for some of the burdens which rest upon her.

Although the decision protected some women, it proved discriminatory in many cases. It assumed that women were weaker and more vulnerable than men. Women were prohibited from practicing law, even when they were fully qualified to do so. They were forbidden to lift weights, even those not heavier than an eighteen-month-old child. Women were forbidden to serve in bars at night, although they were able to work as cleaners or entertainers at the same hour.

These issues, which had been submerged in order to focus on suffrage, now began to come to light more clearly. The women's movement, which had been so united before 1920, now began to show factions among its members: There were those who were pacifists, social feminists, or professional women.

It was into this dilemma that Alice Paul stepped. Born in 1885 of Quaker parents in Moorestown, New Jersey, she had graduated from Swarthmore College in 1905. She went as a student to England, where she had been an active participant in the British suffrage movement. A woman of strong will and ambition, Paul adopted the militant techniques of the British woman suffrage movement. In 1913, she broke with NAWSA, which had always lobbied state legislatures, and founded the Congressional Union for Woman Suffrage to work with Congress in Washington, D.C. This group eventually became known as the National Woman's Party (NWP). In 1917, Paul and the National Woman's Party organized round-the-clock picketing of the White House, and as a result, she was arrested and jailed. This action received international press coverage and was ultimately good for the cause of woman suffrage, but these struggles left Paul ten thousand dollars in debt and without the physical stamina to continue.

However, women realized that the time was ripe for further action on behalf of women, and that they needed Paul's leadership. A ceremony was planned at the Capitol on February 15, 1921, Susan B. Anthony's birthday, both to celebrate women's right to vote and to launch a campaign for the removal of legal disabilities of women. The ceremony took place with representatives of more than one hundred women's organizations. (The only group noticeably absent was NAWSA, which complained that NWP was unconcerned about the problems of working women. NAWSA believed that factory women, for example, still required special legislation.) The idea of an Equal Rights Amendment was conceived during this convention.

Paul took a leave of absence to earn a law degree. She received an LL.B. from Washington College of Law in 1922, an LL.M. in 1927, and a DC.L. in 1928 from American University in Washington. In 1923, the NWP again held a convention, this time in Seneca Falls, New York, where the first equal rights convention had been held in 1848. In memory of Elizabeth Cady Stanton and Lucretia Mott, Paul presented a proposal, originally called the Lucretia Mott Amendment: "Men and women shall have equal rights throughout the United States and in every place subject to its jurisdiction." The proposal was not unanimously accepted. As before, there was a concern that it would invalidate all protective legislation for women, especially laws regarding labor. Paul, however, saw that most protective legislation only furthered discrimination against women. If the women had been able to compromise on these issues, perhaps they could have strengthened their ranks and consolidated their new power, but such was not to be.

Although the majority of women supported the protectionists, the proposal, the Equal Rights Amendment (ERA), was introduced in Congress on December 10, 1923. It read:

Equality of rights under the law shall not be denied or abridged by the United States or by any state on account of sex.

Paul decided that the next step for the National Woman's Party would be to elicit the support of other women's groups. Studies were conducted as to the legal position of women in individual states in relation to divorce, marriage, custody, work,

education, family planning, and career opportunities. The party also planned to reveal the fundamental inadequacy of protectionist legislation. The women lobbied to get representation on an investigative panel of the Department of Labor's Woman's Bureau, which met in January, 1926. However, the gap between the NWP and the rest of the country widened, and antagonisms prevented any progress. In November, 1928, the panel found that legislative protection was good for women.

Despite the passage of the Nineteenth Amendment, the decade of the 1920's was in many ways antifeminist. Women were not considered capable of combining marriage and a career. Prewar feminists were attacked as unfeminine and asexual. Freudian theories, which saw women alternatively as temptresses and slaves, were popular. Feminism did not appeal to many women of the younger generation, which rebelled against repressive, Victorian culture identified with the older generation, which had given birth to the ERA. Despite this milieu, in 1928 the National Federation of Business and Professional Women's Clubs expressed its support of the ERA. Gradually, more groups promoted it. The ERA was publicly championed by the Republican Party in 1940, the General Federation of Women's Clubs in 1943, and the Democratic Party in 1944.

Not until 1959, however, did NAWSA, which by then had become the League of Women Voters, support the amendment. During the 1960's and 1970's, feminist activity was rekindled, and in 1972, the ERA passed the House and the Senate. According to law, it had seven years to be ratified by three-fourths of the states. In her later years, Alice Paul dedicated herself full time to passage of the ERA. She died in 1977, still hoping for its passage. Although Congress extended the deadline to 1982, and many states did ratify the amendment, time ran out before the ERA could become law. —*Winifred O. Whelan*

ADDITIONAL READING:

Gillmore, Inez Haynes. *The Story of Alice Paul and the National Woman's Party*. Fairfax, Va.: Denlinger's, 1977. First published in 1921 as *The Story of the Woman's Party*.

Hammer, Roger A. *American Woman: Hidden in History, Forging the Future*. 2d ed. Vol. 3 in *Hidden America*. Golden Valley, Minn.: The Place in the Woods, 1993. A concise collection of stories about women, both contemporary and historical, including Alice Paul. Illustrations.

Lunardini, Christine A. *From Equal Suffrage to Equal Rights: Alice Paul and the National Woman's Party, 1910-1928*. New York: New York University Press, 1986. Traces the activities of Alice Paul from her work for woman suffrage through her efforts for equal rights.

Pole, J. R. *The Pursuit of Equality in American History*. Berkeley: University of California Press, 1978. Chapter 10 concerns the divisions among women after the passage of the Nineteenth Amendment in 1920.

Woodward, Carolyn. "The Growth of the Modern Women's Movement." In *Changing Our Power: An Introduction to Women's Studies*, edited by Jo Whitehorse Cochran, Donna Lengston, and Carolyn Woodward. 2d ed. Dubuque, Iowa:

Kendall/Hunt, 1991. Describes what happened to the ERA and how it was defeated.

SEE ALSO: 1916, National Woman's Party Is Founded; 1920, League of Women Voters Is Founded; 1920, U.S. Women Gain the Vote; 1982, Defeat of the Equal Rights Amendment.

1924 ■ INDIAN CITIZENSHIP ACT: *confers citizenship on all American Indians born within territorial limits of the United States, thus encouraging the dissolution of tribal nations*

DATE: June 2, 1924
LOCALE: Washington, D.C.
CATEGORIES: Laws and acts; Native American history
KEY FIGURES:
Henry Dawes (1816-1903), author of the General Allotment Act
James Rood Doolittle (1815-1897), Wisconsin senator who opposed granting citizenship to American Indians
John Elk, American Indian who voluntarily separated from his tribe but was denied the right to vote
Homer P. Snyder (1863-1937), author of the Indian Veterans Citizenship Bill and the Indian Citizenship Act

SUMMARY OF EVENT. American Indians hold a unique position in U.S. society and law, so the question of their citizenship was complicated. By the time of the Revolutionary War, it was established practice for European colonial powers to negotiate treaties with American Indian tribes, as they were considered to be independent nations, and this policy was continued by the United States. The Constitution regards tribes as distinct political units separate and apart from the United States, although not foreign nations, so as long as American Indians were members of tribes or nations that negotiated treaties with the United States government as semi-independent political units, they could not be considered U.S. citizens. Two significant rulings made it clear that an act of Congress would be required in order to grant citizenship to American Indians.

The issue of whether American Indians were citizens came into question when the Fourteenth Amendment to the Constitution was adopted in 1868. The amendment stated that "All persons born or naturalized within the United States and subject to the jurisdiction thereof, are citizens of the State wherein they reside." This amendment was intended to grant citizenship to newly emancipated slaves; however, there was a question as to whether it covered American Indians as well. In 1868, Senator James Doolittle of Wisconsin led the opposition to the extension of citizenship to American Indians under the Fourteenth Amendment. Many tribes were not yet settled on reservations, there were ongoing tribal wars in the Great Plains, and Doolittle felt strongly that the natives were not yet prepared for citizenship. There was considerable confusion in the Senate as to whether Indians living with tribal connections

were subject to the jurisdiction of the United States. It was decided that Fourteenth Amendment rights did not extend to American Indians, when the Senate Committee on the Judiciary ruled, in 1870, that tribal Indians were not granted citizenship under the Fourteenth Amendment because they were not subject to the jurisdiction of the United States in the sense meant by the amendment.

Once this matter was settled, issues arose over the status of American Indians who voluntarily severed relationships with their tribe. John Elk, an American Indian who terminated relations with his tribe and lived and worked in Omaha, Nebraska, sought to register to vote in a local election. Elk met all the requirements to vote in the state of Nebraska, but he was refused the right to vote because election officials, and later the courts, ruled that as an American Indian, he was not a United States citizen. In 1884, the United States Supreme Court upheld the lower court decisions; it ruled, in *Elk v. Wilkins*, that an Indian born as a member of a tribe, although he disassociated himself from that tribe and lived among whites, was not a citizen and therefore was ineligible to vote. This ruling indicated it would take a specific act of Congress to naturalize American Indians.

By the 1880's, many persons in the United States sought to end tribal sovereignty, individualize Indians (end their status as tribal members), and grant citizenship to them so they eventually would be amalgamated into the general population. As a means toward this end, Senator William Dawes of Massachusetts, a leader in reform legislation for American Indian issues, sponsored the General Allotment Act, which became law in 1887. This act carried provisions for citizenship as a reward for leaving the tribe and adopting "the habits of civilized life." In part, this meant that American Indians had to accept small plots of land, successfully farm their lands, and learn the English language. Provisions in the General Allotment Act meant that eventually every American Indian could become a citizen, except members of tribes specifically excluded in legislation. Indians in Oklahoma were originally excluded from these provisions, but in 1901, a congressional act granted Indians in Oklahoma Territory citizenship. By 1917, through a variety of federal statutes, as many as two-thirds of all Native Americans were United States citizens. However, it was World War I that reopened the debate about citizenship for American Indians as a whole.

American Indians actively supported the war effort through increased food production, purchase of war bonds, contributions to the Red Cross, and most dramatically, enlistment: Between six and ten thousand Indians, many of whom were not citizens, enlisted for military service. In return for their service to the country, Representative Homer P. Snyder of New York authored the Veterans Citizenship Bill, which became law on November 6, 1919. This law granted any American Indian who had received an honorable discharge from military service during World War I the right to apply for citizenship with no restriction on the right to tribal property. Still, by 1920, some 125,000 American Indians were not citizens. Many people in the United States believed that all Indians should be rewarded for their patriotism in World War I. Therefore, Snyder introduced a bill in Congress proposing to declare all remaining noncitizen Indians born in the United States as citizens. Political maneuverings began at once.

Many people favored citizenship as a way to sever the legal relationship between the tribes and the federal government, and many American Indians were aware that citizenship could alter their tribal governments and possibly dissolve the reservation land base. In particular, full-bloods in many tribes were fearful that citizenship would end tribal sovereignty, bring them under state jurisdiction, and ultimately destroy tribal life and values. Compromise was required to resolve these conflicting views. In January, 1924, Congressman Snyder introduced House Resolution 6355, authorizing the secretary of the interior to grant citizenship to all American Indians, but ensuring that "the granting of such citizenship shall not in any manner impair or otherwise affect the right of any Indian to tribal or other property." The bill was approved by Congress, and the American Indian Citizenship Act, signed into law on June 2, 1924, by President Calvin Coolidge, made Native Americans both citizens of the United States and persons with tribal relations.

Ultimately, citizenship had little impact on American Indian life. The Bureau of Indian Affairs continued its policy of treating tribal members as wards of the government and administering affairs for American Indian citizens. The right to vote was denied to many American Indians until the 1960's, because the states had the power to determine voter eligibility and did not consider tribal members living on reservations to reside in the state. With federal protections in place, American Indians have been granted the right to vote in federal, state, and local elections, and as members of tribes, they also can vote in tribal elections. —*Carole A. Barrett*

ADDITIONAL READING:

Cohen, Felix. *Handbook of Federal Indian Law*. Washington, D.C.: Government Printing Office, 1942. The most complete sourcebook for American Indian legal issues.

Debo, Angie. *A History of the Indians in the United States*. Norman: University of Oklahoma Press, 1989. A comprehensive, in-depth historical survey of Indians of the United States, emphasizing tribal relations with the U.S. government.

Olson, James S., and Raymond Wilson. *Native Americans in the Twentieth Century*. Chicago: University of Illinois Press, 1984. A good text for interpreting major trends, events, and attitudes affecting American Indian peoples, including the myriad issues involved in the citizenship debate.

Prucha, Francis Paul. *The Great Father: The United States Government and the American Indians*. Lincoln: University of Nebraska Press, 1984. A seminal work for understanding federal-tribal relationships and the development of American Indian policy. Traces the controversies surrounding citizenship for Indians.

Smith, Michael T. "The History of Indian Citizenship." In *The American Indian Past and Present*. 2d ed. New York: John Wiley & Sons, 1981. Traces the major factors that made it difficult for American Indians to obtain citizenship.

Washburn, Wilcomb, ed. *Indian-White Relations*. Vol. 4 in *Handbook of North American Indians*. Washington, D.C.: Smithsonian Institution Press, 1988. Discusses the American Indian in the complex federal-tribal context and contains information on citizenship.

SEE ALSO: 1871, Indian Appropriation Act; 1887, General Allotment Act; 1934, Indian Reorganization Act; 1953, Termination Resolution.

1924 ■ IMMIGRATION ACT OF 1924:
Congress restricts immigration by means of a quota system

DATE: July 1, 1924
LOCALE: United States
CATEGORIES: Immigration; Laws and acts
KEY FIGURES:
William Paul Dillingham (1843-1923), U.S. senator from Vermont
Denis Kearney (1847-1907), Irish American who worked for exclusion of Chinese labor
Henry Cabot Lodge (1850-1924), founder of the Immigration Restriction League

SUMMARY OF EVENT. There was no clearly defined official U.S. policy toward immigration until the late nineteenth century. The United States was still a relatively young country, and there was a need for settlers in the West and for workers to build industry. Chinese immigrants flowed into California in 1849 and the early 1850's, searching for fortune and staying as laborers who worked the mines and labored to build the transcontinental railroad.

The earliest immigration restriction focused on Asians. In 1875, the federal government restricted the number of Chinese and Japanese coming into the country. The push for restriction of Asian immigrants was led by U.S. workers. After the depression of 1877, Denis Kearney, an Irish-born labor organizer, helped found the Workingman's Trade and Labor Union of San Francisco, an anti-Chinese and anticapitalist group. Kearney and others believed that lower-paid Chinese workers took jobs away from white workers, and they agitated for expulsion of the Chinese and legal restrictions on future immigrants. Their efforts were successful in 1882, when the Chinese Exclusion Act was passed. The act exempted teachers, students, merchants, and pleasure travelers, and remained in effect until 1943. With the act of 1882, the federal government had, for the first time, placed restrictions on the immigration of persons from a specific country. More specific policy toward European immigration began in the 1880's. In 1882, the federal government excluded convicts, paupers, and mentally impaired persons. Organized labor's efforts also were successful in 1882, with the prohibition of employers' recruiting workers in Europe and paying their passage to the United States.

Federal law became more aggressive by the early twentieth century, with the passage of the Act of 1903, which excluded epileptics, beggars, and anarchists. In 1907, the United States Immigration Commission was formed. This group, also known as the Dillingham Commission, published a forty-two-volume survey of the impact of immigration on American life and called for a literacy test and further immigration restriction. Although several presidential vetoes had prevented a literacy requirement, in 1917, the U.S. Congress overrode President Woodrow Wilson's veto and passed a law requiring a literacy test for newcomers. The test was designed to reduce the number of immigrants, particularly those from southeastern Europe, where the literacy rate was low.

The marked change in official policy and in the view of a majority of people in the United States was caused by several factors. A strong nativist movement had begun after World War I with such groups as the American Protective Association, an organization that began in the Midwest in the 1880's and focused on prejudice against aliens and Catholics. Senator Henry Cabot Lodge organized the Immigration Restriction League in Boston, indicating the addition of U.S. leaders and intellectuals to the restriction movement. The war had brought the United States into position as a major world power, with a resultant view that the United States should be a nation of conformity. Political and economic problems in Europe, including the war and a postwar economic depression, had led to fear of too many immigrants fleeing Europe. Changes in the U.S. economy reduced the need for manual labor, thus creating a fear of lack of job security.

The push for restriction coincided with the most intensive era of immigration in United States history. From the late 1880's until the 1920's, the nation experienced wave after wave of immigration, with millions of persons coming into the country each decade. The growth of new physical and social sciences that emphasized heredity as a factor in intelligence led many people to believe that persons such as Slavs or Italians were less intelligent than western Europeans such as the Norwegians or the English. The belief in genetic inferiority gave credence to the immigration restriction movement and helped sway the government.

At the same time that millions of newcomers were entering the United States, a spirit of reform, the Progressive Era, had grown throughout the country. Americans who saw themselves as progressive and forward-looking pushed for change in politics, society, and education, particularly in the crowded urban areas of the Northeast. Europeans had emigrated in large numbers to the cities, and newer groups, such as Italians and Poles, were seen by many progressive-minded reformers as the root of urban problems. Thus it was with the help of progressive leaders that a push was made at the federal level to restrict the number of immigrants.

In 1921, Congress passed a temporary measure that was the first U.S. law specifically restricting European immigration. The act established a quota system that held the number of immigrants to 3 percent of each admissible nationality living in the United States in 1910. Quotas were established for persons from Europe, Asia, Africa, Australia, and New Zealand. Although only a temporary measure, the Immigration Act of 1921 marked the beginning of a permanent policy of restricting European immigration. It began a bitter three-year controversy that led to the Immigration Act of 1924.

The United States Congress amended the 1921 act with a more restrictive permanent measure in May of 1924, the Johnson-Reid Act. This act, which became known as the National Origins Act, took effect on July 1, 1924. It limited the annual immigration to the United States to 2 percent of a country's population in the U.S. as of the census of 1890. With the large numbers of northern and western Europeans who had immigrated to the country throughout the nation's history, the act effectively restricted southern and eastern European immigrants to approximately 12 percent of the total immigrant population. Asian immigration was completely prohibited, but there was no restriction on immigration from independent nations of the Western Hemisphere.

The new law also changed the processing system for aliens by moving the immigration inspection process to U.S. consulates in foreign countries and requiring immigrants to obtain visas in the native country before emigrating to the United States. The number of visas was held to 10 percent in each country per month and thus reduced the number of people arriving at Ellis Island, leading to the eventual closing of the facility.

The Immigration Act of 1924 reflects a change in the controversy that occurred in the three-year period after the act of 1921. By 1924, the major factor in immigration restriction was racial prejudice. By using the Census of 1890 as the basis for quotas, the government in effect sharply reduced the number of southern and eastern Europeans, who had not begun to arrive in large numbers until after that census year. The passage of the act codified an official policy of preventing further changes in the ethnic composition of U.S. society, and it was to remain in effect until passage of the Immigration and Nationality Act of 1965.   —*Judith Boyce DeMark*

ADDITIONAL READING:

Bolino, August C. *The Ellis Island Source Book*. Washington, D.C.: Kensington Historical Press, 1985. Although focusing on the available resources for family and immigrant history, includes a history of Ellis Island and immigration restriction.

Curran, Thomas J. *Xenophobia and Immigration, 1820-1930*. Boston: Twayne, 1975. A basic overview of the reasons for immigration restriction throughout U.S. history, focusing on nativism and such groups as the Ku Klux Klan.

Divine, Robert A. *American Immigration Policy, 1924-1952*. New Haven, Conn.: Yale University Press, 1957. Reprint. New York: Da Capo Press, 1972. One of the most comprehensive treatments of the history of immigration restriction from the 1924 act through the mid-1950's.

Reeves, Pamela. *Ellis Island: Gateway to the American*

Dream. New York: Crescent Books, 1991. A pictorial history of the major port of entry for new immigrants. Contains a good section on immigration restriction.

Seller, Maxine S. "Historical Perspectives on American Immigration Policy: Case Studies and Current Implications." In *U.S. Immigration Policy*, edited by Richard R. Hofstetter. Durham, N.C.: Duke University Press, 1984. Contains a chronology of the series of events leading up to the Immigration Act of 1924, with a discussion of how those events relate to recent immigration history.

SEE ALSO: 1882, Chinese Exclusion Act; 1892, Yellow Peril Campaign; 1913, Alien Land Laws; 1917, Immigration Act of 1917; 1943, Magnuson Act; 1952, McCarran-Walter Act; 1965, Immigration and Nationality Act.

1924 ■ DAWES PLAN: *the United States develops a plan to assist Germany in recovering from World War I*

DATE: September 1, 1924
LOCALE: Washington, D.C., London, Paris, and Berlin
CATEGORIES: Diplomacy and international relations; Economics
KEY FIGURES:
Charles Gates Dawes (1865-1951), chairman of the first committee of the special commission to investigate the German financial situation
Charles Evans Hughes (1862-1948), U.S. secretary of state who proposed that an international commission be created to deal with Germany's financial difficulties
David Lloyd George (1863-1945), former British prime minister who supported Hughes's plan
Henry M. Robinson (1868-1937) and
Owen D. Young (1874-1962), U.S. financial experts on the special commission
Gustav Stresemann (1878-1929), German foreign minister who supported the Dawes Plan
SUMMARY OF EVENT. In the aftermath of World War I, it appeared that the Treaty of Versailles had raised more problems than it had solved. Among the more pressing and complicated issues were the interrelated problems of German reparations and Allied war debts. By the peace treaty, Germany had been forced to accept blame for the war and to promise to pay damages suffered by the Allies. A special Reparations Commission fixed the sum owed by Germany at 132 million gold marks, about $33 million in gold. Even some members of the commission recognized that Germany would be unable to pay this staggering sum. The Allied governments, especially those of Great Britain and France, expressed a willingness to scale down German reparations if the United States would forgo war debts owed to it by the Allies.

The U.S. government had loaned more than ten billion dollars to twenty nations before and after the armistice, and it refused to forget these debts or to link them with the problem of German reparations. Moreover, while European countries could repay their debts only by selling goods and services in the United States, the latter embarked in the immediate postwar period on a tariff program that represented aggressive economic nationalism and crushed any hope that European goods would be able to compete in the U.S. market. Consequently, the Allies had to press Germany for reparations in order to repay their own debts. The German government made a few token payments, but when faced with catastrophic inflation, it defaulted. In 1923, France occupied the Ruhr, Germany's principal industrial region, and took other steps to coerce the Weimar Republic into resuming payments. The Germans replied with a policy of passive resistance. The crisis was so serious that Europe appeared to be on the verge of financial and political disintegration.

It was to avoid economic disaster in Europe that the United States intervened. Although most people in the United States insisted on repayment of the Allied war debts and refused to accept the Anglo-French argument that reparations and war debts were interdependent, some also saw that European trade was essential to U.S. prosperity. Something had to be done to ensure that trade and financial intercourse be returned to normal channels. Secretary of State Charles Evans Hughes was one of those deeply concerned about the problem, even though he was a tariff protectionist. He could not propose direct U.S. involvement in European financial affairs because of congressional and public opposition; however, unofficial action might help Europe while avoiding serious objections at home.

In a speech before the American Historical Association in December, 1922, Secretary Hughes proposed the creation of a commission of financial experts to investigate Germany's financial situation and to make recommendations concerning how and to what extent reparations should be paid. He did not say that the United States would participate directly in these negotiations, although he did admit, "I have no doubt that distinguished Americans would be willing to serve in such a commission."

Hughes apparently hoped this public proposal would cause the French to postpone occupation of the Ruhr, but the French went ahead with this act in January, 1923, and it appeared that Secretary Hughes's scheme was dead. In the fall of 1923, however, after it had become clear that the Ruhr operation was a failure, David Lloyd George, former prime minister of Great Britain, urged the French government to reconsider the U.S. secretary of state's idea. After further discussion, France agreed to a restricted version of the Hughes proposal. The Reparations Committee in late November created two special commissions; one was to attempt to balance the budget and stabilize the currency of Germany, and the other was to deal with German holdings abroad. The next step was to appoint a battery of experts. Not surprisingly, the Reparations Commission wanted several U.S. representatives to participate in this work. Apparently, the Department of State was asked unofficially to recommend candidates. The names of Charles G.

Dawes, Owen D. Young, and Henry M. Robinson, all noted financial experts, were put forward.

Dawes was appointed chairman of the first committee, and subsequent agreements were called the Dawes Plan. Credit must have gone equally to Hughes. After several months of deliberation, Dawes announced the committee's recommendations on April 9, 1924. Their report recognized two distinct problems: the need for Germany to return to economic solvency, and the need for an acceptable method of transferring surplus revenue to the Allies. The Dawes Committee proposed the reorganization of the Reichsbank under Allied supervision, a loan of $200 million in gold, and the creation of a new monetary unit, the Reichsmark. No precise figure was set for total reparations, but the Dawes Plan posited a sliding scale of payments based on expected German financial prospects. For 1924-1925, the payment was set at $250 million, and it was to rise over a period of five years to $625 million. The German government was committed to making these payments, but provisions were made to ensure that they would not threaten the stability of the German currency. One such provision was the appointment of an Agent General for Reparations Payments to supervise and coordinate financial relations.

The Dawes Plan went into effect on September 1, 1924. Gustav Stresemann, the German foreign minster, persuaded his government that the plan presented Germany with an opportunity to rebuild its economy. Despite criticism from extreme nationalists, he convinced the German people that the plan offered Germany many advantages, freeing Germany from French occupation of the Ruhr and attracting needed foreign investments. In terms of its limited goals, it worked amazingly well. The international loan was oversubscribed, mostly by U.S. investors. An officer of the banking House of Morgan was appointed Agent General. Between 1925 and 1927, all went well and the revival of the German economy seemed assured; only later was the Dawes Plan seen to be a stopgap measure. Only through borrowing from outside was Germany able to meet is obligatory reparations. U.S. loans to Germany under the Dawes Plan and the subsequent Young Plan exceeded $3 billion, while a total of only $2.6 billion was paid by the Allies to the United States during the same period. Despite the obvious connection between German reparations and Allied war debts, the United States continued to repudiate such a relationship.

—Theodore A. Wilson, updated by Leslie V. Tischauser

ADDITIONAL READING:

Adler, Selig. *The Uncertain Giant, 1921-1941: American Foreign Policy Between the Wars.* New York: Harper & Row, 1965. A popular survey of the United States' role in Europe between World Wars I and II.

Craig, Gordon. *Germany: 1866-1945.* New York: Oxford University Press, 1978. Contains a useful discussion of Germany's economic and social problems in the 1920's and an assessment of the impact of the Dawes Plan.

Dawes, Charles Gates. *A Journal of Reparations.* London: Macmillan, 1939. Dawes reviews his role in the investigation of Germany's financial fight.

Schuker, Stephen A. *The End of French Predominance in Europe: The Financial Crisis of 1924 and the Adoption of the Dawes Plan.* Chapel Hill: University of North Carolina Press, 1976. An interpretation of the writing of the plan, with a useful discussion of the role of the United States in the negotiations.

Wilson, Joan Hoff. *American Business and Foreign Policy, 1920-1933.* Lexington: University Press of Kentucky, 1971. Describes the role of the Dawes Plan in the economic rebuilding of Germany.

SEE ALSO: 1919, Treaty of Versailles; 1921, Washington Disarmament Conference; 1928, Kellogg-Briand Pact; 1932, Hoover-Stimson Doctrine; 1935, Neutrality Acts; 1941, Germany and Italy Declare War on the United States; 1945, United Nations Charter Convention; 1945, Potsdam Conference; 1947, National Security Act; 1948, Berlin Blockade.

1924 ■ HALIBUT TREATY: *after five years of negotiation, an agreement is reached to save the fisheries of the North Pacific, displaying U.S.-Canadian cooperation*

DATE: October 21, 1924
LOCALE: Ottawa and Washington, D.C.
CATEGORIES: Canadian history; Environment; Treaties and agreements
KEY FIGURES:
Julian Hedworth George Byng (1862-1935), British governor general of Canada
Charles Evans Hughes (1862-1948), U.S. secretary of state
William Lyon Mackenzie King (1874-1950), Canadian prime minister

SUMMARY OF EVENT. On March 21, 1919, a Canadian-American Fisheries Conference called for a closed season on halibut fishing in the North Pacific every year for the next ten years. The commission, made up of scientists and fisheries experts, reported that halibut would totally disappear from the seas unless fishing were prohibited for at least this period. In October of the same year, the Canadian government sent a draft treaty to the United States secretary of state calling for an end to halibut fishing from November 15, 1920, to February 15, 1921, and similar dates until 1930. Boats violating this season would be seized by either country's navy and their owners suitably punished. The treaty also contained provisions concerning regulations on lobster fishing, tariffs on fish traded between the two nations, rules for port privileges for fishing boats, and a call for a scientific investigation into the life history of the Pacific halibut.

The United States took no immediate action on the proposal. In February, 1921, however, another commission of fisheries experts issued another report predicting disaster unless halibut received protection. This conference report likened the troubles of the halibut industry to the terrible conditions faced by salmon fishermen on the Pacific coast. The value of salmon shipped from U.S. and Canadian canneries had dropped by more than 90 percent since 1913 (from $30 million to $3 million) and was heading quickly toward zero. The halibut industry faced similarly depressed conditions unless something was done quickly to save the fish.

Secretary of State Charles Evans Hughes and Secretary of Commerce Herbert Hoover recognized the need for action on the treaty. President Warren G. Harding sent it to the Senate for ratification, a procedure requiring a two-thirds vote of approval. Senators began debating the various sections of the proposal but refused to ratify it after objections from the governor, members of Congress, and fisheries authorities in Washington State. They claimed the halibut question properly belonged in the hands of state officials, not the federal authorities in Washington, D.C.; thus, the province of British Columbia should be discussing limits with the state of Washington. Canadian authorities argued that the provinces had no jurisdiction over such international questions as fisheries. Therefore, direct negotiations with the state of Washington were not permitted. Another problem had to do with punishing violators of the closed season. Canada suggested that ships caught with halibut during the closed season could be tried in both countries if authorities desired. Several senators argued that this constituted double jeopardy, a violation of the U.S. Constitution. Violators should be tried only once and in only one court for the same crime. Because of these objections, the treaty was withdrawn from Senate consideration in late August. It seemed to have no chance of ratification.

Canadian fisheries experts expressed outrage at the Senate's failure to ratify the treaty and asked whether any modifications would change the results. Secretary Hughes replied that he knew of no modifications that would change the minds of those senators who were opposed. He did suggest a meeting between Washington State officials and Canadian experts in the Pacific Northwest, and both sides agreed to that proposal. In February, 1922, representatives from the Canadian Marine and Fisheries Department met with the Fisheries Board of the state of Washington. They reached no agreement on protecting halibut, although they did decide to stop sockeye salmon fishing totally for five years, so desperately low was the population of that species. Washington State officials refused to give assurance that they would help control halibut fishing.

In August, 1922, the Canadian government, tired of waiting for action by the United States, sent the United States a new draft proposal asking for immediate action. On December 14, the United states agreed in principle to the new treaty, although it still needed Senate approval. The new treaty provided for a closed season on halibut. Violators would be turned over either to the U.S. Department of Commerce or to the Canadian Ministry of Marine and Fisheries of the Dominion of Canada, but not to both agencies. The United States representatives suggested that halibut taken accidentally during the closed season be used only to feed the crew of the detained vessel but not be sold. This provision was added to the final draft.

A new complication arose when the revised treaty was sent back to Canada. In February, 1923, the British Colonial Office in London demanded that the treaty's title be changed before it could be given final approval by the English government. Canada, at this time, was still officially part of the British Empire. The title was to be changed from "A Convention for the Regulation of Halibut Fisheries on the Pacific Coast of Canada and the United States" to "A Convention for the Regulation of Halibut Fisheries on the Pacific Coast of His Majesty the King of the United Kingdom, of Great Britain and Ireland and the British Dominions Beyond the Seas, Emperor of India and the United States." The first version would signify that Canada had the right to negotiate its own treaties, something that had never happened before and that the British wished to ensure never would.

Governor General Julian Byng of Canada suggested that, because the treaty concerned only the United States and Canada, the signature of a Canadian minister should be enough to make it official. The British refused to back down, however, and when the final document was signed in Washington, on March 2, 1923, it included the signature of the British colonial secretary. The closed season was established from November 16 to February 15; halibut taken during this season could be used only for food for the crew. Violators would have their boats seized and would be tried in the courts in the nation from which they came. The treaty also established an International Fisheries Commission of four members to study the life and environment of halibut and present recommendations for future regulations needed to save the fish. The treaty and ban would be in effect for five years and then renewed if both parties agreed.

The Senate began debate on the treaty in March and voted to ratify it with only one change. It added a provision stating that none of the nationals and inhabitants of any other part of Great Britain should engage in halibut fishing. This prohibition included people from all parts of the British Empire. When Canada received this change, it raised an objection. This amendment put the Canadians in an embarrassing position. It seemed to champion the British cause, at the expense of Canada, by insisting that Canada had to secure the consent of the entire British Empire before the treaty could be agreed upon. Canada could not accept this demand; the document would not be presented to the Parliament in Ottawa because it would face certain defeat. The government of William Lyon Mackenzie King wanted to make the point that it could sign treaties without British consent, and they would block passage of the Halibut Treaty if necessary.

In October, the Harding Administration agreed to resubmit the treaty without the offensive reservation. The Senate, however, was not scheduled to meet again until December, too late to approve a closed season for 1923-1924. Canada asked if the president could impose a ban on halibut fishing but was told that such action was beyond the powers of the chief executive of the United States. Halibut fishing had suffered greatly reduced supplies of fish since the first draft treaty had been proposed, more than four years earlier. Still, both sides reluctantly had to announce there would be no closed season that winter either.

By January, 1924, Canadian authorities declared that since the waters off Washington State and southern British Columbia had almost been depleted of halibut, fishing vessels would have to move north to the coast of Alaska. Supplies in that region were more abundant. Still, the halibut industry faced serious trouble and possible bankruptcy if the catching of fish were not halted quickly. Both sides eventually backed down from their positions. The British king, George V, signed the Halibut Treaty on July 31, and Canadian and U.S. officials added their signatures on October 21, 1924. A closed season began in November and has continued into the 1990's.

—*Leslie V. Tischauser*

ADDITIONAL READING:

Clark, Lovell C., ed. *1919-1925*. Vol. 3 in *Documents on Canadian External Relations*. Ottawa: Department of External Affairs, 1970. No single book or article covers the Halibut Treaty in detail. This is the best source of information.

McInnis, Edgar. *Canada: A Political and Social History*. 4th ed. Toronto: Holt, Rinehart and Winston of Canada, 1982. Includes a brief discussion of the treaty.

SEE ALSO: 1936, Reciprocity Treaty.

1924 ■ COOLIDGE IS ELECTED PRESIDENT:
a business-friendly administration triggers the Roaring Twenties

DATE: November 4, 1924
LOCALE: United States
CATEGORY: Government and politics
KEY FIGURES:
Calvin Coolidge (1872-1933), thirtieth president of the United States, 1923-1929
Warren Gamaliel Harding (1865-1923), twenty-ninth president of the United States, 1921-1923
Herbert Clark Hoover (1874-1964), secretary of commerce; later, thirty-first president of the United States, 1929-1933
Andrew William Mellon (1855-1937), secretary of the Treasury

SUMMARY OF EVENT. Calvin Coolidge's famous statement, "The chief business of the American people is business," and Warren Harding's "Less government in business, more business in government," captured the spirit of the United States after World War I. A nation weary of Woodrow Wilson's idealistic crusade to "make the world safe for democracy" and of Progressive attempts to regulate business and individual life elected three consecutive Republican administrations in the 1920's and continued Republican dominance of the Oval Office for all but sixteen years of the period 1860 to 1932. During the decade of the 1920's, the United States reached unparalleled levels of prosperity and sustained a decade without a war.

Technological changes, including the automobile, radio, and widespread use of electrical energy, gave U.S. industry the capability to produce goods and provide employment at unprecedented levels. More than technology accounted for the Roaring Twenties, however: Secretary of the Treasury Andrew W. Mellon created dramatic tax cuts that unleashed the United States' productivity, paid off one-third of the national debt, and resulted in federal budget surpluses for most years in the decade. During the 1920's, unemployment levels dropped to the unequaled level of 1 percent, while confidence in business drove stock prices to new heights.

Warren Harding had won the presidency with his promise to return the U.S. to normality, by which he meant an end to wartime constraints and high levels of taxation. Railroads, telephone, and telegraph systems were returned to private ownership, and the government-built and -owned merchant vessels to the private maritime industry. Harding's administration suffered, however, from scandals such as Teapot Dome and from accusations that he had a mistress. Harding died in June, 1923, bringing New Englander Calvin Coolidge to the presidency.

Coolidge aptly characterized wealth as the product of industry, ambition, character, and untiring effort. Coolidge put people before industry, as when he observed that the country needed a business government, by which he meant not "a government *by* business, not government *for* business, but . . . a government that will *understand* business." Critics, however, maintained that Coolidge merely granted easier access to government for business, and that he ignored antitrust or other regulatory efforts that business disliked. Although Coolidge had no control over the Federal Reserve Board, critics contended that his administration encouraged loose credit policies by the board that resulted in a "speculative bubble" in the stock market.

Coolidge may have represented the era, but it began with the election of Warren Harding in 1920 and was characterized by Harding's appointment of Andrew Mellon as Treasury secretary. Mellon observed that the rich had avoided paying taxes under the high rates, mainly by finding tax shelters. To boost government revenue, Mellon reduced tax rates, especially on the rich, making it less profitable for them to engage in accounting or investment manipulations to avoid taxation. As a result, the rich paid more in taxes than at any previous time in history, both in total dollar amounts and as a share of all taxes paid. Revenues rose as well, with the amount collected from those earning more than one hundred thousand dollars rising from $194 million to $361 million. Mellon's tax cuts benefited the poorest groups the most, as their share of total taxes paid declined from $155 million to $32 million in 1926. Mellon's cuts increased government revenues to such an extent that the government reduced its national debt—not annual deficits—by one-third. "Coolidge prosperity" bathed the nation. Families bought radios, electrical appliances, and other conveniences. Henry Ford, manufacturing Model T's with mass production, cut prices to the extent that an average U.S. family

Calvin Coolidge, thirtieth president of the United States, captured the spirit of the prosperous 1920's in his statement, "The chief business of the American people is business." (Library of Congress)

could acquire an automobile for a year's wages. The widespread expansion of cars and electrical energy made transportation and commerce cheaper and more available, reducing prices on virtually all manufactured goods.

Some did not participate in the "Coolidge prosperity." Wealth inequality during the decade increased, largely because the number of millionaires grew rapidly. Stock manipulations during the Great Bull Market involved more than a few shady characters: Samuel Insull, for example, created a pyramid of utilities that collapsed. Margin buying—seen as contributing to the speculation in the stock market—rose from $1 billion in 1920 to $8 billion in 1929. Many analysts, including the famous economist John Kenneth Galbraith, would argue that the inequities in wealth, stock speculation, and unsustainable consumer demand led directly to the Great Depression.

The fantastic rise in stock prices, however, may have only reflected the real growth of new industries, and not surprisingly, utility, radio, automobile, and steel stocks witnessed some of the most rapid gains. The manufacturing boom also stimulated the stock market, even without assistance from the Federal Reserve or margin buying. Securities pioneers such as Charles Merrill developed sales plans to place securities in the hands of ordinary families, who found that they could own a piece of a major corporation at low cost. The incentive to purchase such stocks was not necessarily brokers' loans, but

the fact that share prices did not fall for more than five years. It was, many people thought, a sure thing.

Coolidge was eligible to run again in 1928, but stepped down. In his place came Secretary of Commerce Herbert Hoover, who had a reputation as a planner who would merge the best parts of government and business. Rather than continuing the Coolidge policies, however, Hoover was a throwback to Wilson—a Progressive who sought to encourage the formation of voluntary trade associations in various industries that would establish quality standards, develop joint advertising campaigns, and force businesses into a net of cooperative efforts at a time when competition had led to the highest standard of living in the world. Nevertheless, business had few reservations about such a policy and welcomed an administration that would return to the World War I era of restricted competition. For example, the large population of small, unit banks supported passage of the McFadden Act of 1927, which essentially stymied the expansion of nationwide branch banking, out of concern that large banks would compete with them in local markets.

Hoover had experience in agriculture and hoped to help the struggling farm economy recover. His administration established the Federal Farm Board to make low-interest loans to farm cooperatives and to absorb surpluses, thus raising prices. Farm income recovered in some spots, but the low-interest loans increased production, lowering prices and contributing to the general business decline by keeping the farm sector in distress.

In other ways, Hoover—who has been criticized as "probusiness"—represented a break from Coolidge and Harding by championing planning as the solution to save the economy, especially after the 1929 stock market crash. The Federal Reserve Board had made a number of critical errors in the management of the nation's banking and monetary system. Misled into thinking that the stock market boom fueled inflation, in 1928, the Federal Reserve Board tightened the money supply, curtailing production and sending international markets further into a tailspin. Congress passed the Hawley-Smoot Tariff in 1930, but key deliberations occurred just days before "Black Thursday," leading many persons to conclude that concern over the ruinous tariff rates (increases up to 34 percent on most goods) prompted the Great Crash. Foreign markets, already in depression, could no longer export to the United States or import U.S. goods; U.S. companies, sensing that their foreign markets were about to clamp shut, laid off workers and liquidated stock to gain capital.

Hoover's other policies represented sharp breaks with the Harding-Coolidge approach to the economy, especially his creation of the Reconstruction Finance Corporation (RFC), which gave loans to troubled banks and businesses. However, the RFC published the names of loan recipients, and the public response was to withdraw money from banks or cease to conduct business with firms on the list. Bank runs accelerated. The policies of the Federal Reserve Board, Hoover, and Congress, combined with the adherence to the gold standard long after other nations had abandoned gold, effectively ended the "Coolidge prosperity." One of Hoover's first attempts to remedy the situation was to raise taxes, marking the final separation from Coolidge and Harding as the Roaring Twenties crashed to an end. —*Larry Schweikart*

ADDITIONAL READING:

Atack, Jeremy, and Peter Passell. *A New Economic View of American History*. 2d ed. Boston: W. W. Norton, 1994. A historiographical look at economists' findings regarding the key economic events of U.S. history. In regard to the Depression, suggests that the monetarist views of Milton Friedman and the case against the gold standard have risen to high levels of acceptability among scholars.

Folsom, Burton, Jr. *The Myth of the Robber Barons*. Herndon, Va.: Young America's Foundation, 1991. Contains an insightful chapter on Mellon and the effects of his tax policies in the 1920's. Includes a criticism of contentions that significant wealth disparities existed during the decade.

Schlesinger, Arthur M., Jr. *Crisis of the Old Order*. Boston: Houghton Mifflin, 1957. An influential book detailing the 1920's from a liberal perspective. Relies heavily on descriptions of Coolidge supplied by William White, whose accounts have not stood the test of time. White, for example, ignored substantial evidence that Coolidge viewed the economy as an integrated force of employees, capitalists, and consumers.

Silver, Thomas B. *Coolidge and the Historians*. Durham, N.C.: Carolina Academic Press, 1982. By far the most balanced book for addressing historical misinformation about Coolidge's policies and words. Provides full quotations for Coolidge's speeches, which other historians have not done.

White, William Allen. *Calvin Coolidge: The Man Who Is President*. New York: Macmillan, 1925. The earliest, and most flawed, interpretation of Coolidge, followed by White's 1938 book, *A Puritan in Babylon: The Story of Calvin Coolidge* (New York: Macmillan, 1938).

Wilson, Joan Hoff. *Herbert Hoover: Forgotten Progressive*. Boston: Little, Brown, 1975. A liberal revisionist portrays Hoover as consistent with the Progressive movement earlier in the century, and argues that Hoover had sharp differences with Coolidge and Harding.

SEE ALSO: 1918, Demobilization After World War I; 1921, Scandals of the Harding Administration; 1928, Smith-Hoover Campaign; 1929, Stock Market Crash; 1929, Great Depression.

1925 ■ SCOPES TRIAL: *a test of one state's prohibition of the teaching of evolution underscores the separation of church and state*

DATE: July 10, 1925-1927
LOCALE: Dayton, Tenneesee
CATEGORIES: Court cases; Education

KEY FIGURES:

William Jennings Bryan (1860-1925), known as "the Commoner," three-time presidential candidate, a staunch religious fundamentalist, and one of the prosecuting attorneys

Clarence Seward Darrow (1857-1938), well-known lawyer and agnostic, member of the defense counsel

Arthur Garfield Hayes, assisting defense attorney

Dudley Field Malone, assisting defense attorney

Henry Louis Mencken (1880-1956), journalist, responsible for much of the trial's sensationalism

John T. Raulston (1868-1956), presiding judge at the trial

John Thomas Scopes (1900-1970), schoolteacher on trial for violation of the Butler Act

A. T. Stewart, prosecuting attorney

SUMMARY OF EVENT. For eleven days in July, 1925, one of the most widely publicized and bizarre legal cases in United States history, *Tennessee v. John Thomas Scopes*, better known as the "Monkey trial," was tried in Dayton, Tennessee.

Scopes, a football coach and science teacher in Dayton's Rhea County High School, was charged with violating the Butler Act, a state law passed in January, 1925, forbidding the teaching in public schools of any theories that denied the story of creation as found in Genesis. This act was written because of the increasing alarm of many fundamentalist Christians who feared the challenge that science and evolutionary theory presented to a literal interpretation of the Bible. Between 1921 and 1929, thirty-seven such bills opposing the teaching of evolution were introduced in twenty states.

Shortly after the passage of the Butler Act, the American Civil Liberties Union (ACLU) offered its services to any teacher in Tennessee who would test the constitutionality of the act. George Rappleyea, a local mining engineer, learned of the ACLU's offer and discussed the possibilities of a test case with Scopes, even though Scopes himself was not teaching biology that year. Since the principal of the school, who actually taught the class, had a family who stood to suffer from the attention that such a trial would invite, Scopes chose to be the defendant. With the reluctant consent of the chairman of the school board and the county superintendent of schools, Scopes was arrested for teaching evolution in his biology class and bound over to the grand jury. The ACLU was immediately notified.

Within a few days, William Jennings Bryan, three-time Democratic presidential candidate and a well-known religious fundamentalist, announced that he would aid District Attorney A. T. Stewart in the prosecution of the case. Bryan, a populist who had been one of the nation's most progressive politicians, advocating women's suffrage, railroad regulation, campaign fund disclosure, and abolition of the death penalty, was obsessed with the social implications of evolution. He was especially outraged at Social Darwinism, an extension of the scientific theory which rationalized neglect of the poor and weak as justified by Charles Darwin's theory of natural selection. Although Darwin had never intended his theory for such nonscientific and immoral use, Social Darwinism had been popularized along with the theories of biological evolution. "Survival of the fittest" went against Bryan's populism and smacked of an elitism he had been fighting all his life.

The lawyers for the defense were led by Clarence Darrow, a well-known agnostic and the most famous trial lawyer in the country. Darrow had not been interested in the case until he learned that Bryan was to be part of the prosecution. The journalist H. L. Mencken happened to be in Richmond with Darrow when word came about Bryan's participation. Mencken persuaded his friend to join the defense. Both Darrow and Mencken considered the trial an opportunity to confront obscurantism, which they saw incarnate in Bryan and the South. Then, Darrow said, "For the first, the last, and the only time in my life, I volunteered my services in a case. I did it because I really wanted to take part in it." Other noteworthy defense lawyers were Dudley Field Malone, a well-known divorce lawyer, and Arthur Garfield Hayes, perhaps the most outstanding civil liberties attorney of the time.

Because of the dramatic nature of the trial and the fame of the opposing attorneys, Dayton became the center of national and even international attention. Mencken was only the most prominent journalist present; the country's major newspapers flooded the small town with reporters. All the wire services had reporters there, and the case was followed daily by millions of readers in both the United States and Europe. Telegraph wires were run into the courthouse and the *Chicago Tribune* installed radio equipment; the trial enjoyed the first broadcast in American history. The town of Dayton assumed a carnival-like atmosphere as the local inhabitants began to prepare for the expected crush of visitors. Soft drink and sandwich stands were built; hotels and boardinghouses were quickly filled. One Daytonian described the scene: "One was hard put to it on the tenth of July to know whether Dayton was holding a camp meeting, a Chautauqua, a street fair, a carnival or belated Fourth of July celebration. Literally it was drunk with religious excitement."

On Friday, July 10, Judge John T. Raulston had the trial opened with a prayer, to which Darrow objected and was overruled. The jury was selected. The state's case as it was presented was simple: Three schoolboys testified that Scopes had taught evolution in the science class and the prosecution rested.

From the beginning it was the defense's goal to put the Butler Act, rather than Scopes, on trial. Darrow wanted to prove that evolution was neither contrary to the Bible nor nonreligious and therefore the Butler Act was unconstitutional and violated the civil rights of all Tennessee teachers. The first controversy surrounded the question of admitting the testimony of "experts" (scientists), who had been assembled by Darrow and Malone for the defense. Each of the experts was both an evolutionist and a Christian whose testimony was to prove that there was no conflict between science and religion. When the first expert was called, Attorney General Stewart objected on the grounds that any interpretation of evolution or the Bible, whether by experts or not, would be opinion rather than fact and should therefore not be admissible as evidence. Further, said Stewart, such testimony would have nothing to do with the case at hand, which was to ascertain whether or not Scopes had taught material that conflicted with the law. At this point, the judge excused the jury until he could rule on whether or not scientific testimony was admissible. The jury was admonished not to stand around in the courtyard where the jurors might hear the trial in progress from the public address system which was broadcasting to the crowd outside.

On Friday, July 17, Judge Raulston, agreeing with the prosecution, refused to permit the scientists to testify, declaring that the only relevant question for the court to decide was whether Scopes had actually taught the theory of evolution. This ruling destroyed the defense's case because it prevented the testing of the questions of the constitutionality of the law and the violation of the defendant's civil liberties, as well as the truthfulness of the doctrine of evolution.

The trial probably would have ended there, for the defense did not deny that Scopes had taught evolution, had not Bryan made the mistake of allowing Darrow to get him on the stand as an "expert" on the Bible. Darrow bore down hard on Bryan's fundamentalist beliefs, and in a grueling and sarcastic hour and a half of cross-examination made a shambles of the "Great Commoner."

DARROW: Do you believe Joshua made the sun stand still?

BRYAN: I believe what the Bible says. I suppose you mean that the earth stood still?

DARROW: Have you ever pondered what would happen to the earth if it suddenly stood still?

BRYAN: No.

DARROW: Don't you know it would have been converted into a molten mass of matter?

BRYAN: I don't think I've ever had the question asked.

* * *

DARROW: Do you believe the story of the flood to be a literal interpretation?

BRYAN: Yes sir.

DARROW: When was the flood?

BRYAN: I would not attempt to fix a date.

DARROW: About 4004 B.C.?

BRYAN: That is the estimate of man that is accepted today. I would not say that it is accurate.

DARROW: But what do you think the Bible, itself, says? Don't you know how it was arrived at?

BRYAN: I never made a calculation.

DARROW: What do you think?

BRYAN: I do not think about things I don't think about.

DARROW: Do you think about things you do think about?

BRYAN: Well, sometimes.

* * *

DARROW: Do you think the earth was made in six days?

BRYAN: Not six days of twenty-four hours.

* * *

BRYAN: Your honor. . . . The only purpose Mr. Darrow has is to slur at the Bible. . . .

DARROW: I object to your statement. I am examining you on your fool ideas that no intelligent Christian on earth believes.

Bryan's admission that he did not really believe in a literal interpretation of the Bible had a shocking effect on many of his fundamental followers. Furthermore, Darrow's cross-examination had a shattering effect on Bryan himself, and many think that it caused his death, which occurred five days later in Dayton. Bryan had prepared a long oration to deliver when he summed up the prosecution's case. He hoped to regain his lost stature by overwhelming the crowd with his oratory, but Bryan never got the chance. Darrow and Malone did not make a final summation for the defense; therefore, none was allowed for the prosecution. Indeed, the defense asked the jury to find their client guilty so that they could appeal its verdict to a higher court.

Scopes was found guilty and fined one hundred dollars. The defense appealed the verdict to the Tennessee State Court of Appeals, and in 1927 Scopes was cleared on a technicality—the lower court had exceeded its authority in fining Scopes. By throwing out Scopes's conviction, the Tennessee Court of Appeals effectively destroyed Darrow's case. His whole plan was to bring the issue to the federal courts in order to get the Butler Act declared unconstitutional. The case never made it to the federal courts and the law remained on the books until 1967. Scopes, dying in 1970, did, however, live to see its repeal.

Because of the Scopes trial, many journalists and educators felt that fundamentalism had suffered a death blow. On the contrary, many school boards throughout the nation then took evolution out of high school curricula. Textbooks were revised quietly to avoid controversy. Tennessee, for example, had textbooks that included evolution as a part of high school biology. Like dozens of other states, no such textbooks were allowed to include evolution until several decades later. It was only in the late 1950's, with the Russian launch of the first artificial satellite, Sputnik, that a concerted attempt was made to strengthen science textbooks in the United States.

—John H. DeBerry, updated by Daniel Brown

ADDITIONAL READING:

Bird, Wendell. *The Origin of the Species Revisited*. New York: Philosophical Library, 1989. An idiosyncratic study of the legal and religious issues involved in the debate.

Ginger, Ray. *Six Days or Forever: Tennessee Versus John Thomas Scopes*. Chicago: Quadrangle Books, 1969. A highly readable, accurate rendition of the trial.

Grebstein, Sheldon N. *Monkey Trial*. Boston: Houghton Mifflin, 1960. A rich, reliable source book for the background and events of the Scopes Trial.

Larson, Edward J. *Trial and Error: The American Controversy over Creation and Evolution*. Oxford: Oxford University Press, 1985. An accurate, careful assessment of the legal, cultural and religious issues involved in the debate.

Scopes, John Thomas, and James Pressley. *Center of the Storm: Memoirs of John T. Scopes*. New York: Holt, Rinehart and Winston, 1967. After a long passage of time, the central figure of the trial reminisces.

Wills, Garry. *Under God: Religion and American Politics*. New York: Simon and Schuster, 1990. Penetrating analysis

and reexamination of American religious history. Chapters 8, 9, and 10 deal with the Scopes trial.

SEE ALSO: 1892, Birth of the People's Party.

1926 ■ LAUNCHING OF THE FIRST LIQUID-FUELED ROCKET: *development of a liquid propellant makes rocketry and space exploration possible*

DATE: March 16, 1926
LOCALE: Auburn, Massachusetts
CATEGORY: Science and technology
KEY FIGURES:
Robert Hutchings Goddard (1882-1945), father of modern rocketry
Hermann Oberth (1894-1989), German scientist and writer who helped to popularize the idea of rockets for space exploration
Konstantin Eduardovich Tsiolkovsky (1857-1935), Russian scientist who laid the theoretical groundwork for modern rocket development
Jules Verne (1828-1905), nineteenth century French writer whose plausible science-fiction stories helped to generate popular interest in space flight

SUMMARY OF EVENT. On a cold winter day in March, 1926, three men and a woman in heavy coats gathered around a small launching stand built of pipes, which had been set up in the snow in a field near Auburn, Massachusetts. Held in place on the stand, which resembled a large metal ladder, was a ten-foot-long rocket. It consisted of a two-foot-long motor at the front, connected by long, slender tubes to two tanks in the rear that contained gasoline and liquid oxygen. The four people gathered in the field were Robert H. Goddard, a physics professor at Clark University who had designed and built the rocket; his wife, Esther Kisk Goddard; P. M. Roope, also of Clark's physics department; and Henry Sachs, the university's instrument maker. The rocket they were about to launch was the product of nearly ten years of research in Goddard's shop and laboratory. Its most unusual feature was its propellant—a combination of gasoline and liquid oxygen fed into the combustion chamber by separate tubes. Up to that time, rockets usually had been fueled with black powder that was stored and ignited in the combustion chamber.

In a few minutes, all was in readiness to begin the test. Mrs. Goddard started her motion-picture camera, and Dr. Goddard touched a blowtorch to an opening near the top of the rocket. There was a steady roar, and a few seconds later, the rocket rose slowly from the launch frame, then shot into the air. It flew 184 feet at a maximum altitude of 41 feet, while achieving a speed of sixty miles an hour. Then it curved sharply to the left and descended, plowing into the ice and snow as it hit the ground at high speed. The flight had lasted fewer than three seconds. There were no speeches and no interviews, and no newspaper reported the event. Yet the rocket's brief flight marked a giant advance toward the exploration of space.

Goddard had received a bachelor of science degree from Worcester Polytechnic Institute in 1908 and a master of arts and doctorate from Clark University in 1910 and 1911, respectively. He had had a lifelong interest in rocketry. Despite a lack of government support, he had continued the research he had begun in the basement of Worcester Polytechnic Institute in 1907 when he fired a powder-fueled rocket.

Goddard's early work developed from an interest in high-altitude weather research. The limitations on balloons led to the development of the mathematical theories of rocketry, as well as two patents, one for a liquid-fueled rocket and the other for a multistage rocket. To prove that rockets could function in the vacuum of space, Goddard had to overcome popular misconceptions of Newton's third law: for every action there is an equal and opposite reaction. His research proved that a rocket engine could deliver propulsion in the vacuum of space.

After initial experiments with solid fuels, in 1921, Goddard switched to the more efficient and cheaper liquid hydrogen and oxygen rocket propellants. By 1924, he had a working engine. Until that year, Goddard had not flown a rocket. Problems with pumps and the size of the combustion chamber needed to be overcome before a flight would be feasible. His work also focused on separating the combustion chamber from fuel storage and changing the exhaust nozzles to increase the velocity.

At the time that Goddard performed his experiment, rockets had been known for several centuries. They were mentioned in Chinese writings as far back as the eleventh century, and they had been used as artillery weapons by European armies at various times between the fifteenth and early nineteenth centuries, until they were finally outmoded by modern long-range artillery. Then in 1918, Goddard developed and tested the bazooka. Even though it came too late for use then, he continued his work, and it became a useful weapon during World War II. Until that time, however, the chief use of rockets seems to have been in staging elaborate fireworks displays.

When interest in interplanetary travel first began early in the seventeenth century, few people thought of the rocket as the most suitable vehicle for the purpose. In Jules Verne's celebrated novel, *From the Earth to the Moon*, published in 1865, the space explorers reached the moon inside a projectile shot out of a gigantic cannon. In 1903, however, a little-known Russian scientist, Konstantin Eduardovich Tsiolkovsky, conclusively demonstrated in a series of articles that the rocket would have to be the vehicle of space exploration. As Tsiolkovsky saw it, the rocket had several peculiar properties that made it the only vehicle capable of carrying a payload into outer space. First, the rocket engine developed more thrust, or push, than any other engine of the same weight; second, because the rocket was a self-contained system carrying its own oxygen supply, it could operate anywhere, even in airless space; third, because the rocket gradually lost weight as its

fuel supply was exhausted, its maximum speed came at the end of its powered flight.

While Tsiolkovsky was developing his ideas, Goddard, unaware of the Russian scientist's work, was reaching the same conclusions. Goddard was interested in designing a vehicle that could be used to carry instruments high into the upper atmosphere for purposes of research. In January, 1920, he published a paper in the *Smithsonian Institution Reports*, entitled "A Method of Reaching Extreme Altitudes," that summed up the conclusions he had reached in the previous ten years regarding the unique suitability of rockets for high-altitude research. In this paper, Goddard demonstrated that it was theoretically possible to design a rocket that would weigh less than ten tons and attain a velocity high enough to reach the moon. That article would have gone unnoticed had it not been for Goddard's suggestion that a rocket fired at the moon should contain flash powder that would ignite on impact, thus marking the landing site for observers on earth and proving that the rocket actually had reached its destination.

Goddard was not only a theoretician; he actually designed and built several rockets. At the time of his experiments, the only rockets he could obtain used the same type of propellant used in the Chinese rockets of the eleventh century, which was black powder. This kind of rocket clearly was unsuitable for the high-altitude flights Goddard had in mind. A high-altitude rocket had to accelerate slowly and at a fairly uniform rate, so that its maximum speed would be reached when it was several miles above the earth, where there is less air resistance. The black-powder rocket, however, exerted its greatest thrust immediately after being ignited and then slowed down as its fuel was exhausted. Some means needed to be found to feed the fuel into the rocket's combustion chamber at a constant and predictable rate, so that the rocket's acceleration would be constant and predetermined. Since this was impractical with solid (powder) fuels, Goddard hit upon the idea of using liquid fuels, such as ether or gasoline, that also would give the rocket a greater exhaust velocity. Because gasoline and similar liquid fuels do not contain oxygen, the rocket also would have to carry its own oxygen supply. Goddard's Auburn rocket contained two separate tanks, one for the gasoline and another for the liquid oxygen. Fuels from both tanks were piped into the combustion chamber.

Having demonstrated the feasibility of the liquid-fueled rocket as a high-altitude vehicle with the Auburn test firing, Goddard went on to conduct successful experiments with other liquid-fueled rockets during the next twenty years. One of his rockets eventually reached a height of seventy-five hundred feet. With another, Goddard achieved the first successful controlled flight of a rocket. His tiny 1926 rocket and the larger ones he built during the 1930's are the direct ancestors of the German V-2's, which in turn were the precursors to the U.S. and Russian rockets that carried the first payloads into Earth orbit.

Despite his many accomplishments, including the first U.S. patent for a multiple-stage rocket and the development of vanes for guidance and gyro control devices, Goddard went unrecognized during his lifetime. He published little for two reasons: First, he was an intensely shy individual; second, he feared the German scientists, with their emphasis on race superiority, and did not want to encourage their work. Today, however, Goddard is recognized as the father of modern rocket technology. In his early work, he theorized the means of landing humans on other celestial bodies. This ability to combine practical research with a vision of spaceflight and rocketry represents his great contribution.

—*Ronald N. Spector, updated by Duncan R. Jamieson*

ADDITIONAL READING:

Arnold, H. J. P., ed. *Man in Space: An Illustrated History of Space*. New York: Smithmark, 1993. Deals more with the results of Goddard's pioneering work than with Goddard.

Coil, Suzanne M. *Robert Hutchings Goddard: Pioneer of Rocketry and Space Flight*. New York: Facts On File, 1992. An account of the life and achievements of a pioneer in rocket science.

Goddard, Robert H. *Rocket Development*. New York: Prentice-Hall, 1948. A selection of Goddard's research notes from 1929-1941, published posthumously.

_____. *Rockets*. New York: American Rocket Society, 1946. Includes Goddard's two most important published papers, "A Method of Reaching Extreme Altitudes" and "Liquid-Propellant Rocket Development."

Lehman, Milton. *This High Man: The Life of Robert H. Goddard*. New York: Farrar, Straus, 1963. A worthwhile study of Goddard as both a visionary scientist and a shy retiring individual.

Williams, Beryl, and Samuel Epstein. *The Rocket Pioneers*. New York: Julian Messner, 1955. Contains good brief accounts of the careers of such early researchers as Tsiolkovsky, Goddard, Oberth, and the erratic German inventor and space-travel enthusiast Hermann Ganswindt.

SEE ALSO: 1903, Wright Brothers' First Flight; 1927, Lindbergh's Transatlantic Flight; 1961, First American in Space; 1969, Apollo 11 Lands on the Moon; 1977, Spaceflights of Voyagers 1 and 2; 1986, *Challenger* Accident.

1927 ■ LINDBERGH'S TRANSATLANTIC FLIGHT: *the first nonstop transatlantic flight from New York to Paris heralds a new era of air transportation and global commerce*

DATE: May 20, 1927
LOCALE: From New York to Paris
CATEGORIES: Cultural and intellectual history; Science and technology; Transportation
KEY FIGURES:
Charles A. Lindbergh (1902-1974), aviator
Harold Bixby (1890-1965), St. Louis banker and one of the primary supporters of *The Spirit of St. Louis*

SUMMARY OF EVENT. Charles Lindbergh was born in Michigan in 1902 and was an adventurous child who did not like school. Barely graduating from high school, he made a failed attempt to study at the University of Wisconsin, and ended up as a flying cadet in the Army. After completing the training and joining the Missouri National Guard instead of choosing active duty, Lindbergh was appointed chief pilot of a new air mail route linking the Midwest with New York City.

Aviation in the 1920's was fairly dangerous, especially flying the air mail. Pilots had to fly with little ground support, unreliable weather reports, and visual ground contact as their only guide. Most aircraft were still unsafe in their own right as well. Because of these problems, Lindbergh and other air mail pilots continually were pushing the Post Office to improve the quality of air facilities. The government did begin providing ground facilities, such as beacons and emergency fields, along contract air mail routes, but would not provide airplanes, money for their purchase, or funding for private aeronautical research. This perpetuated a fundamental problem: Few contractors could afford to provide safe aircraft for their pilots, and there were few outlets to get money to do so. Lindbergh himself knew that safer planes could be built, but he also felt that before money would be made available, aviation had to become a less adventurous way to travel and a more normal, accepted means of transport. How to do this had often crossed his mind, and he was intrigued when he read of a transatlantic flying contest sponsored by millionaire Raymond Orteig.

Orteig had for several years offered a twenty-five-thousand-dollar prize for a nonstop flight linking New York and Paris. René Fonck, a well-known French pilot, had already tried and failed, his plane crashing at the end of his reserved New York runway before takeoff, killing several crew members. Attempting the trip in reverse, two French pilots had departed from Paris but disappeared over the Atlantic. Another group of pilots were caught in a legal entanglement and were forbidden to take off at all. Lindbergh felt that the contest was the perfect way to get aviation into the public eye, and he began preparing for an attempt.

While the other pilots had placed their faith in multiengine biplanes, Lindbergh envisioned a single-engine monoplane. He also wanted to fly alone. Although Lindbergh hated soliciting for support, his plane would cost an estimated ten thousand dollars, and he finally got help from a group of businessmen led by St. Louis banker Harold Bixby. The group produced fifteen thousand dollars to finance Lindbergh's flight, which would be billed as a St. Louis-to-Paris flight, with a stop in New York. Ryan Airlines, Inc., of California was contracted to work with Lindbergh on an aircraft meeting his own specifications. Because Bixby was from St. Louis, he suggested the plane be named *The Spirit of St. Louis*.

The Spirit of St. Louis made its maiden test flight in April, 1927, in California, but the plane would never be fully tested. Lindbergh learned that several other pilots were set to take off from New York on their transatlantic voyages. Lindbergh feared he would be too late if he waited, so despite the lack of test flights, the plane was readied. Lindbergh flew from San Diego to St. Louis and then on to Long Island, New York, where he landed on May 12, 1927.

Upon arriving on Long Island, Lindbergh had his first extensive contact with the press. The Orteig contest was current news, and reporters began calling Lindbergh the "flying fool" because he planned to use a single-engine aircraft and fly solo. He also would not carry a parachute; he needed as much fuel as the plane could carry, and he thought that if he had to bail out over the Atlantic Ocean, he would in any case perish before he could be rescued. Despite disliking the press and considering their attention distracting, the aviator did not want to ignore the media, because he wanted public attention to focus on aviation.

Another problem was that, because Lindbergh had not expected to be in New York so soon, he had not yet cleared all of the eligibility requirements for the contest. Afraid that if he waited he would be beaten across the ocean, Lindbergh contacted his sponsors, who agreed that the flight itself was more important than the prize money. The aviator was given the green light to embark when ready. Bad weather kept Lindbergh from departing immediately, but he finally took off on Friday, May 20, despite not having slept for twenty-three straight hours.

During his solo transatlantic flight, Lindbergh's greatest danger was not inclement weather, fog, low clouds, or even a sizable storm around which he had to detour. The aviator's biggest problem was his desire for sleep. In his later writings, Lindbergh described his experience in surreal terms, with phantoms and other apparitions appearing as he drifted in and out of a state of half-sleep. Lindbergh was able to nap briefly, for as he nodded off, the plane, which did not fly particularly smoothly, would jerk him back awake. After sixteen hours of flying, Lindbergh crossed the southwest coast of Ireland, then passed over Cornwall, England, two hours ahead of schedule and landed at Le Bourget aerodrome outside Paris after thirty-three and a half hours in the air. Lindbergh had been so efficient in his flying that there was still enough fuel in the tanks for a flight to Rome.

In his autobiographical works, Lindbergh admitted that nothing could have prepared him for the conflagration that followed. The aviator had expected to land and spend the day talking to and trading experiences with French pilots. Instead, he was suddenly the world's greatest celebrity. After nearly running over crowds of people who swarmed onto the runway, Lindbergh was literally carried off and welcomed by all manner of people, showered with awards and honors, toasted and praised. There were ceremonies, dinners, parades, meetings with French and U.S. officials, and audiences with royalty. He was no longer the "flying fool" but rather "Lucky Lindy," and he was flooded with telegrams, invitations, and business proposals. Not only had the aviator accomplished a marvelous feat, but people simply liked the polite and modest flyer.

Lindbergh received a similar welcome when he flew on to England, after repairing the parts of his plane that people had torn off as souvenirs.

Lindbergh was taken back to the United States by the Navy, and when he arrived in Washington, D.C., and traveled to New York City, he was busy with dinners, speeches, and receptions. At a dinner with President Calvin Coolidge, the aviator met Dwight W. Morrow, an ambitious but capable politician, and Morrow's three daughters. Although Lindbergh paid the daughters little attention, one, Anne, was to become his future wife. The aviator also was given a huge parade in New York, receiving the city's biggest welcome ever. More than four million people lined the streets, and eighteen hundred tons of ticker tape rained down on the cavalcade bearing Lindbergh. Lindbergh was given the Orteig Prize of twenty-five thousand dollars on June 16, despite the fact that he had never been technically eligible for the contest. Along with more than two million pieces of mail and all manner of business endorsements, Lindbergh was awarded the Congressional Medal of Honor and promoted to the rank of colonel. Lindbergh's later life and career would be filled with all manner of accomplishments, in and out of aviation, but also considerable controversy surrounding his view of Hitler's Luftwaffe just before World War II.

The first solo transatlantic flight was an obvious boost for aviation. It made flying seem slightly more routine and also showed that single-engine craft could make such a journey. The flight was also important as a watershed date in U.S. history. During the 1920's, many people still did not want to accept that the United States was part of a growing global community; the flight forced people to accept that fact, and it helped many begin to look toward the future.

—*Wayne Ackerson*

ADDITIONAL READING:

Lindbergh, Charles A. *An Autobiography of Values*. Edited by William Jovanovich et al. New York: Harcourt Brace Jovanovich, 1978. A lifelong view of the aviator's morals and beliefs.

_____. *The Spirit of St. Louis*. New York: Charles Scribner's Sons, 1953. The best account of the flight, written by the aviator himself.

Milton, Joyce. *Loss of Eden: A Biography of Charles and Anne Morrow Lindbergh*. New York: HarperCollins, 1993. An introduction to the lives of the Lindberghs. Focuses on the couple's relationship, not on specific historical events.

Mosley, Leonard. *Lindbergh: A Biography*. Garden City, N.Y.: Doubleday, 1976. An easy writing style partially makes up for some misrepresentation and misinterpretation of Lindbergh's actions and statements.

Ross, Walter S. *The Last Hero: Charles A. Lindbergh*. New York: Harper & Row, 1976. One of the most balanced account of Lindbergh's life; more objective than most other texts.

SEE ALSO: 1903, Wright Brothers' First Flight; 1926, Launching of the First Liquid-Fueled Rocket; 1961, First American in Space; 1969, Apollo 11 Lands on the Moon.

1927 ■ SACCO AND VANZETTI ARE EXECUTED: *a celebrated example of anti-immigrant feeling during a period of heightened nativism*

DATE: August 23, 1927
LOCALE: Dedham, Massachusetts
CATEGORIES: Court cases; Government and politics; Immigration
KEY FIGURES:
Alvan T. Fuller, governor of Massachusetts
Celestino Madeiros, convicted bank robber and murderer
Fred Moore, chief defense counsel from November, 1920 to November, 1924
Nicola Sacco (1891-1927) and
Bartolomeo Vanzetti (1888-1927), Italian anarchists convicted of and executed for robbery and murder
Webster Thayer, presiding trial judge
William G. Thompson, chief defense counsel from November, 1924, to August, 1927

SUMMARY OF EVENT. One of the most famous U.S. trials of the twentieth century, the robbery and murder case against Nicola Sacco and Bartolomeo Vanzetti, generated worldwide protests, strikes, and riots as it focused the international spotlight on the small town of Dedham, Massachusetts. In order to comprehend the events surrounding the arrest and trial of these two Italian immigrants, it is necessary to understand the prevailing political climate of paranoia that existed in 1919.

In the aftermath of World War I, Europe had undergone a political shuffling that culminated in a communist revolution in Russia. As European immigrants began flooding into the United States, there was fear that this communist ideology and anarchy—the belief that compulsory government should be replaced by voluntary, self-governing groups—would be brought in as well. Many native-born citizens worried about secret plots to undermine the democratic structure of the country, and often anyone who appeared different or foreign was branded as a "Red."

The two events, which may or may not have been connected, that culminated in the arrest of Sacco and Vanzetti began on December 24, 1919, payday for the L. Q. White Shoe Company of Bridgewater, Massachusetts. A truck carrying approximately thirty-three thousand dollars in company payroll was unsuccessfully attacked. Pinkerton Agency detectives investigated the incident, and during eyewitness interviews they determined that one of the suspects appeared to be foreign-born, with a dark complexion and mustache, and that he fled in a large vehicle, probably a Hudson. The identified license plate had been stolen a few days earlier in Needham, Massachusetts, as had a Buick touring car. Thus, despite witnesses to the contrary, the detectives concluded that the Buick likely had been used in the robbery. No suspects were arrested, although tips emerged connecting the getaway car to a group of Italian anarchists.

On April 15, 1920, in nearby South Braintree, the payroll for the Slater and Morrill Shoe Factory was being escorted, on foot, from the office to the factory by two security guards, Frederick Parmenter and Alessandro Berardelli. En route, the guards were attacked, robbed, and murdered by two men who escaped in a waiting vehicle. At the inquest, twenty-three eyewitnesses testified that the assailants appeared to be Italian, but few claimed they could positively identify the men.

Recalling the tip about Italian anarchists storing a car in Bridgewater, police chief Michael E. Stewart traced the lead to Feruccio Coacci, an Italian scheduled for deportation. Coacci revealed that the car belonged to his housemate, Mike Boda, a known anarchist, and that it was currently being repaired in a garage in West Bridgewater. A police guard was planted outside the garage to wait for Boda.

Meanwhile, as a result of the prevalent U.S. attitude toward radicals and in the wake of a national roundup and arrest of aliens, Italians Nicola Sacco and Bartolomeo Vanzetti had decided it would be wise to destroy their anarchist literature. The abundance of material required transportation, and they arranged to borrow Boda's vehicle. Although the trap was laid for Boda, Sacco and Vanzetti were arrested as they attempted to claim the car. Neither man had a police record, but both were armed.

Because the men were not informed of the reason for their arrest, they assumed they were being held as anarchists. Although they were read their rights, the language barrier may have obstructed their complete understanding. They were fingerprinted, their weapons confiscated but not tagged, and they were questioned for seven days without being charged. There was no lineup; the two were paraded in front of witnesses who were asked if they were the men involved in the holdup. On May 12, 1920, Vanzetti was charged with attempted murder and robbery at Bridgewater.

His trial began on June 22, 1920, in Plymouth, Massachusetts, with Judge Webster Thayer presiding. The initial interviews by the Pinkerton detectives were not admitted, and all witnesses for the defense were of Italian origin. After only five hours of deliberation, the jury found Vanzetti guilty of assault with intent to rob and murder. Six weeks later, he was sentenced to twelve to fifteen years for intent to rob. The attempted murder charge was dropped after it was discovered that one of the jurors had brought his own shell casings for comparison.

In September, 1920, Sacco and Vanzetti were charged with the murder of Alessandro Berardelli and Frederick Parmenter during the South Braintree robbery. Each pleaded not guilty. A committee for their defense raised enough money to hire the radical California attorney Fred Moore, who cited the case as an establishment attempt to victimize the working man.

The trial began on May 31, 1921, in Dedham, Massachusetts, once again under Judge Thayer, who, as the presiding judge in Vanzetti's first trial, should have been disqualified. On June 4, the all-male jury was sworn in, and on June 6, Sacco

Bartolomeo Vanzetti (front left) and Nicola Sacco, handcuffed and under guard, arrive at the courthouse to receive their sentence in April, 1927. (AP/Wide World Photos)

and Vanzetti were marched, handcuffed, into the courtroom. Throughout the trial, the prosecution presented a bounty of circumstantial evidence: less-than-convincing "eyewitness" testimony; a cap from the scene, alleged to be Vanzetti's, that was too small; expert testimony qualified with "I am inclined to believe"; no positive identification on the getaway car; ballistic evidence that was technical and confusing; and the accusation of "consciousness of guilt," based on the false statements of the two when they thought they were being held for anarchy. Judge Thayer charged the jury to be "true soldiers," who would display the "highest and noblest type of true American citizenship," while referring to the defendants as slackers. On July 14, once again after a five-hour deliberation, the jury returned a verdict of guilty of first-degree murder. The standard penalty in Massachusetts at the time was death by electric chair.

Sacco and Vanzetti remained incarcerated for six years while motions were filed in their behalf. The presiding judge heard all appeals and each was weighed and denied by Judge Thayer. One motion stated Judge Thayer himself had demonstrated out-of-court prejudice against the two. Despite the growing doubt about the guilt of the men, Thayer remained adamant and his animosity grew toward Moore. On November 8, the defense committee forced Moore to resign and hired William G. Thompson.

While the legal avenues encountered roadblocks, Sacco was slipped a note from another prisoner, Celestino Madeiros, who confessed to the crime. From the note, Thompson traced a link to the Morelli brothers, an Italian gang in Providence. This group had attacked the shoe factory in the past, and one member of the gang bore a resemblance to Sacco. Based on the new evidence, Thompson filed a motion for retrial, which was denied, and in April of 1927, Sacco and Vanzetti were sentenced to die the week of July 10. Due to the public outcry, the date was moved to August 10, and Vanzetti wrote a plea for clemency to Massachusetts governor Alvan T. Fuller. In the letter, he asked not for pardon but for a complete review of the case.

On June 1, the governor appointed a committee to review the case, but after examining their findings, he denied a new trial. On August 10, Sacco and Vanzetti were readied for execution. Thirty-six minutes before the time set for the execution, the governor issued a postponement, awaiting results of a Supreme Court appeal. On August 19, the United States Supreme Court refused to hear the case, citing no authority.

In Europe and South America, mobs rioted and marched on United States embassies. In France, Italy, and the United States, workers struck in protest. Five hundred extra policemen, armed with machine guns and tear gas, barricaded the crowd of thousands outside the jail. Just after midnight, on August 23, 1927, Sacco and Vanzetti were executed.

Doubt still remains as to the unquestionable guilt of the two men. Although no major changes in the judicial process resulted from the case, it can be cited as a history lesson not to be repeated.

—*Joyce Duncan*

ADDITIONAL READING:

Dickinson, Alice. *The Sacco-Vanzetti Case*. New York: Franklin Watts, 1972. An abbreviated overview of the case, including chronology and photos.

Ehrmann, Herbert. *The Case That Will Not Die: Commonwealth vs. Sacco and Vanzetti*. Boston: Little, Brown, 1969. Liberally illustrated account by the case's assistant defense attorney from 1926 to 1927. Maps, time tables, and bibliography.

Frankfurter, Marion Denman, and Gardner Jackson, eds. *The Letters of Sacco and Vanzetti*. New York: Octagon Books, 1971. Correspondence by both men written from prison, including Vanzetti's letter to the governor.

Joughin, G. L., and E. M. Morgan. *The Legacy of Sacco and Vanzetti*. New York: Harcourt, Brace, 1948. Early but masterful analysis of the case.

Russell, Francis. *Tragedy in Dedham*. New York: McGraw-Hill, 1962. Illustrated chronological recitation of events, including a discussion of public temperament.

SEE ALSO: 1919, Red Scare; 1938, HUAC Investigations; 1951, McCarthy Hearings.

1928 ■ SMITH-HOOVER CAMPAIGN: *a presidential election marks the emergence of Northeastern, urban, first-generation Americans in a powerful new Democratic Party*

DATE: 1928

LOCALE: United States

CATEGORY: Government and politics

KEY FIGURES:

James Cannon (1864-1944), influential bishop in the Methodist Episcopal Church South and defender of prohibition

Herbert Clark Hoover (1874-1964), Republican presidential candidate in 1928

Henry Louis Mencken (1880-1956), literary critic and satirist of U.S. mores during the 1920's

John J. Raskob (1879-1950), wealthy industrialist and campaign manager for Smith

Franklin Delano Roosevelt (1882-1945), Democratic candidate for governor of New York in 1928

Alfred Emanuel Smith (1873-1944), Democratic presidential candidate in 1928

SUMMARY OF EVENT. During the 1920's, the United States became an urban nation. The Bureau of the Census reported that for the first time in the nation's history, most of the population resided in areas defined as urban. Statistics cannot convey the disruption that took place as the nation shifted its cultural axis. The was nothing quiet or secret about this "revolt from the village."

Indeed, some of the major literary figures of the period took delight in emphasizing how out of touch with the realities of an increasingly urban nation the rural United States was becoming. *The New Yorker* magazine was founded in 1925 as a weekly periodical for urban sophisticates. Critics such as H. L. Mencken, editor of the *American Mercury*, assailed Puritanism and haughtily proclaimed the superiority of the city-dwellers over the "hicks" and the fundamentalists. On the other side, rural voices cried out against the evil influences of the city. From rural newspapers and from conservative fundamentalist religious leaders such as Methodist bishop James Cannon, Jr., of Virginia, came warnings about the decadence of urban life. To many, the city offered a challenge to Anglo-Saxon dominance in U.S. affairs.

In 1928, these tensions permeated the presidential campaign, primarily because the Democratic candidate, Alfred E. Smith, personified the new urban forces. Al Smith had spent his entire life within the shadow of New York City's skyscrap-

Herbert Hoover, thirty-first president of the United States, would see the nation move from the prosperous Roaring Twenties into a decade of Great Depression. He remained torn between his laissez-faire economic convictions and the need to do something to relieve the rising tide of unemployment and poverty. (Library of Congress)

ers. Although he quit school at the age of fifteen, he became a powerful and vigorous leader because of his abilities and hard work. He was elected governor of New York four times. In 1928, he was nominated by the Democrats to run for the presidency. In the eyes of his followers, Smith was the urban Lincoln. He represented the fulfillment of the American Dream. The son of an immigrant was aspiring to the highest office in the land. With his derby hat, his big cigar, his opposition to prohibition, and his Roman Catholic religion, Smith bore his urban label jauntily and proudly.

The career of Herbert Clark Hoover, the Republican candidate, also resembled a Horatio Alger story. Hoover was born in a small town in Iowa. Initially projected into national prominence through his work as food administrator during World War I and later as a leader of postwar relief work in Europe, he served during the 1920's as secretary of commerce under both Warren G. Harding and Calvin Coolidge. When Coolidge uttered his cryptic statement about not choosing to run in 1928, Hoover was the most outstanding figure in the Republican Party and easily captured the nomination.

As the campaign of 1928 unfolded, a number of vexing problems faced a seemingly prosperous nation. The American farmer had been suffering from unfavorable profit margins since 1921. The nation's Latin American policy had generated considerable antagonism south of the border. The excessive speculation on Wall Street was gradually becoming a source of increasing concern. Some Democrats held that Smith, who had a progressive record as governor of New York, should attack the farm program of the Republicans and promise more positive federal action in general. The more conservative elements warned that radicalism during a period of prosperity would cost the support of the average voter. Smith decided to adopt a cautious platform. Symbolic of this decision was the appointment of John J. Raskob, a General Motors executive, as Democratic campaign manager.

Because the substantive issues that might have distinguished the two candidates on rational grounds became blurred, the campaign soon began to focus upon emotional factors. Smith's antiprohibition stand and his religion, both of which gained support for him in Northeastern urban areas, were bitterly criticized in the West and South. To some, such as Kansas editor William Allen White, Smith's candidacy presented a threat to the long-established political forces dominant in the United States.

Undue emphasis, however, should not be given to Smith's political disadvantages. Probably more decisive in the campaign were Hoover's advantages. The Republican candidate had a distinguished record in public service and was able to project the image of efficiency and industry. Furthermore, he had the overwhelming advantage of Republican prosperity behind him. Although many farmers were suffering financially in 1928, Smith failed to garner the farm vote.

The election count gave Hoover twenty-one million popular and 444 electoral votes. Smith won fifteen million popular votes and only 87 electoral votes. The total popular vote in

1928 was much higher than in 1924. Smith made substantial gains in the nation's large urban centers. This "revolt of the cities" was important in the development of a Democratic majority in 1932.

Immediately after the election, many Catholics and Democrats complained that Smith had been the victim of a whispering campaign of bigotry. Violent anti-Catholicism was exhibited in the election. In retrospect, however, it seems clear that there were factors other than religion that estranged many voters. Smith was a capable statesman and a spokesman for the Northeastern urban areas, but for a majority of the voters he was not an acceptable national symbol. Smith's most significant contribution in 1928 was to arouse the latent political potential of many first-generation Americans in Eastern cities. It remained for Franklin D. Roosevelt to combine this element with a disenchanted farm vote—plus Depression discontent—to produce a winning Democratic coalition in 1932.

—*George Q. Flynn, updated by Michael Witkoski*

ADDITIONAL READING:

Anderson, Kristi. *The Creation of a Democratic Majority, 1928-1936.* Chicago: Chicago University Press, 1979. Examines how the election of 1928 was a turning point in U.S. political life and transformed the Democratic Party into the majority party for almost half a century, with lasting impact on the nation.

Maisel, L. Sandy, ed. *Political Parties and Elections in the United States.* New York: Garland, 1991. An interesting and valuable review of the 1928 campaign and how Smith's candidacy, along with contemporary political trends, helped send the Democrats toward long-lasting victory in U.S. electoral politics.

Reichley, A. James. *The Life of the Parties: A History of American Political Parties.* New York: Free Press, 1992. Helpful review of the role of the party machinery as it first comprehended and then articulated the public mood in the 1928 election. Asserts that Al Smith's candidacy was not an isolated phenomenon but a watershed event in U.S. political history.

Schlesinger, Arthur M., Jr., ed. *1928-1940.* Vol. 7 in *History of American Presidential Elections.* New York: Chelsea House, 1985. The Democratic Party platform, Smith's speeches, and the relevant speeches and remarks of other figures of the time help make the specific circumstances of the election alive and relevant for the reader.

Ward, Geoffrey C. *A First-Class Temperament: The Emergence of Franklin Roosevelt.* New York: Harper & Row, 1989. The relationship between two of the greatest Democratic politicians of the twentieth century was often stormy and ultimately tragic. This biography reveals how Smith's defeat in 1928 was, in many ways, essential for Roosevelt's victory in 1932 and the emergence of the New Deal as the shaping force in modern U.S. history.

SEE ALSO: 1924, Coolidge Is Elected President; 1929, Stock Market Crash; 1929, Great Depression; 1932, Franklin D. Roosevelt Is Elected President.

1928 ■ KELLOGG-BRIAND PACT: *a multi-lateral treaty pledges to renounce war as an instrument of national policy and to maintain peace by common action*

DATE: August 27, 1928
LOCALE: Paris
CATEGORIES: Diplomacy and international relations; Treaties and agreements
KEY FIGURES:
William Edgar Borah (1865-1940), Republican senator from Idaho and chairman of the Senate Committee on Foreign Relations
Aristide Briand (1862-1932), French foreign minister
Frank Billings Kellogg (1860-1951), U.S. secretary of state
Salmon O. Levinson (1865-1941), attorney

SUMMARY OF EVENT. The Kellogg-Briand Multilateral Pact, also known as the Pact of Paris, held out the promise of a new era of international harmony. It was signed on August 27, 1928. The chief architects of the treaty, Aristide Briand and Frank Kellogg, and the other member signatories took a formal pledge "not to have recourse to war as an instrument of national policy, and to settle all disputes arising between them by peaceful means." The treaty was signed originally by fifteen countries and embraced the participation of sixty-four nations by 1934, the exceptions being Argentina, Brazil, and the tiny countries of Andorra, Liechtenstein, Monaco, and San Marino.

The movement to outlaw war was initiated by Salmon Levinson in the United States in the aftermath of the first global war and became a worldwide movement in a few years. This movement was of great importance in bringing about the negotiation and general ratification of the Kellogg-Briand Pact. The idea of a definitive treaty was proposed by Briand on April 6, 1927, when he suggested the conclusion of a bilateral Pact of Perpetual Friendship between France and the United States for the renunciation of war. Briand's aim was to bind the United States—which still remained outside existing international accords, such as the League of Nations' Covenant and the Locarno Pact—to France through a separate bilateral pact, in an effort to reinforce the international movement toward world peace.

At the beginning, the French proposal was ignored completely by Kellogg and the Department of State. It was Nicholas Murray Butler, the president of Columbia University, and Professors J. T. Shotwell and Joseph P. Chamberlain who developed the implications of Briand's offer by drawing up a draft treaty celebrated as the "American Locarno." The idea had an overwhelming impact on both educated and common Americans, creating widespread support for the antiwar idea. Encouraged by these developments, Briand formally presented a "Draft Pact of Perpetual Friendship between France and the U.S." to the Department of State on June 20, 1927.

Levinson's untiring campaign to make the United States the champion of the movement to outlaw war bore fruit. He persuaded William Borah to introduce a resolution in the Senate on December 27, 1927, calling for the outlawing of war. Kellogg, now responding to public enthusiasm, made a new proposition to the French minister: that "the two governments would make a more signal contribution to world peace by joining in an effort to obtain the adherence of all of the principal powers of the world to a declaration renouncing war as an instrument of national policy." There ensued a long period of complex negotiations between France, the United States, the other great powers except Russia, and some lesser powers.

The French did not immediately endorse the suggested alterations to their original proposal. They feared that a new multilateral agreement would conflict with the obligations and machinery of sanctions embodied in the League Covenant and the Locarno Pact. Because the United States was not a signatory to those international accords, France desired only a bilateral pact with the United States. In his reply of February 27, 1928, Kellogg allayed French fears by assuring that the multilateral pact would neither conflict with nor violate the specific obligations of the Covenant and the Locarno Pact. Rather, it would act as an effective instrument for strengthening the foundations of world peace. On March 30, 1928, the French accepted the revised United States proposal to universalize the treaty. It is historically accurate to say that the Briand offer formed the basis of the multilateral Kellogg-Briand Pact, and its wording, with slight modifications, became the wording of the final treaty.

On April 7, 1928, Kellogg secured an understanding with the French ambassador that both France and the United States would separately address the other four great powers—Great Britain, Germany, Italy, and Japan—inviting their opinions and participation. According to *The New York Times* of April 14, 1928, a copy of the U.S. draft treaty and a note were sent to those powers and to France. The U.S. note stated that the United States government "desires to see the institution of war abolished and stands ready to conclude with the French, British, German, Italian, and Japanese governments a single multilateral treaty open to subsequent adherence by any and all other governments binding the parties thereto not to resort to war with one another." The draft treaty contained two articles calling for the renunciation of war as an instrument of national policy and peaceful settlement of all international disputes. The French sent their draft on April 20. The French draft contained six articles, adding other clauses concerning matters such as self-defense, violation and release of obligation by others, and ratification by all before the treaty would be enforced.

The responses of the four great powers to both drafts were more than favorable. The only concern, expressed by the British minister, Sir Austen Chamberlain, was the restrictions that the treaty would place on British freedom of action over its far-flung empire. This fear was lessened by the sovereign right of self-defense implicit in the pact. Every sovereign state,

Kellogg emphasized, possessed the inherent right to defend its territory, and wars fought to repulse aggression would be entirely legal and not a violation of the pact. On the suggestion of the British, other signatories of the Locarno Pact—Belgium, Poland, and Czechoslovakia—were included among the principal signatories, along with India and the five British Dominions of Australia, Canada, the Irish Free State, New Zealand, and South Africa. The U.S. interpretation of the treaty was sent to fourteen governments. The vital element in the fourteen replies received in July was that all the governments had agreed to sign the treaty as proposed by Kellogg.

The diplomatic exchanges thus came to a successful conclusion. This represented a personal triumph for Kellogg, who was awarded the Nobel Peace Prize in 1929. Since December 28, 1927, he had unremittingly pursued the aim of a global multilateral treaty for the renunciation of war as an instrument of national policy, and he had achieved his goal. The other great hero and the original inspiration, Briand, also was awarded the Nobel Peace Prize. He had accomplished everything that he deemed essential for France.

The most important aim of the pact had been to prevent war. The treaty linked the United States to the League of Nations as the guardian of world peace and in turn strengthened the sanctions of the Covenant. It simultaneously enhanced the feeling of security in Europe and in the rest of the world, and abetted the motive for general disarmament. The practical influence of the pact lay in the mobilization of the moral and legal conscience of humankind against aggressive militarism.

The treaty remained permanently flawed, however. Although it outlawed war, it did not codify this into a principle or rule of international law. Hence, a breach of the resolution—many of which happened in subsequent years—was not tantamount to a crime or a violation of international law. Italy's attack on Ethiopia in 1935 and Japanese imperialism in China in the 1930's could not be prevented, as the pact had neither moral sanctions nor any tribunals to enforce its provisions. Moreover, the blanket interpretation of self-defense allowed many a nation to justify its war of aggression. Nevertheless, the pact, although violated many times, was never officially repealed. It acted as the legal basis for the Nuremberg and Tokyo war crimes' trials after World War II.

—*Sudipta Das*

ADDITIONAL READING:

Ferrell, Robert H. *Peace in Their Time: The Origins of the Kellogg-Briand Pact.* New York: W. W. Norton, 1969. An essential source providing superb analyses of the Department of State's stratagems with French diplomats and domestic peace-movers in the shaping of the pact.

Marks, Sally. *The Illusion of Peace: International Relations in Europe, 1918-1933.* London: Macmillan, 1976. General but scholarly coverage of European diplomatic events, with critical analysis of the Kellogg-Briand Pact and its ramifications.

Miller, D. H. *The Peace Pact of Paris: A Study of the Briand-Kellogg Treaty.* New York: G. P. Putnam's Sons, 1928. Detailed and objective study of the shaping and writing of the pact, from both the French and U.S. perspectives. Research based on official documents and firsthand information.

Shotwell, J. T. *War as an Instrument of National Policy and Its Renunciation in the Pact of Paris.* New York: Harcourt, Brace, 1928. An essential, firsthand source on the peace pact. Explains the perspective of the U.S. peace seekers.

Vinson, John C. *William E. Borah and the Outlawry of War.* Athens: University of Georgia Press, 1957. A major contribution to an understanding of the U.S. commitment to promote world peace. Portrays Borah as the spokesperson of the United States and highlights his role in effecting peace plans, especially the Kellogg-Briand Pact.

SEE ALSO: 1912, Wilson Is Elected President; 1919, Treaty of Versailles; 1921, Scandals of the Harding Administration; 1921, Washington Disarmament Conference; 1932, Hoover-Stimson Doctrine; 1940, United States Builds a Two-Ocean Navy.

1929 ■ LEAGUE OF UNITED LATIN AMERICAN CITIZENS IS FOUNDED: *one of the oldest Hispanic advocacy organizations joins different Latino groups in a cohesive front*

DATE: February 17, 1929
LOCALE: Corpus Christi, Texas
CATEGORIES: Civil rights; Education; Latino American history; Organizations and institutions
KEY FIGURES:
José Tomás Canales (born 1877), member of the League of Latin American Citizens
Ben Garza, leader of the Sons of America
Alonso S. Perales (1898-1960), leader of the League of Latin American Citizens
J. Luz Saenz and
Juan B. Lozano, delegates to the first LULAC convention
SUMMARY OF EVENT. The League of United Latin American Citizens (LULAC) was formed in order to unite all Latin American organizations under one title. In 1927, the main Latin American groups were the Sons of America, the Knights of America, and the League of Latin American Citizens, and there were other less well-known groups. The Sons of America had councils in Sommerset, Pearsall, Corpus Christi, and San Antonio, Texas; the Knights of America had a council in San Antonio; the League of Latin American Citizens had councils in Harlingen, Brownsville, Laredo, Peñitas, La Grulla, McAllen, and Gulf, Texas.

As more Anglo-Americans moved into Texas, persons of Spanish or Mexican descent experienced open discrimination and segregation that placed them in the position of second-class citizens. They had been under the rule of six different countries before Texas entered the Union. Most had continued to live and work as they always had, without being assertive about their rights. As time progressed, many Hispanics found

that prejudice and discrimination were becoming less tolerable. Groups began to form to give more impact to requests that these practices cease. The Sons of America Council No. 4 in Corpus Christi, led by Ben Garza, originated a unification plan, believing that if all Hispanic organizations would regroup into one strong, unified, and vocal organization, more attention would be brought to the plight of those who were being discriminated against.

On August 14, 1927, delegates from the Sons of America, the Knights of America, and smaller groups met in Harlingen, Texas, to form LULAC. The resolution that was presented was adopted by those in the meeting. It was expected that the leaders of the major groups—Alonso Perales, Luz Saenz, José Canales, and Juan Lozano of the Rio Grande Valley of south Texas—would be invited by the president general of the Sons of America to begin the unification process. In response to concerns about the merger expressed by some members, Council No. 4 of the Sons of America drafted an agreement between itself and the Knights of America to unite. These two groups waited a year for the merger to be completed. Perales, president general of the Latin American League, stayed in close contact with Garza to maintain interest in the merger among the three main groups. However, the president general of the Sons of America never called the convention. After the long wait, Council No. 4 withdrew from the Sons of America on February 7, 1929. Participants at this meeting again voted to have a general convention for the purpose of unification. On February 17, 1929, invitations were sent to all the groups to meet in Corpus Christi, Texas, to vote on the merger.

Along with interested members of the Hispanic groups, Douglas Weeks, a professor at the University of Texas, attended not only to study the merger but also to open the convention as a nonaligned attendee. Ben Garza was elected chairman pro tem. His popularity as an energetic and fair civic leader made him a good spokesperson for the new group. The assembly had to choose a chairman, plan a single constitution, and select a name that would encompass the goals of the previously separate groups. The committee chosen to select a name included Juan Solis and Mauro Machado of the Knights of America, Perales and Canales of the Latin American League, E. N. Marin and A. de Luna of Corpus Christi, and Fortunio Treviño of Alice, Texas. Machado, of the Knights of America, proposed "United Latin American Citizens." This was amended to read "League of United Latin American Citizens," which was seconded by Canales. On February 17, 1929, LULAC formally came into being at Corpus Christi, Texas.

The naming committee undertook other proposals before coming back to the general convention. Canales proposed a motto, "All for One and One for All," as a reminder of their purpose in uniting and as a basis for their future activities. They set some basic rules to guide the league until the constitutional convention could be held. This meeting was called for May 18 and 19, 1929, with an executive committee made up of Garza, M. C. Gonzales as secretary, and Canales and Saenz as members at large. On May 18, the first meeting under the new title was called. The constitution proposed by Canales was adopted, and new officers were elected. The officers were Garza, president general; Gonzales, vice president general; de Luna, secretary general; and Louis C. Wilmot of Corpus Christi, treasurer general. George Washington's prayer was adopted from the ritual of the Sons of America, and the U.S. flag was adopted as the group's official flag. Now, in union, the new group could work to remove the injustices that had been building for many years. LULAC was chartered in 1931 under the laws of the State of Texas and later in New Mexico, Arizona, California, and Colorado, as other councils were formed. LULAC began issuing *LULAC Notes*, but in August, 1931, the first issue of *LULAC News* was published. In the 1990's, this magazine carried the subtitle "The Magazine for Today's Latino."

In the formative years, auxiliaries were started by women whose husbands were active LULAC members. In August, 1987, LULAC amended its constitution to admit women into the organization. Between 1937 and 1938, junior LULAC councils were formed under the sponsorship of adult councils. In 1940, LULAC councils peaked, but with the beginning of World War II, the councils weakened with the departure of the men to military service. In 1945 and 1946, LULAC began to make great strides as educated, trained men returned from the service. Prestigious positions were filled by Hispanics and discrimination lessened. Non-Hispanics were joining, and LULAC was moving toward its objectives.

When the Civil Rights movement of the 1960's began, other Hispanic groups with a more militant response to discrimination began to form. Leaders such as the charismatic preacher, Reies López Tijerina in New Mexico and Rodolfo Gonzalez in Denver marched in protest of the treatment Hispanics were receiving. César Chávez led farm groups in California on peaceful marches, which frequently erupted into violent confrontations as the number of militant members rose. LULAC did not totally support all these movements. It preferred mediation to resolve serious disagreements and education for all Hispanics as better ways of blending peacefully into the U.S. mainstream.

LULAC has evolved to stress education especially. Parents are encouraged to prepare their children well to enter school. English is encouraged as the primary language, Spanish as the second language. As students mature, they are encouraged to finish high school and enter college. For those who aspire to higher learning, LULAC sponsors many scholarships; it also offers other forms of financial aid and counseling. LULAC Education Centers are located in sixty cities in seventeen states to provide this help. With corporate and federal aid, these centers have made it possible for disadvantaged Hispanic American youth to become productive members of their American communities. —*Norma Crews*

ADDITIONAL READING:

De la Garza, Rodolfo O., ed. *Ignored Voices: Public Opinion Polls and the Latino Community*. Austin: Center for Mexican American Studies, University of Texas at Austin Press,

1987. Argues that the opinions of Hispanic people were virtually ignored, politically and otherwise, except in heavily Hispanic communities.

Garcia, F. Chris, ed. *Latinos and the Political System*. Notre Dame, Ind.: University of Notre Dame Press, 1988. Discusses some of the political problems that prompted the formation of organizations such as LULAC.

Garcia, Mario T. *Mexican-Americans: Leadership, Ideology, and Identity 1930-1960*. New Haven, Conn.: Yale University Press, 1989. A thorough treatise on Hispanic assimilation into the mainstream of U.S. business and community.

Mirande, Alfredo. *The Chicano Experience: An Alternative Perspective*. Notre Dame, Ind.: University of Notre Dame Press, 1985. A view into the life of the less accepted Hispanic, the Chicano. Gives information on La Raza, a more militant group representing Hispanics of the 1960's and 1970's.

Shorris, Earl. *Latinos: A Biography of the People*. New York: W. W. Norton, 1992. A collection of information on Hispanics in the United States, and a general overview of those Hispanics who immigrated and settled during the 1900's.

SEE ALSO: 1930's, Mass Deportations of Mexicans; 1942, Bracero Program; 1954, Operation Wetback; 1965, Delano Grape Strike; 1968, Bilingual Education Act; 1972, United Farm Workers Joins with AFL-CIO; 1982, *Plyler v. Doe*.

1929 ■ STOCK MARKET CRASH: *a cyclical economic downturn, exacerbated by tariffs and federal controls, marks the beginning of the Great Depression*

DATE: October 29, 1929
LOCALE: New York City, New York
CATEGORIES: Business and labor; Economics
KEY FIGURES:
Herbert Clark Hoover (1874-1964), thirty-first president of the United States, 1929-1933
Thomas William Lamont (1870-1948), partner in J. P. Morgan and Company
Charles E. Merrill (1885-1956), founder of the Merrill-Lynch securities brokerage

SUMMARY OF EVENT. During the 1920's, increasing numbers of people in the United States started to invest in the growing economic prosperity of the nation as reflected in the securities market. A combination of new technology (automobiles, electricity, and radios, for example), lower levels of taxation, and generally rising incomes led to the decade known as the Roaring Twenties. At the same time, pioneer securities brokers, such as Charles E. Merrill, marketed stocks to people of average incomes. As more people invested, the already rising prices of stocks accelerated. A popular form of investing, "margin buying," allowed investors to purchase securities on credit from the broker for as little as 15 percent down. Margin buying rose from one billion dollars in 1920 to eight billion dollars in 1929.

The actual cause of the crash, on October 24, 1929, and its subsequent declines through October 29, remains a matter of controversy. The most significant fact is that the 1920's was not a "bubble" or an era of rampant speculation, as some have alleged. Most economists have failed to detect any bubble effect in the economy. The real growth of the economy was nothing less than phenomenal in the 1920's: Unemployment fell as low as 1 percent; Secretary of the Treasury Andrew Mellon's tax cuts lowered the national debt (not deficit) by one-third; and the federal government ran surpluses in most years. Manufacturing productivity reached all-time high levels, and almost every sector except agriculture soared. Stock prices reflected that growth.

The Great Bull Market started to slow, however, in mid-1928, following the election of Herbert Hoover. Despite his public pronouncements, Hoover was less supportive of U.S. business than had been his predecessor, Calvin Coolidge. Overseas, the European economies struggled under the weight of the dislocations caused by World War I, especially the reparation payments on Germany. The German economy had all but collapsed, and the United States intervened with the Dawes Plan. Even the solutions offered under the Dawes Plan could not restore the prewar productivity of the French, British, and German economies. With all the nations of the world on the gold standard, the weakness of one nation was to be offset by gains in neighboring countries, but the Treaty of Versailles had so dislocated some of the major European industries (such as shipbuilding) that no European nation was able to rescue the others. Only the United States remained relatively untouched by the economic problems in Europe.

As the Europeans sought ways out of their difficulties, they tried to stimulate their domestic demand by raising import duties, which slowed U.S. exports. United States legislators investigated ways to retaliate, and developed the Hawley-Smoot Tariff, which started to move through the congressional committees in the fall of 1929. The most significant congressional committee votes on the tariff took place on October 23, the day before the crash.

At that point, a minor cyclical downturn in the economy was accelerated and exacerbated by news that tariffs on virtually all imported products, including raw materials, might soon rise by as much as 34 percent. Industry, already experiencing slowing sales, started to examine ways to brace itself against the expected further drop in sales. Business anticipated higher costs, so it looked to reduce workforces; business needed huge new capital reserves, so it liquidated stocks. The combined effects of those actions resulted in rapidly declining securities prices. When that occurred, those investors who bought on margin suddenly had to sell their stocks, sending prices tumbling still further.

New York bankers attempted to stem the tide of falling prices. Meeting in the office of Thomas W. Lamont, a partner in J. P. Morgan and Company, the banks bought stock in massive amounts, attempting to support the price. They also hoped that the publicity associated with well-known personalities purchasing stocks might have a psychological effect. The bankers' actions, however, were offset by news of further movement on the Hawley-Smoot Tariff. The market suffered its worst drop on October 24, and within two weeks the value of stocks on the exchange declined more than 37 percent. Some fell forty points in a few days.

Meanwhile, a wave of bank failures in the agricultural areas of the Midwest and South, which had accumulated steadily during the 1920's, spread to major banking systems in 1930. The most famous failures involved the Bank of United States in New York City and Caldwell and Company in Tennessee. The two separate streams of economic dislocation—the economic crash and the banking failures—combined when the Federal Reserve Board, attempting to restrict lending on securities, tightened credit and brought on the Great Depression.

Only later, after New Deal legislation was passed that separated investment banking from commercial banking (based on a flawed view of the banks' role in the bull market), did scholars examine the causes of the stock market crash. They discovered that no bubble ever existed; that the banks that had securities affiliates (brokerage houses) were less susceptible to failure than those institutions without securities affiliates; and that margin buying played a much smaller role in the crash than was thought.

—*Larry Schweikart*

ADDITIONAL READING:

Eichengreen, Barry. *Golden Fetters: The Gold Standard and the Great Depression*. New York: Oxford University Press, 1992. Although primarily concerned with the role of the gold standard in causing the international recessions that started in 1928, the author also asserts that Federal Reserve policy caused abrupt changes in purchases of commodities that would have been reflected on Wall Street.

Friedman, Milton, and Anna J. Schwartz. *A Monetary History of the United States, 1867-1960*. Princeton, N.J.: Princeton University Press, 1963. A seminal work that identifies Federal Reserve Board mistakes as causing both the stock market crash and the banking crisis of 1930-1933.

Galbraith, John K. *The Great Crash, 1929*. Boston: Houghton Mifflin, 1955. An engaging book that interprets the stock market crash as resulting from speculation, market flaws, and criminal behavior.

Wanniski, Jude. *The Way the World Works*. New York: Basic Books, 1978. Written by an economist, this book analyzes the relationship between the Hawley-Smoot Tariff and the stock market crash.

White, Eugene N. *The Regulation and Reform of the American Banking System, 1900-1929*. Princeton, N.J.: Princeton University Press, 1983. Significant sections on banks and their securities affliates. Shows that those banks involved in stock market lending were less likely to fail than banks not involved in such activities.

_____. "When the Ticker Ran Late: The Stock Market Boom and Crash of 1929." In *Crashes and Panics: The Lessons from History*. Homewood, Ill.: Dow Jones-Irwin, 1990. Relates the bull market to the expectation that companies would continue paying high dividends; asserts, therefore, that the stock market crash was related to changing expectations, not to Federal Reserve Board policy.

SEE ALSO: 1913, Federal Reserve Act; 1919, Treaty of Versailles; 1924, Dawes Plan; 1924, Coolidge Is Elected President; 1929, Great Depression.

1929 ■ GREAT DEPRESSION: *the worst period of poverty and hardship in the twentieth century, both in North America and abroad*

DATE: October 29, 1929-1939
LOCALE: North America
CATEGORIES: Business and labor; Economics
KEY FIGURES:

Herbert Clark Hoover (1874-1964), thirty-first president of the United States, 1929-1933

Cordell Hull (1871-1955), U.S. congressman and later secretary of state

Hugh S. Johnson (1882-1942), head of the National Recovery Administration

Frances Perkins (1880-1965), U.S. secretary of labor

Franklin Delano Roosevelt (1882-1945), thirty-second president of the United States, 1933-1945

Francis E. Townsend (1867-1960), California physician who led a movement to give a monthly pension to retired elderly persons

Walter W. Waters, World War I veteran and head of the Bonus Army

SUMMARY OF EVENT. Beginning in the summer of 1929, the U.S. economy began a contraction that continued, with minor interruptions, until March of 1933 and from which the nation did not fully recover until 1939. The value of the nation's output of goods and services, or gross national product (GNP), fell from $104 billion in 1929 to $55 billion in 1933, causing a 30 percent decline in the quantity of output and interrupting for more than a decade the historical trend toward increase in per capita production. Industrial production declined 51 percent before reviving slightly in 1932.

Unemployment statistics poignantly revealed the impact of the Depression on Americans. In 1929, the Labor Department reported 1,499,000 jobless persons, or 3.1 percent of all employables. After the crash, the figure soared. At its peak in 1933, unemployment stood at 12,634,000, more than one out of every four people in the labor force. Some estimates placed unemployment as high as sixteen million. By 1933, the annual national income had shrunk from $87.8 billion to $40.2 billion. Farmers, perhaps the hardest hit economic group, saw their income decline from $11.9 billion to $5.3 billion.

The Depression resulted from a severe decline in aggregate demand. One contributing factor was a massive wave of bank failures. As banks failed, the public withdrew large sums of currency, forcing the banks to call in loans and reducing the money supply. Decreased spending drove down prices and wages. Farmers, home buyers, and many business firms found the burden of their debts greatly increased, so bankruptcies and property foreclosures were widespread. The Depression was not limited to North America: It spread across the world, each country buying less from the others. In Germany, for example, the Depression struck sooner and went deeper than it did in the United States.

Political pressures to relieve distress and promote recovery were strong everywhere. For the first two years of the Depression, President Herbert Hoover relied on the voluntary cooperation of business and labor to maintain payrolls and production. In 1929, the government created the Federal Farm Board and gave it authority to make crop loans, which helped keep products off the market and thereby limit price declines. In 1930, Congress adopted the Hawley-Smoot Tariff, which drastically increased U.S. import restrictions, dragging other countries further into the deflationary process. As the crisis deepened, Hoover took positive steps to stop the spread of economic collapse. In 1932, the government established the Reconstruction Finance Corporation (RFC), a loan agency designed to aid distressed firms such as banks, insurance companies, and railroads. This approach to economic recovery was based on Hoover's belief that such government loans would halt deflation, ultimately restoring industry's ability to create jobs, increase the number of wage earners, and thereby increase consumption.

On the relief issue, the president and Congress fought a running battle for months. The Democrats wanted the federal government to assume responsibility for direct relief and to spend heavily on public works. Hoover was willing to see public works spending increase, but he insisted on a massive tax increase in 1932 to pay for it. He argued that unemployment relief was properly the province of local resources, not an appropriate federal activity:

> The proposals of our opponents will endanger or destroy our system. . . . I especially emphasize that promise to promote "employment for all surplus labor at all times." . . . At first I could not believe that anyone would be so cruel as to hold out a hope so absolutely impossible of realization. . . . [a]nd I protest against such frivolous promises being held out to a suffering people. If it were possible to give this employment to 10,000,000 people by the Government, it would cost upwards of $9,000,000,000 a year. . . . It would pull down the employment of those who are still at work by the high taxes and the demoralization of credit upon which their employment is dependent. . . .

After a partisan fight, Hoover did, however, sign the Relief and Construction Act, which expanded the RFC's power to extend loans to states and for the creation of public works projects. Other bills passed in 1932 include the Glass-Steagall Act, which expanded credit to industry and business, and the Federal Home Loan Bank Act, which was designed to limit foreclosures by establishing a series of banks capitalized at $125 million to provide for home construction and long-term mortgages payable in installments.

Despite these efforts, by the end of Hoover's term, the nation's banking system had virtually collapsed, and the economic machinery of the nation was grinding to a halt. Tired and haggard, Hoover left office with the reputation of a do-nothing president, although he had gone far beyond his predecessors in supporting expanded federal responsibilities—even paving the way for the New Deal. His profound belief that promoting government jobs for the unemployed would break the backs of taxpayers, however, had not allowed him to do enough.

What happened to the economy after 1929 left most people baffled and bewildered. The physical structure of business was still intact, undamaged by war or natural disaster. People wanted to go to work, but plants stood dark and idle. Prolonged unemployment created a new class of superfluous people. The jobless sold apples on street corners. They queued up in breadlines and outside soup kitchens. Many lived in "Hoovervilles," shantytowns on the outskirts of large cities. Thousands of unemployed men and boys took to the road in search of work, and the gas station became a meeting place for men "on the bum." In 1932, a crowd of fifty men fought over a barrel of garbage outside the back door of a Chicago restaurant. In northern Alabama, poor families exchanged a dozen eggs, which they sorely needed, for a box of matches.

Despite such mass suffering, there was little violence or support for radical political movements. Farmers suffering from drastic price declines tried to reduce the flow of products to market. In August, 1932, for example, Iowa farmers began dumping milk bound for Sioux City. To dramatize their plight, Milo Reno, former president of the Iowa Farmers Union, organized a strike on the northern plains and cut off all agricultural products from urban markets until prices rose. Several farm states passed moratorium laws preventing the foreclosure of farms for debt. Drought aggravated the problems of farm families in the plains states, where the Dust Bowl made life so difficult that whole families packed up and left for the West Coast. Such "Okies" (named for the state where many originated) flooded into California to take jobs as migrant farm workers, as John Steinbeck vividly depicted in his 1939 novel *The Grapes of Wrath*.

In the summer of 1932, an organized protest occurred when twenty-five thousand World War I veterans, led by former sergeant Walter W. Waters, staged the Bonus March on Washington, D.C., to demand immediate payment of a bonus that was not due until 1945. Congress refused, and Hoover sent troops to disperse the riot that ensued at Anacostia Flats, where the veterans were encamped.

Hoover was resoundingly defeated by Franklin D. Roosevelt in the election of 1932. The political pendulum had swung strongly toward the Democratic Party. Roosevelt's New Deal drastically increased the economic role of the federal government. Roosevelt instituted several major policy

innovations. For example, the dollar was devalued internationally by raising the price of gold from $20.67 to $35 per ounce. This measure opened the way for a large flow of gold from Europe to the United States, raising bank reserves and increasing the money supply. In addition, a "bank holiday" in March, 1933, closed all banks for a few days, then reopened most of them under conditions that restored public confidence in them. Federal insurance of bank deposits was established.

Roosevelt also established a series of relief programs that provided direct transfer payments to the needy. The system evolved from direct handouts under the Federal Emergency Relief Administration to work relief under the Civil Works Administration and the Works Progress Administration (WPA). On the business side, the National Recovery Administration (NRA) was established in 1933 under General Hugh S. Johnson. It attempted to promote industrial recovery by encouraging firms in individual industries and trade groups to get together to formulate "codes of fair competition," which usually tended to reduce competition. For farmers, the Agricultural Adjustment Administration (AAA), also created in 1933, provided a system of production restrictions and price supports for agricultural products that became a permanent part of national policy. The Reciprocal Trade Agreements Act of 1934 enabled Secretary of State Cordell Hull to begin negotiations with other countries to agree on measures to liberalize international trade, beginning another permanent element of national policy. Finally, several measures promoted the establishment and power of labor unions, notably the National Labor Relations Act of 1935. Federal regulation of wages and hours began in 1938, with the Fair Labor Standards Act. Roosevelt appointed the first woman cabinet member, designating Frances Perkins to head the Department of Labor.

Federal government intervention in the economy soared with these measures. For a time, this trend was resisted by the Supreme Court, which on Black Monday, May 27, 1935, rejected the AAA and the NRA as unconstitutional. However, after Roosevelt's landslide reelection in 1936, the Court ceased most of its opposition. The New Deal programs brought a rapid increase in government spending. Although tax rates were frequently increased, toleration of federal deficits became a normal financial policy.

In 1935, Dr. Francis Townsend, a California physician, popularized a proposal to help needy aged persons and stimulate economic recovery by having the government pay a pension of two hundred dollars per month to each person over sixty years of age who agreed to retire. In response, the government developed a comprehensive program of social insurance, adopted in August, 1935, as the Social Security Act. It included a program of unemployment compensation, a separate program of old-age pensions, and a third program of means-tested relief for needy aged, blind, and families with dependent children. With this, the U.S. welfare system of transfer payments came into existence.

The Great Depression was a crisis of the American mind as much as it was an economic disaster. Many people believed that the country had reached all its frontiers and faced a future of limited opportunity. A slowdown of marriage and birth rates expressed this pessimism. The Depression smashed the old verities of rugged individualism, the sanctity of business, and the American preference for limited government. Utopian movements found an eager following. In addition to Townsend's call for an old-age pension system, Charles E. Coughlin, a radio priest of Royal Oak, Michigan, advocated the nationalization of banks, utilities, and natural resources. Senator Huey P. Long led a movement advocating a redistribution of wealth. All these movements tapped a broad vein of discontent among those who felt that they had been left out of the New Deal.

Slowly, however, Americans regained their sense of optimism. The New Deal revived the old faith that the nation could meet any challenge and control its own destiny. Even many intellectuals who had debunked American life in the 1920's began to revise their opinions. By 1936, there were signs of recovery, and by 1937, business indexes were up, some near 1929 levels. The New Deal had eased much of the acute distress, although unemployment remained at around 7.5 million. Although in 1938 the economy again went into a sharp recession, conditions improved by mid-1938. Still, the Depression did not end until the government launched the massive defense spending of World War II.

—Donald Holley, updated by Paul B. Trescott

ADDITIONAL READING:

Allen, Frederick Lewis. *Since Yesterday: The Nineteen-thirties in America, September 3, 1929-September 3, 1939.* New York: Harper & Brothers, 1940. This classic social history provides a vivid picture of Americans' lives in the 1930's.

Bernstein, Irving. *The Lean Years: A History of the American Worker, 1920-1933.* Baltimore: Penguin Books, 1966.

_____. *The Turbulent Years: A History of the American Worker, 1933-1941.* Boston: Houghton Mifflin, 1970. In these volumes, Bernstein provides a readable and dramatic account of employment conditions and the transformation of the labor union movement during the Depression.

Chandler, Lester V. *America's Greatest Depression, 1929-1941.* New York: Harper & Row, 1970. A professional economist explains the quantitative dimensions of the Depression.

Journal of Economic Perspectives 7, no. 2 (Spring, 1993). Symposium on the Great Depression. Articles by four economic historians include updated bibliographies and analysis.

Mitchell, Broadus. *Depression Decade: From New Era Through New Deal, 1929-1941.* New York: Rinehart, 1947. An economic history that blends data and description, incorporating some of the human dimension.

Shannon, David A., ed. *The Great Depression.* Englewood Cliffs, N.J.: Prentice-Hall, 1960. A collection of descriptive materials about the impact of the Depression, reprinted from newspaper and magazine accounts.

SEE ALSO: 1924, Coolidge Is Elected President; 1928, Smith-Hoover Campaign; 1929, Stock Market Crash; 1932, Reconstruction Finance Corporation Is Created; 1932, Bonus

March; 1932, Franklin D. Roosevelt Is Elected President; 1933, The Hundred Days; 1933, Tennessee Valley Authority Is Established; 1933, National Industrial Recovery Act; 1934, The Dust Bowl; 1935, Works Progress Administration Is Established; 1935, Black Monday; 1935, National Labor Relations Act; 1935, Social Security Act; 1937, Supreme Court Packing Fight; 1938, Fair Labor Standards Act; 1939, Mobilization for World War II.

1930's ■ MASS DEPORTATIONS OF MEXICANS: *massive unemployment during the Depression prompts deportation of immigrant workers in order to redistribute jobs to U.S. citizens*

DATE: Early 1930's
LOCALE: Los Angeles, California
CATEGORIES: Business and labor; Economics; Immigration; Latino American history
KEY FIGURES:
William N. Doak (1882-1933), secretary of labor under President Herbert Hoover
Charles P. Visel, chairman of the Los Angeles (City) Citizens Committee on Coordination of Unemployment Relief

SUMMARY OF EVENT. In the early decades of the twentieth century, immigration of Mexican nationals into the United States was a growing phenomenon. It was not viewed as a problem, however, because cheap labor was welcomed, particularly on farms and ranches. U.S. immigration laws generally were enforced selectively with regard to Mexicans. During World War I, at the request of U.S. businesses, the provisions of the Immigration Act of 1917 that required immigrants to pay an eight-dollar "head tax" and prove literacy were waived for Mexican laborers. This special departmental order legitimized U.S. dependence on cheap Mexican labor and institutionalized Mexico's special status.

At the end of World War I, the order was not rescinded; in fact, U.S. companies intensified their recruitment of Mexican farmworkers. Industrial companies in the Northeast and Midwest, such as steel mills and automobile manufacturers, also began recruiting Mexicans from the Southwest, resulting in an expanding migration in terms of both numbers of immigrants and their geographic spread. The Emergency Immigration Act of 1921 and the National Origins Act (Immigration Act of 1924) had each limited immigration from Europe, but no restrictions were imposed on the number of immigrants from countries in the Western Hemisphere. Thus, a large and growing population of Mexican immigrants had established itself in the United States in the first decades of the twentieth century.

In the 1920's, the U.S. government's attitude toward Mexican immigrants gradually changed from lax enforcement to severe restrictions. As social and economic conditions deteriorated on a global scale, the great pool of cheap Mexican labor was increasingly resented by unemployed U.S. citizens. Despite pressure from businesses, laws restricting entry—that is, the head tax and literacy test—began to be strictly enforced against Mexicans by immigration authorities. Two new laws also were passed that had a further chilling effect on Mexican immigration to the United States: the Deportation Act of March 4, 1929, which made entering the United States illegally a misdemeanor punishable by a year in prison or a fine of as much as one thousand dollars, followed by the May 4, 1929, law making it a felony for a deported alien to reenter the United States illegally. These laws, followed within months by the stock market crash that marked the onset of the Great Depression in the United States, set the stage for a period of repressive measures against Mexican nationals in the United States.

As the Depression caused more unemployment, the caseloads of social welfare agencies increased. By 1931, as the pool of unemployed immigrants requiring assistance grew, local agencies intensified their efforts to force repatriation; on the federal level, calls to deport immigrants increased also. President Herbert Hoover endorsed the aggressive efforts to expel aliens, restrict legal immigration, and curtail illegal entry. William N. Doak, who took office as Hoover's secretary of labor in December, 1930, proposed that any alien holding a job be deported. The Bureau of Immigration, at that time a part of the Department of Labor, began an aggressive campaign of rooting out illegal aliens, with the objective of reducing unemployment and thus hastening the end of the Great Depression. Many of the aliens deported under this program, however, were already unemployed.

Although Mexicans were not specifically targeted by the immigration authorities, they were the most affected numerically as a group. The response of the Mexican government to the problem varied: At times, land reform programs were established for repatriating Mexican citizens; at other times, Mexico feared the addition of more unemployed citizens to its labor surplus. Opportunities for Mexican Americans to obtain land in Mexico usually required money to be invested, although occasionally there were programs that offered land to destitute repatriates.

In the southwestern states, particularly, immigration officials aggressively sought deportable Mexicans, and social service agencies encouraged Mexicans to volunteer for repatriation. The most ambitious of these programs was undertaken in Los Angeles County, California, but cities such as Chicago and Detroit, where Mexicans had been recruited by industry in the early 1920's, also were actively attempting to get even legal Mexican residents to leave in the 1930's.

The Los Angeles Citizens Committee on Coordination of Unemployment Relief, headed by Charles P. Visel, had been charged with assisting the unemployed residents of the city, especially through creation of jobs, for which longtime local residents would be given preference. Inspired by Labor Secretary Doak's earlier pronouncements that some four hundred thousand deportable aliens were believed to be in the country,

Visel set out to identify and deport as many illegal aliens from the city of Los Angeles as possible. Visel contacted Doak and requested that a sufficient number of immigration agents be deployed in Los Angeles to create a hostile environment, from which he hoped aliens would flee voluntarily. Visel planned to open his campaign with press releases and a few well-publicized arrests.

Although the plan was not aimed specifically at Mexicans, some statements made by Visel did mention Mexicans as a group to be targeted. The Spanish-language newspapers in Southern California stirred up the Mexican community, both in Los Angeles and in Mexico, by publishing inaccurate stories that virtually all Mexicans were being targeted for deportation. In the first three weeks of February, 1931, immigration agents had investigated several thousand people, 225 of whom were determined to be subject to deportation. Figures released by Visel's committee in March, 1931, indicated that 70 percent of the persons deported up to that time in the Los Angeles campaign were Mexicans. According to the Mexican Chamber of Commerce, which estimated that ten thousand of the more than two hundred thousand Mexicans thought to be living in Los Angeles prior to 1931 had left, many of the repatriates owned businesses and homes in Southern California. It should be noted, however, that the Chamber of Commerce would be more likely to have contact with the more prosperous members of the population than with the unemployed or laborers.

Concurrent with the federal and local campaigns to deport illegal aliens, Los Angeles County officials began attempting to repatriate destitute Mexicans. Many Mexican nationals had entered the United States at a time when penalties for illegal entry were nonexistent or seldom enforced against Mexicans; thus, their legal status was uncertain. With chances of unemployed Mexicans finding employment in the United States slim, welfare officials were beginning to put pressure on alien relief recipients to return to Mexico, at times leading them to believe that if they did not leave voluntarily, they would be cut off from aid immediately.

Frank Shaw, a member of the Board of Supervisors in Los Angeles County, was the first area official to propose paying the cost of transporting families back to Mexico by train. Three hundred fifty Mexicans signed up for the first trip, in March, 1931. Many more trips were made, but statistics on the numbers who were repatriated under the county program are clouded by the fact that the same trains that carried county-aided Mexicans also carried deportees and Mexicans who had made their own arrangements to leave, and accurate records were not kept. Overall, the various efforts to reduce the number of immigrants in Southern California in the early 1930's caused a noticeable, but temporary, reduction of the Mexican population in the area.   —*Irene Struthers*

ADDITIONAL READING:

Cardoso, Lawrence A. "The Great Depression: Emigration Halts and Repatriation Begins." In *Mexican Emigration to the United States, 1897-1931*. Tucson: University of Arizona Press, 1980. Brief discussion of federal deportation efforts and local repatriation efforts in the early 1930's. Includes corridos (ballads) written by returning Mexicans lamenting their plight.

Ehrlich, Paul R., Loy Bilderback, and Anne H. Ehrlich. *The Golden Door: International Migration, Mexico, and the United States*. New York: Ballantine Books, 1978. Introductory chapters on migration in general, and European and Asian immigration into the United States. The rest of the book covers Mexican immigration into the United States until the 1970's. Notes, recommended readings, and index.

Hoffman, Abraham. *Unwanted Americans in the Great Depression: Repatriation Pressure 1929-1939*. Tucson: University of Arizona Press, 1974. Well-researched, comprehensive look at the deportation and repatriation of Mexicans, particularly from Los Angeles County, in the 1930's. Source notes; extensive bibliography, emphasizing sources from the 1930's; index.

Meier, Matt S., and Feliciano Ribera. *Mexican Americans and American Mexicans: From Conquistadors to Chicanos*. Rev. ed. of *The Chicanos*, 1972. New York: Farrar, Straus & Giroux, 1993. Comprehensive history of the Mexican presence in the United States. Pages 153-157 discuss deportation and repatriation in the 1930's. List of acronyms; glossary; suggestions for further readings; index.

Samora, Julian. *"Los Mojados": The Wetback Story*. Notre Dame, Ind.: University of Notre Dame Press, 1971. Discusses illegal immigration from Mexico in the twentieth century, including a chapter by a graduate student assisting the author, who attempted to enter the country illegally. Bibliography; index; useful, if dated, statistical information.

SEE ALSO: 1924, Immigration Act of 1924; 1929, League of United Latin American Citizens Is Founded; 1929, Great Depression; 1933, Good Neighbor Policy; 1942, Bracero Program; 1943, Inflation and Labor Unrest; 1954, Operation Wetback; 1972, United Farm Workers Joins with AFL-CIO.

1930 ■ NATION OF ISLAM IS FOUNDED: *a Muslim religious organization inculcates black pride and helps elevate African Americans' social and economic status*

DATE: Summer, 1930
LOCALE: Detroit, Michigan
CATEGORIES: African American history; Organizations and institutions; Religion
KEY FIGURES:
Wallace D. Fard (c. 1877-1934), first prophet of the Nation of Islam, who established its basic philosophy
Malcolm X (Malcolm Little, 1925-1965), dynamic minister and spokesperson who propelled the organization to national attention
Elijah Muhammad (Elijah Poole, 1897-1975), founder and spiritual leader of the Nation of Islam

SUMMARY OF EVENT. The Nation of Islam (NOI), also known as the Black Muslim movement and the Lost Found Nation of Islam in the Wilderness of North America, is a religious organization that has successfully melded orthodox Islam, black nationalism, and a set of social and economic principles to produce a highly structured way of life for its African American membership. A religious sect founded in 1930 in Detroit, Michigan, the NOI borrowed from earlier movements as it crystallized around three leaders: W. D. Fard, Elijah Muhammad, and Malcolm X.

Orthodox Islam was started in Mecca, Saudia Arabia, by the prophet Mohammad (570-632). A major world religion, Islam may have arrived in America with the Spanish explorers. In 1888, Alexander Russell Webb established an Islamic community in the United States. Members of the Islamic religion are known as Muslims or Moslems. To distinguish between orthodox Muslims and members of the Islamic sect the Nation of Islam, theologian C. Eric Lincoln coined the term Black Muslims. Although the NOI considers itself a branch of orthodox Islam, the majority of its earliest members were affiliated with Christianity.

The Nation of Islam embraces the essential teachings of orthodox Islam: prayer five times daily; belief in one God named Allah; the acceptance of the sacred Islamic book—the Koran or Quran; the coming of the "guided one," known as Mahdi; and a pilgrimage to the holy city of Mecca. Both groups stress cleanliness and a strict moral code, and shun alcohol, drug abuse, and eating pork. Early NOI leaders, however, expanded orthodox Islam because of the historic oppression of African Americans. The Nation of Islam is orthodox Islam customized for the African American experience, with membership solidarity and racial pride being key added features. Black Muslims are required to drop their European last name, associated with enslavement, and adopt the "X" until they earn an Islamic surname. Additional elements, such as advocating a separate nation for its members and teaching about the racist deeds of the "white man," were the source of much outside criticism and prevented the NOI's acceptance into the official fold of orthodox Islam.

During the first half of the twentieth century, African Americans were treated as second-class citizens in the United States, where institutionalized racism made it difficult for their masses to rise above poverty and oppression. In the midst of Great Depression woes and the past specter of slavery, many African Americans at that time were disillusioned and susceptible to philosophies and leaders who promised improvements. Consequently, a number of nationalistic and religious movements developed. The Nation of Islam includes principles that were embedded in two of these movements: Timothy Drew's Moorish Science Temple, founded in 1913, and Marcus Garvey's Universal Negro Improvement Association.

Timothy Drew, known as the Noble Drew Ali, introduced Islam to African Americans. He and his followers adopted the Koran and called themselves Moors, who were an ancient North African people. Drew's church had thousands of members in Northern cities before his unexplained death in 1929. Subsequently, many of Drew's followers joined W. D. Fard's group, which emerged a year later.

The Nation of Islam espoused the political nationalism of Jamaican-born Marcus Garvey, who amassed thousands of followers in the United States from 1916 until his imprisonment in 1923 and subsequent deportation. Garvey advocated a separate African American nation, economic and political solidarity, and racial pride. When W. D. Fard appeared on the American scene during the summer of 1930, the conditions that fostered the acceptance of the ideas of Garvey and Drew were still present, although the original founders were not. Consequently, Fard soon filled a void that, after setbacks, developed into a viable religious sect. The Nation of Islam grew out of the informal visits of Fard to the homes of African Americans in Detroit, where he peddled silk products and discussed orthodox Islam, the African heritage, and the misdeeds of the "white man."

The first prophet of the Nation of Islam is shrouded in mystery. Although believed to be from Mecca, his national origins, his real name, and the circumstances of his 1934 disappearance are not known. In addition to being known as W. D. Fard and Wallace Fard Muhammad, he is referred to as Wali Farrad, F. Mohammad, and other names. Fard's achievements, however, are well documented. In four years during the Great Depression, Fard established the church's basic philosophy, created a security force known as the Fruit of Islam, opened the University of Islam, built its first temple, and amassed about eight thousand followers. Many of his followers, including Elijah Muhammad, thought Fard to be Allah reincarnated as well as the promised Mahdi. After Fard's sudden disappearance Elijah Muhammad became the group's leader.

Elijah Muhammad, born Elijah Poole in Sandersville, Georgia, was respectfully known as the Honorable Elijah Muhammad, the Messenger of Allah. His parents had been slaves and sharecroppers. His father was a Baptist minister. While a teenager, Muhammad moved to Atlanta. He married Clara Evans in 1919, and during the 1920's he and his family migrated to Detroit. It was in Detroit that Muhammad met W. D. Fard and became one of his most devoted converts. He was rewarded by being chosen as Fard's successor, and he transformed Fard's sincere project into a thriving organization.

After Fard's disappearance, rivalry caused some factionalism and a sharp decrease in NOI membership. Muhammad, often the victim of harassment and death threats, was imprisoned. Consequently, Muhammad moved the NOI headquarters

Elijah Muhammad, founder and leader of the Nation of Islam until his death in 1975. (Roy Lewis)

from Detroit to Chicago. Although still confronted with adversities, Muhammad was able to rebuild and strengthen the organization. When Muhammad died in 1975, the Nation of Islam had temples and schools from coast to coast; owned a string of restaurants, apartments, and other businesses and real estate; operated a major printing press; and had a membership of more than one hundred thousand. Much of Muhammad's success, however, can be attributed to one of his ministers, Malcolm X.

Malcolm X was born Malcolm Little in Omaha, Nebraska. His parents Earle and Louise Little, were organizers for Marcus Garvey's Universal Negro Improvement Association. Because of their views, the Littles were forced to move. They eventually settled in East Lansing, Michigan, where Earle apparently was murdered and Louise had a breakdown. Malcolm then lived with his sister and foster families. Later, he wandered between odd jobs and engaged in petty crime. Malcolm was imprisoned from 1946 to 1952, and he married Betty Shabazz in 1958. He was murdered in New York on February 21, 1965.

In prison, Malcolm became self-educated and converted to Islam. After his release, he met Elijah Muhammad, received his X, and trained for the NOI ministry. He headed temples in several cities before becoming the primary spokesperson for the Nation of Islam. His frank speeches and numerous public appearances catapulted the NOI into the national forefront. Membership swelled due to Malcolm's visibility, but his enemies increased also. For unauthorized remarks made about President John F. Kennedy's assassination, Malcolm was suspended from the NOI. Around that time, he changed his name to El Hajj Malik El-Shabazz. He left the NOI in March, 1964, and formed two new organizations, which were curtailed by his death.

After Elijah Muhammad's death, his son, Warith, also known as Wallace, became the NOI leader. Warith's changes forced another NOI split, spearheaded by Louis Farrakhan. The NOI expanded under Farrakhan, a controversial figure for some of his adamant and at times incendiary statements. His nondenominational Million Man March in October, 1995, immensely added to his visibility and to some extent mitigated his controversial image. —*Linda Rochell Lane*

ADDITIONAL READING:

Carson, Clayborne. *Malcolm X: The FBI Files*. New York: Carroll & Graff, 1991. Extracts data from Federal Bureau of Investigation files and provides information on Malcolm X, his family, and the Nation of Islam from 1919-1980. Arranged in time-line format.

Clark, John Henrick, ed. *Malcolm X: The Man and His Times*. Trenton, N.J.: African World Press, 1990. Essays by scholars and personal acquaintances and a chapter in Malcolm's own words. Documents are presented in the appendix.

Frazier, E. Franklin. *The Negro Church in America*. 1963. Reprint. New York: Schocken Books, 1974.

Lincoln, C. Eric. *The Black Church Since Frazier*. New York: Schocken Books, 1974. These two detailed studies, by two noted scholars, have been merged into one volume. While

Frazier's work originally was published separately in 1963, together these studies provide critical background on African American religion.

_____. *The Black Muslims in America*. Boston: Beacon Press, 1961. The first complete academic analysis of the Nation of Islam.

Lippman, Thomas W. *Understanding Islam*. New York: Signet Books, 1982. For those with little knowledge of orthodox Islam, this book is a good start.

Malcolm X with Alex Haley. *The Autobiography of Malcolm X*. New York: Ballantine Books, 1965. This classic is the story of the African American revolutionary and Black Muslim leader.

Muhammad, Elijah. *The Supreme Wisdom*. 2 vols. Brooklyn: Temple of Islam, 1957. The beliefs of the Nation of Islam are explained by its founder.

SEE ALSO: 1909, National Association for the Advancement of Colored People Is Founded; 1917, Universal Negro Improvement Association Is Established; 1965, Assassination of Malcolm X.

1930 ■ BENNETT ERA IN CANADA: *the Conservatives return to dominance after nine years of Liberal rule*

DATE: August, 1930-1935
LOCALE: Canada
CATEGORIES: Canadian history; Government and politics
KEY FIGURES:
Richard Bennett (1870-1947), Conservative prime minister of Canada, 1930-1935
Robert Borden (1854-1937), Conservative prime minister of Canada, 1911-1920
Herbert Clark Hoover (1874-1964), Republican president of the United States, 1929-1933
William Lyon Mackenzie King (1874-1950), Liberal prime minister of Canada, 1921-1930 and 1935-1948
Arthur Meighen (1874-1960), Conservative prime minister of Canada, 1920-1921 and for three days in 1926

SUMMARY OF EVENT. Although Richard Bennett played an active role in Canadian politics throughout the first third of the twentieth century, historians generally believe that he was an uninspired politician who accomplished little during his five years of service as the prime minister of Canada. His ineffectiveness as prime minister made his Conservative Party so unpopular with Canadian voters that the Conservatives would not win another general election in Canada until 1957, when the Conservative John Diefenbaker succeeded the Liberal Louis St. Laurent as prime minister.

Bennett was born in the small town of Hopewell, New Brunswick, in 1870, the son of farmers. He studied law at Dalhousie University in Halifax, Nova Scotia. After his admission to the bar, he moved to Calgary, Alberta, where he became a successful lawyer, and his investments in real estate and various Calgary companies made him a millionaire by the first decade of the twentieth century.

Like his principal political rival, William Lyon Mackenzie King, Bennett never married: Law, business, and politics were Bennett's sole interests. After having served for thirteen years, first in the legislature of the Northwest Territories and then in the legislature in Alberta, Bennett was elected in a Calgary district as a Conservative member of Parliament in Ottawa. He earned the nickname "Bonfire Bennett" because he often spoke in public at more than two hundred words per minute. Prime Ministers Robert Borden and Arthur Meighen both recognized his adminstrative and legal skills. In the government of Robert Borden, Bennett served as the director general of National Service, responsible for encouraging enlistment in the Canadian armed forces during World War I. In 1921, Meighen named Bennett his minister of justice. Bennett was an ethical and effective public servant, which led the Conservatives to conclude that he would lead their party to victory in the general election of 1930.

When the Great Depression began with the U.S. stock market crash on October 29, 1929, the Canadian economy suffered greatly. Businesses failed throughout Canada, and unemployment exceeded 25 percent in many provinces. Canadian voters expected Prime Minister King to do something about this economic and social crisis, but, like the U.S. president Herbert Hoover, King believed that the Depression would not last long. Both leaders also felt that the Depression would worsen if their governments increased spending on social programs. Just before the July, 1930, general election, King made an incredible blunder. During debate in the House of Commons, he stated his unwillingness to send even "a five-cent piece" in unemployment assistance to provincial governments controlled by the Conservative Party. During the election campaign of 1930, Conservative candidates repeatedly referred to King's injudicious remark and suggested that a Conservative prime minister such as Bennett, who already had created many jobs through his Calgary companies, would be more successful than the Liberals in dealing with Canada's economic problems. This argument proved persuasive with Canadian voters, who gave the Conservatives a solid majority in the House of Commons.

Once Bennett assumed power, it became clear that he did not intend to share it, even with fellow Conservatives. In addition to his responsibilities as prime minister, he assigned to himself the posts of secretary of state for foreign affairs and minister of finance. Canadian political commentators of the day drew cartoons depicting Bennett alone and suggested that he was holding a cabinet meeting with himself. His unwillingness to listen to advice from such respected Conservative leaders as former prime ministers Borden and Meighen caused a precipitous decline in the standing of his party in the minds of Canadian voters. His one solution to the economic depression was to impose stiff tariffs on foreign products imported into Canada in an attempt to protect Canadian companies from foreign competition. Other countries retaliated, and the export of Canadian products decreased significantly. The resulting loss of jobs worsened an already alarming unemployment problem throughout Canada.

During his five years as prime minister, the wealthy Bennett lived in an elegant suite in the Chateau Laurier, Ottawa's finest hotel. He spoke repeatedly of the need for personal initiative and hard work in order to solve Canada's economic problem. A strong work ethic had helped Bennett to become a millionaire, and he firmly believed that it sufficed to cure Canada's economic and social problems. He was opposed philosophically to increased spending on social programs, because he believed that the main responsibility of the federal government in Ottawa was to avoid deficits. Although Canadians admired Bennett's integrity and his personal generosity—as shown by his large contributions to charitable organizations—they came to believe that he had no practical ideas for solving Canada's economic and social problems.

Starting in 1932, Bennett spent less time on domestic issues and more on international concerns. At the 1932 Imperial Conference in Ottawa, he persuaded the British government to modify the British North America Act of 1867, which had created Canada, in order to increase Canada's political independence from Great Britain. This was a major accomplishment, but in the minds of Canadian voters, it did not make up for Bennett's unwillingness to recognize the extreme seriousness of the Depression. The Liberals, under the leadership of King, argued for the need for large federal spending to deal with homelessness and unemployment, but such proposals were consistently rejected by the Conservative majority in the House of Commons. Just before the general election of 1935, Bennett suddenly changed his position and argued in favor of increased federal spending on social programs. He presented his new proposals as a Canadian version of Franklin D. Roosevelt's New Deal, but Canadian voters were suspicious of this sudden change in the domestic program of Bennett's Conservative government. The Liberals, under King, won 173 of the 244 seats in the House of Commons.

Bennett reacted bitterly to this defeat. In 1938, he left Canada permanently for England and transferred his allegiance to Great Britain. Thanks to the help of his friend Lord Beaverbrook, Bennett was appointed to the British House of Lords. When he died in 1947, he had been almost forgotten by Canadians, who never understood why a former prime minister of their country would emigrate from Canada. Canadian historians often have compared Bennett to Herbert Hoover, but the comparison is unfair. Neither Bennett nor Hoover succeeded in ending the economic depression, but Hoover was never considered arrogant, and he remained in the United States after his term in office and continued to serve his country as a respected adviser to both Democratic and Republican presidents.

—*Edmund J. Campion*

ADDITIONAL READING:

Bothwell, Robert, Ian Drummond, and John English. *Canada: 1900-1945*. Toronto: University of Toronto Press, 1987.

A well-documented history of the Great Depression in Canada and Bennett's problems in dealing with economic issues.

Canadian History: A Reader's Guide. 2 vols. Edited by M. Brook Taylor and Doug Owram. Toronto: University of Toronto Press, 1994. Contains an annotated bibliography of important studies on the domestic and foreign policies of Bennett.

Creighton, Donald. *Canada's First Century: 1867-1967.* Toronto: Macmillan of Canada, 1970. Describes the terrible effects of the Depression in Canada, especially in Alberta and Saskatchewan, which experienced both high unemployment in private industry and drought conditions in farming regions.

Glassford, Larry. *Reaction and Reform: The Politics of the Conservative Party Under R. B. Bennett: 1927-1938.* Toronto: University of Toronto Press, 1992. Contains a thoughtful analysis of the reasons for Bennett's popularity within the Conservative Party during his six years as leader of the opposition and five years as prime minister.

Hutchison, Bruce. *Macdonald to Pearson: The Prime Ministers of Canada.* Don Mills, Ont.: Longmans Canada, 1967. The chapter on Bennett describes his successful career in business and discusses his inability to understand that Canadians wanted him to spend more money on social programs during the Great Depression.

SEE ALSO: 1867, British North America Act; 1911, Borden Government in Canada; 1920, Meighen Era in Canada; 1921, King Era in Canada; 1929, Great Depression; 1931, Statute of Westminster; 1932, Ottawa Agreements.

1930 ■ JAPANESE AMERICAN CITIZENS LEAGUE IS FOUNDED: *the largest and most influential Japanese American political organization promotes assimilation as the most effective response to racism*

DATE: August 29, 1930
LOCALE: Seattle, Washington
CATEGORIES: Asian American history; Organizations and institutions
KEY FIGURES:

Clarence Takeya Arai (1901-1964), lawyer who convened the first national meeting of the JACL

Wayne Mortimer Collins (1900-1974), attorney who defended Japanese American civil rights during and after World War II

Mike Masaru Masaoka (1915-1991), JACL official and lobbyist who promoted Nisei patriotism

Dillon S. Myer (1891-1982), director of War Relocation Authority during World War II

Franklin Delano Roosevelt (1882-1945), thirty-second president of the United States, 1933-1945

James "Jimmie" Yoshinori Sakamoto (1903-1955), newspaper publisher and early supporter of the JACL

Tokutaro "Tokie" Nishimura Slocum (born 1895), JACL lobbyist for the Nye-Lea Bill granting citizenship to Issei veterans of World War I

Suma Sugi (born 1906), first Nisei lobbyist and JACL lobbyist for amendment of the Cable Act

Thomas Y. Yatabe (born 1897), co-founder of the San Francisco American Loyalty League and the JACL

SUMMARY OF EVENT. In the words of its own historian, Bill Hosokawa, the Japanese American Citizens League (JACL) originated as "a civic and patriotic organization concerned with the well-being and political and economic progress of American citizens of Japanese ancestry." Responding to widespread anti-Asian sentiment in the United States, the JACL promoted assimilation and Americanization as the most effective way for the Nisei (second-generation Japanese Americans) to gain the approval of the general public. Initially a loose federation of loyalty leagues, the JACL's influence was minimal until 1941, when it cooperated with the federal government in carrying out President Franklin Delano Roosevelt's Executive Order 9066, which ordered the internment of Japanese Americans in restricted camps during World War II. Because of that cooperation, it lost the respect of many Japanese Americans. After World War II, the JACL achieved a positive public profile as it lobbied for civil rights legislation. However, it has remained controversial for its insistence on accommodation rather than confrontation in the political arena. Now the largest and most influential Japanese American political organization, the JACL must deal with conflicts within its own ranks regarding its basic goals.

The roots of the JACL can be traced to 1918 in San Francisco, when Thomas Y. Yatabe and a small group of his college-educated friends met to discuss the future of the Nisei in America. Calling themselves the American Loyalty League, they were well aware of the racism blocking the economic progress of Asian immigrants and their families at that time. The Issei (first-generation Japanese Americans) hoped their children, the Nisei, would have opportunities for economic and social advancement. However, as Ronald Takaki has documented in *Strangers from a Different Shore* (1989), widespread discrimination made it very difficult for them to find employment other than manual or menial labor. Yatabe and his friends were among the fortunate few who had achieved professional success; a recent dental school graduate, Yatabe drew into his circle another dentist, a doctor, and an attorney. They realized that Nisei in general still faced an uncertain future. In their view, the best way to gain acceptance by the general public was to define themselves first and foremost as loyal Americans dedicated to advancement of democratic ideals. Individual enterprise, fair play, and respect for law and order were cornerstones of this philosophy.

In 1922, James "Jimmie" Yoshinori Sakamoto founded a similar group, the Seattle Progressive Citizens League. In 1923, Yatabe established the Fresno American Loyalty League, the first statewide league. In 1928, he and Saburo Kido founded the San Francisco New American Citizens

League. All of these groups shared a commitment to being "100% American" in their outlook. Realizing how much more effective they would be if they joined together, Clarence Takeya Arai, who was elected president of the Seattle group in 1928, proposed a national meeting of delegates. He envisioned the formation of a national council of Japanese American citizens leagues which would present a positive public profile. This four-day meeting, called to order by Arai on August 29, 1930, in Seattle, Washington, became the founding convention of the JACL: the first national political organization of Japanese Americans.

The Nisei leadership at the convention represented a special group of college-educated professionals with economically secure, middle-class, urban backgrounds. Mostly in their late twenties and early thirties, they were strikingly unlike the majority of Nisei in America at that time, who were younger (with an average age of seventeen) and from rural, working-class backgrounds. Moreover, they were distinctly different from the Issei, who still held political, economic, and social power in local Japanese American communities through the Japanese Associations, which provided legal aid and other services for immigrants. The Issei usually chose (or were forced by racism) to remain within their own communities; their English skills often were minimal, and their direct interactions with outsiders were limited. Through Japanese Associations and other local organizations—such as prefactural associations, merchants' and farmers' mutual aid societies, vernacular newspapers, and Japanese language schools—the Issei maintained their communities as best they could within the larger American society. The Nisei leadership of the JACL, however, insisted on a completely different approach to finding a secure place for Japanese Americans in the United States. Above all, they stressed assimilation, not ethnicity, underscoring their American aspirations rather than their Japanese heritage.

Therefore, one of the first items of business at the founding convention was to remove the hyphen in "Japanese-Americans," on the basis that any Japanese aspect of Nisei identity had to be subordinated to their American destiny. More than one hundred delegates from five states (Washington, Oregon, California, Illinois, and New York) and the territory of Hawaii approved resolutions asking that Congress address two timely issues: the constitutionality of the 1922 Cable Act and the eligibility of Issei World War I veterans for citizenship. Suma Sugi became their lobbyist for amendment of the Cable Act, which stripped citizenship from any American woman who married an "alien ineligible to citizenship"; through Sugi's efforts and those of the League of Women Voters, Congress changed the law in 1931, so that citizenship could not be revoked by marriage. Tokutaro "Tokie" Nishimura Slocum became their lobbyist for veteran citizenship, which finally was secured by the Nye-Lea Bill in 1935.

During its first decade of existence, however, the JACL had little direct effect on the Japanese American community. This situation changed dramatically in 1941, when President Roosevelt issued Executive Order 9066, authorizing the in-

ternment of Japanese Americans during World War II. The federal government imprisoned virtually all Issei leaders of businesses, schools, and churches on the West Coast. The JACL then took over, directing Japanese Americans not to resist relocation. In fact, the JACL cooperated with the War Relocation Authority (WRA) in identifying community members who might be subversives. Dillon S. Myer, WRA director, worked closely with Mike Masaoka, JACL official, in administering the camps—a relationship intensely resented by the majority of Japanese Americans. Attorney Wayne Mortimer Collins, who stood against popular opinion to defend Japanese American civil rights during and after World War II, went so far as to blame the JACL for much of the suffering that internees endured.

The JACL succeeded in building a positive public profile after the war by lobbying for civil rights legislation such as amendment of the McCarran-Walter Act in 1952, thereby guaranteeing the right of all Issei to naturalized citizenship. To this day, however, it has remained a controversial organization, especially because of its conservative political stance. The JACL now must deal with interfactional conflicts between its "old guard" and younger members who question its basic goals.
—*Mary Louise Buley-Meissner*

ADDITIONAL READING:

Chan, Sucheng. *Asian Americans: An Interpretive History*. Boston: Twayne, 1991. Carefully researched investigation of Asian American socioeconomic, political, educational, and cultural realities. Provides contexts for assessing JACL achievements. Extensive bibliography, index, black-and-white illustrations.

Drinnon, Richard. *Keeper of Concentration Camps: Dillon S. Myer and American Racism*. Berkeley: University of California Press, 1987. Painstakingly researched revisionist history of Myer's administration of War Location Authority, including his collaboration with Mike Masaoka and JACL. Extensive bibliography, index, black-and-white illustrations.

Hosokawa, Bill. *JACL in Quest of Justice*. New York: William Morrow, 1982. History book commissioned by JACL to record its accomplishments. Mainly covers the 1930's and 1940's, emphasizing the organization's patriotic nature. Index, black-and-white illustrations.

Niiya, Brian, ed. *Japanese American History: An A-to-Z Reference from 1868 to the Present*. New York: Japanese American National Museum and Facts On File, 1993. Invaluable resource including narrative historical overview, chronology of Japanese American history, and dictionary entries for that history. Scholarly research accessible to general audience. Index.

Spickard, Paul R. "The Nisei Assume Power: The Japanese Citizens League, 1941-1942." *Pacific Historical Review* 52, no. 2 (May, 1983): 147-174. Argues that early JACL leadership represented Nisei who seized the historical moment to wrest political, economic, and social power from Issei.

Takahasi, Jere. "Japanese American Responses to Race Relations: The Formation of Nisei Perspectives." *Amerasia Jour-*

nal 9, no. 1 (Spring/Summer, 1982): 29-57. Analyzes three major self- and group-concepts developed between 1920 and World War II: cultural bridge, American ideal, and progressive. Discusses JACL history in that context.

Takaki, Ronald. *Strangers from a Different Shore: A History of Asian Americans.* New York: Penguin, 1989. Groundbreaking investigation of Asian American contributions to the United States' socioeconomic and political development. Provides contexts for assessing JACL achievements. Index, black-and-white illustrations.

SEE ALSO: 1892, Yellow Peril Campaign; 1907, Gentlemen's Agreement; 1913, Alien Land Laws; 1922, Cable Act; 1922, *Ozawa v. United States*; 1942, Censorship and Japanese Internment; 1952, McCarran-Walter Act.

1931 ■ SCOTTSBORO TRIALS: *trials of nine young African Americans for rape mirrors both entrenched Southern bigotry and anti-liberal sentiments*

DATE: March 25, 1931-July, 1937
LOCALE: Scottsboro and Decatur, Alabama
CATEGORIES: African American history; Court cases
KEY FIGURES:
Ruby Bates and
Victoria Price, professed rape victims
Olen Montgomery,
Clarence Norris,
Haywood Patterson,
Ozie Powell,
Willie Roberson,
Charlie Weems,
Eugene Williams,
Andy Wright, and
Roy Wright, African Americans accused of rape
James E. Horton, original judge in the trials
Thomas E. Knight (1898-1937), attorney general of Alabama
Samuel Leibowitz (1893-1978), defense counsel
SUMMARY OF EVENT. On March 25, 1931, nine African American boys were pulled off a freight train in Scottsboro, Alabama, after an alleged fight with a group of white youths. As the African Americans were being rounded up by sheriff's deputies, two women riders told onlookers that they had been raped by the entire group. Within a month, the boys were tried in Scottsboro, and eight of them were convicted and sentenced to death; the case of the youngest boy, only thirteen years of age, was declared a mistrial. Because of the speed of the convictions, the questionable nature of much of the testimony, and the hostile atmosphere in which the trial had been held, the case soon attracted widespread attention. Both the International Labor Defense (ILD), an arm of the Communist Party, and the National Association for the Advancement of Colored People expressed concern about the possibility of injustice and

launched an appeal for a new trial. The boys and their parents chose the ILD to manage their defense.

In *Powell v. Alabama* (1932), the Supreme Court overruled the convictions and sent the cases back to a lower court. There followed another series of trials in Decatur, Alabama, beginning in March, 1933, and lasting until December. This time, only three of the boys were tried, all of whom received convictions and death sentences, but the Supreme Court sustained an appeal that irregularities in the selection of jurors invalidated the verdicts. The specific irregularity was that the voting rolls showed no African Americans registered to vote in that county, in spite of a very large population of qualified African Americans. This issue was to appear on several occasions during these trials.

In January, 1936, a third group of trials, held in Decatur, resulted in the conviction of Haywood Patterson, who was sentenced to seventy-five years' imprisonment. After more than a year of delay and behind-the-scenes negotiations between Alabama State officials and a group of the defendants' supporters, the remaining eight were tried in the summer of 1937. One received the death penalty, three were sentenced to long prison terms, and the four others were released without charges. Although the one death sentence was later commuted to life imprisonment, the five convicted Scottsboro boys were unable to obtain a reversal. One of them was paroled in 1943, two more in 1946, and a fourth in 1950. The final prisoner escaped from a work gang in 1948 and managed to reach Michigan, from which the governor refused to extradite him. The former defendant quickly found himself in trouble, committing a murder and being sentenced to Michigan's worst prison. He was unable to escape the environment in which he had spent most of his days, the prison.

It was not simply the length of the Scottsboro trials that accounts for the vast amount of publicity they attracted throughout the 1930's. Most observers outside Alabama and an increasingly large number of people within the state came to believe that the defendants were innocent and were, therefore, the victims of Southern racial injustice. One of the two women accusers, Ruby Bates, had retracted her testimony by 1934 and admitted that she had lied in her original accusations. The other, a prostitute named Victoria Price, presented testimony so full of contradictions that one of the judges in the 1933 trials, Alabamian James E. Horton, overruled the jury's guilty verdict and declared a mistrial. At least one of the defendants was ruled physically incapable of rape, and a physician testified that a medical examination of Bates and Price, performed shortly after the presumed attack, did not support their claims. Although both women were found to have had recent sexual intercourse, there were no contusions or other injuries that would have matched their stories about brutality at the hands of the nine men. None of this had any appreciable effect on the juries, the prosecutors, or Judge William W. Callahan, who presided after Horton was removed from the case. Even the milder sentences meted out in 1937 resulted as much from a desire to end the unfavorable publicity surrounding the trials as from any reevaluation of the evidence. That is

One of the Scottsboro defendants at court during one of the trials. (National Archives)

why four of the defendants were eventually released on the same testimony that convicted the other five.

Besides serving as a symbol of Southern bigotry, the Scottsboro trials attracted attention because of the efforts of the Communist Party to identify the cause of the defendants with their own. Working through the ILD, the Communist Party was one of the first groups to protest the verdicts in the 1931 trials, and it was the only group to offer direct aid at that time. For several years, it engaged in a running battle with the National Association for the Advancement of Colored People (NAACP) and an "American Scottsboro Committee" over the right to manage the boys' defense. The effect of these struggles was to unite many Alabamians against all "reds and foreigners" and make it more difficult to revise the verdicts. The chief defense counsel after 1931 was Samuel Leibowitz, a Jewish attorney from New York who became the target of scurrilous attacks from the prosecutors. Even he, along with Judge Callahan and part of the Alabama press, came to regard the communist support as a liability and sought to dissociate the ILD from the case. In 1935, the NAACP, the American Civil Liberties Union, and the ILD joined to form the Scottsboro Defense Committee (SDC), designed to coordinate support for the de-

fendants and to seek cooperation from moderate Alabamians. Although the ILD played a much smaller role in the case from that point on, there remained enough hostility toward outside interference in Alabama to frustrate the SDC's efforts.

The Scottsboro case mirrored many of the important social currents of the 1930's. While illustrating the extent to which white Southerners would go to defend a system of white supremacy, it also marked a change from the not too distant era when the defendants might well have been summarily lynched. The hysterical attitude with which many Alabamians reacted to outside interest in the case underlined a regional insecurity that had been intensified by the unsettled conditions of the Depression. It was common for both men and women to hop onto freight trains, which the nine men had done, as had the two alleged victims. The Scottsboro boys had gotten into a fight with several white men. In Scottsboro and Decatur, race was on trial, not nine boys and men, much to the lasting chagrin of the state of Alabama. The entire episode ended when, in 1976, the Alabama Board of Pardons and Paroles granted Clarence Norris a full pardon. It had taken forty-five years for justice to be served.

—Courtney B. Ross, updated by John Jacob

ADDITIONAL READING:

Carter, Dan T. *Scottsboro: A Tragedy of the American South.* Rev. ed. Baton Rouge: Louisiana State University Press, 1979. Analyzes the trials and treatment of the nine African Americans and discusses the impact of the events on the South.

Chalmers, Allan Knight. *They Shall Be Free.* Garden City, N.Y.: Doubleday, 1951. An account of the Scottsboro trials from the perspective of one of the defense attorneys who also argued before the U.S. Supreme Court.

Levy, Leonard, et al., eds. *Encyclopedia of the American Constitution.* 4 vols. New York: Macmillan, 1986. Volume 3 provides ancillary but detailed analysis of decisions made by the Supreme Court in these cases.

Norris, Clarence, and Sybil D. Washington. *The Last of the Scottsboro Boys.* New York: Putnam, 1979. The last and most literate of the defendants presents his case. Valuable for its perspective and the view of prison conditions over many years.

Patterson, Haywood, and Earl Conrad. *Scottsboro Boy.* Garden City, N.Y.: Doubleday, 1950. The first book to shed personal light on the plight of the nine, it remains a powerful testament to a decade of injustice.

SEE ALSO: 1866, Rise of the Ku Klux Klan; 1909, National Association for the Advancement of Colored People Is Founded.

1931 ■ EMPIRE STATE BUILDING OPENS:
an engineering marvel becomes the world's tallest building for the next four decades

DATE: May 1, 1931
LOCALE: New York City
CATEGORIES: Economics; Science and technology
KEY FIGURES:

William F. Lamb (1883-1952), New York architect who designed the Empire State Building

Elisha Graves Otis (1811-1861), American inventor of the elevator

John Jacob Raskob (1879-1950), chairman of General Motors and leading participant in construction of the building

Alfred Emanuel Smith (1873-1944), former governor of New York and president of the corporation that built and operated the building

Louis Sullivan (1856-1924), Chicago architect who articulated the aesthetic principles of the skyscraper

SUMMARY OF EVENT. Skyscrapers first appeared in the late nineteenth century when technology made buildings taller than five stories feasible. First the elevator (invented in America by Elisha Graves Otis), then improved water pumping systems, and finally steel skeletons that eliminated the need

for impractically thick load-bearing walls made construction of increasingly taller buildings possible.

Early examples of skyscrapers include Chicago's Home Insurance (1885) and Wainwright (1890) buildings and New York's Flatiron (1902) and Woolworth (1913) buildings. When New York's Chrysler Building, at 984 feet tall, opened in 1930, it stole from Paris' Eiffel Tower the record as the tallest human-made structure. The Chrysler held that distinction only briefly, however; a new skyscraper, already under construction on Fifth Avenue at 34th Street, opened on May 1, 1931, and held the record until the 1970 opening of Chicago's Sears Tower.

In August, 1929, former governor of New York and twice Democratic candidate for the presidency Al Smith announced plans for an eighty-story office tower to be located on the site of Fifth Avenue's world-famous Waldorf Astoria Hotel. This part of "the Avenue" had been home to many of the nation's richest and most powerful families, including John Jacob Astor. In the 1920's, these millionaires began moving away from midtown Manhattan and their mansions were demolished to make room for more profitable office buildings.

The contract for design of Smith's building, known as the Empire State, went to the architectural firm of Shreve, Lamb, and Harmon. William F. Lamb, the principal architect, had been educated at Williams and Columbia colleges and France's École des Beaux-Arts. Other than its shimmering vertical façade, created by a chrome-nickel-steel alloy, and window pairs that were separated by limestone columns, the building had no architectural significance. The land upon which the building stands dictated its design. The owners, led by Smith and John Jacob Raskob, chairman of General Motors, determined that the new building had to contain thirty-six million cubic feet of space, that it had to be completed by May, 1931, that it must cost no more than sixty million dollars, and that the space from window to corridor must be no more than twenty-eight feet. Raskob also wanted a building taller than that of his competitor Walter P. Chrysler. To meet these objectives, Lamb planned an office tower with eighty floors plus five penthouse floors.

Building codes demanded setbacks on the tower to allow light and air to reach the street. Lamb's sixteenth plan resulted in a structure with a five-story base and an eighty-story tower soaring one thousand feet to an observation deck. When examining a scale model, Raskob determined that the building needed a two-hundred-foot mooring mast for transatlantic dirigibles, which would make the building taller than that of Chrysler. Smith sold the plan to government officials in Washington, D.C., giving the building its initial height of 1,250 feet. While two airships did land briefly, the mast, actually a hollow tower, had a far more significant function, containing a second, enclosed observation deck at the 102d story.

Time constraints necessitated standardized techniques of construction. Marble for the lobby had no intricate design, and the limestone facing was delivered in easily handled units. General contractors Starrett Brothers and Eken established and

The Empire State Building c. 1930, close to completion. Erection of a mooring mast for transatlantic dirigibles would make the building taller than the Chrysler Building. It remained the tallest until the opening of Chicago's Sears Tower in 1970. (Library of Congress)

maintained an incredibly tight schedule. The ten million bricks, sixty-four hundred windows, and four hundred tons of stainless steel, along with other building materials, all arrived at the site according to plan and on time.

The excavation phase of the project began while the old Waldorf Astoria was being demolished. Because Manhattan's bedrock is so close to the surface, excavation needed to go down only thirty-three feet, or two floors below street level. Despite the tight schedule, when digging was finished on March 6, 1930, Smith's Irish heritage persuaded him to delay beginning erection of the steel skeleton until March 17, St. Patrick's Day. Within six months a workforce including Mohawk Native Americans, famous as high steel workers, topped out the skeleton on September 9; eight days later, Smith laid the cornerstone containing a time capsule containing, among other items, samples of money totaling one hundred dollars. Besides the speed of its construction, the Empire State achieved a record in safety during construction: As many as five thousand workers labored to build the structure; only five lost their lives on the job.

Smith planned the opening ceremonies for May 1, 1931. A crowd of thousands gathered to see the dignitaries assembled for the event, including Governor Franklin Roosevelt, Mayor James Walker, and the architects. Following the ribbon cutting, President Herbert Hoover pressed a button in Washington, D.C., which turned on the building's lights. The first visitors, Smith's grandchildren, led the guests to a luncheon on the observation deck. At the ceremonies, architect Shreve told the crowd that even though the building weighed six hundred million tons, 220 vertical columns distributed the weight so evenly that each square inch bore no more weight than that supported by a French heel. In speaking of the engineering success, he pointed out that the building was within five-eighths of an inch vertical. Such feats garnered for the architects a gold medal from the New York Architectural League and the Medal of Honor from the New York chapter of the American Institute of Architects.

Planned at the height of the 1920's boom years, the Empire State had opened in the depths of the Great Depression. Only 25 percent of the building's 2,158,000 feet of space was initially rented; funds from the one-dollar fee per visit to the observation deck paid the building's taxes for the first several years.

From its opening, the building attracted attention—not always of the most desirable kind. It had not been open long before someone attempted suicide by jumping from the observation deck. Because he failed to clear the eighty-fourth floor ledge, he fell only a short distance, breaking several bones but remaining alive. In 1933, a despondent young woman was the first successful suicide, followed by a dozen more. Such incidents provoked erection of a wire barricade, but jumpers, parachutists, publicity seekers, and record setters continued their activities: In 1932, the Polish Olympic ski team climbed the stairs to the 102d floor. In 1978, the New York Road Runner Club began sponsoring an annual race to the top. The building became an icon of New York City and motion pictures, first appearing in the 1933 film *King Kong* and later as the famous rendezvous spot in 1957's *An Affair to Remember* and its 1994 remake *Sleepless in Seattle*.

On the morning of July 28, 1945, Air Force colonel William F. Smith piloted a B-25 bomber which crashed into the building between the seventy-eighth and seventy-ninth floors. Witnesses reported that the plane was having rudder problems when it struck the building. Fourteen people died in the incident; survivors reported that the building shook, then settled. The building's design allows it to bend as much as 1.5 inches to withstand such shocks, including high winds: Winds of 186 miles per hour have been recorded at the top.

In 1950, 222 feet were added at the 102d floor when a television tower was erected atop the building. In 1984, a new antenna reduced the building's height by 18 feet, rendering its total height 1,454 feet. The size of such buildings as the Empire State—one of the oldest of the giant skyscrapers—has been debated continually by architects, environmentalists, and sociologists who wonder about the emotional as well as aesthetic impact that such structures have on the human psyche. Nevertheless, such skyscrapers heralded a new urban age brought on by increased population density and the need to bring human and physical resources together.

—Duncan R. Jamieson

ADDITIONAL READING:

Byrne, Robert. *Skyscraper*. New York: Atheneum, 1984. A survey of the history of tall structures.

James, Theodore, Jr. *The Empire State Building*. New York: Harper & Row, 1975. A good overview of the building's design, construction, official opening, and history.

Macaulay, David. *Unbuilding*. Boston: Houghton Mifflin, 1980. A master draftsman dismantles the Empire State from the top down in a series of detailed and technically accurate drawings and text that explain the building's structure and engineering.

Tauranac, John. *The Empire State Building: The Making of a Landmark*. New York: Scribner, 1995. A thorough history of the building and its place in the history of both architecture and New York City.

SEE ALSO: 1883, Brooklyn Bridge Opens; 1893, World's Columbian Exposition; 1906, San Francisco Earthquake; 1959, St. Lawrence Seaway Opens.

1931 ■ STATUTE OF WESTMINSTER: *the establishment of the British Commonwealth of Nations creates the Dominion of Canada*

DATE: December 11, 1931
LOCALE: Canada
CATEGORIES: Canadian history; Government and politics; Laws and acts

KEY FIGURES:

Arthur James Balfour (1848-1930), British prime minister

Julian Hedworth George Byng (1862-1935), governor general of Canada

William Lyon Mackenzie King (1874-1950), Canadian prime minister

SUMMARY OF EVENT. The Statute of Westminster, approved by the British parliament on December 11, 1931, specifically defined the powers of Canada's parliament and those of the other dominions of the British Empire. The statute was a direct result of decades of debate over the issue of self-government for the British dominions. The Statute of Westminster gave legal substance to earlier tentative agreements among Great Britain, Canada, Australia, and New Zealand that the dominions should be considered self-governing communities with autonomous parliaments not subject to control by Great Britain. In effect, the Statute of Westminster allowed the dominion parliaments the freedom to nullify British laws and prevented the British parliament from passing laws affecting the dominions without their legislative consent.

During World War I, the term "commonwealth" was introduced to describe the long-standing imperial relationship between Great Britain and her principal colonies. The newly designated Commonwealth nations, including Canada, were allowed to participate separately in the negotiation and signing of the 1919 Treaty of Versailles, which formally ended World War I. The British government also allowed the Commonwealth nations to join the League of Nations as independent entities. Although the British government assumed that the semi-independent Commonwealth nations would continue solid political support for Great Britain in world affairs, the dominion governments did not share in the overall goals of British foreign policy. The postwar move for Commonwealth independence was initiated primarily by Canada, led by Canadian nationalist William Lyon Mackenzie King, the Liberal Party leader who became prime minister in 1921. King's party, supported by anti-British French Canadians, was a steady proponent of Canadian autonomy and demanded from the prime minister's government a strict policy of "no commitments" in the League of Nations, most particularly regarding possible British imperial schemes in the former Ottoman Empire in the Middle East. In September, 1922, the Turkish government demanded the return of most of the territories stripped from its empire by the Allies following World War I and threatened British forces occupying the Dardanelles. Great Britain called upon the dominions for military support, but Canada refused to send troops. In 1923, Canada led the other dominions in withdrawing support from Great Britain for the Treaty of Lausanne, a proposed agreement between Great Britain and Turkey over British administration of former Turkish provinces in Iraq, Palestine, and the eastern Mediterranean.

Additional divisive incidents between Canada and Great Britain regarding Canadian political independence from the Commonwealth occurred from 1923 to 1926. In 1923, Canada signed the Halibut Fisheries Treaty with the United States without consulting the British Foreign Office and without the formal consent of the British parliament. Canada thus unilaterally negated Great Britain's centuries-old constitutional right to control the foreign relations of a dominion government. Early in 1926, the Canadian Conservative Party uncovered an alleged scandal in Prime Minister King's cabinet. The Conservatives accused the government of accepting bribes from alcohol smugglers who were attempting to violate United States prohibition laws. An independent investigative committee studied the evidence and agreed with the charges. As a result, King, who feared Canadian parliamentary inquiries, requested that the Canadian governor general, Lord Byng, dissolve the Canadian parliament and call an election, as required by the Commonwealth relationship with Great Britain. When Lord Byng refused, King resigned and Byng asked the Conservative Party to form a new government. Following King's successful challenge on constitutional grounds, the Conservative government was defeated by a vote of Parliament and the subsequent election returned King as prime minister. King's Liberal Party later used the "King-Byng affair" as evidence that the governor general's actions had exceeded his powers and threatened Canadian independence.

The result of the King-Byng affair, the Halibut Treaty, the disagreement between Canada and Great Britain concerning the Lausanne Treaty, and additional demands for autonomy by other Commonwealth nations was the convocation of two Imperial Conferences in London, in 1923 and 1926. The 1923 conference adopted new rules for the concluding of treaties affecting the Commonwealth, and a precedent was set for dominion autonomy by creating a system of separate control and responsibility in Commonwealth foreign affairs. Although each dominion was to be responsible for its own international relations without interference from London, a spirit of imperial cooperation was retained; that is, dominion policies were not supposed to harm the interests of any other Commonwealth nation. The new foreign policy guidelines, especially as they affected Canadian relations with the United States, were tantamount to a complete revision of the former practice of subjecting dominion interests to those of Great Britain.

A further erosion of British control of Commonwealth affairs occurred during the Imperial Conference in 1926, attended by political and economic representatives from Canada, Australia, and New Zealand. The conference was forced to address the pressing question of dominion nationalism, in particular the growing movement in Canada for complete autonomy. Although the Australian and New Zealand governments were relatively content with the imperial status quo, Canada, the senior member of the Commonwealth, introduced the question of Commonwealth members' parliamentary status. The specific issue was Canada's constitutional crisis over the King-Byng controversy and the obvious question of conflicting interests: whether a Commonwealth royal governor general, whose interests lay with the British Empire, should continue constitutional supremacy over an elected prime minister's responsibility to government and Parliament. The conference, led by Canada, Australia, and New Zealand, accepted the principle of equality of status with Britain, and a committee was set up to examine the vestiges of British sovereignty and dominion subordination. Formal steps also were taken to modify the authority of the dominion governor general from that of an imperial officer superior to dominion governments to the position of honorary royal representative, subject to appointment based on advice from the respective dominion governments.

With the overwhelming support of the Canadian electorate, King used the forum of the Imperial Conferences to press the issue of complete parliamentary independence for Ottawa. Under the guidance of the British prime minister, Lord Balfour, London was prepared to make further concessions to the dominions over political autonomy. In 1926, the term "commonwealth" was adopted officially to designate the "autonomous communities within the British Empire, equal in status, in no way subordinate one to another in any aspect of their domestic or external affairs, though united by a common allegiance to the crown. . . ." The British parliament also addressed the question of Commonwealth political autonomy by initiating the Statute of Westminster, which was the culmination of decisions reached previously at the Imperial Conferences.

The Statute of Westminster, officially adopted on December 11, 1931, contained two elements central to the issue of self-government in Canada and the other Commonwealth nations. First, the British parliament acceded to the Canadian proposal that it would be inimical to the British constitution for the British government to take any action concerning the affairs of a dominion against the advice tendered by the elected government of that dominion. Second, Great Britain also agreed with the Canadian prime minister's insistence that legislation enacted by the British parliament that applied to a dominion would be applicable only with the parliamentary consent of the dominion concerned. While the Statute of Westminster eliminated most of the limitations on Canadian independence, the Commonwealth retained several basic elements of the old British Empire. While the statute recognized the essentially autonomous character of the Commonwealth nations, London retained the overall responsibility of Commonwealth defense and foreign policy until after World War II.

—*William G. Ratliff*

ADDITIONAL READING:

Barnett, Correlli. *The Collapse of British Power*. New York: William Morrow, 1972. Focuses on the root causes of the decay that reduced Great Britain's control over the Commonwealth nations. Debunks the myth that the British Empire was a source of economic and political strength.

Beloff, Max. *Imperial Sunset*. 2 vols. New York: Alfred A. Knopf, 1970. A comprehensive study of the decline and fall of the British imperial system. Emphasizes economic problems, the rise of colonial nationalism, and Great Britain's preoccupation with European affairs as the prime causes for the collapse.

Holland, Roy F. *Britain and the Commonwealth Alliance, 1918-1939*. London: Macmillan, 1981. Accords Canada a lesser role than other Commonwealth nations in the forging of the Statute of Westminster. A concise, document-based study.

McIntyre, W. David. *The Commonwealth of Nations: Origins and Impact, 1869-1971*. Minneapolis: University of Minnesota Press, 1977. Places little emphasis on economic imperialism and contends that colonial nationalism was the driving force behind the Commonwealth movement. Excellent maps and a comprehensive critical bibliography.

Miller, J. D. B. *Britain and the Old Dominions*. Baltimore: The Johns Hopkins University Press, 1967. A well-documented text that takes the anticolonial, anti-British view in the debate over the structure and functioning of Commonwealth relations in the interwar period.

SEE ALSO: 1867, British North America Act; 1982, Canada's Constitution Act.

1932 ■ HOOVER-STIMSON DOCTRINE:
moral disapproval, lacking military or economic sanctions, fails to deter aggression

DATE: January 7, 1932
LOCALE: United States, China, Japan
CATEGORY: Diplomacy and international relations
KEY FIGURES:
Herbert Clark Hoover (1874-1964), thirty-first president of the United States, 1929-1933
Henry Lewis Stimson (1869-1950), secretary of state

SUMMARY OF EVENT. Some Japanese leaders, especially junior officers of the Kwantung Army stationed in Manchuria, favored expansion. They viewed China's growing nationalism and its progress toward unification under the Nationalist (Kuomintang) government with fear. Their solution was to seize Chinese territory before China became sufficiently strong to defend itself. This policy was especially favored by officers of the Kwantung Army, a unit of the Japanese army created in 1905 to safeguard Japanese imperialist interests in its leased territories and railroads in China's northeastern provinces, known in the West as Manchuria. Officers of the Kwantung Army were prominent in the Black Dragon Society, an ultranationalist officers' organization dedicated to expansion on the Asian mainland. Capitalizing on the devastating floods along the Yangtze River Valley, the communist revolt, and other domestic problems in 1931, Kwantung Army officers, defying an order from the Japanese cabinet to desist, attacked a dozen cities in Manchuria simultaneously on the night of September 18, 1931. Called the September 18, or Manchurian, incident, this was the first shot that culminated in World War II in Asia.

Militarily unready, the Chinese government felt that resistance would have given Japan an excuse to widen its aggression and therefore would have been suicidal. Instead, it appealed to the League of Nations, and to the United States under the 1928 Kellogg-Briand Pact. This pact, cosponsored by then-U.S. secretary of state Frank Kellogg and signed by the United States, China, Japan, and sixty-one other nations, renounced aggressive war as an instrument of national policy. Repeated League of Nations resolutions ordering Japan to halt its advances, agreed to by the Japanese cabinet, were ignored by the Kwantung Army, which completed conquering Manchuria early in 1932.

In response, the United States secretary of state Henry Stimson announced on January 7, 1932, a nonrecognition doctrine, which stated that the United States would not recognize territorial changes created by means contrary to the Kellogg-Briand Pact:

[T]he American Government . . . cannot admit the legality of any situation de facto nor does it intend to recognize any treaty or agreement entered into between [the Japanese and the Chinese governments] . . . which may impair the treaty rights of the United States [or] which may be brought about by means contrary to the covenants and obligations of the Pact of Paris of August 27, 1928 [the Kellogg-Briand Pact].

This Hoover-Stimson Doctrine, better known simply as the Stimson Doctrine, became the cornerstone of U.S. policy in Asia in response to Japanese aggression. In 1932 the League of Nations created a special commission headed by British diplomat Lord Lytton to study the Manchurian incident. The ensuing Lytton Report (1933) charged Japan with aggression, declared the Japanese puppet state of Manchukuo a sham, and demanded that Japan restore Manchuria to China. The report was unanimously endorsed by the League Assembly, and Japan immediately resigned from the league.

Beset by the effects of the Great Depression and by isolationism, the United States did not attempt to force Japan to give up its conquests and lent no more than moral support to China. Burdened by neither military threat nor economic sanctions, Japan ignored international condemnation and continued its aggressions against China and other nations. No nation, except Japan's later Axis allies Germany and Italy, recognized Japan's conquests, and the situation eventually resulted in World War II.   —*Jiu-Hwa Lo Upshur*

ADDITIONAL READING:

Christopher, James W. *Conflict in the Far East: American Diplomacy in China from 1928-33*. Leiden, The Netherlands: E. J. Brill, 1950. A comprehensive review of the period.

Morison, Elting E. *Turmoil and Tradition: A Study of the Life and Times of Henry L. Stimson*. Boston: Houghton Mifflin, 1960. A sympathetic biography.

Rappaport, Armin. *Henry L. Stimson and Japan, 1931-1933*. Chicago: University of Chicago Press, 1963. Details Stimson's limited options in dealing with Japan.

Smith, Sara R. *The Manchurian Crisis, 1931-1932: A Tragedy in International Relations*. New York: Columbia University Press, 1948. This clear, short book looks at all aspects of the crisis.

Stimson, Henry L. *The Far Eastern Crisis: Recollections and Observations*. New York: Council on Foreign Relations, 1936. Firsthand account by the U.S. secretary of state.

Yoshihashi, Takehiko. *Conspiracy at Mukden: The Rise of the Japanese Military*. New Haven, Conn.: Yale University Press, 1963. Documents the Japanese military's flaunting of civilian control.

SEE ALSO: 1928, Kellogg-Briand Pact.

1932 ■ RECONSTRUCTION FINANCE CORPORATION IS CREATED: *the Hoover Administration makes an effort to intervene economically following the onset of the Great Depression*

DATE: January 22, 1932
LOCALE: Washington, D.C.
CATEGORIES: Business and labor; Economics; Government and politics
KEY FIGURES:
Charles Gates Dawes (1865-1951), first president of the RFC
John Nance Garner (1868-1967), Speaker of the House of Representatives
Herbert Clark Hoover (1874-1964), thirty-first president of the United States, 1929-1933
Jesse H. Jones (1874-1956), president of the RFC, 1932-1940
Eugene Meyer (1875-1959), chairman of the Federal Reserve Board
Ogden Livingston Mills (1884-1937), secretary of the Treasury

SUMMARY OF EVENT. After the stock market crash of 1929, the economic conditions in the United States continued to deteriorate, as they were doing all over the world in what would come to be known as the Great Depression. Banks were especially vulnerable, because they had made excessive loans to stockbrokers, dealers in real estate, and the construction industry during the orgy of speculation in the 1920's. An additional factor was the withdrawal of gold by European banks that were facing similar crises. By the end of 1929, some 659 U.S. banks had closed their doors. In 1930, the number grew to 1,352; in 1931, it was 2,294. The problem was complicated by the extreme fragmentation of the U.S. banking system; many banks were very small, almost neighborhood affairs, with minimal capitalization and no resources with which to withstand the collapse in value of the collateral of their loans.

Additional capital had to be found to uphold public confidence in the nation's banks. At first, President Herbert Hoover was opposed to centralizing control of relief in the federal government and urged that voluntary programs be created to relieve the situation by providing incentive capital to industry. If more goods were produced, he reasoned, more jobs would be available and more workers would be earning wages.

When the crisis deepened and the number of bank failures increased, Hoover called upon leading financial figures in the nation to discuss voluntary action with him. Formation, in October, 1931, of the National Credit Corporation, a voluntary cooperative attempt by the strong banks to help the weaker ones, was the logical expression of Hoover's basic ideas about ending the Depression. However, the attempt provided only a brief respite, as the Depression grew worse.

Eugene Meyer, governor of the Federal Reserve Board, urged the president to emulate the earlier success of the War Finance Corporation in creating the industrial capacity needed by the war effort in World War I. On December 7, 1931, President Hoover proposed a broad-scale program to deal with the economic problems of the nation. An integral part of the program was the creation of the Reconstruction Finance Corporation (RFC), modeled on the War Finance Corporation. The bill creating the RFC, drafted by Meyer, was passed by Congress quickly and signed by Hoover on January 22, 1932. The RFC was granted $500 million capital and was authorized to borrow $2 billion more. It was empowered to lend money to banks, insurance companies, railroads, and mortgage and loan associations. Meyer, who had served as a director of the War Finance Corporation during World War I and was governor of the Federal Reserve Board in 1932, was appointed chairman of the governing board of the RFC. Former U.S. vice president Charles G. Dawes was named president.

Many liberals, especially progressives in Congress, remained deeply suspicious of the RFC, which they thought was designed chiefly to bail out troubled banks and other financial institutions but unlikely to do anything to help the ordinary citizen, especially the unemployed. This impression was reinforced by Dawes's early resignation: A Chicago bank with which he had long been closely associated suddenly found itself faced with insolvency; an appeal was made to the RFC for financial help, and Dawes wanted to avoid charges of conflict of interest. The negotiations with the Chicago bank were kept secret at first, which aroused further opposition among liberals and progressives. In the Relief and Construction Act of July 21, 1932, which Congress passed after a long partisan battle, the RFC was required to report monthly on the recipients of its financial assistance. At the same time, it was given autority to lend $1.5 billion to local public works and $300 million to supplement local relief funds.

Despite a rocky beginning, the RFC came to play an important part in the gradual resuscitation of the U.S. economy. Under the leadership of Jesse Jones, an aggressive Texan selected by Franklin D. Roosevelt's administration following his election in 1932, the RFC expanded the kinds of loans it made. In particular, it made many crop loans to distressed dealers in agricultural products, it aided municipalities, and it bought preferred shares in a number of financial institutions. It helped prepare the banking industry for the institution of federal deposit insurance, slated to begin on January 1, 1934. The RFC financed a number of large, revenue-generating public works, such as toll bridges. It provided the initial financing for the Commodity Credit Corporation, designed to lend to the agricultural community to finance its operations.

Practically all the loans made by the RFC were ultimately repaid, and the RFC actually made money through the interest charged on its loans and the dividends on preferred shares it bought in financial institutions. The RFC provided capital investment in 6,104 banks. It established two subsidiaries, the RFC Mortgage Company and the Federal National Mortgage Association, to buy up mortgages that the original grantors could no longer carry. The RFC also granted extensive loans to insurance companies, many of whose assets were tied up in real estate loans that could not be readily turned into cash, and aided many railroads. Altogether, the RFC played a major part in the rescue of the U.S. economy from the ravages of the Great Depression. —*Nancy M. Gordon, based on the original entry by George Q. Flynn*

ADDITIONAL READING:

Ellis, Edward Robb. *A Nation in Torment: The Great American Depression, 1929-1939*. 1970. Reprint. New York: Kodansha International, 1995. A journalistic account of the Depression of the 1930's, with a chapter devoted to the Reconstruction Finance Corporation. Told from a man-in-the-street viewpoint.

Jones, Jesse H. *Fifty Billion Dollars: My Thirteen Years with the RFC (1932-1945)*. New York: Da Capo Press, 1975. Jones was appointed to the board of directors at the time the RFC was created, and he later assumed the presidency. His is the most detailed account of the RFC's accomplishments.

Olson, James Stuart. *Herbert Hoover and the Reconstruction Finance Corporation, 1931-1933*. Ames: Iowa State University Press, 1977. A scholarly and impartial account of the early years of the RFC. Presents the most detailed story of the congressional battles surrounding the agency's creation.

Pusey, Merlo J. *Eugene Meyer*. New York: Alfred A. Knopf, 1974. Treats the full span of Meyer's life and delineates the role he played in suggesting and designing the RFC. Although a political conservative, Meyer had no illusions as to the problems in the U.S. economy that the RFC was created to correct.

Schlesinger, Arthur M., Jr. *The Crisis of the Old Order*. Boston: Houghton Mifflin, 1956. This, the first volume in Schlesinger's trilogy on the Age of Roosevelt, describes Hoover's inability to come to terms with the scope of measures needed to address the deepening Depression. A few pages are devoted to the creation of the RFC and its initial efforts.

SEE ALSO: 1924, Coolidge Is Elected President; 1928, Smith-Hoover Campaign; 1929, Stock Market Crash; 1932, Bonus March; 1932, Franklin D. Roosevelt Is Elected President; 1933, The Hundred Days; 1933, Tennessee Valley Authority Is Established; 1933, National Industrial Recovery Act; 1934, The Dust Bowl; 1935, Works Progress Administration Is Established; 1935, Black Monday; 1935, National Labor Relations Act; 1935, Social Security Act; 1937, Supreme Court Packing Fight; 1938, Fair Labor Standards Act; 1939, Mobilization for World War II.

1932 ■ Ottawa Agreements: *a last attempt to make the British Empire a closed economic system, with dominion economies complementing that of Great Britain, mitigates the effects of the Depression in Canada*

Date: July 21-August 21, 1932
Locale: Ottawa, Canada
Categories: Canadian history; Economics; Treaties and agreements
Key figures:

Richard B. Bennett (1870-1947), Conservative prime minister of Canada

John Alexander Macdonald (1815-1891), Conservative first prime minister of Canada

Franklin Delano Roosevelt (1882-1945), thirty-second president of the United States, 1933-1945

Summary of event. The Great Depression, ushered in by the collapse of the U.S. stock market in October of 1929 and exacerbated by the collapse of the international banking system in 1931, led to dramatic increases in unemployment and to heavy deflation of almost all currencies. All politicans in democratic countries sought ways to mitigate the effects within their borders. One such way was to raise tariff barriers dramatically in an attempt to reserve the "home market" for domestic producers. In Canada, however, the government's ability to provide protection to Canadian industry had been constrained by the determination of Britain to follow a policy of free trade and by the revenue needs of the Canadian government.

In 1879, under Conservative prime minister Sir John Macdonald, the interests favoring protection for Canada's industries were able to abandon the free-trade policy dictated hitherto from London and adopt a National Policy that advocated protective duties. In this campaign they were spurred by the refusal of the United States to grant Canada reciprocity.

The tariff created in the National Policy was actually three tariff schedules: a general tariff, a preference tariff, and a free list. The general tariff was for all countries that did not make special concessions to Canadian exports; the preference tariff was for those countries that granted reciprocity to Canadian goods; and the free list was for those products that did not compete with Canadian products. British goods were covered by the intermediate or preference tariff, even though Britain was rarely able to offer counter-concessions, as the British tariff was gradually converted to a revenue tariff only during the last half of the nineteenth century. Products of the United States, however, were covered by the general tariff because the United States did not grant reciprocity to Canadian goods. Notwithstanding the tariff disincentive, products of the United States for many years dominated Canadian imports, as a result of the low cost of transporting them across the border.

Although the advocates of the National Policy, the Conservative Party in Canada, wanted to provide enough protection to Canadian industries through tariffs on comparable foreign goods to ensure the ability of the Canadian industry to grow, they were held back by one circumstance: import duties remained a major source of government funds. Until the 1930's, 40 percent of the revenue of Canada's federal government came from customs duties. If duties were raised too high, so that imports ceased, the government would suffer a dramatic loss of revenue.

The depression changed conditions affecting the tariffs in many countries. In the United States, it intensified pressure to reserve the U.S. market for U.S. products, and in 1930 Congress passed the Hawley-Smoot Tariff, imposing the highest duties ever on a host of foreign products, including particularly Canadian agricultural products. Canada's prairie provinces, whose agricultural output exceeded Canadian needs and had long been a major Canadian export, demanded relief. The Conservative government of Richard Bennett, elected in the summer of 1930, was ready to respond by raising the Canadian tariff sharply, especially on those goods imported from the United States.

At the same time, in Britain a new "National" Government, dominated by the Conservative Party, formally abandoned the commitment to free trade that had dictated British tariff policy for three-quarters of a century. The British Parliament approved a new tariff that contained significant protection for British goods. The stage was at last set for a serious introduction of imperial preference.

Representatives of all the self-governing dominions met together with British representatives in Ottawa in the summer of 1932, for the frank purpose of creating a system of imperial preferences that would help to reserve the shrunken market for imports in the Empire for goods produced within the Empire. The Ottawa Agreements that resulted consisted of a general agreement between Great Britain and all the self-governing dominions, and special agreements negotiated between individual dominion governments. Canada, for example, besides the agreement with Great Britain, negotiated agreements with South Africa, the Irish Free State, and Rhodesia. Canada had, in 1931 and early 1932, negotiated similar agreements with Australia and New Zealand that formed part of the entire plan. Other dominions negotiated bilateral agreements as well.

Britain itself provided imperial preference for all the dominions based on the new protective tariff established in the Import Duties Act of 1932. This preference was made permanent. It further guaranteed that all items on the free list would remain there for at least five years. Some raw materials, subject to duty if of foreign origin, were made free if originating in the British Empire. Some British duties, levied as a percentage of value, were replaced by specific duties, so as not to erase imperial preference through currency fluctuation. A quota system was set up for imports of meat, designed to encourage imports from the dominions and colonies. These concessions were made firm for five years, after which they could be extended or renegotiated.

Canada agreed that it would provide tariff protection not for all "infant industries" but only for those with some reasonable prospect of success. Duties on British goods would be low enough to ensure that those goods could compete with similar Canadian goods. Revisions would be made in the existing tariff to carry out these principles. The avowed intent was to favor British goods over similar items made in the United States.

There were several consequences of the Ottawa Agreements. Canadian exports and imports did shift somewhat away from the United States to Britain. British imports from the dominions rose from 29 percent of total imports in 1930 to 40 percent in 1938; British exports to the dominions rose from 43 percent in 1930 to 50 percent in 1938. These increases were achieved at the expense of trade with foreign countries. They did, however, help Canada's export industries to recover somewhat from the Depression.

The United States, against which these agreements were largely directed, changed course in the new administration of Franklin D. Roosevelt. Moreover, in Canada the Liberals, less ideologically committed to imperial preference and to the Ottawa Agreements, returned to power in 1935, making possible the negotiation of a treaty of reciprocity between Canada and the United States, which conferred most-favored-nation status on the two parties, thus entitling U.S. exports to Canada's intermediate or preferential tariff. Moreover, reductions were made on items constituting 60 percent of Canadian exports to the United States. This agreement was renewed and expanded in 1938.

Imperial preference remained, however, as part of Britain's tariff. It posed a major problem for Great Britain when that country was considering entrance into the European Economic Community in the 1960's. *—Nancy M. Gordon*

ADDITIONAL READING:

Hancock, William Keith. *Survey of British Commonwealth Affairs.* 3 vols. in 2. Westport, Conn.: Greenwood Press, 1977. A comprehensive survey of the British Commonwealth; volume 2 deals with economic developments.

McDiarmid, Orville John. *Commercial Policy in the Canadian Economy.* Cambridge, Mass.: Harvard University Press, l946. A comprehensive history of the Canadian tariff.

Mansergh, Nicholas. *The Commonwealth Experience.* London: Weidenfeld & Nicolson, 1969. Contains a brief treatment of the Ottawa Agreements, but doubts that they had much significance.

Miller, J. D. H. *Britain and the Old Dominions.* London: Chatto & Windus, 1966. Positive evaluation of the Ottawa Agreements.

Safarian, A. E. *The Canadian Economy in the Great Depression.* Toronto: Toronto University Press, 1959. The role of the Depression in making the agreements possible.

Young, J. H. *Canadian Commercial Policy.* Ottawa: Royal Commission on Canadian Economic Prospects, 1957. Brief treatment of the agreements in the context of Canada's commercial policy.

SEE ALSO: 1867, British North America Act; 1878, Macdonald Returns as Canada's Prime Minister; 1924, Halibut Treaty; 1930, Bennett Era in Canada; 1931, Statute of Westminster.

1932 ■ BONUS MARCH: *at the beginning of the Depression, frustrated World War I veterans demand a promised bonus*

DATE: July 28, 1932
LOCALE: Washington, D.C., and Anacostia Flats, Maryland
CATEGORY: Economics
KEY FIGURES:
Herbert Clark Hoover (1874-1964), thirty-first president of the United States, 1929-1933
Patrick Jay Hurley (1883-1963), secretary of war
Douglas MacArthur (1880-1964), chief of staff of the U.S. Army
Walter W. Waters, elected leader of the Bonus Army

SUMMARY OF EVENT. There were more than three million U.S. veterans of World War I, and they formed the American Legion and other lobbying organizations. Their efforts were effective. One veterans' benefit to be awarded was a bonus that the American Legion defined as "adjusted compensation"—the difference between the pay that was received during military service and what soldiers could have earned outside the military. The first bonus bill passed Congress in 1922 but was vetoed by the president. Congress passed it over the veto of President Calvin Coolidge in 1924. It provided one dollar per day of military service inside the United States and a dollar and a quarter per day outside the United States, but payment was deferred to the year 1945.

Described as endowment insurance, 3.5 million interest-bearing compensation certificates were issued, to expire twenty years later. Each was worth about a thousand dollars, for a total value of $3.5 billion. Pressure by veterans and their organizations continued. The Great Depression was intensifying. In 1931, over President Herbert Hoover's veto, Congress passed a provision that 50 percent of the individual cash value of a certificate could be borrowed at an interest rate of 4.5 percent.

The Great Depression created massive unemployment, and many of the unemployed were veterans. There had been agitation and some violent demonstrations in the early 1930's, and the role of the Communist Party in the United States and abroad was seen by some as significant. At another level, the role of the American Legion and other advocacy groups was also important.

Because of the deteriorating economic conditions, groups of veterans from all over the nation began to demand action. Some traveled great distances to the U.S. Capitol in Washington, D.C., to lobby directly for immediate payment of their bonus. Such a bill was introduced in the 1931 session of

Congress. As a result, approximately fifteen thousand veterans arrived in Washington in the spring of 1932. The elected leader of the veterans was Walter W. Waters. He organized the veterans into military-type units and remained their most identifiable leader. They took up makeshift housing all over the District of Columbia. Some were housed in a group of abandoned government buildings, and others created an encampment consisting of more than two thousand tents and lean-tos across the Anacostia River in Maryland at Anacostia Flats. Many of the tents were provided by the Army.

The assembled veterans, called the Bonus Army or Bonus Expeditionary Force (BEF), exerted increasing pressure on Congress during the spring and summer of 1932 to pass a bonus bill providing cash payments of the appropriate bonus to each veteran who was eligible. Such a bill was introduced by Congressman Wright Patman of Texas. It passed the House of Representatives on June 15 but was defeated in the Senate. Congress adjourned. Most of the veterans then left Washington. A certain amount of money was allocated to assist in paying for transportation home. About two thousand veterans remained.

The high point of the crisis occurred on July 28. A series of demonstrations began on Pennsylvania Avenue and Third and Fourth Streets Northwest. The Board of Commissioners of the District of Columbia asked President Hoover for assistance. By early afternoon, Secretary of War Patrick Hurley had ordered General Douglas MacArthur, chief of staff of the U.S. Army, to bring in previously prepared Army units. MacArthur himself chose to lead the Army units on horseback and dressed in full uniform with medals. There was much confusion during the day. The marchers were driven out of the abandoned government buildings. There is some question about whether Hurley ordered MacArthur to pursue other marchers outside the District of Columbia. In any event, the Army forces pursued the marchers across the river, using copious tear gas but not firing their guns. By midnight, the shantytown at Anacostia Flats was burned. Later tests confirmed that the tear gas then used could initiate fires. In the rioting, there were two deaths and dozens of injuries.

Contemporaneous discussion and subsequent assessments of the episode make much of two factors: the ostentatious role assumed by MacArthur and the role of the Communist Party of the United States. Communist organizers were present, but Waters and others claimed that they had distanced themselves from them. In his memoirs and in partisan biographies, MacArthur insisted that the communists instigated the entire affair. There was even talk that communists had a list of officials to be jailed after the revolution and that MacArthur's name allegedly led the list. Some hagiographic MacArthur biographers have gone so far as to link the Bonus March imbroglio with MacArthur's recall in 1951, claiming the communists were responsible for both.

MacArthur claimed that only one in ten of the Bonus Marchers were legitimate veterans. A survey by the Veterans Bureau, however, concluded that 94 percent were legitimate.

President Hoover, Secretary Hurley, and especially General MacArthur were much criticized in the press for overreacting.

—Eugene L. Rasor

ADDITIONAL READING:

Daniels, Roger. *The Bonus March: An Episode of the Great Depression.* Westport, Conn.: Greenwood Press, 1971. Criticizes Hoover and MacArthur. Enumerates several myths: that the Army fired on and killed veterans, that the marchers had machine guns, and that the BEF was infiltrated by large numbers of communists. Includes the controversial report MacArthur wrote summarizing his actions.

Hunt, Frazier. *The Untold Story of Douglas MacArthur.* New York: Devin-Adair, 1954. One of several hagiographic biographies of MacArthur. Describes the Bonus March as a plot of the U.S. Communist Party, instructed by Moscow to bring about a bloody riot.

James, D. Clayton. *The Years of MacArthur.* 3 vols. Boston: Houghton Mifflin, 1970-1985. The standard and authoritative biography of MacArthur. The Bonus March is covered in volume 1.

MacArthur, Douglas. *Reminiscences.* New York: McGraw-Hill, 1964. A self-serving memoir that should be read with caution. Declares that the Communist Party planned the riot and denies that he was wearing medals.

Waters, Walter W. *B.E.F.: The Whole Story of the Bonus Army.* New York: John Day, 1933. A personal memoir by the most identifiable leader of the Bonus Marchers.

SEE ALSO: 1924, Coolidge Is Elected President; 1928, Smith-Hoover Campaign; 1929, Stock Market Crash; 1932, Reconstruction Finance Corporation Is Created; 1932, Franklin D. Roosevelt Is Elected President; 1933, The Hundred Days; 1933, Tennessee Valley Authority Is Established; 1933, National Industrial Recovery Act; 1934, The Dust Bowl; 1935, Works Progress Administration Is Established; 1935, Black Monday; 1935, National Labor Relations Act; 1935, Social Security Act; 1937, Supreme Court Packing Fight; 1938, Fair Labor Standards Act; 1939, Mobilization for World War II.

1932 ■ FRANKLIN D. ROOSEVELT IS ELECTED PRESIDENT: *dissatisfied with the government's response to the Depression, Americans vote for a New Deal*

DATE: November 8, 1932
LOCALE: The United States
CATEGORY: Government and politics
KEY FIGURES:

James Aloysius Farley (1888-1976), chairman of the National Democratic Committee, Roosevelt's campaign manager

John Nance Garner (1868-1967), Democratic congressman from Texas, Speaker of the House of Representatives, and vice presidential nominee

Herbert Clark Hoover (1874-1964), thirty-first president of the United States, 1929-1933, and Republican candidate for reelection

Louis McHenry Howe (1871-1936), confidant of Roosevelt and his personal secretary

Huey Pierce Long (1893-1935), Louisiana politician

Raymond Moley (1886-1975), leader of an informal group of Roosevelt's advisers known as the Brain Trust

Eleanor Roosevelt (1884-1962), Franklin Roosevelt's wife and a political force in her own right

Franklin Delano Roosevelt (1882-1945), governor of New York and presidential candidate of the Democratic Party

Rexford Guy Tugwell (1891-1979), member of the Brain Trust

SUMMARY OF EVENT. On July 2, 1932, Franklin D. Roosevelt boarded a trimotored airplane at Albany, New York, and flew to Chicago, where the Democratic National Convention had nominated him for president. It was a dramatic gesture. Breaking tradition, Roosevelt became the first presidential candidate ever to make an acceptance speech before a nominating convention. Previously, nominees had awaited official notification via the U.S. mail. In a personal appearance, he could both emphasize his determination to take vigorous action against the nation's economic ills and demonstrate his physical ability to handle the job. His plane bucked strong headwinds and twice had to land in order to refuel. When he at last stood before the sweating delegates in Chicago Stadium, he endorsed the party platform, promising relief for the unemployed, public works, repeal of prohibition, agricultural reform, and tariff reduction. In a ringing conclusion he declared: "I pledge you, I pledge myself, to a new deal for the American people."

Three years of the worst depression in U.S. history, occurring under a Republican administration, had wrecked Republican chances for 1932. An unenthusiastic Republican convention had nominated Herbert Hoover and his vice president, Charles Curtis, for a second term. Republican leaders were under no illusions. Only a sudden upturn in the economy could offer the ticket any hope.

The struggle within the Democratic ranks was intense. As governor of New York, Roosevelt had emerged as the early front-runner. He had support among both urban and rural Democrats, the two factions that had torn the party apart in recent elections; but he lost ground in the late primaries. Al Smith, the titular leader of the party and the 1928 nominee, was the darling of the Eastern political bosses. The most important favorite son was a Texan, John Nance Garner, who had the backing of powerful newspaper publisher William Randolph Hearst. If the anti-Roosevelt coalition had stayed together, the nomination might have gone to a dark horse such as Newton D. Baker, secretary of war in the Wilson cabinet. On the third ballot, the Roosevelt forces were stopped cold, about one hundred votes short of the necessary two-thirds majority. The bandwagon envisioned by Roosevelt's campaign manager, James A. Farley, had not materialized, and the

prize seemed about to slip away. After a brief recess, Texas and California switched to Roosevelt, giving him the necessary majority. Garner himself had made the crucial decision. He was a good Democrat who feared a deadlocked convention and the nomination of a weak compromise choice; to mollify his supporters and balance the ticket, he accepted the vice presidential nomination. Louisiana's governor, Huey P. Long, assisted Garner with Southern delegations.

The flight to Chicago the next day set the tone of the Democratic campaign, but Roosevelt remained vague about the "new deal" he so casually had promised. He spoke in warm but sometimes contradictory generalities, always playing it safe; most of all, he wanted to keep his fractious party together and gather the enormous vote of protest against Hoover. His major farm address at Topeka, Kansas, promised a national

Franklin Delano Roosevelt, thirty-second president of the United States, who remained executive through an unprecedented third term. An entire generation would reach adulthood knowing no other president and considering him a father figure who had brought the United States out of the Great Depression and through World War II. Roosevelt's New Deal marked the birth of the big-government social programs which developed into an American welfare state. (Library of Congress)

program of planned agricultural production without being explicit about how it would work. To the business community, he pledged a 25 percent reduction in federal spending and a balanced budget. The Hoover Administration, he said at Pittsburgh, was "the most reckless and extravagant" peacetime government in history. This speech would haunt him later, but he was thoroughly serious. He left himself one loophole. People would not be allowed to starve, even if the government had to run a deficit. In his address before the Commonwealth Club at San Francisco, he came closest to spelling out his economic philosophy: that government must assume the role of regulator of the common good within the existing economic system.

Hoover's brutal use of the army against the Bonus Marchers that summer—in a demonstration that turned into the Anacostia Flats riots—confirmed the popular image of him as a man insensitive to suffering. On the hustings, Hoover hammered out his speeches without the aid of speechwriters, and his plodding performances contrasted with Roosevelt's ebullience. Sometimes Hoover and Roosevelt sounded strangely alike, but they had fundamental differences. Hoover argued that the causes of the Depression lay in Europe and thus far away from U.S. shores, while Roosevelt emphasized its domestic origins. They also disagreed on tariff policy, the gold standard, prohibition, and public utility regulation. Late in the campaign, Hoover panicked with the fear that U.S. institutions were in jeopardy. If Roosevelt had his way on the tariff, Hoover said, "The grass will grow in the streets of a hundred cities, a thousand towns; the weeds will overrun the fields of millions of farms."

Despite the lack of any real debate of the issues, voters understood that Roosevelt's election meant change, even if it was not clear exactly where he would lead them. Roosevelt amassed 22,821,857 votes to Hoover's 15,761,841, losing only six Northeastern states; he overwhelmingly carried the electoral college by 472 to 59. The Socialist and Communist Parties polled less than a million votes in what should have been a golden opportunity to exploit discontent. Between election day and the inaugural lay another hard winter. While the nation awaited clarification of Roosevelt's New Deal, the Depression reached its nadir.

—Donald Holley, updated by Joseph Edward Lee

ADDITIONAL READING:

Bernstein, Michael. *The Great Depression*. New York: Cambridge University Press, 1987. A provocative study of the causes of the Great Depression.

Brinkley, Alan. *Voices of Protest*. New York: Vintage Books, 1983. Analyzes the criticism that was aimed at the New Deal by Huey P. Long and Father Charles Coughlin.

Friedel, Frank. *Franklin D. Roosevelt: A Rendezvous with Destiny*. Boston: Little, Brown, 1990. In a single volume, one of the most prolific Roosevelt experts examines the president's career.

Garraty, John A., ed. *The Great Depression*. San Diego, Calif.: Harcourt Brace Jovanovich, 1986. A collection of essays exploring the economic collapse from an international perspective.

Lash, Joseph. *Eleanor and Franklin*. New York: W. W. Norton, 1971. Documents the role played by Eleanor Roosevelt in her husband's march toward the White House.

Leuchtenburg, William E. *Franklin D. Roosevelt and the New Deal*. New York: Harper & Row, 1963. An excellent analysis of the implementation of Roosevelt's program.

Terkel, Studs. *Hard Times*. New York: Pantheon Books, 1970. Poignant oral accounts of life during the Great Depression.

SEE ALSO: 1924, Coolidge Is Elected President; 1928, Smith-Hoover Campaign; 1929, Stock Market Crash; 1932, Bonus March; 1931, Empire State Building Opens; 1933, The Hundred Days; 1933, Tennessee Valley Authority Is Established; 1933, National Industrial Recovery Act; 1934, The Dust Bowl; 1935, Works Progress Administration Is Established; 1935, Black Monday; 1935, National Labor Relations Act; 1935, Social Security Act; 1935, Neutrality Acts; 1936, Reciprocity Treaty; 1937, Supreme Court Packing Fight; 1938, Fair Labor Standards Act; 1939, Mobilization for World War II; 1940, United States Builds a Two-Ocean Navy; 1940, Ogdensburg Agreement; 1941, Lend-Lease Act; 1941, Executive Order 8802; 1941, Bombing of Pearl Harbor; 1941, Germany and Italy Declare War on the United States; 1942, Censorship and Japanese Internment; 1942, Manhattan Project; 1942, Invasion of North Africa; 1943, Magnuson Act; 1944, Superfortress Bombing of Japan; 1944, G.I. Bill; 1945, Yalta Conference; 1945, United Nations Charter Convention; 1945, V-E Day.

1933 ■ GOOD NEIGHBOR POLICY: *a new articulation of U.S. relations with Latin American nations replaces military interventionism with mutual respect and cooperation*

DATE: March 4, 1933-1945

LOCALE: Western Hemisphere

CATEGORIES: Diplomacy and international relations; Latino American history

KEY FIGURES:

Herbert Clark Hoover (1874-1964), thirty-first president of the United States, 1929-1933

Cordell Hull (1871-1955), U.S. secretary of state

Franklin Delano Roosevelt (1882-1945), thirty-second president of the United States, 1933-1945

Sumner Welles (1892-1961), U.S. assistant secretary of state and ambassador to Cuba

SUMMARY OF EVENT. In his first inaugural address, President Franklin D. Roosevelt promised that the United States would conduct itself in international relations as a good neighbor. After he applied the term specifically to relations with Latin America and pledged his opposition to armed intervention, the phrase "good neighbor" came to be identified with his Latin American foreign policy.

Following the Spanish-American War (1898), the United States intervened militarily in Central America and the Caribbean. Asserting its right to exercise a police power in the Americas under the 1904 Roosevelt Corollary to the Monroe Doctrine, U.S. presidents sent troops into Cuba, Haiti, the Dominican Republic, Nicaragua, Mexico, and Panama to stabilize conditions, prevent European intervention, and protect U.S. lives and property. After a brief incursion in 1909, a contingent of U.S. Marines was stationed in Nicaragua almost continuously from 1912 to 1933.

Seeking to prevent future interventions, several Latin American jurists proposed the adoption of doctrines against intervention or the use of force or diplomatic recognition to protect the interests of foreign nations in Latin America or to change Latin American governments. At the Sixth Inter-American Conference, held in Havana, Cuba, in 1928, the Latin American representatives tried, but failed, to obtain U.S. support for a nonintervention resolution. There was also increasing opposition in the United States to the policy of sending troops to protect U.S. interests in Central America and the Caribbean.

In 1928, President-elect Herbert Hoover made a series of goodwill trips to Latin America, and in 1930 he repudiated the Roosevelt Corollary to the Monroe Doctrine. Resisting pressure to intervene to protect U.S. investors, Hoover prepared to withdraw troops from Haiti and removed the marines from Nicaragua. His goodwill gestures were undermined, however, by the Great Depression and the high duties imposed by the Hawley-Smoot Tariff act of 1931.

On March 4, 1933, Franklin D. Roosevelt, in his inaugural address, declared that in foreign policy he wished to "dedicate this nation to the policy of the good neighbor . . . who respects himself and . . . the rights of others." After his inauguration, Roosevelt undertook specific measures to improve relations with Latin America and stimulate economic recovery. In 1933, at the Seventh International Conference of American States, in Montevideo, Uruguay, Secretary of State Cordell Hull accepted the principle of nonintervention and signed a convention declaring that no state had the right to intervene in the internal and external affairs of other countries, with a vague reservation. Hull also proposed the reduction of tariffs and trade agreements to stimulate trade. In 1936, at an inter-American conference in Buenos Aires, the United States signed an expanded resolution renouncing intervention and agreed to the principle of consultation in the event of a war between American nations or an external threat to the peace of the Americas.

In 1933, Roosevelt had also dispatched Assistant Secretary of State Sumner Welles to a revolutionary Cuba, where Welles orchestrated the resignation of dictator Gerardo Machado. When Welles's personally designated successor was overthrown by a sergeant's revolt, however, Welles persuaded Roosevelt to withhold recognition from the nationalistic government of Ramón Grau San Martín. With U.S. naval vessels offshore, this policy of nonrecognition encouraged a second revolt, bringing to office a series of presidents controlled by Colonel Fulgencio Batista.

Despite clear interference in Cuban politics, President Roosevelt had refrained from using armed force in Cuba, and in 1934 the United States and Cuba agreed to the removal of the Platt Amendment (1901), which, following the Spanish-American War, gave the United States the right both to intervene in Cuba to protect Cuban independence and to maintain a military base on the island. Similar agreements were concluded with Panama and the Dominican Republic. The United States and Cuba also signed reciprocal trade agreements that lowered duties on Cuban sugar, guaranteed access to the U.S. market for Cuban agricultural exports, and reduced duties on hundreds of U.S.-manufactured goods exported to Cuba.

When Bolivia, Mexico, and Venezuela threatened to nationalize U.S. oil companies in 1937 and 1938, the Good Neighbor Policy faced a direct challenge. President Roosevelt not only resisted the pressure to intervene but also accepted the right of these countries to seize the assets of the companies or increase government revenues from their operations, as long as they made immediate and just compensation. Concerned about the war in Europe, Roosevelt also continued economic assistance and signed new trade agreements with Bolivia and Mexico after a brief suspension. By refusing to intervene to protect the oil companies, Roosevelt demonstrated his adherence to the principle of nonintervention and the concept of the Good Neighbor. In addition to renouncing the use of military force in the Caribbean and Central America, the United States provided credits to struggling countries through the newly created Export-Import Bank and negotiated a series of reciprocal trade agreements to lower barriers to trade between the United States and Latin America.

Because of its renunciation of intervention and the withdrawal of troops, the Good Neighbor Policy fostered an era of good relations and cooperation between Latin America and the United States on the eve of World War II. In a series of agreements drawn up at prewar conferences, nations of Latin America and the United States agreed to cooperate and form an alliance of mutual protection. Following the attack on Pearl Harbor, all Latin American countries but Argentina joined the Allied war effort, cracking down on Axis sympathizers and supplying strategic materials, airbases, and troops for the Allies. Although Argentina was eventually pressured to declare war on the Axis, the public efforts by the U.S. ambassador to influence or change the government in Buenos Aires not only backfired but also raised the specter of past interventions.

While the unity and cooperation between the United States and Latin America survived the war, the death of Roosevelt on April 12, 1945, and the departure of the architects of the Good Neighbor Policy from the State Department contributed to its demise. Differences between Latin America and the United States had already surfaced at wartime and postwar conferences, and with the advent of the Cold War the United States turned its attention to the economic recovery of Europe and the defense of the West.

After 1945, therefore, Latin American requests for economic cooperation and assistance were ignored until the triumph of Fidel Castro's revolution in Cuba in 1959. When the Central Intelligence Agency conducted a covert action to overthrow the democratically elected government of Guatemala in 1954, it appeared that the United States had abandoned nonintervention in favor of military intervention to protect the interests of a U.S. company, thereby ending the era of the good neighbor. Subsequent attempts to overthrow Castro, U.S. invasions of the Dominican Republic, Grenada, and Panama, the overthrow of Salvador Allende in Chile, and the support of military forces in Central America also violated the principle of nonintervention and the Good Neighbor Policy.

The Good Neighbor Policy did not promote freedom and democracy. After the removal of U.S. troops, the commanders of the national guards trained by the United States seized power and established long-term dictatorships. Since these regimes guaranteed stability, protected foreign investments, and were anticommunist, they received U.S. economic and military aid. Although the reciprocal trade agreements stimulated trade, they also reinforced a dependency on the U.S. market and prevented economic development through diversification. Nevertheless, the Good Neighbor Policy fostered a period of goodwill among the nations of the Western Hemisphere, as well as a sense of political hegemony against potential aggressors. The United States demonstrated its growing role in world affairs and safeguarded its long-range interests in both the economic well-being and political autonomy of its Latin American neighbors.   —D. Anthony White

ADDITIONAL READING:

Aguilar Monteverde, Alonso. *Pan-Americanism from Monroe to the Present: A View from the Other Side*. Translated by Asa Zatz. New York: Monthly Review Press, 1968. A Latin American view of Pan-Americanism and U.S. "imperialism."

Blasier, Cole. *The Hovering Giant: U.S. Responses to Revolutionary Change in Latin America, 1910-1985*. Rev. ed. Pittsburgh: University of Pittsburgh Press, 1985. A study of U.S. reactions to revolutionary movements in Mexico, Bolivia, Guatemala, Cuba, Chile, Grenada, and Nicaragua.

Gellman, Irwin F. *Good Neighbor Diplomacy: United States Policies in Latin America, 1933-1945*. Baltimore: The Johns Hopkins University Press, 1979. A thorough study that emphasizes the significance and originality of Roosevelt's policy and the contributions of Cordell Hull and Sumner Welles.

LaFeber, Walter. *Inevitable Revolutions: The United States in Central America*. New York: W. W. Norton, 1984. A critical history of U.S. policy that views conflicts as a consequence of U.S. policy and externally imposed conditions of dependency.

Wood, Bryce. *The Dismantling of the Good Neighbor Policy*. Austin: University of Texas Press, 1985. Traces the gradual dismantling of the Good Neighbor Policy after the death of Roosevelt, ending with the U.S. intervention in Guatemala in 1954.

_____. *The Making of the Good Neighbor Policy*. New York: Columbia University Press, 1961. The definitive study
of the development of the Good Neighbor Policy and its applications, by a prominent historian.

SEE ALSO: 1889, First Pan-American Congress; 1898, Spanish-American War; 1903, Platt Amendment; 1903, Acquisition of the Panama Canal Zone; 1909, Dollar Diplomacy; 1912, Intervention in Nicaragua.

1933 ■ THE HUNDRED DAYS: *a new administration passes a series of acts aimed at bringing hope to millions of Depression-weary Americans*

DATE: March 9-June 16, 1933
LOCALE: Washington, D.C.
CATEGORIES: Economics; Government and politics
KEY FIGURES:
Harry Lloyd Hopkins (1890-1946), head of the Federal Emergency Relief Administration and later Roosevelt's second in command
Raymond Moley (1886-1975), assistant secretary of state in 1933 and member of Roosevelt's Brain Trust
Franklin Delano Roosevelt (1882-1945), thirty-second president of the United States, 1933-1945
Rexford Guy Tugwell (1891-1979), economist from Columbia University, adviser to Roosevelt, member of the Brain Trust
Henry Agard Wallace (1888-1965), secretary of agriculture
SUMMARY OF EVENT. On November 8, 1932, Franklin D. Roosevelt was elected president of the United States. Few people knew what to expect from Roosevelt, a consummate politician who once described himself as "a Christian and a Democrat." One thing, however, was clear: Immediate action of some kind was imperative to stop the nation from slipping further into economic chaos. Perhaps out of desperation, the people were impressed with the expressions of confidence embodied in Roosevelt's inaugural address and his promise of action. The problem facing the new administration was how to sustain this sense of movement and confidence in a new order. On March 9, 1933, a special session of Congress met and sat until June 16. During that period, later to be known as the Hundred Days, fifteen major resolutions became law and the United States underwent a revolutionary change. The legislation was the product of no single person or particular group. The essence of the program was emergency compromise, with Roosevelt standing above the various interests and masterminding them.

The immediate problem was to do something about the paralyzed banking system and to restore business confidence. As a preliminary measure, Roosevelt issued an executive order on March 5, proclaiming a national bank holiday. During the holiday, cash from the Federal Reserve replenished bank vaults. The closing of the banks had the therapeutic effect of convincing many people that, having reached rock-bottom, the situation had to improve. Roosevelt submitted to Congress on March 9, 1933, an Emergency Banking Relief Act, which was passed immediately. The act gave the president power over gold transactions, outlawed hoarding, and provided for the gradual reopening of the banks under the supervision of the secretary of the Treasury. This was followed the next day by the Economy Act, which, despite threatened congressional revolt, reduced federal expenditures drastically by cutting government salaries and veterans' payments. On March 12, Roosevelt gave his first radio address in a series that came to be known as "fireside chats." He emphasized that most of the banks were sound and would reopen in a few days. When the banks did reopen, people rushed to deposit money rather than to make withdrawals. The banking crisis subsided.

Roosevelt next attempted to eradicate some abuses in the nation's banking and financial practices. The Securities Act of May 27, 1933, called for close supervision by the Federal Trade Commission of the issue of new stock, and held stock sellers liable if they provided false information. A complementary measure was the Glass-Steagall Banking Act of June 16, 1933, which differentiated between commercial banking and investment banking. An important corollary of this act was the creation of the Federal Deposit Insurance Corporation (FDIC) to insure individual bank deposits up to five thousand dollars. The insurance on deposits was a significant step in restoring public confidence and bringing currency back into the banks.

Another pressing problem was agriculture. In preparing his legislation, Roosevelt relied heavily upon the advice of his secretary of agriculture, Henry A. Wallace. A former farm editor and horticulturist, Wallace advocated a domestic allotment plan designed to combat overproduction and declining prices by restricting acreage and leasing to the government land left idle. The scale of payments was aimed at establishing parity between farm prices and the cost of manufactured goods, based on figures for the years 1909 to 1914. Not all farming interests accepted this idea of production control; many demanded cheap money as a remedy. When the Agricultural Adjustment Act (AAA) was finally signed into law on May 12, 1933, it provided for various other options to control production besides government leasing of idle land. Additional New Deal legislation provided for loans through the Farm Credit Administration, aid to very poor farmers with the Resettlement Administration, and a means for all rural areas to receive power through the Rural Electrification Administration.

The unemployed and the middle class also received benefits under the new legislation, which later became known collectively as the New Deal. The unemployed were helped through the Civilian Conservation Corps (CCC), one of Roosevelt's most popular measures. The act, passed on March 29, 1933, provided for a civilian army of young men to work in reforestation and conservation projects. In the nine-year life span of the CCC, a total of 250,000 jobless men between the ages of eighteen and twenty-five were given an opportunity to move forward in life. Enactment of the Federal Emergency Relief Act on May 12, 1933, and the subsequent creation of the Federal Emergency Relief Administration (FERA) provided for direct federal grants to states for purposes of relief and brought about a cooperative effort between federal and state agencies. FERA, headed by Harry Hopkins, promoted the idea of work relief instead of the "dole" (as welfare was often called at the time) and stipulated that there would be no discrimination of any kind concerning recipients.

To meet the problems of the middle-class homeowners facing mortgage foreclosures, the Home Owners Refinancing Act, passed in June, 1933, provided for the exchange of defaulted mortgages for guaranteed government bonds, but it appeared to give more assistance to mortgage companies than to hard-pressed homeowners. Homeowners benefited later, when it became government policy to refinance loans where possible instead of taking possession of homes.

One of the most successful programs of the Roosevelt Administration was the enactment of the Tennessee Valley Authority Act (TVA) on May 18, 1933. The act provided for a regional authority that would build dams designed to control disastrous flooding in the states of the Tennessee River basin, bring electricity to rural areas, and replant forests. Eventually, the TVA became the largest utility company in the United States.

When organized labor demanded action to relieve unemployment, Senator Hugo L. Black of Alabama proposed a thirty-hour work week, and his proposal received considerable support from labor interests. Roosevelt regarded the bill proposed by Black to be both unconstitutional and unworkable, but he had to meet the growing demand for relief by industry and industrial workers. He therefore ordered his advisers to prepare an omnibus labor and industry measure to attack the root causes of depression in those fields. A draft was prepared under the direction of Raymond Moley, economist and assistant secretary of state. The passage of the National Industrial Recovery Act (NIRA) on June 16, 1933, provided for industrial self-government through the use of universal codes regulating production, wages, and hours, but negated enforcement of the antitrust laws. Although the program was short-lived, these codes benefited nearly four million women workers through wage and hour provisions. The program did not, however, set up codes for agricultural or domestic laborers, three-fourths of whom were African American. The Roosevelt Administration hoped that the act would eliminate inefficiency and raise prices. The provision that all codes must be submitted for government approval pleased advocates of government control, such as Rexford Guy Tugwell, a member of Roosevelt's Brain Trust—a group of distinguished individuals serving as advisers to the president. Organized labor received legal guarantees that all codes would have to provide for collective bargaining before they could be recognized. Finally, the unemployed were assured of aid from a vast program of public works connected with the NIRA and financed from additional money through increased federal spending.

On June 16, 1933, Congress adjourned after its historic session. Never in the nation's history had so much new legislation been enacted in so short a time. With Roosevelt's support from both houses, bills originating from the president's White House office were passed nearly every day in order to give the country help during the emergency of the Depression. The hasty legislation that was adopted during the Hundred Days helps to explain why so many measures subsequently had to be drastically amended or abandoned altogether.

—*George Q. Flynn, updated by Marilyn Elizabeth Perry*

ADDITIONAL READING:

Davis, Kenneth S. *FDR: The New Deal Years, 1933-1937.* New York: Random House, 1986. A chronicle of the New Deal years combined with the interactions of people and events and their effect on strategy.

Freidel, Frank. *Franklin D. Roosevelt: A Rendezvous with Destiny.* Boston: Little, Brown, 1990. A complete biography of Roosevelt, detailing the Depression and the measures taken to bring recovery.

Leuchtenburg, William E. *Franklin D. Roosevelt and the New Deal, 1932-1940.* New York: Harper & Row, 1963. A one-volume survey of the New Deal period. Excellent bibliography.

Morgan, Ted. *FDR: A Biography.* New York: Simon & Schuster, 1985. Emphasizes Roosevelt's private life and how that influenced his political decisions.

Schlesinger, Arthur Meier. *The Coming of the New Deal.* Vol. 2 in *The Age of Roosevelt.* Boston: Houghton Mifflin, 1959. Re-creating the prevailing atmosphere, attempts to place the Hundred Days within the context of modern U.S. reform.

Sitkoff, Harvard, ed. *Fifty Years Later: The New Deal Evaluated.* Philadelphia: Temple University Press, 1985. Essays outlining the merits and pitfalls of the New Deal.

SEE ALSO: 1924, Coolidge Is Elected President; 1928, Smith-Hoover Campaign; 1929, Stock Market Crash; 1929, Great Depression; 1932, Reconstruction Finance Corporation Is Created; 1932, Bonus March; 1932, Franklin D. Roosevelt Is Elected President; 1933, Tennessee Valley Authority Is Established; 1933, National Industrial Recovery Act; 1934, The Dust Bowl; 1935, Works Progress Administration Is Established; 1935, Black Monday; 1935, National Labor Relations Act; 1935, Social Security Act; 1937, Supreme Court Packing Fight; 1938, Fair Labor Standards Act; 1939, Mobilization for World War II.

1933 ■ TENNESSEE VALLEY AUTHORITY IS ESTABLISHED: *an experiment in federal control over the natural resources of the Tennessee Valley brings economic development to a depressed region*

DATE: May 18, 1933

LOCALE: Alabama, Tennessee, Georgia, Mississippi, North Carolina, Kentucky, and Virginia

CATEGORIES: Economics; Government and politics

KEY FIGURES:

David Eli Lilienthal (1899-1981), attorney and TVA board member

George William Norris (1861-1944), senator from Nebraska and early advocate of public control of natural resources

Arthur Ernest Morgan (1878-1975), engineer and first chairman of the Tennessee Valley Authority (TVA)

Harcourt Alexander Morgan (1867-1950), agronomist and member of the TVA board

Franklin Delano Roosevelt (1882-1945), thirty-second president of the United States, 1933-1945

SUMMARY OF EVENT. The Tennessee River and its tributaries run through the seven southern states of Alabama, Tennessee, Georgia, Mississippi, North Carolina, Kentucky, and Virginia. During the colonial period, this basin was lush with trees and covered with fine topsoil. Much of the land then was controlled by Eastern Woodlands cultures, including the Cherokee, Chickasaw, and Choctaw people. By 1930, however, the region's now mostly white population was visibly impoverished and its resources depleted. Power relationships within the area had made a few people very wealthy, at the expense of both the population and the environment of the area. Agricultural methods emphasized maximum short-term production, depleting the soil's nutrient base. Timbering companies logged the area rapidly, permitting erosion, which washed away precious topsoil. Most people were employed in jobs that depended on extracting the resources of the area without replenishing them. Relatively few sustainable industries capable of improving the long-term living conditions of the area's people took root. The area's high annual rainfall, coupled with the loss of trees that held topsoil in place, contributed to increasingly severe floods that threatened not only the best farmland but also cities such as Chattanooga.

This area had first come to national attention during World War I. Anticipating the curtailment of trade with Germany, which would preclude the importation of nitrates, the United States sought a site upon which to construct a synthetic nitrate plant. The National Defense Act of 1916 authorized the president to establish such a facility at Muscle Shoals on the Tennessee River in northern Alabama. A dam would provide power for the plant. The Army Corps of Engineers did not complete the dam until after World War I was over. By 1922, the plant was complete and idle. Certain private interests, including Henry Ford, realized the potential of the site for the production of nitrates and, more significant, for the generation of electric power. Ford and others repeatedly tried to buy out the government's interest in the site during the 1920's.

Largely because of the work of Senator George W. Norris, the Muscle Shoals site was still government property when Franklin D. Roosevelt became president in 1933. Norris, a longtime proponent of using the federal government to solve economic and environmental problems created by the private sector, envisioned using the site to demonstrate the feasibility and desirability of federal control of natural resources. During the 1920's, Norris used his prestige and position as chairman of the Agriculture and Forestry Committee to ensure that the government would retain ownership of a site that he regarded as admirably located for experimentation in flood control and power production under federal ownership. Twice during the period of Republican ascendancy, Norris submitted bills incorporating his ideas, but both were vetoed. Not until the election of a Democrat in 1932 did Norris make progress in his struggle.

Franklin Roosevelt, an advocate of public control of natural resources, recognized the political potential of the idea. While governor of New York, he had done much to promote more equitable use of public resources. He had long been aware of Norris' plan, and after his election he invited the senator for an inspection tour of the Tennessee Valley. The two men agreed in principle upon a comprehensive planning system that would combine the best of both private initiative and government power. The mission of TVA, as Roosevelt envisioned it, would incorporate reforestation, agricultural education, fertilizer production, and cheap electric power generation under one unified scheme of planning for the entire Tennessee Valley.

When a bill was submitted to Congress during the first hundred days of Roosevelt's administration, it spoke of national planning for a complete river watershed. The severity of the Great Depression had prepared many people for the use of government authority on a wide scale. Roosevelt had declared that the South was the nation's number-one economic problem, and the Tennessee Valley was visible proof of that.

During the first phase of the New Deal, Congress passed an act creating the Tennessee Valley Authority (TVA), which envisioned using the power of the federal government to develop the resources of the river system to promote economic development and responsible environmental conduct. Despite the objections of certain Republicans, who felt the measure was communistic, it passed by a wide margin. Under the act's terms, an independent public corporation was established with a board of three directors and was authorized to build dams, generate electricity for sale to public municipalities, produce cheap fertilizer, and promote the well-being of the area through farm education.

By the 1950's, twenty major dams and many minor ones had been built, and the TVA was vigorously engaged in all fields in which it had been empowered to act. Serving an area of forty thousand square miles, it promoted better living conditions for the people of the valley through its application of modern scientific agriculture and made inexpensive electric power available for industries wishing to move into the area.

Considerable controversy accompanied these accomplishments. One of the major problems faced by the TVA was an internal squabble about its basic aims and goals as understood by the three board members. Arthur E. Morgan, president of Antioch College in Ohio and chairman of the board, viewed the TVA as an experiment in social reconstruction. Criticized by some for his paternalistic approach, Morgan took a large view of his task, incorporating social and political reform as well as economic development.

The other members of the TVA governing board did not share Morgan's vision. Harcourt A. Morgan (no relation to the chairman) was chosen because of his agricultural knowledge and familiarity with the region. David Lilienthal was appointed because of his outstanding work with public utility regulation in Wisconsin. In contrast to the chairman, both H. A. Morgan and Lilienthal were realists who distrusted excessive centralization and realized the importance of good relations with local government and industry. After much arguing, Roosevelt decided to support Lilienthal and dismissed Arthur Morgan in March, 1938.

In addition to this internal dispute, the TVA faced opposition from private power companies. Privately controlled utilities such as Commonwealth and Southern, represented by Wendell Willkie, feared that the TVA would force them out of business. Arthur Morgan attempted to deal with this problem by establishing spheres of influence for both private and TVA power sales. Despite Morgan's friendliness, a number of stockholders in the private companies brought suit against the TVA, claiming that the sale of electricity by a federal corporation was unconstitutional. In *Ashwander v. the Tennessee Valley Authority* (1936), the Supreme Court upheld the constitutionality of such sales, but it was not until 1939 that the full legality of the TVA was settled in favor of the federal government.

Many of those who came to work for the TVA in the early years did so because of the unique reform opportunity the agency presented. Its experimental nature and amorphous organizational structure permitted the agency a great deal of independence in its planning. The TVA needed the support of the existing power structure in order to survive, however, which limited the agency's attempts to reform the region's racial practices. TVA hired African Americans in areas where they were available, but the agency faced tremendous opposition when it attempted to enforce a racial quota system in hiring. The agency built separate housing for black employees and separate visitor facilities for its recreational and tourist areas. African Americans also found themselves displaced, as did many poor whites, by the agency's dam projects. TVA's general land acquisition policy compensated landowners but did little for renters, again because of an unwillingness to challenge the existing power structure.

Along with these shortcomings, the agency has been criticized for exercising both too much influence and too little control over the environmental and socioeconomic development of the region. Nevertheless, the TVA's achievements in providing jobs and building infrastructure at a critical period in U.S. history remain significant contributions.

—*George Q. Flynn, updated by Stephen Wallace Taylor*

ADDITIONAL READING:

Chandler, William U. *The Myth of TVA: Conservation and Development in the Tennessee Valley, 1933-1983*. Cambridge, Mass.: Ballinger, 1984. Economic analysis of the TVA's impact in navigation, flood control, power production, agriculture, and environmental protection concludes that the TVA was a bad investment of tax dollars. The book is flawed in that it uses surrounding non-TVA areas with different economic bases as a control group.

Creese, Walter L. *TVA's Public Planning: The Vision, the Reality.* Knoxville: University of Tennessee Press, 1990. Well-written, lavishly illustrated book demonstrates the relationship between the physical impact of TVA on the visual environment of the region and the policy goals of the agency's leaders.

Grant, Nancy L. *TVA and Black Americans: Planning for the Status Quo.* Philadelphia: Temple University Press, 1990. A scholarly examination of TVA's policies toward black people as employees and residents of the Tennessee Valley. Concludes that TVA's reform impulse effectively was stifled by the need to work within the political establishment.

Hargrove, Erwin C. *Prisoners of Myth: The Leadership of the Tennessee Valley Authority, 1933-1990.* Princeton, N.J.: Princeton University Press, 1994. Examines the mentality of TVA's upper management, their concept of the role TVA should play in the development of the region, and the limitations of that role.

Hubbard, Preston. *Origins of the TVA: The Muscle Shoals Controversy, 1920-1932.* Nashville, Tenn.: Vanderbilt University Press, 1961. Documents the various attempts to deal with the Army Corps of Engineers project at Muscle Shoals. Useful for understanding the roots of TVA in the Progressive ideology of the early twentieth century.

SEE ALSO: 1924, Coolidge Is Elected President; 1928, Smith-Hoover Campaign; 1929, Stock Market Crash; 1929, Great Depression; 1932, Reconstruction Finance Corporation Is Created; 1932, Bonus March; 1932, Franklin D. Roosevelt Is Elected President; 1933, The Hundred Days; 1933, National Industrial Recovery Act; 1934, The Dust Bowl; 1935, Works Progress Administration Is Established; 1935, Black Monday; 1935, National Labor Relations Act; 1935, Social Security Act; 1937, Supreme Court Packing Fight; 1938, Fair Labor Standards Act; 1939, Mobilization for World War II.

1933 ■ National Industrial Recovery Act: *the act encourages firms in industrial sectors to develop codes of fair competition to "do their part" for economic recovery*

DATE: June 16, 1933
LOCALE: Washington, D.C.
CATEGORIES: Business and labor; Economics; Laws and acts
KEY FIGURES:
Clarence Seward Darrow (1857-1938), lawyer and civil libertarian
Harold LeClair Ickes (1874-1952), secretary of the interior
Hugh S. Johnson (1882-1942), administrator of the National Recovery Administration
Franklin Delano Roosevelt (1882-1945), thirty-second president of the United States, 1933-1945

SUMMARY OF EVENT. Between 1929 and 1933, the United States economy descended into its worst economic depression in history. By 1932, one-fourth of the nation's workers were unemployed. Drastic decline in farm prices reduced farm incomes and led to widespread mortgage foreclosures. Banks and other businesses failed by the thousands.

In response, the voters overwhelmingly defeated the efforts of President Herbert Hoover to win reelection and brought into the presidency Franklin D. Roosevelt. Roosevelt had a few specific campaign promises: He would do a better job of balancing the budget, but he favored direct transfer payments for the relief of the unemployed and others suffering hardship. He offered the public a New Deal without giving much detail.

After his inauguration, March 4, 1933, Roosevelt's administration began a whirlwind of activity that came to be known as the Hundred Days. A bank holiday was declared, and the dollar was taken off the gold standard. Representatives of business were called upon to help formulate a program for industrial recovery. From this emerged the National Industrial Recovery Act (NIRA), approved June 16, 1933. It was to be administered by a National Recovery Administration (NRA). Roosevelt quickly appointed General Hugh Johnson to head the NRA. The program began in an explosion of public relations. A dramatic symbol—the Blue Eagle—was adopted, and business firms were encouraged to qualify to display in their windows a blue eagle poster bearing the words "We Do Our Part."

The law encouraged firms in each individual trade and industry sector to join together to draw up a code of fair competition. The assumption was that intense competition was a cause of declining prices, wages, and incomes, and if the intensity of competition were reduced, firms could profit more, produce more, and pay more. Each code was to be submitted to the NRA administrator and, if approved, would have the force of law. Codes were exempted from antitrust prosecution.

Many of the codes contained provisions intended to prevent price cutting and to curtail output. The first code issued was for cotton textiles. It limited machinery operation to two forty-hour shifts per week. It was soon followed by codes for shipbuilding and electrical manufacturing that forbade selling below specified minimum prices. Other codes forbade prices below "cost," where formulas were provided for determining cost. Often firms were required to file price changes so competitors would know about them, a provision intended to deter such changes. Many of the practices forbidden in the codes were genuinely undesirable: misrepresentation, design piracy, commercial bribery, deceptive advertising, false branding, imitation of trademarks or designs.

The NIRA also contained important labor provisions. If businesses were to get higher prices, workers were to get higher wages. Section 7 of the NIRA required that every code contain certain labor provisions. One was "that employees shall have the right to organize and bargain collectively through representatives of their own choosing. . . ." Employers were forbidden to interfere with worker decisions about joining a union. Codes were to provide standards for minimum wages and maximum hours of work. The majority of codes called for a forty-hour work week. Efforts to spread work by reducing hours were somewhat successful; in industries surveyed by the Labor Department, average hours fell from 43.3 to 37.8 per week between June and October, 1933, and the number employed increased by about 7 percent. Minimum-wage provisions generally applied to plant workers but not office workers. Most codes provided for a minimum wage of at least forty cents an hour. Each industry formulated its own wage and hour standards, under pressure from the NRA authorities and sometimes from labor unions. Many codes forbade employment of children less than sixteen years of age.

Even before the codes were put into effect, business firms reacted favorably to the prospect of higher prices. A large increase in inventory purchases helped to stimulate the economy during the summer and autumn of 1933. However, problems and contradictions soon emerged. Many codes were dominated by large firms and were drawn to put small or new competitors at a disadvantage. Each industry was pleased by the prospect of gaining higher selling prices, but displeased by having to pay higher wages and higher prices for inputs. The inventory boom died out by the end of 1933. The NIRA did not end the desire of individual firms to gain more business by offering a lower price. Code enforcement was often slow and difficult.

By the beginning of 1934, NRA codes covered about 90 percent of the industrial labor force. Ultimately, more than 550 codes were adopted. The code approach was based on the false premise that the Depression was caused by overproduction and excessive competition. The real cause was the drastic decline in total spending for goods and services. Another section of the NIRA dealt more directly with this problem. It authorized the creation of a Public Works Administration, which came under the direction of Secretary of the Interior Harold Ickes, to undertake construction projects. Ickes was primarily concerned that projects be useful and that they be constructed efficiently. This often meant they were slow to get under way, and that they did not offer many jobs for which the unemployed could qualify. Between 1933 and 1941, the Public Works Administration spent about $2.5 billion; the highest number of workers employed on its projects was 740,000 in mid-1936. Other government programs, such as the Civil Works Administration and Works Progress Administration, embodied more of a make-work orientation and provided more jobs.

In 1934, a National Recovery Review Board, headed by lawyer Clarence Darrow, strongly criticized the NRA codes as helping large firms oppress smaller firms and consumers. Johnson was forced to resign from the NRA in October, 1934, under fire for heavy drinking and an undiplomatic personality. He was replaced by a five-man board. In May, 1935, the Supreme Court held the code sections of NIRA to be unconsti-

tutional in *Schechter Poultry Corporation v. United States*. The Court ruled that the regulation of industry went beyond the scope of interstate commerce, and the delegation of authority by Congress to the president and NRA administrators was excessive.

Many of the elements of the NRA program were reenacted by Congress in separate pieces of legislation. These included the National Labor Relations Act of 1935; the Fair Labor Standards Act of 1938; regulatory legislation for coal, petroleum, motor transport, and airlines; and laws restricting false and misleading advertising and price discrimination. After momentarily weakening antitrust with NIRA, after 1937, the government shifted to vigorous enforcement, blaming business concentration and inflexible prices for the severity of the Depression.

As a measure to stimulate recovery from the Depression, the NIRA was not very effective, except for the demand stimulation resulting from Public Works Administration activities. Raising prices and wages would tend to reduce output and employment, unless something were done to increase demand. Most economists have been critical of the tendency in the codes to reduce competition and encourage collusion and monopolistic practices. Although consumers were nominally represented in the code-making process, their interests were not protected. However, NIRA began a radical transformation of the work environment by encouraging the spread of labor unions, a process that was continued even more strongly by the National Labor Relations Act of 1935. NIRA also contributed to the reduction of the standard workweek and the extent of child labor. Politically, the measure probably helped to reassure the public that something was being done, and that radical transformation of the political system was not needed.

—*Paul B. Trescott*

ADDITIONAL READING:

Fine, Sidney. *The Automobile Under the Blue Eagle: Labor, Management and the Automobile Manufacturing Code*. Ann Arbor: University of Michigan Press, 1963. Detailed case study. Emphasizes labor aspects of the NIRA; also deals with Henry Ford's resistance to the NIRA.

Hawley, Ellis W. *The New Deal and the Problem of Monopoly*. Princeton, N.J.: Princeton University Press, 1966. Puts the NRA in a broader context of New Deal concern with economic planning and the revival of antitrust after *Schechter Poultry Corporation v. United States*.

Johnson, Hugh S. *The Blue Eagle from Egg to Earth*. Garden City, N.Y.: Doubleday Doran, 1935. A colorful, opinionated account of the top NRA administrator's life and the NRA experience, which he regarded as "a holy thing."

Lyon, Leverett S., ed. *The National Recovery Administration: An Analysis and Appraisal*. Washington, D.C.: Brookings Institution, 1935. An encyclopedic study that carefully examines the contents of the codes in order to assess their effects, arriving at a mostly negative appraisal.

Ohl, John Kennedy. *Hugh S. Johnson and the New Deal*. De Kalb: Northern Illinois University Press, 1985. Lively, objective, scholarly account of Johnson's life and of the achievements and problems of the NRA.

Roos, Charles F. *NRA Economic Planning.* Bloomington, Ind.: Principia Press, 1937. An economist who worked in the NRA tries to assess its relevance to the issue of economic planning. Long, scholarly, and analytical.

Wilcox, Clair, Herbert F. Froser, and Patrick Murphy Malin, eds. *America's Recovery Program.* New York: Oxford University Press, 1934. Four of the nine essays relate to the NRA. Critical view of the NRA's monopolistic tendencies.

SEE ALSO: 1924, Coolidge Is Elected President; 1928, Smith-Hoover Campaign; 1929, Stock Market Crash; 1932, Reconstruction Finance Corporation Is Created; 1932, Bonus March; 1932, Franklin D. Roosevelt Is Elected President; 1933, The Hundred Days; 1933, Tennessee Valley Authority Is Established; 1934, The Dust Bowl; 1935, Works Progress Administration Is Established; 1935, Black Monday; 1935, National Labor Relations Act; 1935, Social Security Act; 1937, Supreme Court Packing Fight; 1938, Fair Labor Standards Act; 1939, Mobilization for World War II.

1934 ■ DEVELOPMENT OF RADAR:
technology that identifies distant objects revolutionizes warfare as well as peacetime industries

DATE: 1934-1945
LOCALE: United States and Europe
CATEGORY: Science and technology
KEY FIGURES:

Christian Hülsmeyer (1881-1957), German engineer acknowledged as inventor of the world's first practical radar system

Guglielmo Marconi (1874-1937), one of the first to experiment with reflected radio waves

Robert M. Page (1903-1992), American physicist who developed a practical technology for pulse radar

Henry Thomas Tizard (1885-1959), British scientist who led a delegation to the United States for cooperative development of radar

Robert Alexander Watson-Watt (1892-1973), Scottish physicist who initiated development of radar in Britain

Leo C. Young (born 1926), American physicist and colleague of Page

SUMMARY OF EVENT. "Radar" is an acronym for *ra*dio *de*tection *a*nd *r*anging. The principle of radar involves the transmission of high-frequency pulses of electromagnetic energy by means of a directional antenna. The pulses are reflected by objects that intercept them. Accordingly, radar receivers pick up the reflections, process them electronically, and convert them into dots of light (blips) on the face of a fluorescent screen that forms part of a cathode-ray tube. In this way, the receivers determine with instant precision the direction, dis-

tance, velocity, altitude, and even form of the targeted object, such as an airplane, ship, submarine, iceberg, body in space, thunderstorm, or landmass.

Radar came into widespread use during World War II and has been credited with changing the course of history, and certainly that of North America. During the 1930's, radar development was pioneered independently and simultaneously in Britain, France, Germany, and the United States. While several proposals to build radar-type detection devices had been made since the late nineteenth century—with a demonstration by Germany's Christian Hülsmeyer in 1904—it was not until the 1930's that the study of radio-echo signals from moving objects was considered important. Early in 1934, Robert M. Page, an American physicist pursuing the theory of his colleague Leo C. Young at the U.S. Naval Research Laboratory, worked out a practical technology for pulse radar. This development marked the beginning of an effective radar program in the United States.

By this time, Britain was becoming increasingly apprehensive of Adolf Hitler's rearming of Nazi Germany. Responding to rumors about a German "death ray" initiated by a speech by the Nazi leader, Scottish physicist Robert A. Watson-Watt wrote a report. In it he demolished the death-ray fiction but observed that the echoes of short-wave pulses could be used to locate approaching aircraft and the like. To boost the British effort, a special committee headed by scientist Henry T. Tizard was formed to give top priority to the systematic research and development of British radar. By 1935, Watson-Watt had completed a practical radar system that was to contribute to the successful outcome of the Battle of Britain five years later. Simultaneously, the French were placing their own version of radar on the luxury liner *Normandie* to assist in the detection of icebergs on its North Atlantic crossings. Thus, by the beginning of World War II, several nations benefited from functioning radar systems. These systems were based on fundamentally different designs. The further diversification of radar designs and their applications by the Allies and Germany would improve the technology considerably by the end of the war. The British won the Battle of Britain by using radar to help intercept the approaching aircraft. When Germany switched to night bombing in 1941, British ground and airborne radar enabled British fighters to zero in on the attackers. Thus, the German threat of invasion was foiled, and Britain in turn became the strategic staging area from which the Allied forces launched their landing in Nazi-held "fortress Europe" in 1944.

In some respects, radar was a typical product of mid-twentieth century scientific technology. It was made possible by two earlier efforts, neither of which had the invention of radar as its purpose. The first was basic research committed solely to an understanding of pertinent scientific phenomena. Two names stand out in this connection: James Clerk Maxwell in Britain, whose mathematical predictions in 1864 regarding the nature of light and electromagnetic phenomena indicated that the latter, like the former, could be reflected, and Heinrich Rudolf Hertz, a German physicist who in 1887 demonstrated experimentally that Maxwell was right. Hertz's efforts were based on the sophisticated understanding of electronics that had formed over three decades of experiments with radio communications. So many individuals were involved in this development that radar—like most scientific break-throughs—can truly be said to have evolved, rather than to have been invented.

That radar did not have any single inventor also flowed from its complexity, design variations, and the number of different components used in radar systems. Moreover, the national emergency of war mandated a total mobilization of resources on the part of all involved. Accordingly, for perhaps the first time in history, scientists, policymakers, military personnel, and others on both sides of the Atlantic became completely devoted to a single research and development project. In tribute, former World War II German Navy head Admiral Karl Doenitz said in 1945, "The one single weapon which defeated the [German] submarine and the Third Reich was the long-range airplane with radar."

In subsequent years, scientists were to focus on technologies that enabled aircraft to avoid radar detection, radar contact with planets and other celestial bodies (radio astronomy), and the use of radar to improve the safety of air travel.

—*Peter B. Heller*

ADDITIONAL READING:

Burns, Russell W., ed. *Radar Development to 1945*. London: Peregrinus, 1988. An illustrated, blow-by-blow account of the development of radar in various countries. Among those writing the history of American radar is one of its principal developers, Dr. Robert M. Page, the retired head of the U.S. Naval Research Laboratory.

De Arcangelis, Mario. *Electronic Warfare: From the Battle of Tsushima to the Falklands and Lebanon Conflicts*. Poole, England: Blandford Press, 1985. Translated from the Italian, this is a fascinating, clearly written account of important military operations involving radar, among other technologies.

Fisher, David E. *A Race on the Edge of Time: Radar, the Decisive Weapon of World War II*. New York: McGraw-Hill, 1988. Another competent account of radar's use during the war, based on interviews with those involved.

Pritchard, David. *The Radar War: Germany's Pioneering Achievement, 1904-1945*. Wellingborough, England: P. Stephens, 1989. A British author traces the development of German radar from Hülsmeyer's demonstration to the end of the war. Photographs of individuals, equipment.

Skolnik, Merrill I. *Introduction to Radar Systems*. 2d ed. New York: McGraw-Hill, 1980. The few pages devoted to radar development prior to World War II survey the efforts of both Allied and Axis powers.

Watson-Watt, Robert A. *The Pulse of Radar: The Autobiography of Sir Robert Watson-Watt*. New York: Dial Press, 1959. A self-centered account by the gifted Scottish pioneer of radar, including a perceptive chapter on why the Americans ignored radar warnings of the impending Japanese attack at Pearl Harbor on December 7, 1941.

1934 ■ TYDINGS-McDUFFIE ACT:

promising Philippine independence from the United States by 1944, the act paves the way for expansion of U.S. economic interests in the islands

DATE: March 24, 1934
LOCALE: Washington, D.C.
CATEGORIES: Asian American history; Economics; Laws and acts
KEY FIGURES:
Harry B. Hawes (1869-1947), former senator from Missouri
John McDuffie (1883-1950), representative from Alabama
Sergio Osmena (1878-1961), vice president of the Philippines
Manuel Luís Quezón (1878-1944), president of the Philippines
Franklin Delano Roosevelt (1882-1945), thirty-second president of the United States, 1933-1945
Millard Tydings (1890-1961), senator from Maryland

SUMMARY OF EVENT. On March 24, 1934, President Franklin D. Roosevelt signed into law the Philippines Commonwealth Independence Act, popularly known as the Tydings-McDuffie Act. The law promised independence to the Philippines islands by 1944, following a ten-year transition period of "commonwealth status." During that time, the islands were to be governed by their own national legislature and executive branches; policy-making power, however, would continue to remain in the United States. This commonwealth system was in place when the Philippines were invaded and occupied by the Japanese in 1942, an event that delayed Philippine independence for two years, until 1946.

Initial support for the Philippine legislation came from particular special interest groups both in the United States and in the Philippines. Striving for their own nationhood, many native Filipino lobbying groups pushed hard for the act's passage. A more economically based pressure came from American beet sugar producers, who sought to eliminate competition from island goods, and from trade union leaders, who wanted to prevent the influx of Filipino workers into the Hawaiian islands and the U.S. mainland. These groups had earlier lent similar support to the legislative predecessor of the Tydings-McDuffie Act, the Hawes-Cutting-Hare Act of 1932. The earlier act's attempt to curb competitive imports from the Philippines was rejected by the U.S. Senate in a close vote.

After the defeat of the Hawes-Cutting-Hare legislation, a new contingent of Filipino supporters of independence traveled to Washington, D.C., where they were joined by those groups of politically influential Americans who supported Philippine autonomy. Sergio Osmena led the Philippine delegation but his call for immediate independence was too drastic for many in the American support group. He was subsequently recalled to Manila. His replacement, Manuel Quezón took a less politically offensive position, emphasizing a gradualist approach to independence for the islands. Thus, he was able to enlist the support of additional American politicians who favored a more moderate approach to Philippine independence. The resulting coalition influenced the passage of the Tydings-McDuffie Act.

Following enactment of the Tydings-McDuffie legislation, the Filipino delegation returned home to draft a constitution and to elect officials who would oversee the gradual transition to Philippine autonomy. Manuel Quezón and Sergio Osmena were elected president and vice president, respectively, of the new Philippines Commonwealth, respectively. Although steps were taken to create a Filipino-based political structure, most of the political decision-making authority still rested with the United States. Filipinos did, however, retain limited control over internal political affairs, but all foreign policy, defense, and monetary matters were defined and implemented in Washington. This political arrangement clearly benefited the United States at the expense of the Filipinos. The commonwealth was prohibited from legislating most of its own economic policies. In particular, legislation was passed which imposed duties on Philippine exports to America.

Under the new commonwealth system the cliental politics and economics of the old colonial structure were perfected. Key provisions of the Tydings-McDuffie Act and of its amendments saw to this. Increasingly, the Philippine presidency came to resemble the office of an American state governor. Quezón was accorded certain discretionary powers, but only where American interests were not affected. He could organize an army but could not deploy it without the consent of President Roosevelt. Travel to foreign lands and discussion of trade agreements with foreign officials could take place but Quezón was powerless to conclude any formal agreement. The enactment of any official Philippine trade agreements remained under the authority of the U.S. high commissioner of the Philippines. This position, strengthened by the provisions of the Tydings-McDuffie Act, protected the interests of the United States in all foreign relations and established official relationships between the Philippines and all other nations.

Looking after American interests abroad required the centralization of political authority in Manila. As a result, domestic policies were often delegated from the top level of Philippine government. It was under such an arrangement that President Quezón increasingly took advantage of his position. As long as his policy initiatives did not conflict with American interests, he wielded immense power, especially toward those who opposed his policies. Quezón often crushed his opposition with American blessings. The elimination of domestic competition greatly increased Quezón's confidence. He began to challenge some of the policies of American commonwealth administrators and even, at times, those of the high commissioner. Chastised at this level, he boldly began to take his conflicts to the American president. While he was successful in protesting the directives of the high commissioner on some occasions, his appeals to President Roosevelt most often produced results that reinforced American hegemony in the Philippines.

Under the structure authorized by the Tydings-McDuffie Act, the goal of true Philippine independence was increasingly circumvented. In the name of independence, American sovereignty over the Philippines continued. American suzerainty was magnified by a commonwealth political system that furthered American economic interests at the expense of the islands' competing in the world market. In the end, the Philippines became increasingly dependent on American economic interests. Commonwealth status destroyed that which the Philippines needed in order to compete economically on a global scale: revenue from the export of duty-free goods to the United States. Without trade revenues the Philippines became increasingly dependent on the United States for loans and investment, made, of course, with the understanding that United States interests came first. As the Philippine treasury emptied, the commonwealth thus became more indebted to its patron, the United States. The implementation of the Tydings-McDuffie Act both initiated and reinforced this condition.

The new relationship between the Philippines and the United States established by the Tydings-McDuffie Act produced a paradox: The closer the Philippines came to political independence from the United States, the more economically dependent upon America it became. In the end, the Tydings-McDuffie Act reinforced the idea that the only kind of independence that would be granted to the Filipinos was the kind that the United States could not grant.   —*Thomas J. Edward Walker, Cynthia Gwynne Yaudes, and Ruby L. Stoner*

ADDITIONAL READING:

Constantino, Renato. *A History of the Philippines.* New York: Monthly Review Press, 1975. A clearly written historical analysis of the Filipino struggle against imperialism. Provides a regional examination of Philippine political, economic, sociocultural, and religious colonization; also includes an intellectual examination of the decolonization process. Excellent non-Western documentation.

Gallego, Manuel. *The Price of Philippine Independence Under the Tydings-McDuffie Act: An Anti-View of the So-Called Independence Law.* Manila: Barristers Book Company, 1939. A Philippine account of the implementation of the act and the evolution of the commonwealth period; provides personal narratives documenting political, economic, and social oppression.

Grunder, Garel A., and William E. Lively. *The Philippines and the United States.* Norman: University of Oklahoma Press, 1951. An overview of the origin and evolution of U.S. policy toward the Philippine islands during the first half of the twentieth century. Explains how such policy affected American Filipino economic relations; examines the evolution of Filipino political institutions; defines the structure of the independence of the Philippine nation.

Hayden, John Ralston. *The Philippines: A Study in National Development.* New York: Macmillan, 1942. A somewhat patronizing account of the Philippine interaction with the United States during the first four decades of the twentieth century. Through primary source materials, provides a positive opinion of U.S. contributions to the development of an independent nation.

Karnow, Stanley. *In Our Image: America's Empire in the Philippines*. New York: Random House, 1989. A journalistic account of the United States' imperial experience in the Philippines. Suggests that the U.S. attempts to remake the Philippines in its own image through the establishment of political, educational, and sociocultural institutions barely affected traditional Filipino values yet such activity resulted in a unique relationship between the two countries. Indexed with bibliography.

Paredes, Ruby R., ed. *Philippine Colonial Democracy*. New Haven, Conn.: Yale University Press, 1988. Analyzes of the patron-client relationship between the United States and the Philippines. Suggests that the interaction was mutually corruptive for both nations: devastating to the evolution of Philippine democracy and detrimental to United States foreign policy. Indexed.

SEE ALSO: 1898, Spanish-American War; 1899, Philippine Insurrection; 1901, Insular Cases; 1944, Battle for Leyte Gulf.

1934 ■ THE DUST BOWL: *a massive drought exacerbates the Great Depression in the plains states and prompts migration westward*

DATE: Peaked April 14, 1934
LOCALE: Great Plains
CATEGORIES: Economics; Environment
KEY FIGURES:

Hugh Hammond Bennett (1881-1960), chief of the Soil Conservation Service

Chester Davis (1887-1975), director of the Agricultural Adjustment Administration

Dorothea Lange (1895-1965), photographer who documented Dust Bowl and "Okie" migration to California

Ferdinand A. Silcox (1882-1939), chief forester of the United States

Franklin Delano Roosevelt (1882-1945), thirty-second president of the United States, 1933-1945

SUMMARY OF EVENT. Farmers all across the Great Plains apprehensively watched the skies during the spring of 1934. Day after day, the weather offered no relief: intense sun, wind, drought, more sun, then gales. Massive clouds of dust blotted out the sun over western Kansas. At first, the wind raced along the surface, tearing at the stunted wheat and licking up the topsoil. Then the dust thickened into low, heavy, dirt-laden clouds. From a distance, the storm had the appearance of a cumulus cloud, but it was black, not white; and it seemed to eat its way along with a rolling, churning motion. As the storm swept toward Oklahoma and Texas, the black clouds engulfed the landscape. Birds and jackrabbits fled before it, and people scurried to safety. For those engulfed in the storm, there was an eerie sensation of silence and darkness. There was little or no visibility, and wind velocity hit forty to fifty miles per hour. That spring was exceedingly hot, with the temperature often above one hundred degrees. On May 10, the wind returned. Unlike the previous storm, these winds whipped up a formless, light brown fog that spread over an area nine hundred miles long. During the next day, an estimated twelve million tons of soil fell on Chicago, and dust darkened the skies over Cleveland. On May 12, dust hung like a pall over the entire Eastern seaboard. These two storms alone blew 650 million tons of topsoil off the plains.

The Dust Bowl was an elusive and constantly moving phenomenon. The entire decade of the 1930's was unusually hot and dry. In 1930, there was a drought in the eastern half of the nation. In 1931, the drought shifted to the northern plains of Montana and the Dakotas, and local level dust storms throughout the plains became more common. The storm that first brought the Dust Bowl to national attention, however, and gave it its name, was the one in May, 1934, which originated mostly on the northern plains and drew the dust high into the atmosphere, allowing the jet stream to deposit it over much of the eastern United States and even into the Atlantic Ocean. After that, the worst storms shifted to the southern plains and were typically more localized in extent. By many statistical measures, 1937 was the peak year for dust storm occurrence and severity, but in popular memory, the worst of the Dust Bowl over the largest area was probably in the early spring of 1934, including the famous "Black Sunday" storm of April 14.

The heart of the Dust Bowl is usually considered to be an area of three hundred thousand square miles in western Kansas, Oklahoma, Texas, and eastern Colorado and New Mexico, although conditions in the northern plains were, at times, equally deserving of the name Dust Bowl. In the hardest-hit areas, agriculture virtually ceased. With successive storms, the wind and the flying dust cut off the wheat stalks at ground level and tore out the roots. Blowing dirt shifted from one field to another, burying crops not yet carried away from the wind. Cattle tried to eat the dust-laden grass and filled their stomachs with fatal mud balls. The dust banked against houses and farm buildings like snow, burying fences up to the post tops. Dirt penetrated into automobile engines and clogged the vital parts. Housewives fought vainly to keep it out of their homes, but it seeped in through cracks and crevices, through wet blankets hung over windows, through oiled cloth and tape, covering everything with grit. Hospitals reported hundreds of patients suffering from "dust pneumonia." The black blizzards struck so suddenly that people became lost and disoriented and occasionally suffocated, some literally within yards of shelter. As a result, more than 350,000 people fled the Great Plains in the 1930's. These "Okies" loaded their meager household goods on flivvers and struck out along Route 66 for California.

Wind and drought alone did not create the Dust Bowl. Nature's delicate balance of wind, rain, and grass had been disturbed by human settlement. Fifty years earlier, a strong

The American heartland began to resemble a beach as sand dunes accumulated during the worst soil erosion of the century, known as the Dust Bowl of the 1930's. In the vicinity of Liberal, Kansas, this farmer's son sits atop a soil drift that threatens to cover his home. (Library of Congress)

protective carpet of grass had covered the Great Plains. The grass held moisture in the soil and kept the soil from blowing away. In dry years, the wind blew out huge craters, later mistakenly called "buffalo wallows"; but as long as the turf remained, the land could recover. After the Civil War, farmers began staking out homesteads in regions once considered too arid for use as anything but range land. Wherever they went, they plowed under the grass. During World War I, the demand for wheat, along with the invention of the tractor, meant plowing larger areas of the virgin grassland. Between 1914 and 1917 the area of wheat planted increased to twenty-seven million acres; more than 40 percent of this land was being plowed for the first time. After the war, the plowing continued. Larger tractors and combines, new machines that could harvest and thresh grain in one operation, inaugurated the age of

the wheat kings. By 1930, there were almost three times as many acres in wheat production as ten years earlier, and the tractors were still tearing open the turf. The plow exposed the land to rain, wind, and sun. By 1932, the earth on the plains was ready to blow.

The Dust Bowl speeded the development of long-range federal programs in the new field of soil conservation. A veteran conservationist, Franklin D. Roosevelt, in late 1933, created the Soil Erosion Service, later the Soil Conservation Service (SCS), with Hugh Bennett as its head. The SCS's task was to supply technical assistance and leadership, while local soil conservation districts carried out Bennett's program of strip crops, contour plowing, stubble-mulch farming, and terracing. In 1934, the Forest Service, under Ferdinand A. Silcox, started planting a shelter belt of trees, within a one-hundred-mile-wide zone, from Canada to the Texas Panhandle. Ten years later, more than two hundred million trees were serving as wind breaks and helping to conserve moisture. In 1936, the Agricultural Adjustment Administration (AAA), directed by Chester Davis, adopted soil conservation as a subterfuge to get around an unfavorable Supreme Court decision; but on the Great Plains, soil conservation was a legitimate part of the AAA program. Farmers received government checks for both acreage reductions and wind control practices.

After 1936, the New Deal added little to its conservation program. Roosevelt did appoint two special committees, one to study Dust Bowl conditions and the other to recommend specific legislation. Congress passed a water storage bill along the lines that the latter committee had suggested, but did little else. In documenting the extent of the Dust Bowl and providing information and arguments to support their own programs, however, federal agencies created a wealth of documentary information on the Dust Bowl, including human responses to it as recorded in the photographs of Dorothea Lange.

There has continued to be a lively debate over who or what—government programs, conservation practices of individual farmers, or Mother Nature—should receive most of the credit for bringing the Dust Bowl to an end, with the majority of scholars placing the greatest responsibility with nature. In any case, by 1938, the scale of wind erosion had dropped dramatically, and by 1941, temperature and rainfall levels had returned to near or above normal and the Dust Bowl had effectively disappeared. More to the point is the question of its possible recurrence. In the 1970's, Great Plains farmers were once again plowing "fence row to fence row" for export, grasslands were plowed up for irrigation farming, and the shelter belt had mostly been destroyed or allowed to deteriorate. Whether the government and the people of the plains learned the appropriate lessons from the terrible experience of the Dust Bowl remains an open question.

—Donald Holley, updated by Kent Blaser

ADDITIONAL READING:

Bonnifield, Mathew Paul. *The Dust Bowl: Men, Dirt, and Depression*. Albuquerque: University of New Mexico Press, 1979. Emphasizes the roles of nature and government policy in creating the Dust Bowl, and the efficacy of grass-roots human responses in alleviating the problem.

Gregory, James N. *American Exodus: The Dust Bowl Migration and Okie Culture in California*. New York: Oxford University Press, 1989. A more academic study of the migration made famous by Lange's photography.

Hurt, R. Douglas. *The Dust Bowl: An Agricultural and Social History*. Chicago: Nelson-Hall, 1981. An impressive overview, with a generally positive view of New Deal actions to combat the Dust Bowl.

Lange, Dorothea, and Paul Taylor. *An American Exodus: A Record of Human Erosion*. New York: Reynal and Hitchcock, 1939. Lange's stunning photographs of the Dust Bowl and migration to California provide some of the most famous images available of those events.

Svobida, Lawrence. *An Empire of Dust*. Caldwell, Idaho: Caxton Printers, 1940. Reprint. *Farming the Dust Bowl: A First-Hand Account from Kansas*. Lawrence: University Press of Kansas, 1986. A classic account of the Dust Bowl, written by a Kansas farmer who battled the Dust Bowl conditions for almost a decade.

Worster, Donald. *Dust Bowl: The Southern Plains in the 1930's*. Oxford: Oxford University Press, 1979. Classic modern account with a strong environmentalist perspective. Places much of the blame for the Dust Bowl on human activities.

SEE ALSO: 1924, Coolidge Is Elected President; 1928, Smith-Hoover Campaign; 1929, Stock Market Crash; 1932, Reconstruction Finance Corporation Is Created; 1932, Bonus March; 1932, Franklin D. Roosevelt Is Elected President; 1933, The Hundred Days; 1933, National Industrial Recovery Act; 1935, Works Progress Administration Is Established; 1935, Black Monday; 1935, National Labor Relations Act; 1935, Social Security Act; 1937, Supreme Court Packing Fight; 1938, Fair Labor Standards Act; 1939, Mobilization for World War II.

1934 ■ INDIAN REORGANIZATION ACT: *one of the most important pieces of legislation affecting Native Americans reverses policies of forced assimilation and promotes tribal self-government*

DATE: June 18, 1934
LOCALE: Washington, D.C.
CATEGORIES: Laws and acts; Native American history
KEY FIGURES:
John Collier (1884-1968), head of the Bureau of Indian Affairs, 1934-1945
Edgar Howard (1858-1951), congressman who co-sponsored the Indian Reorganization Act
Burton K. Wheeler (1882-1975), senator who co-sponsored the Indian Reorganization Act

SUMMARY OF EVENT. The New Deal policy toward American Indians in the 1930's and early 1940's and its centerpiece, the Indian Reorganization Act, were a reaction to the controversies generated by past federal policies toward American Indians. From the 1870's through the 1920's, tribal peoples were confined to government-controlled reservations and subjected to a policy aimed at bringing them into the dominant society's mainstream through forced assimilation. Government and church-run schools attempted to eradicate native languages and religion, customs and dress, tribalism and group loyalty, and replace them with Christian values, traditions, and institutions. To foster individualism and undermine tribalism, congressional legislation allotted the tribal communal domain to small individual holdings and opened surplus land for public sale.

This ambitious social experiment did not work as its original reform-minded advocates had intended. Under allotment, American Indians lost most of their lands to whites, while the educational experience undermined or destroyed indigenous peoples' heritage and culture without providing a viable substitute. The common results were demoralization, loss of identity, abject poverty, poor health, and defective education. These conditions, documented by independent studies, sparked a high-level, decade-long debate in the 1920's about American Indian policy. Congress, the Department of the Interior, and the authoritarian management style of the department's Bureau of Indian Affairs (BIA) came under sharp criticism.

The political upheaval wrought by the Great Depression and the election of Franklin D. Roosevelt in 1932 provided reformers with an opportunity to reshape American Indian policy. In 1933, John Collier, a persistent critic of the BIA, became Commissioner of Indian Affairs and directed the bureau until 1945.

Collier, a former social worker in New York City, had been introduced to the Pueblo cultures of the Southwest in 1920. Collier had experienced a native society that had maintained its communal and group traditions. Collier believed that he had discovered a "Red Atlantis," whose communal life and harmonious relationship with the natural world contained lessons and hope for the regeneration of Western society through a cooperative commonwealth.

After taking office, Collier began to reverse past government policy by initiating the Indian New Deal through executive orders and lobbying activities. In January, 1934, he forbade interference with traditional Native Americans' religious practices, declared their culture equal to all others, and encouraged the revival of native languages. Next, Collier ended forced attendance at Christian religious exercises by American Indian children at boarding schools. The commissioner persuaded Congress to repeal espionage and gag rules that restricted free speech and other civil liberties on reservations. Collier also decreased BIA controls and interference with tribal courts and tribal law. Finally, he placed a moratorium on the further sale of tribal lands.

Collier then sought to implement his goals of American Indian cultural freedom and political self-determination through legislation. He and his associates drew up a forty-eight-page document containing four sections aimed at replacing the agency's authoritarian approach with a new bilateral relationship between the tribes and the federal government. Title I dealt with the restoration of tribal self-government and economic revitalization to make tribal society viable. Tribes would petition for home-rule elections, adopt constitutions, and charter a tax-exempt corporation to set up businesses, manage property, and borrow from a federal revolving loan program. Title II, which focused on education, promoted the study of American Indian civilization and traditional arts and crafts, provided scholarships, and appropriated funds for primary and secondary education. Title III, which concerned Indian lands, ended allotments, returned previously allotted lands to tribal ownership, and restored unsold surplus reserva-

tion lands to tribal control. The federal government also was authorized to provide tribes with funds to rebuild their lost land base. Title IV proposed setting up a federal Court of Indian Affairs that would have original jurisdiction in cases involving Native Americans. In Congress, Representative Edgar Howard of Nebraska and Senator Burton K. Wheeler of Montana agreed to sponsor this initial version of what was to become the Indian Reorganization Act (IRA).

The proposed legislation immediately encountered opposition from both Indian and non-Indian sources. Few American Indians were consulted when the proposal was drawn up, which gave rise to suspicion and concern about some provisions. Those Native Americans who were most affected by assimilation policies over the last half century saw the act's provisions as taking a step backward. Some who held private allotments were concerned about losing them. Tribal leaders who viewed their sovereignty as inherent and some groups that already had constitutions or intact traditional political structures argued that the proposed BIA constitutional guidelines provided no new rights and, in fact, restricted tribal sovereignty. BIA constitutions resembled U.S. governmental bodies rather than traditional forms of tribal government. Some clergy and missionaries denounced the promotion of traditional culture as anti-Christian and pagan. A growing conservative coalition in Congress did not share Collier's radically progressive views on the restoration of traditional tribal cultures and the establishment of politically independent tribal nations.

In the end, Collier had to compromise. Getting the legislation out of the congressional committee in which it was stalled required the strong support of both President Roosevelt and Secretary of the Interior Harold Ickes. In the bill's final version, which passed on June 18, 1934, Title II, concerning Native American culture, and Title IV, which provided for an American Indian court, were deleted. The amount of funding to assist the establishment of tribal governments was cut back significantly. Other modifications greatly reduced the number of tribal peoples to be covered under the act. Senator Wheeler insisted on subjecting tribal self-government to the approval of the secretary of the interior and excluded from the act American Indians who were not members of tribes, as well as those tribes located in Oklahoma and Alaska. Another amendment by Howard required that each tribe hold a referendum to accept or reject the IRA.

In referenda held between 1933 and 1945, 174 tribes accepted the act while 73 voted against ratification, including the largest American Indian nation, the Navajo. However, only 92 of the tribes that voted in favor adopted IRA constitutions, and 71 took the next step of incorporating for the purpose of obtaining federal economic development loans. American Indians living in Oklahoma and Alaska were placed under the IRA by legislation passed in 1936.

Collier reluctantly accepted these changes, emphasizing the breakthrough represented by those parts of his original proposal that were retained. The commissioner also attempted to implement many of his goals through administrative actions and orders. The failure of Congress to appropriate the full amounts authorized in the IRA, continuing opposition to some of Collier's goals, and the commissioner's own misjudgments and administrative shortcomings were some of the factors that prevented his dream of a Red Atlantis from becoming reality. In the decade following the New Deal era, federal American Indian policy temporarily adopted an assimilationist and anti-tribal orientation.

Nevertheless, the IRA was a landmark in federal American Indian policy, with some noteworthy results. Many scholars consider it the single most important piece of federal American Indian legislation. Accomplishments of the IRA and the Indian New Deal included halting the disappearance of the tribal land base and restoring several million acres to various reservations. The act permitted many tribes to assume a degree of economic and political control over their affairs. The restoration of religious freedom and traditional ceremonies were also important measures. With few exceptions, those tribes that received government loans used them to improve economic conditions on reservations and made repayment. American Indians were given preference for positions in the BIA. Many tribes have taken advantage of IRA provisions to defend sovereignty and survive. Most important, the reversal of past policies awakened hope and pride in being American Indian.   —*David A. Crain*

ADDITIONAL READING:

Fey, Harold E., and D'Arcy McNickle. *Indians and Other Americans: Two Ways of Life Meet*. Rev. ed. New York: Harper & Row, 1970. Good account of the Collier years from a pro-IRA perspective. McNickle, a Montana Blackfoot, was a BIA employee during this era.

Kelly, Lawrence C. "The Indian Reorganization Act: The Dream and the Reality." *Pacific Historical Review* 44 (August, 1975): 291-312. Balanced look at what the IRA failed to achieve in contrast to the claims of some proponents. Discusses Collier's strong points and shortcomings as American Indian commissioner during the New Deal era.

Kelly, William H., ed. *Indian Affairs and the Indian Reorganization Act: The Twenty Year Record*. Tucson: University of Arizona Press, 1954. A collection of scholarly essays on this subject.

Parman, Donald L. *The Navajos and the New Deal*. New Haven, Conn.: Yale University Press, 1976. A study of the troubled relations between the American Indian policy reformers in the Roosevelt Administration and the nation's largest tribe.

Philp, Kenneth R. *John Collier's Crusade for Indian Reform, 1920-1954*. Tucson: University of Arizona Press, 1977. A detailed, objective account of Collier's achievements and shortcomings as a policy critic, activist, reformer, and administrator.

Taylor, Graham D. *The New Deal and American Indian Tribalism: The Administration of the Indian Reorganization Act, 1934-1945*. Lincoln: University of Nebraska Press, 1980.

Argues that the IRA, although enlightened compared to previous policies, was weakened by its emphasis on tribal reorganization and its mistaken assumptions about contemporary American Indian societies.

SEE ALSO: 1929, Great Depression; 1953, Termination Resolution; 1968, Indian Civil Rights Act; 1978, American Indian Religious Freedom Act.

1935 ■ WORKS PROGRESS ADMINISTRATION IS ESTABLISHED: *a new agency administers a nationwide program of public works to alleviate unemployment*

DATE: April 8, 1935
LOCALE: Washington, D.C.
CATEGORIES: Business and labor; Economics; Organizations and institutions
KEY FIGURES:
Henry G. Alsberg (1881-1970), director of the Federal Writers' Project
Holger Cahill, head of the Federal Art Project
Hallie Flanagan (1890-1969), director of the Federal Theater Project
Harry L. Hopkins (1890-1946), former social worker who became director of the Works Progress Administration
Harold L. Ickes (1874-1952), secretary of the interior, 1933-1946, and head of the Public Works Administration under the National Industrial Recovery Act
Franklin Delano Roosevelt (1882-1945), thirty-second president of the United States, 1933-1945
Frank Walker (1886-1959), head of the Application and Information Division of the Federal Relief Program
Aubrey Willis Williams (1890-1965), former social worker who became director of the National Youth Administration
SUMMARY OF EVENT. The history of the New Deal's relief policy is essentially one of hopeful experimentation. President Roosevelt was reluctant to engage in a full-scale program of deficit spending implicit in direct relief and public works, yet he was deeply committed to relieving the nation's unemployment. The National Industrial Recovery Act (NIRA), passed in June, 1933, had provided for the creation of a Public Works Administration, under Secretary of the Interior Harold L. Ickes, for the purpose of spending some $3.3 billion to relieve unemployment. Ickes, however, had approached his task with such caution that it had little effect. Also, to relieve the growing unemployment problem, Roosevelt had established the Federal Emergency Relief Administration (FERA) in May, 1933, with an appropriation of five hundred million dollars to make direct grants to the states for relief services.

The director of this agency was Harry L. Hopkins, a former social worker. Hopkins soon realized that his agency was making little progress on the national unemployment problem. With Roosevelt's assistance he succeeded in establishing a temporary Civil Works Administration (CWA) in October, 1933. The primary purpose of this agency was to provide employment for some four million men and women in a complete federal make-work project. Nationwide, the CWA engaged in such tasks as repairing or building in excess of five hundred thousand miles of roads, one thousand airports, forty thousand schools, and more than thirty-five hundred playgrounds and athletic fields. The CWA also employed fifty thousand teachers. In the winter of 1933-1934, Hopkins employed more than three million persons and spent $933 million. At its peak, in mid-January, 1934, the program employed 4,230,000 individuals. According to historian William E. Leuchtenburg, "The CWA got the country through the winter." By March of 1934, however, the president was disturbed at the rate of expenditure; more important, he did not want the work relief program to become a permanent form of dole to the unemployed. The CWA was terminated, and once again the FERA took up major responsibility for relief, including those projects left unfinished by the CWA.

An evaluation of the programs persuaded Roosevelt that something else was needed to combat the problem of unemployment. Neither FERA, which generally provided direct relief, nor the CWA, which had provided a disguised dole, had made much of an impact on the constantly expanding unemployment problem. Both the president and Hopkins wanted to keep the federal government out of direct relief; instead, they wanted to concentrate on a vast public employment program which would provide honest jobs for the needy. It was this reasoning that led Roosevelt to call for a new emergency relief appropriation in January, 1935. The subsequent Emergency Relief Appropriation Act, passed April 8, 1935, provided $5 billion with few strings attached.

The appropriation of the money, however, was only one of the problems facing Roosevelt in his new work relief program. Of immediate concern was the appointment of a director for the new program. Hopkins had much to recommend him for the task. Roosevelt sympathized with Hopkins' desire to place major emphasis on benefits for the workers. Yet at times the president seemed disturbed by the fantastic rate at which Hopkins spent federal funds. Another leading contender for the job was Ickes, who desired an expansion of his Public Works Administration. With both men campaigning for the job, and feeling unable himself to disregard either for fear of seeming to repudiate their past accomplishments, Roosevelt effected a compromise by creating an incredibly complex organization to spend the money and by bringing in Frank Walker, an old and tactful friend, to serve as mediator between the two men.

Despite the elaborate organization, Hopkins managed to dominate the new relief program, primarily because the president, liking his approach better than that of Ickes, provided loopholes in the rules and certain strategic assistance. Hopkins' new agency, called the Works Progress Administration (WPA), proceeded to expand into the most gigantic federal works operation ever seen in peacetime. Originally designed for the unskilled worker, the WPA was soon engaged in a variety of projects, constructing more than six hundred thousand miles of highways, roads, and streets, repairing and constructing more than a hundred thousand bridges, a hundred thousand public buildings, thousands of parks and airfields, and thousands of recreational facilities. In these activities Hopkins was guided by the idea of providing legitimate employment and making sure that most of the money went into wages rather than material expenses.

The WPA also aided thousands of artists, writers, actors, and students. A Federal Theater Project was established under the direction of Hallie Flanagan, a Guggenheim Fellow and head of Vassar College's theater. The project employed many gifted people and engaged in considerable experimentation until it was abruptly terminated by Congress in 1939. During a period of four years, live drama was brought to an audience totaling thirty million in thousands of small towns that hitherto had seen no better than the small traveling tent show. A Federal Writers' Project directed by Henry Alsberg, a former director of the Provincetown Theater, employed college professors, journalists, and other literary persons to record local and regional history. More than a thousand state and territorial guides, picture books, and other works of historical interest were written. Under the direction of Holger Cahill, a Federal Art Project provided employment for thousands of local artists whose artistic endeavors still grace hundreds of local post offices and libraries throughout the United States.

In addition to these projects, the National Youth Administration (NYA) was created to assist the young men and women of the United States unable to find jobs. Under the direction of former Alabama social worker Aubrey Williams, the NYA sought and found part-time employment for more than six hundred thousand college students and more than 1.5 million high school students over a five-year period.

The WPA, effective as an emergency measure, had its weaknesses. At no time did Hopkins employ more than four million people, less than half of the ten million unemployed at the time. Political problems arose because of his opposition to the use of the WPA for patronage purposes, and there was mounting concern that the jobs created by the program were in fact a dole. When Congress succeeded in gaining control of WPA appropriations, Hopkins was forced to change his approach. Corruption was to some degree inevitable, but when the immensity of the unemployment problem posed by the Depression and the novelty of the remedy is considered, the WPA represented a gigantic effort on the part of the federal government to bring immediate succor to the country's jobless. It also proved to be a forerunner and the introductory phase of the nation's attempt to deal effectively with the ever-growing problem of unemployment and public welfare with all the accompanying complications.

—George Q. Flynn, updated by Liesel Ashley Miller

Additional reading:

Adams, Henry H. *Harry Hopkins*. New York: G. P. Putnam's Sons, 1977. This biography of the director of the Works Progress Administration provides insight into both the private and public lives of Hopkins. Photographs, extensive bibliography, index.

Braeman, John, Robert H. Bremner, and David Brody, eds. *The New Deal: The National Level.* Columbus: Ohio State University Press, 1975. A total of eleven essays in this work include titles ranging from "The New Deal and the Negro" to "Fiction and the New Deal."

Brinkley, Alan. *The End of Reform: New Deal Liberalism in Recession and War.* New York: Alfred A. Knopf, 1995. Brinkley sees the New Deal not merely as a reform movement, but "as part of a long process of ideological adaptation" in the United States.

Conkin, Paul K. *The New Deal.* 2d ed. Arlington Heights, Va.: Harlan Davidson, 1975. A concise overview in which Conkin argues that the New Deal did not go far enough with reform efforts, nor did it address the fundamental problems of economic cycles.

Leuchtenburg, William E. *Franklin D. Roosevelt and the New Deal: 1932-1940.* New York: Harper & Row, 1963. Explores Roosevelt's role in the New Deal. Chapter 6 focuses on efforts of the Works Progress Administration to relieve unemployment.

Schlesinger, Arthur, Jr. *The Coming of the New Deal.* Boston: Houghton Mifflin, 1959. An essential and timeless study, this comprehensive and detailed work cannot be overlooked in any thorough examination of New Deal legislation and policies.

White, Graham, and John Maze. *Harold Ickes of the New Deal: His Private Life and Public Career.* Cambridge, Mass.: Harvard University Press, 1985. Looks at the career of Ickes as the temperamental interior secretary and head of the Public Works Administration in the context of the New Deal.

SEE ALSO: 1924, Coolidge Is Elected President; 1928, Smith-Hoover Campaign; 1929, Stock Market Crash; 1932, Reconstruction Finance Corporation Is Created; 1932, Bonus March; 1932, Franklin D. Roosevelt Is Elected President; 1933, The Hundred Days; 1933, Tennessee Valley Authority Is Established; 1933, National Industrial Recovery Act; 1934, The Dust Bowl; 1935, Black Monday; 1935, National Labor Relations Act; 1935, Social Security Act; 1937, Supreme Court Packing Fight; 1938, Fair Labor Standards Act; 1939, Mobilization for World War II.

1935 ■ BLACK MONDAY: *a business-oriented Supreme Court renders a series of decisions that undermine the New Deal*

DATE: May 27, 1935
LOCALE: Washington, D.C.
CATEGORIES: Court cases; Economics
KEY FIGURES:
Louis D. Brandeis (1856-1941),
Pierce Butler (1866-1939),

Benjamin N. Cardozo (1870-1938),
Willis Van Devanter (1859-1941),
James C. McReynolds (1862-1946),
Owen J. Roberts (1875-1955),
Harlan Fiske Stone (1872-1946), and
George Sutherland (1862-1942), associate justices
Charles Evans Hughes (1862-1948), chief justice of the United States
Franklin Delano Roosevelt (1882-1945), thirty-second president of the United States, 1933-1945

SUMMARY OF EVENT. In the spring of 1935, Franklin Delano Roosevelt was in the last year of his first term as president of the United States. He had taken office in 1933 and had labored to end the Great Depression, which had begun with the stock market crash of October, 1929. His initiatives had resulted in an unprecedented assertion of presidential power and made inevitable a conflict with the United States Supreme Court. Decisions on the constitutionality of legislation and executive action are based on nine sitting judges' interpretation of the U.S. Constitution, a document written in general terms at a time when the complexities of twentieth century governing bodies could not have been imagined.

The president received what he may not have recognized as a portent on January 7, 1935, when the Court ruled unconstitutional the provision of the National Industrial Recovery Act (NIRA) by which the president could prohibit interstate transportation of oil exceeding production quotas. By an eight-to-one vote, the Court ruled that the president had usurped legislative power—a violation of the first section of Article I of the Constitution.

By May, it began to be clear that the NIRA as a whole was in trouble. As often happens, the Court was considering a case that on the surface seemed to have small and merely local interest: violations of the Live Poultry Code by a Long Island firm that supplied chickens for New York-area kosher markets. The code was part of the National Recovery Administration's code-making authority, through which the Roosevelt Administration was striving to pull the nation out of the Great Depression.

While the administration awaited the decision on this matter, the Court, by a five-to-four margin, on May 6 declared the Railroad Retirement Act of 1934 a violation of the Fifth Amendment property rights of the railroads, because the law required that the railroads (as well as their employees) contribute to the retirement fund. Retirement, said the Court, had nothing to do with the government's legal right to regulate interstate commerce. Because the Roosevelt Administration was keenly interested in a much larger retirement program that had not yet passed the Senate—the one familiar today as Social Security—the decision on the railroad pension arrangement threatened Social Security even before it could be enacted.

Three weeks later, on Monday, May 27—a day that came to be known as Black Monday—the Court handed down a series of decisions. The first, crucial one unanimously declared that

President Roosevelt had acted unconstitutionally by removing a Republican appointee, William E. Humphrey, from the Federal Trade Commission (FTC) without cause. From the president's point of view, the cause was clear enough: Humphrey had been obstructing Roosevelt's policies at the FTC. In its decision, the Court in effect reversed a 1916 decision that had justified a similar exercise of presidential power.

Next, an amendment to the National Bankruptcy Act that aimed at relieving farmers who had defaulted on their mortgages was unanimously ruled in violation of the "due process" clause of the Fifth Amendment. Although not, strictly speaking, a part of Roosevelt's New Deal, the act had been signed into law the year before. Here again, the Court was hedging the combined legislative power of Congress and the president and making it more difficult to deal with the economic crisis.

Finally, in the case of *Schechter Poultry Corporation v. United States*—the "sick chicken" case, as some had termed it—Chief Justice Charles Evans Hughes read a unanimous decision in favor of the former. The conviction of the Schecter brothers by a lower court for selling diseased poultry was thrown out, because the Supreme Court ruled the applicable federal code was an unconstitutional delegation of legislative power to the executive branch. This decision was significant because it voided the hundreds of other NIRA codes. Again, the previously accepted power to regulate interstate commerce was abridged. Only activities that the Court considered as having direct effects on interstate commerce could be regulated.

This decision dealt a devastating blow to the administration's recovery program. While opponents of the New Deal rejoiced, many industries that appeared destined to be affected by the decision had much to worry about. The textile manufacturers of New England, for example, now were stripped of possible government protection from Southern competitors who paid significantly lower wages. More than anything else, it was that aspect of the decision abridging government's power to regulate interstate commerce that made May 27 Black Monday, for the Court's narrow interpretation of "interstate" in the interests of local industry suggested that the Court viewed most of what had commonly been regarded as interstate commerce as only indirectly interstate. If all industry was local, because it occurred in a particular locality, the government would be virtually powerless to effect economic recovery nationally.

The Court was acting sincerely as guardian of the Constitution, but its decisions were standing between the New Deal and the economic recovery that everyone wanted but that the federal government alone seemed in a position to promote. A decisive majority in Congress had been willing to accept the NIRA codes, but Hughes argued that the legislative branch had no right to abdicate or transfer to the executive the powers constitutionally vested in Congress.

At issue also was the matter of emergency powers. The issue had come before the Court in 1934 in *Home Building and Loan Association v. Blaisdell*, when the judgment had suggested that emergencies justified enlargement of the government's ordinary constitutional powers. In the eyes of Roosevelt and his aides, the economic situation in 1935 constituted a national emergency, but the Hughes court seemed to back away from that opinion in the Black Monday decisions. One possible explanation for this seeming inconsistency is the common background of the Court's members at this time. The Court was split then, as it often is, between philosophical liberals and conservatives, but the fact that eight of the nine justices had backgrounds in corporate law disposed even relative liberals, such as Louis Brandeis and Harlan Stone, to affirm the property rights of business interests. In the eyes of the administration, the Court's stalwart defense of these property rights was blocking attempts to protect the livelihoods of millions of jobless people, many of whom had already lost all the property they owned.

Far from being discouraged by the Court's most recent actions, President Roosevelt called a news conference four days later in which he attacked the Court's "horse-and-buggy definition of interstate commerce." Shortly thereafter, his administration began to redesign the National Recovery Administration programs to evade similar Supreme Court obstructions of the New Deal in the future. The Court, however, continued to strike at pillars of his reforms, such as the Agricultural Adjustment Act; Justice Owen Roberts delivered the majority decision in January, 1936, again employing the argument that the government was trying to regulate local enterprises that fell under the jurisdiction of the states.

The tide began to turn in 1937. Despite stern popular opposition to Roosevelt's attempt to "pack" the Court with his own appointees by raising the number of justices, the now more circumspect Court upheld the Wagner National Labor Relations Act and the Social Security Act, two of the most vital reforms to emerge from Roosevelt's second term. In that year, the first of Roosevelt's nemeses on the Court, Roberts, retired. By 1941, the president had named replacements for all but one of the 1935 justices.

—*Robert P. Ellis*

ADDITIONAL READING:

Cope, Alfred Haines, and Fred Krinsky, eds. *Franklin D. Roosevelt and the Supreme Court*. Boston: D. C. Heath, 1952. Contains a variety of relevant writings fro the 1930's, including selections from primary sources.

Davis, Kenneth S. *F.D.R.: The New Deal Years, 1933-1937—A History*. New York: Random House, 1986. Part of a multivolume biography, this book offers a carefully documented and evenhanded account of the series of clashes between President Roosevelt and the Supreme Court.

Hendel, Samuel. *Charles Evans Hughes and the Supreme Court*. New York: King's Crown Press, 1951. A study of the man who, as chief justice, epitomized judicial opposition to New Deal innovations. Contains extended discussion of Black Monday as viewed by Supreme Court justices.

Jackson, Percival E. *Dissent in the Supreme Court: A Chronology*. Norman: University of Oklahoma Press, 1969. Discusses dissents of Justices Hughes and Cardozo in two of the 1935 cases.

Leuchtenburg, William. *The Supreme Court Reborn: The Constitutional Revolution in the Age of Roosevelt*. New York: Oxford University Press, 1995. Although focused on developments in Roosevelt's second term, this work includes detailed chapters on the Black Monday railroad pension decision and the Humphrey case.

SEE ALSO: 1924, Coolidge Is Elected President; 1928, Smith-Hoover Campaign; 1929, Stock Market Crash; 1932, Reconstruction Finance Corporation Is Created; 1932, Bonus March; 1932, Franklin D. Roosevelt Is Elected President; 1933, The Hundred Days; 1933, Tennessee Valley Authority Is Established; 1933, National Industrial Recovery Act; 1934, The Dust Bowl; 1935, Works Progress Administration Is Established; 1935, National Labor Relations Act; 1935, Social Security Act; 1937, Supreme Court Packing Fight; 1938, Fair Labor Standards Act; 1939, Mobilization for World War II.

1935 ■ NATIONAL LABOR RELATIONS ACT:
the federal government accepts the right of labor to use collective bargaining, marking the birth of "big labor"

DATE: July 5, 1935
LOCALE: Washington, D.C.
CATEGORIES: Business and labor; Economics; Laws and acts
KEY FIGURES:
Lloyd K. Garrison (1897-1991), first head of the temporary National Labor Relations Board and supporter of the Wagner Act
Hugh Samuel Johnson (1882-1942), administrator of the National Recovery Administration
Donald Randall Richberg (1881-1960), successor to Johnson and opponent of the Wagner Act
Franklin Delano Roosevelt (1882-1945), thirty-second president of the United States, 1933-1945
Robert Ferdinand Wagner (1877-1953), Democratic senator from New York and sponsor of the National Labor Relations Act

SUMMARY OF EVENT. A commonly repeated fallacy relative to the New Deal is that Franklin Delano Roosevelt, almost immediately after his inauguration in 1933, turned his back on the nation's business interests and instead cultivated and indulged those of labor. This misleading bit of fiction would have one believe that the president gave organized labor immense power in exchange for its support at the polls. The weakness of this interpretation becomes apparent when one studies the creation of what is described as the "Magna Carta of modern unionism." The National Labor Relations Act (Wagner-Connery Act), mainly the work of Senator Robert F. Wagner of New York. Its adoption must be credited more to Wagner's perseverance than to any support received from the president or his administration.

When the New Deal started, organized labor was in serious retreat. During the 1920's, a combination of general prosperity, vigorous business attacks, and weak leadership had seriously depleted the ranks of trade unions. The Depression was merely an additional burden. The union movement achieved a small victory on March 23, 1932, when Congress passed the Norris-La Guardia Act, which prohibited courts from granting management injunctions against union activities. The law, interpreted as disallowing employers from proscribing workers from becoming involved in union activities, had no teeth, however.

In 1933, the National Industrial Recovery Act (NIRA) included a provision requiring all industries submitting codes to the government to pledge themselves to the recognition of labor's right to collective bargaining. In practice, however, this section proved worthless, because of the promotion of company unions and the plurality of bargaining units in any one industry.

The main difficulty in reforming NIRA's labor policy was the attitude of the Roosevelt Administration. General Hugh S. Johnson, administrator of the National Recovery Administration (NRA), looked upon strikes in a code industry as similar to treason. Both Johnson and Roosevelt believed that business recovery had first priority. The president hardly could be described as pro-union but rather as reflecting a paternalistic approach. He sympathized with the worker, but he apparently had no desire to use the federal government to build up the strength of unions.

Labor grew increasingly restive under this situation, and during 1934, a number of serious strikes broke out. Senator Wagner, a leading union supporter, recognized the ineffectiveness of the NIRA's labor provision and took steps to remedy this condition. he succeeded in establishing a National Labor Board to hear grievances of workers and was named by Johnson to head the body. However, this board had no power to execute its decisions. Wagner believed that the situation was critical, because in his mind, economic recovery and stability could come only when the U.S. worker shared extensively in the benefits of increased productivity. The only hope for the survival of capitalism, in his opinion, was a complete redistribution of wealth. Wagner was convinced that this redistribution would come about only when the worker had gained the power of collective bargaining, and that this level of trade unionism could develop only with the assistance of the federal government.

In March, 1934, Wagner introduced a bill into Congress to prevent unfair labor practices and to put teeth into the labor provisions of the NIRA. The president, however, was not inclined to support such a measure. Instead, on June 29, 1934, he established the National Labor Relations Board to replace the NRA's National Labor Board. Lloyd K. Garrison, dean of the Wisconsin Law School, was appointed chairman. Designed to hear workers' grievances, the board depended upon the cooperation of the NRA and the Department of Justice for its effectiveness. By November, 1934, most people realized that the board was useless. Neither General Johnson nor his successor, Donald R. Richberg, indicated any intention of cooperating with the board. Recovery was still most important, and the administration theme was cooperation with business.

The congressional election of 1934 swept away the right wing of the Republican Party. With the failure of the temporary National Labor Relations Board, the American Federation of Labor, finally recognizing the importance of Wagner's efforts in Congress, began a gigantic lobbying campaign. Finally, the Supreme Court appeared to be no longer hostile to New Deal legislation.

Senator Wagner now moved to resubmit his original bill. With the support of both Biddle and Garrison, and aided by the effective lobby of the American Federation of Labor, Wagner introduced a measure in the Senate in February, 1935. It had a number of important provisions. First, all workers employed in industries that were engaged in interstate commerce were to be granted the right to join a union of their own choice and to bargain collectively. Second, the union that won majority support in a secret ballot election was to be granted sole bargaining privileges in that industry. Third, employers would be required to reorganize this union and to bargain in good faith. Fourth, the existing National Labor Relations Board was to be reestablished as an independent agency with the power to conduct elections to determine bargaining units and to prevent certain unfair labor practices by means of subpoenas, cease and desist orders, and court action. Fifth, to implement provisions of the act, management was asked to engage in affirmative action, a new term that was understood to mean that the burden of voluntary compliance was on management, such as reinstating workers with back pay who had been discharged from engaging in union activity, now protected by the law. The term next appeared in the text of Executive Order 10925, which President John F. Kennedy issued in 1961, requiring contractors to desegregate voluntarily as a condition of doing business with the federal government.

The bill had a stormy but quick passage through Congress. A number of Southern senators attempted to persuade Roosevelt to intervene against the bill, but Wagner succeeded in keeping the White House neutral. Business interests insisted that the bill threatened U.S. recovery. Violent opposition also came from the American Communist Party. Despite this opposition and the lack of backing from the Roosevelt Administration, the bill passed the Senate by a vote of 63 to 12.

One week later, on May 24, 1935, Roosevelt belatedly announced his support for the Wagner Bill. Three days after that, the Supreme Court declared the NIRA unconstitutional. It is still not clear why Roosevelt decided to come to the support of Wagner at that time. It is probably that, being a political realist, he was impressed by the wide margin by which the bill passed the Senate. On June 27, 1935, with backing from the administration, the bill easily passed the House by voice vote, and on July 5, 1935, Roosevelt signed it. The Wagner Act meant that the federal government was now behind the drive for the unionization of U.S. labor. Coming at the same time that labor itself was undergoing the internal revolution that spawned the militant Congress of Industrial Organizations, the National Labor Relations Act symbolized the birth of "big labor."

Soon after the Wagner Act passed, a challenge appeared in federal court. In *National Labor Relations Board v. Jones & Laughlin Steel Corporation* (1937), the act was declared unconstitutional. Nevertheless, guarantees in the National Labor Relations Act have been whittled down by two major amendments—the Labor Management Relations Act (Taft-Hartley Act) of 1947 and the Labor-Management Reporting and Disclosure Act (Landrum-Griffin Act) of 1959.

With the decline in union membership in the 1980's, the heyday of the National Labor Relations Act seems in the distant past. Formed primarily to protect workers with limited educational backgrounds, whose employment alternatives were limited, the union movement since has been diminished because many workers have enough education to shift jobs, and work requiring less educational preparation either is being replaced by machines or is being exported by multinational corporations to less developed countries at significantly lower wages. —*George Q. Flynn, updated by Michael Haas*

ADDITIONAL READING:

Bernstein, Irving. *The New Deal Collective Bargaining Policy*. Berkeley: University of California Press, 1950. A history of the National Labor Relations Act of 1935.

Derber, Milton, and Edwin Young, eds. *Labor and the New Deal*. Madison: University of Wisconsin Press, 1957. Ten essays on labor during the Roosevelt years, showing that union pressure and political pragmatism were more responsible for favorable New Deal attitudes toward labor than was ideology.

Hardin, Patrick, ed. *The Developing Labor Law*. 3d ed. Chicago: Bureau of National Affairs, 1992. Compiled by the American Bar Association's Section on Labor and Employment Law, this book provided the most comprehensive statement of rights under the National Labor Relations Act.

Millis, Harry A., and Emily C. Brown. *From the Wagner Act to Taft-Hartley: A Study of National Labor Policy and Labor Relations*. Chicago: University of Chicago Press, 1950. A general survey of legislation and government policy toward labor from 1932 to 1947.

SEE ALSO: 1924, Coolidge Is Elected President; 1928, Smith-Hoover Campaign; 1929, Stock Market Crash; 1932, Reconstruction Finance Corporation Is Created; 1932, Bonus March; 1932, Franklin D. Roosevelt Is Elected President; 1933, The Hundred Days; 1933, Tennessee Valley Authority Is Established; 1933, National Industrial Recovery Act; 1934, The Dust Bowl; 1935, Works Progress Administration Is Established; 1935, Black Monday; 1935, Social Security Act; 1935, Congress of Industrial Organizations Is Founded; 1937, Supreme Court Packing Fight; 1938, Fair Labor Standards Act; 1939, Mobilization for World War II; 1955, AFL and CIO Merge.

1935 ■ SOCIAL SECURITY ACT: *authorization of the United States' first national program of economic protection during retirement, unemployment, and disability*

DATE: August 14, 1935
LOCALE: Washington, D.C.
CATEGORIES: Economics; Laws and acts; Social reform
KEY FIGURES:
Frances Perkins (1882-1965), secretary of labor and chair of the Committee on Economic Security
Franklin Delano Roosevelt (1882-1945), thirty-second president of the United States, 1933-1945
Francis Everett Townsend (1867-1960), leader of a private lobby for the establishment of a federal old-age pension
SUMMARY OF EVENT. Although Social Security in the United States is most often associated with a program for older, re-tired persons, the creators of the 1935 legislation viewed old-age dependency in the larger context of major changes in the economy and in family structure. They tended to believe that if economic security could be assured to the oldest members of society, such security could also be made a reality for other citizens. The original legislation did not profess to solve deep structural problems of unemployment and poverty—it was designed to provide the first links in the safety net that would protect U.S. citizens from future economic disasters. From the beginning, social welfare programs reflected an uncertainty of purpose between adequacy—a concept that benefits should be based on the needs of the recipients, and equity—a notion that benefits should reflect contributions made by the participants.

By the 1930's, most of the nations of Western Europe had enacted some kind of social insurance legislation providing for old-age care and unemployment compensation. For a number of reasons, however, the United States had lagged behind in such efforts. It was not until the administration of Franklin Delano Roosevelt that the United States adopted an effective social security measure. The general economic de-pression of the decade undoubtedly contributed to the momen-tum needed to pass social security legislation, for during the Great Depression, many people in the United States came to see economic insecurity as a social problem, not merely a matter of individual virtue and responsibility. By 1934, con-siderable support had developed for utopian schemes, such as that developed by Dr. Francis E. Townsend, whose Old-Age Revolving Pension Club was lobbying for a monthly grant of two hundred dollars for every citizen over sixty years of age.

There was nothing radical about a plan for old-age pen-sions. Both private pensions and veterans' benefits existed long before the New Deal. Partly because such plans proved inadequate during the Depression, the Democratic platform of 1932 called for public retirement pensions and for unemploy-ment compensation. By the 1930's, almost half the states had some kind of old-age pension, but these were generally limited in scope. Only Wisconsin had a working unemployment com-pensation plan. In 1932, Senator Robert F. Wagner of New York and Representative David J. Lewis of Maryland intro-duced bills in Congress calling for a federal unemployment plan patterned after that of Wisconsin. The same year, Senator Clarence C. Dill of Washington and Representative William P. Connery of Massachusetts introduced a bill providing for fed-eral grants to those states establishing old-age pensions.

It was not until 1934 that President Roosevelt decided to take the initiative in the field of social insurance legislation. He asked Congress to delay action on the existing bills while he appointed a special committee to look into all aspects of social security, with the aim of presenting a comprehensive measure at the 1935 congressional session. In June, 1934, he established the Committee on Economic Security, with Secre-tary of Labor Frances Perkins as chair. Perkins took a broad view of her job and aimed to bring U.S. social insurance up to that of advanced European countries. She soon discovered, however, that there were divergent opinions, especially on the subject of how unemployment compensation should be han-dled. The debate centered on whether the compensation should be strictly a national operation. On one side of the question stood a group of Wisconsin social workers, such as Paul Rauschenbush and his wife Elizabeth Brandeis Rauschenbush. They advocated a joint state-national plan that would allow for greater experimentation and variety. They also pointed out that a joint approach would be more likely to meet constitutional objections. Others, such as Rexford G. Tugwell, Abraham Epstein, former secretary of the American Association of Old-Age Security, and Professor Paul Douglas of the University of Chicago recommended a solely national system to avoid un-equal coverage and protect the highly mobile U.S. worker. Perkins sided with the Wisconsin group, and the final recom-mendation of the committee followed the decentralized ap-proach: unemployment compensation would be financed by a federal tax on total payrolls, with 90 percent of the tax going to the states to implement the program. The report also advocated a contributory national program of old-age pensions. Roose-velt accepted the committee's report.

The Social Security bill was submitted to Congress in Janu-ary, 1935, by Senator Wagner and Congressman Lewis. The air was filled with warnings that the act would destroy in-dividual responsibility and the principles of self-help, but it was passed in the Senate by 76 votes to 6, and in the House by 371 votes to 33. On August 14, 1935, Roosevelt signed the measure.

Money to fund the old-age insurance plan was to come from a tax to be levied on employees' wages and employers' pay-rolls. Benefits would be payable at sixty-five years of age. The unemployment compensation provisions followed the recom-mendations of the Perkins Committee. In addition, the federal government would extend grants to the states for the care of the destitute elderly not covered by Social Security, and pro-vide aid on a matching basis to states for the care of dependent mothers, children, and the blind, and for public health services.

A Social Security Board was set up to administer the various provisions of the act.

While clearly innovative for its time, the Social Security Act was considered inadequate by many of its planners. The idea that a worker should pay one-half the cost of his own retirement stopped far short of most of the European plans. As Tugwell pointed out in 1934, the worker would already be paying a disproportionate share as a consumer, because the employer's payroll tax in the program would immediately be passed on in the form of higher prices. Roosevelt defended the payroll tax by pointing to the political strength it gave the program. Because workers contributed to the pension fund, they built up equity in it. The sense that workers had earned a right to future benefits would make it difficult, if not impossible, for subsequent administrations to deny coverage or to dismantle the program. A weak feature of the law was its

limited scope: It omitted farmworkers and domestics from unemployment compensation and contained no health insurance provisions of any kind. The law also reflected the assumptions of its framers that men were the principal wage earners and that women were economically dependent. Nevertheless, the act represented the beginning of a growing belief that the federal government had a responsibility to ensure certain benefits to its citizens. It provided a floor of basic economic protection and a greater level of uniformity of assistance among the states.

By the end of the twentieth century, a number of problems in the social security system demanded attention. Since the system began, a large workforce contributed payroll taxes to support payments to a relatively small number of retirees. As the large number of "baby boomers"—those born in the two decades following World War II—reached retirement age,

Needy elderly were able to apply for aid at the local Public Welfare Office after passage of the Social Security Act of 1935. The act created a safety net that saved many elderly from destitution and public institutions; in the latter half of the twentieth century, unprecedented population growth and budget deficits threatened the system's survival. (National Archives)

however, the proportion of citizens eligible for benefits increased more rapidly than the workforce. Amendments to the Social Security Act passed in 1983 anticipated the situation and raised taxes to create a surplus of funds in the system, but the program was still foreseen to be depleted by the year 2030. Younger workers feared that the social security system would be bankrupt before they became eligible for benefits.

Although most politicians were reluctant to propose major changes in the popular program, several types of reforms were suggested, including privatization of the system by allowing workers to invest in their own retirement accounts, thereby abolishing the social security trust fund. Others advocated a series of more modest changes: diverting some of the payroll taxes into savings accounts, increasing payroll taxes in small increments, raising the retirement age, limiting cost-of-living adjustments, or a combination of these.

—*George Q. Flynn, updated by Mary Welek Atwell*

ADDITIONAL READING:

Achenbaum, W. Andrew. *Social Security: Visions and Revisions*. New York: Cambridge University Press, 1986. Discusses the evolution and adaptation of the social security system in the face of changing economic and demographic realities.

Berkowitz, Edward D. *America's Welfare State: From Roosevelt to Reagan*. Baltimore: The Johns Hopkins University Press, 1991. Interprets the development and history of Social Security as a series of reasonable and pragmatic responses to political and economic conditions.

Haber, Carole, and Brian Gratton. *Old Age and the Search for Security: An American Social History*. Bloomington: Indiana University Press, 1993. Emphasizes the importance of Social Security in replacing intrafamilial support for the aged with an intergenerational public strategy.

Louchheim, Katie, ed. *The Making of the New Deal: The Insiders Speak*. Cambridge, Mass.: Harvard University Press, 1983. Includes an explanation of the social security legislation by its creators.

Miller, Dorothy C. *Women and Social Welfare: A Feminist Analysis*. New York: Praeger, 1990. Examines how social attitudes about the appropriate roles of men and women have had an impact on the structure of programs such as Social Security.

Perkins, Frances. *The Roosevelt I Knew*. New York: Viking Press, 1946. An insider's account of the debate over the provisions of the Social Security Act.

SEE ALSO: 1921, Sheppard-Towner Act; 1924, Coolidge Is Elected President; 1928, Smith-Hoover Campaign; 1929, Stock Market Crash; 1932, Reconstruction Finance Corporation Is Created; 1932, Bonus March; 1932, Franklin D. Roosevelt Is Elected President; 1933, The Hundred Days; 1933, Tennessee Valley Authority Is Established; 1933, National Industrial Recovery Act; 1934, The Dust Bowl; 1935, Works Progress Administration Is Established; 1935, Black Monday; 1935, National Labor Relations Act; 1937, Supreme Court Packing Fight; 1938, Fair Labor Standards Act; 1939, Mobilization for World War II.

1935 ■ NEUTRALITY ACTS: *strong isolationist sentiment during the 1930's prompts legislation to prevent foreign entanglements*

DATE: August 31, 1935-November 4, 1939
LOCALE: Washington, D.C.
CATEGORIES: Diplomacy and international relations; Laws and acts
KEY FIGURES:
William Edgar Borah (1865-1940), isolationist senator from Idaho
Cordell Hull (1871-1955), secretary of state
Hiram Warren Johnson (1866-1945), isolationist senator from California
Gerald Prentice Nye (1892-1971), isolationist senator from North Dakota
Franklin Delano Roosevelt (1882-1945), thirty-second president of the United States, 1933-1945

SUMMARY OF EVENT. Foreign policy was of secondary importance in the estimation of most people in the United States during the early 1930's, as the nation was preoccupied in the struggle to recover from the Depression. By 1935, however, a congressional movement had been initiated to formulate legislative safeguards that would prevent the United States from becoming involved in foreign entanglements. President Franklin D. Roosevelt and Secretary of State Cordell Hull supported such safeguards, so long as the chief executive retained discretionary power in their application. Ignoring the president's wishes, Congress passed a series of neutrality acts in 1935, 1936, 1937, and 1939, limiting presidential options. Although these acts demonstrated the strength of isolationist sentiment, they could not keep the United States out of a second world war.

The neutrality acts stemmed, in large part, from a reevaluation of the reasons for the United States' entry into World War I. Noteworthy in this regard was Senator Gerald P. Nye, a North Dakota Republican, who chaired the committee investigating the munitions industry and seeking evidence of possible economic pressures leading to the nation's involvement in World War I. Supported by a vigorous peace lobby in 1934, Nye dramatically publicized the thesis that the United States had been duped into entering World War I to assist unscrupulous armaments producers and bankers, so-called merchants of death, who stood to profit financially by an Allied victory. This conclusion strengthened an existing feeling that some kind of neutrality legislation, which included an arms embargo, was needed to prevent such a catastrophe in the future.

In March, 1935, with public opinion staunchly against involvement in any future war, Roosevelt asked the Nye Committee to study the neutrality question and formulate appropriate legislation. Entrusted with this new task, Nye and his colleagues proposed several resolutions, one of which prohibited the export of arms and ammunition to all belligerents.

Because Nye's resolutions did not give the president the authority to distinguish between aggressors and victims or to embargo the sale of arms to aggressors exclusively, Roosevelt had the Department of State draft legislation that did so. The State Department measure was lost when the Senate Foreign Relations Committee, dominated by two isolationist senators, William E. Borah of Idaho and Hiram W. Johnson of California, produced its own bill. The Foreign Relations Committee measure, approved by both the Senate and the House, was to last six months. It provided for an impartial arms embargo to nations engaged in a conflict recognized by the president, prohibited U.S. ships from carrying war materiel to belligerents, and recommended that U.S. citizens be warned against traveling on belligerent ships. Roosevelt opposed the mandatory embargo and regretted that the act did not apply to nonmunitions war materials. Nevertheless, he accepted the bill on August 31, fearing that a failure to do so would adversely affect domestic reforms then under consideration in Congress and believing that he could persuade the legislators to revise the act by the time it expired on February 29, 1936.

Unfortunately for Roosevelt, a State Department neutrality resolution of January 3, 1936, which gave the president discretionary authority to limit the sale of raw materials to belligerents, ran into serious opposition from Nye, Borah, Johnson, and other isolationists. With the expiration date of the 1935 measure fast approaching, Congress, in mid-February, passed a new act slightly more stringent than the first. Extending the basic provisions of the first act, the Second Neutrality Act also required the president to extend the arms embargo to any third party that became involved in a conflict and forbade loans by U.S. citizens to belligerents. Recognizing that there was no chance for the State Department measure and wary of creating an antiadministration issue in an election year, Roosevelt signed the Second Neutrality Act on February 29, 1936.

Like its predecessor, the Second Neutrality Act carried an expiration date: May 1, 1937. When Congress began to debate a new measure in early 1937, neither the wisdom of the basic principle of keeping the United States out of war nor the implementation of this goal through an arms embargo was questioned. As the nation emerged from the Depression, however, pressure mounted for some kind of compromise that would permit business as usual with Europe, even in wartime. Bernard M. Baruch, a noted financier, suggested that a practical solution would be a cash-and-carry formula. He reasoned that if U.S. businesses could sell goods, with the exception of arms, on the basis of immediate delivery and payment by the buyer, the risk of U.S. involvement in war would be minimized. Both Roosevelt and the advocates of strict neutrality favored the cash-and-carry plan, the president believing it would favor Great Britain, the European state controlling the sea. The new, permanent neutrality bill that emerged in April retained the mandatory embargo on arms, the ban on loans, and the prohibition on travel; but it gave the president discretion, until May 1, 1939, to place all belligerent trade except arms under the cash-and-carry formula. On May 1, the Third

Neutrality Act, having passed both the House and the Senate, was signed by Roosevelt.

Two months later, in the first test of this act, the futility of legislating for unforeseen diplomatic contingencies was revealed. In July, 1937, without a declaration of war, Japan launched a full-scale attack against China. Adherence to the neutrality act would work to the advantage of the aggressor, Japan, whose powerful navy dominated the seas off the coast of China. Therefore, Roosevelt made no official recognition of the conflict, and the neutrality act was not implemented in East Asia.

In the months that followed, Roosevelt had little reason to suspect that isolationism was losing strength. Public reaction to his call for collective security, given in his Chicago "Quarantine Speech" of October 5, 1937, was mixed. The Ludlow Amendment, requiring a favorable national referendum before a declaration of war, was only narrowly defeated in the House on January 10, 1938. Alarm in the United States at the ominous trend of events in Europe and the Far East must be attributed to the nation's relaxation of its policy of strict neutrality. In March, 1938, Adolf Hitler's Germany annexed Austria and began to make demands on Czechoslovakia. Meanwhile, the Japanese extended their aggression in China.

By the beginning of 1939, Roosevelt had concluded that the neutrality act of 1937 needed revision. On January 4, in his state of the union address, the president warned of increasing threats to peace and pointed out that U.S. neutrality laws could operate unfairly, giving aid to aggressors and denying it to victims. Although he knew that Congress would not agree to a discretionary arms embargo, Roosevelt hoped it might agree to modify the law allowing for the sale of arms on a cash-and-carry basis. While Germany and other aggressors would be eligible, the administration anticipated that Great Britain and France would benefit most, because of their control of the sea. In April, with the president's approval, Senator Key Pittman of Nevada introduced a resolution providing for the repeal of the arms embargo and the placing of all trade with belligerents on a cash-and-carry basis. Congress, under the influence of Borah, Johnson, and Nye, who were adamant in their opposition, rejected the proposal.

Congress' attitude toward a revision of the 1937 law changed after Germany's assault on Poland on September 1, 1939. Learning from discussions with a number of legislators that a repeal of the arms embargo might be possible, Roosevelt called Congress into special session on September 23. Reiterating his belief that the existing law aided aggression, the president requested that the sale of all goods, including arms, be placed on a cash-and-carry basis. By shrewdly courting Southern conservatives, dispensing patronage, and securing indefatigable public relations work by internationalists, the president succeeded in pushing his revision through Congress by a close vote. On November 4, 1939, Roosevelt signed the Fourth Neutrality Act, and the United States took its first step toward becoming the arsenal of democracy.

—George Q. Flynn, updated by Bruce J. DeHart

ADDITIONAL READING:

Cole, Wayne S. *Roosevelt and the Isolationists, 1932-1945*. Lincoln: University of Nebraska Press, 1983. Discusses the relationship between Roosevelt and the isolationists from the perspective of the latter.

Dallek, Robert. *Franklin D. Roosevelt and American Foreign Policy, 1932-1945*. New York: Oxford University Press, 1995. Defends Roosevelt's foreign policy, showing the president as a master politician who had to consider both domestic and diplomatic objectives.

Davis, Kenneth S. *FDR: The New Deal Years, 1933-1937* and *FDR: Into the Storm, 1937-1940*. New York: Random House, 1986 and 1993. Volumes 2 and 3 of a multivolume biography bring to life the people and issues involved in the passage of the neutrality acts.

Divine, Robert A. *The Reluctant Belligerent: American Entry into World War II*. New York: John Wiley & Sons, 1965. Although older, this remains a valuable source of information about the neutrality acts.

SEE ALSO: 1917, Espionage and Sedition Acts; 1921, Scandals of the Harding Administration; 1921, Washington Disarmament Conference; 1928, Kellogg-Briand Pact; 1932, Hoover-Stimson Doctrine; 1933, Good Neighbor Policy; 1937, Embargo on Arms to Spain; 1941, Lend-Lease Act; 1941, Bombing of Pearl Harbor; 1941, Germany and Italy Declare War on the United States.

1935 ■ CONGRESS OF INDUSTRIAL ORGANIZATIONS IS FOUNDED: *a militant congress of trade unions organizes both skilled and unskilled workers regardless of race or gender*

DATE: November 10, 1935
LOCALE: United States
CATEGORIES: Business and labor; Organizations and institutions; Social reform
KEY FIGURES:
David Dubinsky, head of the International Ladies' Garment Workers
William Green (1873-1952), president of the American Federation of Labor
William L. Hutcheson, head of the Carpenters' Union
John Llewellyn Lewis (1880-1969), president of the United Mine Workers
Homer Martin (1901-1968), president of the United Auto Workers
Frank Murphy (1890-1949), Democratic governor of Michigan
Philip Murray (1886-1952), head of the Steel Workers' Organizing Committee
Myron C. Taylor (1874-1959), chairman of the board of the United States Steel Corporation

SUMMARY OF EVENT. The struggle which produced the Congress of Industrial Organizations (CIO) revolved around a disagreement over labor tactics and philosophy. The American Federation of Labor (AFL), founded in 1886, was organized on a craft basis and did not include the skilled and unskilled workers in mass production industries. By 1934, however, some members of the AFL wanted to form one union for an entire industry to include these mass production workers. To William Green, president of the AFL, and the generally conservative members of its executive council, industrial unionism was associated with violence and radicalism. Leadership in the move for more militant unionism came primarily from John L. Lewis, president of the United Mine Workers and vice president of the AFL. Lewis criticized the voluntarism preached by Green and argued that it was imperative that the AFL become active in politics and in industrial unionism. Sidney Hillman, president of the Amalgamated Clothing Workers, and David Dubinsky of the International Ladies' Garment Workers were the other leading figures in this insurgency.

At the 1934 convention of the AFL, Lewis and other industrial union supporters succeeded in receiving an endorsement for the chartering of unions in a number of industries, including auto and rubber. In addition, there had been a promise made to organize steel. However, little was done in the following months to implement the resolution. The next year, the AFL leadership rejected appeals for help in instituting a more active movement among the industrial workers. Lewis addressed the convention, pleading to "organize the unorganized" and thereby make the AFL the "greatest instrumentality . . . to befriend the cause of humanity." His resolution failed by a substantial majority. The frustrated Lewis confronted the head of the Carpenters' Union, William L. Hutcheson, who was quelling dissent among some of the workers, and started a fistfight. Lewis knocked Hutcheson to the floor, disrupting the convention; afterward, a new image became popularized of a "battling Lewis" who fought for industrial organizing.

Rebuffed by the convention, Lewis, Hillman, and others proceeded to meet separately, and on November 10, 1935, they formed what was originally called the Committee for Industrial Organization. Ostensibly this group was working within the AFL to promote organization of the mass production industries. Green and his executive council, however, quickly concluded that such activity was in disregard of majority AFL sentiment as expressed at the convention and could easily lead to dual unionism. An order went out from the council calling upon the Committee for Industrial Organization to disband. The unions now involved in this revolt included the United Mine Workers, the United Auto Workers, the Amalgamated Clothing Workers, the United Textile Workers, the International Ladies' Garment Workers, and some five smaller organizations. The AFL request was ignored, and in August, 1936, the entire group was suspended. A peace conference between Green and Lewis was arranged, but it collapsed—a result primarily of the latter's uncompromising attitude. In March,

1937, the insurgent group was formally expelled from the AFL. Green also announced that the AFL itself would begin an immediate campaign to organize the mass production industries. In 1938, Lewis' group changed its name to the Congress of Industrial Organizations (CIO).

The decision of the AFL to move into mass production industry unionism was probably prompted by the remarkable success of the CIO. Initially the insurgent unions had approximately 1,800,000 members, but in seven months the CIO claimed to represent some 3,750,000 workers. This growth resulted from organizational victories in the steel and automobile industries. In 1935, Lewis appointed Philip Murray, vice president of the United Mine Workers, to head the Steel Workers' Organizing Committee. Before Murray could start activities, however, a crisis arose in the automobile industry which demanded attention from the CIO leadership. Under the AFL, the United Auto Workers (UAW) had been losing members, and local leadership was completely intimidated by management. In 1936, Homer Martin, a former minister, took over the union and began to work closely with the CIO. Although Lewis would have preferred to attack steel first, he rushed to the support of the now militant UAW when on December 28, 1936, it began a dramatic sit-down strike in the Flint, Michigan, plant of General Motors.

Although utilized on a limited scale before, the dramatic effect of thousands of men refusing to work but remaining in their plant took the public by surprise. Following normal procedure, General Motors immediately requested government assistance. An injunction was issued by a local judge, but the sheriff refused to serve it and was backed up by Michigan governor Frank Murphy, a Democrat who supported the rights of the workers and strove for a compromise settlement. Management, realizing that little support could be expected from Washington, constantly being prodded by Murphy to go to the bargaining table, and faced with a considerable loss of profits, decided to meet with the UAW. On February 11, 1937, a contract was signed providing for the dismissal of the injunction, recognition of the UAW as the sole bargaining unit, and procedures for collective bargaining on wages and hours. The other companies, with the exception of Ford, which held out until 1941, quickly fell into line.

In the meantime, Murray was conducting his campaign to organize the steel industry, though in the end steel was broken from the top down. Myron C. Taylor, chairman of the board of the United States Steel Corporation, desiring to avoid a work stoppage that would jeopardize a lucrative foreign contract and anticipating inevitable union recognition, invited Lewis to private talks that lasted for three months. The result was the signing of a contract on March 2, 1937, which granted union recognition, provided for a ten percent wage increase, a forty-hour week, and time-and-a-half for overtime. Many other companies followed Taylor's lead, but three of the "Little Steel" companies, under the moral leadership of Tom M. Girdler of Republic Steel, fought unionization successfully, culminating in the May 30, 1937, Memorial Day Massacre,

when union demonstrators were fired upon by police before the South Chicago plant of Republic Steel. It was not until World War II that the entire industry was finally "organized."

Nevertheless, within the space of one month, the CIO had achieved a remarkable victory over two huge industries which had long been immune to unionization. The drive of men such as Lewis, Murray, and Martin, and the reasonableness of men such as Taylor, were important in this advance. Yet, the attitude of the government on both the state and federal levels was also of critical importance. Without the fair-minded attitude and support of Governor Murphy, the UAW would have been driven from the General Motors plant. Although Lewis and President Franklin Roosevelt were soon to be enemies, the White House placed considerable pressure on the employers to negotiate. Finally, the work of the National Labor Relations Board and the revelations by a Senate subcommittee, headed by pro-labor senator Robert M. La Follette, Jr., of the unsavory antiunion tactics used by employers, helped the CIO to consolidate and expand its gains in the year ahead.

By the end of the 1930's, union membership had increased to 30 percent of all workers. The CIO's commitment and democratic initiatives to bring workers into the union organization regardless of skill, job, race, or sex, as well as a policy of inclusion on the part of the mass production industries, revolutionized unionization. Although not completely removed from discrimination, hundreds of thousands of black workers were able to join unions. Women, despite obstacles to their gaining key union leadership roles, nevertheless were instrumental in building the forces of the CIO, especially in issues specifically relating to women.

—George Q. Flynn, updated by Marilyn Elizabeth Perry

ADDITIONAL READING:

Dubofsky, Melvyn, and Warren Van Tine, eds. *Labor Leaders in America*. Urbana: University of Illinois Press, 1987. A collection of biographies on labor's most influential leaders, including Green, Lewis, and Murray.

Gabin, Nancy F. *Feminism in the Labor Movement: Women and the United Auto Workers, 1935-1975*. Ithaca, N.Y.: Cornell University Press, 1990. The contributions made by women to building the CIO.

Galenson, Walter. *The CIO Challenge to the AFL: A History of the American Labor Movement, 1935-1941*. Cambridge, Mass.: Harvard University Press, 1960. The history of the CIO in what the author calls a revolutionary era marked by a radical change in the power structure of American labor.

Howe, Irving, and B. J. Widick. *The UAW and Walter Reuther*. New York: Random House, 1949. Study of a leading figure in the founding of the CIO who continued to be active until his untimely death in 1970.

Zieger, Robert H. *The CIO, 1935-1955*. Chapel Hill: University of North Carolina Press, 1995. The history of the CIO prior to its merger with the AFL, incorporating archival records and oral histories

SEE ALSO: 1886, American Federation of Labor Is Founded; 1929, Great Depression; 1935, National Labor Relations Act; 1938, Fair Labor Standards Act; 1943, Inflation and Labor Unrest; 1955, AFL and CIO Merge.

1936 ■ RECIPROCITY TREATY: *the first reciprocal trade agreement between the United States and Canada since 1854*

DATE: November 11, 1936
LOCALE: United States and Canada
CATEGORIES: Canadian history; Diplomacy and international relations; Economics; Treaties and agreements
KEY FIGURES:
Cordell Hull (1871-1955), U.S. secretary of state
William Lyon Mackenzie King (1874-1950), Liberal Canadian prime minister
Franklin Delano Roosevelt (1881-1945), thirty-second president of the United States, 1933-1945

SUMMARY OF EVENT. A reciprocal trade agreement between two nations provides for both countries to reduce tariffs on trade goods. Such agreements between the United States and Canada date to 1854. British diplomats had begun negotiations with Washington two years earlier. They were unable to reach a conclusion at the time, however, because of a dispute over fishing rights off the eastern coast of Canada. Negotiations continued until the fisheries dispute was resolved and a reciprocity treaty was signed on June 6, 1854. This treaty allowed fishermen from the United States the right to catch fish in the Atlantic coastal fisheries off Newfoundland, which were then the richest fishing grounds in the world. British fishing boats were granted permission to operate in U.S. coastal waters off Maine. The agreement also created a list of free goods, such as timber, wheat, and corn, that both countries would not tax. Trade increased rapidly after ratification of this treaty.

In 1866, because of complaints from U.S. farmers, the United States repealed its part of the agreement. The Civil War had ended a year earlier, which enabled many veterans to resume farming; they protested loudly against free importation of Canadian grain, so reciprocity was ended. The Canadians wanted a new agreement, however, and in 1871 sent a delegation to Washington, D.C., to open trade talks. Nothing came of the talks, and the 1871 Treaty of Washington barely mentioned reciprocity.

The issue was not raised again until 1911. Canada's finance minister, William S. Fielding, told the House of Commons that negotiations with the United States would begin immediately. The goal was to obtain as much free trade as possible, and Fielding suggested that once that was accomplished, the Canadian economy would flourish and unemployment would decline rapidly. A loud protest from workers and industrialists in Ontario indicated that many Canadians did not agree. These protesters argued that reciprocity and free trade would be a tremendous advantage for powerful industries in the United States, such as steel and textile companies, who would flood Canada with huge amounts of goods, driving Canadian industries into bankruptcy and costing thousands of jobs. Trade became the major issue in the election of that year. Conservatives denounced reciprocity in the campaign and won the election, bringing an end to discussions of free trade with the United States.

In 1923, both nations signed a treaty limiting halibut fishing off the coast of Washington and British Columbia, but reciprocity talks continued to flounder. Republican administrations in the United States wanted only one thing from the Canadians, an agreement to construct the St. Lawrence Seaway linking the Great Lakes with the Atlantic Ocean. This massive project would make it easier to ship grain from the Midwest to Europe and, it was hoped, greatly improve the prosperity of farmers in the region. By 1932, it seemed as if negotiations on this project were about completed. President Herbert Hoover signed an agreement in July with the Canadians, but the Senate was unable to get the two-thirds majority required by the Constitution for ratification. The major opposition came from senators opposed to the seaway's projected high costs. The seaway would not be constructed for another twenty-five years.

Canadian-U.S. relations improved greatly after the inauguration of President Franklin Delano Roosevelt in 1933. He promoted a Good Neighbor Policy with all nations in the Western Hemisphere, which included support for reciprocal trade agreements. Talks with Canada began in 1934 but were not concluded until two years later. Roosevelt had signed the Trade Agreements Act of 1934, significantly lowering tariffs on many items. This bilateral agreement was not satisfactory, however, to the newly elected Liberal government of Prime Minister William Lyon Mackenzie King. King, a fervent advocate of reciprocal trade agreements, led a delegation to Washington to discuss such an agreement with representatives of the Department of State. Secretary of State Cordell Hull headed the U.S. negotiating team.

Hull favored reducing trade restrictions with as many nations as possible, but he faced considerable criticism for his position within his own Democratic Party and especially from conservatives in the Republican Party. He knew it would be difficult to win the two-thirds majority vote in the Senate for approval of any bill reducing tariffs. Many conservatives in both parties thought higher tariffs rather than lower presented the best opportunity for protecting jobs. The Great Depression, they argued, made it necessary for countries to protect themselves from competition from outside states by building a high tariff wall.

The U.S. secretary of state wanted Canada and the United States to reach an agreement quickly. This, he explained to the Canadians, would demonstrate to the rest of the world, especially the Europeans, that persons of goodwill could still sit down and negotiate peacefully. The Germans, Italians, and Japanese seemed to prefer war or economic suicide to any attempt to discuss seriously the mutual sacrifices required by reciprocal trade treaties. The United States and Canada could show world leaders an alternate course for resolving economic problems. Friendly nations had to show that talking still could produce results. The fact that the King government recently had signed a bilateral agreement with the German Nazis angered Hull, but he indicated that it would not stand in the way of the current discussions. It was hoped that reciprocal trade agreements could reduce conflict in the world and provide an alternative to cut-throat methods of bilateral trading, with each nation looking out only for its own narrow self-interest.

Hull believed that unless freer world trade was provided for, the nations of Europe and the Far East would face continued economic strife and chaos. Economic disaster would affect all countries and bring about an even worse financial collapse than the Great Depression. Only a broad program to remove excessive trade barriers, he told the Canadian delegation, could save the situation. The world needed a policy of equal treatment for all nations and a method to promote and protect fair trade methods and practices. If nations such as the United States and Canada refused to take the first steps in this direction, catastrophic consequences awaited the peoples of the world.

Such warnings of the terrible consequences of failure encouraged a quick end to negotiations. The final result, the Reciprocal Trade Act of 1936, produced far fewer reductions in trade barriers than had been gained in 1854, but it proved satisfactory to both sides. The United States agreed to admit limited amounts of cream, cattle, lumber, and potatoes with significantly reduced rates. In return, Canada accepted more manufactured goods from the United States. Liberals hoped that this trade would produce higher incomes for Canadian farmers, loggers, and ranchers. They also predicted it would reduce Canada's economic dependence on the United States. As it turned out, it made little difference. Both policies, the high tariffs favored by Conservatives in the 1920's and the Liberal support for freer trade, had the same result: They increased Canadian economic dependence on the United States.

From 1923 to 1935, the period of the highest tariffs on U.S. manufactured goods, the number of U.S.-owned factories and businesses in Canada increased from 524 to 816. U.S. goods were kept out, but corporations bought the factories or built new ones in Canada rather than pay the increased rates. As one Canadian economist expressed the situation, it made little difference whether Canadians were buried by U.S. exports or U.S. branch plants—they would lose control of their economy either way. The 1936 agreement remained in effect until 1948, when both nations signed a general agreement that superseded prior trade treaties.
—*Leslie V. Tischauser*

ADDITIONAL READING:

Corbett, Percy E. *The Settlement of Canadian-American Disputes: A Critical Study of Meetings and Results*. New Haven: Conn.: Yale University Press, 1937. Covers treaty and tariff negotiations from the 1840's to 1936. Detailed discussion of trade policies of both nations.

McInnis, Edgar. *Canada: A Political and Social History*. Toronto: Holt, Rinehart and Winston, 1990. Contains a useful discussion of Canadian trade policy in the 1930's. Includes a brief discussion of the treaty.

U.S. Department of State. *British Dominions and Canada*. Vol. 1 in *Papers Relating to the Foreign Policy of the United States, 1936*. Washington, D.C.: Government Printing Office, 1951. Contains the complete record of the discussions and negotiations.

Welles, Sumner. *Seven Decisions That Shaped History*. New York: Harper, 1951. Discusses the secretary of state's views on trade relations and his belief that freer trade would prevent a future war. Written by a participant in the 1936 negotiations with Canada.

SEE ALSO: 1871, Treaty of Washington; 1924, Halibut Treaty; 1933, Good Neighbor Policy.

1937 ■ EMBARGO ON ARMS TO SPAIN: *the United States continues an isolationist foreign policy of disengagement and appeasement*

DATE: January 6, 1937
LOCALE: United States
CATEGORY: Diplomacy and international relations
KEY FIGURES:
Manuel Azaña y Diaz (1880-1940), president of the Spanish Republic
Francisco Franco (1892-1975), leader of the Nationalist forces rebelling against the Spanish Republic
Cordell Hull (1871-1955), secretary of state
Franklin Delano Roosevelt (1882-1945), thirty-second president of the United States, 1933-1945

SUMMARY OF EVENT. As the Depression of the 1930's deepened and economic hardship increased, most people in the United States, including President Franklin D. Roosevelt, placed major emphasis on domestic problems. In 1935, a neutrality law was passed that provided for a mandatory embargo of U.S. arms shipments to all belligerents. Despite U.S. desires, however, international events were developing in a way that eventually would frustrate any hopes of noninvolvement. In Europe, Adolf Hitler had begun his career in Germany and Benito Mussolini was elaborating the Fascist system that he had established for Italy in 1922. As the decade unfolded, it had become apparent that these nations were on the move, dissatisfied with the results of World War I and dedicated to a change in the status quo. The two main champions of the Treaty of Versailles, the settlement that had concluded the war, were England and France, both of which, because of numerous factors such as internal economic problems, were willing to accept a limited expansion on the part of both Germany and Italy as the best means of preserving peace.

It was in such a historical setting that the Spanish Civil War began in 1936. Seldom has a particular event represented the culmination of so many complex and long-range forces as did the decision of General Francisco Franco and his Nationalist forces to revolt against the Spanish Republic in July, 1936. Spain had become a republic in April, 1931, and was torn by dissension from the very beginning. In broad terms, by 1936, the Spanish Republic had come to represent the liberal, anti-clerical forces of the nation and was dedicated to agrarian reform and disestablishment of the Roman Catholic church. However, large segments of the population, represented by the army and monarchists on the right and by the Anarcho-Syndicalists on the left, rejected this republican government and by spring, 1936, civil disorder was widespread.

The immediate reaction of England and France to the civil war was the fear that it might spread into a general European conflict. To avoid this threat, France sponsored a British-authored plan for the establishment of a Non-Intervention Committee to see that the struggle in Spain remained localized. This solution soon developed into a farce, as Germany, Italy, and Russia—all members of the committee—began extending aid to different parties of the civil war. The amazing myopia of England and France, which were unwilling to acknowledge or to prevent this aid, can be explained by several factors: concerns that a leftist revolutionary Spain might open the door to social revolution and Soviet involvement in Western Europe, a desire not to permit relations with Fascist Italy to deteriorate further, and the haunting fear of a local war leading to a general European conflagration.

In the United States, events had once more demonstrated the futility of trying to legislate for all contingencies in international affairs. The Neutrality Act in force at that time made no mention of civil wars, and the Spanish Republic (Loyalists) immediately requested military aid from the United States. Even before England and France decided upon their Non-Intervention Committee, President Roosevelt and Secretary of State Cordell Hull had agreed that noninvolvement would be the best course for the United States to follow. Supporting this decision the Department of State was strictly neutralist, as were William Bullitt, the ambassador to France, and Joseph Kennedy in London, two heavy contributors to Roosevelt's electoral campaign. Urging support for the Loyalists was Ambassador Claude Bowers in Madrid, who warned that a fascist state in Spain could have a fascist "domino effect" in Latin America. Bowers' input into policy formulation was largely ignored by Roosevelt and Hull. The administration announced that, although not legally binding, the arms embargo should be considered as extending to the Spanish situation.

Roosevelt and Hull had many reasons for this action. This seemed an opportunity whereby the United States could act in unity with England and France to preserve the peace by promoting noninterference in Spain, and at the same time serve the cause of noninvolvement, the dominant attitude of Congress, the American people, and the administration. It would permit continuance of the policy of complete disengagement from situations involving foreign wars. This initial decision met with almost universal approval by the American people. Unfortunately, the unofficial embargo proved inadequate to the situation. The desire for profit led one entrepreneur to export \$2,777,000 worth of aircraft equipment to the Loyalists despite the disapproval of President Roosevelt, and it appeared that others were eager to follow this example. This situation forced the administration into requesting from Congress a special amendment to the existing Neutrality Act, which would legalize the embargo on arms to Spain. Passed on January 6, 1937, by overwhelming majorities in both houses, the joint resolution soon became the focal point for a vigorous national debate, as the tide of battle turned decidedly in favor of the Axis-supported Nationalists under Franco.

On January 9, 1937, a liberal weekly, *The Nation*, printed an editorial condemning the embargo resolution as being "pro-fascist neutrality." This particular line of reasoning soon was adopted by a wide segment of the American public, representing in most cases the liberal, professional, and well-educated classes. Ranged on the other side of the controversy were many who felt the embargo was a good assurance of U.S. noninvolvement, and a minority who were anxious for a Franco victory. Numerous U.S. public opinion polls during the period indicated that most people favored the Loyalists in the civil war, but an even larger majority favored noninvolvement. Of those groups most vigorous in support of retaining the embargo, an especially large number were Roman Catholics. During 1937 and 1938, the debate on the wisdom of the administration's policy continued. Liberal weeklies such as *The Nation* and *The New Republic* consistently debated the question with Catholic periodicals.

A concerted lobbying campaign was undertaken in the spring of 1938 to end the arms embargo. Twenty-eight hundred volunteers from the United States went to Spain to aide the Republic, most serving in the Lincoln and Washington Brigades. Some were African Americans such as Lincoln Brigade commander Oliver Law. About nine hundred Americans, including Law, died in Spain for the Republican cause. The embargo was never lifted, however, and by March, 1939, Franco was in complete control of Spain.

Many different theories have been advanced to explain why President Roosevelt failed to initiate a change in the embargo policy toward Spain. Some scholars assert that Roosevelt retained the embargo because he feared the alienation of Roman Catholic Democrats, a bulwark of the party. Others point to a divided cabinet and Roosevelt's ignorance about Spanish affairs. Still others emphasize that the president desired to cooperate with the noninvolvement policy of France and England. U.S. military aid to one side in the Spanish Civil War would have flouted the International Non-Intervention Committee and placed the United States in the company of Germany, Italy, and Russia. Finally, some authors assert that retention of the embargo was simply another reflection of the predominant attitude of isolationism that controlled U.S. opinion during the 1930's. —*George Q. Flynn, updated by Irwin Halfond*

ADDITIONAL READING:

Alpert, Michael. *A New International History of the Spanish Civil War*. London: Macmillan, 1994. A well-researched analysis of foreign policy formulation in the era of the Spanish Civil War.

Bolloten, Burnett. *The Spanish Civil War: Revolution and Counter-Revolution*. Chapel Hill: University of North Carolina Press, 1991. This extensively documented study uses new materials from the Spanish archives and is an end product of lifelong work on the topic.

Falcoff, Mark, and F. Pike, eds. *The Spanish Civil War, 1936-1939: American Hemispheric Perspectives*. Lincoln: University of Nebraska Press, 1982. A collection of scholarly analyses of reactions to the Spanish Civil War in the United States and major Latin American nations.

Little, Douglas. *Malevolent Neutrality: The U.S., Great Britain and the Origins of the Spanish Civil War*. Ithaca, N.Y.: Cornell University Press, 1985. Provides an in-depth, critical evaluation of motivations underlying U.S. foreign policy objectives during the Spanish Civil War.

Thomas, Hugh. *The Spanish Civil War*. Rev. ed. Harmondsworth, Middlesex, England: Penguin Books, 1977. An updated, expanded version of the highly readable seminal study of the war and its impact on both individual lives and nations.

Traina, Richard. *American Diplomacy and the Spanish Civil War*. Bloomington: Indiana University Press, 1968. Reprint. Westport, Conn.: Greenwood Press, 1980. A standard work on U.S. policy, which should be consulted for any research on the subject.

SEE ALSO: 1935, Neutrality Acts.

1937 ■ SUPREME COURT PACKING FIGHT: *the executive and judicial branches of the U.S. government confront each other over social legislation*

DATE: February 5-July 22, 1937
LOCALE: Washington, D.C.
CATEGORY: Government and politics
KEY FIGURES:
Homer S. Cummings (1870-1956), U.S. attorney general
Charles Evans Hughes (1862-1948), chief justice of the United States
Owen J. Roberts (1875-1955), associate justice in the Supreme Court
Joseph Taylor Robinson (1872-1937), senator from Arkansas
Franklin Delano Roosevelt (1882-1945), thirty-second president of the United States, 1933-1945
Burton Kendall Wheeler (1882-1975), senator from Montana
SUMMARY OF EVENT. In November, 1936, Franklin Roosevelt was returned to office by one of the widest election margins in history. Even conservative journalists spoke of a mandate for further New Deal reform. Indeed, the president's second inaugural address spoke of the problems with "one-third of a nation ill-housed, ill-clad, ill-nourished." In what was a surprise to many, including some members of his own party,

however, the president's first message to Congress on February 5, 1937, called not for social programs but for adjustments to the Supreme Court. By July, 1937, the president had been defeated in his attempts to reorganize the Court, and he was faced with the growing disintegration of congressional support for his other legislative initiatives.

If the public was surprised at the "court packing" proposal, the idea of judicial reform had long appealed to some members of the administration. A number of considerations led to Roosevelt's decision to place judicial reorganization ahead of social legislation. The Supreme Court, as then composed, favored a conservative interpretation of the Constitution, but the president and others had hoped that the Court would make allowances for the emergency atmosphere when considering New Deal legislation.

The Court which was sitting in judgment on Roosevelt's reform measures consisted of pre-New Deal appointees. Roosevelt had not had an opportunity to appoint a single justice during his first term. James C. McReynolds, George Sutherland, Willis Van Devanter, and Pierce Butler (known as the Four Horsemen) were all staunch conservatives who considered private property sacred and laissez-faire the best policy. The liberal wing of the Court consisted of Louis D. Brandeis, Benjamin N. Cardozo, and Harlan Fiske Stone. Chief Justice Charles Evans Hughes and Associate Justice Owen J. Roberts were both Republicans, and although they did not share the uncompromising laissez-faire attitude of the conservative bloc, they were reluctant to see an expansion of government involvement in the economy.

However, in 1935, the Court delivered a series of decisions which virtually overturned the early New Deal's recovery programs. In January, the Court, by an 8 to 1 vote, invalidated parts of the National Industrial Recovery Act (NIRA). At that point, the president was ready to attack the Court's power of judicial review publicly as "unconscionable" if they ruled against the government's power to regulate the currency in the Gold Clause cases. Confrontation was temporarily averted when the justices sustained the administration's monetary policy by a vote of 5 to 4. Three months later the Court, also dividing 5 to 4, declared the Railway Retirement Act of 1934 unconstitutional. New Dealers feared that their programs would be destroyed by a narrowly divided court, especially if Justice Owen Roberts, an unpredictable jurist, had permanently joined the conservatives.

Their worst fears were confirmed when, on Black Monday, May 17, the Court handed down three unanimous anti-administration decisions. In *Louisville Bank v. Radford*, they declared the Frazier-Lemke Act (Farm Bankruptcy Act), which provided mortgage assistance to farmers, unconstitutional. The Court limited the president's power to remove members of regulatory bodies in *Humphrey's Executor v. United States*, and in *Schechter v. United States*, they found that the NIRA was unconstitutional because of an illegal delegation of legislative authority to the executive branch of the government in the form of code-making procedures. In the latter case, the

Court also narrowly defined Congress' power to regulate interstate commerce. In a press conference, Roosevelt criticized the ruling, calling it a "horse and buggy definition of commerce." Also to some advisers, he expressed a brief interest in a constitutional amendment that would limit the Court's power of judicial review.

In early 1936, in *United States v. Butler* the Court ruled that the Agricultural Adjustment Act (AAA) was also unconstitutional. In a 6 to 3 decision, the Court held that the AAA involved an illegal use of federal taxing power. Finally, during the summer of 1936, in the *Tipaldo* decision, the Court struck down a New York State minimum wage by a 5 to 4 vote in terms which seemed to indicate that the National Labor Relations Act (NLRA) and the recently passed Social Security Act were both in danger. The president accused the Court of creating a regulatory "no man's land," where neither states nor the federal government was allowed to function. During 1936 more than one hundred bills that would curb the Court's power were introduced in Congress without Roosevelt's endorsement.

Even before the election of 1936, Roosevelt too had undoubtedly decided to take some action to protect his program from judicial nullification. His advisers believed that it was an opportune time to act, but there was disagreement about the best method to employ. A constitutional amendment was rejected because it would be too difficult to draft and ratification would take too long. Change needed to occur before the Court had an opportunity to decimate more New Deal programs.

Furthermore, Roosevelt was convinced that the real problem with the Court was one of personnel. The method finally selected was designed to foil the conservative bloc by an out-flanking strategy. Ironically it incorporated an approach once advocated by Justice McReynolds, the most intractable of the "Four Horsemen" on the Court. The administration bill, which was drawn up by Attorney General Homer S. Cummings, provided that whenever a federal judge failed to retire after reaching the age of seventy, the president could appoint a new judge to that bench. The number of new appointments, however, was limited to six on the Supreme Court and forty-four in the lower federal courts. The chief attraction of this plan, according to Roosevelt, was that it emphasized efficiency in the entire federal judicial system rather than singling out the high court or dwelling on politics and personalities. The president made reference to the overcrowded dockets of the federal courts and the resulting expense and delay to litigants. He claimed that younger judges could handle the courts' business with more vigor and new vision. Although many people shared FDR's frustration with the Court, opposition to the bill developed immediately from Republicans, anti-New Deal Democrats, members of the bar, and newspaper editors. More serious was the resistance from party regulars and liberals such as Senator Burton K. Wheeler.

Chief Justice Hughes soon applied ample evidence to Senator Wheeler that the Court was not behind in its business. Wheeler had been a supporter of many New Deal measures in the past but was now heading the opposition to the bill from his post on the Senate Judiciary Committee. In addition, the president's oblique slap at people over the age of seventy was resented by many elder statesmen. One of these was the most liberal member of the bench, Justice Brandeis, who was eighty years old. Helping to strengthen this opposition were the almost incredibly clumsy political tactics employed by the administration. Keeping even the floor leaders in ignorance until the last minute, Roosevelt did little to prepare Congress for the measure. Finally, the administration was surprised at the level of reverence many Americans expressed for the judiciary as a guardian of personal liberties and the separation of powers.

In the midst of the debate, the Supreme Court itself spoke out in a manner which did much to undermine the president's already faltering support in Congress. In March, 1937, in *West Coast Hotel Co. v. Parrish*, the Court, seeming to reverse its *Tipaldo* ruling, upheld a Washington state minimum wage law by a 5 to 4 vote. In April, *National Labor Relations Board v. Jones & Laughlin Steel* upheld the Wagner Act (NLRA) by the same margin. On May 24, 1937, the Court upheld the Social Security Act in all particulars. It was clear that at least one member of the court, Justice Owen Roberts, had shifted from opposition to support of the New Deal legislation. Roberts' move, which appeared to seal the doom of the court packing bill, is often referred to as "the switch in time that saved nine."

In addition, Justice Van Devanter announced his plans to retire. Roosevelt would at last be presented with the opportunity to nominate a member of the Court with a philosophy compatible with the New Deal, and presumably to assure approval of his legislation by a 6 to 3 margin.

While the president publicly announced his great satisfaction with the Court's apparent change of ideology, the news actually helped to kill his floundering Court Reform Bill. He was also acutely aware of the dissension the bill was creating within the Democratic Party. The Court Reform Bill gave conservative Democrats (who had been temporarily intimidated by the Depression) an opportunity to take a popular stand and at the same time to free themselves from the irritating confines of the presidential directions. When Senate majority leader Joseph T. Robinson of Arkansas, who was guiding the bill through Congress, died suddenly, the future of the legislation became hopeless. On July 22, 1937, the Senate sent the bill back to committee. It was never seen again.

Many historians have commented that Roosevelt lost the battle over the court packing law but won the war to achieve a more compatible Supreme Court. Before he left office, Roosevelt would name eight justices and one chief justice. In the process of winning the war, however, he may have lost his army, for after the court fight, an anti-New Deal coalition formed. After 1937, Roosevelt was never again able to count on widespread congressional support for his social reform programs. —*George Q. Flynn, updated by Mary Welek Atwell*

ADDITIONAL READING:

Abraham, Henry J. *Justices and Presidents: A Political History of Appointments to the Supreme Court.* 3d ed. New

York: Oxford University Press, 1992. How and why justices
are nominated for the Court. Bibliography.

Baker, Leonard. *Back to Back: The Duel Between FDR and
the Supreme Court*. New York: Macmillan, 1967. Details the
politics of the court fight.

Burns, James Macgregor. *Roosevelt: The Lion and the Fox*.
New York: Harcourt, Brace & World, 1956. Still the classic
political biography of Roosevelt.

Hall, Kermit L. *The Magic Mirror: Law in American History*. New York: Oxford University Press, 1989. A chapter on
the New Deal court puts it into the context of legal thought and
culture.

Leuchtenburg, William E. *The Supreme Court Reborn: The
Constitutional Revolution in the Age of Roosevelt*. New York:
Oxford, 1995. The definitive study of court packing.

SEE ALSO: 1924, Coolidge Is Elected President; 1928,
Smith-Hoover Campaign; 1929, Stock Market Crash; 1932,
Reconstruction Finance Corporation Is Created; 1932, Bonus
March; 1932, Franklin D. Roosevelt Is Elected President;
1933, The Hundred Days; 1933, Tennessee Valley Authority Is
Established; 1933, National Industrial Recovery Act; 1934,
The Dust Bowl; 1935, Works Progress Administration Is Established; 1935, Black Monday; 1935, National Labor Relations Act; 1935, Social Security Act; 1938, Fair Labor Standards Act; 1939, Mobilization for World War II.

1938 ■ HUAC INVESTIGATIONS: *the Dies Committee launches a crusade against subversive activity in the U.S. government, spreading its investigations to unions, educational institutions, and the media*

DATE: Beginning June, 1938
LOCALE: Washington, D.C.
CATEGORY: Government and politics
KEY FIGURES:

Martin Dies, Jr. (1900-1972), Texas congressman who
founded the House Special Committee on Un-American
Activities

John P. Frey (1871-1957), president of the Metal Trades
Department of the American Federation of Labor

Harry Lloyd Hopkins (1890-1946), adviser to President
Franklin D. Roosevelt, who was accused of associating
with radicals

Harold LeClair Ickes (1874-1952), secretary of the interior,
accused of allowing communists into his department

Robert La Follette, Jr. (1895-1953), U.S. senator from
Wisconsin who headed the HUAC-opposed Senate Civil
Liberties Committee

Frances Perkins (1882-1965), labor secretary in the
Roosevelt Administration

Franklin Delano Roosevelt (1882-1945), thirty-second
president of the United States, 1933-1945

SUMMARY OF EVENT. Inspired by the failure of the country to
emerge from the Great Depression, the ebbing of the New
Deal, the reemergence of the Republican Party in the electoral
process, the successful growth of trade unionism, and the
uneasiness of international political affairs, loyalty probes by
the Congress of the United States started to take center stage
during the late 1930's in a delicate political process. Attempting to expose real and perceived conspiracies, a congressional
committee was organized to investigate the affairs of individuals and groups who, it was alleged, were engaged in attempts
to overthrow the existing social and political order of the
nation.

On May 26, 1938, the House Special Committee on Un-American Activities, popularly known as the House Un-American Activities Committee (HUAC), chaired by conservative Democrat Martin Dies, Jr., of Texas, was established; in
June, it began hearings to seek out subversive activities against
the government of the United States. Members of the committee included Democrats John J. Dempsey of New Mexico,
Arthur D. Healey of Massachusetts, and Joe Starnes of Alabama; and Republicans Noah M. Mason of Illinois, Harold G.
Mosier of Ohio, and J. Parnell Thomas of New Jersey. While
the committee was up to the task of ferreting out subversives,
it was also quick to lend itself to uncovering communist activity. First on HUAC's list for investigation were the Federal
Theater Project and Federal Writers' Project. Born in New
Deal legislation, these programs became an early target for
Republican strategists in the congressional electoral campaigns of the late 1930's. Representative Thomas led the way,
determining that evidence received from committee investigators clearly indicated that the Federal Theater Project was a
branch of the Communist Party. Actual evidence in support of
the specific allegations against the project failed to materialize.

Next, HUAC investigated labor unions. Testifying before
the committee, John P. Frey, president of the Metal Trades
Department of the American Federation of Labor (AFL), accused all but one member of the leadership of the Congress of
Industrial Organizations (CIO), a rival labor organization, of
being either members of the Communist Party or sympathetic
to its cause. Only John L. Lewis, president of the United Mine
Workers, was exempted from this charge. Regardless of the
accusations, no cross-examination of the witness took place
and no subpoenas against those accused were issued. Charges
were made in the presence of a supportive gallery of witnesses.
Frey's indictment of the CIO leadership later was amended to
state that the rank and file of the union were not being accused,
only its leadership. Newspapers elaborated Frey's charges. By
the end of his testimony, 280 CIO union leaders had been
charged with communist activity. In only a few cases was there
any corroborating material to support the allegations.

Walter S. Steele of the *National Republic*, chairman of the
American Coalition Committee on National Security, claimed
to have documented evidence that more than six and a half
million Americans were engaged in conspiratorial activities
against the government of the United States. Steele did not

Anticommunist sentiment had a long history in the United States, beginning with the Red Scare of 1919-1920. Precedents for the 1938 HUAC investigations were set by such congressional committees as the Immigration Committee in 1930 (above), which probed communist activities in the United States in the expectation of strengthening the deportation laws. Left to right, seated, are Representative Samuel Dickstein, New York Police Commissioner Grover Whalen, Representative Albert Johnson, and the chairman, Representative John C. Box.

have to support his claim. By the end of the committee's first hearings, 640 separate groups, 483 newspapers, and 280 labor unions had been labeled as communist organizations.

Included in these organizations was the American Civil Liberties Union (ACLU), which had recently been involved in the Senate Civil Liberties Committee hearings. The Senate's committee had been organized to investigate official abuses of civil rights in trade union organizing activities during the decade. According to HUAC, both the Senate Committee and the ACLU had fallen under the influence of the Communist Party. Other groups receiving HUAC's ire were pacifist organizations, which were seen as dupes of the communist conspiracy; the media, which, according to the committee, supported trade unionism at the expense of business; and institutions of higher education, which the committee said were rife with communists and radicals encouraging racial strife and anti-fascist activities. The motion picture industry received special atten-

tion; accusations against screen stars and writers such as James Cagney, Clark Gable, Dorothy Parker, Robert Taylor, and Shirley Temple were written into the records.

Despite HUAC assurances that all those accused would be given a chance to clear their names, only a small number received that opportunity. Writer Heywood Broun read a prepared statement and then was asked to leave. Witness after witness was paraded before the committee, supporting the idea that there were communists in government positions, higher education, the media, and labor. By the 1938 election, public opinion had become divided on some of the committee's methods but not on the idea that there was a role for the committee in government.

HUAC's charges changed the nation's legislative agenda. The Republican success in the 1938 election, its first major success in almost a decade, had brought down New Dealers such as Michigan and Wisconsin governors Frank Murphy and

Philip La Follette. At the national level, eight new Republican senators and eighty-eight new Republican members of the House of Representatives helped point to the fact not only that the New Deal was in trouble but also that there was a need for government to ferret out subversives in the United States.

Despite Roosevelt's support, the Senate Civil Liberties Committee came to an end in 1940, after only four years in operation. On the other hand, HUAC went on for another thirty-five years. Dies's initial confrontation with those on the political left helped lay the groundwork for the killing of the Senate's committee, by electing those who would support the loss of its funding. Dies's committee also laid the foundation for the evolution of the McCarthy hearings of the 1950's and for government police operations such as the Federal Bureau of Investigation, an early investigative arm of HUAC, and the Counter Intelligence Program (Cointelpro) of the 1960's and 1970's.

Dies's attack on communists eventually led to his attack on trade unionism, civil rights movements, and liberal agendas in particular. He called for the resignation of government officials with whom he disagreed, such as Hopkins, Ickes, and Frances Perkins. His accusations that there were thousands upon thousands of communists in the federal government conspired against New Deal programs and personalities alike. In his book *The Trojan Horse* (1940), Dies institutionalized the idea that communism was an organized fifth column that had brought on the Great Depression and made Roosevelt's New Deal its tool. He went on to accuse the president's wife, Eleanor, of being the Communist Party's most valuable asset in Washington, D.C. Once again, no evidence of these accusations ever materialized.

Dies set up the rules for official government action that, in the end, ruined lives and careers, denied due process of law to those accused, and insinuated guilt by association. In the process, his committee produced a thorough challenge to the democracy it was attempting to protect. —*Thomas J. Edward Walker, Cynthia Gwynne Yaudes, and Ruby L. Stoner*

ADDITIONAL READING:

Dies, Martin. *Martin Dies' Story*. New York: Bookmailer, 1963. Besides providing personal insight into Dies's life, this book is valuable for its informative appendices.

Gellermann, William. *Martin Dies*. New York: Da Capo Press, 1972. Discusses Martin Dies's beliefs and how they were shaped into totalitarianism.

Goodman, Walter. *The Committee: The Extraordinary Career of the House Committee on Un-American Activities*. New York: Farrar, Straus & Giroux, 1968. A narrative as well as an investigation into how collective behavior influences political activity.

Ogden, August Raymond. *The Dies Committee: A Study of the Special House Committee for the Investigation of Un-American Activities, 1938-1944*. Washington, D.C.: Catholic University of America Press, 1945. Discusses the antecedents to committee, its formation, and its process of investigation.

Sexton, Patricia Cayo. *The War on Labor and the Left:*

Understanding America's Unique Conservatism. Boulder, Colo.: Westview Press, 1991. Analyzes how the use of power has evolved in government and legal institutions, economic policies, and the media.

SEE ALSO: 1919, Red Scare; 1935, Works Progress Administration Is Established; 1951, McCarthy Hearings.

1938 ■ FAIR LABOR STANDARDS ACT:
legislation establishes the federal minimum wage, a compulsory overtime system, and the prohibition of most child labor

DATE: June 25, 1938
LOCALE: Washington, D.C.
CATEGORIES: Business and labor; Laws and acts; Social reform
KEY FIGURES:
Hugo L. Black (1886-1971), Supreme Court justice
William P. Connery, Jr. (1888-1937), congressman from Massachusetts
Herbert Clark Hoover (1874-1964), thirty-first president of the United States, 1929-1933
Frances Perkins (1882-1965), secretary of labor and first woman cabinet member
Franklin Delano Roosevelt (1882-1945), thirty-second president of the United States, 1933-1945

SUMMARY OF EVENT. Beginning with Massachusetts in 1912, seventeen U.S. states had adopted minimum-wage laws by 1923. For constitutional reasons, their coverage was limited to women (and perhaps children), excluding adult men. However, the Supreme Court ruled such laws unconstitutional in *Adkins v. Children's Hospital* (1923).

The disastrous Great Depression that followed 1929 brought radical economic changes under President Franklin D. Roosevelt's New Deal. Drastic deflation had induced a substantial decline in wage rates and a great increase in unemployment. Presidents Herbert Hoover and Roosevelt both favored higher wages to try to increase workers' purchasing power. There was widespread support for measures to shorten hours of work, in order to spread the work around. Bills to reduce work hours were introduced into Congress in 1933 by Senator Hugo Black and Congressman William Connery. Secretary of Labor Frances Perkins favored efforts to support or raise wages by industry boards. All of these ideas were reflected in the administration of the National Industrial Recovery Act (NIRA) of 1933. Each of the 585 codes of fair competition adopted under NIRA contained minimum-wage provisions; although varying from one industry to another, they generally were thirty cents per hour or more and applied to men as well as women. In about one-fourth of the codes, lower minimums were provided for women. However, the NIRA was ruled unconstitutional in 1935. A number of states enacted new minimums and were aided by a Supreme Court decision in

1937 that largely reversed the Adkins doctrine (*West Coast Hotel Co. v. Parrish*). Of the twenty-nine state laws in force by 1941, all but two applied only to women.

An administration wage-hour bill developed by Secretary Perkins was introduced in Congress in May, 1937. Traditional opposition by organized labor to minimum-wage legislation had been reduced by the formation of an independent Congress of Industrial Organizations (CIO) in 1935. The wage-hour bill, also sponsored by Senator Black and Congressman Connery, proposed a labor standards board to set industry-specific provisions relating to wages, hours, and child labor. A new bill in 1938 provided for more uniform statutory provisions, but with some discretionary authority to be lodged in the Wage-Hour Division of the Department of Labor.

As finally adopted, the Fair Labor Standards Act (FLSA) contained two types of minimum-wage provisions. In Section 6, statutory minimum rates were set at twenty-five cents per hour for the first year, thirty cents per hour for the following six years, and forty cents per hour beginning in 1945. Sections 5 and 8 authorized the "wage-hour administrator" to establish industry wage committees that could recommend minimum hourly rates to be at least twenty-five cents in the first year and thirty cents thereafter, but not to exceed forty cents. The committees, composed of representatives of employers, workers, and government officials, would make recommendations to the administrator. Through 1940, such committees had made recommendations for a dozen industries, mainly involving clothing and textiles. However, the rapid rise in wages during World War II rendered them obsolete, and they were abolished in 1949.

The minimum-wage provisions applied generally to employees "engaged in commerce or in production of goods for commerce." Many sectors were exempted, notably agriculture and local retailing and service trades. Partial coverage applied to construction, wholesale trade, and agricultural processing. The administrator was empowered to permit subminimum wages for learners, apprentices, messengers, and workers with disabilities. No differentials were permitted between men and women. However, a large proportion of female workers were excluded by the exemption of trade and services.

Actions to enforce the law against employers paying low wages could be initiated either by the affected worker (or a union representing him or her) or by the government. Workers could sue employers for the amount they should have been paid and could collect damages of an equal amount, totaling to double damages. The Wage-Hour Division of the Department of Labor could initiate actions against employers, seeking either civil or criminal penalties.

It is estimated that in 1941, more than fourteen million workers were covered, about one-fourth of the labor force. An estimated 350,000 covered workers were paid less than the twenty-five-cent minimum in 1938 and about 900,000 received less than the thirty-cent minimum in 1939.

One goal of the law was to shorten the number of hours worked by individual workers, so that work could be spread more widely to help reduce unemployment. The law provided that employers had to pay one and a half times the basic hourly rate for hours worked by an individual in excess of forty-four per week in the first year, forty-two per week the second, and forty per week beginning in 1940. However, many categories of administrative and professional workers were excluded from these provisions. Industries with pronounced seasonal patterns of operation could obtain from the administrator permission to have individuals work as much as fifty-six hours per week and twelve hours per day for as much as fourteen weeks without paying overtime.

The law also brought to completion a long effort to secure federal legislation limiting child labor. Most states had some restrictions on the employment of children, particularly in night work or hazardous industries. A federal law in 1916 had prohibited shipment in interstate commerce of goods produced in violation of detailed child labor conditions regarding age, employment sector, and hours worked. The Supreme Court ruled this unconstitutional in 1918 (*Hammer v. Dagenhart*). Congress responded by reenacting similar provisions to be enforced by a tax, but this also was struck down by the Supreme Court (*Bailey v. Drexel Furniture*, 1922). Congress then passed a constitutional amendment authorizing federal regulation of child labor, but by 1941, only twenty-eight states had ratified it.

Encouraged by the changed tone of Supreme Court rulings in 1937, Congress enacted Section 12 of the FLSA to forbid interstate shipment of goods produced using workers under sixteen years of age, with the exception of children working for their parents or working in sectors designated by the administrator as acceptable. Supreme Court approval came in *U.S. v. Darby Lumber Co.* (1941).

The inflation of the 1940's carried actual wages well above the minimum. Many workers benefited from the premium pay for overtime, as wartime prosperity increased employment and work hours. Congress raised the minimum wage in 1949 and numerous times thereafter, bringing the level to $4.35, beginning in 1989. In 1996, Congress voted to increase the level to $5.25. For most of its history to that time, the minimum wage was 40 to 50 percent of average wages. Large increases in coverage were mandated in 1961 and 1967. Coverage of private, nonfarm employment rose from about 61 percent in 1950 to 69 percent in 1961, 83 percent in 1967, and 86 percent in 1978. Most sectors with concentrated female employment were covered by then. By 1977, coverage of domestic service reached 64 percent of workers, other services 74 percent, and retail trade 79 percent. State laws extended coverage still further. However, enforcement against small firms was loose, and employers of waitpersons were permitted to claim anticipated tips as part of their compliance. In addition, the mid-1980's saw a decline of an annual minimum-wage income to below the poverty level as defined by the U.S. government.

Some economists believe that the statutory minimum wage tends to raise wage levels slightly but to decrease employment opportunities. The requirement to pay higher wages can drive some firms out of business, cause others to decrease output and employment, and encourage others to find labor-saving procedures. Wages in uncovered sectors can be reduced by workers displaced from the covered sector. Thus, women's wages may have been adversely affected prior to the late 1970's. Studies in the 1990's suggested impacts only on teenage workers of both genders. —*Paul B. Trescott*

ADDITIONAL READING:

Bernstein, Irving. *A Caring Society: The New Deal, the Worker, and the Great Depression*. Boston: Houghton Mifflin, 1985. Gives a good narrative history of the adoption of the FLSA in the context of political personages and economic depression.

Card, David, and Alan B. Krueger. *Myth and Measurement: The New Economics of the Minimum Wage*. Princeton, N.J.: Princeton University Press, 1995. Controversial study that reports interview data suggesting that an increase in the minimum wage did not decrease employment.

Daugherty, Carroll R. *Labor Problems in American Industry*. 3d ed. Boston: Houghton Mifflin, 1941. This older college text gives a comprehensive overview of government regulation of wages, hours, and child labor.

Levitan, Sar A., and Richard S. Belous. *More than Subsistence: Minimum Wages for the Working Poor*. Baltimore: The Johns Hopkins University Press, 1979. Presents narrative, analysis, and advocacy. Brief and clearly written.

Peterson, John M. *Minimum Wages: Measures and Industry Effects*. Washington, D.C.: American Enterprise institute, 1981. Good information on the extension of coverage in successive legislation.

Rottenberg, Simon, ed. *The Economics of Legal Minimum Wages*. Washington, D.C.: American Enterprise Institute, 1981. Twenty-eight essays on different aspects of minimum-wage laws, some highly technical.

SEE ALSO: 1929, Great Depression; 1933, National Industrial Recovery Act; 1935, Works Progress Administration Is Established; 1935, National Labor Relations Act; 1935, Congress of Industrial Organizations Is Founded; 1943, Inflation and Labor Unrest; 1955, AFL and CIO Merge.

1938 ■ FIRST XEROGRAPHIC PHOTOCOPY:
a technological breakthrough creates a revolution in the maintenance of records and the transmission of information

DATE: October 22, 1938
LOCALE: Astoria, New York
CATEGORY: Science and technology
KEY FIGURES:
William E. Bixby (born 1920), scientist at the Battelle Memorial Institute
Chester F. Carlson (1906-1968), physicist and patent attorney who invented the process of electrophotography

John H. Dessauer (born 1905), scientist and director of research and engineering at Xerox Corporation
Otto Kornei (born 1903), engineer who assisted in the earliest experiments on electrophotography
Roland Michael Schaffert, scientist at the Battelle Memorial Institute
Joseph C. Wilson (1909-1971), president of Xerox Corporation

SUMMARY OF EVENT. In Astoria, New York, stands an unpretentious building with a bronze plaque on a central wall commemorating an event that occurred on October 22, 1938, when Chester F. Carlson and Otto Kornei produced the first dim copy of an image by a process called "electrophotography." The text of the copy was simply "10-22-38 Astoria." Carlson patented the process and, after considerable additional work, also patented a working model of a copying machine based on electrophotography. Carlson had come to New York from California, where he had earned his bachelor's degree in physics at the California Institute of Technology in 1930, and was employed by the patent department of P. R. Mallory Company. His experimental work was carried out in his spare time and entirely at his own expense; he hired Otto Kornei, an unemployed engineer recently arrived from Germany, to assist him.

Carlson's invention may be contrasted with ordinary photography, in which an image is produced by the effect of light on a film or plate coated with a silver compound. In electrophotography, the light-sensitive element is a reusable plate of metal coated with a layer of sulfur and electrostatically charged before exposure. When the plate is exposed, electrical charge leaks away from the illuminated areas in proportion to the light that falls. The image is trapped as an invisible pattern of static charges which may be rendered visible by dusting the plate with fine powder which adheres to the charged areas. The copying process ends when the powder pattern is transferred to paper and permanently bonded by heat or solvent vapors. In conventional photography, the image is developed by bathing the film in successive chemical liquids which darken the exposed areas and remove unexposed silver compounds. The advantage of electrophotography lies in the speed and convenience of dry developing, and in the economy resulting from having a reusable plate, thus avoiding the consumption of expensive silver compounds.

In modern xerographic equipment, most of the technical details are different from the ones used by Carlson and Kornei, but the principles are essentially the same. The light-sensitive plate is usually coated with a thin layer of selenium, which is much more sensitive than the original sulfur; and electrostatic charging is accomplished by a corona discharge instead of by simply rubbing the plate with cloth or fur, as was the practice in 1938. The corona discharge is generated in a shielded wire maintained at a high voltage and moved across the selenium-coated plate prior to exposure. The clinging powder image was formerly transferred to paper by pressing, thus causing the powder to stick to the paper. A more efficient method is now used in which the paper is given an electrical charge opposite to that of the powder, causing the image to be transferred as the powder clings preferentially to the paper.

For six years Carlson was unable to obtain financial backing for further research and development of his invention, despite repeated attempts. In 1944, he demonstrated his process in Columbus, Ohio, at the Battelle Memorial Institute. When asked for his opinion of the demonstration, Dr. R. M. Schaffert, then head of the Graphic Arts division at Battelle, wrote a memorandum favoring the new idea, and support was granted. In the years that followed, Battelle scientists, including W. E. Bixby, R. M. Schaffert, L. E. Walkup, C. D. Oughton, J. F. Rheinfrank, and E. N. Wise, improved the process and patented further inventions related to it. The work attracted additional support from the United States Signal Corps and from the Haloid Company of Rochester, New York, a small company that needed a new product to bolster earnings in the period following World War II. During this time many other companies were approached and offered a share in the new process in exchange for their support of the research at Battelle, but none was interested.

After 1947, research began to be directed toward the production of a practical copying device that could be sold commercially. In 1948, work had progressed far enough for a demonstration to be held at a meeting of the Optical Society of America in Detroit. The date was October 22, 1948, the tenth anniversary of Carlson's first copy, and for the occasion a new word, "xerography" (from the Greek, meaning "dry-writing"), was coined to replace the more technical term "electrophotography": The demonstration was a success, but Haloid could not immediately benefit from the publicity. Two more years of developmental work were necessary before the Model A copier, the first commercial xerographic copier, could be brought out in 1950. The Model A was successful mainly for preparation of multilith masters; it was not particularly successful as a document copier.

Not until 1960, after a long, expensive, and difficult period of development, did the Xerox Model 914 copier become available ("Xerox" and "914" are registered trademarks of the Xerox Corporation, Stamford, Connecticut). Many people contributed to the success of Model 914 (so-called because it used 9-by-14-inch paper), but prominent mention should be made of Dr. John H. Dessauer, Haloid's vice president in charge of research and product development, and Joseph C. Wilson, the company president. Soon after the introduction of the new copier, Haloid adopted a new name: Xerox Corporation.

Model 914 weighed about six hundred pounds and could make up to four hundred copies an hour. It was reliable and simple to operate. These virtues soon made it very popular: so much so that people began to speak and write of a "copying revolution." Many other companies began to develop and market competitive models, and in the latter part of the 1960's, copiers became smaller and boasted increased copying rates. By 1975 it was estimated that seventy-eight million copies were being made annually in the United States, and that 2.3 million copying machines were in use. Extrapolation of the growth of the copying led to the expectation that the volume would double within five years, which proved to be short of actual use, and by the middle 1990's volume had soared beyond a billion copies annually.

The easy availability of multiple copies of documents, periodicals, and books led to many benefits, and also to some problems. In a government study of photocopying, 21,280 libraries were surveyed with regard to their copying practices. It was found that in 1976, a total of 114 million copies were made, of which 54 million were of copyrighted materials. Authors and publishers were becoming concerned about their rights, while libraries, always desirous of providing service at low cost, found copying irresistible. Eventually there were lawsuits, including the case of *Williams and Wilkins* (a publisher) *v. the United States*. The United States Supreme Court reached a tie vote on the case, in which the publisher sought royalties from a library which had reproduced copyrighted materials. In 1976, President Gerald Ford signed into law a new copyright bill that went into effect, January 1, 1978. Under the new law, publishers would receive royalties for some of the copies made in libraries, but limited royalty-free "fair-use" library copying was still allowed. During the next five years Congress amended the law four times, one of which was to give U.S. adherence to the Berne Convention, a multilateral copyright treaty of 1989.

The technical development of xerography continues to the present time. The entire xerographic process can be completed in less than five seconds, and is comparatively inexpensive. Other recent achievements include color copying, enlarging and reducing, copying on both sides of the paper, sorting, collating, and even stapling. Problems concerning copyright conflicts and other societal impacts remain, complicated in recent years by the widespread use of personal computers that permit downloading and printing of information that, in turn, can be photocopied. —*Elizabeth Fee, updated by P. Ann Peake*

ADDITIONAL READING:

Dessauer, John H. *My Years with Xerox: The Billions Nobody Wanted.* Garden City, N.Y.: Doubleday, 1971. Written by an employee of the Haloid Corporation (later known as Xerox) from 1935 to 1970, serving as executive vice president and head of the research and engineering division. Although trained as an organic chemist, Dessauer nevertheless wrote a nontechnical account of the growth of the Xerox Corporation, including material on the development of xerography and the people who made it possible; the farsighted business decisions that allowed the company to succeed; and the sociological implications of xerography.

Golembeski, Dean J. "Struggling to Become an Inventor." *American Heritage of Invention & Technology* 4, no. 3 (1989): 8-15. Recounts the life and work of Chester F. Carlson, who discovered xerography, and traces the subsequent commercial development of that process into modern copy machines.

Gundlach, R. W. "Xerography from the Beginning." *Journal of Electrostatics* 24, no. 1 (November, 1989): 3-9. Surveys the history of xerography with focus on the inventor Chester F.

Carlson and scientists at Battelle, like Bill Bixby, who made substantive improvements in the process. Also champions the uncommonly good management of J. C. Wilson for Xerox's business success.

Schaffert, Roland Michael. *Electrophotography*. New York: Halstead Press, 1975. Schaffert was a scientist at Battelle Memorial Institute whose research of electrophotography began in the 1940's. This book is concerned largely with technical matters, with only about seven pages out of a total of nearly a thousand devoted to introductory and historical material.

Strong, William S. *The Copyright Book: A Practical Guide*. 3d ed. Cambridge, Mass.: MIT Press, 1990. Discusses the 1976 copyright law and congressional amendments to it, including adherence to the Berne Convention, and provides guidelines to rights and responsibilities of those affected by the law.

SEE ALSO: 1981, IBM Markets the Personal Computer.

1939 ■ DEBUT OF COMMERCIAL TELEVISION: *business and technology join to exploit a visual medium that will dominate the second half of the twentieth century*

DATE: April 30, 1939
LOCALE: New York
CATEGORIES: Communications; Cultural and intellectual history; Science and technology
KEY FIGURES:
John L. Baird (1888-1946), early television inventor
Philo T. Farnsworth (1906-1971), early inventor and developer of commercial television
C. Francis Jenkins (1867-1934), early television inventor
Franklin Delano Roosevelt (1882-1945), thirty-second president of the United States, 1933-1945, who made the first commercial telecast in 1939
David Sarnoff (1891-1971), president of the Radio Corporation of America (RCA), and a determined television planner
Vladimir Zworykin (1889-1972), television camera developer
SUMMARY OF EVENT. American commercial television made its long-awaited public debut at the New York World's Fair on April 30, 1939. It was unfortunate timing because the beginning of World War II was to force immediate postponement of further development of this new medium. The public was enthusiastic and expressed astonishment at the fair's television programs; military strategists were equally enthusiastic over the possibilities of a new secret weapon, radar, which used the same technological innovations as television. By the time the war ended, radar was no longer unknown, and television seemed little more than a wistful memory from the New York World's Fair.

Television would not have made its debut when it did had it not been for the dedication and persistence of one of its chief backers, David Sarnoff, president of the Radio Corporation of America (RCA), who as a member of the World's Fair planning committee was determined to start the exploitation of the new medium by beginning commercial programming at the fair in full view of the millions in attendance. The first experimental program successfully emanated from the unfinished fairgrounds on February 26, 1939, foreshadowing a pattern that would be long-standing—the use of the best entertainers from radio. For the official opening of the fair, however, and the start of commercial television broadcasting, Sarnoff was to engage the president of the United States himself; President Franklin Delano Roosevelt was on hand for the first program.

Television's development had been quietly proceeding for some time and on several fronts. Experimentation on the transmission of transient visual images began in the 1870's, but it was only in 1925 that C. Francis Jenkins in the United States and John L. Baird in Great Britain successfully demonstrated the technology's feasibility. These demonstrations, employing heavy, awkward mechanical devices, served as catalysts for further work. By 1928, practicality had been demonstrated with low-definition fuzzy pictures produced. The 1930's were marked by the development of higher-definition all-electronic systems and experimental broadcasting. Perfected by 1939, the issue of the final development phase was authorization of commercial broadcasting.

Philo T. Farnsworth, an early experimenter, came from a large Mormon family and had started experimenting on his own without benefit of formal training. He astonished his high school science teacher in 1922 with a request for advice on an electronic television set he had been designing. Later while he was working on his design, Farnsworth's San Francisco apartment was raided by police who thought the tubes were part of an illegal distillery. By 1927 Farnsworth was able to transmit on his primitive television screen a dollar sign as a test pattern, a film of the Dempsey-Tunney fight, and some Mary Pickford films. In that year, he filed for a patent on his image dissector tube.

Meanwhile, RCA's Vladimir Zworykin worked at developing his Iconoscope camera. He had begun experimenting with television as early as 1917 with the Russian Wireless and Telegraph Co. After the Bolshevik Revolution, Zworykin, who had been educated at the Saint Petersburg Institute of Technology and the Collège de France, came to America and joined Westinghouse in 1920.

In 1923, he demonstrated an electronic pickup tube, but its poor definition and contrast showed that much work was needed to make an all-electronic system feasible. A patent was not then pursued and Westinghouse lost interest. Converting electricity was the easy part, but converting light to electricity was difficult, and it eluded Zworykin.

After a series of disappointments, Zworykin finally succeeded in perfecting a practical photoelectric tube for television transmittal, which he called the Iconoscope—effectively a mosaic of tiny photoelectric cells and capacitors, allowing the image to be scanned. The kinescope, or cathode-ray picture tube for the receiver, had been easier to develop. There were claims that Zworykin "stole" some of the ideas from Farnsworth, whom he visited in 1930. By then, Zworykin and Sarnoff had been introduced, and Zworykin joined RCA as a research engineer when RCA and Sarnoff took over both General Electric's and Westinghouse's radio and television research in 1930. The high point of television research was reached in 1932, when RCA had sixty people working in television, and the National Broadcasting Company (NBC) was already transmitting experimental programs. In 1934, RCA began demonstrating its all-electronic television system.

Eventually the Zworykin and the Farnsworth inventions became the subject of U.S. Patent Office hearings. Zworykin failed to convince the patent examiners that the Iconoscope was similar to his 1923 device, so it was concluded that Farnsworth had developed electronic transmission first. This forced RCA to seek out cross-licensing agreements with Farnsworth. By May, 1935, Farnsworth and Zworykin had greatly improved their respective systems, and RCA began work on a new Empire State Building transmitter which, by the following year, was successfully transmitting television signals to points over forty-five miles away.

In 1935, RCA allocated an additional million dollars for television tests. Farnsworth had won Philco's backing and from Philadelphia continued his experiments. Meanwhile, in Los Angeles, the Don Lee group and Allen Dumont were conducting independent testing of television systems. RCA used its Empire State Building transmitter to broadcast experimental programs from Radio City's Studio 3H.

The first television receiving sets at the New York World's Fair were as primitive as the broadcasts. The sets used five-inch or nine-inch tubes, and later twelve-inch tubes were introduced with prices ranging from about two hundred to six hundred dollars. One program a day originated from the Radio City Studio and one came from the mobile unit that roamed the city looking for news. By the end of 1939, the Columbia Broadcasting System (CBS) and Dumont were also telecasting in New York, and by May, 1940, there were twenty-three stations in the nation. In 1940, a National Television Standards Committee was created to recommend broadcast standards; a 525-line system was approved in 1941. The limited commercial licensing allowed by the Federal Communications Commission (FCC) was rescinded early in 1940, and when commercial programming began again in 1941, it was limited to only four hours per station per week.

The monochromatic television system was now ready for vigorous marketing with full commercial service on July 1, 1941. The first commercial television station, WNBT in New York City, began broadcasting to about forty-seven hundred set owners, including regular newscasts with Lowell Thomas. Also in New York, CBS station WCPW began experimental color broadcasting. During World War II, however, only six stations were on the air and many sets were inoperative due to a lack of parts. Although the war delayed the promotion of the system, in 1947 the television boom began in earnest. In the

United States, the number of television sets increased tenfold between 1949 and 1951 (from 1 to 10 million), and then climbed to 50 million by 1959. Many foreign countries initiated television broadcasting services during the 1950's.

—Richard H. Collin, updated by Stephen B. Dobrow

ADDITIONAL READING:

Abramson, Albert. *The History of Television, 1880-1941.* Jefferson, N.C.: McFarland & Company, 1987. Covers the technological and business aspects of the early developmental days of television.

Barnouw, Eric. *The Golden Web: 1933-1953.* Vol. 2 in *A History of Broadcasting in the United States.* New York: Oxford University Press, 1968. This second volume of a planned three-volume history of American broadcasting covers the development of radio through its ascendancy in the 1930's and begins the history of the development of commercial television. Well documented.

Gross, Lynne S. *Telecommunications: An Introduction to Electronic Media.* 4th ed. Dubuque, Iowa: Wm. C. Brown, 1992. Good overview of electronic mass media, including history.

Maclaurin, W. Rupert. *Invention and Innovation in the Radio Industry.* New York: Macmillan, 1949. An invaluable history of technical and entrepreneurial innovation in the broadcasting business. Especially useful in tracing the Zworykin-Farnsworth patent disputes.

Ritchie, Michael. *Please Stand By: A Prehistory of Television.* Woodstock, N.Y.: Overlook Press, 1994. Covers the period before 1948.

Shulman, Arthur, and Roger Youman. *How Sweet It Was: Television, a Pictorial Commentary.* New York: Shorecrest, 1966. Useful for its 1,435 photographs.

Udelson, Joseph H. *The Great Television Race: A History of the American Television Industry, 1925-1941.* Tuscaloosa: University of Alabama Press, 1982. Covers the heart of television's technological development.

SEE ALSO: 1876, Bell Demonstrates the Telephone; 1879, Edison Demonstrates the Incandescent Lamp; 1893, World's Columbian Exposition; 1920, Commercial Radio Broadcasting Begins; 1981, IBM Markets the Personal Computer; 1990's, Rise of the Internet.

1939 ■ MOBILIZATION FOR WORLD WAR II: *the prospect of involvement in war prompts conversion of domestic production to meet military needs*

DATE: Beginning August, 1939
LOCALE: United States
CATEGORIES: Business and labor; Economics; Government and politics
KEY FIGURES:
James Francis Byrnes (1879-1972), director of the Office of Economic Stabilization

William Martin Jeffers (1876-1953), head of the Government Rubber Board

William Signius Knudsen (1879-1948), head of the Office of Production Management

Emory Scott Land (1879-1971), head of the United States Maritime Commission

Henry J. Morgenthau, Jr. (1891-1967), secretary of the Treasury

Donald Marr Nelson (1888-1959), head of the War Production Board

Franklin Delano Roosevelt (1882-1945), thirty-second president of the United States, 1933-1945

Harry S Truman (1884-1972), senator from Missouri and chairman of the committee investigating defense spending

SUMMARY OF EVENT. In June, 1940, German forces overran France. U.S. industrial mobilization became necessary when large British orders for military supplies were received. European events also aided the Roosevelt Administration in passing a number of military appropriations bills. Although more money was becoming available for war production, U.S. industry was reluctant to exploit this market. Conditioned by the static economic situation of the Depression, many capitalists expected such conditions to return after the war.

Expanding plants for wartime production was seen as a risky, short-term investment. The Roosevelt Administration tried in various ways to persuade industrialists that this was not true. The federal government offered to finance expansion through low-interest loans from the Reconstruction Finance Corporation. The Revenue Act of 1940 provided an incentive in the form of a 20 percent per year depreciation of new defense plants, instead of the former 5 percent tax write-off. Most important, however, was the "cost-plus" provision incorporated into government defense contracts. Private industry was guaranteed the cost of producing particular military hardware, plus a profit of a certain percentage of the cost. This plan proved lucrative to industry but led to excessive waste in production. Eventually, Senator Harry S Truman of Missouri led a special investigation into the waste and corruption in defense work, the revelations of which resulted in improved efficiency.

Roosevelt wrestled desperately with the problem of centralizing control of industrial mobilization. Drawing upon his experiences during World War I, he first established a War Resources Board (WRB) in August, 1939. The WRB drew up a plan of mobilization providing for rigid government controls. Roosevelt rejected this plan for political and personal reasons and permitted the WRB to be dissolved in October, 1939, after organized labor accused it of being prejudiced in favor of big business. A pattern of establishing an agency with a vague mandate and then reorganizing it when its attempts to operate provoked criticism was repeated during succeeding years.

The next attempt at central direction was the establishment of the National Defense Advisory Commission on May 28, 1940. Composed of representatives of labor, industry, the armed services, and the consuming public, the commission was under the direction of a former General Motors executive,

William S. Knudsen. Knudsen was expected to balance these various interests. The most vexing problem was the assignment of priorities to the various manufacturers for the acquisition of scarce materials. Ideally, such materials ought to have gone to factories in proportion to the relative importance of their finished products to the health of the economy as a whole. Knudsen never solved this problem but permitted the Army-Navy Munitions Board to gain great power in acquiring scarce materials.

On January 7, 1941, Roosevelt tried another reorganization. The Office of Production Management (OPM) was set up, with Knudsen and Sidney Hillman of the Congress of Industrial Organizations (CIO) as joint directors. The OPM did succeed in beginning the shift toward a war economy, but it placed strains on domestic needs and shortages developed in the electric power, aluminum, steel, and railroad equipment industries. By August 28, 1941, Roosevelt was ready for another change. At first, a slight adjustment was made by creating a Supplies Priorities and Allocation Board headed by Sears Roebuck executive Donald M. Nelson. Within a few months, the OPM had gone the way of the WRB, and Nelson was called to the White House to head an entirely new organization, the War Production Board (WPB).

Established on January 16, 1942, the WPB was to have supreme command over the entire economy. Nelson, however, proved inadequate for the job; he permitted the military to regain control over priorities and seemed to favor big corporations in the allocation of contracts. He also permitted the economy to develop unevenly. Ship factories were built at a pace far exceeding the ability of the steel industry to supply material for ship construction. Nelson remained as head of the WPB until 1944, but long before then control of economic mobilization had been assigned to yet another agency.

Recognizing that problems were developing under the WPB, Roosevelt asked Supreme Court associate justice James F. Byrnes to head the new Office of Economic Stabilization (OES). This new office replaced the WPB as supreme arbiter of the economy. Byrnes did solve the problems of priorities and brought order to the entire mobilization scheme. He seemed to have the political astuteness required to make the OES work. In May, 1943, his agency's official title was changed to Office of War Mobilization, and in October, 1944, it became the Office of War Mobilization and Reconversion.

Despite such frequent reorganization of the government's regulatory bodies, U.S. industry performed fantastic feats of production during the war years. Statistics tell part of the story. In 1941, the United States produced approximately eight and one-half billion dollars' worth of military equipment. Using the same dollar value, in 1944 the sum was sixty billion dollars. Included in these gross figures was an increase in the annual production of planes from 5,865 in 1939 to almost 100,000 in 1944. Ship tonnage rose from one million tons in 1941 to nineteen million in 1943. Certain parts of the economy performed miracles. As public director of WPB, William M. Jeffers, president of the Union Pacific Railroad, directed the creation of a great synthetic rubber industry; Admiral Emory S. Land, head of the United States Maritime Commission, prodded the shipping industry into building ships in fewer than ten days; comparable production feats were achieved by other industries.

Probably most significant in the long run was the fact that this remarkable production was accomplished with little effect on the basic corporate structure of the economy. Shortages existed in the civilian community during World War II, and rationing was introduced for foodstuffs, including meat and sugar. While restraints were imposed on free enterprise, outright government seizure of private industry was never attempted. For the most part, government gave businessmen exceptional latitude in what they could produce and how, as long as it met national goals. The government let contracts for a wide variety of experimental or unusual projects, such as the famous *Spruce Goose* developed by Howard Hughes's engineers. Government allowed exceptional industrialists, such as Andrew Jackson Higgins, Preston Tucker, and Henry Kaiser, to mass-produce patrol torpedo (PT) boats and landing craft, gun turrets, and ships with little interference and with almost no concern for cost. Kaiser, for example, cut the production time of a Liberty Ship (a basic freighter crucial to the war effort) from 120 days to 4.5 days. As British historian Paul Johnson observed, the war "put back on his pedestal the American capitalist folk-hero."

The efforts of the War Production Board also involved businesses in planning future economic activities more than ever before, and persuaded many that government could and should play a role in that planning. The size of government has never returned to its pre-Depression levels, and only in the administration of Ronald Reagan did the military share of the gross national product remain at less than 6 percent for more than a year. Ironically, many business leaders took from the war the exact opposite message from what it had taught. Rather than reaffirming the phenomenal productive capacity of the United States, business left the war expecting special favors and government considerations.

—*George Q. Flynn, updated by Larry Schweikart*

ADDITIONAL READING:

Catton, Bruce. *The War Lords of Washington.* New York: Harcourt, Brace & World, 1948. Argues that the war failed to produce the social revolution that started with the New Deal, because putting industrialists in charge ended the opportunity for social reform. Given the extraordinary production of the system, Catton's thesis does not convince.

Civilian Production Administration. *Industrial Mobilization for War, 1940-1945.* Washington, D.C.: Government Printing Office, 1947. The official government record of mobilization.

Higgs, Robert. *Crisis and Leviathan: Critical Episodes in the Growth of American Government.* New York: Oxford University Press, 1987. Examines the War Production Board and dozens of other government agencies as agents of government expansion during wartime. Hypothesizes that wars and other critical episodes created a ratchet effect that caused government power and scope to increase.

Janeway, Eliot. *The Struggle for Survival.* New Haven, Conn.: Yale University Press, 1951. This brief volume in the *Chronicles of America* series is a convenient treatment of the economic mobilization for the general reader.

Johnson, Paul. *Modern Times: A History of the World from the Twenties to the Nineties.* Rev. ed. New York: HarperCollins, 1991. A vast, interpretive history of the modern world. Devotes more than two chapters to World War II and spends several pages celebrating the efforts of U.S. business.

Nelson, Donald M. *Arsenal of Democracy: The Story of American War Production.* New York: Harcourt, Brace & World, 1946. A personal account of the WPB's achievements by its director. Depicts the difficult decisions about strategy that the WPB had to make and praises the free enterprise system for its efficiency and productivity.

Novick, David, Mevin Anshen, and W. C. Trappner. *Wartime Production Controls.* New York: Columbia University Press, 1949. An older but useful study of the problems faced by Nelson and his associates in allocating priorities.

Rockhoff, Hugh. *Drastic Measures: A History of Wage and Price Controls in the United States.* New York: Cambridge University Press, 1984. Argues that controls kept inflation under wraps during the war, but only postponed the effects until after the war.

SEE ALSO: 1917, Mobilization for World War I; 1929, Great Depression; 1932, Reconstruction Finance Corporation Is Created; 1940, United States Builds a Two-Ocean Navy; 1941, 6.6 Million Women Enter the U.S. Labor Force; 1941, Lend-Lease Act; 1941, Executive Order 8802; 1941, Bombing of Pearl Harbor; 1941, Germany and Italy Declare War on the United States.

1940 ■ UNITED STATES BUILDS A TWO-OCEAN NAVY: *on the eve of World War II, the U.S. government begins construction of warships that will dominate both the Atlantic and the Pacific*

DATE: Beginning June 14, 1940
LOCALE: The United States
CATEGORIES: Government and politics; Wars, uprisings, and civil unrest
KEY FIGURES:
Carl Vinson (1883-1981), chairman of the House Naval Affairs Committee
Franklin Delano Roosevelt (1882-1945), thirty-second president of the United States, 1933-1945
Harold Raynsford Stark (1880-1972), chief of naval operations
Park Trammel (1876-1936), chairman of the Senate Naval Affairs Committee

SUMMARY OF EVENT. The goal of establishing a two-ocean fleet was a powerful, if elusive, force in determining the nature of the United States Navy before the Japanese attack on Pearl Harbor plunged the United States into war in 1941. In the late 1930's, the two-ocean standard became the latest in a succession of rallying cries designed to gain popular support for naval expansion. Its appeal originated in a growing recognition that vital U.S. interests were being threatened simultaneously by Germany and Japan. This two-ocean focus was an extension of threat perceptions and arguments dating back to the 1890's and made more pressing with the Anglo-Japanese alliance of 1902 and Japan's victory over Russia in the 1904-1905 Russo-Japanese War. With the collapse of naval arms limitations in 1936, the rearmament of National Socialist Germany, and the naval buildup and military adventurism of Japan, the necessity of creating fleets capable of fighting independently in widely separated theaters seemed evident. Congress, responding to the change in popular attitude, passed legislation between 1938 and 1941 designed to translate the ideal of a two-ocean fleet into reality.

U.S. naval policy has been a mirror of national ambition. In the 1890's, and especially after the Spanish-American War, the horizon of that ambition increased measurably. At a single stroke, the United States became both a Caribbean and a Pacific power. U.S. control of the Philippines was perplexing for many people in the United States but exciting for navalists and imperialists. Together with Hawaii, which was annexed in 1898, the Philippines provided U.S. commerce with a toehold in the fabled China trade. Distant possessions seemed to mandate an increased fleet, and an increased fleet required overseas bases, setting the foundation for a self-perpetuating expansion of the military and naval establishment.

For better or worse, expanded interests called for expanded responsibilities, and President Theodore Roosevelt, an enthusiastic convert to U.S. imperialism, led the movement to secure those interests. Between 1905 and 1909, Congress authorized the construction of sixteen new battleships of the all-big-gun, dreadnought style by which international naval power was measured. Meanwhile, work on the Panama Canal, which was intended to provide much-needed flexibility for the fleet, continued toward its completion in 1914.

By the time of Theodore Roosevelt's presidency, Japan and especially Germany were seen as the most important potential threats to U.S. commerce and possessions. Tension caused by the treatment of Japanese nationals living in the United States was the primary reason for congressional approval of the last six new battleships authorized during Roosevelt's administration. The attention of most U.S. naval experts was fixed on Germany, where an ambitious twenty-year naval construction program had been announced in 1900. While the German fleet law was intended as a challenge to British naval supremacy, it was also perceived as a threat to U.S. interests by a host of United States congressmen and naval authorities. That traditional German concerns were continental and that the German navy had a nearer rival in Great Britain seemed to make no

difference. Those guiding U.S. naval policy believed that it would be a mistake for the United States to allow itself to be surpassed in naval power by any nation that also maintained a great standing army. This growing U.S. fear of Germany was also reflected in the concentration of the fleet. Long a dictum of the United States' most distinguished naval strategic synthesizer, Captain A. T. Mahan, the concentration of naval forces was adopted by Roosevelt as a cardinal principle of fleet deployment. Throughout his presidency, and Taft's as well, the main fleet remained posted in the Atlantic Ocean.

After 1914, the prewar desire to improve the United States Navy to second place behind the British fleet was replaced by a determination to build a navy second to none. This challenge to British naval superiority, the first ever by the United States, was engendered by British arrogance toward neutral United States shipping and a fear of the naval landscape in the postwar world. President Woodrow Wilson and Congress joined in the $588 million naval construction act of 1916, which mandated ten new superdreadnought battleships and six battle cruisers. Wilson called for a similar program in 1918 to strengthen the U.S. bargaining position at the Versailles Conference.

By 1924, the United States Navy would be the most powerful in the world, a dismaying prospect to the British government. U.S. naval ascension was delayed by the decision to shift battleship construction assets to the production of anti-submarine warships, such as destroyers, and to merchant ships to counter losses to German submarines. In the three years that followed the signing of the armistice ending World War I, the United States built more warships than all the rest of the world combined. In taking dead aim at British naval superiority, the United States also revealed apprehension concerning Japan's being linked to Britain by the ten-year renewal of the Anglo-Japanese alliance in 1911. Between 1917 and 1921, Japanese naval appropriations tripled, undoubtedly affected by the upsurge in U.S. construction. It is not surprising that with the demise of German naval power in 1919, concern in the United States shifted from the Atlantic to the Pacific. In the summer of that year, the battle fleet was divided, with the newer and heavier units being sent to the West Coast.

Fear of a costly, all-out naval race in the immediate postwar period served to induce a certain amount of moderation. In Washington, D.C., in 1921-1922, the five leading naval powers adopted a system of restrictions on individual capital ships (battleships and battle cruisers) and aircraft carriers as well as on the aggregate tonnages of capital war fleets. By the terms of the Five-Power Treaty, Great Britain and the United States were to share the first rank of naval power, Japan was assigned the second rank (approximately 60 percent of capital ship parity with the first-rank powers), while France and Italy were relegated to the third rank. In 1930, this agreement was augmented by the London Treaty, which established similar kinds of restrictions on the noncapital construction (cruisers, destroyers, and submarines) of Great Britain, the United States, and Japan. Thus, from 1922 through 1936, the size and nature of the United States war fleet was restricted by international agreement.

Domination of the Imperial Japanese Navy by the hardliners of the so-called Fleet Faction, who chafed at Japan's second-rank status under the treaties, resulted in significant pressure on the Japanese government to demand equal status with the United States and Great Britain at the London Naval Conference of 1935. When Great Britain and the United States demurred, the Japanese government provided the requisite notice that it would no longer abide by the naval treaties after December, 1936. Japan's subsequent penetration of China in 1937 and Hitler's annexation of Austria and absorption of the Sudetenland in 1938 seemed to provide ample proof for the proposition that unilateral restraint by the United States was a dangerous policy. The issue of naval preparedness became correspondingly less controversial.

In 1932, U.S. naval officers applauded the election of navalist Franklin D. Roosevelt to the presidency after the lean years of Republican naval and military expenditures. They were not disappointed. On the same day he signed the National Industrial Recovery Act (NIRA) into law in June, 1933, Roosevelt signed an executive order using $238 million of NIRA public works funds for construction of new warships. This first step in building the U.S. Navy up to "treaty limits" was followed by congressional moves to improve the status of the war fleet. Spearheaded by the navalist chairman of the House Naval Affairs Committee, Carl Vinson, and the aging chairman of the Senate Naval Affairs Committee, Park Trammel, this movement's objective was the replacement of all the fleet's obsolete warships, or "floating coffins," to use Vinson's words. The resulting Vinson-Trammel bill which became law in March of 1934, also known as the Vinson Naval Parity Act, envisioned the replacement of almost a third of the existing tonnage of the Navy, including practically all the destroyers and submarines. The act did not appropriate funds for construction but served as a blueprint for U.S. naval policy. The clear intention of this action was the establishment of a fighting force that would be the equal of any in the world. Both the NIRA-funded ships and the Vinson-Trammel Act exacerbated strategic concerns in Japan, which was approaching its warship treaty limits and now faced new, qualitatively superior, U.S. warships.

By 1938, many isolationists, hemispherists, and internationalists were in agreement that a powerful navy was an indispensable adjunct to a free United States. Thus, another authorization bill swiftly passed through Congress. The second Vinson-Trammel bill, the Naval Expansion Act, or Vinson Naval Act, sought the creation of a navy 20 percent larger than that permitted by the former limitation treaties. As Europe plunged into war, the last restraints on full-scale naval construction disappeared. On June 14, 1940, the day that Paris fell to the German Blitzkrieg, President Roosevelt signed into law a naval expansion bill that authorized an 11 percent increase in appropriations. Three days later, Admiral Harold R. Stark, chief of naval operations, asked Congress for an additional four billion

dollars in order to bring the fleet up to the two-ocean standard. This bill, which was passed the following month, was the largest single naval construction program ever undertaken by any country. It provided for a 70 percent increase in combat tonnage to be constructed over a period of six years.

Franklin Roosevelt largely acted as his own navy secretary and shared most admirals' perception that the battleship defined naval power. While additional aircraft carriers were authorized in the late 1930's, the main focus of the Roosevelt naval buildup was the production of the seventeen new battleships authorized prior to U.S. entry into World War II.

Despite the flurry of construction authorizations, U.S. naval power was insufficient to protect the Atlantic and Pacific interests of the United States in the wake of Pearl Harbor. A full year prior to that catastrophe, the Navy, pressured by the president, had been forced to shift its strategic focus from an offensive action against Japan to a position that in any future war would include both Germany and Japan; the fleet would take the offensive in the Atlantic while assuming a defensive posture in the Pacific. Even this severe modification of the strategy implicit in the two-ocean standard did not achieve satisfactory results for a disconcertingly long period of time. While the success of Japan's surprise attack on Pearl Harbor might well be considered the result of a failure of specific rather than general preparedness, the inability of U.S. naval resources to provide adequate protection against the onslaught of Germany's U-boat attack during all of 1942 provides convincing evidence that the Atlantic fleet had not achieved even a one-ocean capability at that time. This was an outgrowth of the myopic battleship strategic paradigm that restricted movement toward true capabilities in air, surface, and subsurface warfare. It was not until early 1943 that U.S. naval forces began to gain the upper hand in the Atlantic and Pacific theaters of the war.

—Meredith William Berg, updated by William M. McBride

ADDITIONAL READING:

Davis, George T. *A Navy Second to None: The Development of Modern American Naval Policy.* New York: Harcourt Brace, 1940. A useful scholarly study of U.S. naval policy and armaments, and the relation of naval power to commerce.

Hagan, Kenneth J. *This People's Navy: The Making of American Sea Power.* New York: Free Press, 1991. Excellent concise history of the United States Navy.

O'Connell, Robert. *Sacred Vessels: The Cult of the Battleship and the Rise of the U.S. Navy.* Boulder, Colo.: Westview Press, 1991. A readable, cautionary account of naval strategic weapons and the profession in which they evolved.

Pelz, Stephen E. *Race to Pearl Harbor: The Failure of the Second London Naval Conference and the Onset of World War II.* Cambridge, Mass.: Harvard University Press, 1974. An excellent tracing of the naval policies of the great sea powers from the end of arms limitations to Pearl Harbor, using United States, Japanese, and British sources.

Tuleja, Thaddeus V. *Statesmen and Admirals: Quest for a Far Eastern Naval Policy.* New York: W. W. Norton, 1963. An excellent examination of the interwar relationship between the naval policies of the United States and Japan.

Wheeler, Gerald. *Prelude to Pearl Harbor: The United States Navy and the Far East, 1921-1931*. Columbia: University of Missouri Press, 1963. A clear discussion of the attitudes of senior naval officers, Congress, the executive branch, and the U.S. public during an important period of naval limitation.

SEE ALSO: 1933, National Industrial Recovery Act; 1939, Mobilization for World War II.

1940 ■ OGDENSBURG AGREEMENT: *the United States and Canada come to an agreement on hemispheric defense*

DATE: August 16, 1940

LOCALE: Ogdensburg, New York

CATEGORIES: Canadian history; Diplomacy and international relations; Treaties and agreements

KEY FIGURES:

Winston Leonard Spencer Churchill (1874-1965), British prime minister

William Lyon Mackenzie King (1874-1950), prime minister of Canada

J. L. Ralston (1881-1948), Canadian defense minister

Franklin Delano Roosevelt (1882-1945), thirty-second president of the United States, 1933-1945

SUMMARY OF EVENT. After only slight hesitation, Canada had followed the mother country, Great Britain, in going to war against Germany in 1939. Canada's southern neighbor, the United States, was sympathetic to Great Britain and her allies but avowed to remain neutral.

The situation changed drastically after the Germans conquered France in June, 1940. The German armies seemed invincible, and there was a real threat that they might cross the English Channel and conquer Great Britain. The United States, realizing the gravity of the world situation, became more concerned about its security and that of the Western Hemisphere. The British prime minister, Winston Churchill, developed a contingency plan to have the royal family, in the event of a German takeover, flee Britain and take sanctuary in Canada. Clearly, the Atlantic Ocean was no longer a barrier to world conflict.

Franklin D. Roosevelt, the president of the United States, was worried about both Western Hemisphere security and Great Britain's ability to stay in the war. He wanted to help Great Britain and prepare his own country for the war he knew it would one day enter, but he believed that the U.S. public was not ready for full-fledged participation. Roosevelt therefore conceived the lend-lease policy to address both issues. Under lend-lease, Great Britain would lease certain military bases in the Western Hemisphere (in Newfoundland, Bermuda, and elsewhere) to the United States for ninety-nine years. In return, the United States would lend surplus aircraft and other military equipment to Great Britain. Thus, the British military would be strengthened, and the United States would gain control of bases that would help it defend the Western Hemisphere against potential German aggression.

Canada was not consulted under this agreement. Although a close ally and associate of Great Britain, since the Statute of Westminster in 1931 Canada had been a sovereign nation. The Canadian prime minster, William Lyon Mackenzie King, had been slow to recognize the threat posed by Nazi Germany. King, indeed, was ambivalent about his country's entry into the European war until the very last moment. There were many political pressures on King not to enter the war, ranging from Francophones in Quebec, whose fierce opposition to Britain made them reluctant to enter the war even though their own mother country, France, was on the British side, to isolationist farmers in the prairie provinces, who saw no apparent need to intervene in foreign disputes. Most Canadians, however, supported King when he decided to commit Canada to the war effort at the side of Great Britain.

Once engaged in the war, King shared the concerns of Roosevelt and Churchill regarding Western Hemisphere security, and was heartened by the lend-lease agreement. Nevertheless, he was concerned about Canadian national sovereignty as affected by the accord, especially in the case of Newfoundland. Newfoundland's close geographical proximity to Canada put it in the natural Canadian sphere of influence. Newfoundland had been an independent, self-governing dominion for sixty years, until the 1930's, when, because of its inability to handle the economic depression of that era, it had been taken over by Great Britain. King and the majority of the Canadian public expected that one day Newfoundland would join the rest of Canada (as, in fact, it did in 1949). He thus was unwilling to accept the permanent transfer of bases in Newfoundland to U.S. sovereignty.

Roosevelt was friendly toward Canada and knew the country well from his summer visits to the Canadian island of Campobello. Recognizing King's concern over the situation, Roosevelt advised the Canadian leader that he would be reviewing troops in the town of Ogdensburg, located in northern New York State close to the Canadian border, on August 16. King decided that it would be to Canada's advantage for him to meet Roosevelt at Ogdensburg. In deference to Canadian public opinion, he made no public announcement of the visit, fearing that it would be seen as an act of submission or surrender to the United States.

King did his best to keep the meeting a secret. Even J. L. Ralston, the Canadian minister of defense, whose responsibilities were vitally concerned with the situation, learned of the meeting only through reading the next day's newspapers. On the morning of August 16, Roosevelt arrived in Ogdensburg, accompanied by the U.S. ambassador to Canada, J. Pierrepont Moffat. Roosevelt met King, and the two men together reviewed U.S. troops. Roosevelt and King then repaired to a railway carriage, where the substantive discussions were held. The two men were very different. King was a mystic who regularly held séances in order to communicate with the spirit of his dead mother. Roosevelt, on the other hand, was regarded by many as the ultimate political opportunist, although his fierce commitment to democracy and liberalism never wavered. Nevertheless, the two men, who knew each other from previous meetings, had established a good working rapport, and they quickly reached a broad consensus.

The centerpiece of this consensus was the so-called Continental System. The Continental System provided that Canada and the United States would regularly consult each other about military conditions. It also stipulated that the two countries would prepare themselves to mount a common defense of the Western Hemisphere. It even allowed for the possibility of temporary U.S. bases being established on Canadian soil. This was the aspect of the Continental System most disagreeable to Canadian nationalists. The U.S. bases, however, were only in the context of Canadian involvement in the lend-lease policy. Although King and Canada had not been involved in the formulation of this policy, Roosevelt's briefing apprised the Canadian prime minister of the lend-lease initiative, of which King wholeheartedly approved. King and Roosevelt also reached agreement on the status of Newfoundland. Roosevelt abjured any possible U.S. intent to control or annex Newfoundland permanently and stated that the future status of Newfoundland was up to the inhabitants of the island themselves, in consultation with the Canadian and British governments.

The most important achievements of the Ogdensburg meeting were not in the precise terms hammered out between Roosevelt and King but in the general spirit of understanding and mutual support built between the two men. Canada and the United States had been friends for many years, but the two countries had never really been allies. The Ogdensburg Agreement prepared Canada and the United States for the alliance that would exist between them when the United States entered World War II in 1941 and that would continue through the postwar years.

The Ogdensburg Agreement also represented a shift on the part of Canadian military and defense policy from a primary orientation toward Great Britain to a similar orientation toward the United States. By 1940, Canadian independence had been fully achieved. Canada, large in area but small in population, would inevitably have to engage in cooperation and alliance with another, more powerful country. Canada previously had been wary of the United States, since the latter country was so much larger in population. The dominance of the United States on the North American continent had caused observers periodically to wonder if Canada might eventually be annexed by the United States. Although the Ogdensburg Agreement might have seemed to subordinate Canada to U.S. defense policy, it had the countervailing effect of firmly enshrining the interests of an independent Canada within a North American defense context. This reaffirmation of Canadian independence substantially assisted U.S.-Canadian cooperation after the United States entered the war. It also smoothed the way for eventual Canadian participation in two postwar

defense alliances led by the United States: the North Atlantic Treaty Organization (NATO) and the North American Air Defense Pact (NORAD).

Predictably, King faced considerable outcry in the Canadian nationalist press once he returned to Ottawa and his meeting with Roosevelt was revealed to the public. However, his achievement in the Ogdensburg meeting was considerable, helping cement Allied cooperation in the long and determined struggle against Nazi Germany and its threat to democracy and freedom. —*Nicholas Birns*

ADDITIONAL READING:

Gibson, Frederick, and Jonathan G. Rossie, eds. *The Road to Ogdensburg*. East Lansing: Michigan State University Press, 1993. Analyzes developments in Canadian-U.S. relations leading up to the agreement.

Kimball, W. F. *The Most Unsordid Act: Lend-Lease, 1939-1941*. Baltimore: The Johns Hopkins University Press, 1969. Provides background on British-U.S. relations.

Pickersgill, J. W. *The Mackenzie King Record*. Toronto: University of Toronto Press, 1960. A comprehensive archive of King's tenure as prime minister.

Stacey, C. P. *Arms, Men, and Governments: The War Policies of Canada, 1939-1945*. Ottawa: Queen's Printers, 1970. A history of Canadian defense policy.

Teatero, William. *Mackenzie King: Man of Mission*. Don Mills, Ont.: Nelson, 1979. An elementary biography of the prime minister.

SEE ALSO: 1931, Statute of Westminster; 1936, Reciprocity Treaty; 1941, Lend-Lease Act; 1949, North Atlantic Treaty.

1941 ■ 6.6 MILLION WOMEN ENTER THE U.S. LABOR FORCE: *wartime depletion of the male labor force opens nontraditional employment and new social roles to women*

DATE: 1941-1945
LOCALE: United States
CATEGORIES: Business and labor; Economics; Social reform; Women's issues

SUMMARY OF EVENT. With the advent of U.S. participation in World War II, employment opportunities for women increased dramatically, in both scope and number. As early as the summer of 1940, the U.S. government began to strengthen military and defense capabilities in preparation for war. Industry responded to this increased demand for war materials and, practically overnight, the rampant unemployment of the Depression years turned into a labor shortage. The entry of the United States into the war, prompted by the Japanese attack on Pearl Harbor in December, 1941, greatly increased the need for workers. Unemployment, which stood at 17.2 percent in 1939, plummeted to 4.7 percent in 1942, the first full year of U.S. mobilization. By 1944, at the war's peak, it was at a twentieth

century low of 1.2 percent. By 1942, both government officials and industry leaders realized that, in order to maintain
productivity, they must turn to the labor supply at
hand—women. In 1940, 11,970,000 women worked outside
the home. As a result of war-related employment, their numbers had increased to 18,610,000 by 1945. These women
worked in aircraft production, munitions, shipbuilding, and
other arenas traditionally dominated by men.

This rise in female employment in the 1940's was in stark
contrast to the previous decade—a decade dominated by economic depression. Historically, women had been tolerated in
the workforce as long as they continued to fulfill their primary
duties as wife, mother, and homemaker. In the 1930's, because
of widespread unemployment and economic hardship, that
tolerance existed only if a woman worker did not displace a
man. Depression-era policies in both the private and public
sectors encouraged employers to lay off women before men.
Section 213 of the 1933 Economy Act, for example, mandated
that federal agencies reducing personnel must first release
employees married to other federal workers. Seventy-five percent of those whom such agencies subsequently dismissed
were women. Many city and state governments, private employers, and school districts practiced similar policies during
the 1930's. Because men were the primary breadwinners, their
jobs were viewed as sacrosanct.

Despite the labor shortage in the early war years, the shift to
women workers did not come easily. Only by overcoming or
setting aside numerous cultural biases could Americans in the
1940's readily accept women workers in factories. There was
a stigma attached to women, especially married women, working outside the home; in addition, many employers feared that
factory work would be too physically challenging for "the
weaker sex." Women themselves often believed they lacked
the stamina to succeed at such heavy work, and some even felt
that physical labor was beneath their dignity.

The media played a large role in allaying these fears. From
films to advertisements, working women were shown supporting their fighting men by filling in at jobs back home. Although women were called upon to make sacrifices equal to
those made by men overseas, they were expected to do so
without sacrificing their femininity. Rosie the Riveter, a glamorous beauty in hard hat and work clothes, became the symbol
for a nation of women laboring to help win the war and bring
their men safely home. Such portrayals assured women that
they could best serve their husbands and families by serving
their country, and that so doing would not jeopardize their
womanliness. By emphasizing that such service was only until
the war ended, the media also reminded women that their
traditional roles as full-time wives and mothers had only been
temporarily suspended.

As women followed "Rosie's" example and entered the
workforce, they did so in new and challenging occupational
arenas. Before 1940, one in every four female workers was
employed as a domestic servant. During the war, however, this
was the only segment of the female labor force that stagnated.

Women became pilots, scientists, professors, and factory
workers in record numbers. Such professional fields as engineering, an almost exclusively male enclave before the war,
began to open to women. By the war's end, the number of
female defense workers had increased by 460 percent. Women
flocked to these more upwardly mobile careers, leaving most
service-oriented businesses facing labor shortages.

This new female presence in industry helped chip away at
some legal obstacles that had long stymied women. Between
1941 and 1945, four state legislatures passed equal pay laws,
mandating that women receive the same pay as men for the
same work. For the first time in history, Congress debated both
an equal pay bill and an equal rights amendment to the Constitution. In 1942, the National War Labor Board required that
women receive equal pay when the work they did was substantially the same as that of men. Several states passed laws
protecting married women from employment discrimination.
Under the provisions of the Lanham Act, passed early in 1942,
federally subsidized child care was made available to some of
the mothers who had taken jobs. Although such centers were
not widely available, at one point, there were three thousand
centers providing care for 130,000 children.

Although women were employed in much greater numbers
during World War II, some of them still faced discrimination.
Initially, married women were discouraged from joining their
unmarried sisters in the workforce. Their duties at home were
still considered too pressing. Economic realities, however,
soon forced employers and the government to rethink this
position. By 1944, for the first time in recorded U.S. history,
married women workers outnumbered those who were single.
The wives of men who were serving overseas were three times
more likely to work than those whose husbands remained at
home. Despite the continued labor shortage, many companies
were reluctant to employ older women, often refusing to hire
women older than thirty-five years of age. Black women,
however, experienced the most discrimination. Employers
who hired black men and white women still refused to hire
black women. When black women registered with federal
employment agencies, they were, almost without exception,
referred to such positions as domestic servants, waitresses,
laundresses, and cooks.

Although World War II temporarily altered women's labor
history, it did not permanently change its course. More women
did remain in the workforce in the immediate postwar years
than during the Depression. Many of them, however, lost their
jobs in industry and were compelled to return to traditional
female occupations such as clerical work, service, and sales.
Between June and September of 1945, one in four women who
had held factory jobs was dismissed. During the war years,
women held 25 percent of all jobs in the automobile industry;
by April, 1946, they were filling only 7.5 percent of those
same positions. After the war ended, society mandated that
women's patriotic duty be replaced by familial duty. Many
women who had carried double burdens of home and job
while their husbands were overseas eagerly embraced their

traditional role as homemaker. With the return of so many men from the war, the nation's birthrate soon skyrocketed, expanding many women's child-rearing responsibilities. The media continued to play an active part as a cultural mediator by encouraging women to ease the returning veterans' adjustment to civilian life by resuming their prewar roles. Still, some changes remained in effect. Pay scales for women generally improved, and the door that had opened to allow women a greater range of career choices did not completely close again.

—*Jane M. Gilliland*

ADDITIONAL READING:

Anderson, Karen. *Wartime Women: Sex Roles, Family Relations, and the Status of Women During World War II*. Westport, Conn.: Greenwood Press, 1981. Examines women's wartime experiences in the defense industry centers of Baltimore, Detroit, and Seattle.

Chafe, William. *The Paradox of Change: American Women in the Twentieth Century*. New York: Oxford University Press, 1991. Three chapters are devoted to women's experiences in World War II, including those in the workforce.

Gluck, Sherna. *Rosie the Riveter Revisited: Women, the War, and Social Change*. Boston: Twayne, 1987. Based on interviews with ten women who worked in the aircraft industry during World War II.

Hartmann, Susan M. *The Home Front and Beyond: American Women in the 1940's*. Boston: Twayne, 1982. Sets women's work experience in the context of a decade that began with war and ended by ushering in the postwar decorum of the 1950's.

O'Brien, Kenneth P., and Lynn H. Parsons, eds. *The Home Front War: World War II and American Society*. Westport, Conn.: Greenwood Press, 1995. Several articles in this collection of papers by noted World War II scholars discuss the female workforce.

Sealander, Judith. "The Reaction to Rosie the Riveter: War Policy and the Woman Worker in World War II." In *As Minority Becomes Majority: Federal Reaction to the Phenomenon of Women in the Work Force, 1920-1963*. Westport, Conn.: Greenwood Press, 1983. Summarizes federal policy regarding, and legislative reaction to, the expanded presence of women workers.

SEE ALSO: 1920, U.S. Women Gain the Vote; 1923, Proposal of the Equal Rights Amendment; 1963, Equal Pay Act.

1941 ■ LEND-LEASE ACT: *the United States finds a way to support Great Britain during wartime while maintaining official neutrality*

DATE: March 11, 1941
LOCALE: Washington, D.C.
CATEGORIES: Diplomacy and international relations; Laws and acts; Wars, uprisings, and civil unrest

KEY FIGURES:

Winston Leonard Spencer Churchill (1874-1965), prime minister of Great Britain

Franklin Delano Roosevelt (1882-1945), thirty-second president of the United States, 1933-1945

SUMMARY OF EVENT. Nazi Germany's invasion of Poland on September 1, 1939, plunged Europe into a second major war within twenty-five years—a war that would prove to be the worst in human history. As in the beginning of World War I, the United States hoped to remain neutral, although popular sentiment weighed heavily toward Great Britain and France. With memories of World War I still fresh in the minds of most Americans, isolationist views prevailed.

For six years prior to Germany's move against Poland, the United States watched developments in Europe with concern. Adolf Hitler, whose Nazi Party governed Germany, made no attempt to conceal his intentions to break with the Treaty of Versailles, rearm Germany, and expand Nazi control throughout Europe. At the same time, Italy's Benito Mussolini advanced aggressively against Ethiopia, and Japan continued military operations in China.

Keenly aware of these developments, the United States Congress in 1935 legislated the first in a series of neutrality laws. A six-month renewable act, the legislation prohibited the United States from selling arms or transporting munitions to belligerent nations. When it was renewed, a ban against making loans to warring nations was included. Congress and the president believed such a foreign policy would prevent the United States from slipping into another European war, should one arise.

The following year, developments in Europe proved peace to be but an illusion. Hitler's forces moved unopposed into the Rhineland, a French territory; in 1937, Germany involved itself in the Spanish Civil War and sealed the Rome-Berlin alliance. The United States responded with the Neutrality Act of 1937, which retained the principal features of the 1935 act but, at Roosevelt's urging, allowed presidential discretion to sell military goods to belligerents on a "cash and carry" basis, provided the material was not transported on U.S. ships. The altered policy pleased manufacturers who wanted to profit while the nation remained officially neutral and apart from the European crisis. The new policy also pleased those in the United States who thought it essential to aid the country's traditional allies.

Germany's expansion continued, and in his state of the union address, on January 4, 1939, President Roosevelt announced his dismay over the course of European affairs and his dissatisfaction with existing neutrality laws. He believed that the 1937 act benefited Hitler more than it did France or Great Britain. If Hitler's enemies were unable to acquire sufficient material for defense, Germany would find the Western nations unable to halt Nazi aggression. Surely, the president hinted, the United States could devise methods short of war to aid British and French military defense preparations.

Early that summer, the British government made a direct

appeal to Roosevelt for military supplies, and in June, the president suggested revision of the Neutrality Act of 1937 to broaden the cash-and-carry provision. Fearful that such a program of support for Great Britain would cast the United States in an image of cobelligerent, isolationists in Congress blocked Roosevelt's efforts. Germany's invasion of Poland on September 1, and the British-French declaration of war that followed, changed the congressional mood. By year's end, revisions to the 1937 act were sanctioned, making it easier for Britain to obtain needed supplies.

France fell to the Nazis in June, 1940. Great Britain was the sole surviving power in Europe. Many thought that the United States should provide direct military aid to the British, the United States' front line against Germany. If Britain collapsed, the United States would become Hitler's next target. Others contended that the United States needed to strengthen its own defenses in preparation for Nazi actions in the Western Hemisphere. Roosevelt chose to follow both courses. He gained approval from Congress to appropriate funds for U.S. rearmament and for a peacetime compulsory military training law. In June, using executive authority, Roosevelt authorized the supply of outdated aircraft and rifles to Great Britain; in September, he arranged with Britain the exchange of fifty U.S. naval destroyers for leases of British naval bases.

Great Britain's financial reserves dwindled as autumn faded. In December, Prime Minister Winston Churchill informed Roosevelt that the cash-and-carry system needed modification. Roosevelt understood that Great Britain could not withstand further Nazi attacks without direct U.S. aid and that the United States' own security was largely dependent on British resistance to Hitler. In mid-December, Roosevelt conceived the idea of lend-lease: War goods would be provided Allied nations and either returned or paid for at war's end. In both a press conference and a radio "fireside chat," Roosevelt stated that the best defense for the United States was a strong Great Britain. Every step short of war should be taken to help the British Empire defend itself. Great Britain's inability to pay cash for U.S. supplies should not relegate the empire to Nazi conquest. To lend or lease the necessary goods would provide for Great Britain's immediate war needs and indirectly benefit the United States by making Great Britain the United States' front line of defense. Roosevelt presented an analogy to clarify the proposal: "Suppose my neighbor's home catches fire, and I have a length of garden hose four hundred or five hundred feet away. If he can take my garden hose and connect it up with his hydrant, I may help him to put out his fire." If the hose survived the fire, it would be returned. Should it be damaged, the neighbor would replace it. Military aid would be treated in the same way. The United States must become the "arsenal of democracy" and provide the goods necessary to halt Nazi expansion.

To secure permission and funding to aid Great Britain, Roosevelt introduced into the House of Representatives the Lend-Lease bill. The bill generated intense debate. Opponents said the measure would move the United States from neutral-

ity to the status of active nonbelligerent and risk war with Germany. They believed that it would be more logical to plan to build the United States' own defenses. Supporters argued that Hitler posed a real, direct threat to the United States, and that aiding Great Britain would make U.S. entry into the war less likely. Public opinion favored the president. Although 82 percent of Americans believed war was inevitable, nearly 80 percent opposed entry unless the nation were directly attacked.

After two months of congressional debate, the Lend-Lease Act was passed on March 11, 1941. It permitted the president to lend or lease war materiel to any nation whose defense was deemed critical to the United States, and it authorized an immediate appropriation of seven billion dollars for Great Britain. In June, following Germany's invasion of Russia, Roosevelt extended lend-lease to the Soviet Union. The Lend-Lease Act retained official U.S. neutrality, but the measure also placed the United States more squarely in opposition to Nazi Germany. In March, 1941, the United States teetered on the brink of war.

By war's end, in 1945, the United States appropriated slightly more than fifty billion dollars under the lend-lease program. Great Britain received twenty-seven billion dollars of aid, the Soviet Union was provided ten billion dollars, and the remaining funds supplied goods to other Allied nations.

Roosevelt's contemporaries and postwar scholars have questioned the president's prewar direction of U.S. policy, particularly with regard to lend-lease. Some have argued that Roosevelt desperately wanted U.S. entry into the war long before Pearl Harbor but was restrained by popular opinion and political realities. Therefore, they argue, Roosevelt worked within the system to place the United States on an ever-advancing course toward war by molding public opinion, relaxing neutrality laws, and securing lend-lease. Others contend the president hoped to avoid intervention in Europe's war. Lend-lease thus was a practical method for the United States to aid the Allies while remaining a nonbelligerent. Regardless of Roosevelt's motives, Japan's attack on Pearl Harbor on December 7, 1941, sealed the United States' fate. War came to the United States. 　　　　　　　　　—*Kenneth William Townsend*

ADDITIONAL READING:

Dobson, Alan P. *U.S. Wartime Aid to Britain, 1940-1946*. New York: St. Martin's Press, 1986. Investigates the economic relationship between the United States and Great Britain.

Herring, George C., Jr. *Aid to Russia, 1941-1946: Strategy, Diplomacy, the Origins of the Cold War*. New York: Columbia University Press, 1973. While U.S. aid to the Soviet Union was meager and a slow process initially, it came to symbolize the cooperative Allied spirit in war.

Jones, Robert Huhn. *The Roads to Russia: United States Lend-Lease to the Soviet Union*. Norman: University of Oklahoma Press, 1969. Asserts that lend-lease aid was critical to Soviet survival but at war's end, became a central issue in decaying Soviet-United States relations.

Kimball, Warren F. *The Most Unsordid Act: Lend-Lease, 1939-1941*. Baltimore: The Johns Hopkins University Press,

1969. Shows the slow legislative process involved in securing passage of the Lend-Lease Act. Examines the issue of whether the act made United States entry into the war inevitable.

Langer, William L., and S. Everett Gleason. *The Unde-clared War, 1940-1941*. Gloucester, Mass.: Peter Smith, 1968. Chapters 8 and 9 are centered on the origin and enactment of lend-lease.

Van Tuyll, Hubert P. *Feeding the Bear: American Aid to the Soviet Union, 1941-1945*. New York: Greenwood Press, 1989. Examines U.S. lend-lease aid to the Soviet Union and its promises of continued aid following the war.

SEE ALSO: 1935, Neutrality Acts; 1939, Mobilization for World War II; 1940, Ogdensburg Agreement.

1941 ■ EXECUTIVE ORDER 8802: *a major step in the advancement of African American civil rights prohibits discrimination in the military*

DATE: June 25, 1941
LOCALE: Washington, D.C.
CATEGORIES: African American history; Civil rights
KEY FIGURES:
Asa Philip Randolph (1889-1979), president of the
   Brotherhood of Sleeping Car Porters
Eleanor Roosevelt (1884-1962), First Lady of the United
   States
Franklin Delano Roosevelt (1882-1945), thirty-second
   president of the United States, 1933-1945
Harry S Truman (1884-1972), thirty-third president of the
   United States, 1945-1953
SUMMARY OF EVENT. Ever since the Revolutionary War, the United States had experienced difficulty in bringing African Americans into its military. Although one of the victims of the Boston Massacre, Crispus Attucks, was an African American, and black soldiers were with George Washington when he made his famous 1776 Christmas crossing of the Delaware to attack the Hessians at Trenton and Princeton, it was not until the Civil War that African American troops were recruited officially into the United States Army. Even then, however, a rigid policy of segregation was maintained. In the two wars that followed, the Spanish-American War and World War I, both the Army and Navy had black troops, but largely in supporting roles, and always as separate, segregated units. In addition, black troop strength was kept deliberately low, partly to avoid offending white soldiers and partly because the military establishment had a low opinion of the abilities of African American troops.

During the 1930's, however, under the presidency of Frank-lin Delano Roosevelt, these prejudiced traditions began to change. Roosevelt's New Deal, which had been put into place to fight the ravages of the Great Depression, also addressed a number of social conditions, including civil rights. Although

civil rights were never at the forefront of Roosevelt's agenda, his administration was more committed to them than any previous presidency had been, and his wife, the redoubtable Eleanor Roosevelt, was an especially strong and capable advocate for racial equality and justice. In addition, the shrewdly realistic president, who foresaw the coming struggle with Nazi Germany, realized that the U.S. military needed every capable citizen, of whatever color or background. The policy of "Jim Crowism," or rigid segregation of blacks and whites, remained largely in place, however.

Correctly estimating the extent and depth of prejudice against African American participation in the military, especially in positions of responsibility, Roosevelt moved cautiously. He had been assistant secretary of the Navy under President Woodrow Wilson during World War I; now, Roosevelt prodded and encouraged the Navy high command to enlist additional African Americans and to place them in positions of greater responsibility than stewards or mess servers. Gradually and slowly, the Navy responded. A similar broadening took place in the Army in 1935, when the president insisted that African American medical officers and chaplains be called up from the reserves. On October 9, 1940, Roosevelt announced a revised racial policy for the armed forces; its intent was to bring more African Americans into the military and to place them in positions of trust and responsibility. At a glacial but perceptible pace, the United States military was becoming more receptive to African Americans.

The progress was not sufficiently rapid for many African Americans, among them A. Philip Randolph, president of the Brotherhood of Sleeping Car Porters, one of the strongest and most effective African American unions in the country. Randolph, who well understood that black voters had become an essential part of the Democratic Party's electoral base, calculated that Roosevelt would need to respond to African American demands, especially as the 1940 presidential elections approached. Randolph's logic and timing were correct.

In 1940, Roosevelt ran for an unprecedented third term as president. Randolph, along with former Republican city councilman Grant Reynolds of New York City, began a campaign against the Jim Crow practices still prevalent in the United States military. Randolph and Reynolds also called for greater opportunities for African American workers in the rapidly growing defense industries, which had arisen as the United States rearmed against the threat from Nazi Germany and imperialist Japan. As the campaign intensified, Roosevelt faced a difficult situation that threatened his Southern, conservative support at the same time that it endangered his urban, liberal allies. When Randolph announced plans for a march on Washington, scheduled for July 1, 1941, Roosevelt knew he must act. His determination was steeled by the resolve of his wife Eleanor, who had long been a champion of equal rights for African Americans, and whose contacts with the black community were strong and deep.

On June 25, 1941, Roosevelt issued Executive Order 8802, which enunciated a broad policy of racial equality in the armed forces and the defense industry. The order was clear and sweeping in its intent:

> In offering the policy of full participation in the defense program by all persons regardless of color, race, creed, or national origin, and directing certain action in furtherance of said policy . . . all departments of the government, including the Armed Forces, shall lead the way in erasing discrimination over color or race.

President Roosevelt backed up the policy by establishing the Fair Employment Practices Commission, which was charged with monitoring and enforcing compliance among civilian contractors. It is estimated that Roosevelt's executive order, combined with the work of the commission, helped to bring fifty-three thousand African American civilians into defense industry jobs they otherwise would not have held.

The timing of the policy was impeccable. Randolph and the other campaign leaders, satisfied that the Roosevelt Administration was sincere in its commitment to civil rights, called off the march on Washington. Political conservatives, who otherwise might have challenged the president's order, had to admit that it would not be proper to expect African Americans to serve in the military without allowing them to hold responsible positions and achieve corresponding rank. Black voters responded enthusiastically to the Roosevelt re-election campaign, helping him to sweep to victory in the November balloting.

Inevitably, there were racial tensions and outbreaks of violence, especially in lower- and middle-class Northern neighborhoods. In 1943, for example, tension between black and white workers led to open violence at a park on Belle Isle near Detroit; in the end, federal troops had to be called in to restore order, and twenty-five African Americans and nine whites had been killed. Similar, if less bloody, events took place in other cities. Still, the transition to a more equitable situation continued in both civilian and military life.

However, the traditional segregation remained. During World War II, black units still were kept separate and apart from white troops, and generally reserved for support and logistical duties rather than combat. When the difficulties and emergencies of battle required it, African American units were brought into the fighting line; generally, they acquitted themselves well. By the end of the war, African Americans had distinguished themselves as ground soldiers, sailors, and pilots in both combat and noncombat situations. After the surrender of the Axis powers in 1945, there was a sense of inevitable change ahead for the United States military. The question of whether it would be a peaceful, productive change remained.

Harry S Truman, who assumed the presidency in 1945 after the death of Franklin Roosevelt, was determined to make the change in a proper fashion. He assembled a special Civil Rights Committee which, on October 30, 1947, issued its report, *To Secure These Rights*. Clearly and unhesitatingly, the report called for the elimination of segregation in the United States military.

As the 1948 presidential elections approached, the issue of African Americans in the military affected the political atmosphere. Truman and the national Democratic Party, as heirs of the Roosevelt New Deal, had strong connections with the Civil Rights movement and its leaders; at the same time, much of the traditional Democratic strength was in the South, where civil rights issues were strongly opposed by the entrenched establishment. Southern politicians, such as Strom Thurmond of South Carolina, threatened to bolt the party if the Democrats adopted a strong civil rights platform at their convention; however, inspired by the passionate appeal of Mayor Hubert H. Humphrey of Minneapolis, the Democrats did indeed adopt a positive plank on civil rights. The Southerners stormed out, nominating Thurmond to run on the "Dixiecrat" ticket, and Truman went on to win a come-from-behind victory in November.

One element of that victory was his own Executive Order 9981, issued on July 26, 1948, just after the Democratic Party convention. Truman's order was similar to but stronger than Roosevelt's: It required equal opportunity in the armed forces of the United States, regardless of race, and called upon the military services to move immediately to implement the directive. The Air Force reacted promptly and soon achieved remarkable integration of black and white troops; the Navy and Marines were more hesitant in their acceptance. In the end, however, all branches of the armed forces responded, making them among the most egalitarian and equitable of U.S. institutions.

—Michael Witkoski

ADDITIONAL READING:

Dalifiume, Richard. *Desegregation of the U.S. Armed Forces: Fighting on Two Fronts, 1939-1953*. Columbia: University of Missouri Press, 1969. Although its emphasis is on the role of African Americans as soldiers, sailors, and airmen, this volume brings additional light to Roosevelt's order and its impact.

Nalty, Bernard C. *Strength for the Fight: A History of Black Americans in the Military*. New York: Free Press, 1986. A comprehensive narrative of the relationship between African Americans and the U.S. armed forces. Factual and balanced in its approach, it places the issues in historical context. Illustrated.

Stillman, Richard J. *Integration of the Negro in the U.S. Armed Forces*. New York: Frederick A. Praeger, 1968. Provides a specialized, in-depth examination of the way in which African Americans were gradually brought into the U.S. armed forces. Especially good discussion of the Roosevelt and Truman policies regarding blacks in the military.

U.S. Department of Defense. Office of the Deputy Assistant Secretary of Defense for Civilian Personnel Policy/Equal Opportunity. *Black Americans in Defense of Our Nation*. Washington, D.C.: Government Printing Office, 1991. This pictorial documentary covers all branches of the armed forces and include defense- and military-related occupations as well.

Woodward, C. Vann. *The Strange Career of Jim Crow*. 2d rev. ed. New York: Oxford University Press, 1966. Has remained the definitive work on legal, official segregation in

American life. A valuable resource that places the Roosevelt and Truman executive orders in historical perspective.

SEE ALSO: 1943, Urban Race Riots; 1970's, Rise of Women's Role in the Military.

1941 ■ BOMBING OF PEARL HARBOR:
Japan's surprise attack on the United States' Pacific Fleet forces U.S. entry into World War II

DATE: December 7, 1941
LOCALE: Pearl Harbor, Oahu, Hawaiian Islands
CATEGORY: Wars, uprisings, and civil unrest
KEY FIGURES:
Cordell Hull (1871-1955), secretary of state
Husband Edward Kimmel (1882-1968), commander, U.S. Pacific Fleet
George Catlett Marshall (1880-1959), chief of staff of the U.S. Army
Kichisaburo Nomura (1887-1964), Japanese ambassador to the United States
Franklin Delano Roosevelt (1882-1945), thirty-second president of the United States, 1933-1945
Walter Campbell Short (1880-1949), commander, Hawaiian Department, United States Army
Harold R. Stark (1880-1972), chief of naval operations
Hideki Tojo (1884-1948), prime minister of Japan
Isoroku Yamamoto (1884-1943), creator of the plan to launch a surprise air attack on Pearl Harbor
SUMMARY OF EVENT. The surprise attack by Japanese naval air forces upon the huge United States naval base at Pearl Harbor, Hawaii, has become synonymous with duplicity and cunning. Nevertheless, the circumstances of the attack engendered bitter controversy over the reasons for the failure of U.S. leaders to anticipate and to defend themselves against this devastating blow.

In retrospect, Pearl Harbor can be explained without recourse to a "devil theory of war"—that Japan, unprovoked by the United States, deliberately and wantonly struck the Navy's Pacific command center. Given the Japanese military and political situation and the dictates of Japanese strategic thinking, the attack was the logical result of a series of confrontations between Japan and the United States. Although U.S. interest was focused primarily on Europe between 1939 and 1941, events in the Far East aroused increasing concern in Washington, D.C., as Japan carried forth its ambitious creation of a Japanese-dominated Greater East Asia Co-Prosperity Sphere, which championed "Asia for Asians." Much of China had fallen under Japanese control by 1939. Japan officially became an Axis power in September, 1940, with the signing of the Tripartite Pact—a "defensive" alliance among Germany, Italy, and Japan. By the summer of 1941, Japan had gained concessions in Indochina and was threatening to engulf Thai-

land, Russia's Siberian provinces, the British bastion of Singapore, Burma, the Dutch East Indies, and the Philippines.

The United States opposed this Japanese expansion primarily with moral and economic sanctions. Throughout the 1930's, as Japan seized Manchuria and moved against China, the United States proved unable or unwilling to oppose Japan by force. Although sympathetic toward China, President Franklin Delano Roosevelt was more concerned about Germany than about Japan. Supported by navy spokesmen who feared that a two-ocean war would lead the United States to disaster, Roosevelt adopted a policy of caution toward Japanese expansion in the hope that liberal Japanese leaders would wrest power from the more militant imperialists and reverse Japan's course. Despite British and Dutch pressure, the United States was slow to accept the necessity of economic sanctions until August, 1940, when Roosevelt imposed an embargo on aviation gasoline. Restrictions on the export of scrap iron and steel followed in September, 1940, and Japanese assets in the United States were frozen in July, 1941.

Japanese leaders, almost all of whom supported the program of expansion and differed only on how it should be accomplished, came to believe that Japan was being encircled by the Western powers. If Japanese demands were not achieved by diplomacy, military force would become necessary. Economic sanctions by the United States, Great Britain, and the Netherlands—especially the embargo—meant that Japan had to choose between peace and war within a year, before its oil reserves were exhausted. In July, 1941, an advance into Southeast Asia for oil and other resources was approved by the Japanese Imperial Council, even if it meant war with the United States. On September 6, an Imperial Conference set what amounted to a time limit on diplomatic efforts for the settlement of negotiations with the United States. Negotiations continued, with neither side offering concessions. Roosevelt and Secretary of State Cordell Hull were pessimistic but believed that discussions should continue, in order that the United States might gain time for defense preparations.

Meanwhile, Army and Navy intelligence at Pearl Harbor and in Washington, D.C., learned that Japan might be planning to mount a surprise attack, but the evidence was fragmentary. U.S. military planners knew from intercepted messages that things would happen automatically if the U.S. rejected a final Japanese proposal, but most indications pointed to an attack somewhere in Southeast Asia. Ambassador Kichisaburo Nomura of Japan presented to Hull what was to be the final Japanese proposal for peace on November 10. Hull declared it unacceptable and on November 26 made a counteroffer, which he knew from intercepted Japanese messages would be rejected. Diplomacy proved futile. On Sunday, December 7, while Japanese planes were making their bomb runs over Pearl Harbor, a Japanese diplomatic note was handed to the secretary of state; it implied disruption of relations, but it was not a declaration of war.

Japan's preparations for the attack on Pearl Harbor had begun with tactical planning in the early months of 1941.

Japanese strategists recognized that an advance into Southeast Asia would likely generate a U.S. military response. Destruction of the United States Pacific Fleet based in Hawaii was essential if Japan's move into the region was to succeed. A daring plan by Admiral Isoroku Yamamoto to destroy or crip-ple the fleet at anchor in Pearl Harbor was at first considered impractical, if not suicidal, but the proposal was later accepted when table-top games proved it workable and Yamamoto exerted his powerful influence in favor of it. Pilots began training in September, and all objections were overcome. To cope with

Pearl Harbor, Hawaii. In the background, smoke rises from Hickam Field in this captured Japanese aerial photograph taken during the bombing. (National Archives)

the shallow waters of Pearl Harbor, wooden-finned torpedoes were devised, together with a new method of delivering them on target; elaborate precautions were undertaken to preserve secrecy; and abundant intelligence was gathered concerning the movements of the U.S. Pacific Fleet.

Under the command of Vice Admiral Chuichi Nagumo, a special task force of thirty-one vessels, including six aircraft carriers that carried 432 airplanes—fighters, dive-bombers, high-level attack bombers, and torpedo planes—left Japanese ports in early November. On November 22, this force gathered in the Southern Kuriles. Four days later, it headed out to sea for a run of 3,500 miles to a rendezvous point 275 miles north of Pearl Harbor. The strike force was not to attack until final clearance for action was issued from the Japanese high command. On December 2, the signal "Climb Mount Niitaka" was received by Nagumo and the date of attack confirmed. Early on December 7, the strike force reached position, so that the first Japanese planes were flying over Pearl Harbor by 7:55 A.M., local time.

The weather was ideal for an attack, and Pearl Harbor was caught totally unprepared. The blow was deliberately planned for Sunday morning, when the ships of the Pacific Fleet were moored in perfect alignment and their crews were ashore, having breakfast, or relaxing on board ship. There was no advance warning in Hawaii. An operator at a temporary U.S. radar post observed the oncoming Japanese squadrons at 7:02 A.M.; he reported the blips shown on the radar screen, but the watch officer did not pass on the information, thinking they were a group of U.S. bombers expected to arrive that morning from the West Coast.

The Japanese planes swooped to the attack. Fighters and dive-bombers strafed and bombed the neat rows of aircraft at Wheeler Field and the Naval Air Station. Torpedo planes and dive-bombers also attacked Battleship Row in the devastating first phase, which lasted thirty minutes. After a fifteen-minute lull, the Japanese launched high-level bombing attacks on the harbor, airfields, and shore installations, followed by more attacks by dive-bombers, which pressed through mounting antiaircraft fire. The last planes withdrew at 9:45 A.M., less than two hours after the attack had begun.

They left behind a scene of destruction and carnage without parallel in U.S. history. Casualties were 2,403 dead and 1,178 wounded. Three battleships—the *West Virginia*, *Arizona*, and *California*—were sunk; the *Oklahoma* lay capsized; and the *Tennessee*, *Nevada*, *Maryland*, and *Pennsylvania* suffered varying degrees of damage. Several smaller warships were sunk, and others were seriously crippled. Almost all combat aircraft on the islands were damaged or destroyed. Twenty-nine Japanese airplanes were lost, along with one full-sized submarine and five midget submarines.

The U.S. forces in Hawaii fought courageously and recovered quickly from their initial shock. However, they were tragically unprepared to repel the skillful blows rained down by the Japanese strike force. The Japanese were successful far beyond the expectations of their high command; the United

States Pacific Fleet lay grievously wounded and would not, Japan believed, be able to undertake offensive operations for months. The attack failed, however, in two particulars. First, the Japanese missed their prime targets: the aircraft carriers *Lexington* and *Enterprise* (both of which were at sea), and *Saratoga* (which was in dry dock on the West Coast). Second, the Japanese failed to destroy the huge oil storage facilities, without which the Pacific Fleet would have been forced to retire to the West Coast. While historical debate continues regarding the necessity of the attack for Japan and the United States' lack of preparedness, the Pearl Harbor attack unified the U.S. people and eliminated whatever isolationist sentiment still existed in 1941. Within a few days, the United States was at war with Japan, and, because of the Tripartite Pact, with Germany as well. —*Theodore A. Wilson, updated by Kenneth William Townsend*

ADDITIONAL READING:

Layton, Edwin T. *"And I Was There": Pearl Harbor and Midway—Breaking the Secrets.* New York: William Morrow, 1985. A personal recollection of one U.S. naval officer in Hawaii during the Pearl Harbor attack.

Prange, Gordon. *At Dawn We Slept: The Untold Story of Pearl Harbor.* New York: McGraw-Hill, 1981. An objective study of the principal participants of Pearl Harbor, both Japanese and American. The book provides an examination of personalities and events as they unfolded over a span of two years.

_____. *Pearl Harbor: The Verdict of History.* New York: McGraw-Hill, 1986. Examines the Pearl Harbor attack to determine responsibility for the United States' loss and Japan's victory.

Satterfield, Archie. *The Day the War Began.* Westport, Conn.: Praeger, 1992. A reexamination of the events leading to and following the attack on Pearl Harbor.

Toland, John. *Infamy: Pearl Harbor and Its Aftermath.* New York: Berkeley Books, 1982. Presents the events leading to Pearl Harbor from both Japanese and U.S. perspectives. Includes numerous interviews with officers, strategists, and general personnel of both military forces. Presents a conspiracy theory to explain the U.S. defeat at Pearl Harbor.

Weintraub, Stanley. *Long Day's Journey into War: December 7, 1941.* New York: Dutton, 1991. Covers the Sunday morning Japanese air assault and the day's developments in Hawaii following the attack, with emphasis on popular reactions.

Wohlstetter, Roberta. *Pearl Harbor: Warning and Decision.* Stanford, Calif.: Stanford University Press, 1962. The story of Pearl Harbor, grounded in the position that the U.S. loss was the result of human error.

SEE ALSO: 1939, Mobilization for World War II; 1940, United States Builds a Two-Ocean Navy; 1941, Lend-Lease Act; 1942, Censorship and Japanese Internment; 1942, Battle of Midway; 1942, Manhattan Project; 1942, Battle of Guadalcanal; 1944, Superfortress Bombing of Japan; 1944, Battle for Leyte Gulf; 1945, Atomic Bombing of Japan.

World War II: The Fight for Europe

Sept. 1, 1939	Germany invades Poland.
Sept. 3, 1939	Great Britain declares war on Germany. President Franklin D. Roosevelt declares U.S. neutrality.
Sept. 10, 1939	King George VI declares war on Germany on behalf of Canada. Although Canada was technically at war upon Britain's entry, this independent declaration confirms de facto Canadian sovereignty.
Oct. 3, 1939	DECLARATION OF PANAMA: Inter-American Conference announces zones in the Western Hemisphere where belligerents are warned to refrain from military action.
Nov. 4, 1939	FOURTH NEUTRALITY ACT: Authorizes U.S. exports of arms to belligerents on a cash-and-carry basis.
Apr. 9, 1940	Germany invades Norway.
May 10, 1940	Germany invades Luxembourg, the Netherlands, and Belgium.

World War II: The European Theater

May 11, 1940	British prime minister Neville Chamberlain is succeeded by Winston Churchill.
May 28-June 11, 1940	DUNKIRK EVACUATION: Nearly 350,000 French and British troops leave France.
June 5, 1940	BATTLE OF FRANCE: Germans invade France across the Somme River and the Aisne-Oise canal.
June 10, 1940	Italy declares war on France and Great Britain. Italian forces enter southern France.
June 14, 1940	Germany enters Paris.
July 20, 1940	Roosevelt signs into law U.S. legislation authorizing funds for a two-ocean navy to defend the United States and the Western Hemisphere. *See* **1940, United States Builds a Two-Ocean Navy.**
Aug. 8-Oct. 31, 1940	BATTLE OF BRITAIN: Germany bombs Great Britain in preparation for a land invasion; despite great losses on both sides, British repulse German air power and avoid German occupation.
Aug. 16, 1940	OGDENSBURG AGREEMENT: United States and Canada establish the Continental System, whereby Canada and the United States mount a common defense of the Western Hemisphere and the United States is allowed to build military bases on Canadian soil.
Sept. 27, 1940	Germany and Italy sign the Tripartite Pact, a mutual defense agreement with Japan.
Oct. 8, 1940	Germany occupies Romania.
Oct. 28, 1940	Italy invades Greece.
Jan., 1941	United States establishes Office of Production Management to mobilize defense production. Roosevelt's stated objective is to make the United States the "arsenal of democracy."
Jan. 6, 1941	Roosevelt delivers his "Four Freedoms" speech to Congress, listing freedom of expression, freedom of religion, freedom from want, and freedom from fear. The same speech recommends aid to the Allies by means of lend-lease.
Feb.-May, 1941	BATTLE OF THE ATLANTIC: Germany mounts a naval campaign against Allies and neutral powers, using submarines as well as battleships. Germans sink U.S. merchant vessel *Robin Moor* off the coast of Brazil on May 21.
Mar. 11, 1941	LEND-LEASE ACT: Lend-lease makes it possible for U.S. arms to continue to flow to Great Britain, despite its inability to pay. Britain's defense is judged vital to U.S. interests. *See* **1941, Lend-Lease Act.**
Mar. 24, 1941	German general Erwin Rommel begins a North African campaign forcing British to retreat to Egypt.
Apr. 17, 1941	Yugoslavia falls to the Germans.
Apr. 23, 1941	Greece falls to the Germans.
Apr. 27, 1941	United States, the Netherlands, and Great Britain make alliance in the event of Japanese aggression.
June 18, 1941	French general Charles de Gaulle pledges continued French resistance against coming Vichy dictatorship.
June 22, 1941	France under Henri Philippe Pétain signs a German-French armistice; a similar armistice with Italy is signed two days later. Pétain is installed at Vichy as French dictator on July 10.
June 22, 1941	Germany invades the Soviet Union; occupies Ukraine, then Leningrad, then Sevastopol, reaching Moscow by November.
Sept. 4, 1941	Germany attacks USS *Greer*; on Oct. 17, USS *Kearny* is torpedoed by a German submarine; on Oct. 30, Germany sinks USS *Reuben James*. Congress repeals parts of the Fourth Neutrality Act to allow arming of merchant vessels.
Sept. 24, 1941	Fifteen nations have endorsed the anti-Axis Atlantic Charter, drawn up by Roosevelt and Churchill during secret talks conducted aboard U.S. and British ships in August.
Nov. 1, 1941	United States extends lend-lease credit to the Soviet Union.
Dec. 7, 1941	PEARL HARBOR BOMBING: Japan's aggression ensures the United States' entry into the war. *See* **1941, Bombing of Pearl Harbor.**
Dec. 11, 1941	Germany and Italy declare war on the United States, and United States responds with its own declaration. *See* **1941, Germany and Italy Declare War on the United States.**

Jan. 20, 1942	Russians begin German counteroffensive.
May 30, 1942	Allies begin their thousand-bomber air raids on Germany.
Sept. 13, 1942	Germans enter Stalingrad.
Nov. 4, 1942	BATTLE OF EL ALAMEIN: British victory forces a German retreat from Egypt. British go on to take Bardia, Tobruk, and Bengasi by Nov. 20.
Nov. 8, 1942	OPERATION TORCH: U.S. and British amphibious forces land in North Africa at Casablanca, Oran, and Algiers. Allies make armistice with Vichy leader in North Africa, Jean Louis Darlan (Nov. 11), but he is soon assassinated (Dec. 24).
Jan. 24, 1943	British take Tripoli. *See* **1942, Invasion of North Africa.**
Feb. 2, 1943	Germans surrender at Stalingrad.
Feb. 14, 1943	Rostov falls to the Russians.
Feb. 16, 1943	Kharkov falls to the Russians.
Mar. 9, 1943	Rzhev falls to the Russians.
Apr. 7, 1943	U.S. and British lines meet in North Africa.
May 7, 1943	Tunis falls to the British. Bizerte falls to the United States.
May 13, 1943	Axis surrenders in North Africa.
July 10-Aug. 17, 1943	OPERATION HUSKY: Allies invade and occupy Sicily.
July 25, 1943	Italian dictator Benito Mussolini resigns, replaced by Pietro Badoglio as head of the Italian government. Badoglio dissolves the Fascist Party on July 28.
Aug. 4, 1943	Russians take Orel and Belgorod.
Sept. 3, 1943	British invade Italy.
Sept. 8, 1943	Italy surrenders unconditionally.
Sept. 9, 1943	OPERATION AVALANCHE: United States begins campaign against German-occupied Italy, landing amphibious forces at Salerno. *See* **1943, Western Allies Invade Italy.**
Sept. 25, 1943	Russians take Smolensk.
Oct. 9, 1943	Yugoslavians under Marshal Josip Broz Tito begin their campaign against Axis powers.
Dec. 25, 1943	Allied invasion of Italy has reached the Sangro River.
Jan. 3, 1944	Russians enter Poland.
Jan. 11-May, 1944	Allied air raids of the Continent from Great Britain begin to soften Normandy for a ground-force invasion.
Jan. 16, 1944	U.S. general Dwight D. Eisenhower, former leader of Allied forces in North Africa, arrives in England as Supreme Commander of the Allied Expeditionary Forces.
Jan. 22, 1944	Allied amphibious forces land south of Rome at Anzio beachhead and begin an assault on Germans in central Italy. Monte Cassino falls on May 18.
Jan. 29, 1944	Russians have evacuated German troops from the Moscow-Leningrad region.
Apr. 10, 1944	Russians take Odessa.
May 9, 1944	Russians take Sevastopol.
June 4, 1944	Allied liberation of Rome.
June 6, 1944	OPERATION OVERLORD: Crossing the English Channel, massive Allied amphibious forces invade Normandy along the coast between the Orne River and the Cotentin Peninsula. With an initial force of more than 150,000 troops, 4,000 invasion craft, 600 warships, and 11,000 airplanes, the invasion is the largest amphibious campaign in history. *See* **1944, Operation Overlord.**

June 14, 1944	Germans launch V-1 pilotless aircraft to bomb England.
June 23, 1944	Russians begin a counteroffensive south of Leningrad.
June 27, 1944	U.S. forces capture Cherbourg.
July 9, 1944	Caen falls to the British.
July 20, 1944	Failed attempt to assassinate German chancellor Adolf Hitler.
July 25, 1944	BATTLE OF FRANCE: U.S. "breakout" of Normandy at St. Lô launches the Allied thrust into Brittany, ending the Normandy invasion and initiating the campaign to secure the interior of France.
Aug. 12, 1944	Florence, Italy, falls to British.
Aug. 15, 1944	OPERATION DRAGOON: U.S. forces invade southern France and begin to move up the Rhone River Valley.
Aug. 25, 1944	Liberation of Paris.
Sept. 4, 1944	Liberation of Brussels and Antwerp.
Sept. 7, 1944	Germans launch V-2 rockets toward London.
Sept. 8, 1944	Bulgaria surrenders to the Allies.
Sept. 11, 1944	Liberation of Luxembourg.
Sept. 12, 1944	BATTLE FOR GERMANY begins when the United States enters Germany near Trier and Eupen.
Sept. 22, 1944	Russians take Tallinn.
Oct. 2, 1944	Polish forces surrender to Germany. In Germany, the United States begins the battle for Aachen.
Oct. 9, 1944	Canadians begin to secure the Scheldt Estuary to allow Allied use of Antwerp's port.
Oct. 20, 1944	Russians and Yugoslavs take Belgrade.
Oct. 21, 1944	United States takes Aachen.
Nov. 22, 1944	United States takes Metz.
Nov. 23, 1944	United States takes Strasbourg.
Dec. 16-26, 1944	BATTLE OF THE BULGE: Along an eight-mile front in the Ardennes region of France, the Germans launch a surprise attack, advancing nearly to the Meuse River, where they are stopped by the Allies. The United States suffers approximately 77,000 casualties. *See* **1944, Battle of the Bulge.**
Dec. 29, 1944	Russians enter Budapest.
Jan. 17, 1945	Warsaw falls to the Russians.
Jan. 19, 1945	Lodz falls to the Russians.
Feb. 8, 1945	British offensive in the Netherlands.
Feb. 22, 1945	United States crosses the Saar River, reaching the Ruhr Valley the next day.
Mar. 7, 1945	Fall of Cologne and Düsseldorf.
Mar. 23, 1945	U.S. forces cross the Rhine River.
Apr. 11, 1945	United States reaches Elbe River in Germany.
Apr. 21, 1945	Fall of Nuremberg and Bologna.
Apr. 25, 1945	U.S. forces, coming from the west, and Russian forces, from the east, meet at Torgau.
Apr. 28, 1945	U.S. forces invade the Po River Valley in Italy. Italian partisans assassinate Mussolini.
May 2, 1945	Fall of Berlin. German forces in Italy surrender.
May 4, 1945	German forces in Denmark and the Netherlands surrender.
May 7, 1945	Germany surrenders unconditionally. The next day is declared V-E ("victory in Europe") day. *See* **1945, V-E day.**

1941 ■ GERMANY AND ITALY DECLARE WAR ON THE UNITED STATES: *by declaring war on the United States, Hitler and Mussolini transform the Pacific and European conflicts into one global war*

DATE: December 11, 1941
LOCALE: Berlin, Rome, and Washington, D.C.
CATEGORY: Wars, uprisings, and civil unrest
KEY FIGURES:
Adolf Hitler (1889-1945), chancellor of Germany
Benito Mussolini (1883-1945), Italian dictator and head of the Salo Republic
Franklin Delano Roosevelt (1882-1945), thirty-second president of the United States, 1933-1945

SUMMARY OF EVENT. On December 11, 1941, four days after the Japanese attack on Pearl Harbor, the governments of Germany and Italy issued declarations of war against the United States of America. Although both the Germans and the Italians had pledged Japan their aid in the event of a conflict between Japan and the United States, their declarations cited President Franklin D. Roosevelt's anti-Axis attitude and hostile U.S. actions as reasons for their decision to declare war. In response, Congress passed two joint resolutions affirming a state of war against Germany and Italy. With these events, the war in Europe and the war in the Far East merged to become World War II.

That the United States would become involved in a war in Europe seemed highly unlikely from 1936 to 1940, because during these years, the U.S. government and people were strongly isolationist. Moreover, Nazi Germany was preoccupied in Europe and not primarily interested in the Western Hemisphere. Although most Americans were opposed to Benito Mussolini's invasion of Ethiopia, the United States government did no more than invoke the first Neutrality Act, which included an arms embargo designed to weaken Italy. By 1936, it became clear that Germany and Italy were bent on territorial revisions. The Rome-Berlin Axis was formed in 1936, and Japan joined Germany and Italy in the Anti-Comintern Pact in 1937. In response, the United States government extended the Neutrality Act in 1937.

Despite their desire to stay out of war, President Roosevelt and his advisers grew increasingly concerned about the dangers of foreign aggression and human rights violations in both Europe and the Far East during the last years of the 1930's. In November, 1938, Roosevelt responded to the German riots against Jews during *Kristallnacht* (literally, "night of broken glass") by replacing the U.S. ambassador in Berlin with a chargé d'affaires; in April, 1939, the president sent letters to Adolf Hitler and Mussolini asking for assurances that they would refrain from aggression and suggesting discussions on armaments reductions. Hitler's invasion of Poland on September 1, 1939, increased the Roosevelt Administration's belief that Germany posed a real threat to U.S. security.

The year 1940 marked a turning point in U.S. foreign policy. The fall of France seriously alerted people in the United States to the might of Nazi Germany, while England's dogged resistance to Hitler, exemplified in the Battle of Britain, resulted in increased U.S. aid to the English. During the last six months of 1940, the United States responded to the Nazi Blitzkrieg in Europe with billions of dollars for defense, destroyers for England, and the first peacetime Selective Service Act in U.S. history. In addition, Roosevelt, after winning an unprecedented third term in office in November, 1940, proclaimed the United States "the great arsenal of democracy" and announced his intention to secure congressional approval of a Lend-Lease Act to aid all countries fighting to preserve freedom.

During 1941, the United States inched ever closer to war with Germany. In January, the Joint Chiefs of Staff of the U.S. armed forces met with their British opposite numbers and discussed how to coordinate military actions in the event of U.S. entry into the war. It was decided that the defeat of Germany should be given top priority. On March 11, the United States Congress passed the Lend-Lease Act, authorizing Roosevelt to provide arms, equipment, and supplies to "any country whose defense the President deems vital to the defense of the United States." In a speech on May 27, Roosevelt stressed the German danger to the Western Hemisphere and declared a state of national emergency. In August, Roosevelt and British prime minister Winston Churchill issued the Atlantic Charter against the Axis powers. Serious naval incidents occurred in September and October, when German submarines torpedoed the U.S. destroyer *Greer* and sank the *Reuben James*. In November, the president extended lend-lease to the Soviet Union, which had been attacked by Germany on June 22, while Congress modified the Neutrality Act to permit the arming of U.S. merchant ships. It is clear that by the fall of 1941, Roosevelt believed Germany was bent on world domination, was a great threat to the Western Hemisphere, and that war was a strong possibility.

In spite of the increased U.S. presence in the European conflict, the ultimate initiative for war lay with Germany and its ally Japan. By 1941, Hitler, who had first mentioned the possibility of a conflict with the United States in his 1928 unpublished sequel to *Mein Kampf* (1925-1927), clearly intended to wage war against the United States at some undetermined point in the future. Hitler believed the United States was culturally and racially decadent and underestimated its industrial capacity and willingness and ability to fight a war. In this connection, he was impressed by the strength of U.S. isolationism. Thus, unlike many German diplomats, Hitler failed to grasp the implications of U.S. power. Hitler's contempt for the United States turned to hostility when Roosevelt expressed his opposition to Nazi totalitarianism and aided Great Britain and the Soviet Union.

Despite Hitler's intention to fight, Germany developed no military plans. The Nazi dictator wanted to postpone war with Washington until Germany could construct a navy large enough to win what would certainly be a naval conflict. Consequently, Hitler ordered the German navy to avoid any incidents with U.S. ships in the Atlantic that might bring on war sooner than desired. Nevertheless, incidents did occur, the result being that an undeclared, limited naval war between the United States and Germany existed by the autumn of 1941.

Germany's caution in the Atlantic was offset by her reckless support of Japanese ambitions in the Far East. Hoping that the Japanese would exacerbate Great Britain's already difficult position and help check the United States commitment to Europe, Hitler began in 1940 to urge Tokyo to expand into southeast Asia. To encourage the Japanese, the Nazi dictator and Mussolini entered into a defense mutual assistance agreement, the Tripartite Pact, with Japan on September 27, 1940. Six months later, on April 4, 1941, the Nazi dictator went further, assuring Japan of his full support in the event of a Japanese-American war, no matter who was the aggressor.

The Japanese attack on Pearl Harbor on December 7, 1941, came as a pleasant surprise to both Hitler and Mussolini. Believing that Japan would weaken the British, Soviet, and U.S. war efforts, the Nazi dictator decided the time had come for war with the United States. Hitler took the initiative for this conflict, ordering all-out submarine attacks on U.S. ships and, along with his Italian ally, declaring war on the United States.

In declaring war on the United States at a time when Axis military forces found themselves bogged down in the Soviet Union and under attack by the British in North Africa, Hitler and Mussolini may have made the most fatal blunder of their careers. When the Nazi dictator said that his declaration of war on the United States would be "decisive not only for the history of Germany, but for the whole of Europe and indeed for the world," he was right. With their declaration of war, Germany and Italy not only unleashed a global war but also went a long way toward guaranteeing their own ultimate defeat and the postwar superpower ascendancy of the United States.   —Leon Stein, updated by Bruce J. DeHart

ADDITIONAL READING:

Hearden, Patrick J. *Roosevelt Confronts Hitler: America's Entry into World War II.* De Kalb: Northern Illinois University Press, 1987. While admitting that Roosevelt opposed the Nazi regime for both economic and ideological reasons, argues that the United States and Hitler's Germany were primarily economic rivals.

Heinrichs, Waldo. *Threshold of War: Franklin D. Roosevelt and American Entry into World War II.* New York: Oxford University Press, 1988. Focusing on the period from March to December, 1941, shows how strategic and operational considerations helped transform Roosevelt's policy toward Nazi Germany from neutrality to belligerence.

Herzstein, Robert E. *Roosevelt and Hitler: Prelude to War.* New York: Paragon House, 1989. Traces Roosevelt's evolution into the "most purposeful and consequential anti-Nazi leader of his time."

Jäckel, Eberhard. "Hitler Challenges America." In *Hitler in History.* Hanover, N.H.: University Press of New England, 1984. Argues that Hitler's declaration of war on the United States was motivated by a desire to guarantee that Japan would not make a separate peace.

Weinberg, Gerhard L. "From Confrontation to Cooperation: Germany and the United States, 1917-1949." In *Germany, Hitler, and World War II: Essays in Modern German and World History.* New York: Cambridge University Press, 1995. Argues that Hitler saw Japan's attack on Pearl Harbor as the perfect time to begin a war he believed Germany would have to fight sooner or later.

_____. "The World Turned Upside Down" and "The Expanding Conflict, 1940-1941." In *A World at Arms: A Global History of World War II.* New York: Cambridge University Press, 1994. Establishes the strategic context of Hitler's declaration of war by discussing and explaining Germany's efforts, in 1940 and 1941, to persuade Japan to expand into southeast Asia.

SEE ALSO: 1935, Neutrality Acts; 1939, Mobilization for World War II; 1940, United States Builds a Two-Ocean Navy; 1941, Lend-Lease Act; 1941, Bombing of Pearl Harbor; 1942, Censorship and Japanese Internment; 1942, Invasion of North Africa; 1943, Western Allies Invade Italy; 1944, Operation Overlord; 1944, Battle of the Bulge; 1945, Yalta Conference; 1945, V-E Day; 1945, Potsdam Conference.

1942 ■ CENSORSHIP AND JAPANESE INTERNMENT: *the Roosevelt Administration authorizes repressive wartime measures to prevent internal subversion*

DATE: February 19, 1942-1945

LOCALE: United States

CATEGORIES: Asian American history; Civil rights; Government and politics

KEY FIGURES:

Elmer H. Davis (1890-1958), veteran foreign correspondent and head of the Office of War Information

John L. De Witt (1880-1962), commander of the Western Defense Command

Mike Masaru Masaoka (1915-1991), national secretary of the Japanese American Citizens League

James Matsumoto Omura (1912-1994), Japanese American journalist and editor

Byron Price (1891-1981), Associated Press correspondent and director of the Office of Censorship

Franklin Delano Roosevelt (1882-1945), thirty-second president of the United States, 1933-1945

SUMMARY OF EVENT. During World War II, few people in the United States were confused about the basic questions that might affect loyalty and cooperation in terms of waging the war. Because of the strong public support for the nation's war effort, the Roosevelt Administration considered few measures to protect the United States' military commitment from internal subversion. Their most notable repressive policy was the in-

The Takemoto family's living quarters at Manzanar, one of the main internment camps for Japanese Americans during World War II. Scrap wood provided material for the chair on which Mr. Takemoto is sitting. (National Archives)

ternment of individuals of Japanese descent on the West Coast.

President Franklin Delano Roosevelt cautiously approached the sensitive problems of censorship and war propaganda. He and many of his advisers had vivid memories of the hasty and sensational decrees of the Creel Committee during World War I, and they wanted to avoid making the same mistakes again. Roosevelt recognized that the majority of people in the United States believed that the Germans and the Japanese were clear aggressors in this war. Because of Adolf Hitler's actions in Europe and the Japanese attack on Pearl Harbor, the administration needed to do little to foster a sense of public unity for the war effort. Indeed, it was sometimes difficult to keep public resentment under control. Nongovernmental sources of public information, such as the motion-picture industry, often treated the enemy in a sensational manner and did not hesitate to fan the flames of hatred.

Immediately after Pearl Harbor, the president took steps to gain control over public information that might prove to be of value to the enemy. In December, 1941, he established the

Office of Censorship and appointed an Associated Press correspondent, Byron Price, as its director. Taking a tolerant view of his responsibilities, Price permitted most government agencies, including the armed services, to continue operating their own information services. Censorship of war information usually was left to the discretion of the news media, and only in doubtful instances was Price consulted. The U.S. press generally was responsive and cooperative. Military censors in war zones exercised strict control over outgoing mail, and on the whole, World War II had more accurate press coverage than any prior conflict.

Price's office did not place restraints on the sharp competition that developed between the Army and the Navy, each of which was seeking to establish major credit for winning the war. It was perhaps with this rivalry in mind that Roosevelt decided to reorganize the government's role in public relations and press coverage. On June 13, 1942, he called upon Elmer Davis, veteran journalist, foreign correspondent, and radio commentator, to head a new government agency, the Office of

War Information (OWI). Davis was assigned the problem of news control, part of which was the assuring of continued public support for the administration's war effort. By this reorganization, the OWI took over functions of the Office of Facts and Figures, the Division of Information of Emergency Management, and the Foreign Information Service. Using pamphlets and other media, Davis experienced little difficulty in explaining to the U.S. public why the nation was at war. His most serious problem arose when a number of Republicans in Congress accused his agency of being a propaganda machine for the reelection of Roosevelt. Despite such charges, Davis had great success on the domestic front, and long before the war ended, he had shifted his major emphasis toward shaping civilian attitudes in Axis-held territory.

In comparison to government actions in World War I, the administration treated pacifists with more understanding during World War II. The military services recognized sincere conscientious objectors and provided them with an opportunity to work in civilian public service camps or in noncombatant medical service. The Supreme Court also placed limits on the government's ability to control suspected dissenters. For example, in 1940, the Alien Registration Act had been passed, giving the Federal Bureau of Investigation authority to control enemy aliens. After war was declared, thousands of aliens suspected of subversive activity were detained and questioned, and a number were confined for the duration of the conflict. In *Hartzel v. United States* (1944), however, the Supreme Court held that under the law, the government must prove subversive intent in order to convict. A protracted legal battle ensued, which resulted in the case being dismissed in 1946.

In contrast to its treatment of other groups, however, the government severely repressed the basic liberties of Japanese Americans on the West Coast. After the Japanese invasion of Pearl Harbor, the West Coast was thrown into a state of racist hysteria, exacerbated by military and government officials who preferred to blame "fifth column" activities for the attack of Pearl Harbor, rather than U.S. military incompetence. Top military officials originally decided to evacuate only a few aliens from militarily sensitive areas, citing cost and the constitutional rights of citizens for not interning the entire West Coast Japanese population. In the end, a small group of military bureaucrats and Pacific coast special interest groups—motivated by racial and economic reasons—convinced military and civilian leaders that mass evacuation of all U.S. Japanese and their families was a necessary defense measure.

On February 19, 1942, Franklin D. Roosevelt signed Executive Order 9066, which authorized Lieutenant General John L. De Witt, commander of the Western Defense, to evacuate people of Japanese ancestry from the West Coast. Although the majority of Americans supported the removal of the Japanese from the West Coast—some even noting the side benefit for Japanese Americans of protecting them from xenophobic extremists in the wartime atmosphere of paranoia—they did not support the wholesale internment of Germans and Italians, and only a small group of Italian and German aliens

were interned during the war. Confused, the Japanese American leadership did not know whether to resist or stoically accept the evacuation as a means of demonstrating their loyalty. In the end, many of the leaders, especially those associated with the Japanese American Citizens League (JACL), chose to cooperate with the government. Given only a few days' notice, West Coast Japanese were ordered to sell their possessions and prepare for evacuation.

By November 3, 1942, approximately 120,000 people of Japanese ancestry were interned; most of the internees passively accepted their imprisonment, although some resisted. Mike Masaoka, the national secretary of JACL, opted for an accommodationist policy, while James Omura, journalist and editor, challenged both government policy and the JACL's position. While some of the internees resisted through protest or civil disobedience, others challenged the legality of the evacuation in court. Two key court cases—*Hirabayashi v. United States* (1943) and *Korematsu v. United States* (1944)—challenged the legality of the evacuation. The Supreme Court, in a 9-0 decision in the *Hirabayashi* case and a 6-3 decision in the *Korematsu* case, supported the government's evacuation policies, citing the existence of "the gravest imminent danger to the public safety."

From September of 1943, the repression of Japanese Americans began to be eased. In part, this shift was a result of the changes in the national images of Japanese Americans, most significantly affected by the heroism of segregated Japanese American combat units. Moreover, the government began to feel the effects of the court cases. After the war, a small group of white liberals began working for some form of redress for the internees, an action that the JACL would later actively demand. On February 19, 1979, President Gerald Ford revoked Executive Order 9066, and in 1988, President Ronald Reagan signed redress legislation authorizing monetary reparations to each of the sixty thousand surviving former internees.

—George Q. Flynn, updated by Sandra K. Stanley

ADDITIONAL READING:

Christgau, John. *"Enemies": World War II Alien Internment.* Ames: Iowa State University Press, 1985. Focuses on the stories of several German aliens, and one Japanese American who initially renounced his citizenship, interned during World War II.

Corwin, Edward S. *Total War and the Constitution.* New York: Alfred A. Knopf, 1947. Studies the judicial problems created by the necessary extension of executive power during wartime.

Daniels, Roger. *Concentration Camps, North America: Japanese in the United States and Canada During World War II.* 1981. Reprint. Malabar, Fla.: Robert E. Krieger, 1989. A major source of information concerning the Japanese American evacuation and internment.

Hatamiya, Leslie T. *Righting a Wrong: Japanese Americans and the Passage of the Civil Liberties Act of 1988.* Stanford, Calif.: Stanford University Press, 1993. Traces the redress efforts of the Japanese American community, specifically focusing on legislative action.

Masaoka, Mike, with Bill Hosokawa. *They Call Me Moses Masaoka: An American Saga.* New York: William Morrow, 1987. Masaoka tells the story of his leadership role in the JACL, his decision to accommodate the administration's internment policies, and his efforts to seek redress.

Sibley, Mulford Q., and P. E. Jacob. *Conscription of Conscience: The American State and the Conscientious Objector, 1940-1947.* Ithaca, N.Y.: Cornell University Press, 1952. A generally sympathetic treatment of the problem of individual conscience versus social obligation.

See also: 1930, Japanese American Citizens League Is Founded; 1938, HUAC Investigations; 1939, Mobilization for World War II; 1941, Bombing of Pearl Harbor.

1942 ■ Congress of Racial Equality Is Founded: *a leader in the nonviolent direct-action movement will fight for civil rights using tactics such as the Freedom Rides*

Date: June, 1942
Locale: Chicago and United States
Categories: African American history; Civil rights; Organizations and institutions
Key figures:
James Farmer (born 1920), founder of CORE and first national chairman
Roy Innis (born 1934), selected as national director of CORE in 1966
John Lewis (born 1940), CORE member and Freedom Rider
Krishnalal Shridharani (1911-1960), author of *War Without Violence*

Summary of event. The "Big Five" civil rights organizations in America—the National Association for the Advancement of Colored People (NAACP), the Urban League, the Student Nonviolent Coordinating Committee (SNCC), the Southern Christian Leadership Conference (SCLC), and the Congress of Racial Equality (CORE)—utilized different approaches in their quest for racial equality. The NAACP excelled in both litigation and lobbying, while the Urban League focused on economic development. SNCC, SCLC, and CORE all utilized techniques of nonviolent direct action. Although the SCLC was the best known of these groups due to the media savvy of its leader, the Reverend Dr. Martin Luther King, Jr., CORE pioneered the technique and was using it for two decades before SCLC and SNCC were created.

Founded in Chicago in 1942, CORE attempted to apply the nonviolent techniques of Mohandas K. Gandhi to the racial problems in America. Skeptical of the approaches of the NAACP and the Urban League, CORE members believed that discrimination had to be confronted directly, without hatred and violence but also without compromise. All CORE members were required to read Krishnalal Shridharani's book *War Without Violence* (1939), which described Gandhi's philosophy and methods.

Growing out of the religious radicalism of the 1930's, CORE was dominated by Methodist leaders in its early years. Many were socialists, and most were pacifists. Three of the six individuals most responsible for the formation of CORE either spent time in jail or served in Civilian Public Service camps because they were conscientious objectors to military service. CORE leaders were admirers of the industrial unions and copied their "sit-down" strikes. In fact, the first CORE "sit-ins" were actually called sit-downs.

The belief in nonviolence was for both religious and practical reasons. Since many of the early members were ministers or divinity students, nonviolence was merely an extension of their Christian beliefs blended with the Hindu philosophy of Mohandas Gandhi. Pragmatically, nonviolence was viewed as the only appropriate approach to resolving racial problems. A minority group utilizing violence would likely be assisting in their own demise. CORE leaders expressed concerns about movements of black militancy and retaliation and believed that nonviolent direct action was the most reasonable approach to furthering racial equality.

CORE was founded as an interracial organization; four of its founders were white and two were black. James Farmer, a charismatic leader with a divinity degree from Howard University, was CORE's first national chairman and later served as national director from 1961 to 1966. The first major project that CORE undertook was to help black students obtain housing in neighborhoods surrounding the University of Chicago. White members of CORE secured property with restrictive covenants attached to the property. These covenants prevented African Americans from renting or buying the property. The white CORE members then leased the property to blacks, and integrated housing was established.

During its first two decades of operation, CORE concentrated on integration of public accommodations. A 1946 project, the Journey of Reconciliation, captured national attention for CORE. In order to test compliance with a recent Supreme Court decision outlawing segregation in interstate travel, CORE decided to take a two-week interracial trip into the South. Eight black and eight white CORE members rode Trailways and Greyhound buses into Virginia, North Carolina, and Kentucky. CORE challenged the segregated seating on the buses but did not challenge segregation in bus stations, restrooms, or restaurants. Twelve arrests were made. The Journey of Reconciliation served as a forerunner to the better-known Freedom Rides in 1961.

During the 1940's and 1950's, CORE's membership was small, mostly non-Southern, and usually located in university towns. Efforts to establish chapters in the South failed due to fears of economic reprisals or violence. While CORE had twenty chapters in 1950, the number of chapters dropped to half a dozen by the mid-1950's. There were several reasons for CORE's membership problems. Since most chapters were on college campuses, members would graduate and leave. The

McCarthyism of the early 1950's, which brought any political leftist organization under suspicion, helped to suppress membership. CORE also lacked a strong national organization and a staff to help recruit and retain membership. A final problem, and a common one in most interracial groups, was the complaint that whites dominated the leadership structure. Membership became such a problem for CORE that only seven individuals attended the organization's 1957 national convention.

With the advent of the sit-in movement in Greensboro, North Carolina, on February 1, 1960, CORE found an issue to rejuvenate its membership and become a leading force in the Civil Rights movement. With the return of James Farmer as national director of CORE in 1961, CORE decided to take on its most challenging project. Farmer and CORE decided to launch the Freedom Ride of 1961.

In 1960, the United States Supreme Court, in *Boynton v. Virginia*, extended the prohibition against segregation in interstate travel to cover terminal accommodations as well as trains and buses. Thirteen CORE members, seven blacks and six whites, boarded Trailways and Greyhound buses in Washington, D.C., and headed into the Deep South. James Farmer and John Lewis were among the riders. (Lewis would soon become chairman of the Student Nonviolent Coordinating Committee and later serve as a member of Congress from Georgia.) It did not take long for arrests and violence to occur. The first arrest took place in Charlotte, North Carolina, and the first extensive violence occurred in Anniston, Alabama. A white mob with chains, sticks, and rocks broke bus windows and slashed tires. The Greyhound bus was fire-bombed, while the Trailways bus was boarded by a white mob who severely beat the Freedom Riders. One CORE member suffered permanent brain damage from his beating. The buses were attacked again in Montgomery, Alabama. Most of the original Freedom Riders were either in jail or in hospitals, so new riders were recruited in Montgomery. Members of CORE, SNCC, and the Southern Christian Leadership Conference continued the ride to Jackson, Mississippi, where 360 were arrested. In September of 1961 the Interstate Commerce Commission issued a rule banning segregated facilities in interstate travel. Although ignored in many parts of the Deep South, CORE had won a major moral victory.

The success of the Freedom Ride revitalized the Southern Civil Rights movement and elevated CORE to the forefront of civil rights organizations. Farmer was thrust into national prominence, and CORE chapters sprang up all over the nation. CORE members felt vindicated that their philosophy of nonviolent direct action had produced a major victory and mobilized thousands of blacks and whites to work together in seeking racial justice.

After the Freedom Rides, CORE continued to participate in direct action campaigns throughout the Deep South, but the organization was never able to match the success of the Freedom Rides. As CORE efforts continued to be met with violence, many members began to reexamine the organization's philosophy. The murders of CORE workers Michael Schwerner and James Chaney in Mississippi in 1964 caused many members to abandon the group's nonviolent philosophy. Black members also questioned the value of interracial membership, with many coming to the conclusion that only blacks should remain members.

In 1965, CORE was so fundamentally different from what it had been when it was established that Farmer decided to resign. In 1968, Roy Innis took over as national director. In 1978, Washington journalist Jack Anderson accused Innis of ordering the shooting of a former colleague and the beating of another. Also in 1978, former CORE leader James Farmer unsuccessfully tried to oust Innis as CORE director. Farmer charged that Innis had fraudulently raised millions of dollars using CORE's name and that Innis had made himself into a "permanently installed dictator." Innis attacked Farmer for leaving the organization in a shambles and contended that Innes had raised millions of dollars for inner-city community development projects. —*Darryl Paulson*

ADDITIONAL READING:

Chong, Dennis. *Collective Action and the Civil Rights Movement.* Chicago: University of Chicago Press, 1991. A theoretical study of the dynamics of collective action within the Civil Rights movement.

Farmer, James. *Freedom—When?* New York: Random House, 1965. The national director of CORE describes the dilemmas confronting CORE and other civil rights groups.

_____. *Lay Bare the Heart: The Autobiography of the Civil Rights Movement.* New York: New American Library, 1985. An eyewitness account of the Freedom Rides and other civil rights events. Highlights the strengths and weaknesses of the movement.

Meier, August, and Elliott Rudwick. *CORE: A Study in the Civil Rights Movement, 1942-1968.* New York: Oxford University Press, 1973. The most thorough account of the founding and philosophy of CORE.

Morris, Alden. *The Origins of the Civil Rights Movement.* New York: Free Press, 1984. Describes the interrelationships of leading civil rights groups, both tensions and cooperation.

SEE ALSO: 1909, National Association for the Advancement of Colored People Is Founded; 1954, *Brown v. Board of Education*; 1955, Montgomery Bus Boycott; 1957, Southern Christian Leadership Conference Is Founded; 1957, Little Rock School Desegregation Crisis; 1960, Civil Rights Act of 1960; 1962, Reapportionment Cases; 1964, Civil Rights Act of 1964; 1965, Voting Rights Act; 1965, Watts Riot; 1967, Long, Hot Summer; 1968, Assassinations of King and Kennedy.

1942 ■ BATTLE OF MIDWAY: *a U.S. naval victory ends Japanese dominance in the Pacific theater during World War II*

DATE: June 3-5, 1942
LOCALE: Pacific Ocean near Midway Island
CATEGORY: Wars, uprisings, and civil unrest

KEY FIGURES:

Frank Jack Fletcher (1885-1973), commander of the U.S. Naval Carrier Striking Force

Chester William Nimitz (1885-1966), commander in chief of the U.S. Pacific Fleet

Chuichi Nagumo (1887-1944), commander of the Japanese First Carrier Striking Force

Raymond Ames Spruance (1886-1969), commander of U.S. Naval Task Force 16

Isoroku Yamamoto (1884-1943), commander in chief of the Japanese Combined Fleet

SUMMARY OF EVENT. From December, 1941, until the spring of 1942, Japanese forces conquered British, Dutch, and U.S. possessions in East Asia and the Pacific Ocean. Fast aircraft carriers enabled them to project their power far into the Pacific, and the December 7 strike by their carrier-based aircraft on the U.S. naval base at Pearl Harbor, Hawaii, had crippled the United States Pacific Fleet. Six months later, Japanese planners prepared for another strike toward Hawaii. They intended to neutralize the remaining vessels in the U.S. fleet and occupy Midway, an island located a thousand miles east of Hawaii that could serve as the springboard for future operations in the Hawaiian chain proper. With Midway and Hawaii in their hands, the Japanese believed they could force the United States to retreat to California.

The commander in chief of the Japanese Combined Fleet, Admiral Isoroku Yamamoto, sought to initiate the operation before the overwhelming U.S. industrial capacity began to play a decisive role in the conflict. Yamamoto put together the largest fleet the Japanese ever had assembled; it included eleven battleships, headed by the *Yamato*, Japan's newest and the world's largest battleship; four heavy and four light carriers; twenty-one cruisers; sixty-five destroyers; more than fifty support and smaller craft; and nineteen submarines. In a serious strategic error, Yamamoto dispersed these vessels in many groups so widely scattered that they could not be mutually supporting. The Northern Force—comprising two light carriers, eight cruisers, thirteen destroyers, and six submarines—sped toward the Aleutian Islands of Alaska in order to divert the U.S. forces and capture Kiska and Attu, which might be used as the springboards for future operations. The islands were successfully occupied, but the operation was secondary in nature, and the ships could have been used more effectively for the main thrust toward Midway.

Japanese forces were badly divided within the main strike force, as well. From the southwest came the Midway Occupation Group, supported by the Second Fleet with two battleships, eight cruisers, a light carrier, and a dozen destroyers. Approaching Midway from the northwest was Yamamoto with the Main Body and the Carrier Striking Force. His main force was organized around three battleships and a light carrier. Split off to the north in order to move either to the Aleutians or to Midway, but in actuality too far from either, was the Guard Force of four battleships and a screen of cruisers and destroyers. In the van was the First Carrier Striking Force under Vice

Admiral Chuichi Nagumo, with four heavy carriers, *Akagi*, *Kaga*, *Soryu*, and *Hiryu*, and their screen and support vessels.

Nagumo's carriers were to attack Midway on June 4 and destroy the United States' airfields and planes preparatory to the landings; when the Americans sortied from Pearl Harbor, the Main Body would move in and destroy them. Previous successes had made Japanese planners arrogant. They made no plans for what to do if the U.S. response unfolded in a different manner from the one they anticipated.

United States naval intelligence teams had advance warning of Japanese plans from official Japanese Navy messages that had been intercepted. The intelligence unit at Pearl Harbor, under Commander Joseph J. Rochefort, Jr., decided, on the basis of incomplete information and brilliant analysis, that Midway was the primary target. Admiral Chester W. Nimitz, commander in chief of the Pacific Fleet, called in all of his available carriers and could come up with only three: the *Enterprise* and the *Hornet*, commanded by Rear Admiral Raymond A. Spruance, and the wounded *Yorktown*, commanded by Rear Admiral Frank Jack Fletcher. The carriers were screened by a total of eight cruisers and fourteen destroyers. Nimitz ordered the extensive reinforcement of Midway to a total of 120 planes, antiaircraft guns, and 3,632 defenders. The three carriers lay in wait for the Japanese, northeast of Midway, as ready as forewarning could make them.

Confirmation that the intelligence guesses were correct came early on June 3, when a scout plane sighted the invasion force six hundred miles to the southwest. Army and Marine pilots attacking from Midway scored no significant hits. Unaware that U.S. ships were anywhere nearby, Nagumo launched an attack with half of his planes (108) before dawn on June 4; the other half he held back, in case the United States fleet threatened. Searches by Nagumo's own planes were inadequate.

The Midway defenders put all of their planes in the air and took heavy punishment, but were not knocked out. Defending planes were totally outclassed, but they and the antiaircraft guns still inflicted losses on the Japanese Zeros. By 7:00 A.M., the first raid was over and the Japanese flight leader radioed Nagumo that another attack was required.

Before the second attack could be launched, the Japanese carriers were scattered repeatedly by Marine and Army pilots from Midway, none of whom scored hits and nearly all of whom died trying. In the midst of these attacks, a Japanese scout plane reported a U.S. carrier within range. Rather than immediately launching the second wave of planes that were being rearmed for another attack on Midway, Nagumo decided to recover his first wave and rearm the second for fleet action. By 9:18, all was ready, although the haste meant that bombs and torpedoes were piled around the carrier decks.

At that point, forty-two slow-moving, low-level U.S. torpedo bombers arrived unescorted by fighters and began nearly suicidal attacks, in which thirty-eight planes were lost. None scored hits, but the defending Zeros were drawn down to low levels to attack them. At the end of these attacks, thirty-three high-altitude SBD Dauntless dive bombers, led by Lieutenant Commander C. Wade McCluskey, by chance managed to locate the *Kaga*, *Akagi*, and *Soryu*. McCluskey's planes soon were joined by another group of dive bombers, led by Lieutenant Commander Maxwell Leslie. The Zeros were flying too low to intercept the U.S. planes before the damage was done. In only five minutes, U.S. pilots made fatal hits on the three Japanese carriers. With poor fire management policies on their ships, the Japanese were unable to prevent the sinking of the carriers. Later the same day, the *Hiryu* was also fatally hit and sunk by U.S. pilots. While Yamamoto wanted to engage the U.S. surface fleet in a nighttime battle, a U.S. course change prevented him from doing so.

The Japanese had lost four aircraft carriers, 275 planes, about three thousand military personnel, and their four largest carriers in the Battle of Midway. The United States, by contrast, lost one carrier (the *Yorktown*), one destroyer, 150 planes, and 307 personnel. Many of Japan's best pilots were lost in the battle, and the balance of power in the Pacific had shifted in favor of the United States.

—Charles W. Johnson, updated by William E. Watson

ADDITIONAL READING:

Belote, James H., and William M. Belote. *Titans of the Seas: The Development and Operations of Japanese and American Carrier Task Forces During World War II*. New York: Harper & Row, 1975. Contrasts U.S. and Japanese carrier doctrines.

Fuchida, Mitsuo, and Masatake Okumiya. *Midway: The Battle That Doomed Japan: The Japanese Navy's Story*. Annapolis, Md.: Naval Institute Press, 1955. Offers the perspective of two Japanese participants.

Lord, Walter. *Incredible Victory*. New York: Harper & Row, 1967. A standard popular work based on interviews with four hundred participants in the battle.

Morison, Samuel Eliot. *Coral Sea, Midway and Submarine Actions, May 1942-August 1942*. Vol. 4 in *History of United States Naval Operations in World War II*. Boston: Little, Brown, 1950. The standard scholarly work on Midway.

Smith, William Ward. *Midway: Turning Point of the Pacific*. New York: Thomas Y. Crowell, 1966. A good account written by an American participant.

SEE ALSO: 1941, Bombing of Pearl Harbor; 1942, Battle of Guadalcanal; 1944, Superfortress Bombing of Japan; 1944, Battle for Leyte Gulf; 1945, Atomic Bombing of Japan.

1942 ■ MANHATTAN PROJECT: *the United States develops the world's first nuclear weapon*

DATE: June 17, 1942-July 16, 1945
LOCALE: United States
CATEGORIES: Government and politics; Science and technology; Wars, uprisings, and civil unrest

KEY FIGURES:
Vannevar Bush (1890-1974), director of the Office of Scientific Research and Development, 1941-1946
James Bryant Conant (1893-1978), president of Harvard University and director of the National Defense Research Council
Franklin Delano Roosevelt (1882-1945), thirty-second president of the United States, 1933-1945
Alexander Sachs (1893-1973), Russian-born economist and occasional presidential adviser
Leo Szilard (1898-1964), Hungarian-born refugee physicist

SUMMARY OF EVENT. The building by the United States of an atomic bomb was not the result of a single decision, but of a series of decisions taken over more than two years. Although President Franklin D. Roosevelt held the ultimate responsibility, his attitudes were shaped by scientific advisers whose reasoned conclusions and best guesses persuaded him that it was possible to construct a nuclear fission device "of superlatively destructive powers," as a 1941 report termed it.

Research had been going on in the 1920's and 1930's, primarily by European physicists, including James Chadwick in Great Britain, Enrico Fermi and Emilio Segrè in Italy, Lise Meitner and Otto Frisch, who in 1938 fled Austria for Denmark, (where Niels Bohr was working), Hungarians such as Leo Szilard, the Frenchman Frédéric Joliot-Curie, and Otto Hahn and Fritz Strassmann at the Kaiser Wilhelm Institute in Berlin. Their research indicated the possibility of bombarding the nucleus of the uranium atom, splitting it into lighter fragments, and releasing tremendous amounts of energy. A significant number of these scientists fled Fascism for the United States or England. Many of them gathered with U.S. physicists in January, 1939, at the fifth Washington Conference on Theoretical Physics to hear Bohr recount the exciting atomic discoveries. Within the year, nearly one hundred papers had been published in scholarly journals expanding on and confirming this new work.

In March, 1939, Fermi, Szilard, and a number of other émigré physicists who feared that the Nazis were developing an atomic bomb began a lengthy effort to arouse in both their U.S. colleagues and the United States government some sense of their own urgent concern. After a direct approach by Fermi to the Navy, made on March 17, failed to generate any active interest, and after the Germans forbade further export of uranium ore from the Joachimstal mines in recently conquered Czechoslovakia, Szilard became convinced that Albert Einstein was the only scientist in the United States with enough fame and prestige to garner a sympathetic hearing from the U.S. government. Visiting Einstein on Long Island in mid-July, 1940, Szilard exacted from his old friend a promise to write, or at least sign, any letter or letters that might be needed to attract the attention of the U.S. government. Einstein's promise in hand, Szilard and fellow émigré physicist Eugene Wigner wrote a letter addressed to President Roosevelt. Dated August 2, 1939, and signed "A. Einstein," this letter, detailing the dangers and possibilities of atomic energy, was presented

The atomic bomb, product of the intensive and top-secret Manhattan Project, would unleash the possibility of nuclear devastation that both ended World War II and threatened the future safety of the world. (National Archives)

to Roosevelt on October 11 by Alexander Sachs, an occasional presidential adviser who had eagerly agreed to serve as the intermediary for Szilard.

Sachs and the Einstein letter convinced the president that the situation should be explored. Accordingly, he established the Advisory Committee on Uranium. Headed by Lyman Briggs, director of the National Bureau of Standards, and including representatives from the Army, the Navy, and the scientific community, this attempt to draw federal support into scientific research for the national defense produced few early results. The committee met infrequently, and its financial support involved only a six-thousand-dollar research grant.

Research on the explosive potential of uranium, which was being conducted at some twenty university laboratories scattered across the country, pointed in two main directions. One involved the separation of the fissionable isotope U-235 from the much more common U-238 by a variety of methods, including gaseous or thermal diffusion, electromagnetic separation, and the centrifuge. The other sought to transmute uranium into a new fissionable element, plutonium (U-239), through a controlled chain reaction in an atomic pile. It was not until 1942 that either a chain reaction or the separation of more than a few micrograms of U-235 would be accomplished.

As the Germans drove into France in May and June, 1940, others in the scientific community, including Hungarian-born émigré physicist Edward Teller, grew increasingly concerned. Responding to that concern, on June 15, President Roosevelt established the National Defense Research Council (NDRC) under the leadership of Vannevar Bush, president of the Carnegie Institute. Creative and highly capable, Bush and his able deputy, Harvard president James Conant, played key roles in the decision to make the bomb.

While support for the Advisory Committee on Uranium and other scientific defense research grew during the next year, Bush believed that the work lacked the necessary urgency. On June 28, 1941, acting on Bush's advice, Roosevelt created the stronger Office of Scientific Research and Development (OSRD), with Bush as the head. Conant moved up to head the NDRC, and the Uranium Committee, strengthened and enlarged, became the S-1 Section of OSRD.

Although the establishment of OSRD represented a significant organizational step, it did not signify a decisive commitment to the building of an atomic bomb. Key figures in the U.S. government—Roosevelt, Vice President Henry Wallace, Secretary of War Henry L. Stimson, and Army Chief of Staff George C. Marshall—members of the OSRD, and members of the U.S. scientific community remained skeptical about both the cost and feasibility of developing an atomic weapon. This skepticism, however, began to give way during the second half of 1941. At that time, the British government, based on the recent ideas of Otto Frisch and Rudolf Peierls, refugee physicists working at Cambridge, reported to the OSRD its belief that an atomic bomb could be developed within two years. Another push to the U.S. atomic effort was provided by Mark Oliphant, the Australian-born head of the physics department

at the University of Birmingham. During a visit to the United States in August, 1941, Oliphant pressed upon Bush the British conviction that a bomb really could be made.

With the Japanese attack on Pearl Harbor and the German and Italian declarations of war on the United States in December, 1941, Roosevelt had to choose between committing to the construction of a weapon that might win the war in the long run or cutting back on an unproven program to concentrate valuable resources to the more immediate goal of not losing the war in the short run. On March 9, 1942, Bush informed the president that a major industrial effort might produce an atomic weapon in 1944, but that a decision had to be made soon. After receiving additional encouraging news, Roosevelt decided on June 17, 1942, that the United States would build an atomic bomb.

Having committed itself to the construction of an atomic weapon, the U.S. government had to determine how to produce sufficient quantities of fissionable materials. After learning from S-1 Section researchers that four methods—gaseous diffusion, the centrifuge, electromagnetic separation, and controlled chain reactions in uranium piles—were at comparable stages of development, it was decided to make an all-out effort on all four fronts, rather than explore a single method that might prove a dead end.

The U.S. atomic bomb program—code-named the Manhattan Project and headed by General Leslie R. Groves (appointed September 17, 1942)—involved highly secret research at Los Alamos, New Mexico, where basic bomb development took place; Oak Ridge, Tennessee, where U-235 was separated from U-238 by gaseous diffusion and electromagnetic techniques; and Hanford, Washington, where plutonium was produced in graphite piles. At a cost of nearly two billion dollars, the Manhattan Project ultimately paid dividends: The first bomb was successfully detonated on July 16 at Alamogordo, New Mexico, and there followed production of the weapons that ended World War II in August, 1945, and that enabled the United States to lead the world into the Atomic Age.

—Charles W. Johnson, updated by Bruce J. DeHart

ADDITIONAL READING:

Hewlett, Richard G. *A History of the United States Atomic Energy Commission.* Vol. 1 in *The New World, 1939-1946*, by Richard G. Hewlett and Oscar E. Anderson, Jr. University Park: Pennsylvania State University Press, 1962. The early chapters detail the major steps that produced the Manhattan Project.

Jones, Vincent C. *Manhattan: The Army and the Atomic Bomb.* Washington, D.C.: Government Printing Office, 1986. Discusses the Army's role in the development of the bomb.

Rhodes, Richard. *The Making of the Atomic Bomb.* New York: Simon & Schuster, 1986. Provides a wealth of scientific information and integrates it with the decision-making process.

Sherwin, Martin J. *A World Destroyed: The Atomic Bomb and the Grand Alliance.* New York: Alfred A. Knopf, 1975. Part 1 details major developments in physics and the critical political decisions.

Stoff, Michael B., Jonathan F. Fanton, and R. Hal Williams, eds. *The Manhattan Project: A Documentary Introduction to the Atomic Age*. New York: McGraw-Hill, 1991. Contains key documents, including Einstein's letter of August 2, 1939.

SEE ALSO: 1944, Superfortress Bombing of Japan; 1945, Atomic Bombing of Japan; 1952, Hydrogen Bomb Is Detonated.

1942 ■ BATTLE OF GUADALCANAL: *one of the first military campaigns to use air, land, sea, subsurface, and amphibious forces together, this conflict turns the tide in the Asian-Pacific war*

DATE: August 7, 1942-February 9, 1943
LOCALE: Solomon Islands
CATEGORY: Wars, uprisings, and civil unrest
KEY FIGURES:
Frank Jack Fletcher (1885-1973), commander of the invasion and naval support forces at Guadalcanal
Robert Lee Ghormley (1883-1958), commander of the South Pacific Area until October, 1942
William Frederick Halsey (1882-1959), Ghormley's replacement as commander of the South Pacific Area
Kiyotake Kawaguchi, commander of the Japanese armed forces on Guadalcanal
Ernest Joseph King (1878-1956), chief of naval operations
Douglas MacArthur (1880-1964), commander in chief, Southwest Pacific Area
Gunichi Mikawa, commander of Japanese naval forces during the Battle of Savo Island
Chester William Nimitz (1885-1966), commander in chief, Pacific Ocean Areas
Richmond Kelly Turner (1885-1961), commander of the amphibious force at Guadalcanal
Alexander Archer Vandegrift (1887-1973), commander of the U.S. Marine landing force
SUMMARY OF EVENT. During the first half of 1942, the Japanese achieved spectacular expansion and the Allies were in desperate straits in all theaters of World War II. The global strategic priority was Germany first, so resources were scarce. The Guadalcanal and larger Solomon Islands campaigns were fought under these challenging circumstances, and the Allied situation was reversed.

The Battle of Midway set the stage for the Battle of Guadalcanal, one of the most important struggles during the war in the Pacific. The engagement at Midway had taken place in early June, 1942. It was a spectacular air engagement, in which the Japanese lost 4 aircraft carriers, 275 planes, and one hundred first-line pilots. Land-based Army Air Force planes also participated, although they achieved little. This stunning defeat forced Japan onto the defensive and gave the Allied powers a badly needed reprieve. As a result of the Battle of

Midway, U.S. planners soon decided to launch a limited offensive in the area of the Pacific Ocean where the Central Pacific and Southwest Pacific commands overlapped.

The logical initial objective was the Solomon Islands. This chain of islands was located within easy bombing range of the great Japanese air base at Rabaul on New Britain Island and the important Allied base of Port Moresby in southern New Guinea. Furthermore, the Japanese had begun construction of a bomber field on Guadalcanal—one of the southernmost islands in the Solomons. Whoever controlled Guadalcanal and finished the airfield would hold an important advantage in the Pacific war.

Acting from the initiative of Admiral Ernest King, chief of naval operations, the Joint Chiefs of Staff ordered Admiral Chester Nimitz and General Douglas MacArthur, theater commanders, to gather all available forces and equipment for an amphibious operation in the Solomon Islands against the adjoining islands of Guadalcanal and Tulagi. The invasion, planned in conjunction with a renewed attack in New Guinea and an attempt to seize Rabaul, was to begin on August 1, but delays and a lack of supplies dictated that the Solomons operation be postponed until August 7. The Allied forces included U.S. air, marine, army, naval, and submarine units, and various other forces from Australia and New Zealand, native coast-watcher units coordinated by the Royal Australian Navy, and intelligence agencies modeled on British methods. The U.S. forces were largely ignorant of the islands that they were to invade and had little time to work out plans for the landings. The combined force, consisting of eighty-two ships carrying the First Marine Division, elements of the Second Marine Division, and other contingents, met near the Fiji Islands in late July.

Early on August 7, a U.S. carrier task force took position south of Guadalcanal. Under its protection, the first support ships and landing force, commanded by Rear Admiral Richmond K. Turner, slipped along the west coast of Guadalcanal. After a heavy shore bombardment, Major General Alexander A. Vandegrift's Marines waded ashore. The landings were practically unopposed on Guadalcanal, although strong resistance was encountered on Tulagi. On August 8, the Marines seized their primary objective, the unfinished airfield soon to be named Henderson Field. Japanese forces on Guadalcanal were fewer than twenty-five hundred, and within a few days there were approximately sixteen thousand Marines on the island. Other factors, however, intervened to prevent a swift Allied victory.

The Japanese were able to respond quickly to the attack by dispatching reinforcements to Guadalcanal and initiating steps designed to gain naval superiority in the area. They were assisted by U.S. timidity regarding the safety of the carrier task force. Vice Admiral Frank J. Fletcher, commander of the invasion, withdrew his carriers on August 8. Thereafter, the beachhead received almost no air protection, and heavy Japanese bombing attacks began. The withdrawal of the carriers emboldened the Japanese to send a strong surface force, in the hope of destroying U.S. warships and transports and thereby isolating the Marines. The Japanese striking force of five heavy cruisers, two light cruisers, and a destroyer slipped past Allied patrol vessels and entered Iron Bottom Sound at 1:00 A.M. on August 9. Carefully trained for night action, the Japanese sank four Allied cruisers and won a tremendous victory, although their commander, Vice Admiral Gunichi Mikawa, erred in not attacking the unprotected support ships and the beachhead itself. The defeat caused Rear Admiral Turner to withdraw his amphibious force, leaving behind sixteen thousand Marines who were insufficiently supplied for the task of maintaining their positions on Guadalcanal. However, their enemy had even more serious logistical problems.

From mid-August, 1942, until early February, 1943, when Allied forces finally cleared the entire island, Japanese and Allied forces were locked in bitter conflict. Both sides made desperate efforts to reinforce their numbers in this struggle of attrition and to deny supplies and reinforcements to the other. After initial success, the Marines encountered stubborn resistance and made little progress for several months. The Japanese launched several offensives, but inaccurate information about the strength of the Allied forces caused them to fail. The most notable engagements were the Battle of the Tenaru River, in which one thousand Japanese were virtually wiped out, and the Battle of Bloody Ridge on September 13 and 14, at which a Japanese force of six thousand troops under Major General Kiyotake Kawaguchi was cut to pieces. By the time the Japanese high command realized that large reinforcements were required, Allied naval and air defenses were much improved. After mid-September, the Marine foothold was secure, and reinforcements and supplies were coming in on a continual basis.

Final victory could not be won, however, until one side achieved naval dominance in the area. The struggle between Allied and Japanese naval forces continued through the autumn, with the Imperial Navy controlling the waters around Guadalcanal at night and the Allies—because of Henderson Field's aircraft, mostly with Marine pilots—commanding the area during the day. A number of important but indecisive carrier and ship-to-ship engagements occurred, such as the Battle of the Eastern Solomons and the Battle of Cape Esperance. The latter was the result of a desperate Japanese effort to reinforce Guadalcanal. Although it was considered an Allied victory, the Japanese moved ahead, bombing Henderson Field and dispatching a battleship force to bombard Allied positions. On October 15, forty-five hundred Japanese soldiers were landed, raising their total on the island to twenty thousand, and the Imperial Army prepared for a victorious offensive.

The Marines suffered from low morale, malaria and other diseases, and exhaustion. With more than half the planes on Henderson Field rendered non operational, a defeatist feeling spread throughout the chain of command. On October 16, Vice Admiral William F. Halsey replaced Vice Admiral Robert L. Ghormley as commander of the Southwest Pacific forces. Halsey was convinced that control of Guadalcanal was essen-

tial, and the Joint Chiefs had reached the same conclusion.

The main Japanese attacks came on October 24 and 25, but these frontal assaults against fortified U.S. positions resulted in costly defeats. In November, both sides attempted to bring in reinforcements. The Allies were successful, but the Japanese, having lost a crucial naval engagement in the middle of the month, were able to land only about four thousand soldiers, who were badly equipped and poorly supplied.

In December, U.S. Army units replaced the exhausted Marines, and these fresh forces soon launched a powerful attack, assisted by air strikes from Henderson Field and from aircraft carriers. The Japanese held on grimly until January 4, 1943, when Tokyo ordered the evacuation of Guadalcanal within thirty days. Operating brilliantly under constant pressure from the Allies, the Imperial Army command evacuated more than eleven thousand troops by destroyers February 9. The bitter six-month struggle for Guadalcanal ended on this note of indecisiveness. Allied casualties were sixteen hundred and forty-two hundred wounded. Fourteen thousand Japanese were killed or missing, nine thousand dead from disease, and approximately one thousand captured.

Later disclosures concerning intelligence, communications, and reconnaissance have shed additional light on events. The coastwatchers rightly have received major credit. One reason the Japanese cruisers that annihilated the Allied naval forces at Savo Island were a surprise was a communication breakdown between regional commands. An Australian reconnaissance aircraft sighted and reported the Japanese, but the message was lost between command centers. The Allies benefited frequently from intercepts and analysis of signals intelligence. The Japanese achieved complete surprise when they withdrew more than ten thousand troops at the end. Indeed, the Allies were expecting a Japanese offensive.

Guadalcanal received much interest on the home front, and a new vocabulary arose: Guadalcanal, Henderson Field, the Tokyo Express (Japanese reinforcements), Iron Bottom Sound (a bay north of Guadalcanal, where naval and air forces were destroyed and sunk), the Long Lance torpedo (a superior Japanese weapon), and Starvation Island (the Japanese name for Guadalcanal). The fiftieth anniversary commemorations of events of World War II paid tribute to Guadalcanal through several publications, a reenactment, an entire summer of events involving underwater searches and the discovery of wrecks, and a symposium.

—Theodore A. Wilson, updated by Eugene L. Rasor

ADDITIONAL READING:

Frank, Richard B. *Guadalcanal: The Definitive Account of the Landmark Battle*. New York: Penguin, 1992. A scholarly study using sources from all perspectives. Stresses unique, multidimensional aspects—air, land, sea, subsurface, and amphibious—and credits the contribution of the coastwatchers. Argues that Admiral King initiated the campaign and the result was a decisive turning point of the Pacific war.

Griffith, Samuel B. *The Battle for Guadalcanal*. Philadelphia: Lippincott, 1963. Emphasizes the operations of the

U.S. Marines and neglects other forces. Sees World War II as having two bases—continental and oceanic—and presents Guadalcanal as the decisive battle of the oceanic phase. Preface by Admiral Chester Nimitz.

Isely, Jeter Allen, and Philip A. Crowl. *The U.S. Marines and Amphibious War: Its Theory and Its Practice in the Pacific*. Princeton, N.J.: Princeton University Press, 1951. An ambitious work explaining many of the questions arising from operations in the Solomon Islands. A valuable interpretive account of the war in the Pacific.

Koburger, Charles W. *Pacific Turning Point: The Solomons Campaign, 1942-1943*. Westport: Conn.: Praeger, 1995. Treats the entire campaign for the Solomon Islands, a joint effort of Nimitz's Central Pacific command and MacArthur's Southwest Pacific command.

Miller, John. *Guadalcanal: The First Offensive*. Washington, D.C.: Government Printing Office, 1949. One of eighty volumes in the highly acclaimed official Army history series. Clear, detailed, and balanced survey of the campaign. Emphasizes U.S. Army operations, but covers activities of other forces.

Morison, Samuel Eliot. *The Struggle for Guadalcanal, August 1942-February 1943*. Boston: Little, Brown, 1949. The fifth of the fifteen volumes of the official U.S. naval history of World War II by the Pulitzer Prize-winning official historian. Discusses and assesses more than a dozen naval battles and several amphibious landings of the campaign.

Rasor, Eugene L. *The Solomon Islands Campaign, Guadalcanal to Rabaul: Historiography and Annotated Bibliography*. Bibliographies of Battles and Leaders. Westport, Conn.: Greenwood Press, 1996. A comprehensive historiographical and bibliographical survey of the literature on the campaign; 544 annotated entries and extensive critical analysis and integration of those sources in the historiographical narrative section.

Tregaskis, Richard. *Guadalcanal Diary*. New York: Random House, 1943. A moment-by-moment narrative of the campaign by an on-the-spot journalist-correspondent. A popular account that was distributed to all troops in the field and much read at home.

SEE ALSO: 1941, Bombing of Pearl Harbor; 1942, Battle of Midway; 1944, Superfortress Bombing of Japan; 1945, Atomic Bombing of Japan.

1942 ■ BRACERO PROGRAM: *labor shortages during World War II prompt a plan to import agricultural workers from Mexico*

DATE: September 29, 1942-1964
LOCALE: Northwestern, Southwestern, Southeastern United States
CATEGORIES: Business and labor; Economics; Immigration; Latino American history; Treaties and agreements

KEY FIGURES:
Ignacio Pesqueira, Mexican consulate delegate, who acted on behalf of migrant workers
Claude R. Wickard (1893-1967), secretary of agriculture, who assumed control of the farm labor supply program
SUMMARY OF EVENT. The bracero program was created by the United States to meet a labor shortage caused by World War II. Many men and women left to fight in the war, and many workers left agricultural pursuits to fill job vacancies in factories. Braceros (a term that comes from the Spanish word *brazos*, meaning "arms" or "helping arms") were predominantly Mexican migrant workers who were employed in agriculture. By 1942, U.S. farmers were complaining about the labor shortages farms faced and demanded that workers be brought in to help plant, harvest, and distribute their agricultural products. In Idaho alone, more than fifteen hundred workers were needed to harvest crops.

As a result of this need for agricultural workers, the U.S. and Mexican governments created the bracero program, also known as the Mexican Farm Labor Program (MFLP). There were many provisions in this program for both the farmers and the braceros. Because many Mexicans were afraid of being forced into the United States' military upon arrival in the country, one provision was that no Mexican contract workers could be sent to fight in the U.S. military. Another provision was that Mexican laborers were not to be subjected to discriminatory acts of any kind. The United States agreed that the contract laborers' round-trip transportation expenses from Mexico would be paid and adequate living arrangements for them in the United States would be provided. There was also a provision that the braceros would not displace local workers or lower their wages.

From these provisions, various guidelines were established. The braceros were to be employed only in the agricultural realm, and on the basis of a contractual agreement (in English and Spanish) between the braceros and their employers. The farmers agreed to pay the braceros wages equal to those prevailing in the area of employment, and no less than thirty cents an hour, for a minimum of three-quarters of the duration of the contract. The braceros also were granted the right to organize. Ten percent of the braceros' earnings would be deducted and deposited in a savings fund, payable upon their return to Mexico. Finally, the braceros would be given sanitary housing conditions. In 1943, braceros would be granted the right to have a Mexican consul and Mexican labor inspectors intervene in disputes on their behalf. With these provisions and guidelines intact, on September 29, 1942, the first fifteen hundred braceros were transported to California by train.

In Mexico, people wanted to work in the United States as braceros for several reasons. One was that Mexicans were desperate for work. The United States was viewed as the achievement of a dream, where there were many jobs, good wages, and little discrimination. This image was exacerbated by the returning braceros from the 1942 farming season, who exaggerated the benefits of the program. Furthermore, many

Mexicans came from extremely rural, minimally developed, isolated areas, where the majority of inhabitants were of a low socioeconomic class, with life experiences tied to their own localities. The chance to go to the United States and work for what was perceived to be a great amount of money seemed to be a great opportunity.

Still, braceros encountered a variety of problems in the United States. Although their contracts were explained to them before they signed them, many braceros did not have a basic understanding of the contract's terms and conditions. Workers often understood little beyond the fact that they were going to work in the United States. The move from Mexico to the

The bracero program, which took advantage of Mexican farmworkers during a period of labor shortage in the United States, set specific guidelines to ensure fairness in wages and working conditions for Mexican nationals but was subject to abuses by growers who hired the migrant workers. (Library of Congress)

United States was difficult and brought culture shock. Many workers were unprepared for the cooler temperatures, having only lightweight, thin clothing. In addition, when the braceros arrived in the United States, they were not given time to orient themselves to their new surroundings—they were required to report for work the following day.

Farmers were skeptical of the MFLP because the farmers viewed it as infringing on their own welfare and traditional independence. Written contracts covering conditions of employment and having to provide adequate housing were not compatible with the farmers' deep-seated attitudes toward labor. Farmers tended to reject the idea of providing such concessions to labor in general, but in particular to imported workers, because it was a drastic departure from previous policy. The farmers would have preferred a return to an open border policy based on need per farm in place of the MFLP. The farmers wanted the federal government to provide braceros in order to grant relief from the labor crisis, but they wanted it to be done on their own terms. However, the labor shortage crisis was so severe that the farmers consented to the government's program.

Despite initial misgivings about the program, farmers eventually gained local control over the program. Once the braceros were consigned to their employers, the binational agreement between Mexico and the United States was followed weakly, if at all, by the farmers. The farmers had much more power and control than the Mexican labor inspectors did. The farmers basically had full say and could do as they pleased with the workers and their contracts.

For example, the bracero program was structured in such a way that the imported workers served as emergency workers, who could be sent quickly to other areas in need of workers. As contract laborers, they were expected to adapt to and stay on the job under adverse conditions from which local workers would have turned away. The intrinsic value of the bracero workforce was a low-paying job market that used the Mexicans for the heaviest and worst-paid jobs. This meant that the bulk of the imported workforce was fixed largely in the production and harvesting of crops that required large numbers of temporary, seasonal laborers for hard stoop work. The braceros were considered a blessing, because local workers refused to do stoop labor. The farmers used the argument that Mexicans were better suited for back-bending labor than were the local workers to justify their claim that they could not continue farming without the braceros. This type of work and mentality exploited and sadly disappointed braceros. Braceros frequently were treated and referred to as animals. Despite the ill treatment and harsh conditions, many braceros continued to migrate in order to find work and much-needed money,

Between 1942 and 1945, the braceros aided the war effort considerably by harvesting needed crops such as sugar beets, tomatoes, peaches, plums, and cotton. They worked in twenty-one states, and in 1944 alone, braceros harvested crops worth $432 million. During those same years, the federal government appropriated more than one hundred million dollars for the labor importation program and recruited workers by the thousands: four thousand in 1942, fifty-two thousand in 1943, sixty-two thousand in 1944, and one hundred twenty thousand in 1945.

By entering into an agreement with Mexican workers and the federal government in 1943, agriculture began a dependency on braceros that continued after World War II had ended. Within a year of the program's inception, braceros had in many areas become a mainstay in farm production.

After World War II ended, the Migratory Labor Agreement was signed with Mexico to continue encouraging the seasonal importation of farmworkers. Between 1948 and 1964, some 4.5 million Mexicans were brought to the United States for temporary work. Braceros were expected to return to Mexico at the end of their labor contract, but often they stayed. While the United States government sanctioned this importation of Mexican workers, it shunned the importation of workers during times of economic difficulties. During the 1953-1954 recession, the government mounted a campaign called Operation Wetback to deport illegal entrants and braceros who had remained in the country illegally. Deportations numbered in excess of 1.1 million. As immigration officials searched out illegal workers, persons from Central and South America, as well as native-born U.S. citizens of Central or South American descent, found themselves vulnerable to this search. Protestations of the violation of their rights occurred, but to little effect.

Although the jobs reserved for the braceros were generally despised, they were nevertheless essential first links in the robust war food production chain. In this capacity, the Mexican workers made a vital and measurable contribution to the total war effort. —*Kristine Kleptach Jamieson*

ADDITIONAL READING:

Copp, Nelson Gage. *"Wetbacks" and Braceros: Mexican Migrant Laborers and American Immigration Policy, 1930-1960*. San Francisco: R and E Research Associates, 1971. Provides detailed accounts of emigration and immigration policies affecting migrant agricultural workers from Mexico.

Craig, Richard B. *The Bracero Program: Interest Groups and Foreign Policy*. Austin: University of Texas Press, 1971. Discusses the political agreement between the United States and Mexico regarding migrant laborers.

Galarza, Ernesto. *Merchants of Labor: The Mexican Bracero Story*. Santa Barbara, Calif.: McNally and Loftin, West, 1978. Discusses the treatment of braceros and the effects of the bracero program in California.

Gamboa, Erasmo. *Mexican Labor and World War II: Braceros in the Pacific Northwest, 1942-1947*. Austin: University of Texas Press, 1990. A detailed history of the life, conditions, and social policy affecting migrant workers from Mexico in the United States.

Valdes, Dennis Nodin. *Al Norte: Agricultural Workers in the Great Lakes Region, 1917-1970*. Austin: University of Texas Press, 1991. An in-depth discussion of the Mexican migration to and settlement in the upper Midwest regions.

SEE ALSO: 1924, Immigration Act of 1924; 1929, League of United Latin American Citizens Is Founded; 1929, Great Depression; 1930's, Mass Deportations of Mexicans; 1933, Good Neighbor Policy; 1943, Inflation and Labor Unrest; 1954, Operation Wetback; 1972, United Farm Workers Joins with AFL-CIO.

1942 ■ INVASION OF NORTH AFRICA: *an Allied campaign designed to force the Germans out of North Africa provides a training ground for U.S. forces in World War II*

DATE: November 7-8, 1942
LOCALE: French North Africa
CATEGORY: Wars, uprisings, and civil unrest
KEY FIGURES:
Winston Leonard Spencer Churchill (1874-1965), prime minister of Great Britain
Jean Louis Darlan (1881-1942), commander in chief of the French forces at Vichy
Dwight David Eisenhower (1890-1969), commander of Allied forces in Northwest Africa
Henri-Honoré Giraud (1879-1949), French general in North Africa
George Catlett Marshall (1880-1959), chief of staff of the U.S. Army
Bernard Law Montgomery (1887-1976), commander of the Eighth Army in North Africa
George S. Patton (1885-1945), commander of U.S. forces in Morocco
Henri Philippe Pétain (1856-1951), head of the French puppet government at Vichy
Erwin Rommel (1891-1944), German general defeated by the Allies in North Africa
Franklin Delano Roosevelt (1882-1945), thirty-second president of the United States, 1933-1945

SUMMARY OF EVENT. On December 11, 1941, Germany and Italy declared war on the United States. Thereafter, the United States devoted its chief efforts to defeating its European enemies. Officers of the U.S. Army, however, disagreed with their British counterparts about how this aim should be accomplished. General George C. Marshall, chief of staff of the U.S. Army, wanted to build up air and ground forces in the British Isles and then launch a cross-channel invasion into France, aimed ultimately at Berlin. He hoped to be ready to invade late in 1942 and certainly by early 1943. The British leaders, especially Prime Minister Winston Churchill, favored a peripheral strategy designed to wear down Germany and Italy through air attacks and by striking at weak points on the frontiers of their empires. Churchill argued that only when the enemy was exhausted should the Allies cross the English Channel and confront the German army directly.

President Franklin D. Roosevelt and Marshall also believed that by concentrating on a cross-channel operation, they could achieve several objectives. First, the operation would satisfy Russia's Joseph Stalin, who was pressuring the Allies for a second front in Europe, which would take pressure off the beleaguered Russians. Second, such an attack would take the Germans by surprise and stimulate French resistance. In the long run, it was unrealistic to attack the powerful Germans on their home ground without preparation. The dangers of defeat were great, but it was imperative that the United States show its colors somewhere.

Roosevelt insisted that U.S. troops be in action against the Germans somewhere before the end of 1942. Invasion of France was not possible in 1942 because of a lack of landing craft and trained troops to staff them, so the Allies had to find an easier target. Churchill won the argument when the Allies decided that French North Africa was ideal for invasion. There were no German troops in that area, and it was probable that the Vichy French forces (set up as part of the French puppet state after France had surrendered to the Germans in June, 1940) would put up only token resistance against British and U.S. invaders. At the other end of the North African landmass, the British Eighth Army was fighting General Erwin Rommel's Afrika Korps. An Allied landing in French North Africa would relieve the pressure on the British in Egypt and, it was hoped, make it possible to force the Germans out of North Africa altogether. Allied possession of North Africa would free the Mediterranean Sea for British shipping, so that oil from the Near East and supplies from India could come to the British Isles by the most direct route. Marshall argued that a landing in North Africa would delay an invasion of northern France by two years because of the drain on supplies, but Roosevelt overruled him.

The planning for the invasion, called Operation Torch, proved to be difficult. The United States preferred simultaneous landings in Morocco and Algeria, while the British wanted the operation to focus on the Algerian coastline alone. Both sides had good reasons. The United States wanted a foothold in Morocco, near Casablanca, if things went poorly in Algeria. Casablanca also would give the Allies a port that would not be subject to Axis air attacks. On the other hand, the British argued that if the landings did not include eastern Algeria, the Germans and Italians could quickly occupy all of Tunisia, using it as a base for air attacks and for a solid defensive position that would take many Allied lives to reduce.

By the end of August, the plans were in place, and General Dwight David Eisenhower was firmly entrenched as the overall commander of the operation. In October, 1942, Major General Mark Clark and diplomat Robert Murphy were sent on a secret mission into North Africa to gauge the sentiments of the French forces there. Clark and Murphy ran head-on into French politics in North Africa. One problem was deciding which French general would lead the defection from Vichy and from collaboration with the Axis. It was clear that maverick General Charles de Gaulle would be unacceptable to

French military leadership in North Africa. Admiral Jean Darlan, commander in chief of Vichy forces, was suspect because of his previous support for Vichy. It was agreed that General Henri-Honoré Giraud would announce the landings and order Vichy troops not to resist the Allies. In another undercover operation, Giraud was brought to Gibraltar to confer with Eisenhower on the eve of the invasion. In the long run, Giraud's selection did not settle French political problems in North Africa.

In the early morning of November 8, 1942, Eisenhower's troops landed at Casablanca, Oran, and Algiers. General Giraud's orders not to resist too often were ignored by French officers unaware of Giraud's new role in French North Africa, and the aged Marshal Henri Philippe Pétain, head of the Vichy government, ordered his forces to resist. Eisenhower, contacting Admiral Darlan, made the following arrangements: Darlan was to assume control of French North Africa and then would order his troops to cease fire preparatory to a later attack on the Germans. The U.S. press criticized Eisenhower for coming to terms with a pro-Fascist, but Churchill and Roosevelt supported him, especially when Eisenhower explained that the deal was necessary to avoid fighting the French and to begin the real job of fighting the Germans.

In November and early December, Eisenhower made a dash for Tunis, hoping to seize that port before the Germans could pour troops into Tunisia. Rain, superior German tank tactics, and German air superiority stalled his offensive before it reached its objective. The British Eighth Army, under General Bernard L. Montgomery, was driving Rommel back. By February, 1943, Rommel had crossed Libya and reached southern Tunisia. He then turned against Eisenhower's troops and inflicted a sharp blow on them at Kasserine Pass. The Allies, however, were building up their force, while the Germans received no significant reinforcements. By May 13, the last resistance had ended, and Eisenhower had captured nearly three hundred thousand prisoners in Tunisia.

As Marshall had feared, the large troop commitment to North Africa made a cross-channel invasion in 1943 impossible. Because the troops and landing craft were already in the Mediterranean, they had to be used there. Despite Marshall's concerns, Operation Torch did have a number of beneficial results. First, it established Eisenhower as a military planner and as an officer who could be diplomat as well as warrior. Second, it gave Eisenhower's staff valuable training in planning and executing a complex mission that involved air, land, and sea components. Third, Operation Torch and subsequent fighting in North Africa allowed U.S. Army troops to train in realistic conditions. Fourth, Operation Torch was carried out successfully less than one year after the attack on Pearl Harbor, thereby showing the United States' resilience, resolve, and combat potential.

On July 10, 1943, Anglo-American forces invaded Sicily, and the Allies soon captured the island. The fall of Sicily and the Allied bombing of Rome led to the downfall of the Italian head of government, Benito Mussolini, on July 25, 1943, and

ultimately to an Italian surrender. Before the negotiations could be planned, however, the Germans had occupied the country. In September, U.S. troops invaded Italy. The progress of the Allied forces up the peninsula was slow; not until June 4, 1944, did the U.S. Fifth Army liberate Rome. The campaign that began with the invasion of North Africa had accomplished much, principally the freeing of the Mediterranean Sea and the elimination of Italy from the war.

—*Stephen E. Ambrose, updated by James J. Cooke*

ADDITIONAL READING:

Howe, George F. *The Mediterranean Theater of Operations, Northeast Africa: Seizing the Initiative in the West.* Washington, D.C.: Center of Military History, 1991. Official operational history that contains great detail about Operation Torch.

Jackson, W. G. F. *The Battle for North Africa.* New York: Mason/Charter Press, 1975. A survey of military operations in North Africa.

Langer, William L. *Our Vichy Gamble.* New York: Alfred A. Knopf, 1947. A classic and useful work on this topic.

Murphy, Robert D. *Diplomat Among Warriors.* Garden City, N.J.: Doubleday, 1964. These memoirs of a participant are invaluable to understanding the political and military nuances of Operation Torch.

Pogue, Forrest C. *George C. Marshall: Ordeal and Hope, 1939-1942.* New York: Viking Press, 1966. Contains a short but good analysis of Marshall and Operation Torch.

SEE ALSO: 1941, Germany and Italy Declare War on the United States; 1943, Western Allies Invade Italy.

1943 ■ INFLATION AND LABOR UNREST: *in the face of wartime limits on wages, labor turns to mass disruption and strikes*

DATE: April 8, 1943-June 23, 1947

LOCALE: United States

CATEGORIES: Business and labor; Economics; Wars, uprisings, and civil unrest

KEY FIGURES:

William Green (1873-1952), president of the American Federation of Labor, 1925-1952

John Llewellyn Lewis (1880-1969), president of the United Mine Workers, 1920-1960

Philip Murray (1886-1952), president of the Congress of Industrial Organizations, 1941-1952

Walter Philip Reuther (1907-1970), emerging voice of the Auto Workers Union after World War II

Rolland J. Thomas (1900-1967), president of the United Auto Workers, 1939-1946

Harry S Truman (1884-1972), thirty-third president of the United States, 1945-1953

SUMMARY OF EVENT. In examining the crisis in U.S. labor relations that followed World War II, one is confronted not by a single dramatic event but by a series of interrelated industrial struggles. Between 1945 and 1948, concerns about the postwar economy and labor reorganization swelled into a nationwide wave of strikes that influence all levels of employment. The strikes occurred in the political vacuum created by divisions within the U.S. workforce, the shift in industrial production from a wartime to a peacetime economy, and the legacy of wartime governmental intervention into labor activities.

During the war, government intervention into industrial relations had been deemed necessary to ensure uninterrupted production of war materials. Beginning in 1940, under the slogan National Unity, the government enforced a policy of uneasy collaboration between unions and employers. William Green of the American Federation of Labor (AFL) and Philip Murray of the Congress of Industrial Organizations (CIO) pledged that for the duration of the war, there would be no work stoppages or walkouts, which had characterized the prewar era during the rise of the CIO. Furthermore, they voluntarily renounced many of their administrative decision-making powers to a War Labor Board.

Composed of four members each from labor, management, and the public, the board's primary duties were to regulate wages and settle disputes between labor and management. In such disagreements, the board not only was the final arbiter but also set limits on what the disagreeing parties could negotiate voluntarily. Thus in July of 1942, the War Labor Board implemented the "Little Steel" formula, which set a relatively severe restriction on the wages of employees of national steel industries. On April 8, 1943, President Franklin D. Roosevelt issued an order to freeze wage increases to a percentage equal to the estimated rise in the cost of living since January 1, 1941: 15 percent. Employees who had already received 10 percent in increases could bargain for only 5 percent more. Eventually applied to the entire industrial sector, the ultimate effect of the Little Steel formula was that wartime abundance of overtime work was prevented from raising actual levels of take-home pay in basic industries.

Despite these governmental efforts to create economic stability, commodity prices rose 33 percent. Inflation rates were severe enough to provoke strikes during the war, against the "no-strike" pledges of most wartime industrial union leaders. In 1943, almost five thousand unauthorized work stoppages occurred, affecting more than two million laborers. During the same year, John L. Lewis, president of the United Mine Workers, urged his followers to strike, despite recriminations from the government and from some fellow unionists. In the end, Lewis' miners won "portal to portal" pay—a formula whereby the War Labor Board circumvented its own wage freeze, granting Lewis' people pay for the time it took them to arrive at their workstations.

That such a major walkout could take place given the harsh wartime restrictions made many labor analysts predict chaos after the peace declaration—and many of their concerns were realized. The dissolution of the War Labor Board following the United States' victory over Japan in 1945 brought on a massive wave of strikes. With the end of national price controls, the already high inflation rate soared to unprecedented heights, yet employee wages, held by the Little Steel formula, showed little growth. To overcome the gap between prices and wages, unions attempted to negotiate wage increases. When negotiations failed, strikes were called.

Beginning in 1946, the United Auto Workers requested a 30 percent increase in wage rates without a price increase at General Motors. In response, the company offered a 10 percent cost-of-living increase and would not allow union discussion of industry price rates. In April, United Auto Workers president R. J. Thomas and lead negotiator Walter Reuther were urging union members toward a settlement that could be reached without a work stoppage, but by early September some auto plants around Detroit were already on strike, and the national union decided to call for a strike vote. When General Motors failed to respond to a union offer to have all issues settled by arbitration if the company would open its books for public examination, 225,000 workers walked out on November 21, led by newly elected president Reuther.

The auto strikers were soon joined by workers throughout industry. On January 15, 1946, 174,000 electrical workers struck General Electric. The next day, 93,000 meat packers struck. On January 21, 750,000 steelworkers struck U.S. Steel. At the height of these and 250 lesser disputes, 1.6 million workers were on strike. On April 1, 340,000 of Lewis' coal miners struck again, causing a nationwide brown-out. A May 23 railroad strike by engineers and trainmen over work-rule changes brought an almost complete shutdown of the nation's commerce. The strike wave, however, was not limited entirely to industrial workers. Strikes were widespread among teachers and municipal workers, and there were more strikes in transportation, communication, and public utilities than in any previous year. In short, the first six months of 1946 marked the most concentrated period of labor-management strife in U.S. history, with 2.97 million workers involved in strikes—and by the end of the year, that figure had risen to 4.6 million.

Spurring the strikers was the idea of counter-power over such management decisions as the speed of work, numbers of workers per task, what foremen were acceptable, and how the work was organized. The real uniting factor for the unions, however, was the long-standing push for higher wages. In 1947, the government moved quickly to contain the strike movement. In the auto dispute, President Harry Truman appointed a fact-finding board and appealed to the strikers to return to work pending its decision; similar boards were created for numerous other industries. In most cases, however, the findings of the strike boards were insufficient to satisfy union demands. Where fact-finding boards were unable to set limits on the strike wave, the government turned to direct seizure of industries, still authorized under wartime powers.

Overall, unions made little effort to combat the government's attack. Except for Lewis' United Mine Workers, fined $3.5 million for insubordination, all returned to work when the government seized their industries. In most cases, unions accepted the conclusions of the government's fact-finding boards, although by 1947 this often meant a decline in wages to below wartime levels. Indeed, by March of that year, auto and steel workers' salaries were 25 percent less than two years before.

The final settlement of the strike wave granted wage increases of only 17 percent, not enough to keep up with lost income from cutbacks in overtime. Contract language regarding control over the workplace strengthened management at the expense of the workers, and wage increases with no bar against price hikes meant that unions' gains came at the expense of the consumer.

The labor unrest was finally quelled by the conservative political response to the strikes of 1943 and 1946, combined with the emerging conservatism of the Cold War. Passed on June 23, 1947, the Taft-Hartley Act contained provisions that restricted labor unions from organizing aggressively or conducting militant activities. To enforce these restrictions, the law included strict anti-communist oaths for union officers. Elimination of domestic communists from the trade union movement was seen not only as a way to prevent another massive strike wave but also as an essential ingredient of the larger anti-communist crusade typified by Joseph McCarthy and the House Committee on Un-American Activities.

—Edward A. Zivich, updated by Thomas J. Edward Walker and Cynthia Gwynne Yaudes

ADDITIONAL READING:

Barnard, John. *Walther Reuther and the Rise of the Auto Workers*. Boston: Little, Brown, 1983. A complete biography of the celebrated union organizer; discusses his view of the place of labor in the U.S. economy.

Brecher, Jeremy. *Strike!* San Francisco: Straight Arrow Books, 1972. Narrates and analyzes rank-and-file labor struggles; discusses the major strikes of U.S. workers between 1877 and 1970, including the 1946 strike wave. Index.

DeCaux, Len. *Labor Radical: From the Wobblies to the CIO*. Boston: Beacon Press, 1970. A "personal history," which spans the period from 1910 to the 1960's. As a participant in the labor movement, DeCaux provides a unique perspective on the 1940's strike wave. Index.

Lens, Sidney. *The Crisis of American Labor*. New York: Sagamore Press, 1959. A political and social analysis of post-World War II labor unrest. Focuses on key labor leaders, including John L. Lewis and Walter Reuther. Index.

Lipsitz, George. *Class and Culture in Cold War America*. South Hadley, Mass.: J. F. Bergin, 1981. Analyzes the effects of the collective actions and aspirations of workers after World War II on the United States' economic, political, and social identity. Contains a chapter chronicling the strike wave of 1946. Bibliography, index.

Zieger, Robert. *John L. Lewis: Labor Leader*. Boston: Twayne, 1988. Describes in detail Lewis' rise through the ranks of the United Mine Workers; compares Lewis' goals for the labor movement with those of Walter Reuther. Index.

SEE ALSO: 1886, American Federation of Labor Is Founded; 1894, Pullman Strike; 1902, Anthracite Coal Strike; 1905, Industrial Workers of the World Is Founded; 1935, National Labor Relations Act; 1938, Fair Labor Standards Act; 1941, 6.6 Million Women Enter the U.S. Labor Force; 1955, AFL and CIO Merge.

1943 ■ URBAN RACE RIOTS: *racial tensions peak as minorities and whites compete for jobs and social services during World War II*

DATE: May-August, 1943

LOCALE: Mobile, Beaumont, Harlem, Detroit, and Los Angeles

CATEGORIES: Business and labor; Economics; Wars, uprisings, and civil unrest

KEY FIGURES:

Ross Dickey, chief of police for Beaumont, Texas

Edward J. Jeffries (1900-1950), mayor of Detroit

Robert W. Kenny, California's attorney general

Fiorello H. La Guardia (1882-1947), New York City mayor

John LeFlore (1911-1976), executive secretary of the Mobile NAACP

Charles "Little Willie" Lyon, African American youth who led a group on a violent spree that triggered the Detroit riots

Burton R. Morley (1898-?), Mobile area director for the War Manpower Commission

Walter F. White (1893-1955), African American leader in New York City

SUMMARY OF EVENT. The urban race riots in the summer of 1943 did not occur spontaneously. A pattern of violence throughout the nation, similar to the racial conflicts that occurred during World War I, had been escalating since 1940, as urban areas swelled with workers drawn to wartime industries. The lack of interracial communication, the failure of local, state, and federal agencies to comprehend the severity of the racial environment, challenges against established Southern racial traditions, and extreme shortages of housing and social services created frustration, which manifested itself in racial violence.

Mobile, Alabama's tremendous growth in population caused severe problems in housing and city services. These shortages, combined with the competition for jobs, created racial tension. Whites jealously protected what they considered to be white-only, high-paying, skilled jobs. The largest wartime contractor in Mobile was ADDSCO, the Alabama Dry Dock and Shipbuilding Company. ADDSCO, like numerous other industries, employed African Americans only for unskilled or semiskilled positions. Unable to find enough skilled welders and to appease the local National Association for the Advancement of Colored People (NAACP), led by John LeFlore and Burton R. Morley of the War Manpower

Commission, ADDSCO agreed to employ African American welders. On May 24, 1943, black welders reported for work on the third shift at the Pinto Island Yard. No racial incidents occurred during the night, but the next morning, after additional black welders reported for work, violence erupted.

Between five hundred and one thousand whites attacked black workers and drove them from the yards. Governor Chauncey Sparks ordered the Alabama State Guard to intervene, and by noon the rioting had ended. Federal troops occupied the shipyards, and local city and county government ordered all bars and liquor stores closed until the tension eased. Mobile police eventually charged three whites with felony assault, intent to murder, and inciting a riot. On June 5, 1943, the Alabama State Guard pulled out and on June 10, 1943, federal troops returned to their base at Brookley Field.

As emotions in Mobile calmed, racial tensions in Los Angeles exploded. On June 3, 1943, servicemen from area bases began attacking Mexican American youths known as "zoot-suiters" in response to rumors that the youths had assaulted female relatives of military personnel. Servicemen, accompanied by civilians, roamed the streets, sometimes in taxicabs, in search of zoot-suiters. Streetcars and buses were stopped and searched, and zoot-suiters found in stores and theaters were disrobed and beaten.

In retaliation, gangs of Mexican American adolescents attacked military personnel. Police arrested reported zoot-suit leaders Frank H. Tellez and Luis "the Chief" Verdusco in an effort to stop Mexican American violence against whites. Fighting reached a climax on June 7, 1943, when a mob of more than a thousand servicemen and civilians moved down Main Street in downtown Los Angeles to the African American neighborhood at Twelfth and Central, and then through the Mexican American neighborhood on the east side, looking for zoot-suiters. The Mexican ambassador to the United States lodged a formal complaint with Secretary of State Cordell Hull, and California governor Earl Warren appointed Attorney General Robert Kenny to investigate the riots. While the riots officially ended on June 7, violent incidents continued throughout the city for the rest of the summer.

As rioting in Los Angeles subsided, racial violence returned to the South. Beaumont, Texas, located between Houston and the Louisiana border, had experienced tremendous wartime growth because of its petroleum production facilities and shipbuilding operations. With emotions already frayed from an earlier suspected rape of a white woman by a black ex-convict, the reported rape of a young white woman by a black man on June 15, 1943, set off a violent reaction among white workers at the Pennsylvania Shipyards. In the early evening, approximately two thousand workers marched on downtown Beaumont. Police Chief Ross Dickey convinced the mob not to lynch any black prisoners.

Around midnight, mobs converged on black neighborhoods in north Beaumont and along Forsythe Street. At the Greyhound bus station, about three hundred whites assaulted fifty-two African American army draftees. Whites looted and burned local businesses and assaulted African Americans until the next morning. Killed during the evening's violence were Alex Mouton and John Johnson, African Americans, and Ellis C. Brown, a white man. Local law enforcement tried diligently to stop the rioting. More than two hundred whites and six African Americans were arrested during the rioting. Martial law was declared on June 16 and lifted on June 20. Although calm had been restored to Beaumont, the violence compelled approximately twenty-five hundred blacks to leave soon after the riots.

One of the worst riots in the summer of 1943 occurred in Detroit. On Sunday, June 20, 1943, more than one hundred thousand Detroiters, a large percentage of them African American, had gone to the Belle Isle Amusement Park. A group of black teenagers led by Charles "Little Willie" Lyon began attacking whites. A fight broke out between white sailors and young African Americans on the bridge connecting Belle Isle with the city. The fighting spread, and by 11:00 P.M., an estimated five thousand people were fighting on and around the Belle Isle Bridge.

Rumors of atrocities against African Americans circulated in the Paradise Valley ghetto. Black rioters stoned passing cars of whites and destroyed white-owned businesses. By early morning, whites along Woodward Avenue had retaliated by beating African Americans. Mayor Edward J. Jeffries asked Governor Harry F. Kelly to request federal troops, but Kelly hesitated until Monday evening, and federal troops did not arrive until Tuesday morning. As African Americans rioted along the east side of Woodward Avenue, whites continued congregating along Woodward Avenue. Detroit remained under a curfew and martial law for the following week, and federal troops remained for two weeks. After two days of intense rioting, the Detroit riots were over. Authorities reported thirty-four people, mostly African Americans, killed and more than seven hundred injured. Property damage estimates ranged around two million dollars.

As the situation calmed in Detroit, tensions were mounting in Harlem, New York. On August 1, 1943, in the late afternoon, Robert Bandy, an African American soldier on leave from the army, argued with James Collins, a white policeman, over the arrest of a black woman at the Braddock Hotel on West 126th Street. A fight ensued, and Collins shot Bandy, inflicting a superficial wound. Rumors quickly spread that a black soldier trying to protect his mother had been killed by a white policeman. Crowds of angry African Americans gathered at the Braddock Hotel and the twenty-eighth police precinct, and by midnight, rioting had started.

The rioting centered in Harlem and never directly involved confrontations between blacks and whites. Mayor Fiorello H. La Guardia acted swiftly to confine the violence by using extra police, firefighters, black Office of Civilian Defense volunteers, and National Guardsmen. African American civic leaders such as Walter White worked alongside city officials to calm Harlem residents. The all-night looting and burning of white-owned businesses left Harlem looking like a war zone.

By the time peace was restored, after twelve hours of rioting, six African Americans had been killed by police and National Guard troops, and almost two hundred people reported injuries. Property damage was estimated to be as high as five million dollars. The racial violence of the summer of 1943 had ended, but the problems that triggered riots and violence across the nation remained. *—Craig S. Pascoe*

ADDITIONAL READING:

Blum, John Morton. *V Was for Victory: Politics and American Culture During World War II.* New York: Harcourt Brace Jovanovich, 1976. A study of politics and culture that examines established segregation and prejudice in the United States during World War II.

Capeci, Dominic J., Jr. *The Harlem Riot of 1943.* Philadelphia: Temple University Press, 1977. Examines race relations in New York from 1933 to 1943. Argues that African Americans became disillusioned with social gains that were meager compared with their contributions to the war effort.

Grimshaw, Allen D. *Racial Violence in the United States.* Chicago: Aldine Publishing, 1969. Discusses the historical, sociological, and psychological factors of racial violence in the United States.

Lee, Alfred McClung. *Race Riot, Detroit 1943.* 1943. Reprint. New York: Octagon Books, 1968. Firsthand account of the Detroit riots. Analyzes the reasons for rioting and discusses measures needed to avoid future urban violence.

McWilliams, Carey. *North from Mexico: The Spanish-Speaking People of the United States.* 1948. Reprint. New York: Greenwood Press, 1990. Offers an insight into the Mexican American experience; includes a section on Los Angeles.

SEE ALSO: 1866, Rise of the Ku Klux Klan; 1866, Race Riots in the South; 1965, Watts Riot; 1967, Long, Hot Summer; 1992, Los Angeles Riots.

1943 ■ WESTERN ALLIES INVADE ITALY:
Germans are forced to use troops and resources that might have been used in northern France

DATE: July 9-September 19, 1943
LOCALE: Sicily and the Italian mainland
CATEGORY: Wars, uprisings, and civil unrest
KEY FIGURES:

Harold R. L. George Alexander (1891-1969), commander of the Fifteenth Army Group
Pietro Badoglio (1871-1956), prime minister of Italy, 1943-1944
Mark W. Clark (1896-1984), commander of the U.S. Fifth Army
Dwight David Eisenhower (1890-1969), supreme commander of the Allied Expeditionary Force
Albert Kesselring (1885-1960), German commander in chief, South

Bernard Law Montgomery (1887-1976), commander of the British Eighth Army
Benito Mussolini (1883-1945), prime minister of Italy, 1922-1943
George Smith Patton, Jr. (1885-1945), commander of the U.S. Seventh Army

SUMMARY OF EVENT. One of the decisions made by President Franklin D. Roosevelt and Prime Minister Winston Churchill at the Casablanca Conference in February of 1943 was to occupy the island of Sicily in order to assure the safety of Allied shipping lines in the Mediterranean. At the time, no decision was made as to an invasion of the Italian mainland. General Dwight Eisenhower was given overall military command of the Mediterranean theater, while General Harold R. L. George Alexander was in command of the invasion force, the Fifteenth Army Group.

The invasion of Sicily was preceded by the capture of a small garrison on the island of Pantelleria on June 11, 1943. The Germans were not convinced that the capture of this island pointed to an invasion of Sicily, but were tricked by a British ruse that suggested that an Allied invasion of Sardinia was forthcoming.

Following a monthlong bombardment of Axis air bases, the Fifteenth Army Group, consisting of the British Eighth Army under General Montgomery and the U.S. Seventh Army commanded by General George S. Patton, carried out two separate landings on the southern coast of Sicily on July 9 and July 10, 1943. Supported by naval gunfire and airborne operations, the Allies landed 160,000 men on the island. The Allies benefited greatly from superior air power, having thirty-seven hundred planes as opposed to sixteen hundred Axis aircraft. Although the landing itself went relatively smoothly, tragedy struck when U.S. airborne drops encountered friendly fire. Montgomery's forces ran into some stubborn German resistance south of Catania, while Patton, whose forces had landed on the left flank, first moved through western Sicily and later assisted the British. On August 17, both forces arrived in Messina, on the northern tip of the island. In spite of complete Allied air superiority, the Germans had managed to evacuate more than a hundred thousand troops and a considerable number of vehicles to the Italian mainland.

The fall of Sicily was a major factor in the collapse of Benito Mussolini's government. The Fascist leadership had become increasingly disenchanted with Mussolini, in particular with his alliance with Adolf Hitler. A meeting between Mussolini and Hitler, in which Mussolini requested the transfer of Italian divisions from the Russian front to be used in the defense of Italy, had brought no results. During a subsequent meeting of the Fascist Grand Council on July 24, Mussolini was handed a vote of no confidence. On the following day, he was dismissed from office by the king of Italy, Victor Emmanuel III, arrested, and spirited away to a hotel on the Gran Sasso in the Abbruzzi Mountains.

Mussolini was succeeded as prime minister by Marshal Pietro Badoglio, a former Fascist leader whose emissaries had negotiated secretly with the Allies in Lisbon and Madrid. Badoglio's problem was to make peace with the Allies and extricate Italy from the war, while preventing the Germans from defending Italy against an expected Allied invasion.

The collapse of the Fascist government in Italy brought to the fore the still unresolved issue of the entire purpose of the Italian campaign. U.S. military planners had insisted all along that the Italian campaign was to be no more than a secondary effort, insisting that the primary Allied effort had to be Operation Overlord, the Normandy invasion. In their view, the purpose of the Italian campaign was merely to force the Germans to commit troops and resources in the Italian theater to prevent their use on the Eastern Front and, more important, against an Allied invasion in Normandy. On the other hand, British military planners—perhaps with an eye toward postwar settlements in the Balkans—assigned far greater importance to the Italian theater. The conflict of opinion was reflected in the fact that it took until the end of July to authorize an invasion of the Italian peninsula.

September 3, 1943, an armistice was signed between Italy and the Allies. By mid-October, the Badoglio government had declared war on Germany and was recognized by the Allies as a cobelligerent. Although the announcement of the Italian capitulation took many Germans by surprise, Hitler had prepared for such an eventuality ever since Mussolini's overthrow by ordering troops to assemble for possible entry into Italy. Thus, by the beginning of September, the Germans had eight divisions in readiness in the north of Italy, in addition to Field Marshall Albert Kesselring's forces in southern Italy.

The invasion of the Italian mainland began on September 3. It involved the movement of two British divisions under General Bernard Montgomery across the narrow Straits of Messina into Calabria. On September 9, another British division landed at Taranto. The Italians were unprepared for the invasions, but the Germans reacted quickly, occupying Rome and airfields in the vicinity, thereby putting an end to any hopes for a possible Allied airborne operation in the area.

Unlike the invasions in Calabria and Taranto, which met with virtually no resistance, Allied landings at Salerno (Operation Avalanche) on September 9 met with stiff resistance. An invasion force of 55,000 troops for the initial landings, with another 115,000 to follow, was confronted by a much smaller contingent of German defenders. Lieutenant General Mark Clark, who had intended to surprise the defenders by forgoing preparatory naval bombardment, was faced with counterattacks from the Germans that almost turned the entire invasion into a disaster. Only with the help of skillful naval gunnery, artillery, and considerable air support could the invasion force maintain its precarious positions on the beach. By September 18, the beachhead was at last secured and the German offensive could be checked. Montgomery, after some prompting to accelerate, at last had managed to make contact with the beachhead on September 16.

The Germans realized that their failure to drive the Allies back into the sea left them only one option: a gradual withdrawal northward beyond Naples, where they had established a strong defensive zone, the so-called Winter Line or Gustav Line. The Allied campaign to penetrate this line met with little success. In an effort to break the stalemate, the Allies, on January 22, 1944, resorted to a landing behind the German lines on the beaches at Anzio. In spite of initial successes, the effort bogged down, and during four months on the beachhead, the Allies had to evacuate more than thirty thousand casualties. Following a combined air-ground offensive, a breakthrough was at last effected, and Allied troops entered Rome on June 4, 1944, two days before the Normandy invasion.

The Allied drive toward the new German defensive positions south of Bologna—the so-called Gothic Line—again bogged down, and the offensive could not be resumed until the spring of 1945. Bologna fell on April 21, only a few days before Mussolini was captured and executed by partisans. In fact, since March, 1945, SS General Karl Wolff secretly had been negotiating surrender terms for the German forces in Italy with Allen Dulles, the chief of the American Office of Strategic Services in Switzerland. Fighting in Italy ceased on May 2, 1945, five days before the final capitulation of Germany.

—*Helmut J. Schmeller*

ADDITIONAL READING:

Breuer, William B. *Drop Zone Sicily: Allied Airborne Strike, July 1943*. Novato, Calif.: Presidio Press, 1983. An account of airborne operations, based largely on interviews with participants. Photographs, maps, index.

Clark, Mark W. *Calculated Risk*. New York: Harper Brothers, 1950. Memoirs of General Clark, covering the period from July, 1940, to the Moscow Conference of 1947. Forceful description of the Italian campaign. Photographs, maps, index.

Graham, Dominick, and Shelford Bidwell. *Tug of War: The Battle for Italy, 1943-1945*. New York: St. Martin's Press, 1986. Comprehensive, lucid account of a campaign that assumed unintended proportions. Maps, index, chronology.

Hickey, Des, and Gus Smith. *Operation Avalanche: The Salerno Landings, 1943*. New York: McGraw-Hill, 1984. A day-by-day account, based on eyewitness reports and historical documentation. Discusses tactical conceptions of Clark and Kesselring. Photographs, maps, index.

Keegan, John. "Italy and the Balkans." In *The Second World War*. New York: Viking, 1989. Analyzes the war periodically and thematically; focuses on strategic dilemmas faced by Axis and Allied leaders. Photographs, maps, index.

Kitchen, Martin. "Italy and the Balkans." In *A World in Flames: A Short History of the Second World War in Europe and Asia, 1939-1945*. New York: Longman, 1990. Concise, up-to-date interpretation that places military events in a broader political context. Maps and index.

Liddell Hart, B. H. *History of the Second World War*. New York: G. P. Putnam's Sons, 1971. Comprehensive, authoritative analysis of the strategic and tactical aspects of the war.

More than fifty excellent maps; general and subject index.

See also: 1941, Germany and Italy Declare War on the United States; 1942, Invasion of North Africa; 1944, Operation Overlord; 1944, Battle of the Bulge; 1945, Yalta Conference; 1945, V-E Day; 1945, Potsdam Conference.

1943 ■ Magnuson Act: *repeat of Asian exclusion laws opens the way for further immigration reforms*

Date: December 17, 1943
Locale: Washington, D.C., and China
Categories: Asian American history; Immigration; Laws and acts
Key figure:
Franklin Delano Roosevelt (1882-1945), thirty-second president of the United States, 1933-1945

Summary of event. The passage by Congress of the Immigration Act of 1943 and President Franklin D. Roosevelt's signing it into law ended the era of legal exclusion of Chinese immigrants to the United States and began an era during which sizable numbers of Chinese and other Asian immigrants came to the country. It helped bring about significant changes in race relations in the United States.

The first wave of Chinese immigrants came from the Pearl River delta region in southern China. They began coming to California in 1848 during the gold rush and continued to come to the western states as miners, railroad builders, farmers, fishermen, and factory workers. Most were men. Many came as contract laborers and intended to return to China. Anti-Chinese feelings, begun during the gold rush and expressed in mob actions and local discriminatory laws, culminated in the Chinese Exclusion Act of 1882, barring the immigration of Chinese laborers for ten years. It was renewed in 1892, applied to Hawaii when those islands were annexed by the United States in 1898, and made permanent in 1904. Another bill, passed in 1924, made Asians ineligible for U.S. citizenship and disallowed Chinese wives of U.S. citizens to immigrate to the United States. As a result, the Chinese population in the United States declined from a peak of 107,475 in 1880 to 77,504 in 1940.

The passage of the Magnuson Act of 1943, which repealed the Chinese Exclusion Act of 1882, inaugurated profound changes in the status of ethnic Chinese who were citizens or residents of the United States. It made Chinese immigrants, many of whom had lived in the United States for years, eligible for citizenship. It also allotted a minuscule quota of 105 Chinese persons per year who could enter the United States as immigrants. The 1943 bill was a result of recognition of China's growing international status after 1928 under the Nationalist government and growing U.S. sympathy for China's heroic resistance to Japanese aggression after 1937. It also was intended to counter Japanese wartime propaganda aimed at

discrediting the United States among Asians by portraying it as a racist nation.

World War II was a turning point for Chinese-U.S. relations. After Japan's attack on Pearl Harbor in December, 1941, China and the United States became allies against the Axis powers. Madame Chiang Kai-shek, wife of China's wartime leader, won widespread respect and sympathy for China during her visit to the United States; she was the second female foreign leader to address a joint session of Congress. In 1943, the United States and Great Britain also signed new equal treaties with China that ended a century of international inequality for China. These events and the contributions of Chinese Americans in the war favorably affected the position and status of Chinese Americans. The 1943 act also opened the door for other legislation that allowed more Chinese to immigrate to the United States. In the long run, these laws had a major impact on the formation of Chinese families in the United States.

The War Brides Act of 1945, for example, permitted foreign-born wives of U.S. soldiers to enter the United States and become naturalized. Approximately six thousand Chinese women entered the United States during the next years as wives of U.S. servicemen. An amendment to this act, passed in 1946, put the Chinese wives and children of U.S. citizens outside the quota, resulting in the reunion of many separated families and allowing ten thousand Chinese, mostly wives, and also children of U.S. citizens of Chinese ethnicity, to enter the country during the next eight years. The Displaced Persons Act of 1948 granted permanent resident status, and eventually the right of citizenship, to 3,465 Chinese students, scholars, and others stranded in the United States by the widespread civil war that erupted between the Chinese Nationalists and Communists after the end of World War II. The Refugee Relief Act of 1953 allowed an additional 2,777 refugees to remain in the United States after the civil war ended in a Communist victory and the establishment of the People's Republic of China. Some Chinese students from the Republic of China on Taiwan, who came to study in the United States after 1950 and found employment and sponsors after the end of their studies, were also permitted to remain and were eligible for naturalization.

The four immigration acts passed between 1943 and 1953 can be viewed as a result of the alliance between the United States and the Republic of China in World War II and U.S. involvement in the Chinese civil war that followed. In a wider context, they were also the result of changing views on race and race relations that World War II and related events brought about. Finally, they heralded the Immigration Act of 1965, which revolutionized U.S. immigration policy in ending racial quotas. Its most dramatic consequence was the significant increase of Asian immigrants in general, and Chinese immigrants in particular, into the United States.

The new immigrants changed the makeup of Chinese American society and caused a change in the way the Chinese were perceived by the majority groups in the United States.

Whereas most of the earlier immigrants tended to live in ghettoized Chinatowns, were poorly educated, and overwhelmingly worked in low-status jobs such laundrymen, miners, or railroad workers, the new immigrants were highly educated, cosmopolitan, and professional. They came from the middle class, traced their roots to all parts of China, had little difficulty acculturating and assimilating into the academic and professional milieu of peoples of European ethnicity in the United States, and tended not to live in Chinatowns. The latter group was mainly responsible for revolutionizing the way Chinese Americans were perceived in the United States.

—*Jiu-Hwa Lo Upshur*

ADDITIONAL READING:

Chan, Sucheng, ed. *Entry Denied, Exclusion and the Chinese Community in America, 1882-1943*. Philadelphia: Temple University Press, 1991. Articles from nine scholars on different facets of the era.

Chen, Jack. *The Chinese of America*. San Francisco: Harper & Row, 1980. A comprehensive summary with tables, graphs, and maps.

Min, Pyong Gap, ed. *Asian Americans Contemporary Trends and Issues*. Thousand Oaks, Calif.: Sage Publications, 1995. A collection of essays that gives an overall picture of Asian American issues.

Riggs, Fred W. *Pressure on Congress: A Study of the Repeal of Chinese Exclusion*. 1950. Reprint. Westport, Conn.: Greenwood Press, 1972. A detailed account of the reasons for the repeal.

Steiner, Stanley. *Fusang, the Chinese Who Built America*. New York: Harper & Row, 1979. This book is sympathetic toward the Chinese; it is suitable for both laypersons and students.

Sung, Betty Lee. *Mountain of Gold: The Story of the Chinese in America*. New York: I Company, 1967. A good overview on Chinese immigration.

Tung, William L. *The Chinese in America, 1870-1973: Chronology and a Fact Book*. Dobbs Ferry, N.Y.: Oceana, 1974. Useful and informative.

SEE ALSO: 1849, Chinese Immigration; 1882, Chinese Exclusion Act; 1882, Rise of the Chinese Six Companies; 1895, Chinese American Citizens Alliance Is Founded; 1917, Immigration Act of 1917; 1924, Immigration Act of 1924; 1952, McCarran-Walter Act.

1944 ■ SMITH V. ALLWRIGHT: *the U.S. Supreme Court rules that disfranchisement of African Americans in state primary elections is unconstitutional*

DATE: April 3, 1944
LOCALE: Washington, D.C.
CATEGORIES: African American history; Civil rights; Court cases

KEY FIGURES:

Richard Randolph Grovey, complainant in the 1935 case testing the constitutionality of the Texas white primary
William Hastie (1904-1976), dean of the Howard Law School and co-counsel in the case
Thurgood Marshall (1908-1993), NAACP legal counsel
L. A. Nixon, El Paso doctor, NAACP member, and litigant in two tests of the Texas white primary
Stanley Reed (1884-1980), Supreme Court associate justice who wrote the majority opinion
Lonnie Smith, Houston dentist, NAACP member, and complainant

SUMMARY OF EVENT. In 1923, the Texas legislature sought to disenfranchise African American voters in the state by passing a resolution that "in no event shall a Negro be eligible to participate in a Democratic primary. . . ." Since the 1890's, in Texas as in all other Southern states, nomination in the Democratic primary was tantamount to election; therefore, while African Americans would be permitted to vote in the general election, they would have no meaningful role in the political process.

Almost immediately after the Texas legislature barred African Americans from participating in the Democratic primary, the National Association for the Advancement of Colored People (NAACP) secured a plaintiff, Dr. L. A. Nixon, to test the constitutionality of the legislative act. In *Nixon v. Herndon* (1927), the United States Supreme Court, in an opinion written by Justice Oliver Wendell Holmes, Jr., held that the Texas statute violated the equal protection clause of the Fourteenth Amendment to the U.S. Constitution by discriminating against African Americans on the basis of race. He also ruled, however, that it was unnecessary to strike down the white primary as a denial of suffrage "on account of race [or] color" repugnant to the Fifteenth Amendment.

The Texas legislature reacted defiantly to the Supreme Court decision. On June 7, 1927, the legislature passed a new resolution granting to the state executive committees of every political party the authority to establish the qualifications of their members and to determine who was qualified to vote or otherwise participate in the party. In turn, the Democratic Party State Executive Committee limited participation in its primary to white voters in Texas.

Once again Nixon filed suit, this time against James Condon, the election officer who refused to give him a ballot in the 1928 Democratic primary. In *Nixon v. Condon* (1932), the Supreme Court struck down this new Texas statute as a violation of the equal protection clause. The vote was five to four.

The Democratic Party State Executive Committee immediately rescinded its resolution prohibiting African Americans from voting in its primary, but the state party convention voted to limit participation in its deliberations to whites, and Nixon and the NAACP, after two Supreme Court cases and an expenditure of six thousand dollars, were once more back at the beginning. In July, 1934, Richard Randolph Grovey in Houston, Texas, was refused a ballot to vote in the Democratic primary. On April 1, 1935, in *Grovey v. Townsend*, Justice Owen J. Roberts ruled that the Democratic Party was a private organization, and that its primary, although held under state law, was a party matter paid for by the Democrats. Since Roberts could find no state action in the process by which Democrats nominated their candidates, there was, he said, no violation of the Fourteenth Amendment.

There the matter rested. The primary was held not to be part of the general election, so there was presumably no relationship to the Fifteenth Amendment's protection of suffrage. Because the Democratic Party was a private organization, it was free to establish membership qualifications, and there was not sufficient state involvement to invoke the guarantees of the Fourteenth Amendment.

It seemed there was no way to contest the validity of the Texas white primary. In 1941, however, in *United States v. Classic*, a case that ostensibly had nothing to do with African Americans or the white primary, the Supreme Court held for the first time that the right to vote was protected in a primary as well as in the general election, "where the state law has made the primary an integral part of the process of choice or where in fact the primary effectively controls the choice."

United States v. Classic dealt with a Louisiana primary in which there had been fraudulent returns, but otherwise there was no way to distinguish the Texas primary from the one held in the neighboring Southern state. In Texas, as in Louisiana, in 1941 as in 1923, Democratic Party nomination in its primary was a virtual guarantee of election, and the general election was a mere formality.

The NAACP was back in action. Lonnie Smith, a Houston dentist and NAACP member, sued a Texas election official for five thousand dollars for refusing to give him a ballot to vote in the 1940 Democratic congressional primaries. The NAACP's legal counsel, Thurgood Marshall, and William Hastie, dean of the Howard Law School, brought *Smith v. Allwright* to the United States Supreme Court.

In April, 1944, mindful of Southern sensibilities but intent upon overruling the nine-year-old precedent in *Grovey*, the Court chose Stanley Reed, a Democrat from Kentucky, to write its opinion. Justice Reed's opinion made it clear that the Court, except for Justice Roberts (the author of the *Grovey* decision), had concluded that the primary was an integral part of a general election, particularly in the Southern states. The *Classic* decision, wrote Justice Reed, raised the issue of whether excluding African Americans from participation in the Democratic Party primary in Texas violated the Fifteenth Amendment. The answer was in the affirmative, and *Grovey v. Townsend* was expressly overruled. "If the state," Reed said, "requires a certain election procedure, prescribing a general election ballot made up of party nominees so chosen, and limits the choice of the electorate in general elections for state officers . . . to those whose names appear on such a ballot, it endorses, adopts, and enforces the discrimination against Negroes practiced by a party entrusted by Texas law with the

determination of the qualifications of participants in the primary. This is state action within the meaning of the Fifteenth Amendment."

The long litigative battle against the Texas white primary seemed to be over—but it was not. In Fort Bend County, Texas, the Jaybird Democratic Party, organized after the Civil War, held primaries closed to African American voters; its candidates consistently won county offices. In spite of *Smith v. Allwright*, the Jaybirds refused to open their primary to African Americans, arguing that they did not operate under state law or use state officers or funds. Nevertheless, in *Terry v. Adams* (1953), the Supreme Court held that the Jaybird primary violated the Fifteenth Amendment, because it controlled the electoral process in Fort Bend County.

It took twenty-one years for the United States Supreme Court to rule that the Texas white primary violated the right to vote guaranteed by the Fifteenth Amendment. It would take another twenty-one years before the Voting Rights Act of 1965 finally secured the ballot for African Americans in the South. In the interim, the fall of the white primary had the practical effect of increasing African American registrants in the Southern states from approximately 250,000 in 1940 to 775,000 seven years later. African Americans were still intimidated and defrauded of their suffrage rights, but *Smith v. Allwright* was an important landmark on the road to uninhibited enfranchisement. It also was a symbol that the Supreme Court would examine the reality behind the subterfuge and act to protect African Americans in the enjoyment of their civil rights.

—David L. Sterling

ADDITIONAL READING:

Fassett, John D. *New Deal Justice: The Life of Stanley Reed of Kentucky*. New York: Vantage Press, 1994. A biography of the conservative Democratic justice who wrote the majority opinion in *Smith v. Allwright*.

Hine, Darlene Clark. *Black Victory: The Rise and Fall of the White Primary in Texas*. Millwood, N.Y.: KTO Press, 1979. An examination of the background of the white primary and the struggle to bring about its demise.

Kluger, Richard. *Simple Justice: The History of "Brown v. Board of Education" and Black America's Struggle for Equality*. New York: Alfred A. Knopf, 1976. An eminently readable analysis of another landmark Supreme Court case in African American history.

Lawson, Steven F. *Black Ballots: Voting Rights in the South, 1944-1969*. New York: Columbia University Press, 1976. Traces the development of African American enfranchisement from *Smith v. Allwright* to the Voting Rights Act of 1965 and its aftermath. Includes a chapter on the white primary.

Powledge, Fred. *Free at Last: The Civil Rights Movement and the People Who Made It*. Boston: Little, Brown, 1991. A popular account of the struggle for equality during the 1960's, with numerous human interest stories.

SEE ALSO: 1868, Fourteenth Amendment; 1890, Mississippi Disfranchisement Laws; 1902, Expansion of Direct Democracy; 1960, Civil Rights Act of 1960; 1965, Voting Rights Act.

1944 ■ OPERATION OVERLORD: an amphibious invasion of northern France begins the liberation of Western Europe from Nazi control

DATE: June 6, 1944
LOCALE: Normandy, France
CATEGORY: Wars, uprisings, and civil unrest
KEY FIGURES:

Omar Nelson Bradley (1893-1981), commander of the U.S. First Army

Dwight David Eisenhower (1890-1969), commander in chief of Allied Forces in Western Europe

Adolf Hitler (1889-1945), German chancellor and Nazi Party leader

Bernard Law Montgomery (1887-1976), commander of Allied ground forces in northern France

Erwin Rommel (1891-1944), second in command of German forces in Western Europe

Karl Rudolf Gerd von Rundstedt (1875-1953), German commander in chief in Western Europe

SUMMARY OF EVENT. The Allied invasion of German-occupied France in June, 1944, remains one of the most famous events in World War II history. Crossing the English Channel from England to the French coast of Normandy, the forces waging the attack constituted the largest amphibious operation undertaken in military history.

To command this challenging effort, Western Allied leaders appointed General Dwight David Eisenhower as commander in chief of Allied Forces in Western Europe. Arriving in England in January, 1944, to oversee the complicated project, he spent many months directing the planning for the cross-channel invasion. Excellent cooperation between the Western Allies was essential for successfully planning and implementing the attack. The second highest military appointment was, therefore, assigned to a prominent British general, Bernard Montgomery.

Defining the attack's size, scope, and location required careful consideration. Normandy was selected because of its proximity to Great Britain. German defenses in Normandy were weaker than elsewhere on France's northern coast, although Field Marshal Erwin Rommel had strengthened his fortified positions in early 1944. Beach and tide characteristics also made Normandy a likely choice. The original plan for "Overlord," the operation's code name, designated three army divisions for the initial invasion. Eisenhower and Montgomery expanded the size of the target area and increased the divisions to five for the coastal attack: two U.S. divisions, two British, and one Canadian.

Allied deception played an important role before the attack. Adolf Hitler and most German military leaders predicted an invasion would occur in the Pas de Calais region to the northeast. Significant German forces therefore were positioned there, and did not play a role when the actual invasion began. Allied schemes increased Hitler's belief that the Pas de Calais was the intended target. Phantom armies were "located" in eastern England and fake radio transmissions misled the Germans. Eisenhower also ordered widespread air attacks on railroad centers, bridges, and other transportation targets within France to hinder German reinforcements from reaching the coast when the invasion eventually began. The Normandy attack was therefore nearly a complete surprise.

The plan required the landings to begin at dawn, so troops would have a full day to establish a beachhead and begin to move inland. Other requirements included a full moon the night before, so parachute forces could be dropped in predawn hours behind enemy lines to cut communication lines and control key bridges and road junctions; a low tide at dawn, so beach obstacles could be cleared; and a fairly calm sea, as soldiers had to land from small assault craft. Early June would meet these requirements, assuming favorable weather. General Eisenhower selected June 5 as D day for the attack. The right combination of tide and moon would not occur again for several weeks, and planners did not wish to postpone the invasion.

In early June, soldiers boarded ships in English embarkation ports, but bad weather on June 3 and June 4 made the scheduled June 5 invasion impossible. An updated weather forecast indicated a break in the storm might occur the night of June 5-6. Eisenhower decided on June 5 to take the risk. The weather improved, and more than five thousand ships, carrying more than a hundred thousand troops, headed for the continent. Paratroopers dropped inland during the night, the first Allied soldiers to land in occupied France. By daylight on June 6, bombers and fighter planes were flying overhead, as ground forces moved toward the beaches. Warships pounded German fortifications with heavy artillery from the sea. Each of the five army divisions had an assigned coastal sector (identified by a code name) to attack and secure: "Utah" and "Omaha" were assigned to the United States, "Gold" and "Sword" to the British, and "Juno" to the Canadians. The landings succeeded in the face of heavy German resistance, although the United States troops at "Omaha Beach" had the greatest difficulty and highest casualties. By the end of the first day, approximately 150,000 soldiers had landed in Normandy.

The invasion forces gradually consolidated and expanded their positions. By the end of June, more than 850,000 Allied troops were in France. The Germans, because of the disruption of their transportation systems from air attacks, could not bring sufficient units to launch effective and sustained counterattacks. Rommel's preferred strategy favored using all available German forces to drive the Allies into the sea. However, Hitler in Berlin and Field Marshal Gerd von Rundstedt adopted a policy of using their forces on a more selective basis. Thus, the German defense was not well coordinated at the highest levels.

German forces occasionally succeeded in blocking Allied advances from the beachhead. British and Canadian troops on

Montgomery's left flank were unable to capture the city of Caen, a D day objective, until mid-July. On the right flank, General Omar Bradley's U.S. First Army finally succeeded in capturing the port of Cherbourg on June 27 but was unable to break out of the Cotentin Peninsula quickly.

Greater Allied firepower, both on the ground and in the air, finally broke the impasse. By August 1, Bradley's troops were in open country, and General George Patton's U.S. Third Army headed to the south and east. The German Seventh Army, nearly cut off in the "Falaise pocket," sustained major losses of troops and equipment by mid-August. U.S. and French forces liberated Paris on August 25.

Casualty figures for Operation Overlord vary, in part because of incomplete data. Considering the large numbers of

General Dwight D. Eisenhower gives orders to paratroopers somewhere in England just before Operation Overlord and the invasion of Normandy: "Full victory—nothing else." (Library of Congress)

troops in the operation, contradictory totals seem inevitable. Tallies of battle losses also differ according to the period included in any tabulation. Descriptions of the Normandy campaign often cover the weeks between June 6 and the Allied breakout into the French interior by the end of July. Some figures include the liberation of Paris in late August. Casualties on D day (June 6) alone are estimated to be between 10,000 and 10,500 for the Allies and 6,500 for the Germans. Eisenhower referred to 60,000 casualties in three weeks. Another source placed casualties from June 6 to the end of August at approximately 84,000 British and Canadian, 126,000 U.S., and 200,000 German.

Relations between Eisenhower and Montgomery eroded during the campaign. Eisenhower believed the British commander was overly cautious in advancing toward Caen. Montgomery favored holding German forces there while urging Bradley to break out to the west. Eisenhower was displeased when Montgomery did not push his British forces toward Falaise, where, if they had linked with U.S. forces advancing from the west, they would have cut off an entire German army. In both cases, Montgomery believed he had acted correctly and resented Eisenhower's assessment.

Western scholars emphasize the significance of the Normandy invasion in the overall history of World War II. Veterans and the general public correctly interpret Operation Overlord as a major step toward the ultimate defeat of Nazi Germany. In June, 1994, on the fiftieth anniversary of the battle, an elaborate commemoration of the campaign was held in the locale where this dramatic and violent conflict had occurred.   *—Stephen E. Ambrose, updated by Taylor Stults*

ADDITIONAL READING:

Ambrose, Stephen E. *D-Day, June 6, 1944: The Climatic Battle of World War II.* New York: Simon & Schuster, 1994. Comprehensive account by a leading U.S. historian.

Eisenhower, David. *Crusade in Europe.* Garden City, N.Y.: Garden City Books, 1948. Eisenhower's memoirs provide his account of Operation Overlord.

_____. *Eisenhower at War, 1943-1945.* New York: Random House, 1986. Detailed and scholarly assessment from Operation Overlord's commander.

Hallion, Richard P. *The U.S. Army Air Forces in World War II: D-Day 1944, Air Power over the Normandy Beaches and Beyond.* Washington, D.C.: U.S. Air Force, 1994. A brief illustrated account of an essential element of the Allied invasion.

Keegan, John. *Six Armies in Normandy: From D-Day to the Liberation of Paris, June 6-August 25, 1944.* New York: Viking, 1982. A British scholar explains the military operations.

Ryan, Cornelius. *The Longest Day: June 6, 1944.* New York: Simon & Schuster, 1959. First-rate account of D day from the viewpoint of individual participants.

Speidel, Hans. *Invasion 1944: Rommel and the Normandy Campaign.* Westport, Conn.: Greenwood Press, 1971. Rommel's chief of staff provides a German interpretation.

SEE ALSO: 1941, Germany and Italy Declare War on the United States; 1942, Invasion of North Africa; 1943, Western Allies Invade Italy; 1944, Battle of the Bulge; 1945, Yalta Conference; 1945, V-E Day; 1945, Potsdam Conference.

1944 ■ SUPERFORTRESS BOMBING OF JAPAN: *a raid on Yawata marks the beginning of the American strategic bombing campaign against the Japanese home islands*

DATE: June 15, 1944
LOCALE: Chengtu, China; and Yawata, Japan
CATEGORY: Wars, uprisings, and civil unrest
KEY FIGURES:
Henry Harley "Hap" Arnold (1886-1950), commander of the U.S. Army Air Corps
Franklin Delano Roosevelt (1882-1945), thirty-second president of the United States, 1933-1945
LaVerne "Blondie" Saunders (born 1903), commander of the Fifty-eighth Bombardment Wing
Kenneth B. Wolfe (1886-1971), commander of the Twentieth Bomber Command

SUMMARY OF EVENT. The Doolittle raid against Tokyo on April 18, 1942, was the first air raid by United States bombers on the Japanese home islands and the only one for the next two years. The rapid Japanese advance in the Pacific and the Japanese hold on the Asian mainland drove U.S. forces from any bases close enough to carry out air raids on Japan. The available heavy bombers, the B-17 Flying Fortress and the B-24 Liberator, did not have adequate range. The B-29 Superfortress, however, brought to bear new technology that made possible a devastating strategic bombing campaign against the Japanese home islands.

The Army had shown interest in the new long-range, high-altitude bomber that the Boeing Company had begun to develop in 1938. Although the prototype, the XB-29, was not test-flown until September 21, 1942, the Air Corps had already ordered 250 planes from Boeing, which built an entire new plant to produce the new bomber exclusively. Far larger than the B-17, the Superfortress measured 99 feet in length, with a wing span of 141 feet. It weighed more than sixty tons fully loaded and had a top speed of up to 375 miles per hour. Powered by four twenty-two-hundred-horsepower Wright Duplex Cyclone engines, it had a combat radius of sixteen hundred miles fully loaded. Three separate pressurized compartments meant that its crew of eleven could cruise at the plane's service ceiling of 31,800 feet without needing oxygen masks. The aircraft was armed with twelve .50-caliber machine guns, or ten machine guns and a 20-millimeter cannon, all mounted in power-driven turrets. Under ideal conditions, it could carry a bomb load of ten tons.

Plans by the Air Force for the plane's use had taken various forms, including its commitment in Europe. By the time significant numbers of the planes could be ready, however, British and U.S. bombers flying from England had made the B-29 less than essential for the war against Germany. By the end of 1943, Air Force chief General H. "Hap" Arnold, was committed to its use against Japan. United States air bases in the Aleutian Islands, however, were too far from Japan. The islands in the Mariana group that could provide bases (Saipan, Tinian, and Guam) were not projected to be in U.S. hands until the winter of 1944. Thus, Air Force planners, wanting to get the new Superfortresses into operation as soon as possible, looked to China.

On Arnold's orders, Brigadier General Kenneth B. Wolfe drew up a plan. Submitted to the Air Force Chief on October 11, 1943, Wolfe's plan called for basing the new B-29's in India and staging them through fields in China. Approved by Arnold, the plan then went to President Franklin D. Roosevelt. Desiring to do something for China and fearing that China's leader, Chiang Kai-shek, might quit the war if he did not receive some tangible help against the Japanese, Roosevelt proved a receptive audience and approved the plan, known as Operation Matterhorn, in November, 1943.

The idea of an independent, powerful, strategic bombing force had long been a dream of U.S. flyers. Supplying itself with all the necessities of war, this command could, it was believed, bludgeon any enemy into surrender by strategic bombing without the necessity of invasion. Perhaps the Superfortress was the weapon.

Having committed itself to a strategic bombing campaign against the Japanese home islands, in April, 1944, the United States Joint Chiefs of Staff established a special organization, the Twentieth Air Force, to direct all B-29 operations. General Arnold, acting as executive agent of the Joint Chiefs of Staff, was selected to command this new force and given control over the employment of the Superfortresses. Neither the British commander in the area, Lord Louis Mountbatten, nor United States Army commander Lieutenant General Joseph W. Stilwell exercised any authority over the deployment and use of the B-29's in the China-Burma-India theater of operations, except in an emergency. However, they would see a significant amount of the very limited tonnage that was flown over the Hump into China diverted to the B-29 bases at Chengtu.

Implementation of Operation Matterhorn was entrusted to Wolfe's Twentieth Bomber Command, which originally was made up of the Fifty-eighth and the Seventy-third Bombardment Wings. The Seventy-third was detached in April, 1944, to go to the Mariana Islands, whose date of capture had been advanced to June, 1944. A wing contained 112 bombers plus replacement ships, and slightly more than three thousand officers and eight thousand enlisted men. Support, service, and engineer personnel brought the total strength of the Twentieth Bomber Command to approximately twenty thousand troops.

Because all supplies for Chinese bases had to be flown in, stockpiling was difficult. B-29s from India had to fly seven round trips to bring enough gasoline and other necessities to make possible one mission over Japan. With the loss of the Seventy-third Wing, the Fifty-eighth Wing could not supply

itself for raids of one hundred planes or more, the hoped-for number, more than a few times each month. This, combined with the high rate of engine failure, the loss of planes because of inexperienced crews, and the other faults to be expected in a new weapon meant that the first raid on Japan could not be launched until June 15, 1944.

The Army Air Force's Committee of Operations Analysts had suggested that an appropriate strategic target for B-29s would be the coke ovens that supplied Japan's steel mills. Consequently, the first strike was directed against the coke ovens of the Imperial Iron and Steel Works at Yawata. Located on the island of Kyushu, at the edge of the bomber's combat range, the Yawata plant produced 24 percent of Japan's rolled steel and was considered the most important target in the Japanese steel industry.

Beginning on June 13, ninety-two planes left the Bengal fields in India, seventy-nine of which reached the Chengtu bases. Each came loaded with two tons of five-hundred-pound bombs and needed only to refuel in China. Commanders in Washington, D.C., who had picked the target, ordered a night mission with bombs to be dropped from between eight thousand and eighteen thousand feet. On June 15, the same day that Marines went ashore on Saipan, sixty-eight planes, led by Wing Commander Brigadier General LaVerne "Blondie" Saunders, left the fields. Four were forced back by engine trouble, and one crashed immediately after take-off. Forty-seven Superfortresses bombed Yawata that night, thirty-two using radar because of an effective blackout of the city compounded by haze and smoke. The other planes did not make it over Yawata for a variety of reasons, most of them mechanical. Six planes were lost, one to enemy fighters on the return trip. Fighter opposition over the target and antiaircraft fire had been light.

Photo reconnaissance showed little damage, the only significant hit being on a power station thirty-seven hundred feet from the coke ovens. This was not a massive fire-bomb raid of the type that would begin in March, 1945, from the Mariana islands. The AAF was still concentrating on high-altitude, precision bombing. The Fifty-eighth Wing averaged two raids a month until March, 1945, when it was moved to Saipan. Operating under a very difficult logistical situation, Operation Matterhorn had been a stimulant for Chinese morale and had provided a necessary shakedown for the new bombers and crews. Matterhorn was not a success, nor was the first raid on Japan; but both presaged a more destructive future for the Superfortress.

—*Charles W. Johnson, updated by Bruce J. DeHart*

ADDITIONAL READING:

Craven, Wesley F., and James L. Cate. *The Pacific: Matterhorn to Nagasaki, June 1944 to August 1945*. Vol. 5 in *The Army Air Forces in World War II*. Chicago: University of Chicago Press, 1953. This volume in the U.S. Air Force's official history provides a wealth of information about the people, machines, and events that were part of Operation Matterhorn.

Larrabee, Eric. "LeMay." In *Commander in Chief: Franklin Delano Roosevelt, His Lieutenants, and Their War*. New York: Simon & Schuster, 1987. A concise account of the role of General Curtis LeMay, the man who assumed leadership of the Twentieth Bomber Command in August, 1944, in the strategic bombing offensive against Japan. Discusses both the Yawata raid and subsequent assaults from China.

Morrison, Wilbur H. *Point of No Return: The Story of the Twentieth Air Force*. New York: Times Books, 1979. Chapters 1 through 13 of this narrative history cover in detail the development of the B-29, the debates about its employment, and Operation Matterhorn.

Pimlott, John. *B-29 Superfortress*. Englewood Cliffs, N.J.: Prentice-Hall, 1993. Provides detailed information about the Superfortress itself. Excellent drawings and illustrations.

United States. Strategic Bombing Survey. *The Strategic Air Operations of Very Heavy Bombardment in the War Against Japan (Twentieth Air Force)*. Washington, D.C.: Government Printing Office, 1946. The reports that make up this survey contain extensive statistical material about the impact of strategic bombing on Japan.

SEE ALSO: 1941, Bombing of Pearl Harbor; 1942, Battle of Midway; 1942, Manhattan Project; 1942, Battle of Guadalcanal; 1944, Battle for Leyte Gulf; 1944, Battle of the Bulge; 1945, Atomic Bombing of Japan.

1944 ■ G.I. BILL: *federal subsidies for the education of veterans boost reintegration of military personnel into the U.S. economy after World War II*

DATE: June 22, 1944
LOCALE: United States
CATEGORIES: Education; Laws and acts
KEY FIGURES:
Franklin Delano Roosevelt (1882-1945), thirty-second president of the United States, 1933-1945
George F. Zook (1885-1951), president of the American Council on Education

SUMMARY OF EVENT. World War II had a twofold effect on education in the United States. In the short run, the existence of many colleges and universities was seriously jeopardized. Both students and faculty members were removed by the selective service draft and by patriotic volunteering. Small private colleges, often perilously close to financial ruin, were among the institutions most severely affected. In the long run, however, the war served as a tremendous impetus in convincing people that the national government had a role to play in assuring that all citizens were given an opportunity to pursue formal education to the limit of their natural ability. The first tangible sign of this new concern was the passage in 1944 of the Serviceman's Readjustment Act, familiarly known as the G.I. Bill of Rights, which was concerned with the federal

financing of educational opportunities for returning veterans. While this particular act undoubtedly was affected by wartime sentiments, the concept of federal responsibility in education soon enjoyed wide support.

President Franklin D. Roosevelt and others began thinking about the interrupted education of many U.S. soldiers and sailors soon after Pearl Harbor. In 1942, a report entitled *Statement of Principles Relating to the Educational Problems of Returning Soldiers, Sailors, and Displaced War Industry Workers* was published by the Institute of Adult Education of Teachers College, Columbia University. The report emphasized the need for some sort of postwar vocational and educational program for veterans, financed by the national government. In July, 1942, Roosevelt discussed the matter with President George F. Zook and other officials of the American Council on Education. Convinced of the federal responsibility in this area, Roosevelt initiated a Conference on Postwar Readjustment of Civilian and Military Personnel, which in June, 1942, submitted a recommendation for action. This "Demobilization and Reconversion" report indicated that the following action was needed: the development of a vocational training program for returning veterans; the establishment of special courses at regular colleges and universities for returnees; the financing of such educational services by the federal government; and the cooperation of local and state agencies with the federal government in the execution of this program. Roosevelt charged the War and Navy departments with establishing precise guidelines and recommendations for the implementation of these goals. The report that the War and Navy departments issued on October 27, 1943, became the basis for the G.I. Bill.

Roosevelt's legislative proposal to Congress was assisted by a number of factors. Of primary concern was the patriotic sentiment engendered by persons such as newspaper columnist Ernie Pyle, who insisted that the country owed its veterans something. The American Legion also lobbied in support of the bill. In addition, a number of government planners saw problems in the demobilization of an estimated fifteen million service people into the civilian economy.

It seemed reasonable to spread the returning veterans among educational institutions of many different kinds— vocational schools and especially colleges. Draft statistics that indicated that U.S. education had been failing significantly in the prewar years were another important factor. The selective service studies provided a unique opportunity to measure the educational progress of a vast segment of the American public. To the chagrin of professional educators, the government announced that more than 676,000 men were disqualified from military service because they lacked the minimum of four years of formal schooling. Furthermore, it became clear that U.S. education also had failed to produce enough qualified mathematicians, scientists, and foreign-language experts. The problems of too few schools, too few competent teachers, and too few course offerings all pointed to one conclusion in the eyes of many educators and politicians: Only a major injection of federal funds could enable U.S. education to meet the idealistic goals established for it. The first hesitant steps in this direction were taken during World War II. On March 24, 1943, President Roosevelt signed into law the Vocational Rehabilitation Bill, which provided federal funds for the retraining and rehabilitation of disabled veterans and workers in the civilian defense industry. This was followed on June 22, 1944, by the Serviceman's Readjustment Act.

Under the provisions of the G.I. Bill, veterans were defined as those individuals with more than ninety days of active service after September 16, 1940, who possessed an honorable discharge. These persons were to receive an opportunity to further their education on a full-or part-time basis at any approved educational or training institution of their selection. The course of study could range from graduate work to elementary courses and had to be completed within a four-year period. The university or college was free to pass on the veteran's eligibility to enroll in any of its programs, and normal standards were to be considered in force. The federal government would pay all tuition and fees required by the university. In addition, the veteran was entitled to a subsistence check each month. The amount of the check varied with the number of dependents and was increased to keep pace with inflation. By 1947, a veteran with one or more dependents was entitled to ninety dollars per month. A single veteran received sixty-five dollars per month. The act also provided money for new veterans' hospitals and guaranteed unemployment compensation of twenty dollars per week for a period of one year after separation. Finally, low-interest loans were made available to veterans interested in purchasing a home or farm or establishing a new business.

The implications of this act were tremendous. The national government was guaranteeing the educational opportunity of more than fifteen million citizens. The responsibility for this education was to be shared by the individual, the institution, and the national government. The flood of returnees soon swamped both public and private institutions in the United States. Schools that had been facing bankruptcy soon found themselves engaged in building programs. Special married student dormitories sprang into existence to accommodate this new type of student. Altogether, the veterans caused a revolution in the techniques and status of U.S. higher education. At its crest in 1947, the flood of veterans represented more than one million students out of a total student population of two and one-half million. In 1952, a new G.I. Bill was passed for veterans of the Korean War; later, the Vietnam War became the occasion for a further extension.

The original G.I. Bill of 1944 brought a different type of student to college campuses. Some had had their education interrupted by the war. Others never had envisioned receiving a college education, because of the cost. Thus, the campuses swelled with so-called nontraditional students, that is, students older than the usual eighteen- to twenty-two-year-old. Their maturity and experiences added markedly to the academic activity. The sheer numbers of students also strained the college facilities and the stamina of faculty and staff. Year-round programs, night classes, and academic counseling became necessary. Much to the dismay of conservative academics, the schools provided program acceleration and credit for experiential learning. Many of these changes became standard parts of the educational experience at most institutions of higher learning. Continuing education (adult learning) for either credit or educational enrichment became commonplace at both secondary and higher-education institutions. The G.I. Bill is also credited with providing African Americans with greater opportunities for higher education, as well as helping to improve the quality of education at traditionally African American institutions.

The numbers of veterans taking advantage of the several federal programs has varied with the different conflicts. For example, 51 percent of World War II veterans, 43 percent of Korean War veterans, and 60 percent of Vietnam veterans received some training benefits. Schools located near large military installations attracted the largest numbers of veterans, especially for older veterans with families and those approaching retirement who sought a second career.

—George Q. Flynn, updated by Albert C. Jensen

ADDITIONAL READING:

Kandel, Issac L. *The Impact of the War upon American Education.* Chapel Hill: University of North Carolina Press, 1948. Written during the height of the G.I. Bill's initial impact, this study examines the state of U.S. education before, during, and after World War II.

Montgomery, G. V. "The Montgomery G.I. Bill: Development, Implementation, and Impact." *Education Record* 75, no. 4 (Fall, 1994): 49-54. The Mississippi congressman chronicles the first peacetime veterans' education legislation, which became effective in 1985.

Rose, Amy D. "Significant and Unintended Consequences: The G.I. Bill and Adult Education." *Education Record* 75, no. 4 (Fall, 1994): 47-48. Describes the G.I. Bill as providing a laboratory for adult education services.

Tiedt, Sidney W. *The Role of the Federal Government in Education.* New York: Oxford University Press, 1966. A survey of the problem of federal aid to education, including the pros and cons of government involvement.

Wilson, Reginald. "G.I. Bill Expands Access for African Americans." *Education Record* 75, no. 4 (Fall, 1994): 32-39. Asserts that federal programs of educational aid for veterans are revolutionary and radical legislation that have been especially beneficial to African American veterans.

Zook, Jim. "As G.I. Bill Marks Its Fiftieth Year, Use of Educational Benefits Rises." *Chronicle of Higher Education* 40, no. 41 (June 15, 1994): A27. A brief review of legislation for veterans' educational benefits and the positive influences on the nation, the institutions, and the veterans.

SEE ALSO: 1941, 6.6 Million Women Enter the U.S. Labor Force; 1942, Censorship and Japanese Internment; 1945, War Brides Act; 1946, Employment Act.

WORLD WAR II: THE FIGHT FOR THE PACIFIC

Sept. 27, 1940	Japan signs a pact with Germany and Italy, becoming a member of the Axis powers.
July 24, 1941	Japan occupies French Indo-China (modern Vietnam). U.S. halts trade with Japan, sends General Douglas MacArthur to oversee military forces in the Philippines.
Nov. 25, 1941	During U.S.-Japanese negotiations, Japanese forces leave Kurile Islands, headed for Pearl Harbor.
Dec. 6, 1941	Japanese-U.S. negotiations, conducted since Oct. 18, break down.
Dec. 7, 1941	PEARL HARBOR: Japanese bomb Pearl Harbor in the Hawaiian Islands, sinking or disabling five of eight U.S. battleships, as well as other ships and airplanes. Nearly 2,500 persons, including 68 civilians, are killed. Japan simultaneously attacks Guam, the Philippines, Midway Island, Hong Kong, and the Malay Peninsula. *See* **1941, Bombing of Pearl Harbor.**
Dec. 8, 1941	United States declares war on Japan.
Dec. 8-25, 1941	Japan invades Thailand and Malaya; sinks British ships in the South China Sea; occupies the Philippines, then Guam, Wake Island, Hong Kong.
Jan., 1942	MacArthur establishes headquarters at "The Rock," Corregidor on the Bataan Peninsula.
Jan. 24-27, 1942	BATTLE OF MACASSAR STRAIT: Allies inflict heavy damage on the Japanese in the first major Pacific confrontation.
Feb. 15, 1942	Singapore falls to Japan.
Feb. 27-Mar. 1, 1942	BATTLE OF THE JAVA SEA: severe U.S. losses; Japan occupies Java.
Mar. 9, 1942	Japan occupies Rangoon, Burma, cutting off Allied access to China.
Mar. 17, 1942	MacArthur leaves Bataan Peninsula to take command of the Allied forces in the Southwest Pacific.
May 6, 1942	Bataan Peninsula and Corregidor fall to the Japanese.
May 7-8, 1942	BATTLE OF THE CORAL SEA: For first time in history, all fighting in a naval battle is conducted by planes launched off aircraft carriers. Japanese advance into Australia is halted.
June 3-5, 1942	BATTLE OF MIDWAY: Japan's advance across the Pacific is stopped, and Japan suffers severe losses. Turning point in the Pacific war. *See* **1942, Battle of Midway.**
June 3-21, 1942	Japan bombs Alaska, occupies the Aleutian Islands, and shells the Oregon coast.
Aug. 7, 1942	GUADALCANAL OFFENSIVE BEGINS: Victory in the Battle of Midway prompts Allies to launch a limited offensive in the area of the Pacific Ocean where the Central Pacific and Southwest Pacific commands overlap. U.S. Marines land at Guadalcanal in the Solomon Islands on Aug. 7. *See* **1942, Battle of Guadalcanal.**
Aug., 1942	BATTLE OF THE TENARU RIVER: One thousand Japanese are disabled.
Aug. 9, 1942	BATTLE OF SAVO ISLAND: Japanese victory.
Aug. 23-25, 1942	BATTLE OF THE EASTERN SOLOMONS: U.S. inflicts severe damage on Japanese ships.
Sept. 13-14, 1942	BATTLE OF BLOODY RIDGE: Six thousand troops under Kiyotake Kawaguchi are routed.
Oct. 11-12, 1942	BATTLE OF CAPE ESPERANCE: Japanese move ahead, bombing Henderson Field on Guadalcanal and dispatching a battleship force to bombard Allied positions; 4,500 Japanese soldiers are landed. On Oct. 24-25, Japanese attacks fail to take Henderson Field.
Oct. 26-27, 1942	BATTLE OF SANTA CRUZ: Japanese suffer heavy losses of ships.
Nov. 12-15, 1942	BATTLE OF GUADALCANAL: U.S. prevents Japanese from landing reinforcements, ensuring Allied conquest of Guadalcanal. Japanese evacuate Guadalcanal on Feb. 9, 1943.
July 6, 1943	BATTLE OF KULA GULF: first U.S. victory in South Pacific.
Aug. 15, 1943	U.S. regains Aleutians.
Nov. 2, 1943	BATTLE OF EMPRESS AUGUSTA BAY: Japanese defeat in South Pacific secures Solomons for the Allies.

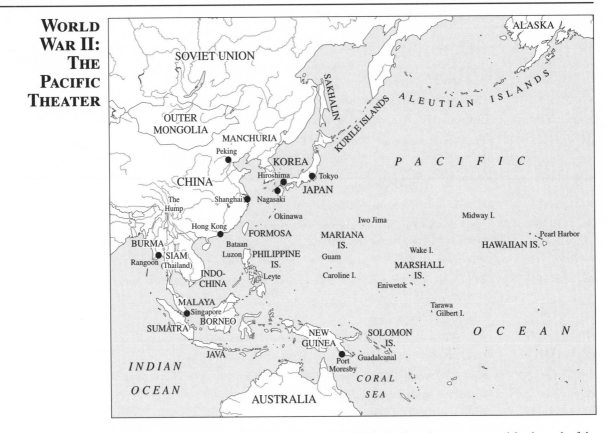

WORLD
WAR II:
THE
PACIFIC
THEATER

Nov. 21, 1943	CENTRAL PACIFIC OFFENSIVE: Admiral Chester W. Nimitz begins advance to secure islands north of the Solomons.
Jan. 31-Nov. 25, 1944	U.S. takes Marshall Islands, Mariana Islands, Guam, and the Palaus.
Mar. 1-Apr. 22, 1944	U.S. takes Admiralty Islands and Hollandia in Dutch New Guinea.
May 17-Aug. 3, 1944	Allies take Myitkyina, Burma.
June 15, 1944	B-29's, "Superfortresses," begin bombing Kyushu in Japan. *See* **1944, Superfortress Bombing of Japan.**
June 19-20, 1944	BATTLE OF THE PHILIPPINE SEA: inflicts severe losses on Japan, of both sea vessels and airplanes.
July 18, 1944	Premier Tojo and his cabinet resign.
Oct. 23-26, 1944	BATTLE FOR LEYTE GULF: In three major naval engagements, U.S. destroys remaining Japanese naval forces and takes control of Philippines. The greatest naval battle in history, based on number of ships involved. *See* **1944, Battle for Leyte Gulf.**
Nov. 24, 1944	Superfortress bombings of Tokyo begin; especially intense during Feb., 1945.
Mar. 17, 1945	BATTLE OF IWO JIMA: U.S. Marines, having landed on Iwo Jima on Feb. 19, occupy that island by Mar. 17.
Apr. 1, 1945	BATTLE OF OKINAWA: U.S. invades Okinawa, occupying it by June 21. Japanese suicide flights contribute to making this the costliest battle of the war, with nearly 45,000 casualties (more than 11,000 killed).
Apr. 5, 1945	Premier Koiso and his cabinet resign.
July 26, 1945	U.S. and Britain demand Japan's unconditional surrender; Japan refuses on July 29.
Aug. 6, 1945	U.S. DROPS ATOMIC BOMB: Four square miles of Hiroshima are decimated; casualties total 160,000. Another atomic bomb follows on Aug. 9, this time on Nagasaki. *See* **1945, Atomic Bombing of Japan.**
Aug. 14, 1945	JAPAN SURRENDERS: Aug. 15 is declared V-J ("victory in Japan") day.

1944 ■ BATTLE FOR LEYTE GULF: *the largest naval engagement of World War II secures control of the seas surrounding the Philippine Islands and breaks Japanese naval power*

DATE: October 23-26, 1944
LOCALE: Leyte Gulf, Surigao Strait, San Bernardino Strait, and Cape Engaño in the Philippines
CATEGORY: Wars, uprisings, and civil unrest
KEY FIGURES:

William Frederick Halsey (1882-1959), commander of the U.S. Third Fleet

Thomas C. Kinkaid (1888-1972), commander of the U.S. Seventh Fleet and Allied naval forces in the Southwest Pacific

Takeo Kurita (1889-1977), commander of the Japanese Central Force

Douglas MacArthur (1880-1964), supreme commander of Allied Forces in the Southwest Pacific

Chester William Nimitz (1885-1966), commander in chief of the U.S. Pacific Fleet

Jesse Oldendorf (1887-1974), commander of the Seventh Fleet's Fire Support Force

Jisabuto Ozawa (1886-1986), commander of the Japanese decoy Northern Force

Clifton A. F. Sprague (1896-1955), commander of the Seventh Fleet's Taffy 3 escort carrier group

SUMMARY OF EVENT. The Battle for Leyte Gulf, October 23-26, 1944, was history's largest naval engagement. Its 282 vessels (216 U.S., 2 Australian, and 64 Japanese) outnumbered the ships of the 1916 Battle of Jutland. The battle in Leyte Gulf involved almost two hundred thousand men and encompassed an area of more than one hundred thousand square miles. It saw all aspects of naval warfare—air, surface, submarine, and amphibious—as well as the use of the largest guns ever at sea, the last clash of the dreadnoughts, and the introduction of kamikazes. The battle was also distinguished by fine planning and leadership, brilliant deception, failed intelligence, and great controversies.

The invasion of Leyte Island, beginning on October 20, 1944, was the first phase of an Allied campaign to liberate the Philippine Islands from the Japanese. The Philippines occupied a strategically important position between Japan and its important resources base of the East Indies. Leyte is in the middle of the Philippine archipelago.

The Japanese anticipated a U.S. offensive and had plans to combat it; Shō Ichi Go (Operation Victory One) covered defense of the Philippines, to which the Japanese decided to commit the entire Combined Fleet. The Combined Fleet commander, Admiral Soemu Toyoda, knew the operation would be a gamble. He said after the war, "If things went well, we might obtain unexpectedly good results; but if the worst should happen, there was a chance that we would lose the entire fleet. But I felt that chance had to be taken." Toyoda knew that should the Americans retake the Philippines, even with the fleet left, the shipping lane to the south would be completely cut off, so that if the fleet came back to Japanese waters, it could not obtain fuel. If the fleet remained in southern waters, it could not receive supplies of ammunition and arms. In Toyoda's opinion, there would be no reason to save the fleet at the expense of the Philippines.

The Allied armada that advanced toward Leyte in mid-October comprised more than seven hundred ships. The U.S. Third Fleet also was available for strategic support of the operation. Under the command of Admiral William F. Halsey, the Third Fleet was given two tasks: to cover the Leyte landings and, if the opportunity arose, to destroy the Japanese fleet.

Opposing the Allied forces were four Japanese naval forces. The Northern Force, commanded by Vice Admiral Jisabuto Ozawa, consisted of one heavy carrier, three light carriers, two hybrid battleship-carriers, three cruisers, and eight destroyers. It was to serve as a decoy, drawing Halsey's Third Fleet toward the north and away from the beaches. The most powerful of the Japanese units was Central Force (First Division Attack Force), commanded by Admiral Takeo Kurita. It included the two super battleships, *Musashi* and *Yamato*. With their 18.1-inch guns, these 862-foot long, 70,000-ton behemoths were, at the time, the largest warships ever built. Kurita also had three older battleships, twelve cruisers, and fifteen destroyers. Kurita's ships were to slip through San Bernardino Strait. Meanwhile, Southern Force (C Force)—comprising two battleships, one heavy cruiser, and four destroyers, commanded by Vice Admiral Shoji Nishimura—would strike eastward through the Sulu Sea in an effort to force its way through Surigao Strait between the islands of Leyte and Mindanao. It was trailed by the Second Division Attack Force, commanded by Vice Admiral Kiyohide Shima, which had one light and two heavy cruisers and four destroyers. These two prongs would then converge simultaneously on the landing area in the Leyte Gulf and destroy Allied shipping there. At the same time, Japanese shore-based aircraft were to inflict maximum damage on U.S. forces assisting the landings. The main strength of the Japanese fleet lay in its naval gunnery, because its carrier- and land-based aircraft had largely been destroyed in earlier battles and by U.S. Army and Navy air raids during September and early October. Any chance the Japanese had for success lay in using their huge battleships to shell the Leyte beaches. Shō Ichi Go was, at best, a long shot.

Opposing the Japanese were two U.S. fleets: the Seventh Fleet, commanded by Admiral Thomas C. Kinkaid and operating under General MacArthur's Southwest Pacific Command, and Admiral William F. Halsey's Third Fleet, under Admiral Chester Nimitz at Pearl Harbor. Leyte was the first landing to involve two entire U.S. fleets and the first landing without unified command. Divided command had unfortunate consequences.

Seventh Fleet was divided into three task groups. The first consisted of Rear Admiral Jesse Oldendorf's six old battleships, sixteen escort carriers, four heavy cruisers, four light cruisers, thirty destroyers, and ten destroyer escorts. The other two elements were amphibious task groups carrying out the actual invasion. Seventh Fleet had escorted the invasion force to Leyte and now provided broad protection for the entire landing area. As most of Halsey's amphibious assets had been loaned to Kinkaid, Third Fleet consisted almost entirely of Admiral Marc Mitscher's Task Force (TF) 38: fourteen fast carriers (with more than one thousand aircraft) organized into four task groups containing six battleships, eight heavy cruisers, thirteen light cruisers, and fifty-seven destroyers. Third Fleet's orders called for it to secure air superiority over the Philippines, protect the landings, and maintain pressure on the Japanese. If the opportunity to destroy a major part of the Japanese fleet presented itself or could be created, that destruction was to be Third Fleet's primary task.

First contact between the rival forces was made on October 23. In the Battle of the Sibuyan Sea, U.S. submarines sighted the Central Force and sank two Japanese heavy cruisers, one of which was Kurita's flagship, *Atago*. When reports of Nishimura's Southern Force reached Admiral Halsey, he issued a preliminary order detailing a battle line of battleships known as Task Force 34, to be commanded by Vice Admiral Willis A. Lee. Admiral Kinkaid was aware of that signal and assumed TF 34 had been established. Kinkaid ordered the fire-support portion of Seventh Fleet, commanded by Rear Admiral Jesse Oldendorf, to assume a blocking position at the lower end of Leyte Gulf to halt any Japanese attempt to force Surigao Strait; Seventh Fleet escort carriers guarded the eastern entrance to Leyte Gulf. Halsey, meanwhile, ordered his own fleet carriers to launch air strikes against enemy units then steaming through San Bernardino Strait. These planes concentrated on the *Musashi*. She took nineteen torpedoes and nearly as many bombs before finally succumbing. Half of her nearly 2,200-man crew perished with her. Several other Japanese ships were damaged. On the afternoon of October 25, U.S. pilots reported that Kurita had reversed course and was heading west; Halsey incorrectly assumed that this part of the battle was over.

Meanwhile, Japanese land-based planes from the Second Air Fleet attacked U.S. ships supporting the land invasion. Most were shot down, but they sank the light carrier *Princeton* and damaged the cruiser *Birmingham*. Unknown to Halsey, after nightfall Kurita's force changed course and resumed heading for San Bernardino Strait.

Halsey broke off the engagement in order to pursue what appeared to be a more tempting target. U.S. scout planes had sighted the Northern Force, and Halsey, believing it to be the most powerful Japanese threat, turned his carrier task forces northward. Several of Halsey's subordinates registered reservations about his decision, but the admiral would not be deterred. Compounding the error, Halsey failed to inform Admiral Kinkaid, who still assumed that TF 34 was protecting the

strait. Halsey's decision left the landing beaches guarded only by Seventh Fleet's Taffy 3 escort carrier group commanded by Rear Admiral Clifton A. F. Sprague. Taffy 3 was one of three such support groups operating off Samar. Sprague had six light escort carriers, three destroyers, and four destroyer escorts. This was precisely what the Japanese had intended; for the U.S. forces, it was a grave tactical error, because it enabled the Japanese Central Force to sail undisturbed through the San Bernardino Strait toward the landing area.

Late on the evening of October 24, battleships and cruisers of the Seventh Fleet engaged the Southern Force. The October 24-25 Battle of Surigao Strait was a classic example of "crossing the T" in naval warfare. The PT boats discovered the Japanese moving in line-ahead formation, but Nishimura's force easily forced the PT boats back. While the battleships often get the credit for the Surigao Strait victory, it was U.S. destroyers that inflicted most of the damage. Two converging torpedo attacks sank a battleship and three destroyers. The Japanese then ran into the line of Oldendorf's battleships. The Allies won a great victory at little cost to themselves; when it was over, the sole survivors of the Southern Force and Second Division Attack Force were five destroyers and a heavy cruiser.

The U.S. escort carriers operating north of Leyte were not as fortunate. Early on October 25, the Central Force emerged from San Bernardino Strait, headed for Leyte Gulf, and surprised the U.S. ships. Crew members of the U.S. destroyers and pilots of escort carriers of Taffy 3, brilliantly commanded by Admiral Sprague, fought a courageous but apparently hopeless battle. The Japanese sank the *Gambier Bay*, the only U.S. carrier ever lost to gunfire, and also sank the destroyers *Hoel* and *Johnston*, and destroyer escort *Samuel B. Roberts*. Although Japanese guns were registering repeated hits and Kurita was in position to secure a crushing victory, he abruptly broke all contact and retired north toward the San Bernardino Strait. This puzzling action allowed the transports and troops at the beachhead to escape certain destruction.

Kurita believed he was under attack by aircraft from Halsey's fleet carriers. Kurita's decision was strengthened by the fact that the southern attacking force had been destroyed. After the war, Kurita said, "The conclusion from our gunfire and antiaircraft fire during the day had led me to believe in my uselessness, my ineffectual position, if I proceeded into Leyte Gulf where I would come under even heavier air attack." Several days of nearly incessant attacks may also have frayed Kurita's nerves. Kurita hoped to join Ozawa's force to the north but changed his mind and exited through San Bernardino Strait. Sprague later noted that the failure of Kurita's force "to completely wipe out all vessels of this Task Unit can be attributed to our successful smoke screen, our torpedo counterattack, continuous harassment of the enemy by bomb, torpedo, and strafing air attacks, timely maneuvers, and the definite partiality of Almighty God." The four ships lost by Taffy 3 were the only U.S. warships sunk by Japanese surface ships in the Battle for Leyte Gulf.

Meanwhile, Admiral Sprague's escort carriers and Oldendorf's force returning from the Battle of Surigao Strait came under attack from land-based kamikaze aircraft, the first such attacks of the war. These sank the escort carrier *St. Lô* and damaged several other ships.

After the major issues of the battle had been decided, Halsey's Third Fleet caught the Japanese Northern Force off Cape Engaño. By nightfall, U.S. aircraft, a submarine, and surface ships had sunk all four Japanese carriers of Ozawa's force as well as five other ships. This blow ended Japanese carrier aviation. Ironically, the entire Northern Force would have been destroyed if Halsey had not yielded to urgent appeals to turn back to intercept the Central Force. The Third Fleet failed to catch up with Kurita and the remainder of Northern Force was able to get away.

Including retiring vessels sunk on October 26 and 27, Japanese losses in the battle were twenty-nine warships (four carriers, three battleships, six heavy and four light cruisers, eleven destroyers, and a submarine) and more than five hundred aircraft. Japanese personnel losses amounted to some 10,500 seamen and aviators dead. The U.S. Navy lost only six ships (one light carrier, two escort carriers, two destroyers, and a destroyer escort) and more than two hundred aircraft. About twenty-eight hundred Americans were killed and another one thousand wounded. The Battle for Leyte Gulf ended the Japanese fleet as an organized fighting force. —*Spencer C. Tucker, based on an original entry by Theodore A. Wilson*

ADDITIONAL READING:

Cannon, M. Hamlin. *Leyte: The Return to the Philippines.* Washington, D.C.: United States Army, Center of Military History, 1993. The Army's official history provides good coverage of the Leyte battle.

Cutler, Thomas J. *The Battle of Leyte Gulf, 23-26 October 1944.* New York: HarperCollins, 1994. Well balanced between Japanese and U.S. accounts of the battle, placing it in its proper context.

Field, James A., Jr. *The Japanese at Leyte Gulf: The Shō Operation.* Princeton, N.J.: Princeton University Press, 1947. Useful for its presentation of the Japanese perspective.

Halsey, William F. *Admiral Halsey's Story.* New York: Whittlesey House, 1947. A helpful memoir by one of the chief participants in the Leyte operation, although Halsey never admitted responsibility for errors in the battle.

Morison, Samuel Eliot. *Leyte: June, 1944-January, 1945.* Vol. 12 in *The History of United States Naval Operations in World War II.* Boston: Little, Brown, 1963. The classic U.S. Navy official history, stressing description of events.

Potter, E. B. *Bull Halsey.* Annapolis, Md.: Naval Institute Press, 1985. Excellent biography of the controversial admiral.

U.S. Strategic Bombing Survey. *United States Strategic Bombing Survey: Compaigns of the Pacific War.* New York: Greenwood Press, 1969. Contains interviews with Japanese commanders in the battle.

Woodward, C. Vann. *The Battle for Leyte Gulf.* New York: Macmillan, 1947. Competent survey of the complex action,

placing the battle in the context of the war in the Pacific.

SEE ALSO: 1899, Philippine Insurrection; 1901, Insular Cases; 1934, Tydings-McDuffie Act; 1941, Bombing of Pearl Harbor; 1942, Battle of Midway; 1942, Manhattan Project; 1942, Battle of Guadalcanal; 1944, Superfortress Bombing of Japan; 1945, Atomic Bombing of Japan.

1944 ■ BATTLE OF THE BULGE: *German forces are defeated in a desperate campaign to halt advancing Allied armies*

DATE: December 16-26, 1944
LOCALE: Belgium and Luxembourg
CATEGORY: Wars, uprisings, and civil unrest
KEY FIGURES:

Omar Nelson Bradley (1893-1981), commander of the U.S. Twelfth Army
Dwight David Eisenhower (1890-1969), supreme commander of the Allied Expeditionary Force
Adolf Hitler (1889-1945), German chancellor and Nazi Party leader
Bernard Law Montgomery (1887-1976), commander of the British Twenty-first Army
George Smith Patton, Jr. (1885-1945), commander of the U.S. Third Army
Karl Rudolf Gerd von Rundstedt (1875-1953), commander in chief of the German forces

SUMMARY OF EVENT. In December, 1944, six months after the successful landing at Normandy, Allied forces were closing in on Germany's western frontier. The advance across France was so rapid as to overstretch the Allied supply lines that ran five hundred miles back to Normandy and the English Channel. Faced with growing fuel shortages, the supreme Allied commander, General Dwight D. Eisenhower, gave fuel supply priority to the advancing British forces under Field Marshal Sir Bernard Law Montgomery as they drove toward the Low Countries and the port city of Antwerp. The U.S. advance farther south ground to a halt as a result of the lack of fuel. As the Allied assault on Germany stalled, Adolf Hitler saw a chance to alter the course of the war by launching a great counteroffensive against the Western Allies. He announced his intentions on September 16 at a conference held at his East Prussian headquarters, the Wolf's Lair.

Hitler's plan was bold and desperate. It called for an attack against the rugged Ardennes sector, thinly held by U.S. forces. Hoping for a repeat of the highly successful 1940 campaign that led to the fall of France, Hitler aimed at splitting the Allied forces—U.S. troops to the south and the British and Canadians to the north. The German thrust first would obtain the Meuse River and then advance on the strategically important city of Antwerp. Speed and the ability of the advancing German forces to capture key road junctions in the Ardennes were critical ingredients for success. Once this was achieved, the

Allied forces (chiefly British and Canadian), north of a line running from Antwerp to the Ardennes, would be destroyed. Hitler hoped that, if the plan worked, the Allied coalition would fall apart, leading to a negotiated peace. It might at least be possible to transfer troops to the Eastern Front to meet the Russian threat.

Hitler's generals were less confident of success. They argued that Germany did not have sufficient resources in troops and materiel to carry out such an attack. Nevertheless, by tremendous exertion, two new Panzer armies, the Sixth SS Panzer and Fifth Panzer, were assembled. More than twenty-five German divisions were gathered for the attack along a fifty-mile front opposite five U.S. divisions. Two largely infantry armies, the Fifteenth and Seventh, were to provide support on the right and left flanks, respectively, of advancing Panzer armies. Two hundred thousand troops were mustered, along with six hundred tanks and nineteen hundred guns. Opposite, the U.S. front was held by eighty thousand troops, supported by four hundred tanks and four hundred guns. Special commando units composed of English-speaking Germans dressed in U.S. uniforms were assembled to spread chaos behind the U.S. lines.

As the Germans marshaled their forces for the attack, strict secrecy was imposed on all involved. Poor weather and the rugged territory of the Eifel region opposite the U.S. sector covered German preparations. Radio traffic directly mentioning the impending counteroffensive was banned. Although the Allies had various clues that something was being planned, underestimation of German potential led Allied intelligence to disregard the accumulating evidence of a possible enemy winter offensive. Allied intelligence considered the broken terrain of the Ardennes region unsuitable and therefore unlikely to be attacked. Intercepted German radio traffic that mentioned fuel shortages was interpreted as a positive indicator that the Germans were incapable of launching an attack. In reality, fuel was being prioritized for the assembled German forces in the Eifel.

On the morning of December 16, advancing out of the winter gloom, the German forces under General Karl von Rundstedt obtained complete tactical surprise as the great offensive began. Two U.S. divisions, depleted by earlier fighting, were shattered by the initial blow. Rapid gains were made by the attacking Germans, as they drove on the key road junctions at St. Vith and Bastogne. Yet the German advance immediately ran into difficulty. Even cut-off and surrounded U.S. units continued to fight with a ferocity unanticipated by the Germans. If the Allies underestimated the German ability to launch a great counteroffensive, Hitler also seriously erred by underestimating the fighting abilities of the U.S. troops.

For six days, U.S. troops at St. Vith held the critical road junction against German attacks. The 101st Airborne Division encircled at Bastogne held on in the face of tremendous pressure from the Fifth Panzer Army. The commander of the division responded to a surrender demand from the Germans with the famous reply, "Nuts!" To the north, the Eighty-second Airborne Division held on to the shoulder of the bulge. The Germans were unable to widen their initial breech in the Allied line. In the most infamous moment of the battle, on December 17, elements of the First SS Panzer Division participated in the murder of eighty-six U.S. prisoners at Malmedy. A number of the German officers and men involved were later charged with war crimes. The German attack was canalized and proved unable to widen the initial breakthrough that had managed to create only a bulge in the Allied line, from which the famous battle receives its name.

The Allied response to the German attack was swift. Eisenhower halted all offensive operations along the front and concentrated all available Allied forces to stop the German advance. With communications sliced, Lieutenant General Omar Bradley's troops north of the salient were put under the command of Field Marshal Montgomery. In a remarkable feat, Lieutenant General George S. Patton's Third Army halted the Germans' advance into the Saar and, after a ninety-degree turn north, moved to relieve Bastogne. By Christmas Day, staunch U.S. resistance and critical fuel shortages had stopped the German momentum more than five miles short of the Meuse River, the first objective of Hitler's battle plan, and one hundred miles from the primary objective of Antwerp. A long but narrow bulge had been created in the Allied lines that was forty miles at the base and nearly sixty miles in depth. The clearing of the skies over the battlefield opened the way for massive Allied air attacks on the German forces. More than five thousand planes moved to cut off the German supply line and support the hard-pressed Allied ground forces. Not until January 21, 1945, did the Allies manage to retake the lost ground.

The Battle of the Bulge, perhaps the greatest battle in the history of the U.S. Army, took staggering tolls: The Germans lost 120,000 men either killed, wounded, or missing, along with six hundred tanks and assault guns. Air strikes to cover the retreating German forces had cost the Luftwaffe (the German air force) more than fifteen hundred aircraft. Allied casualties, chiefly from the United States, totaled 8,000 killed, 48,000 wounded, and 21,000 captured or missing. Nearly 740 tanks and tank destroyers were lost. Among the soldiers, 4,500 African Americans saw action.

Hitler's great gamble had failed without achieving any of its objectives. The Germans, using up their strategic reserves, lost irreplaceable men and equipment that hastened the end of the war. At most, the Germans had merely slowed the Allied advance by weeks. With the destruction of Germany's reserves, little was left to stop the Russian New Year offensive on the Eastern Front and the Allied advance across the Rhine into the heart of Germany.

—*Van M. Leslie*

ADDITIONAL READING:

Cole, Hugh M. *The Ardennes: Battle of the Bulge*. Washington, D.C.: Office of the Chief of Military History, Department of the Army, 1965. Detailed official U.S. Army history, essential for any study of the battle. Black-and-white illustrations, maps.

Eisenhower, Dwight D. *Crusade in Europe*. Garden City, N.Y.: Doubleday, 1948. An account of the battle from the commander of Allied forces in Western Europe.

Fuller, J. F. C. *The Second World War, 1939-1945*. 1948. Reprint. New York: Da Capo Press, 1993. A critical strategic and tactical assessment of the conduct of the war.

Liddell Hart, B. H. *History of the Second World War*. New York: G. P. Putnam's Sons, 1971. An interpretative study that includes a chapter on the battle by one of the great military historians.

MacDonald, Charles B. *A Time for Trumpets: The Untold Story of the Battle of the Bulge*. New York: William Morrow, 1984. Account of the battle written from the perspective of the front-line infantry soldier, written by a rifle company commander. Black-and-white illustrations, maps, order of battle.

Stokesbury, James L. *A Short History of World War II*. New York: William Morrow, 1980. Excellent general history that places the battle within the wider context of the war.

Weinberg, Gerhard L. *A World at Arms: A Global History of World War II*. Cambridge, England: Cambridge University Press, 1994. Provides valuable insights on Hitler and Germany during the period leading up to and after the battle.

SEE ALSO: 1941, Germany and Italy Declare War on the United States; 1942, Manhattan Project; 1942, Invasion of North Africa; 1943, Western Allies Invade Italy; 1944, Operation Overlord; 1945, Yalta Conference; 1945, V-E Day; 1945, Potsdam Conference.

1945 ■ YALTA CONFERENCE: *the most important meeting of the "Big Three" powers marks the height of Allied cooperation but reveals conflicting agendas*

DATE: February 4-11, 1945
LOCALE: Livadia Palace, Yalta, Crimea, Soviet Union
CATEGORIES: Diplomacy and international relations; Wars, uprisings, and civil unrest
KEY FIGURES:
Winston Leonard Spencer Churchill (1874-1965), prime minister of Great Britain
Anthony Eden (1897-1977), British secretary of state for foreign affairs
William Averell Harriman (1891-1986), U.S. ambassador to the Soviet Union
Vyacheslav M. Molotov (1890-1986), people's commissar for foreign affairs of the Soviet Union
Franklin Delano Roosevelt (1882-1945), thirty-second president of the United States, 1933-1945
Joseph Stalin (Joseph Vissarionovich Dzhugashvili, 1879-1953), Marshal of the Soviet Union and secretary of the Communist Party
Edward Reilly Stettinius, Jr. (1900-1949), U.S. secretary of state
SUMMARY OF EVENT. In February, 1945, the armies of the Soviet Union moved rapidly toward Berlin with the Nazis in full retreat. In the West, British and U.S. forces, commanded by General Dwight D. Eisenhower, prepared to invade Germany. The unconditional surrender of Germany was expected in a matter of weeks. In the Far East, U.S. forces moved steadily from island to island across the Pacific toward a final invasion of the Japanese home islands. The possibility of using an atomic bomb to end the war remained questionable. Military experts did not believe the bomb could be made ready before the end of the year.

With the defeats of Germany and Japan a certainty, the Big Three Allied leaders—Prime Minister Winston Churchill of Great Britain, Communist Party secretary Joseph Stalin of the Soviet Union, and President Franklin D. Roosevelt of the United States—met to plan the postwar world. It was the last time the three would see one another, for Roosevelt died on April 12, 1945, just two months after the conference ended and less than a month before Germany surrendered. At Stalin's request, the Allies gathered at Livadia Palace (once a summer home of Czar Nicholas II) at Yalta on the Crimean Peninsula of the Black Sea. The conference lasted from February 4 to February 11, 1945.

Yalta represented the height of Allied cooperation. The Big Three spoke happily of the end of the fighting, but conflicting aims and conflicting personalities led to compromises in the spirit of cooperation that failed to satisfy any of them. Four major issues were discussed, and in spite of much talk of cooperation, no comprehensive settlement proved possible. The future of Germany, the future of Poland, the nature of a world organization to replace the discredited League of Nations, and the Soviet Union's formal entrance into the war against Japan were all highly controversial issues that needed to be settled by the Big Three.

Upon the defeat of Germany, Stalin wanted to divide that country into permanent zones of occupation; and he wanted reparations in kind (food and industry) to compensate for the nearly twenty million Russian dead and the Nazi destruction of one thousand Russian towns and cities. Stalin demanded a harsh policy to prevent Germany from ever making war again. Churchill agreed to divide Germany, but not permanently. He insisted that a healthy Europe depended upon a prosperous Germany. Roosevelt's position was somewhere between these two views. Stalin's reparations demands were incorporated into the conference's final protocol, and the three powers called for Germany's "dismemberment" into occupation zones during the period following surrender. A U.S. proposal granting France the status of an occupying power gained Stalin's reluctant approval. The details of Allied occupation policy, however, as well as the precise amount of reparations, were deferred to a later meeting.

In addition to a neutralized Germany, Stalin wanted the security of a friendly Polish government. He sought boundaries giving Russia territory from eastern Poland, while compensating the Poles with part of eastern Germany. The Soviet Union recognized the provisional Polish government in Warsaw (the so-called Lublin Poles), but both Great Britain and

In an official photo of the Big Three meeting at Yalta in February, 1945, Britain's Winston Churchill (left), the United States' Franklin D. Roosevelt (center), and the Soviet Union's Joseph Stalin are seated in the foreground. Roosevelt shows the wear of illness and the stress of his wartime presidency, and in fact he would die only two months later, shortly before V-E day and before the end of the Pacific war. (AP/World Wide Photos)

the United States insisted that the Polish government-in-exile in London also participate in the political rebuilding of Poland after the war. The Big Three agreed on a formula calling for the reorganization of the Lublin government with open elections, worded in such a way that both sides could see their respective interests maintained. The question of Poland's postwar boundaries also found a compromise solution. Ignoring the protests of the London Poles, the Big Three set the Curzon Line as the basis for Poland's eastern border, thereby sanctioning Russian reacquisition of areas lost in the fighting during the Russian Civil War of 1918-1921. As compensation, the Poles would receive substantial accessions of territory in the north and west, but the precise delineation of the new German frontier was left to the peace conference.

Primarily at U.S. insistence, discussion of a world organization to maintain the postwar peace enjoyed a high priority at Yalta. The Big Three planned an international conference to be held in San Francisco in April, at which the United Nations would be formed. Stalin, Roosevelt, and Churchill reached agreements on several points concerning membership and voting in the new body. Churchill resented U.S. proposals for

United Nations trusteeships of colonial territories, which the British prime minister interpreted as an attempt by Roosevelt to dismantle the British Empire. Stalin exploited the disagreement over trusteeships between the Western Allies to gain Churchill's support for his own plan to have two Soviet republics recognized as independent voting members of the new United Nations. The atomic bomb was still a somewhat vague conception at Yalta, and so it was assumed that the Soviets would be needed to defeat Japan. Stalin promised that in return for Russian territory ceded to Japan under Russia's czarist imperial government, he would declare war on Japan within three months of Germany's surrender. The agreement on the Far East was not made public in February, 1945.

The agreements at Yalta could have become the basis for an amicable peace, for the spirit of the conference was one of hope and trust. In the spring and summer, however, charges of bad faith and double-dealing began to replace the spirit of compromise. Serious disagreements that heralded the Cold War to come were soon in evidence, and within a short time, the good will that marked the Yalta Conference had vanished.

—*Burton Kaufman, updated by William Allison*

ADDITIONAL READING:

Buhite, Russell D. *Decisions at Yalta: An Appraisal of Summit Diplomacy.* Wilmington, Del.: Scholarly Resources, 1986. Examines the use of summit diplomacy based on the model of Yalta and other meetings between the Big Three.

Clemens, Diane Shaver. *Yalta.* New York: Oxford University Press, 1970. A thorough account of the Yalta meeting and its aftermath.

Gardner, Lloyd C. *Spheres of Influence: The Great Powers Partition Europe, from Munich to Yalta.* Chicago: Ivan R. Dee, 1991. Traces the partitioning of Europe between Eastern and Western spheres of influence during World War II.

Snell, John L., ed. *The Meaning of Yalta: Big Three Diplomacy and the New Balance of Power.* Baton Rouge: Louisiana State University Press, 1956. A solid early account of Yalta and the world created by the Big Three.

Theoharis, Athan G. *The Yalta Myths: An Issue in U.S. Politics, 1945-1955.* Columbia: University of Missouri Press, 1970. A revisionist examination of the results of the decisions made at Yalta.

SEE ALSO: 1945, United Nations Charter Convention; 1945, Potsdam Conference; 1945, Atomic Bombing of Japan; 1947, Truman Doctrine; 1948, Berlin Blockade; 1949, North Atlantic Treaty.

1945 ■ UNITED NATIONS CHARTER CONVENTION: *birth of a global international organization for conflict resolution and maintenance of world peace*

DATE: April 25-June 26, 1945
LOCALE: San Francisco
CATEGORY: Diplomacy and international relations
KEY FIGURES:

Winston Leonard Spencer Churchill (1874-1965), prime minister of Great Britain

Tom Connally (1877-1963), chairman of the Senate Committee on Foreign Relations and member of the U.S. delegation

Cordell Hull (1871-1955), secretary of state, 1933-1944

Franklin Delano Roosevelt (1882-1945), thirty-second president of the United States, 1933-1945

Joseph Stalin (Joseph Vissarionovich Dzhugashvili, 1879-1953), marshal of the Soviet Union and general secretary of the Central Committee of the Communist Party

Edward Reilly Stettinius, Jr. (1900-1949), Hull's replacement as secretary of state, 1944-1945, and chairman of the U.S. delegation to the Charter Convention

Harry S Truman (1884-1972), thirty-third president of the United States, 1945-1953

Arthur Hendrick Vandenberg (1884-1951), Republican senator from Michigan and member of the U.S. delegation

SUMMARY OF EVENT. On January 1, 1942, Franklin D. Roosevelt, Winston Churchill, Maxim Litvinov (Russian ambassador to the United States), and representatives of twenty-three other nations signed the Declaration of the United Nations, pledging themselves to a continued alliance in the struggle against the Axis and to uphold the principles enunciated in the Atlantic Charter. This latter document was a joint statement made by Roosevelt and Churchill on August 14, 1941, which spoke of the need to establish a permanent organization for collective security. Eventually, this commitment to permanent collective security led to the establishment of the United Nations on June 26, 1945, in San Francisco, as a successor to the League of Nations, which had rested on similar principles but had failed to achieve consensus from all the great powers.

Throughout the evolution of the United Nations, initiative came from the Western powers, particularly the United States. From its inception, the United Nations was a Western idea, but the United States believed that Soviet participation was absolutely essential. Yet it was not until October, 1943, that the Soviet Union agreed, in the Moscow Declaration of Foreign Ministers, to a statement making firm the commitment to establish a general international organization. In August, 1944, the Big Four—the United States, the Soviet Union, China, and Great Britain—at last met to discuss the actual structure of the postwar security organization. At the invitation of President Roosevelt, the delegates assembled at a suburban Washington, D.C., estate, Dumbarton Oaks, to review proposals. By October 7, the conferees had reached agreement on a number of vital points. There were a number of outstanding problems after the convention adjourned, however, the most notable of which was a disagreement between the United States and the Soviet Union over the veto power. The Soviet Union insisted that the Big Four be permitted an absolute veto over issues in which they were involved. Roosevelt appealed directly to Stalin in hopes of modifying this position, but without success. The president decided to accept the progress that had been made and reserve a final decision on the veto question until after he had an opportunity to discuss the matter with the Soviet leader in person.

On paper, Roosevelt had every reason to feel that he had achieved his goal after the conclusion of the Yalta Conference of February, 1945. Although concerned with many different topics of far-reaching implications, the Yalta meeting of Stalin, Roosevelt, and Churchill did produce a temporary accord on the veto question. Stalin accepted the U.S. proposition that those issues that were defined as procedural could not be vetoed by any member of the organization, but would require a majority vote of the Security Council. It was further agreed that in certain cases a disputant to an issue—even if one of the Big Four—must abstain from voting. Finally, it was decided that all nations that declared war on the Axis by March 1, 1945, would be considered charter members of the United Nations.

At the invitation of the Big Four, forty-six other nations assembled in San Francisco in April, 1945, to establish the United Nations. President Roosevelt had chosen the U.S. delegation with great care. Recalling the unfortunate experiences of Woodrow Wilson and the Paris convention, Roosevelt picked a bipartisan delegation. At the head of the group was Edward R. Stettinius, Jr., newly appointed secretary of state. He was joined by a number of other delegates, most notable of whom were Senator Arthur H. Vandenberg, a Michigan Republican who had moved from an isolationist position to one of full support of the president, and Senator Tom Connally, a Texas Democrat who was chairman of the Senate Foreign Relations Committee. The president did not live to see the convention open: He died of a stroke on April 12, 1945, only two months before World War II ended.

Harry S Truman, Roosevelt's successor, was firmly committed to the same sort of program as Roosevelt and endorsed the delegation. At the convention, the U.S. representatives immediately became bogged down in a number of disputes. Russia already was creating tensions within the Allied coalition by its supposed intransigence regarding Poland. It was only at Truman's insistence that Stalin, who viewed the entire San Francisco affair as a Western production, permitted Vyacheslav Molotov, Soviet foreign minister, to attend the convention in place of a lower-ranking official. In San Francisco, the United States and Russia again disagreed over voting procedure. Seeking to revoke the decision made at Yalta, Molotov now insisted that a Big Power be granted the veto over the discussion of an issue before the Security Council. Truman appealed to Stalin personally and finally was able to persuade him that a decision to discuss an issue was a procedural question and therefore not subject to a simple veto.

On another issue, however, the United States found itself in complete agreement with the Soviet Union. As conceived by the Big Four in pre-San Francisco meetings, the United Nations was to operate through the domination of the five major powers, which now included France. It was agreed by all major powers that only unanimity among themselves could keep the peace. This met stiff resistance from the smaller powers, both before and during the U.N. Conference at San Francisco. Latin American representatives met at Mexico City in early 1945 and called for a more powerful General Assembly and International Court, and insisted on a greater role for regional organizations in the maintenance of peace. Small powers expressed resentment at San Francisco concerning the veto provisions insisted upon by the major powers, but the latter held firm on their dominant role in the Security Council.

On a host of other points, concessions were made to the smaller powers, which resulted in a strengthening of provisions for regional collective security in cooperation with the Security Council and in the elaboration of an extensive set of articles dealing with decolonization and trusteeship arrangements for non-self-governing territories. The Dumbarton Oaks proposals developed by the great powers had been largely silent on these issues, so the details of these initiatives had to be sketched out at San Francisco. The result was a U.N. structure with six major organs instead of the four anticipated at Dumbarton Oaks. To the Security Council, the General Assembly, the Secretariat, and International Court of Justice were added the Economic and Social Council (ECOSOC) and the Trusteeship Council.

While the Security Council was created to deal with the major U.N. goal of maintaining global peace and security and punishing acts of aggression under chapters 6 and 7 of the charter, the General Assembly was granted even broader authority not only to discuss peace and security matters (although it could make no recommendations on such matters while the Security Council was engaged in deliberations concerning them) but also to coordinate U.N. efforts to eliminate the underlying causes of conflict. ECOSOC and the Trusteeship Council, as well as mechanisms established to promote decolonization under General Assembly oversight, were established to address these underlying causes of conflict, which were attributed to the lack of self-determination, poverty, violations of human rights, and other social pathologies. The General Assembly, unlike the Security Council, was open to all member states, with equal voting rights. The General Assembly could make recommendations only with regard to areas under its purview, while the Security Council could bind U.N. members under the provisions of Chapter 7 for enforcement of international peace and security.

Almost immediately after the creation of the United Nations, the Cold War deepened and the Allied consensus Roosevelt had hoped would furnish the basis for effective global management of conflict evaporated. Security Council action was often frustrated by the threat or use of the veto. Apart from the Korean War, when the Soviet Union was boycotting Security Council sessions, thus enabling the latter to deploy U.N. forces to resist the North Korean aggression, the Security Council was unable to invoke its collective enforcement powers. This led to the development of roles for the General Assembly and the Secretariat in pursuing peacekeeping initiatives that the Security Council itself eventually adopted, short of using economic sanctions or military force. After the demise of the Cold War in the late 1980's, followed by the collapse of the Soviet Union and of Soviet communism, the Security Council undertook a number of classic enforcement actions. No longer stymied by the Soviet veto, and in a climate of great-power consensus to restore order in regional conflicts in the early 1990's, the Security Council deployed forces in the Persian Gulf to free Kuwait from Iraqi occupation, in Somalia to provide humanitarian aid and restore order, and in Haiti to oversee the reestablishment of democracy. In these actions, the Security Council belatedly fulfilled the role anticipated for it by the framers of the United Nations Charter, at the same time stirring suspicion among American isolationists and nationalists.

—George Q. Flynn, updated by Robert F. Gorman

Additional reading:

Bennett, A. LeRoy. *International Organizations: Principles and Issues.* 6th ed. Englewood Cliffs, N.J.: Prentice-Hall, 1995. A comprehensive treatment of the origins, genesis, and historical development of the United Nations in the context of wider developments in international organization.

Claude, Inis L., Jr. *Swords into Plowshares: The Problem and Progress of International Organization.* 3d rev. ed. New York: Random House, 1964. A standard history of the early development of the United Nations.

Goodrich, Leland M., Edvard Hambro, and Anne P. Simons. *Charter of the United Nations: Commentary and Documents.* 3d ed. New York: Columbia University Press, 1969. Although dated, an invaluable, article-by-article analysis of the actual practice of the United Nations in its first two decades of implementing charter provisions.

Mingst, Karen A., and Margaret P. Karns. *The United Nations in the Post-Cold War Era.* Boulder, Colo.: Westview Press, 1995. Traces the development of the United Nations and its prospects for renewed activity in global peacekeeping and economic development.

The United Nations Conference on International Organization, San Francisco, California, April 25 to June 26, 1945. Selected Documents. U.S. Department of State Conference Series 83. Washington, D.C.: Government Printing Office, 1946. Contains a wealth of documents, reports, verbatim records, and summaries of meetings leading up to and including the U.N. Conference in San Francisco.

Weiss, Thomas, David P. Forsythe, and Roger A. Coate. *The United Nations and Changing World Politics.* Boulder, Colo.: Westview Press, 1994. Examines the theory of collective security and its applicability to U.N. efforts at peacekeeping and the protection of human rights in the late twentieth century.

SEE ALSO: 1919, Treaty of Versailles; 1945, Yalta Conference; 1945, Potsdam Conference; 1948, Berlin Blockade; 1949, North Atlantic Treaty; 1950, Korean War; 1950, Truman-MacArthur Confrontation; 1991, Persian Gulf War; 1992, U.S. Marines Intervene in Somalia.

1945 ■ V-E DAY: *the defeat of Nazi Germany marks the transfer of international power from the center of the European continent to two world powers at Europe's flanks*

DATE: May 8, 1945
LOCALE: Rheims, France
CATEGORY: Wars, uprisings, and civil unrest
KEY FIGURES:
Omar Nelson Bradley (1893-1981), U.S. commander of the Twelfth Army Group
Winston Leonard Spencer Churchill (1874-1965), prime minister of Great Britain
Dwight David Eisenhower (1890-1969), commander in chief of Allied forces in Western Europe
Adolf Hitler (1889-1945), chancellor of Germany and Führer
Bernard Law Montgomery, first Viscount Montgomery of Alamein (1887-1976), British commander of the Twenty-first Army Group

Franklin Delano Roosevelt (1882-1945), thirty-second president of the United States, 1933-1945
Joseph Stalin (Joseph Vissarionovich Dzhugashvili, 1879-1953), marshal of the Soviet Union and general secretary of the Central Committee of the Communist Party
Harry S Truman (1884-1972), thirty-third president of the United States, 1945-1953

SUMMARY OF EVENT. After repelling the German counterattack in the Ardennes during the Battle of the Bulge in December, 1944, the commander in chief of Allied forces in Western Europe, General Dwight D. Eisenhower, prepared for the final offensive into the heart of Germany. He planned two major crossings of the Rhine in the spring of 1945—one on the north by Field Marshal Bernard Law Montgomery's Twenty-first Army Group, consisting mainly of British and Canadian troops, and the U.S. Ninth Army; another in the center by General Omar N. Bradley's Twelfth Army Group; and a third in the south by the U.S. Third and Seventh Armies. Adolf Hitler, the Führer of Germany, had ordered his commanders to defend every inch of ground, and as a result of this directive, Eisenhower was able to destroy much of the German Army in battles west of the Rhine in February, 1945. He also was able to capture the Ludendorff railroad bridge over the Rhine at Remagen on March 7, so that he had a bridgehead in the center; consequently, he abandoned plans to cross the river on his left and right flanks, and instead he rushed troops across the Rhine at Remagen.

By March 28, Bradley's forces had passed through Remagen and reached Marburg, where they were ready to swing northward to link up with Montgomery's Twenty-first Army Group, which also had crossed the Rhine and had cut off German Army Group B, assigned to defend Germany's main industrial area, the Ruhr Valley. Eisenhower informed Montgomery that once the latter's encirclement of German units had been completed, the U.S. Ninth Army (which had been fighting with Montgomery's Twenty-first Army Group) would revert to General Bradley's Twelfth Army Group for the final thrust into Germany. This administrative shift was a major change in Eisenhower's overall strategy. Before the capture of the railroad bridge at Remagen, he had intended that Montgomery should spearhead the major military effort east of the Rhine, with Berlin as the primary target; now he was shifting the emphasis to General Bradley's Twelfth Army Group headed for Dresden. On March 28, Eisenhower informed Soviet dictator Joseph Stalin of his intentions, implying that he would leave capture of the German capital to the Soviet armies advancing from the East.

The prime minister of Great Britain, Winston Churchill, was furious. He considered Eisenhower's shift in emphasis uncalled-for from the military point of view and held that Berlin should remain the prime objective for both the British and U.S. forces. Eisenhower insisted that Berlin was no longer important, because no German armies or government agencies of any significance remained in the capital. The Supreme Allied Commander wanted to end the war as soon as possible; to do so he had to destroy the remaining armed forces of Germany, which were concentrated in southern Germany. Churchill insisted that politically it was essential for the British and Americans to capture Berlin, for if the Soviets were allowed to capture the capital, they would gain an exaggerated opinion of their contribution to the common victory. Churchill also implied that if the British-U.S. forces took Berlin, they could hold the city for the purpose of making postwar deals with the Soviets.

The division of Germany into zones of occupation already had been decided, and Berlin was located within the territory allotted to the Soviet zone. Berlin itself was to be divided into sectors among the Allies. Eisenhower held that it would be foolish to waste U.S. and British lives in taking a city that would have to be handed over by prior agreement to the Soviets because it was to be allocated to their zone. At no time did Churchill advocate repudiating earlier agreements with the Soviets concerning the division of Germany, although he did want "to shake hands as far east as possible" with the Red Army.

Churchill could not give orders to Eisenhower; that prerogative was reserved for the combined chiefs of staff of the United States and Great Britain, or the president of the United States. The chief of staff of the U.S. Army, General George C. Marshall, saw to it that Eisenhower was given a free hand in field operations. Churchill appealed to President Roosevelt, but Roosevelt's foreign policy was to make every effort to attain good relations with Stalin, and he refused to order Eisenhower to race the Soviet Army to Berlin. After Roosevelt's death on April 12, 1945, the new president, Harry S Truman, adopted the same policy. Eisenhower was free to do as he thought fit, and he sent his armies into central and southern Germany, avoiding Berlin. The Soviets captured the German capital in late April. Eisenhower's forces reached the Elbe River in central Germany between April 19 and May 2. On April 25, U.S. and Russian patrols met near Torgau and cut Germany in half. Hitler committed suicide on April 30; his successor, Admiral Karl Doenitz, began negotiations for surrender on May 4. Doenitz wanted to hand over German forces to the Western Allies, hoping thereby to avoid punishment from the Soviets for German crimes in the east, but Eisenhower refused to comply. Doenitz, his country in ruin, agreed to the immediate unconditional surrender of all Germany's armed forces. German and Allied representatives met at Eisenhower's headquarters in Rheims, France, on May 7, 1945, and signed the necessary documents that made the surrender effective the following day. Truman declared that day, May 8, to be V-E day (victory in Europe day).

It soon became evident that the documents signed at Reims were not the correct versions previously agreed upon by the Allies. Confusion reigned. The documents had not been approved formally by the Soviets, did not make provisions for authoritative Russian translations, and were signed by an obscure Soviet general without Stalin's knowledge. Although the United States tried to downplay the mistake, the Soviets insisted upon a second surrender ceremony with the proper

documents and different representatives in Berlin. That ceremony took place on May 9, a date that Soviets subsequently commemorated as the "true" V-E day. The Soviets had achieved a symbolic victory over the United States, as the second signing ceremony bolstered Moscow's dark intimations that the Western allies sought to marginalize the Soviet Union in the postwar order. As much as marking the end of the war against Germany, V-E day also can be seen as the opening of the Cold War.

—*Stephen E. Ambrose, updated by Steve D. Boilard*

ADDITIONAL READING:

Churchill, Winston S. *Triumph and Tragedy.* Vol. 6 in *The Second World War.* Boston: Houghton Mifflin, 1953. In this final volume of his history of World War II, Churchill examines and reflects upon the victory in Europe.

Gilbert, Martin. *The Day the War Ended: May 8, 1945, Victory in Europe.* New York: H. Holt, 1995. One of the better works to come out at the fiftieth anniversary of V-E day. Includes photos and bibliography.

Lucas, Jones Sidney. *Last Days of the Third Reich: The Collapse of Nazi Germany, May 1945.* New York: William Morrow, 1986. Examines the events leading up to V-E day, incorporating maps and diagrams. Divided into sections that focus on the different military fronts of the war.

Short, K. R. M., and Stephen Dolezel, eds. *Hitler's Fall: The Newsreel Witness.* London: Croom Helm, 1988. A collection of essays that examines how the struggle with and victory over Germany was portrayed by the media at the time. Essays are drawn from several countries and focus on commercial and governmentally controlled newsreel films.

Weinberg, Gerhard. "The Final Assault on Germany." In *A World at Arms: A Global History of World War II.* Cambridge, England: Cambridge University Press, 1994. An engaging and authoritative chapter in a lengthy book by a prominent scholar. Includes notes.

SEE ALSO: 1941, Germany and Italy Declare War on the United States; 1942, Manhattan Project; 1942, Invasion of North Africa; 1943, Western Allies Invade Italy; 1944, Operation Overlord; 1944, Battle of the Bulge; 1945, Yalta Conference; 1945, Potsdam Conference.

1945 ■ POTSDAM CONFERENCE: *the third and final "Big Three" meeting plans a peace settlement at the conclusion of World War II*

DATE: July 17-August 2, 1945
LOCALE: Potsdam, near Berlin, Germany
CATEGORIES: Diplomacy and international relations; Wars, uprisings, and civil unrest
KEY FIGURES:
Clement Richard Attlee (1883-1967), prime minister of Great Britain, 1945-1951

Winston Leonard Spencer Churchill (1874-1965), prime
   minister of Great Britain, 1940-1945, 1951-1955
Harry S Truman (1884-1972), thirty-third president of the
   United States, 1945-1953
Joseph Stalin (Iosif Vissarionovich Dzhugashvili,
   1879-1953), premier of the Soviet Union, 1924-1953

SUMMARY OF EVENT. There were only three occasions when
all three of the heads of state of the Allies met face to face:
Teheran, November-December, 1943; Yalta, February, 1945;
and the Potsdam Conference, July 17-August 2, 1945. At the
Potsdam Conference—the third and last Big Three summit
conference during World War II—the Allied leaders attempted,
but failed, to resolve outstanding disagreements and to conclude a final peace settlement of the war. In addition to peace,
the disposition of Germany, Eastern Europe, and the Japanese
surrender were on the agenda.

The personalities involved at the first two conferences were
President Franklin Roosevelt, Prime Minister Winston Churchill, and Premier Joseph Stalin. Roosevelt died in April, 1945,
and was succeeded by Vice President Harry Truman. The
results of the general election of Great Britain were announced
on July 26, after the Potsdam Conference began. Churchill,
head of the Conservative Party, and Clement Attlee, head of
the Labour Party, both attended the conference until the announcement was made that the Labour Party had won. Only
Attlee returned. Stalin was the only Big Three leader in power
before, during, and after the war. Thus, at Potsdam, Stalin
enjoyed some advantage because of his experience and the
enormous power he wielded as dictator of the Soviet Union.

The war in Europe had ended with the unconditional surrender of Germany in May, 1945, the Italians having previously surrendered in 1943. The war in the Pacific, to which
the Soviet Union was not a party, continued, and at the time of
the Potsdam Conference there appeared to be no immediate
prospect for ending it. At the Yalta Conference, Stalin had
promised to break the Soviet-Japanese neutrality pact concluded earlier and enter the Pacific war within two or three
months after the Germans surrendered.

The strategic bombing campaign against Japan, and its ultimate dimension, the use of the atomic bomb, was being developed by the United States, with important British contributions.
This effort involved massive resources and enormous costs,
however. By the summer of 1945, sufficient materials for a
small number of bombs were ready for use. Testing occurred
successfully in New Mexico on July 15. President Truman was
informed of this while en route to Potsdam. Materials for at
least two additional bombs were assembled and rushed to Tinian
in the Marianas Islands, from where superbombers could reach
Japan. Much has been made of the fact that Truman, in an
almost casual manner, informed Stalin of the fact that a bomb
with massive destructive potential had been developed. Stalin
urged him to use it against Japan. The British, who already
knew of the project and its results, also urged the bomb's use.

The Big Three leaders assembled at Potsdam, south of
war-torn Berlin, where the extensive palace complex of the

former Hohenzollern rulers of Prussia was located. The official conference took place at the Cecilienhof Palace on the
shores of Lake Griebnitz. At the time, the Soviet Union occupied all of Germany east of the Elbe River, including Berlin
and its environs. Stalin and the Russians therefore acted as
host of the conference and made all of the arrangements.

At the first of thirteen plenary sessions, Stalin nominated
Truman as chairman. Truman was pleased to serve and had
already prepared an agenda. The Yalta agreements were reaffirmed and elaborated upon. Previously, the European Advisory Committee had overseen Allied international issues in the
European war. At Potsdam, the decision was made to replace it
with the Council of Foreign Ministers, charged with preparation for peace terms in Europe, initially for Italy, Romania,
Bulgaria, Austria, Hungary, and Finland. Other items included
the political and economic principles that would govern Germany, continued discussion of the question of German reparations, German disarmament and military occupation, provisions for punishment of war criminals, and the disposition of
Poland and other Eastern European states.

The disposition of Germany was perhaps the most important,
pressing, and controversial issue on the table of the Big Three.
At Yalta, a general agreement had been reached that Germany
would be occupied by Allied forces. After much deliberation
and debate, the Attlee Plan, named for the then vice prime
minister of Great Britain, was accepted. Germany was to be
temporarily divided into three zones—the Northwest, the Southwest, and the East—to be militarily occupied by Great Britain,
the United States, and the Soviet Union respectively. Berlin,
the old capital, located about one hundred miles inside the
Soviet zone, was also to be divided into three zones.

Originally, there were to be three occupiers, and zones of
occupation were drawn up. However, at the Yalta Conference,
after much persuasion, Stalin reluctantly had agreed with the
Roosevelt-Churchill recommendation that France participate.
Subsequently, the French did participate and a French zone was
carved out contiguous to the French border. However, the French
were bitter and disappointed because they were not a party to
the arrangements, and they had not been invited to Potsdam.

War reparations was another sensitive issue harking back to
the previous treaties at Vienna and Versailles. Stalin consistently pressured for huge amounts to be extracted from Germany, rightly pointing out that Russia, more than any other
power, deserved to be compensated for massive destruction of
its homeland caused by the Germans. Roosevelt and Churchill
acknowledged that, but also recalled the imbroglio caused by
the reparations question after World War I. They effectively
renounced all claims on Germany. A tentative arrangement
was initialed stating that Russia was eligible for the equivalent
of ten billion dollars worth of reparations from Germany.
Further discussion and much debate ensued on how, and especially from which zones of occupation, in-kind reparations
could be obtained. Anglo-American leaders insisted that the
future viability of the German economy must be considered.
Reparations remained a contentious issue between the Soviet

Union and the Anglo-Americans, and final amounts and other details were not decided until later.

The central authority that was to administer occupied Germany was the Allied Control Council. Its objective was to disarm, demobilize, demilitarize, de-Nazify, and democratize Germany. Trials of Nazi war criminals were prepared and conducted at Nuremberg. Certain limits were placed on reparations if a threat to the future of the German economy was indicated.

Complications abounded. The Potsdam Declaration came out of the Potsdam Conference, published on July 26. This was a joint statement to Japan calling for immediate surrender, signed by Truman, Churchill, and a representative of Chiang Kai-shek, the Chinese head of state. Since the Soviet Union was not, at that time, an official belligerent in the Pacific war, she was not a signatory. —*Eugene L. Rasor*

ADDITIONAL READING:

Feis, Herbert. *Between War and Peace: The Potsdam Conference*. Princeton, N.J.: Princeton University Press, 1960. This Pulitzer Prize-winning work by an eminent historian, who had special access to official sources, documents the deterioration of the wartime coalition between the time of the German and the Japanese surrenders.

Leahy, William. *I Was There*. New York: Whittlesey, 1950. An informative memoir of Fleet Admiral Leahy, the long-term chief of staff to Roosevelt and Truman. Contains much detail on the preparations and participation of Truman at the conference.

Mee, Charles. *Meeting at Potsdam*. New York: Evans, 1975. Considers the conference a failure. Blames the Cold War on all sides, asserting that all three powers were opportunists.

Truman, Harry S. *Memoirs*. 2 vols. Garden City, N.Y.: Doubleday, 1955-1956. The personal memoirs of Truman, who was pleased with his performance at the conference under the circumstances.

United States Department of State. Historical Office. *The Conference of Berlin (The Potsdam Conference), 1945*. 2 vols. Washington, D.C.: Government Printing Office, 1960. The official U.S. account of the conference.

SEE ALSO: 1944, Operation Overlord; 1944, Battle of the Bulge; 1945, Yalta Conference; 1945, United Nations Charter Convention; 1945, V-E Day; 1945, Atomic Bombing of Japan; 1947, Truman Doctrine; 1948, Berlin Blockade; 1948, Truman Is Elected President; 1949, North Atlantic Treaty.

1945 ■ ATOMIC BOMBING OF JAPAN: *the use of powerful new weapons against civilian populations precipitates the end of World War II and unleashes the nuclear age*

DATE: August 6 and 9, 1945
LOCALE: Hiroshima and Nagasaki, Japan
CATEGORIES: Science and technology; Wars, uprisings, and civil unrest

KEY FIGURES:

James Francis Byrnes (1879-1972), special assistant to the president, later secretary of state

Leslie Richard Groves (1896-1970), head of the Manhattan Project, which developed the atomic bomb

Henry Lewis Stimson (1867-1950), secretary of war, 1940-1945, and chairman of the Interim Committee on Atomic Policy

Harry S Truman (1884-1972), thirty-third president of the United States, 1945-1953, who ordered the dropping of the bomb on Hiroshima

SUMMARY OF EVENT. At 2:45 A.M. on August 6, 1945, a U.S. B-29 bomber, the *Enola Gay*, took off from the island of Tinian in the Mariana Islands, carrying an atomic bomb. Shortly after 8:15 A.M., from an altitude of about 31,600 feet, the bomb was released over Hiroshima, Japan. It exploded with terrible fury over the center of the city, immediately killing more than eighty thousand people and maiming thousands more. The searing heat that resulted from the explosion set the city afire and utterly destroyed it. Two days later, on August 8, the Soviet Union declared war on Japan. On August 9, over Nagasaki, Japan, at 11:00 A.M., the United States dropped a second atomic bomb, which killed more than forty thousand of the city's inhabitants.

The destruction of Hiroshima and Nagasaki was a shock to the Japanese, but the Soviet Union's declaration of war was devastating, for it removed all hope of Soviet mediation with the West to end the war. Moreover, it necessitated that the Kwangtung Army—the force that Japanese extremists were hoping to bring home to face the anticipated Allied invasions—remain in Manchuria to protect the region from Soviet invasion. Throughout the day and into the night of August 9, the Japanese Supreme War Council met in grim deliberation. At 2:00 A.M., on August 10, the Japanese prime minister asked Emperor Hirohito to decide Japan's future. Speaking softly, the emperor told his ministers that he wished the war brought to an end. That day, Japan announced that it would accept the terms of surrender that the Allies had demanded in the Potsdam declaration, with the addition of a sole condition not contained therein: that the position of the emperor be protected. The Japanese accepted the Allies' terms on August 14, 1945, now known as V-J (for "victory in Japan") day.

The dropping of the atomic bomb by the United States was one of the most portentous events in history. Development of the bomb had begun in 1939, after a small group of scientists persuaded the U.S. government that such a weapon was feasible and that Germany was already conducting experiments in atomic energy. The research program that began in October, 1939, ultimately developed into the two-billion-dollar Manhattan Project, which was headed by Leslie R. Groves. The project's goal was to produce a bomb before the Germans did. Few U.S. political or military officials ever doubted that such a bomb, if produced, would not be used. Yet before the first bomb was perfected and tested, Germany surrendered. Only Japan remained at war with the Allies. Early in 1945, as the first bomb

The devastation wreaked on the Japanese city of Nagasaki, which suffered the effects of the second atomic bombing by the United States, would be felt not only in physical destruction but also in radiation-related illnesses for years to come. (National Archives)

neared completion, some scientists began to have doubts about using it. The wave of horror that might follow its use and the moral burden of unleashing such an awesome weapon might, they thought, offset any immediate advantage the bomb could provide. Several options were possible: The United States might demonstrate the new weapon on a barren island before representatives of the United Nations, who could then warn the Japanese of its destructive power; the bomb might be dropped on a military target in Japan after giving a preliminary warning; or the United States could refuse to drop it at all.

While the scientists pondered such choices, military officials prepared to use the bomb. By the end of 1944, possible targets in Japan had been selected, and a B-29 squadron had begun training for the bomb's delivery. Two weeks after President Roosevelt died in 1945, Secretary of War Henry L. Stimson, on April 25, met with the new president, Harry S Truman, informed him about the bomb, and predicted that in four months it would be available for use. Upon Stimson's recommendation, Truman appointed a special Interim Committee on Atomic Policy to consider use of the bomb. On June l, 1945,

the committee recommended to the president that the bomb be used against Japan as soon as possible, be used against a military target, and be dropped without prior warning. By early July, 1945, as Truman left for the Potsdam Conference in Germany to discuss postwar settlements with Great Britain and the Soviet Union, he had decided to use the bomb once it was perfected. On July 16, in the Trinity Flats near Alamogordo, New Mexico, the first atomic bomb was successfully tested. The United States now had its weapon, although the war in the Pacific had already driven Japan to the brink of surrender. As early as September, 1944, the Japanese had sought to sound out the Allies concerning peace terms. On the eve of the Potsdam Conference, the Japanese ambassador in Moscow asked the Soviet government to mediate with the Allies to end the war. Japan could not accept unconditional surrender, but the Japanese appeared ready to surrender under terms that would allow them to preserve the position of the emperor in the Japanese system. This the Allies would not accept.

The Truman Administration faced difficult problems. Total defeat and unconditional surrender of Japan might require a costly and prolonged invasion of the Japanese home islands. The Soviets, as they had promised at Yalta in February, 1945, were scheduled to enter the Pacific war in early August. Although their support had been eagerly sought until the spring of 1945, it now appeared less vital; indeed, Truman now hoped to defeat Japan before the Soviet Union could effectively enter the war and gain any control over the postwar settlement with Japan. Also, use of the atomic bomb in Japan would indicate to the Soviets just how powerful the United States was. On July 26, from Potsdam, the Allies called upon Japan to surrender unconditionally or suffer "the utter devastation of the Japanese homeland," a veiled reference the significance of which only the Allies fully understood. The Potsdam declaration did not mention the atomic bomb and did not offer Japan any terms. The Japanese government chose not to reply to the declaration, while it waited for a reply to the peace overtures it had made through the Soviet government. For home consumption, the Japanese government called the Potsdam declaration "unworthy of public notice."

In the Mariana Islands, two bombs had been readied for use, and the B-29 crews were standing by. Truman ordered the U.S. Air Corps to drop them. When they were dropped, the age of atomic warfare and the Cold War began.

During the fiftieth anniversary of the dropping of the bomb on Hiroshima, there was considerable controversy in the United States concerning why the first bomb over Hiroshima was dropped. The Smithsonian Institution first proposed an exhibit that would have the *Enola Gay* as its centerpiece with four side displays, two of which would depict the devastation of the Japanese cities of Hiroshima and Nagasaki. With these displays, it intended to depict the Japanese as victims. Veterans' groups and Congress complained, pointing out that the bomb was dropped not only to end the war but also to retaliate for the Japanese attack on Pearl Harbor, which produced U.S. victims. In spite of the efforts of various scholars, the exhibit ultimately simply contained the *Enola Gay*. Thus, the significance of dropping the bomb on Hiroshima, the start of the Cold War and the atomic age, is by no means uncontroverted. The question still remains: Was it necessary to drop the bomb in the first place?   —*Burl L. Noggle, updated by Jennifer Eastman*

ADDITIONAL READING:

Alperovitz, Gar. *The Decision to Use the Atomic Bomb and the Architecture of an American Myth*. New York: Alfred A. Knopf, 1995. A detailed account of the decisions of political leaders and others in considering whether to drop the bomb. Argues that the decision was unnecessary.

Gardner, Lloyd C. *Architects of Illusion: Men and Ideas in American Foreign Policy, 1941-1949*. Chicago: Quadrangle Books, 1970. Discusses ten U.S. policymakers during the years just before and after the bomb appeared as an element in U.S. foreign policy. Valuable in placing the 1945 decision in a broader setting.

Hachiya, Michihiko. *Hiroshima Diary: The Journal of a Japanese Physician, August 6-September 30, 1945*. Translated and edited by Warner Wells. Chapel Hill: University of North Carolina Press, 1955. Hachiya, director of a hospital in Hiroshima, was badly wounded in the explosion, but kept a diary of his own case and of events following the blast. Offers much medical detail and reveals the full horror of the bomb, especially regarding the slow and horrible deaths of some who survived the initial impact.

Hersey, John. *Hiroshima*. New York: Alfred A. Knopf, 1946. This story of the effect of the atomic bomb upon six survivors at Hiroshima is a classic of World War II reporting, by a journalist who was there soon after the explosion.

LaFeber, Walter. *America, Russia, and the Cold War, 1945-1971*. 2d ed. New York: John Wiley & Sons, 1972. One of the most judicious and comprehensive of the "revisionist" studies on the origins of the Cold War. Assigns more responsibility for the Cold War to the United States than do earlier books.

Lifton, Robert Jay, and Greg Mitchell. *Hiroshima in America: Fifty Years of Denial*. New York: G. P. Putnam's Sons, 1995. Interesting psychological profiles of some of the people involved in the decision to drop the bomb. The thesis that the Hiroshima bomb has profoundly affected the U.S. psyche negatively for the subsequent half century is less persuasive.

Rosenblatt, Roger. *Witness: The World Since Hiroshima*. Boston: Little, Brown, 1985. Includes the differing perspectives of a Hiroshima victim, a physicist, and President Richard Nixon in discussing how the bomb has affected people's lives since it was dropped.

Wyden, Peter. *Day One Before Hiroshima and After*. New York: Simon & Schuster, 1984. Emphasizes the physicists who created the bomb and their complex interactions with one another.

SEE ALSO: 1942, Manhattan Project; 1944, Superfortress Bombing of Japan.

1945 ■ WAR BRIDES ACT: *immigration regulations are waived to allow foreign-born spouses and children of U.S. military personnel to settle in the United States*

DATE: December 28, 1945
LOCALE: United States
CATEGORIES: Immigration; Laws and acts
SUMMARY OF EVENT. Between 1939 and 1946, more than sixteen million U.S. servicemen, primarily single and between eighteen and thirty years of age, were deployed to war theaters in foreign lands. Although the U.S. government discouraged servicemen from marrying at all—believing the single soldier, without distractions, would be of more value to the war effort—one million marriages to foreign nationals occurred during and shortly after the war. Aware of the potential for these romantic liaisons, the United States War Department had issued a regulation requiring personnel on duty in any foreign country or possession of the United States to notify their commanding officer of any intention to marry

at least two months in advance. Enacted in June, 1942, the regulation demanded strict adherence and the waiting period was waived rarely, with the possible exception for the pregnancy of the bride-to-be. Usually, permission to marry was granted; however, certain couples, for example U.S.-German, U.S.-Japanese, and those of different races, either encountered longer waiting periods or were denied permission completely.

Many of those couples who had been granted permission and had married were separated for two to three years. In October, 1945, the Married Women's Association picketed for transport to allow their families to reunite. Evidently, the three thousand members' voices were heard, for on December 28, 1945, the Seventy-ninth Congress passed an act to expedite the admission to the United States of alien spouses and alien minor children of U.S. citizens who had served in or were honorably discharged from the armed forces during World War II. These spouses had to meet the criteria for admission under the current immigration laws, including a thorough medical examination, and the application had to be filed within three years of the date of the act.

Following passage of the War Brides Act, thirty vessels, primarily hospital ships and army troopships, were selected to transport the women, children, and a few men ("male war brides") to the United States. Even the *Queen Elizabeth* and the *Queen Mary* were recruited for the task, because of their capacity to carry large groups of people. Transportation requests were prioritized by the military as follows: dependents of personnel above the fourth enlisted grade, dependents of personnel already placed on orders to the United States, wives of prisoners of war, wives of men wounded in action, and wives of men hospitalized in the United States. At the bottom of the priority pool were fiancés and spouses in interracial marriages.

Before debarking, the spouse (usually a woman) had to present her passport and visa, her sworn affidavit from her husband that he could and would support her upon arrival, two copies of her birth certificate, two copies of any police record she might have, any military discharge papers she might have, and a railroad ticket to her destination from New York. The families who saw them off knew they might never see their children and grandchildren again.

The American Red Cross was officially requested by the War Department to function as a clearinghouse for the brides, and many of their volunteers served as "trainers" for the women in how to become American wives. Since many did not speak English, the Red Cross also offered classes to aid in practical communication skills.

On January 26, 1946, the first war bride ship, the SS *Argentina*, left Southampton, England, with 452 brides, 173 children, and 1 groom on board. Lauded as the "Pilgrim Mothers" or "The Diaper Run," the voyage was highly publicized. Many of the brides, upon arriving in the United States on February 4, were greeted by the U.S. press.

In Germany and Japan, permission to marry had not easily been attained and often was not granted at all. The ban on marriage to Germans was lifted on December 11, 1946, with twenty-five hundred applications submitted by the end of the year; in Japan, the ban lingered much longer.

During the first months of occupation, a half-million U.S. soldiers had been stationed in or near Yokohama. Many young women, fearing for their lives, hid from these "barbarians," but since the U.S. military was often the only source of employment, the women were forced to venture out. The country was in a cultural flux, resulting from economic deprivation, matriarchal predominance and female enfranchisement, and the abjuration of divinity by Emperor Hirohito. As the U.S. soldiers and Japanese women worked together, romantic relationships often developed, and because official permission to marry could not be obtained, many such couples were wed in secret in traditional Japanese ceremonies.

Although as many as one hundred thousand Japanese brides were deserted, others sought immigration to the United States. However, one proviso of the War Brides Act was that émigrés could not be excluded under any other provision of immigration law. The Oriental Exclusion Act of 1924 was still in place, and although Public Law 199 had overridden the act to allow Chinese immigration, the Japanese were still excluded. Many were not allowed admission to the United States until July, 1947, when President Harry Truman signed the Soldier Brides Act, a thirty-day reprieve on race inadmissibility.

In many cases, life for the war brides in the United States was not what they had expected. Many were treated poorly by isolationists who placed personal blame on all foreigners for U.S. involvement in the war, and many had to tolerate the scorn of former sweethearts who had jilted them. Because of the influx of soldiers returning to the civilian population, available housing and jobs were limited. Often the brides found themselves in the middle of a family-run farm, with some as sharecroppers. Frequently, when adjustment to civilian life was difficult for the former military man, he would rejoin his outfit, leaving the bride behind with his family— strangers who were sometimes hostile to the foreigner in their midst. Many of the marriages made in haste soured just as quickly through homesickness, promises unkept, or abuse. War brides who were unhappy or abused often stayed in their marriages, however, from fear of losing their children or of being deported.

Marriage did not confer automatic citizenship on foreign brides. They were required to pass exams to be naturalized, and many were still incapable of communicating in any but their native tongue. Public assistance was unavailable for these women.

Within one year of the mass exodus from Europe and Asia, one out of three of the war marriages had ended in divorce, and it was predicted that by 1950, the statistics would be two out of three. This prediction proved incorrect, however. Many of the war brides not only preserved their marriages but also became valuable members of their communities and contributors to American culture. In April, 1985, several hundred of these women, men, and children journeyed to Long Beach, California, for a reunion, appropriately held aboard the dry-docked *Queen Mary*.
—*Joyce Duncan*

ADDITIONAL READING:

Hibbert, Joyce. *The War Brides*. Toronto: PMA Books, 1978. Discussion of the mobilization and acclimation of war brides.

Kubat, Daniel, et al. *The Politics of Migration Policies*. New York: Center for Migration Studies, 1979. Discusses immigration laws and the political control behind them.

Michener, James. *Sayonara*. New York: Ballantine, 1954. Fictional work that casts light on the occupation of Japan.

Moravia, Alberto. *Two Women*. New York: Playboy, 1981. A novel that recounts the lives of two war brides.

Shukert, Elfrieda Berthiaume, and Barbara Smith Scibetta. *War Brides of World War II*. Novato, Calif.: Presidio Press, 1988. The definitive work on the topic; includes interviews with the brides.

SEE ALSO: 1922, Cable Act; 1924, Immigration Act of 1924.

1946 ■ EMPLOYMENT ACT: *Congress passes legislation to stimulate the economy following World War II*

DATE: February 20, 1946
LOCALE: Washington, D.C.
CATEGORIES: Business and labor; Economics; Laws and acts
KEY FIGURES:

John Maynard Keynes (1883-1946), British economist who advocated demand management to achieve full employment and economic stability

Leon Hirsh Keyserling (1908-1987), vice chairman, later chairman, of the Council of Economic Advisors

James Edward Murray (1876-1961), senator from Montana who initiated the full-employment bill

Edwin Griswold Nourse (1883-1974), economist and first chairman of the Council of Economic Advisors

SUMMARY OF EVENT. During the last months of World War II (1941-1945), people in the United States looked ahead anxiously to the nation's postwar economy. Their gravest worry was the possibility of a catastrophic depression. When the war ended, the nation would face the immediate task of demobilizing eleven million members of the armed forces and reconverting the economy to a peacetime basis. As soon as possible, a war-weary nation hoped to scrap price controls and rationing, cut taxes, and turn industry back to the production of consumer goods, such as automobiles. Still, the memory lingered of the Great Depression of the 1930's, with its mass unemployment, farm foreclosures, bank failures, and idle factories. Perhaps the sudden end of wartime spending would again plunge the nation back into depression. By early 1945, many economists were predicting eight to ten million unemployed when the returning troops were released from service. However, the levels of production, income, and employment reached during the war had given the United States a taste of a full-production economy. After the sacrifices of war, people were determined to settle for nothing less. In 1944, the Demo-

cratic platform pledged to guarantee full employment after the war, and the Republicans made virtually the same promise.

Only a month after Hiroshima, as hostilities ceased, the new president, Harry S Truman, urged the passage of full-employment legislation then pending before Congress. The outcome was the Employment Act of 1946. On January 22, 1945, Senator James E. Murray had introduced a full-employment bill. The bill asserted that "all Americans able to work and seeking work have the right to useful, remunerative, regular, and full-time employment. . . ." Furthermore, it was the government's responsibility "to provide such a volume of Federal investment and expenditure as may be needed to assure continuing full employment. . . ." The president was directed to present a forecast of aggregate demand for goods and services throughout the economy, compare it with the level needed for full employment, and recommend changes in federal spending to remedy any shortfall or excess.

Murray's Full Employment Bill passed the Senate (with amendments) on September 28, 1945, by a vote of 71 to 10, and was endorsed by President Truman. Over the next year, however, the Murray bill underwent a drastic metamorphosis. Congressional conservatives cut out any federal guarantee of the right to a job or of full employment. They also reduced the force of the government's commitment to forecasting and eliminated specific mention of public works and other kinds of compensatory spending. The ultimate result was the Employment Act, signed into law by President Truman February 20, 1946.

The final law contained two main provisions. The first committed the government "to promote maximum employment, production, and purchasing power." In practice, this strange wording came to be seen as a mandate to avoid significant depression or inflation. Second, two agencies were established to carry out the commitment. Congress set up a Council of Economic Advisors (CEA), consisting of three economists, to assist the president in drawing up an annual report on the state of the economy. In Congress, a Joint Committee on the Economic Report (later renamed the Joint Economic Committee—JEC) was to review the president's report and make recommendations of its own. President Truman soon appointed Edwin Nourse, Leon Keyserling, and John D. Clark as the first Council of Economic Advisors.

The Employment Act was a statutory expression of what the United States had learned during the Great Depression and World War II. The act's spiritual father was British economist John Maynard Keynes. In 1936, Keynes had published his landmark work *The General Theory of Employment, Interest, and Money*. Keynes did not endorse fashionable proposals for nationalization or economic planning of specific industries. Rather, he argued that government could help a free market to work well if it used monetary and fiscal measures to help stabilize the aggregate demand for goods and services. A nation, Keynes argued, could actually pull itself out of a depression if the government stimulated the economy through deficit spending for public works and other purposes. As supporting evidence, many people pointed to the rapidity with which the

U.S. economy was restored to full employment when federal defense spending skyrocketed from 1940 on. The ambitious provisions of the original Full Employment Bill assumed that government economists could accurately forecast undesirable declines or increases in aggregate demand, and that government could easily offset these with fiscal measures, such as spending increases or tax-rate changes. Well-founded skepticism about both of these propositions lay behind the scaling down of the bill's scope.

From the end of World War II through the end of the twentieth century, every president has used the philosophy and machinery of the Employment Act to keep the economy from falling into a dangerous boom-and-bust cycle. In the immediate postwar years, Truman faced a confusing economic situation that was just the reverse of what experts had predicted—shortages instead of surplus and inflation instead of depression and deflation. These problems became acute during the Korean War, and both the CEA and the JEC contributed significantly to research on managing the economy under renewed war conditions. Their influence helped persuade Congress to increase tax rates so that the war did not lead to large federal deficits.

Experience soon demonstrated some problems inherent in the workings of the Employment Act. The first chairman, Edwin Nourse, visualized the CEA as a relatively nonpolitical body reflecting the technical expertise of professional economists. Realistically, however, the CEA had no clientele or constituency of its own, and therefore no real political power, except in relation to the president; therefore, CEA members have been chosen for conformity with the outlook of the president. This has meant that the likelihood that the CEA will shape the president's economic views is not great. A second issue arises because the Federal Reserve System, which has potentially a large influence on demand management policies, is relatively independent of the president and therefore of the CEA.

The CEA has involved many prominent professional economists, such as James Tobin, Herbert Stein, Walter Heller, Martin Feldstein, and Alan Blinder. The agency has produced significant research and commentary, but has not been a major policy influence. Nor has the JEC, which does not initiate legislation in its own right.

In 1978, the Employment Act was significantly extended by the Full Employment and Balanced Growth Act (Humphrey-Hawkins Act), which established nonbinding targets of 4 percent for unemployment and 3 percent for inflation, to be achieved by 1983. The unemployment target generally was recognized as unrealistic. Good economic performance in the 1980's and 1990's usually involved getting unemployment below 6 percent. However, the inflation target was eventually fulfilled in the early 1990's. The Humphrey-Hawkins Act directly addressed the issue of Federal Reserve Board policy, instructing the Federal Reserve to report directly to Congress concerning the relationship between its policy targets and the goals articulated by the act.

After 1946, by a combination of good luck and good man-agement, the United States economy achieved a record of economic stability far superior to earlier times. The principal blemish on this record was the severe inflation that raised consumer prices an average of 8 percent per year in the decade ending in 1982. Beginning in 1982, however, the economy entered a phase of economic expansion, which was interrupted by only a brief, mild recession in 1990-1991 before continuing on through 1995. During this period, demand management and business-cycle policy ceased to be a major focus of concern in government economic policy.

—*Donald Holley, updated by Paul B. Trescott*

ADDITIONAL READING:

Bailey, Stephen K. *Congress Makes a Law: The Story Behind the Employment Act of 1946*. New York: Columbia University Press, 1950. Very few pieces of congressional legislation have been so meticulously documented. Captures the personalities and interest-group infighting, and discusses the role of economic analysis.

Canterbury, E. Ray. *The President's Council of Economic Advisors: A Study of Its Functions and Its Influence on the Chief Executive's Decisions*. New York: Exposition Press, 1961. Describes the council's growing importance during the 1950's and 1960's.

Flash, Edward S. *Economic Advice and Presidential Leadership: The Council of Economic Advisors*. New York: Columbia University Press, 1965. A political scientist examines both the structure of the CEA within the government and the personal roles of Keyserling, Arthur Burns, and Heller.

Nourse, Edwin G. *Economics in the Public Service: Administrative Aspects of the Employment Act*. New York: Harcourt, Brace and World, 1953. The first chairman of the CEA explains the conflict between detached expertise and political partisanship and describes conflicts within the CEA between himself and Keyserling.

Stein, Herbert. *The Fiscal Revolution in America*. Chicago: University of Chicago Press, 1969. Stein, a member of the CEA under President Richard Nixon, effectively describes the impact of Keynesian ideas on the management of government financial policies.

SEE ALSO: 1944, G.I. Bill; 1950, Korean War.

1947 ■ CANADA'S CITIZENSHIP ACT: *the first legal definition of Canadian citizenship, reflecting a growing Canadian nationalism*

DATE: January 1, 1947
LOCALE: Ottawa, Ontario
CATEGORIES: Canadian history; Laws and acts
KEY FIGURES:
John George Diefenbaker (1895-1979), Conservative
    member of Parliament and a principal critic of the act
William Lyon Mackenzie King (1874-1950), prime minister
    and Liberal Party leader

Paul Joseph James Martin (1903-1992), cabinet member responsible for the Citizenship Act

SUMMARY OF EVENT. Before passage of the 1947 Canadian Citizenship Act there were, in the strict legal sense, no Canadian citizens. Legally, Canadians were British subjects. British subjects born outside Canada, unless specifically prohibited, became Canadians upon establishing permanent residence in Canada without need of any formalities.

The only legislation defining Canadian nationality was in various immigration and naturalization acts, a situation that failed to satisfy the growing nationalism of twentieth century Canada. Non-British subjects had to meet the provisions of laws and bureaucratic decisions designed to implement a "white Canada" policy. Canada's Chinese Exclusion Act of 1885 barred immigration from that country. The Immigration Act of 1910 continued and extended that policy, by authorizing the cabinet minister responsible for immigration control to exclude any race deemed unsuitable to the climate or requirements of Canada. Although the 1952 act would substitute "ethnic group" for "race," not until 1962 did Canada finally end racial discrimination in admissions.

Unlike the United States, which set numerical quotas designed to limit or exclude nationalities deemed undesirable, Canada left it to ministerial and bureaucratic discretion to reject or approve applicants for admission. Pre-World War II immigration policy encouraged immigration from Britain, the United States, and the countries of Western Europe. Italians, Slavs, Greeks, and Jews were thought of as less assimilable and less desirable; their access to Canada was limited or denied. Asians were barred. By government policy, all blacks appearing at Canada's border with the United States were refused admission on medical grounds, a decision from which there was no appeal.

Non-British subjects lawfully admitted to permanent residence in Canada who were more than twenty-one years of age and had resided in Canada for five years could apply to the nearest court for naturalization, where they would be asked to produce evidence that they were of good character and met the requirements of the immigration laws. If the court agreed, the candidate would, upon renouncing all foreign allegiances and taking an oath of allegiance to the monarch of Great Britain, be naturalized as a British subject and Canadian national.

This situation failed to satisfy the feelings of Canadian nationalism that had been growing from the time Canada became a self-governing dominion in 1867 and that were intensified as Canada began to develop its own foreign policy and sent an army to fight in World War II. Nationalists wanted a definition of Canadian nationality that expressed the country's uniqueness and removed all vestiges of the colonial past. Paul Martin, the son of an Irish father and a French Canadian mother, had been powerfully affected by the sacrifices of Canadian troops during World War II. When he became secretary of state in the Liberal Party administration of William Lyon Mackenzie King in 1945, the first piece of legislation Martin undertook to move through Parliament was a law that would define Canadian citizenship specifically. He clearly hoped that a Canadian citizenship separate from that of Great Britain would serve as a unifying symbol for the nation, one that would overcome sectional differences among the provinces and bring together French- and English-speaking Canadians. John Diefenbaker led the Conservative Party opposition to the bill, arguing that distinguishing Canadian citizens from other British subjects would lead to dissension and an undesirable split in the British Commonwealth of Nations. With the strong support of King, the objections of opponents were overcome, and the bill became law on July 1, 1946, to take effect on January 1, 1947.

All persons who had been born in Canada or on a Canadian ship, except for children of foreign diplomats, were declared to be natural-born citizens of Canada, entitled to a certificate to that effect. King proudly accepted the first such certificate on January 3, 1947, in an elaborate ceremony inaugurating the act.

Children born outside Canada before January 1, 1947, to fathers who had been born in Canada, or were British subjects with permanent residences in Canada, or had been naturalized under Canadian law, also would be considered to be natural-born Canadian citizens. A person born outside Canada after December 31, 1946, would be a natural-born citizen if the father were a Canadian citizen, the child's birth were registered with the appropriate authorities by the age of two years, and the child either established residency in Canada or filed a declaration of retention of Canadian citizenship before reaching twenty-one years of age.

The act provided that all who had been included in a certificate of naturalization before January 1, 1947, as well as all British subjects with a permanent residence in Canada, were now Canadian citizens. The new act treated citizenship as a personal and individual right of women. A woman who was a Canadian citizen would no longer lose her nationality upon marriage to an alien, nor would marriage to a Canadian citizen confer Canadian nationality. Previously, women had gained or lost nationality by marriage.

Aliens, as well as British subjects who were not already Canadian citizens, had to fulfill certain requirements to be naturalized. The person had to be twenty-one years of age, have been lawfully admitted to permanent residency, and have lived in Canada for at least five years, be of good character, have an adequate knowledge of either English or French, and demonstrate knowledge of the responsibilities and privileges of Canadian citizenship. A certificate of citizenship would be issued when the applicant, in open court, renounced all conflicting allegiances and took an oath to bear true allegiance to the monarch of Great Britain, to uphold faithfully the laws of Canada, and to fulfill all duties of a Canadian citizen.

Not until the Citizenship Act of 1976, which came into effect on February 15, 1977, was the 1947 act replaced. Distinctions between the citizenship status of men and women were eliminated; children born abroad to Canadian mothers, as well as Canadian fathers, would now count as natural-born Canadian citizens. Persons born outside Canada to a Canadian mother and a non-Canadian father between January 1, 1947, and February 14, 1977, who had not been able to claim Canadian citizenship under the previous act, could apply for citizenship certificates under the 1976 act.

Other provisions permitted persons to apply for naturalization after they had been resident legally for at least three of the previous four years and as early as eighteen years of age. Applications went to a citizenship court that judged whether a candidate met the requirements on language proficiency and knowledge of Canada. If accepted, the candidate took a prescribed Oath of Citizenship, promising allegiance to Canada's monarch, pledging respect for Canadian laws, and promising to fulfill all duties of a citizen. There were no special privileges for British subjects, and the law spoke of Canadians as also "citizens of the Commonwealth" rather than British subjects.

Other developments in the years after 1947 also strengthened the sense of Canadian nationality. Canadian participation independent of Great Britain in the United Nations and the North Atlantic Treaty Organization (NATO), the appointment from 1952 on of Canadians rather than British aristocrats as governor general of Canada, the change in the royal title to Queen of Canada in 1953, and adoption of the red maple leaf Canadian flag in 1964, all helped reinforce and confirm belief in Canadian uniqueness. With the passage of a Canadian Constitution in 1982, which included a Charter of Rights and Freedoms, the country had total independence from Britain.

The main challenge to this idea of nationality came from the province of Quebec, where belief in the special character of French Canadian culture led to demands, first for autonomy, and then for establishment of a separate sovereign nation to protect that culture. Although referenda in the province in 1980 and 1995 failed to produce majorities for separation from the rest of Canada, the relationship between Quebec and Canada has remained unsettled. Until this issue can be put to rest, the ideal of a single, unique Canadian citizenship uniting a bilingual and multicultural Canada cannot be achieved.

—Milton Berman

ADDITIONAL READING:

Bothwell, Robert, Ian Drummond, and John English. *Canada Since 1945: Power, Politics, and Provincialism.* Rev. ed. Toronto: University of Toronto Press, 1989. Includes valuable information on the development of Canadian nationalism and Quebec separatism.

Brubaker, William Rogers, ed. *Immigration and the Politics of Citizenship in Europe and North America.* Lanham, Md.: University Press of America, 1989. Articles compare the impact of postwar mass immigration on citizenship policies on both sides of the Atlantic.

Cairns, Alan, and Cynthia Williams. *Constitutionalism, Citizenship, and Society in Canada.* Toronto: University of Toronto Press, 1985. Explores the relationship between citizenship, social change, and the evolution of political communities in Canada.

Hawkins, Freda. *Canada and Immigration: Public Policy and Public Concern.* 2d ed. Kingston, Ont.: McGill-Queens University Press, 1988. Examines changes in immigration regulations that reflect changing concepts of who is acceptable as a Canadian.

Martin, Paul. *Far from Home.* Vol. 1 in *A Very Public Life.* Ottawa, Ont.: Deneau, 1983. The autobiography of the 1947 Canadian Citizenship Act's sponsor contains a detailed description of the passage of the act.

SEE ALSO: 1867, British North America Act; 1931, Statute of Westminster; 1982, Canada's Constitution Act.

1947 ■ TRUMAN DOCTRINE: *following World War II, the president articulates the cornerstone of forty years of subsequent U.S. foreign policy*

DATE: March 12, 1947
LOCALE: Washington, D.C.
CATEGORY: Diplomacy and international relations
KEY FIGURES:
James Francis Byrnes (1879-1972), secretary of state
Winston Leonard Spencer Churchill (1874-1965), prime minister of Great Britain
George F. Kennan (1904-1995), official in the U.S. State Department
George Catlett Marshall (1880-1959), secretary of state
Harry S Truman (1884-1972), thirty-third president of the United States, 1945-1953

SUMMARY OF EVENT. Soon after the conclusion of World War II, the United States was faced with the necessity of finding a new approach to the problem of peaceful stabilization in international affairs. Franklin D. Roosevelt's concept of a postwar peace based on cooperation between the United States and the Soviet Union proved to be ineffective. The Soviet army occupied most of Eastern and Central Europe, and it was made clear that the Soviet Union would not tolerate independent regimes there. Despite the agreements made at the Yalta Conference, Joseph Stalin, the Soviet dictator, unilaterally imposed communist regimes on Poland, Hungary, Bulgaria, Czechoslovakia, and Romania. The protests of the United States and Great Britain did not alter this policy of Soviet control. Furthermore, the Soviet government attempted to expand into areas where it had no military control, including Greece, Turkey, and Iran.

In confronting these emergencies, the United States at first tried ad hoc measures which, although essentially successful in achieving their immediate objectives, failed to establish policy guidelines for the postwar world. In Iran, the Soviet Union refused to withdraw its occupation forces and made demands through diplomatic channels for exclusive oil and mineral rights. The United States and Great Britain joined in a strong protest, which implied the threat of Western military assistance to counter Soviet pressure. In March, 1946, Soviet troops began a complete withdrawal, and the Iranian government succeeded in stabilizing its rule. In the case of Turkey, the Soviet Union sent several diplomatic notes in 1945 and 1946 that demanded the cession of border territory and a joint administration of the Dardanelles. These demands were to be ratified in a treaty that also would provide for the leasing of navy and army bases in the Dardanelles to the Soviets to implement joint control. Following a second Soviet note, the United States sent a strong naval fleet into the Mediterranean, the first U.S. warships to be sent into those waters during peacetime since 1803. A week later, Great Britain joined the United States in rejecting Soviet demands on Turkey. Meanwhile, in Greece, only extensive British military and economic aid prevented a complete collapse of the war-torn country and a coup d'état by communist guerrillas.

Following extensive domestic debate, the United States formally abandoned its traditional peacetime isolationist approach to world affairs and adopted a long-range policy intended to deal with Soviet expansionism. One position in the debate was dramatized by Winston Churchill, the former prime minister of Great Britain, in a speech at Fulton, Missouri, in early 1946. There, with President Truman on the platform, Churchill characterized the Soviet Union as an expansionist state that would react only to a strong counterforce. Soviet expansion, Churchill believed, could be prevented only by a collaboration between the United States and Great Britain to preserve the independence of Europe and to prevent the extension of what came to be called the Iron Curtain. A contrasting attitude was expressed by Secretary of Commerce Henry A. Wallace, who declared that only American-Soviet cooperation could prevent another war. He pointed out that the Soviet desire for control of areas on its borders was understandable and reasonable, and that the United States had long acted to secure its own hemispheric security. Substantial segments of U.S. public opinion supported either Churchill or Wallace. However, the State Department sought a middle ground. Rejecting both the Soviet-expansion position of Churchill and the sphere-of-influence concept of Wallace, Secretary of State James F. Byrnes urged that the Soviet Union adopt a more cooperative diplomatic policy. The United States, he said, should pursue a policy of firmness and patience and wait for the Soviets to see the reasonableness of negotiation. It appeared to many, including President Truman, that the United States was the one that was always being reasonable, not the Soviet Union. By 1947, the administration had adopted the position that the revolutionary postulates of the Soviet regime made traditional diplomacy impossible.

The first step in the development of the new policy toward the Soviet Union appeared in response to the continuing Soviet threat to Greece and Turkey. In February, 1947, Great Britain informed the State Department that His Majesty's Government could no longer continue to support the regime in Greece. Great Britain, like all Western Europe, was suffering from grave economic problems. As the British Empire retreated, the United States stepped forward. Within the next few weeks, President Truman decided that the independence of Greece and the recovery of Europe were crucial for the security of the United States. On March 12, 1947, the president appeared before a joint session of Congress and presented what became known as the Truman Doctrine. He outlined the desperate situation in both Greece and Turkey and called upon the American people to "help free peoples to maintain their free institutions and their national integrity against aggressive movements that seek to impose upon them totalitarian regimes." Most important, he pointed out, was the fact that such totalitarian aggression was a direct threat to the security of the United States. In response, Congress appropriated four hundred million dollars for economic aid to both Greece and Turkey. Additionally, the president was authorized to dispatch civilian and military advisers to help both nations defend their sovereignty.

The next step in this new policy was to bring the same consideration to bear upon Western Europe, an even more critical area. There is debate over the degree to which the Marshall Plan was motivated by the desire to contain Soviet influence in Western Europe; nevertheless, to proponents of this new internationalism in U.S. foreign policy, it clearly seemed axiomatic that if aid to Greece and Turkey could be justified because of their strategic importance, the United States must aid other European countries where the situation was equally desperate. Great Britain was suffering from the wartime destruction of its factories and the loss of its capability to export manufactured goods. Germany was in ruins and virtually incapable of feeding its population. In France and Italy, the Communist Party had wide support within the industrial laboring class and was working by both overt and covert means for a radical change in the government of both countries. A further difficulty was that the winter of 1946-1947 was the most severe experienced by Europeans for generations.

From a military viewpoint, new weaponry made it essential that European control of the Atlantic gateways be in friendly hands. In terms of trained technicians, industrial capacity, and raw materials, Western Europe was a potential giant worth keeping in the U.S. camp. These factors led to an announcement by the new secretary of state, George C. Marshall, at Harvard University in June, 1947, of what came to be known as the Marshall Plan. Assuming that the European countries could develop a cooperative approach to their economic problems, the United States, said Marshall, would assist in their recovery. Congress eventually authorized a grant of seventeen billion dollars to the Organization for European Economic Cooperation over a four-year period. A total of about twelve billion dollars was actually spent. Although aid was offered to all European nations, including the Soviet Union, the Soviet-dominated areas were not permitted to cooperate because that would have meant revealing Soviet economic secrets and sacrificing Soviet economic control. Success of the Marshall Plan emerged quickly; in 1952, Europe exceeded its prewar production figures by some 200 percent.

A discussion of the theory behind the policy embodied in the Truman Doctrine and the Marshall Plan appeared in an unsigned article on the subject of containment in the July, 1947, issue of *Foreign Affairs*. The author, it was later disclosed, was George F. Kennan, a high-ranking member of the State Department. Kennan's essay proposed that the antagonism that existed between the United States and the Soviet Union was merely the logical extension of certain basic Soviet assumptions. The United States, Kennan maintained, could count on Soviet hostility because the rhetoric of the Bolshevik Revolution demanded war against capitalist states. World War II had submerged this antagonism only temporarily. "These characteristics of Soviet policy," he wrote, "like the postulates from which they flow, are basic to the internal nature of Soviet power, and will be with us . . . until the nature of Soviet power is changed."

The immediate question, Kennan insisted, was how the United States should counter this new ideological crusade and power drive that threatened to engulf Europe. In Kennan's view, the United States should adopt a policy of "long-term, patient, but firm and vigilant containment." To counter the Soviet policy, the United States should adopt a long-range course of diplomacy toward the Soviet Union and pursue it consistently. This containment, or the counterapplication of force wherever Soviet expansion threatened, had a negative aspect, because it put a tremendous burden on U.S. consistency and steadfastness. On the positive side, through containment, the United States could help to work changes within the Soviet system and help modify the revolutionary zeal of the regime. If expansionist dynamics were constantly frustrated, Kennan reasoned, the forces must be expended within the system itself, and this would mean some modification of totalitarian control.

Although many persons in the United States remained vocally critical of it, containment became the official Cold War policy of the United States until the Soviet Union began its public collapse in the summer of 1991. In the words of former national security adviser and secretary of state Henry Kissinger, history has shown that "Kennan came closest, and earliest, in his predicting of the fate that would befall Soviet power."

—George Q. Flynn, updated by Joseph R. Rudolph, Jr.

ADDITIONAL READING:

Acheson, Dean. *Present at the Creation: My Years in the State Department.* New York: Norton, 1969. Written by Truman's last secretary of state, an often poignant, immensely interesting accounting of the years during which United States foreign policy shaped the postwar world.

Jones, Howard. *"A New Kind of War": America's Global Strategy and the Truman Doctrine in Greece.* New York: Oxford University Press, 1989. A detailed analysis of the effect of the containment policy on politics in its first beneficiary.

Jones, Joseph M. *The Fifteen Weeks (February 21-June 5, 1947).* New York: Viking Press, 1955. A good account of the crucial weeks during which the Truman Administration committed itself to first the containment doctrine and then the Marshall Plan.

Lieberman, Sanford R., et al., eds. *The Soviet Empire Reconsidered.* Boulder, Colo.: Westview Press, 1994. Many of the generally excellent essays address the impact of the containment policy on postwar Soviet foreign policy.

McGhee, George Crews. *The U.S.-Turkish-NATO Middle East Connection: How the Truman Doctrine Contained the Soviets in the Middle East.* New York: St. Martin's Press, 1990. An excellent regional study of containment at work.

Rees, David. *The Age of Containment: The Cold War, 1945-1965.* New York: St. Martin's Press, 1967. A view of the coldest days of the Cold War from a British perspective.

SEE ALSO: 1945, Yalta Conference; 1945, Potsdam Conference; 1948, Berlin Blockade; 1948, Truman Is Elected President; 1949, North Atlantic Treaty; 1950, Korean War.

1947 ■ NATIONAL SECURITY ACT: *a new U.S. defense policy avoids costly duplication of effort and allows for flexibility in times of national emergency*

DATE: July 26, 1947
LOCALE: Washington, D.C.
CATEGORIES: Diplomacy and international relations; Laws and acts
KEY FIGURES:
Omar Nelson Bradley (1893-1981), chairman of the Joint Chiefs of Staff, 1949-1953
James Vincent Forrestal (1892-1949), secretary of the U.S. Navy and the first secretary of defense
Louis A. Johnson (1891-1966), Forrestal's successor as secretary of defense
George Catlett Marshall (1880-1959), former secretary of state and Johnson's successor as secretary of defense
Robert Porter Patterson (1891-1952), secretary of war
Harry S Truman (1884-1972), thirty-third president of the United States, 1945-1953

SUMMARY OF EVENT. As steps were taken to strengthen the U.S. commitment to European security by means of the Truman Doctrine and the Marshall Plan, it became increasingly clear that measures were needed at home to increase the efficiency of the United States military establishment. A major impetus to the reorganization of the U.S. defense system had come from the obvious weaknesses revealed during World War II. One prime example of such weaknesses was the military disaster at Pearl Harbor. The war also had revealed numerous cases of duplication of effort among the various services. Another new factor that needed to be considered was that Cold War diplomacy required close collaboration between military and diplomatic elements, a condition that had hardly existed during the war. Therefore, many officials, including President Harry S Truman, thought that the need for a more efficient system of defense was obvious.

On July 26, 1947, the Truman Administration accomplished one of its more outstanding contributions, the passage of the National Security Act, but reaching an agreement on the exact details of the reorganization and centralization of the military establishment had not been an easy task. As early as 1945,

President Truman had submitted a plan for reorganization to Congress, but it took two years to settle the differences of opinion among the three branches of the armed forces. The Navy was especially reluctant to sacrifice its independence to what it feared would be a defense establishment dominated by the Army. In particular, the Navy feared that the new system might mean the abolishment of the Marines, or at least their transferral to the Army. Another sensitive area of dispute centered on the Navy's newly acquired air capability. Having become firmly convinced of the value of aircraft carriers during World War II, the Navy wanted to expand its air arm, which would include the construction of super-carriers able to accommodate the newly designed jet planes. Many admirals feared that an Army-dominated defense system might mean an emphasis of land-based, long-distance bombers. During 1946 and 1947, President Truman worked to bring together the Army, represented by Secretary of War Robert P. Patterson, and the Navy, represented by Secretary of the Navy James V. Forrestal. In this campaign, Truman was assisted especially by Forrestal, who, although entirely sympathetic to the Navy's point of view, did work for a reasonable compromise.

As a result of these meetings, agreements were reached that culminated in the National Security Act of 1947. The act created a Department of Defense (called the National Military Establishment until 1949) with a secretary holding cabinet rank. The Department of the Army, the Department of the Navy, and a new Department of the Air Force were made into separate subcabinet agencies in the Department of Defense. The act also gave legal recognition to the Joint Chiefs of Staff, with a rotating chairman. Each of the three services would be represented on this committee, which was to be responsible for providing close military coordination, preparing defense plans, and making strategy recommendations to another new agency, the National Security Council, which was to be chaired by the president of the United States. The other members of the National Security Council were to include the vice president, the secretary of state, the secretary of defense, the secretaries of the three services, and the chairman of the board of another new agency, the National Security Resources Board. The president could designate additional persons to serve on the Security Council; under Truman, the council had twenty members. Critics labeled the council "Mr. Truman's Politburo," because it attempted to blend diplomatic and military considerations at the highest level of national interest. Finally, the act created the Central Intelligence Agency as an independent source of security information.

This impressive reorganization plan had barely gotten under way when serious problems arose. In some instances, these problems were merely carryovers from the traditional competition between the Army and the Navy; the new system did little to eliminate interservice rivalry, despite the outstanding work of Forrestal as first secretary of defense. Some opponents pointed out that the new system merely created one more contending party, the Air Force. The three services soon were engaged in conducting separate, elaborate publicity and con-

gressional lobbying campaigns to gain increased shares of money for defense purposes. The Navy championed the merits of its super-carrier program, while the Air Force pointed to the new B-36 bomber as the best defense investment. Secretary Forrestal tried to mediate this struggle, but the issues seemed to be beyond the capacity of any one person to control. In failing health, the secretary resigned on March 3, 1949. Although interservice rivalry still existed, Forrestal had reported prior to his resignation that the new defense system had already saved the U.S. taxpayer more than $56 million.

The new secretary of defense appointed by President Truman was Louis A. Johnson of West Virginia, who approached his job with a pugnacious attitude that may have been a result of his lack of administrative experience at a comparably high level of government employment. He soon plunged into the interservice rivalry by favoring the Air Force. The building of new naval aircraft carriers was suspended, and considerable amounts of money went into expanding the strength of the Air Force. Although this executive policy saved money, some critics claimed that it weakened national defense. The State Department joined in the growing criticism of Johnson because it resented the new secretary's unilateral approach to national security. Apparently it was not long before Truman had reason to regret his appointment of Johnson, and in September, 1950, he turned to General George C. Marshall, former secretary of state, to take over the Department of Defense. The simultaneous appointment of Marshall's service colleague, General Omar N. Bradley, as chairman of the Joint Chiefs of Staff helped to make operations smoother within the Defense Department.

Equally important were congressional modifications of the original system. In 1949, the Hoover Commission, appointed by President Truman to investigate government administration and efficiency, reported that changes were needed in the Department of Defense. In August, 1949, a new bill was passed that gave the secretary of defense more power in dealing with the individual services. In July, 1958, the "Battle of the Pentagon" was further resolved with the passage of the Defense Department Reorganization Act.

The full implications of the new diplomatic and military structures created by the National Security Act became evident during the administration of Richard Nixon. Nixon's national security adviser and secretary of state, Henry A. Kissinger, established the supremacy of those two positions over the rest of the foreign-policy-making apparatus. Although efforts were made to decentralize foreign-policy decision making after Kissinger's departure, his legacy continued into subsequent administrations. The overall result of the National Security Act was to create a U.S. foreign-policy-making system that fit the country's new and unprecedented role as a global superpower. The demise of the Cold War at the end of the 1980's helped to spur a reexamination of that system, including the budgetary priority accorded the Department of Defense and the powers and effectiveness of the Central Intelligence Agency.

—George Q. Flynn, updated by Steve D. Boilard

ADDITIONAL READING:

Destler, I. M. "National Security Advice to U.S. Presidents: Some Lessons from Thirty Years." *World Politics* 29, no. 2 (January, 1977): 143-176. An analysis and critique of the foreign policy advisory system created by the National Security Act. Although thorough and based on three decades of experience, the analysis is now somewhat dated.

Hoxie, R. Gordon. "James V. Forrestal and the National Security Act of 1947." In *Command Decision and the Presidency: A Study in National Security Policy and Organization.* New York: Readers Digest Press, 1977. Discusses the origins and provisions of the National Security Act; provides particular detail on the 1949 amendment to the act. Written in a narrative style. Notes and bibliography.

Leffler, Melvyn P. *A Preponderance of Power: National Security, the Truman Administration, and the Cold War.* Stanford, Calif.: Stanford University Press, 1992. Places the National Security Act within the larger context of the Cold War. See especially chapter 4, "From the Truman Doctrine to the National Security Act, November 1946-July 1947." Notes and bibliography.

Rosati, Jerel A. "Presidential Management and the NSC Process." In *Politics of United States Foreign Policy.* Fort Worth, Tex.: Harcourt Brace Jovanovich, 1993. Discusses the foreign-policy-making system created by the National Security Act. Clear and well organized. Tables, charts, and bibliographic essay.

Theoharis, Athan G., ed. *The Truman Presidency: The Origins of the Imperial Presidency and the National Security State.* Stanfordville, N.Y.: Earl M. Coleman Enterprises, 1979. A compilation of extracts from declassified memos, addresses, letters, and analyses, with commentary by the editor. The chapter on the political and legislative history of the National Security Act and the 1949 amendments is especially useful. Notes and bibliography.

SEE ALSO: 1947, Truman Doctrine.

1947 ■ INVENTION OF THE TRANSISTOR: *a key technological advance gives birth to a new era of solid-state electronics and computers*

DATE: December 23, 1947
LOCALE: Bell Telephone Laboratories at Murray Hill, New Jersey
CATEGORIES: Communications; Science and technology
KEY FIGURES:
John Bardeen (1908-1991),
Walter Houser Brattain (1902-1987), and
William Bradford Shockley (1910-1989), physicists at Bell Telephone Laboratories who invented the transistor
Lee De Forest (1873-1961), inventor of the three-element vacuum tube

Mervin J. Kelly (1894-1971), director of research at Bell Telephone Laboratories

SUMMARY OF EVENT. The invention of the transistor in December, 1947, revolutionized the fledgling electronics industry and paved the way for a postwar explosion in communications and computer technology. The invention of the transistor was also one of the most significant productions of industrial scientific research laboratories, first established by the electrical and chemical industries to organize and direct the process of scientific research toward the needs of the sponsoring corporations.

The Bell Telephone Laboratories (Bell Labs), which produced the transistor, were first established in 1925 to serve the research and development interests of their co-owners, the American Telephone and Telegraph Company and the Western Electric Company. The Bell laboratories were systematically organized into research sections, each concentrating on an aspect of the communications industry. Their primary corporate goal was the improvement and expansion of existing communications equipment.

Before the invention of the transistor, the expansion of the telephone system had depended on the vacuum tube. The main problem in sending telephone messages over long distances was that the signal lost its strength as it traveled, so that the message became increasingly faint. The invention of the three-element vacuum tube (triode) in 1906 by a young inventor, Lee De Forest, had permitted the amplification and reamplification of the voice signal; with further improvements, the vacuum tube had made possible the first transcontinental telephone call between New York and San Francisco in 1915.

By 1936, Mervin Kelly, director of research at Bell Labs, had become concerned about the limitations of the vacuum tube. Long-distance telephone transmission required huge numbers of vacuum tubes as amplifiers. These tubes had serious drawbacks: They were fragile, bulky, gave off too much heat, consumed too much electrical power, and failed frequently, disrupting service. Because the tubes did not last very long, circuits that used a great many of them were costly to operate and maintain. As a result, Bell Labs hired scientists and engineers explicitly to form a special interdisciplinary solid-state research team to develop a better technology.

Kelly approached a young physicist working at Bell Labs, William Shockley, with the problem of finding a cheap and efficient replacement for the vacuum tube. Shockley had been working on semiconductors, which he thought might have the potential for amplifying electrical signals. (Semiconductors, such as germanium and silicon, have conduction properties intermediate between those of insulators, such as glass, and conductors, such as copper.) Shockley began exchanging ideas with Walter Brattain, another young Bell Labs physicist, who also had been working with semiconductors. World War II interrupted their research, however, and it was not until late in 1945 that they were able to return to the problem. After the war, they were joined by John Bardeen, one of Bell Labs' theoretical physicists. The three decided to begin their investigations with germanium and silicon, two semiconductor solids that had been widely used during the war for signal detection.

Shockley and Brattain tried to understand why the semiconductors allowed current to flow at points of contact with certain other metals. Shockley thought that the electrical fields set up by the current at these points of contact might be made to control the amount of current flowing through the semiconductor. If so, a small electrical charge at the contact point could be made to generate a large current in the semiconductor, thus producing amplification.

The team's first experimental device consisted of a tiny slab of germanium mounted close to, but insulated from, a piece of metal. It failed, and continued to fail, although many design changes were tried. Following these failures, John Bardeen developed a theory explaining the peculiar movements of electrons on the surface of a semiconductor. In an absolutely pure state, a crystal of germanium does not easily carry an electric current, because of the stability of the electron-sharing pattern (covalent bonds) between germanium atoms. If an impurity is present, however, this electron-sharing pattern is altered. Depending upon the atomic structure of the impurity, various numbers of electrons are freed to migrate whenever an electrical charge reaches the crystal. This electron movement allows the electrical current to flow across the germanium without changing its structure.

When Bardeen had formulated the solid-state theory, Brattain began experiments to confirm it. Months of experimenting went by, as the team pursued what Shockley came to call the "creative failure methodology." On November 17, 1947, the last phase of discovery began. Following the suggestion of a colleague, Robert B. Gibney, Shockley, Brattain, and Bardeen tried generating an electrical current perpendicular to the semiconductor. They set their germanium crystal in contact with two wires two-thousandths of an inch apart. When the current reached the semiconductor, it amplified more than forty times. The "transistor effect" had been discovered. (The word "transistor" is short for transfer resistor, because the circuit transfers current from a low-resistance circuit to a high-resistance circuit.)

By December 23, 1947, the three men were ready to demonstrate a working model to their colleagues. Their little device looked primitive. Bardeen had pressed two tiny strips of gold leaf, to act as contacts, onto a germanium crystal, which he then put on top of a piece of metal. This was the first transistor. It was a solid-state device, because it had neither moving parts nor a vacuum. It would bypass the limitations of the vacuum tube.

For six months, the invention was kept a secret while improvements were made and patents drawn up. On July 1, 1948, Bell Labs reported the discovery. The unheralded announcement went virtually unnoticed by the general public. After an initial period of concern over the cost involved in switching production technology, the electronics industry ultimately responded.

Impure semiconductors can be of a positive or negative charge type. Shockley's subsequent sandwiching of minuscule impure semiconductors with a piece of one type in between pieces of the other type yielded the junction transistor in 1951; it proved to be more useful. In the early days, both kinds of transistors were limited in their applicability, easily damaged, unreliable, and expensive. Development of techniques to manufacture semiconductor materials of sufficient purity would require time and money.

In 1952, when Bell first offered the developed transistor in a licensing arrangement, all the major vacuum tube manufacturers took out licenses and soon began production. Realizing the potential of the device for military electronics, the Department of Defense sponsored further research, development, and production of transistors. Private capital was injected into the field as well, leading to new types of junction transistors with new materials such as silicon; transistors for specific applications, such as power transistors; and somewhat different technology in several types of field effect transistors. Transistors were used not only in the telephone network but also in radios, recorders, computers, calculators, instrumentation, and medical electronics; new, unexpected products hit the market. The transistor was internationalized with both the devices themselves and whole systems made overseas; it opened up the Japanese consumer electronics industry. Further development led to integrated circuits that can combine millions of transistors on a single chip.

Creation of the point-contact transistor resulted in the awarding of the Nobel Prize in Physics to the three Bell Labs scientists, Bardeen, Brattain, and Shockley. As a result of the transistor, all electronic products could be made much smaller, could run on much less power, and could be made much more cheaply. A new technology and new industries were built on the tiny crystal, including personal computers.

—*Elizabeth Fee, updated by Stephen B. Dobrow*

ADDITIONAL READING:

Braun, Ernest, and Stuart MacDonald. *Revolution in Miniature*. 2d ed. Cambridge, Mass.: Cambridge University Press, 1982. An excellent account of the development of transistors.

Dorf, Richard C., ed. *Electrical Engineering Handbook*. Boca Raton, Fla.: CRC Press, 1993. A handy technical reference on transistors and related areas.

Gregor, Arthur. *Bell Laboratories: Inside the World's Largest Communications Center*. New York: Charles Scribner's Sons, 1972. A popular, illustrated history of Bell Laboratories.

Kelly, Mervin J. "The First Five Years of the Transistor." In *Bell Telephone Magazine* 32 (Summer, 1993): 73-86. Explains the early types of transistor design and their applications.

Mabon, Prescott C. *Mission Communications: The Story of Bell Laboratories*. Murray Hill, N.J.: Bell Telephone Laboratories, 1975. This official history of Bell Labs, written by a corporate official, mixes useful information with a heavy dose of public relations.

Marcus, Alan, and Howard Segal. *Technology in America: A Brief History*. San Diego: Harcourt Brace Jovanovich, 1989. A good overview of the history of technology in the United States.

Noble, David F. *America by Design: Science, Technology, and the Rise of Corporate Capitalism.* New York: Alfred A. Knopf, 1977. Analyzes the development of modern technology in the context of corporate capitalism.

SEE ALSO: 1981, IBM Markets the Personal Computer; 1990's, Rise of the Internet.

1948 ▪ ORGANIZATION OF AMERICAN STATES IS FOUNDED: *creation of a vehicle for all nations in the Americas to work toward common goals*

DATE: March-May, 1948
LOCALE: Bogotá, Colombia
CATEGORIES: Diplomacy and international relations; Latino American history; Treaties and agreements
KEY FIGURES:
Jorge Eliécer Gaitán (1902-1948), leader of the Liberal Party of Colombia
George Catlett Marshall (1880-1959), U.S. secretary of state and chief U.S. delegate to the Bogotá conference
Harry S Truman (1884-1972), thirty-third president of the United States, 1945-1953
SUMMARY OF EVENT. After World War II, the traditional preeminence of Latin American countries in United States diplomacy was replaced by the demands of Europe and the Far East upon U.S. money and military strength. Latin America was not forgotten, but the United States concentrated on the communist threat to Western Europe and gave highest priority to economic and military aid in that region. This change would lead to difficulties with Latin America. In the years between 1945 and 1948, the United States was interested primarily in hemispheric security, whereas the Latin American nations wanted help to further their own internal economic development.

This principle of hemispheric defense had been confirmed by the Act of Havana in July, 1940. The agreement, signed by the twenty-one republics of the Pan-American Union, provided that the American republics, individually or collectively, should control and administer any European possession in the Western hemisphere threatened by any act of aggression. After the bombing of Pearl Harbor by the Japanese on December 7, 1941, most Latin American nations had declared war on Germany and Japan, thus causing pan-Americanism to be strengthened. This wartime cooperation was continued by such agreements as the Act of Chapultepec on March 3, 1945, which recognized that aggression against any American nation was aggression against all of them. Two years later, negotiations were undertaken for the purpose of creating a permanent defensive alliance. On June 3, 1947, President Harry S Truman announced that the United States was willing to negotiate an inter-American mutual defense pact. Working to secure this end, in August, 1947, a conference of twenty-one American nations convened at Rio de Janeiro, Brazil. Secretary of State

George C. Marshall spoke for the United States. Faced by clamor demanding a Marshall Plan for Latin America, the secretary of state asked that such economic questions be postponed temporarily. The principal result of the conference was the signing, on September 2, of the Inter-American Treaty of Reciprocal Assistance providing for active cooperation in the event of any attack on an American nation. Members agreed to consult together if the threat of aggression arose against any of their number, and eventually all twenty-one American republics ratified the treaty. This pact became the model for later mutual security agreements, but it failed to set up methods by which signatories of the pact could be convened or make decisions and carry out resolutions. The questions left unanswered at the Rio de Janeiro conference were held over for the Ninth International Conference of American States, which met at Bogotá, Colombia, in the spring of 1948. This conference resulted in the formation of the Organization of American States.

Soon after the delegates arrived for the Bogotá conference, riots broke out in the Colombian capital, which almost disrupted the meeting. Secretary of State Marshall, who again headed the U.S. delegation, addressed the second plenary session. Describing the tremendous economic, military, and humanitarian responsibilities that the United States was undertaking all over the world, Marshall confessed that U.S. resources were limited. He bluntly admitted that a Marshall Plan for Latin America was not possible. Europe was the critical front, and success there would ensure universal economic stability.

The most important topic at Bogotá was the establishment of permanent machinery for hemispheric cooperation. Discussions of this important matter were interrupted abruptly on April 9, when Jorge Eliécer Gaitán, leader of the opposition Liberal Party in Colombia, was assassinated in downtown Bogotá. The violence provoked a riot that soon spread out of control. For several days, the visiting delegations were besieged in their embassies and hotel rooms. Much of Bogotá lay in ruins by the time that the Colombian army gained control of the situation. On April 14, the conference was able to resume its meetings in a boys' school near the United States embassy.

The major achievement of the conference was the creation of the Organization of American States (OAS), which was accomplished by renaming and reorganizing an existing organization, the sixty-year-old Pan-American Union. The charter of the OAS consolidated into one organization what previously had been an informal association acting on matters of common concern, but it replaced the flexibility of the former inter-American system with a rigid, more coherent pattern of rights and obligations. Although the OAS was not an entirely new inter-American organization, there were clear distinctions in theory and in practice between the OAS and the old Pan-American Union. Under the OAS charter, all American nations that ratified it agreed to certain basic principles: international law and order govern inter-American relations, especially the idea of equality of member states; an act of aggression against one will be considered to be aggression against all; any controversy between states shall be decided by peaceful means; and the well-being of the American peoples depends on social justice, political democracy, economic welfare, and mutual respect for national cultural values. The most important provisions of the charter were those that created the machinery for carrying out its principles. Six organizations were established: the Inter-American Conference, the Meeting of Consultation of Ministers of Foreign Affairs, Specialized Conferences, the OAS Council, the Pan-American Union, and Specialized Organizations. The first three bodies were given responsibility for issues of a political, economic, or general nature. The Meeting of Consultation of Foreign Ministers was an emergency assembly reserved for matters of extreme urgency, such as an armed threat to hemispheric peace.

The organization thus created was less than an autonomous international body. The OAS could exercise authority only in limited areas; it was the creature of those nations that brought it into existence. Nevertheless, formation of the Organization of American States did strengthen cooperation among the republics of the Western Hemisphere, and increasingly it has become the vehicle for majority action in the political and military realm.

Although the OAS was founded in 1948, its charter actually took force in December of 1951. Since that time, as economic, social, and political views have evolved, the OAS has restructured, reformed, and modernized to stay abreast of events and address issues as they arise. In 1967, the Protocol of Buenos Aires enabled the inclusion of new ideas in economic, social, educational, scientific, and cultural fields. In 1985, the Protocol of Cartagena called for representative democracy within the already established policy of nonintervention. An example of this in action was the organization's efforts to assure peaceful and democratic elections in Haiti in December, 1995. An OAS Electoral Observation Mission spent a month in Haiti before the elections, observed voting throughout the country on election day, and monitored the vote counts. The Managua Protocol, which was adopted June 10, 1993, calls for a cooperative effort to encourage development and eliminate abject poverty from the Western Hemisphere; this policy was ratified upon the approval of two-thirds of the members and was officially put in place on January 29, 1996.

Other measures of great interest within the OAS include human rights, the rights of women, an end to domestic violence, and an end to the use of violence as a way to overthrow governments. The Protocol of Washington, which was adopted in 1992, calls for suspending the rights of any member of the organization's councils if that member's government has been overthrown by force. This protocol, still awaiting two-thirds acceptance of the membership, is designed to pressure countries into settling disagreements and ousting unpopular or corrupt governments by peaceful means, such as through the ballot box.   —*Theodore A. Wilson, updated by Kay Hively*

ADDITIONAL READING:

Cornell-Smith, Gordon. *The Inter-American System.* New York: Oxford University Press, 1966. An informative study of

how the inter-American system works, and a good presentation of the original Bogotá meeting in 1948.

Matthews, Herbert L., ed. *The United States and Latin America.* Englewood Cliffs, N.J.: Prentice-Hall, 1963. A thorough look at the United States and its relationship with members of the OAS in Latin America.

Mower, A. Glenn. *Regional Human Rights: A Comparative Study of the Western European and Inter-American Systems.* New York: Greenwood Press, 1991. Looks at human rights, a subject of increasing importance in international relations.

Muñoz, Heraldo. *The Future of the OAS.* New York: Twentieth Century Free Press, 1993. Discusses the role of the OAS in the next century.

Palmer, Bruce. *Intervention in the Caribbean: The Dominican Crisis.* Lexington: University Press of Kentucky, 1989. A thoughtful look at one of the most important crises that faced the OAS and how it was handled.

Stoetzer, O. Carlos. *The Organization of American States: An Introduction.* New York: Praeger Press, 1965. An easy-to-understand look at the OAS.

SEE ALSO: 1933, Good Neighbor Policy.

1948 ■ BERLIN BLOCKADE: *faced with Soviet attempts to cut off West Berlin from the Western Allies' zones in Germany, the United States and Britain respond with a successful airlift*

DATE: March, 1948-May, 1949
LOCALE: Berlin, Germany
CATEGORY: Diplomacy and international relations
KEY FIGURES:
Lucius du Bignon Clay (1897-1978), U.S. military governor in Germany and commander of U.S. forces in Europe
George Catlett Marshall (1880-1959), U.S. secretary of state
Ernst Reuter (1889-1953), lord mayor of West Berlin
Joseph Stalin (Joseph Vissarionovich Dzhugashvili, 1879-1953), marshal of the Soviet Union and general secretary of the Central Committee of the Communist Party
Harry S Truman (1884-1972), thirty-third president of the United States, 1945-1953

SUMMARY OF EVENT. The most important and dramatic confrontation between the United States and the Soviet Union in the formative period of the Cold War was the blockade of Berlin and the resulting airlift. The Soviet challenge to the West's rights of access to Berlin seems to have been designed not only to expel the Western powers from the former German capital but also to prevent the creation of a workable West German government. President Harry S Truman, General George Marshall, and General Lucius Clay, however, recognized that the continued Western presence in Berlin was a test of the determination of the Western powers regarding the

German question. Therefore, they made it clear that the United States would not submit to Stalin's demands.

The problem in Berlin arose from the wartime agreements among the Allies for the postwar administration of Germany. Zones of occupation were agreed upon for Germany itself. Although Berlin was deep within the Soviet zone, the Allies also arranged sectors in Berlin. U.S., British, and French authorities dutifully assumed their responsibilities in the ruined capital, seeking to cooperate with the Soviet authorities in the Allied Control Council (for all of Germany) and the Kommandatura (for Berlin). Soviet obstructionism, however, convinced U.S. leaders that the Soviet Union sought to dominate all of Berlin and eventually, the whole of Germany. The climax of this struggle was the municipal election of October 20, 1946, in greater Berlin. The result was an overwhelming victory for the Social Democrats and defeat for the Soviet-backed Socialist Unity Party. Soviet-inspired political and economic pressure on Berlin increased during 1947.

In early 1948, Great Britain and the United States developed plans to merge their two zones in western Germany economically, and the French were encouraged to cooperate. The Soviet Union protested these actions bitterly and responded by putting more economic pressure on the western sectors of Berlin. A communist coup in Czechoslovakia in February, 1948, incurred Western suspicions of Soviet intentions in Germany. In March, the London Conference (which included the United States, the United Kingdom, France, Holland, Belgium, and Luxembourg) recommended that West Germany be united to form a federal state and that it take part in the Marshall Plan of economic recovery. In response, the Soviet Union withdrew its representatives from the Allied Control Council in Berlin. On April 1, the Soviet Union began the "small Berlin blockade," by restricting land access and deliveries of food and fuel to Berlin.

U.S. leaders realized that should the Soviets cordon off Berlin entirely, the situation of the city's inhabitants and the token Western garrisons would be desperate. The Western sectors were entirely dependent upon provisions shipped in by rail, truck, and canal. There was no written agreement guaranteeing free access to Berlin by surface transportation, merely oral understandings. There was a specific agreement on air access between Berlin and West Germany, but few people believed that the needs of 2,250,000 people could be met by air transport alone.

Aware of the West's dilemma, the Soviets pushed forward with plans to isolate the city. Apparently, their goal was to discourage the economic and political unification of West Germany, and eventually to take control of Berlin, by demonstrating that the Western powers were unwilling or unable to protect their rights. The Western powers nevertheless went ahead with economic and currency reform in their zones of Germany, introducing the deutsche mark to replace the worthlessly inflated old currency, beginning on June 20, 1948. The full-scale Soviet blockade of West Berlin followed on June 24.

General Lucius Clay organized an immediate but modest airlift to keep the Western garrisons supplied, and he returned to Washington, D.C., to consult with President Truman in July. Clay favored forcing the issue with the Soviet Union by sending an armed transport convoy along the main highway from western Germany into the city. Secretary of State George Marshall favored an expanded airlift instead, coupled with a direct but informal approach to Stalin. Truman decided on the airlift rather than the armed convoy, and he told the U.S. ambassador in Moscow to contact Joseph Stalin, the Soviet dictator.

An airlift to ferry all necessary supplies for more than two million people was a most difficult undertaking. The logistic triumph would have proven fruitless if it had not been for the dogged determination of the people of West Berlin. Berliners knew Soviet troops could take over the city in a few hours. The Western allies had only sixty-five hundred combat troops in Berlin to face more than three hundred thousand troops in the Soviet zone. Yet the Berliners refused to give in to fear, hunger, or discouragement. In December, Ernst Reuter, a Social Democrat and staunch opponent of communist rule, was elected lord mayor of West Berlin. During the blockade, many non-communist professors abandoned Humboldt University in the Soviet sector and, with aid from the United States, established the Free University of Berlin in the U.S. sector. Reuter's leadership and the Free University became a rallying points for the Berliners, strengthening their resolve.

The airlift proved more and more successful. Tons of fuel and food staples, and enough luxuries such as fish, coffee, and children's candies, arrived each day to buoy popular spirits. Politically, the blockade and airlift brought unintended and unwelcome results for the Soviet Union. Rather than forcing a humiliating retreat on the Western powers, the blockade showed the West to be a solid ally of the Berliners, willing to pay any price to save the people from either Soviet domination or war. West Germany continued on its way to becoming a unified state and eventually an ally of the North Atlantic Treaty Organization, rather than merely a conquered enemy. Truman, who was facing a difficult election campaign at home, emerged as a hero, willing to face up to communist threats without actually going to war. He not only ordered the full power of U.S. transport aircraft into the airlift but also moved B-29 bombers, capable of carrying atomic weapons, to British bases within range of Moscow. Soviet attempts to intimidate the U.S. and British fliers on airlift duty by holding "air maneuvers" along the approaches to the West Berlin airfields were brushed aside, and deliveries continued to increase, even in the bad winter weather.

At the same time, Truman made behind-the-scenes diplomatic efforts in an attempt to bring an end to the crisis. In August, 1948, the U.S. ambassador in Moscow spoke directly to Stalin about Berlin. At times, Stalin appeared reasonable, remarking that the United States and the Soviet Union were still allies. At other times, Stalin seemed elusive and belligerent, and Truman commented privately in September that he feared that the United States and the Soviet Union were slipping toward war.

Airmen unload bottles of milk from a U.S. Air Force transport, to be delivered to isolated sections of Berlin during the blockade of 1948. (Library of Congress)

By February, 1949, it had become clear that the Western powers could sustain the airlift indefinitely and that the blockade was driving the Germans into the arms of the West. Stalin hinted to a Western newsman that he was willing to give up his objections to the use of the West German deutsche mark in West Berlin and eventually drop the blockade. Soviet and U.S. diplomats soon began meeting secretly at the United Nations in New York.

In early May, the secret talks at the United Nations were nearing successful completion. Simultaneously, the West German parliamentary council was moving toward approval of the constitutional document that would establish the Federal Republic of Germany. On May 10, 1949, the Soviets published the orders for lifting their restrictions, and the next day, electrical power began flowing into West Berlin from East German power plants. The gates were lifted and the Berlin blockade was over. The airlift had lasted a total of 321 days, from June 24, 1948, until May 12, 1949, and brought into Berlin 1,592,787 tons of supplies. The achievements of the airlift were not without cost. It was a heavy burden for U.S. and British taxpayers—approximately $200 million—and the Berliners had to make do with very short rations. Moreover, accidental deaths did occur. Twenty-four planes crashed, and seventy-six persons lost their lives.

Although additional Berlin crises would occur, including the building of the Berlin Wall in 1961, the Berlin blockade and the airlift response had been a clear turning point in the history of post-World War II Europe. War had been avoided, the Soviet Union was forced to back down, and West Germany and West Berlin were clearly linked to the United States and Western Europe for the remainder of the Cold War. In addition, the United States had solidified its role as a world power willing to commit its resources to the advancement of democracy.

—*Theodore A. Wilson, updated by Gordon R. Mork*

ADDITIONAL READING:

Clay, Lucius D. *Decision in Germany*. Garden City, N.Y.: Doubleday, 1950. The U.S. commander in Germany recounts his personal experiences.

Ferrell, Robert H. *George C. Marshall*. The American Secretaries of State and Their Diplomacy, vol. 15. New York: Cooper Square, 1966. An exhaustive study of Marshall's tenure at the Department of State. The author relies on memoirs and other published information for most of his information.

Grathwol, Robert P., and Donita M. Moorhus. *American Forces in Berlin: Cold War Outpost, 1945-1994*. Washington, D.C.: Department of Defense, 1994. Partly a commemorative booklet, partly an illustrated documentary history, this well-illustrated book adds significant details to the U.S. achievements in Berlin.

McCullough, David. *Truman*. New York: Simon & Schuster, 1992. Portrays Truman's staunch response to the Berlin blockade crisis as one of the finest aspects of his presidency. Puts the whole matter into the context of U.S. political history.

Shlaim, Avi. *The United States and the Berlin Blockade, 1948-1949: A Study in Crisis Decision-Making*. Berkeley: University of California Press, 1983. A scholarly analysis of United States decision making, step by step, during the crises of the blockade and airlift.

Tusa, Ann, and John Tusa. *The Berlin Airlift*. New York: Atheneum, 1988. A well-documented narrative account of the blockade and the airlift within the context of Cold War diplomacy.

SEE ALSO: 1945, Yalta Conference; 1945, United Nations Charter Convention; 1945, Potsdam Conference; 1947, Truman Doctrine; 1948, Berlin Blockade; 1948, Truman Is Elected President; 1949, North Atlantic Treaty.

1948 ■ TRUMAN IS ELECTED PRESIDENT: *a new administration brings World War II to a close and seeks to shield liberal social programs from the attacks of conservatives*

DATE: November 2, 1948

LOCALE: United States

CATEGORY: Government and politics

KEY FIGURES:

Alben William Barkley (1877-1956), Truman's running mate in 1948

Thomas Edmund Dewey (1902-1971), governor of New York and Republican presidential candidate in 1944 and 1948

Franklin Delano Roosevelt (1882-1945), thirty-second president of the United States, 1933-1945, who died in office and was succeeded by Truman

James Strom Thurmond (born 1902), presidential candidate on the States' Rights Party (Dixiecrat) ticket

Harry S Truman (1884-1972), thirty-third president of the United States, 1945-1953

Henry Agard Wallace (1888-1965), vice president of the United States, 1941-1945, and presidential candidate on the Progressive Party ticket, 1948

Earl Warren (1891-1974), Dewey's running mate in 1948

SUMMARY OF EVENT. When Harry S Truman took the presidential oath of office in April, 1945, upon the death of President Franklin Roosevelt, a great majority of the people in the United States rallied behind him. He seemed to be an ordinary man who was trying to do the best he could, and his simple humility evoked the sympathy of the citizens. That summer, he presided over the momentous decisions involved in ending World War II and adopted a tough stand toward the Soviet Union. On September 6, only four days after the formal surrender of Japan, Truman sent Congress a broad domestic program that revived the spirit of President Roosevelt's New Deal. Truman called for the expansion of social security, a higher minimum wage, full-employment legislation, a permanent Fair Employment Practices Commission to protect African American workers, public housing, and slum clearance. In a series of subsequent messages, he expanded his requests, but the Truman "honeymoon" was quickly over. Congress, dominated by a coalition of Republicans and conservative Democrats, gave him the truncated Employment Act of 1946 but little else. In the meantime, Truman bungled the task of reconverting the nation's economy from war to peace. All the postwar uncertainties—inflation, strikes, shortages, price controls on food and products, problems with the Soviet Union, controversy over the use of atomic weapons—eroded his personal popularity and that of his party. "To err is Truman," people joked; "I wonder what Truman would do if he were alive."

By the fall of 1946, Republicans were asking, "Had enough?" The question caught the mood of the country. The Republicans swept the mid-term elections, winning both houses of Congress for the first time since 1928. The size of the victory was the real surprise; their margin was 245 to 188 in the House of Representatives and 51 to 45 in the Senate. The new Eightieth Congress was even less receptive to Truman's domestic proposals than the previous Congress had been.

As the 1948 election approached, Republicans seemed complacently certain of victory. When their national convention met, they passed over Robert A. Taft, the conservative senator from Ohio, and again nominated New York governor Thomas E. Dewey. Earl Warren, the popular governor of California, received the vice presidential nomination.

The Democratic Party seemed to disintegrate, losing first its left wing and then the South. In late 1947, Henry A. Wallace,

Harry S Truman, thirty-third president of the United States, helped the nation return to a peacetime economy at the same time that he oversaw the birth of the Cold War and conflict in Korea. (Library of Congress)

recently expelled from Truman's cabinet, announced that he would run on a third-party ticket. The dissident Northern liberals who supported him were dissatisfied with the slow pace of domestic reform, and they favored greater cooperation with the Soviet Union. Other Democrats sought a glamorous candidate to replace Truman. The first choice of the "dump Truman" movement was General Dwight D. Eisenhower, whose party affiliation was not yet known. He was flattered but not interested. At Philadelphia, a gloomy convention accepted Truman for lack of any alternative; Senator Alben Barkley was named as his running mate. When a liberal faction inserted a civil rights plank into the platform, Southern diehards bolted the party. Meeting at Birmingham, Alabama, they formed the States' Rights Party (Dixiecrats), with J. Strom Thurmond of South Carolina as their candidate.

Confident that the prize would be his, Dewey campaigned as though he had already won. The polls showed him far ahead. His speeches were polished and statesmanlike, although he aroused little enthusiasm among the Republican rank and file. He accused the Truman Administration of corruption, but he tacitly accepted the New Deal reforms and even promised to administer them more efficiently. In contrast, Truman entered the contest in a fighting mood. Ignoring Dewey, he lashed out at the "no-account, do nothing" Eightieth Congress and identified the Republican Party with selfish special interests. Hurling himself into strenuous whistle-stop tours that covered 31,700 miles and included 356 speeches, he took on the role of an indomitable fighter, a scrappy underdog making an uphill fight. His extemporaneous style of speaking captivated his audiences. "Give 'em hell, Harry," voices called out. To the consternation of almost everyone, he defeated Dewey by 24,105,812 to 21,970,065 votes. The electoral score was Truman, 303; Dewey, 189; Thurmond, 39. Wallace and Thurmond each received about 1,150,000 votes, far below predictions. The Democrats also regained control of both houses of Congress. Truman had pulled off one of the most stunning upsets in the history of presidential politics.

Once he was president in his own right, Truman resumed the fight for his domestic program, incorporating the phrase "fair deal" in his state-of-the-union speech on January 4, 1949. Truman's Fair Deal proposals were dedicated to increasing economic growth, redressing the problems of unequal wealth and opportunity, and providing abundance for all. Specifically, Truman wanted a more progressive tax structure; the repeal of the Taft-Hartley Act, which outlawed industrywide strikes, the closed shop, and mass picketing; higher wages; and subsidized farm prices. He also proposed the establishment of anti-inflation control measures; expanded resource development and public power programs; national health insurance; federal aid to education; and extensive housing and civil rights legislation.

After seven years, however, the tangible results were slim: enactment of the National Housing Act of 1949; an increase in the minimum hourly wage to seventy-five cents; establishment of a social security law that boosted benefits and extended coverage to more people; and passage of more liberal immigration laws. Congress turned down Truman's requests for civil rights legislation, national health insurance, a new system of agricultural subsidies, and federal aid to education.

The failure to obtain passage of most of the Fair Deal programs in Congress was primarily a result of perennial congressional factionalism that Truman could not control, even within his own party. Truman—noted for holding grudges against key congressional leaders and insulting others—was his own worst enemy in shepherding his legislation through Congress. More important, the public became increasingly conservative; they were more concerned with inflation, the war boom of the Korean War, and the rise of McCarthyism in the wake of the communist menaces of Russia and China.

Truman did succeed in accelerating the civil rights gains for African Americans. Although he failed to get a broad civil rights program through Congress, he used executive authority to desegregate the armed forces. His Justice Department participated in important civil rights cases before the Supreme Court. Under his direction, the Civil Service Commission eliminated discrimination in government agencies. Thus, Truman preserved New Deal reforms and modestly extended some of its programs. His best proposals constituted the unfinished business of U.S. reform for the next two decades.

—*Donald Holley, updated by Richard Whitworth*

ADDITIONAL READING:

Ferrell, Robert H. *Choosing Truman: The Democratic Convention of 1944.* Columbia: University of Missouri Press, 1994. Tells the unbelievable but true story of how Senator Harry Truman became the running mate of President Franklin Roosevelt in 1944. Fascinating political anecdotes.

_____. *Harry S. Truman: A Life.* Columbia: University of Missouri Press, 1994. Chronicles Truman's early life and how he rose to the presidency. Chapter 14 explores Truman's Fair Deal and its importance to future generations.

Hamby, Alonzo L., ed. *Harry S. Truman and the Fair Deal.* Lexington, Mass.: D. C. Heath, 1974. Offers essays, pro and con, on the various programs of Truman's Fair Deal. Also includes selected Truman speeches on civil rights and domestic reforms.

McCullough, David G. *Truman.* New York: Simon & Schuster, 1992. Compelling story of Truman as an "ordinary" man who became an extraordinary president. Captures both the complex man and the times in which he lived.

Miller, Richard L. *Truman: The Rise to Power.* New York: McGraw-Hill, 1986. Details Truman's life up the day he assumed the presidency in 1945; demonstrates how Truman's character was formed. A gritty reinterpretation of Truman.

Pemberton, William E. *Harry S. Truman: Fair Dealer and Cold Warrior.* Boston: Twayne, 1989. Sketches events after Truman assumed the presidency. Includes a helpful chronological outline of major events; lists more than four hundred manuscripts in the Truman Library collection.

SEE ALSO: 1949, North Atlantic Treaty; 1950, Korean War; 1950, Truman-MacArthur Confrontation.

1948 ■ St. Laurent Succeeds King: *the retiring King is replaced by a new head of the Liberal Party and a new prime minister*

DATE: November 15, 1948
LOCALE: Ottawa, Ontario
CATEGORIES: Canadian history; Government and politics
KEY FIGURES:
James Garfield Gardiner (1883-1962) and
Charles Gavan Power (1888-1968), candidates for the leadership of the Liberal Party in 1948
Clarence Decatur Howe (1886-1960), influential member of the Liberal Party and King's cabinet supported St. Laurent's candidacy
William Lyon Mackenzie King (1874-1950), Liberal prime minister of Canada 1921-1926, 1926-1930, and 1935-1948
Louis St. Laurent (1882-1973), minister of external affairs under King, Liberal Party leader, and prime minister of Canada, 1948-1957

SUMMARY OF EVENT. The retirement of William Lyon Mackenzie King as leader of the Liberal Party and prime minister of Canada in 1948 was not merely the end of a political career, but the closing of an era. King had been a part of the Canadian government since joining the civil service in 1900, in preference to an academic post at Harvard University. In 1908, he resigned from the civil service in order to stand for Parliament. King assumed the leadership of the Liberal Party in 1919, following the death of the much-loved Wilfred Laurier, first becoming prime minister in 1929. In all, King had served as prime minister for twenty-two years.

Perhaps the most important part of his long career was his leadership of Canada during World War II and in the years immediately following. Having served as Leader of the Opposition during the worst of the Great Depression, King was again elected prime minister in 1935. As prime minister, King oversaw Canada's massive contribution to the war, overcoming Canadians' mixed feelings about the war and crises over conscription. At the close of the war, the continued popularity of the Liberals assured King's victory in the election of 1945. The government's plans for social welfare programs that raised the standard of living for all Canadians became part of King's legacy. Although he was, perhaps, more respected than beloved, his leadership during the war guaranteed that his departure from politics would be a turning point for Canada.

In January, 1948, worn out by the stress of wartime leadership and now in his seventies, King announced his decision to retire. A Liberal Party convention, the first since 1919, was called for August to choose his successor. The most likely of the candidates was Louis St. Laurent, an intelligent and successful corporate lawyer, fluent in French and English. St. Laurent, then sixty-six years of age, was a relative newcomer to federal politics, having been elected to Parliament for Que-

Modern Canada, 1949

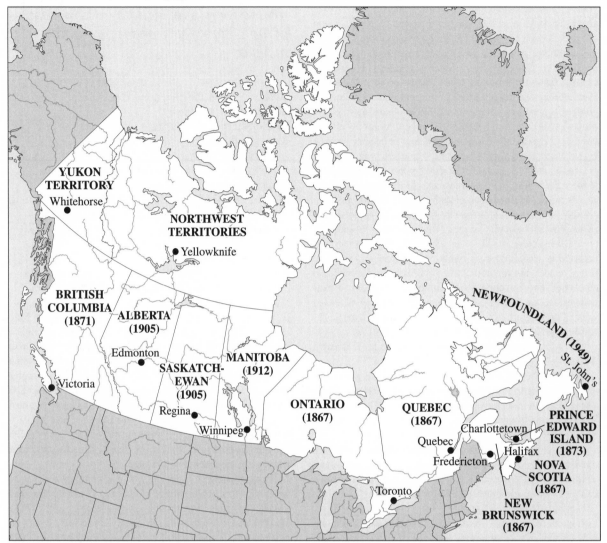

One of the most important developments of St. Laurent's term took place on April 1, 1949, when Newfoundland joined the Canadian Confederation, completing the modern confederation of provinces that compose Canada. Current provinces, dates of admission to the confederation, territories, and capital cities appear above.

bec East in 1942. Since that time, he had served as minister of justice and minister of external affairs, and he had been asked by King to consider himself as the next leader of the Liberal Party. For King, the similarities between St. Laurent and the late Wilfred Laurier represented a chance to repair the rift between French Canadians and the Liberal Party, caused primarily by the issue of conscription. The other candidates were James Gardiner, minister of agriculture, and Charles "Chubby" Power, who had been elected to Parliament for Quebec South and served in the Senate. Of these two, only Gardiner was a serious contender.

On August 5, the national Liberal Convention opened at the Ottawa Coliseum. In the course of the convention, three events took place: King took formal leave of his party, a new platform was debated and resolved, and voting for a new leader was carried out. St. Laurent eventually was elected to lead the party, with 848 votes; Gardiner and Power received 323 and 56 votes, respectively. On Monday, November 15, 1948, St. Laurent took the oath of office as prime minister.

The following year, a federal election confirmed the popularity of St. Laurent and his Liberal government. The Liberals won 50 percent of the vote, taking 193 seats in Parliament. The major opposition came from Progressive Conservatives, led by George Drew, which won forty-one seats in Parliament. Running a close third came the Cooperative Commonwealth Federation, which won thirteen seats. Liberal victory was, in part, the result of a healthy economy and a fiscal surplus that allowed a reduction in income tax and a continuation of Liberal plans for social services.

One of the most important developments of St. Laurent's term took place on April 1, 1949, when Newfoundland joined the Canadian Confederation. Newfoundland had long declined to join in the union of the provinces begun more than eighty years earlier, but postwar prosperity gave Newfoundland confidence that it could join Canada while maintaining its distinct identity. In July, 1948, a referendum was held approving union with Canada, and the terms of union were worked out in the first weeks of St. Laurent's term in office.

St. Laurent would serve as prime minister for nine years, until the first Liberal defeat in five federal elections. In this time, St. Laurent's stewardship of the nation saw several key developments in Canada. First, Canada began to find its place in world affairs, both in direct relations with the great powers and in international cooperation through the United Nations. Canada also redefined its relationship with its great allies, the United States and Great Britain, strengthening its economic and political ties to the former and lessening its dependence on the latter. In this period, Canada was increasingly urban, wealthy, and nationalist, working to define its own cultural and political identity. The Royal Commission Report on National Development in the Arts, Letters and Sciences—known as the Massey Report after its chairman, Vincent Massey—investigated the state of Canadian culture. The report concluded that Canada had been too much shaped by outside influences, and that government should take steps to encourage a unique Canadian culture. Manufacturing converted from wartime to peacetime production without losing its pace, and Canadian goods and natural resources found ready markets at home and around the globe.

The postwar boom in Canada was the source of the continued success of the Liberals under the leadership of St. Laurent. Following the landslide victory of 1949, the Liberals were confirmed by a slightly less vigorous victory in the election of 1953. Their victory was a measure of the comparative weakness of the opposition and the popularity of the latest round of social welfare works, including the old-age pensions, unemployment insurance, and family allowances.

The power of the Liberal government weakened in the mid-1950's, when a combination of forces made change seem appropriate. First, there was a growing sense that the Liberals had been in power for too many years, and that their long years in power had made them complacent and out of touch. Second, a controversy over the funding for the Trans-Canada Pipe Line and the manner in which debate on the issue was shut down in Parliament brought loud and vigorous criticism to the government. Finally, regional dissatisfaction, particularly in the Western and Atlantic provinces, convinced many that the government did not care about regional interests. In the election of June, 1957, a revitalized Progressive Conservative Party under the leadership of John Diefenbaker defeated St. Laurent's Liberal Party, taking 112 seats to the Liberals' 105. The election

marked the beginning of a change in the Liberal Party, which increasingly seemed to rely on support from Ontario and Quebec and was seldom able to win seats in the West. In January, 1958, a national Liberal Convention was held, and St. Laurent was replaced by Lester B. Pearson as head of the Liberal Party and Leader of the Opposition. Pearson, winner of the Nobel Peace Prize in 1957 and former president of the United Nations, became prime minister in April, 1963. —*Kelley Graham*

ADDITIONAL READING:

Bothwell, Robert, and William Kilbourn. *C. D. Howe: A Biography*. Toronto: McClelland and Stewart, 1979. An engaging biography of the man who was a major power in the Liberal Party.

Bothwell, Robert, Ian Drummond, and John English. *Canada Since 1945: Power, Politics, and Provincialism*. Toronto: University of Toronto Press, 1981. Presents a comprehensive look at postwar Canada. One chapter covers the beginnings of St. Laurent's leadership.

Feigert, Frank. *Canada Votes, 1935-1988*. Durham, N.C.: Duke University Press, 1989. Offers both a statistical breakdown and an analysis of federal elections in Canada.

Pickersgill, J. W. *My Years with Louis St. Laurent: A Political Memoir*. Toronto: University of Toronto Press, 1975. Provides an insider's look at the transfer of power from King to St. Laurent.

Pickersgill, J. W., and D. F. Forster. *1947-1948*. Vol. 4 in *The Mackenzie King Record*. Toronto: University of Toronto Press, 1970. Drawing from King's speeches and personal memoranda, this work gives insight into the last part of King's political career.

Thomson, Dale C. *Louis St. Laurent: Canadian*. New York: St. Martin's Press, 1968. A general, rather than scholarly, study of the political career of St. Laurent.

SEE ALSO: 1921, King Era in Canada; 1930, Bennett Era in Canada; 1952, Massey Becomes Canada's First Native-Born Governor General; 1957, Diefenbaker Era in Canada.

1949 ■ NORTH ATLANTIC TREATY: *twelve democracies, including the United States and Canada, establish an association for mutual defense against the Soviet Union*

DATE: April 4, 1949
LOCALE: Western Europe and Washington, D.C.
CATEGORIES: Diplomacy and international relations; Treaties and agreements
KEY FIGURES:
Dean Acheson (1893-1971), U.S. secretary of state, 1949-1953
Ernest Bevin (1881-1951), foreign secretary of Great Britain
Dwight David Eisenhower (1890-1969), U.S. general and commander of NATO forces
George Catlett Marshall (1880-1959), U.S. secretary of state, 1947-1949

Robert Schuman (1886-1963), French minister of foreign affairs

Joseph Stalin (Joseph Vissarionovich Dzhugashvili, 1879-1953), general secretary of the Communist Party of the Soviet Union

Harry S Truman (1884-1972), thirty-third president of the United States, 1945-1953

Arthur Hendrick Vandenberg (1884-1951), senator from Michigan and leader of the movement for a bipartisan foreign policy

SUMMARY OF EVENT. On April 4, 1949, the United States and eleven other nations (Belgium, Canada, Denmark, France, Great Britain, Iceland, Italy, Luxembourg, the Netherlands, Norway, and Portugal) signed a treaty of alliance establishing the North Atlantic Treaty Organization (NATO), committing the signatories to the principle of common security on a regional basis. By joining, the United States under President Harry S Truman took a precedent-shattering step; it had never before concluded a military alliance in peacetime with any European state. Participation in NATO meant that the United States had modified one of its oldest principles, which stemmed from the advice of George Washington and Thomas Jefferson: to avoid entangling alliances.

The genesis for such an alliance emerged from the Truman Administration's containment policy, with the fundamental objective of opposing Soviet expansionist efforts in Europe after World War II. The United States had committed itself in the 1947 Truman Doctrine to assisting European nations facing civil war or external threats from the Soviet Union. The United States extended military and economic aid to Greece and Turkey that year (April 23) to counter Soviet ambitions in the region, as those countries were too weak to be self-sustaining.

Also in 1947, Secretary of State George Marshall proposed the more ambitious European Recovery Program. Economic aid through this costly effort, often called the Marshall Plan, greatly assisted the European economy after the program began in 1948. There was widespread belief in the United States, however, that Europe's full economic and psychological recovery would not be possible until Europeans believed themselves safe from the threat of the Red Army. Thus, military security was essential for continued economic recovery.

Several major events in 1948 revealed the widening Cold War in Europe. A communist coup d'état in Czechoslovakia, the Soviet blockade of Berlin (lasting into 1949), and other Soviet actions convinced the Truman Administration of the need for more extensive, long-term U.S. involvement in Europe. Despite appeals from European leaders for the creation of a common front, however, Truman was not sufficiently confident of public and congressional support to move directly toward an alliance. In June, 1948, the Senate approved the Vandenberg Resolution by a vote of sixty-four to four, which declared support for U.S. participation in regional arrangements for "continuous and effective self-help and mutual aid." This pronouncement was interpreted by some as an attempt to limit presidential power in foreign affairs rather than as

a sincere expression of support for collective security. Only after the presidential election of 1948 and cautious discussions with the principal European nations did the Truman Administration act to move the United States away from its traditional isolationism.

In March, 1948, five European nations—Great Britain, France, Belgium, the Netherlands, and Luxembourg—signed the Brussels Pact, a fifty-year defensive alliance. Its terms obligated the signatories to come to the aid of any member attacked by an aggressor. The Brussels Pact nations invited the United States to participate, but there were numerous obstacles to concerted action at that time, even though the Vandenberg Resolution showed U.S. interest in a mutual security system. In January, 1949, more positive support was expressed in Truman's inaugural address, which promised that the United States would contribute to the defense of friendly nations.

The United States began negotiations with a number of European states, with the aim of creating a cooperative system of military security against the presumed Soviet threat to Western Europe. These discussions were criticized by some people in the United States and especially by communist authorities in Moscow. They accused the United States of undercutting the United Nations and jeopardizing world peace by forming a bloc of states for aggressive purposes. The United States answered this accusation by pointing out that Article 51 of the U.N. Charter allowed for regional defense pacts, and that the proposed alliance clearly was defensive in character.

Dean Acheson, who succeeded Marshall as secretary of state in early 1949, believed that the United States should look to military and diplomatic arrangements to meet the communist challenge rather than rely upon the institutional procedures of the United Nations, which could be blocked by a Soviet veto. Negotiations achieved the desired objective of an expanded association of democratic states. In ceremonies in Washington, D.C., on April 4, 1949, the North Atlantic Treaty was signed by representatives of twelve nations—Belgium, Canada, Denmark, France, Iceland, Italy, Luxembourg, the Netherlands, Norway, Portugal, the United States, and the United Kingdom. They reaffirmed their support of the United Nations, vowed to cooperate in the maintenance of the stability and well-being of the North Atlantic region, and promised to work together for collective defense and the preservation of peace and general security.

Although the pact bound its members to settle international disputes by peaceful means, Article 5 stated that "the Parties agree that an armed attack against one or more of them in Europe or North America shall be considered an attack against them all." Any attack would be met by armed force, if necessary. Each member state was permitted to adopt its own response to aggression after consultation with its allies. The treaty provided for the establishment of the NATO council, on which each of the signatory states was to be represented. The council created a defense committee and other departments to develop measures for the nations' common defense. No signatory was committed absolutely to go to war, but the treaty was a powerful moral commitment to aid members threatened by aggression. The treaty was to be in effect for at least twenty years, and could be renewed.

Senate hearings on the North Atlantic Treaty, while not endangering its chances of ratification by the United States, resulted in sometimes bitter debate concerning the wisdom of U.S. involvement. Prominent national political figures, such as Senator Robert Taft, warned against the United States assuming major long-term responsibilities. These discussions revealed that the Truman Administration could not anticipate all the military implications of the new alliance. Nevertheless, on July 21, 1949, the Senate approved the North Atlantic Treaty by a vote of 82-13. Eleven of the thirteen who voted "no" were Republicans, but both Republicans and Democrats supported the treaty. By late August, following ratification by member governments, the North Atlantic Treaty Organization officially went into effect. The next two years saw the creation of the alliance's administrative structure and the planning for military cooperation under the NATO system.

The adoption of the pact demonstrated the signatories' willingness to make military commitments for their common security. Although NATO was never used in actual combat with the Soviet Union, its formation illustrated the unity of spirit and dedication of its Western democracies. Members who entered NATO later included Greece and Turkey (1952), West Germany (1955), and Spain (1981). NATO succeeded in fulfilling its primary purpose of creating a viable military counterweight to Soviet power.

With the collapse of communist systems in the states of Eastern Europe in 1989, followed by the disintegration of the Soviet Union in 1991, the relevance and functions of NATO had to be considered. Despite the apparent ending of the Cold War, all member governments agreed that the organization still served the primary objective of promoting stability within Europe, even as new problems (such as the Yugoslav civil war) appeared on the horizon. Several East European states formerly associated with the Soviet Union applied during the 1990's for NATO membership, fearful of the possibility of a resurgence of Russian expansionism. Moscow consistently opposed those overtures, however, which in turn provided renewed credibility of the need for this defensive alliance system to exist against potential Russian aggression in the twenty-first century.

—*Theodore A. Wilson, updated by Taylor Stults*

ADDITIONAL READING:

Acheson, Dean. *Present at the Creation: My Years in the State Department*. New York: W. W. Norton, 1969. Memoirs of the U.S. secretary of state.

Feis, Herbert. *From Trust to Terror: The Onset of the Cold War, 1945-1950*. New York: W. W. Norton, 1970. Provides a detailed account of the issues and crises during the Cold War in the later 1940's.

Kaplan, Lawrence S. *NATO and the United States: The Enduring Alliance*. New York: Twayne, 1988. Solid survey of the United States' relationship with its NATO partners.

Rose, Clive. *Campaigns Against Western Defence: NATO's Adversaries and Critics*. New York: St. Martin's Press, 1985. An unusual perspective on NATO, assessing its opponents.

Sherwen, Nicholas, ed. *NATO's Anxious Birth: The Prophetic Vision of the 1940's*. New York: St. Martin's Press, 1985. Diverse topical essays discuss the formative period of the alliance.

Truman, Harry. *Memoirs: Years of Trial and Hope, 1946-1952*. Garden City, N.Y.: Doubleday, 1956. The president's personal account of the events and negotiations leading to the Western alliance in the late 1940's.

Vandenberg, Arthur H. *The Private Papers of Senator Vandenberg*. Boston: Houghton Mifflin, 1952. Observations of a prominent supporter of Western defense.

SEE ALSO: 1945, Yalta Conference; 1945, United Nations Charter Convention; 1945, Potsdam Conference; 1947, Truman Doctrine; 1948, Berlin Blockade; 1948, Truman Is Elected President.

1950 ■ KOREAN WAR: *the first test of the U.S. policy of containment articulated in the Truman Doctrine, the conflict escalated from a U.N.-led "police action" to a confrontation between the United States and the People's Republic of China*

DATE: June 25, 1950-July 27, 1953
LOCALE: Korean Peninsula
CATEGORY: Wars, uprisings, and civil unrest
KEY FIGURES:

Dwight David Eisenhower (1890-1969), thirty-fourth president of the United States, 1953-1961

Kim Il Sung (1912-1994), premier of the Democratic People's Republic of Korea

Douglas MacArthur (1880-1964), commander in chief of the Far East and supreme commander of United Nations forces

Syngman Rhee (1875-1965), president of the Republic of Korea

Joseph Stalin (Iosif Vissarionovich Dzhugashvili, 1879-1953), marshal of the Soviet Union and general secretary of the Central Committee of the Communist Party

Harry S Truman (1884-1972), thirty-third president of the United States, 1945-1953

SUMMARY OF EVENT. At the end of World War II, Korea was a nation divided to allow for occupation by several members of the victorious Allied coalition. The so-called Hermit Kingdom, which had been under Japanese control for many years, was occupied by Soviet and U.S. forces, and the thirty-eighth parallel was set as a temporary line of demarcation. In their zone north of the parallel, the Soviets organized a communist regime, which was named the Democratic People's Republic of Korea (North Korea) in 1948. An old-time communist, Kim Il Sung, was its first premier. In the south, various elements struggled for power until the party of the "father of Korean nationalism," Syngman Rhee, won a United Nations-sponsored election. On August 15, 1948, Rhee became president of the Republic of Korea (South Korea).

Both Korean governments were determined to achieve unification on their own terms. Large-scale guerrilla incursions into the south were supported by the North Koreans, and retaliatory raids by South Korean forces kept the divided country in a state of crisis. Despite this situation, U.S. troops were withdrawn in June, 1949, leaving behind only a small group of technical advisers. South Korea, whose army was small, ill-trained, and poorly equipped, faced an adversary that possessed an army of 135,000 men equipped with modern Russian weapons. North Korea also had between 150 and 200 combat airplanes.

Although South Korean leaders and some in the United States feared that North Korea might attack across the thirty-eighth parallel at any time, Secretary of State Dean Acheson gave further evidence of the United States' disinterest by stating on January 12, 1950, that South Korea was not within the "defense perimeter" of the United States in the Pacific. Some authorities have suggested that Acheson's remarks sent misleading signals to North Korea about the United States' commitment to the security of South Korea. As yet, there is no documentary evidence to determine if these remarks had any effect on either North Korea or the Soviet Union. However, after the fall of the Soviet Union, historians found evidence to suggest that Joseph Stalin was deeply involved in planning the initial invasion and secretly supplied North Korea with Soviet pilots to counter U.S. air power.

The attack came on June 25, 1950. North Korean armed forces—armored units and mechanized divisions supported by massed artillery—struck without warning across the demarcation line. Meeting only uncoordinated resistance, North Korean tanks were moving into the outer suburb of Seoul, the capital of South Korea, within thirty-six hours. Contrary to communist expectations, the United States reacted swiftly and with great determination. With U.S. encouragement, the United Nations Security Council met in special session on the day of the attack. The Soviet Union was boycotting the council at the time, and a resolution calling for an immediate end to hostilities and withdrawal of North Korean forces to their former positions on the thirty-eighth parallel was passed unanimously.

When the United Nations resolution was ignored by North Korea, the Security Council convened on June 27, and adopted a resolution that recommended that members "of the United Nations furnish such assistance to the Republic of Korea as may be necessary to repel the armed attack." President Harry S Truman ignored recommendations of caution and acted to enforce the U.N. resolutions. On June 27, he committed U.S. air and naval forces to the conflict, as well as ground forces previously stationed in Japan.

These commitments were inadequate to stem North Korean advances. By the end of June, more than half of South Korea's army had been destroyed, and U.S. units were forced to fight countless rearguard actions in a retreat southward. In early August, a defense perimeter was created around the important port of Pusan, and after intense fighting, a stable defense line was assured. As U.S. forces and contingents from fifteen other nations arrived, General Douglas MacArthur, commander in chief of the Far East and supreme commander of U.N. forces, decided to employ his troops not in a frontal offensive from Pusan but in a daring amphibious landing at Inchon, a west coast port just miles from Seoul. This brilliantly conceived but risky operation, launched on September 15, 1950, was a great success. The North Korean Army, threatened with encirclement, was forced to retreat back across the thirty-eighth parallel.

With the North Korean forces in retreat, the U.N. command was forced to make the single most important decision of the war: Should the retreating North Koreans be chased across the demarcation line? Pressed by public demands for total victory, the Truman Administration cited the Security Council's resolution and gave MacArthur authorization to pursue the Northern troops across the thirty-eighth parallel. MacArthur already had decided to take this step. He was confident that the North Korean Army was effectively destroyed and that the Soviet Union and China would not risk a confrontation with U.N. forces led by the United States. The first crossing took place on October 1. United Nations and South Korea forces sped north, and by late November they were nearing the Yalu River boundary between North Korea and the People's Republic of China.

The seesaw struggle was reversed once again by the entry of Chinese "volunteers" into the war. Chinese leaders had warned that they would not allow North Korea to be invaded and would come to the aid of their communist allies. U.S. intelligence services and MacArthur had dismissed these threats as rhetoric, but it soon became clear that Beijing was not bluffing. By late October, thousands of Chinese soldiers had crossed the Yalu River. A month later, they struck at the exposed flank and rear of MacArthur's overextended armies. By early December, U.N. troops were again in headlong retreat, a withdrawal marked by great heroism but accounting for near-disaster for the U.N. forces.

In the United States, there was widespread fear of an expanded war in Korea. A Gallup poll estimated that 55 percent of the people in the United States believed that World War III had begun soon after the Chinese entry into the war. A new line was organized south of the thirty-eighth parallel, and through the remaining winter and early spring months, the lines fluctuated from south of Seoul to north of the thirty-eighth parallel. On April 11, Truman relieved MacArthur of his U.N. and U.S. commands, after MacArthur publicly questioned Truman's prohibition on U.S. bombing of North Korean supply depots inside China. MacArthur's support of a wider war against the People's Republic of China had long been opposed by Truman, who feared an even greater conflict with the Soviet Union.

KOREAN WAR, 1950-1953

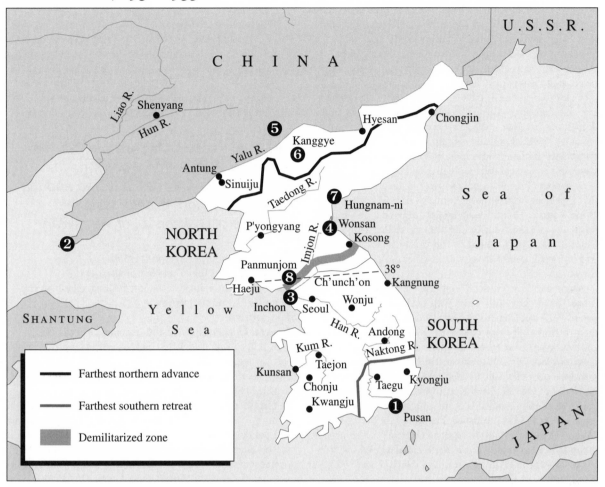

(1) Main U.N. base. (2) Russian-Chinese naval installation. (3) Sept. 15, 1950, U.N. forces land. (4) Oct. 26, 1950, U.N. forces land. (5) Nov. 26, 1950, Chinese attack. (6) Dec., 1950, Battle of the Reservoir. (7) Dec. 9, 1950, U.N. forces evacuate. (8) July 27, 1953, armistice signed.

Military stalemate was finally reached in July, 1951. The conflict deteriorated into trench warfare, which was marked by indecisive but bloody fighting, at which the Chinese were particularly adept. The situation lasted for two cruel years. During this time, more than a million U.S. troops served in Korea. For much of this period, talks went on, seeking a cease-fire and armistice. On June 10, 1951, communist and U.N. delegations began negotiations, talks initiated by the North Koreans and welcomed by the majority of people in the United States. Most of the talks took place in the city of Panmunjom, located in the no-man's-land between the two armies. The talks broke down repeatedly because of antagonism generated by North Korean accusations of germ warfare, disputes over prisoner of war exchanges, and other issues.

The stalemate was a source of mounting frustration in the United States, where it influenced both the rise of McCarthyism and the election of Republican Dwight Eisenhower to the presidency. Eisenhower won support by promising to go to Korea if elected. He kept his pledge, but the visit had no noticeable effect on the success of the peace talks. The North Korean and Chinese negotiators ultimately modified their position on forcible repatriation of prisoners, and an armistice agreement was signed at Panmunjom on July 27, 1953. It provided for a cease-fire and for withdrawal of both armies two kilometers from the existing battle line, which ran from coast to coast from just below the thirty-eighth parallel in the west to thirty miles north of it in the east. The agreement also provided for the creation of a Neutral Nations Supervisory Commission to carry out the armistice terms. It further called for a political conference to settle all remaining questions, including the fate of prisoners who refused to return to their homelands. The political conference was never held, and relations between North and South Korea deteriorated because of both Koreas' claims on "unification" with the other.

The Korean war had lasted three years and one month and taken more than four million lives. There was little celebration in the United States. Upon signing the armistice in Panmunjom, U.S. Commander Mark Clark declared, "I cannot find it in me to exalt at this hour." General Omar Bradley later observed that the conflict was "the wrong war, in the wrong place, at the wrong time, with the wrong enemy." Some commentators did commend the United States' resolve in containing communism and defending South Korea, but after the deaths of fifty-four thousand troops, a hundred thousand wounded, eight thousand missing in action, and a cost of twenty-two billion dollars, most people in the United States were simply relieved that the fighting had ceased.

A symbol of the war's unique status in history was the fact that President Truman never formally had declared war on North Korea or China. Truman simply referred to the military hostilities in Korea as a United Nations "police action." Because it was soon followed by the United States' protracted war in Vietnam, the Korean War soon became known as "the forgotten war."

After the 1953 armistice, both the United States and the Soviet Union moved to fortify their positions on the Korean peninsula. Apart from isolated incidents at the border between the two Koreas, the two sides avoided open military conflict. Lacking an agreement to end hostilities, North and South Korea have remained in a state of war, and more than a million troops guard the 150-mile demilitarized zone. The United States has continued to provide South Korea with military aid. In 1995, more than thirty thousand U.S. troops remained in South Korea to ensure the 1953 armistice. The same year, President Bill Clinton praised the "never surpassed courage" of U.S. troops at the dedication of the Korean War Memorial in Washington.

—*Theodore A. Wilson, updated by Lawrence I. Clark*

ADDITIONAL READING:

Blair, Clay. *The Forgotten War: America in Korea, 1950-1953*. New York: Times Books, 1987. A well-researched, comprehensive examination of the origins and conduct of the Korean War. Index.

Hastings, Max. *The Korean War*. New York: Simon & Schuster, 1987. An in-depth examination of military operations of the nations involved in the Korean War, from a British military historian. Chronology of the war, bibliography, index.

Hoyt, Edwin P. *The Day the Chinese Attacked: Korea, 1950*. New York: McGraw-Hill, 1990. An investigation of the misperceptions and policy failures in the United States and China that led to the Chinese entry into the Korean War in October, 1950. Bibliography, index.

James, D. Clayton, and Anne S. Wells. *Refighting the Last War: Command and Crisis in Korea, 1950-1953*. New York: Free Press, 1993. Provides a detailed examination of the conduct of the leadership, personalities, and viewpoints of President Truman, Douglas MacArthur, Matthew B. Ridgeway, Mark Clark, and Turner Joy. Index.

Stokesbury, James L. *A Short History of the Korean War*. New York: William Morrow, 1988. A brief introduction to the

sources, conduct, and outcome of the Korean War. Suggested readings, index.

Whelan, Richard. *Drawing the Line: The Korean War, 1950-1953*. Boston: Little, Brown, 1990. Using declassified documents, this detailed examination of the war focuses mainly on the war's roots and the effects of U.S. politics on the Korean War.

SEE ALSO: 1947, Truman Doctrine; 1948, Truman Is Elected President; 1950, Truman-MacArthur Confrontation; 1951, McCarthy Hearings; 1952, Eisenhower Is Elected President.

1950 ■ TRUMAN-MACARTHUR CONFRONTATION: *a disagreement between the head of military forces in Korea and the U.S. commander in chief tests the principle of civil control of the military*

DATE: October 14, 1950-April 11, 1951
LOCALE: Korea, Tokyo, and Washington, D.C.
CATEGORIES: Diplomacy and international relations; Wars, uprisings, and civil unrest
KEY FIGURES:
Douglas MacArthur (1880-1964), commander in chief of U.S. forces in the Far East and supreme commander of U.N. forces in Korea
Harry S Truman (1884-1972), thirty-third president of the United States, 1945-1953

SUMMARY OF EVENT. General Douglas MacArthur of the U.S. Army was a powerful military leader and a highly controversial politician, having been a Republican Party contender in the presidential campaigns of 1944, 1948, and 1952. As the overseer of the occupation of Japan, he was the obvious choice as commander of all United Nations forces when the Korean War broke out in June, 1950.

The Korean War challenged the willingness of the U.S. people to accept the burden of a discouraging and dirty struggle in order to check communist aggression. It was a war being fought for limited ends, without hope of total victory. This was the first war to be carried forward under the policy of containment initiated by President Harry S Truman. A cause of serious dispute was whether the brand of military strategy dictated by the containment policy would prove workable or would be tolerable to the public and to Congress. In the first year of the Korean War, the question of how communist expansion should be met found expression in a personal, political, and constitutional struggle between President Truman and General MacArthur. MacArthur's flouting of a strategy that had presidential approval resulted in his dismissal. A tremendous public outcry ensued. The MacArthur-Truman confrontation was one of the most serious threats in the nation's history to the basic principles of civilian control over the military.

The circumstances in which the Korean War began guaranteed that MacArthur would have a commanding role. In June, 1950, MacArthur, after a long and illustrious military career,

President Truman pins a Distinguished Service Medal on the shirt of General Douglas MacArthur during ceremonies on an airstrip on Wake Island, October 14, 1950. The stern looks of both men suggest the confrontation to come. (AP/Wide World Photos)

was serving as Supreme Commander for the Allied Powers (SCAP). Since September, 1945, MacArthur had governed Japan, exercising the functions and enjoying much of the prestige of a head of state. For some time, MacArthur had disapproved of the Far Eastern policy of the Truman Administration. MacArthur believed that Asia would be the supreme test of communist expansion, not Europe.

When North Korea invaded South Korea in June, 1950, President Truman responded and gained United Nations' sanction. MacArthur was appointed supreme commander of U.N. forces in Korea. Operating out of his headquarters in Tokyo and using staff officers who were personally devoted to him, MacArthur began to plan a bold offensive counterstrike that would place the United Nations on the way to a complete victory. This plan called for amphibious landings at Inchon, the port on Korea's west coast a few miles from Seoul, and was carried forward against strong opposition from some military and naval leaders. MacArthur dismissed all objections, revealing a pattern of authoritarianism that was to become clearer as the weeks and months passed. He believed that Korea provided priceless opportunity for the United States to recoup lost prestige and to stop Asian communism once and for all. He also saw this war as an outstanding opportunity to conclude a brilliant military career.

As the U.N. forces approached China in the North, rumors of Chinese intervention abounded. MacArthur downplayed them. He advocated, if necessary, a preventive war against China, including the dropping of twenty or thirty atomic bombs on Chinese cities. He supported a policy of encouraging the Chiang Kai-shek regime on Formosa and employing part of Chiang's army in Korea. This was in direct opposition to Truman's aim of preventing any widening of the war. MacArthur's outspokenness about Formosa caused the first dispute with Truman, and apparently led the president to give serious thought to firing the general. Instead, Truman ordered MacArthur to withdraw the statement, which MacArthur did.

President Truman was forced to move carefully in his relations with MacArthur because of MacArthur's great popularity and the power of his political supporters. The stunning success of the Inchon landings added to the general's reputation. Military success also allowed the Truman Administration to expand its political goals in Korea. For a time, Truman and MacArthur worked toward the same ends. The administration's initial aim had been the restoration of the thirty-eighth parallel as the boundary between North and South Korea, but in September, Truman approved MacArthur's proposal that United Nations and South Korean forces move into North Korea and occupy the entire country. This action followed a

National Security Council recommendation that all North Korea be occupied, unless Soviet or Chinese troops were encountered. The thirty-eighth parallel was crossed on October 7, and the campaign proceeded without difficulty. By mid-November, advance units were nearing the Yalu River. MacArthur's headquarters was supremely confident that complete victory was assured and discounted growing rumors of military intervention by the Chinese communists.

At this point, an extraordinary conference took place. Truman flew to remote Wake Island for a meeting with MacArthur on October 14. The fact that the president would travel so far to meet with a subordinate was evidence of the delicacy of the relationship between the two men. The Wake Island conference glossed over the differences between them. MacArthur provided assurances that the Chinese would not intervene, but was in error. On November 26, Chinese forces crossed the Yalu River and attacked the exposed flanks of MacArthur's forces. There followed a numbing retreat, and by Christmas, 1950, United Nations forces were once again fighting below the thirty-eighth parallel.

Truman and MacArthur now took opposing positions. The Truman Administration, thoroughly frightened by China's action, moved to limit the war. MacArthur pressed for attacks against the Chinese troops and supplies in Manchuria and, implicitly, for expansion of the war into China proper. The president refused and decided to allow only the Korean side of the Yalu River bridges to be bombed. This was a compromise that infuriated MacArthur.

MacArthur became increasingly belligerent. In January, 1951, he recommended a naval blockade of China, air attacks to destroy Chinese military and industrial capabilities, and the use of Nationalist Chinese forces in Korea. The president again restrained him, arguing that the worldwide threat of the Soviet Union made a war of containment necessary in Korea. The fact that Lieutenant General Matthew Ridgway, MacArthur's deputy in Korea, was being dealt with directly by the White House and the Pentagon, and was making a success of limited war, made MacArthur's position more difficult.

The final phase of the MacArthur-Truman confrontation began when the general attempted to bypass the president in order to gain support for his program from Congress and the U.S. people. MacArthur's practice of making public his differences with the president and Washington policymakers angered and embarrassed Truman on several occasions. The break came in late March, 1951. When MacArthur learned that President Truman planned to issue a peace offer, he released a military appraisal, a document that amounted to an ultimatum to the Chinese. It destroyed any hope of a negotiated settlement and precipitated Truman's decision to dismiss MacArthur. "By this act," Truman stated, "MacArthur left me no choice—I could no longer tolerate his insubordination." Henceforth, the president was concerned only about the timing of the act, but the timing was to be decided by MacArthur and his allies in Congress. On April 5, Representative Joseph Martin read a letter from MacArthur on the floor of the House of Repre-

sentatives. MacArthur again rejected the limited war policy and called for total victory in Asia. A series of meetings began in the White House the following day. On April 11, President Truman cabled MacArthur in Tokyo and, at the same time, informed the press that the general was being relieved of his commands because he was unable to give wholehearted support to the president's policies.

General MacArthur returned to the United States a triumphant hero. He addressed a joint session of Congress. Across the nation, there was a tremendous surge of support for him. A joint Senate committee conducted hearings during the rest of the summer. Truman rode out the emotional reaction, secure in the conviction that his decision had been correct. He was supported openly by his military advisers. Powerful foreign leaders praised his courage. After two months of hearings, the committee issued no report.

—Theodore A. Wilson, updated by Eugene L. Rasor

ADDITIONAL READING:

James, D. Clayton. *Command Crisis: MacArthur and the Korean War.* Colorado Springs: U.S. Air Force Academy, 1982. Contends that the Truman-MacArthur confrontation had been overemphasized. Argues that poor communication seems to have been as important as policy disputes.

_____. *The Years of MacArthur, 1880-1964.* 3 vols. Boston: Houghton Mifflin, 1970-1985. A definitive biography of MacArthur, based on more than twenty years of research and hundreds of interviews. Balanced and restrained. The third volume covers the confrontation with Truman.

McCullough, David. *Truman.* New York: Simon & Schuster, 1992. A Pulitzer Prize-winning biography of Truman. Concludes that the Korean War was Truman's worst ordeal and asserts that the timing of the decision to remove MacArthur was crucial.

Rasor, Eugene L. *General Douglas MacArthur, 1880-1964: Historiography and Annotated Bibliography.* Bibliographies of Battles and Leaders 12. Westport, Conn.: Greenwood Press, 1994. A comprehensive compilation of writings and publications about MacArthur. Includes a historiographical narrative and an annotated bibliography of 759 individual publications.

Rovere, Richard H., and Arthur M. Schlesinger, Jr. *General MacArthur and President Truman: The Struggle for Control of American Foreign Policy.* New Brunswick, N.J.: Transaction, 1992. Originally published in 1951 as *The General and the President*, this negative critique of MacArthur and his actions in Korea concludes that MacArthur challenged the doctrines of collective security and of civilian authority.

Spanier, John W. *The Truman-MacArthur Controversy and the Korean War.* New York: Norton, 1959, 1965. A scholarly assessment of the controversy, emphasizing the decision that the United Nations forces should cross the thirty-eighth parallel and MacArthur's end-of-the-war offensive of November, 1950. Detached appraisal and support for Truman's decision.

Truman, Harry S. *Years of Trial and Decision.* Vol. 2 in *Memoirs.* New York: Doubleday, 1955-1956. Includes recollections and rationale for the Wake Island conference, the decision to recall MacArthur, and the Senate hearings in the summer of 1951. Describes MacArthur as a mercurial character and argues that the Joint Chiefs of Staff unanimously supported Truman.

SEE ALSO: 1947, Truman Doctrine; 1950, Korean War.

1951 ■ MCCARTHY HEARINGS: *Cold War paranoia tests the principles of democracy, threatening the civil rights of U.S. citizens*

DATE: March 21, 1951-December, 1954
LOCALE: Washington, D.C.
CATEGORIES: Civil rights; Government and politics
KEY FIGURES:
Roy M. Cohn (1927-1986), chief counsel to the Senate's Permanent Investigating Subcommittee
Alger Hiss (1904-1996), former State Department official accused of being a communist spy
Owen Lattimore (1900-1989), professor of Far Eastern affairs
Joseph Raymond McCarthy (1908-1957), senator from Wisconsin and chair of the Senate Permanent Investigating Subcommittee
Margaret Chase Smith (1897-1995), senator from Maine
Harold R. Velde (1910-1985), congressman from Illinois and chair of HUAC during the entertainment investigations
Arthur V. Watkins (1886-1973), senator from Utah

SUMMARY OF EVENT. On February 9, 1950, Senator Joseph R. McCarthy of Wisconsin addressed the Ohio County Women's Republican Club of Wheeling, West Virginia. He said, "While I cannot take the time to name all of the men in the State Department who have been named as members of the Communist Party and members of a spy ring, I have here in my hand a list of two hundred and five that were known to the Secretary of State as being members of the Communist Party and who nevertheless are still working and shaping the policy of the State Department." Later McCarthy revised his figures downward to fifty-seven, but the shocking allegations were that the secretary of state knew of these persons, and that they continued nonetheless to shape U.S. government policies.

McCarthy was exploiting a sensitive and emotional issue, for it was a known fact that there had been communists in the government, the labor movement, certain intellectual circles, and "popular front" organizations shortly before, during, and after World War II. Communist cells had functioned in Washington, D.C., during the 1930's, numbering among their members government officials such as Alger Hiss, whom an admitted communist agent, Whitaker Chambers, had named on August 3, 1948, as a prewar member of the Communist Party. Hiss brought a libel suit but was eventually indicted on charges of perjury and sentenced to five years in prison. Hiss had been highly regarded, and his conviction fueled growing Cold War fear that if he could be a communist, almost anyone might be guilty of such subversion.

Fear of communism, to be sure, had existed well before World War II. In the early 1920's, in the wake of the Bolshevik Revolution of 1917, Attorney General A. Mitchell Palmer and a young J. Edgar Hoover had led the charge against "foreign" elements in public life, resulting in such phenomena as the Red Scare of 1919-1920. Boom and depression also encouraged people to look for enemies outside the mainstream "American" ideals of motherhood, apple pie, and patriotism. America-first movements manifested themselves in a variety of ways, from Huey P. Long to Father Coughlin to the Ku Klux Klan. Anti-communist fervor seemed justified by events such as the Russian purge trials and executions of 1936-1938 and, more important, the signing of the Russo-Nazi Pact in August, 1939. After World War II, the Soviet determination to build a world power led President Harry S Truman to form his policy of containment and, on March 22, 1947, to institute a "loyalty order" to ensure detection and removal of subversive elements within the government. Bolstered by the Smith Act of 1940—which required that aliens in the United States register with the government and which made it unlawful for anyone to preach the overthrow of the U.S. government—such policies led to the conviction and sentencing of communist spies but also threatened innocent people with unfashionable political affiliations. Lives were being ruined, such as those of the "Hollywood Ten," a group of film writers and directors who in 1947 appeared before the House Committee on Un-American Activities (popularly, HUAC), chaired by Harold R. Velde, and refused to "name names"; they were supported by a cadre of famous actors who flew to Washington for the event. The Ten were subsequently blacklisted by Hollywood executives and did not work in their chosen profession for years afterward. Some in the entertainment community did inform, but many more—actor Zero Mostel and folksinger Pete Seeger among them—appeared at the hearings and denounced HUAC's investigations, refusing to inform. Although many Americans recognized the dangers of a growing paranoia, others wanted action to eradicate what seemed a communist "conspiracy" in their midst.

Thus, when the specter of a home-grown communist conspiracy was raised, a fearful nativist element existed to give it legitimacy, and Joseph McCarthy, the Republican senator from Wisconsin, appeared as the incarnation of that nativism and the nemesis of communism. After his appearance before the women's club in Wheeling, McCarthy—unable to name two hundred five, eighty-five, or even fifty-seven communists in the State Department—shifted his attack to Professor Owen Lattimore, whom he called "the top espionage agent" in the United States, and to certain diplomats. Some Republicans thought that McCarthy had struck a rich vein that might yield political treasures (perhaps the presidency in 1952), but other Republicans, including Senator Margaret Chase Smith, disagreed. She did not want the Senate being used for "selfish political gain at the sacrifice of individual reputations and national unity." A committee headed by Millard Tydings, Democratic senator from Maryland, investigated McCarthy's accusations and concluded that McCarthy had perpetuated "a fraud and a hoax" on the Senate and the American people, and that his statements represented "perhaps the most nefarious campaign of half-truths and untruth in the history of the Republic." McCarthy's defenders rushed to his support, and he was able to continue his crusade for another four years.

In 1953, as head of the Senate Permanent Investigating Subcommittee, McCarthy became more sensational, strident, and unbelievable, now associating the Democratic Party with communist tendencies. He denounced Charles E. Bohlen's appointment as ambassador based on his close alignment with the foreign policy of Franklin D. Roosevelt and Harry Truman (Bohlen was confirmed anyway), and then claimed that the Democratic Party was a perpetrator of twenty years of treason. McCarthy caused his own downfall in the late spring of 1954, however, when he displayed ruthlessness during the nationally televised Army-McCarthy hearings before an audience of more than twenty million people. McCarthy had charged Secretary of the Army Robert T. Stevens, along with Brigadier General Ralph W. Zwicker, of covering up espionage activities at Ft. Monmouth's Signal Corps Engineering Laboratories. The Army countercharged that McCarthy and Roy M. Cohn, counsel to McCarthy's Senate subcommittee, were attempting to exert pressure on the Army and the War Department. Cohn resigned on July 20, although McCarthy was cleared. Finally, on September 27, a Senate committee headed by the venerable Arthur V. Watkins of Utah recommended that McCarthy be censured. McCarthy's reign of terror was effectively ended in December of 1954, when the Senate condemned him for bringing the Senate "into dishonor and disrepute" and thus impairing that institution's "dignity."

It was later proven that many communist cells had as many double agents working for the United States as there were die-hard converts. In the 1990's, moreover, questions surrounding Hiss's conviction showed it to have been flawed. Perhaps the ultimate lesson of the McCarthy hearings is that, when a people allows the freedoms they cherish to be compromised by innuendo, fear, and finger-pointing, those freedoms may be in greater danger from their supposed defenders than from their perceived threats.

—*William M. Tuttle, updated by Paul Barton-Kriese*

ADDITIONAL READING:

Cohn, Roy. *McCarthy*. New York: New American Library, 1968. Written by one of McCarthy's main associates, this book proffers a flattering account of McCarthy's rise and fall.

Cook, Fred J. *The Nightmare Decade: The Life and Times of Senator Joe McCarthy*. New York: Random House, 1971. Cook, a former FBI agent, sees McCarthy as a person who was able to twist fact and fiction together to create the type of reality he wanted, and needed, to see.

Fried, Richard. *Nightmare in Red: The McCarthy Era in Perspective*. New York: Oxford University Press, 1990. A study of the anticommunist movement in the United States after World War II up to the beginning of Dwight D. Eisenhower's presidency in 1952.

Navasky, Victor S. *Naming Names*. New York: Viking

Press, 1980. The editor of the liberal periodical *The Nation* provides a meticulously researched history of the HUAC hearings in this "moral detective story" that seeks answers to the question, "What happens when a state puts pressure on its citizens to betray their fellows?"

Newman, Robert. *Owen Lattimore and the "Loss" of China*. Berkeley: University of California Press, 1992. One of the major suspected "spies" accused by McCarthy and the political and ideological storms waged around him. An excellent picture of life in the United States during the McCarthy years.

Schrecker, Ellen. *The Age of McCarthyism: A Brief History with Documents*. Boston: St. Martin's Press, 1994. An excellent overview of the McCarthy years, collecting many important primary documents.

SEE ALSO: 1919, Red Scare; 1938, HUAC Investigations.

1952 ■ DEVELOPMENT OF A POLIO VACCINE: *a paralytic disease is nearly eradicated in one of the greatest medical victories in history*

DATE: 1952-1956
LOCALE: Various research centers in the United States
CATEGORIES: Health and medicine; Science and technology
KEY FIGURES:

John Franklin Enders (1897-1985), researcher who demonstrated the growth of poliovirus in laboratory cultures of tissue

Thomas F. Francis, Jr. (1900-1969), director of the Poliomyelitis Vaccine Evaluation Center, which directed the 1954 Salk vaccine field trial

Oveta Culp Hobby (1905-1995), secretary of health, education, and welfare in 1955

Basil O'Connor (1892-1972), president of the National Foundation for Infantile Paralysis

Albert Bruce Sabin (1906-1993), developer of an effective oral polio vaccine

Jonas Edward Salk (1914-1995), developer of the poliomyelitis vaccine that bears his name

Leonard Andrew Scheele (1907-1993), surgeon general of the United States in 1955

SUMMARY OF EVENT. Although poliomyelitis is an ancient disease, dating to the time of the Pharaohs in ancient Egypt, little was known about it until the twentieth century. In 1908, Karl Landsteiner and Erwin Popper discovered that the disease was caused by a virus rather than bacteria. This discovery itself presented new problems, for viruses could not be grown for experimental purposes as readily as bacteria. Another problem was the nature of the disease itself. It was mistakenly assumed that polio was a disease of the nervous system—an understandable error, in view of its symptoms. As late as 1937, various useless, and in at least one case harmful, immunization measures were tried that were based upon such erroneous ideas. The discovery that polio is actually the product of an infection of the intestinal tract brought about through contaminated food or water provided the real breakthrough upon which the development of an effective vaccine rested. The National Foundation for Infantile Paralysis ("infantile paralysis" was a common name for poliomyelitis in the 1930's and 1940's) was formed in 1938 with the support of President Franklin Roosevelt, who (unbeknownst to much of the American public during his long presidency) had lost the use of both his legs to the disease. Basil O'Connor was appointed president of the foundation. Funded through the famous March of Dimes program, the foundation was dedicated solely to the eradication of polio, and its enormously successful publicity and fund-raising programs played a great part, both positively and negatively, in the development of the Salk vaccine.

By the end of World War II, significant progress had been made in polio research. First was the demonstration that only three strains of the polio virus existed, despite a much larger number of isolates. The key technological advance, however, was the demonstration by Doctors John Enders, Thomas Weller, and Frederick Robbins that poliovirus could be grown in cultures of nonnervous human tissue in the laboratory. It would now be technologically possible to test a putative vaccine in a relatively rapid and convenient procedure outside the human body. In 1954, the three Harvard scientists were awarded the Nobel Prize for Medicine for their work. By 1952, the three types of poliovirus were under study, and it had been discovered that the virus was disseminated from the intestinal tract to the nervous system through the bloodstream. It appeared that the production of a suitable vaccine was within sight, but the important question that had plagued earlier researchers—whether to develop a killed or a live vaccine—remained. Each type had its advantages and disadvantages. The National Foundation for Infantile Paralysis, the chief funder of polio research, finally decided to put its resources behind the killed virus approach, and Professor Jonas Salk of the University of Pittsburgh was selected to take charge of the project.

Salk had considerable experience in virus research and had been working with the polio virus for a long time. As the first order of business in his new position, Salk arranged for the production of each of the three strains of the virus by the Connaught Medical Research Laboratories in Toronto. He elected to use formalin in the crucial virus-killing process. Although a seemingly simple procedure, there were very real problems to overcome. Dr. Salk had to be sure that the virus had been exposed to formalin long enough for complete killing, but not so much longer that the potency of the resultant vaccine suffered. In his research, Salk had determined that exposure to the killing solution for three days reduced the amount of live virus to an immeasurable level. He then assumed that an exposure for a total of six days would effectively kill all the viruses, yet retain their immunization potential. As later events proved, his system was less than perfect.

Within a year, the vaccine was ready for testing. The first tests were conducted upon subjects who had previously con-tracted the disease and were thus immune to further infection. In these tests, Salk hoped merely to obtain an indication of the ability of his vaccine to raise the antibody count in the subjects' bloodstreams. In this respect, the tests were a success. The next step was to test the vaccine on subjects who had not previously had paralytic polio but who did have immunity to the disease through childhood exposure—the kind of exposure that only rarely results in the actual contracting of polio but produces immunity nonetheless. These tests were successful in producing higher antibody counts as well.

Although professional opinion was divided on the ultimate usefulness of his vaccine, events were soon to propel Salk into the public arena. In early 1953, he presented a confidential report of his progress to the National Foundation for Infantile Paralysis. Leakage of this report to the press created a considerable stir, and the foundation then unwisely exploited the publicity by holding a press conference at which glowing reports of progress were made to the nation. Although such publicity undoubtedly aided fund-raising, it also created an impatient expectation among the public that resulted in an increasing pressure for speedy development and release of the vaccine. Salk tried to temper these expectations with a press conference of his own, but the effect of his appearance actually was to make things worse. Instead of lessening the tension, his press conference made him into a scientist-hero overnight, and pressure continued to mount for quick development of his vaccine. A short while later, Salk successfully tested the vaccine upon individuals who had no immunity to polio. The public now seemed totally convinced that further delays were unnecessary.

Salk was now more optimistic himself, and it only remained to test the vaccine on a large scale. Basil O'Connor created a vaccine advisory committee to handle the details of contracting with several pharmaceutical companies for the preparation of the vaccine. The field trial was scheduled for the spring of 1954, and Dr. Thomas Francis, Jr., of the University of Michigan, was appointed to head a Poliomyelitis Vaccine Evaluation Center funded by the foundation to organize, administer, and interpret the results of the test.

Not everyone was sure that the vaccine was ready for such large-scale testing, however. Some researchers had difficulty in killing the polio virus with the Salk method and felt that the vaccine might therefore prove dangerous. The six pharmaceutical firms that had contracted to produce the vaccine had difficulty in preparing adequate supplies, and no one could determine why so many lots of vaccine failed the potency and safety tests and had to be discarded. This situation seemed to support the view of those who thought that the Salk vaccine was as yet unsuitable for mass trial. O'Connor and the foundation, however, feeling the pressure of public demand, which their own propaganda had helped to create, concluded that such manufacturing difficulties were not altogether unusual with a new vaccine and were thus no cause for alarm. The federal government had not been much involved in all of these developments, preferring instead to let private enterprise run its course. At this juncture, the Public Health Service simply directed that more rigorous processing controls be adhered to by the manufacturers.

Under these circumstances the field tests began on April 26, 1954. The tests were of two kinds, involving "observed areas" and "placebo control areas." In the first type, the incidence among vaccinated children was simply compared with that of unvaccinated children. In the second areas, a more scientifically valid method of study was employed.

The trials in the observed areas generally indicated that things were going well, thus furthering the public's desire for the vaccine. Dr. Francis announced, however, that the results from the placebo control areas would not be available until mid-1955, delaying release of the vaccine until that time, and this disappointing word added to an already dramatic situation. The National Foundation for Infantile Paralysis was in a difficult position. The public was clamoring for release of the vaccine, and the pharmaceutical companies were eager to get production under way. In August, before the test results were known, O'Connor took the risk of placing orders with the companies for twenty-seven million doses of vaccine. To the public, this seemed like a heroic thing to do.

The release of the Francis report on April 12, 1955, added to the unnecessarily dramatic aura surrounding the whole project. Rather than submit the results of the tests to a scientific journal for publication and then hold a press conference to answer questions, Dr. Francis, the University of Michigan, and the foundation jointly decided that the report would be presented at a public reading to which leading physicians, public health officials, and virus researchers would be invited. In addition, the presentation would be televised nationwide via closed circuits for the benefit of physicians everywhere. Press releases were given to representatives of the news media one hour before this stage show began, but rather than waiting an hour as they had been asked, the journalists immediately contacted their respective news media. A somewhat inaccurate version of the Francis report was thus being broadcast before the actual presentation had begun. Needless to say, this slipshod method of presentation did little to calm the popular excitement. The report was generally favorable, although not nearly as favorable as most people seemed to think. It indicated that the vaccine had been only 60 to 90 percent effective, and that there appeared to be no indications that the vaccine was dangerous. The duration of immunity, however, was still largely unknown.

Although Dr. Salk rather testily maintained that his vaccine was safe, some virologists were still doubtful. At any rate, public demand for the vaccine was higher than ever before, and the immediate problem of supplying this great demand was presented. The vaccine had been officially licensed for manufacture by the federal government on the same day that Dr. Francis had revealed his findings, and President Dwight D. Eisenhower completed the process by announcing that the Salk vaccine would be made available to any country—even the Soviet Union—that wished it.

Meanwhile, the six pharmaceutical houses had run into difficulty in manufacturing the millions of doses of the vaccine ordered by O'Connor. The lack of time before the onset of the summer polio season and the great quantities of vaccine under preparation resulted in the inability of the United States Laboratory of Biologics Control to test all lots of the vaccine thoroughly, so the manufacturers themselves were instructed to test their products according to government specifications. This was not an unusual procedure at the time. The specifications proved to be hard to meet, and large quantities of the vaccine had to be discarded. Because there was no requirement for the drug companies to reveal information about such discarded material, the existing control system offered no indication that things were not going well. By April 27, 1955, only some 10.5 million doses of the 27 million doses had been approved for use.

On April 26, the Laboratory of Biologics Control was notified of five cases of paralytic poliomyelitis in California among a group of children who had received vaccine manufactured by Cutter Laboratories. The fact that all these children were paralyzed in the left arm, the arm that had been injected with the vaccine, made coincidence appear unlikely. A similar case was reported in Chicago, and another California case was reported during the night. After consultation with the staff of the National Institutes of Health, Surgeon General Leonard Scheele requested that Cutter Laboratories withdraw their vaccine. The firm did so at once. The Public Health Service immediately began a study of the Cutter vaccine and manufacturing methods. A special Poliomyelitis Surveillance Unit, established at the Communicable Disease Center in Atlanta, was directed to investigate all reported cases and report daily to the Surgeon General and other health officials. By April 30, there were seventeen vaccine-linked cases of polio. The Laboratory of Biologics Control suspended approval of further quantities of the vaccine and awaited the action of the National Institutes of Health. A special committee met there on May 5-6 and concluded that minimum production standards for the vaccine needed to be revised and that any further use of the Salk vaccine should be postponed until new testing and inspection procedures could be implemented. At this meeting, the Public Health Service first learned that Cutter's manufacturing problems had been shared by the other five companies as well. On May 7, 1955, the surgeon general formally recommended that the use of the Salk vaccine be suspended.

This tragic situation practically destroyed public confidence in the vaccine, but fixing responsibility for the disaster was not easily done. It was obvious that the Cutter Laboratories had done its job as well as could have been expected. It was widely believed that the whole program had been rushed unnecessarily, and the dispute among professionals regarding the relative merits of killed and live vaccines rose to new levels of intensity. It was increasingly believed that the federal government had not played an active enough role in the development and testing processes. Dr. Albert Sabin, who was working on a live type of vaccine, was especially critical and urged that the entire killed vaccine program be abandoned. Basil O'Connor refused to succumb to this pressure, and work on the Salk vaccine continued. The resignation of the Secretary of Health, Education, and Welfare, Oveta Culp Hobby, at this point did much to relieve tensions all around.

Revision of testing standards and manufacturing methods finally enabled the Salk vaccine to be put to use. It had been discovered that the viruses had clumped together in processing and that those in the center of the clumps had not always been killed by the formalin solution. The answer was simply to filter the virus material before its treatment with the killing solution. Other improvements were made so that by 1956 the Salk vaccine was thoroughly safe and reliable, although still less than 100 percent effective and difficult to administer in some field situations.

Despite its difficulties, the vaccine trial ultimately proved to be a triumph of technology over disease. The trial arguably involved the largest peacetime mobilization in U.S. history, with participation of nearly two million children from 213 cities and counties in forty-four states. Findings from placebo control areas, in which the incidence of polio among vaccinated children was compared with that in children receiving an inactive injection, indicated a success rate of between 80 and 90 percent.

The Salk vaccine was superseded by an attenuated version developed by Albert Sabin later in the decade; the inactivated form ceased being manufactured in the United States in 1965. However, the Salk vaccine remains an important component of the fight against polio elsewhere in the world. Its success is found in the numbers: The last natural case of polio in the United States was in 1979. By the early 1990's, polio had been eradicated in the Western Hemisphere. Worldwide use of both the Salk and Sabin vaccines has led to a realistic goal for the World Health Organization: the complete, worldwide elimination of polio. —*Terrill J. Clements, updated by Richard Adler*

ADDITIONAL READING:

Carter, Richard. *Breakthrough: The Saga of Jonas Salk.* New York: Pocket Books, 1967. A biography of Jonas Salk, combined with a detailed account of the polio vaccine story.

Francis, Thomas F., Jr., et al. "Evaluation of the 1954 Field Trials of Poliomyelitis Vaccine: Summary Report." *American Journal of Public Health* 45, no. 1 (May, 1955): supplement. Report of the Salk vaccine trials, as presented at the University of Michigan on April 12, 1955.

Garrett, Laurie. *The Coming Plague.* New York: Farrar, Straus & Giroux, 1994. Detailed discussion of the conditions associated with the spread of viruses and other microbes. Includes descriptions of the spread of polio.

Karlen, Arno. *Man and Microbes.* New York: G. P. Putnam's Sons, 1995. Studies the interactions between humans and microbes. Presents history of the spread of disease.

Salk, Jonas E. "Vaccination Against Paralytic Poliomyelitis: Performance and Prospects." *American Journal of Public Health* 45, no. 1 (May, 1955): 575-596. Salk's presentation on results of the field trials, as delivered April 12, 1955, at the University of Michigan.

Smith, Jane S. *Patenting the Sun: Polio and the Salk Vaccine.* New York: William Morrow, 1990. Contains a thorough discussion of Thomas Francis and the conducting of the Salk vaccine trial.

SEE ALSO: 1900, Suppression of Yellow Fever; 1912, U.S. Public Health Service Is Established; 1981, First AIDS Cases Are Reported.

1952 ■ MASSEY BECOMES CANADA'S FIRST NATIVE-BORN GOVERNOR GENERAL: *appointment of the first native Canadian to hold the office since the nation's founding bolsters Canadian nationalism*

DATE: February 28, 1952
LOCALE: Canada
CATEGORIES: Canadian history; Government and politics
KEY FIGURES:
Viscount Alexander (1891-1969), last British governor general of Canada
George VI (1895-1952), king of Great Britain and Canada
Charles Vincent Massey (1887-1967), first native-born Canadian governor general

SUMMARY OF EVENT. Vincent Massey's appointment by the British crown, on February 28, 1952, as Canada's first native-born governor general honored a Canadian who had given distinguished service to both Canada and Great Britain and also recognized growing Canadian nationalism at the conclusion of World War II. By appointing a Canadian governor general, the Crown looked toward strengthening its ties to Canada by ending British overseas appointments that could be interpreted internationally as treating Commonwealth countries more like colonies than equal partners.

Charles Vincent Massey was born in Toronto on February 20, 1887. The Massey family owned and managed Massey-Harris, a company, founded by Vincent Massey's great-grandfather Daniel in 1847, that was the largest manufacturer of farm implements in the Commonwealth. Massey's younger brother, Raymond, became a distinguished actor of the stage and motion pictures in both Canada and the United States.

Massey was educated at the University of Toronto, receiving his bachelor of arts degree in 1910, and then received the master of arts degree from Balliol College, Oxford, in 1913. He then became a lecturer at Victoria College at the University of Toronto (1913-1915). During World War I, Massey served as a captain in the army's University Officers Corps, eventually earning the rank of lieutenant colonel.

Massey entered public life in 1918 as the associate secretary of the War Committee of the Cabinet in Ottawa. In 1919, he was promoted to secretary of the government's Repatriation Committee. From 1921 to 1925, Massey was president of Massey-Harris Company, Ltd. He resigned in 1925 to join Prime Minister William Lyon Mackenzie King's cabinet as a

Minister Without Portfolio, but Massey's failure to win a seat in the Canadian Parliament forced his resignation.

Conservative Canadian governments appointed Massey as Canada's first minister to the United States (1926-1930), Canadian High Commissioner to Great Britain (1935-1946), Canadian delegate to the League of Nations (1936), and Privy Councilor of the United Kingdom (1941). However, some Canadian prime ministers contended that Massey excelled more in the social side of his political appointments than in diplomatic negotiations affecting imperial issues.

At the end of World War II, Massey returned to Canada and accepted the post of chancellor of the University of Toronto (1947). He founded the National Council of Education and served on the board of governors for Ridley College and Upper Canada College. During his lifetime, Massey was awarded fifteen honorary degrees from colleges and universities in Canada and Great Britain.

Vincent Massey's career in diplomacy and education led to his 1949 appointment as the head of Canada's Royal Commission on National Development and the Arts, Letters, and Sciences. The commission found Canadian culture to be anemic and dependent upon the United States. The commission's Massey Report recommended government financial aid to cultural institutions, the arts, and the universities; a permanent Council for the Arts, Letters, Humanities, and Social Sciences; and retaining the Canadian Broadcasting Corporation as a public radio and television corporation regulating private stations.

Because Canada's military and financial contribution during World War II enhanced Canada's international reputation, Canadians increasingly demanded the recognition of their own identity separate from Great Britain and the United States. In 1950, cabinet minister Lester Pearson approached Massey about becoming governor general of Canada when British-born Viscount Alexander's term ended. Massey agreed to consider the position seriously. Alexander's term was extended twice, perhaps because Massey's wife died in 1950, and the work of the commission that Massey chaired remained uncompleted. By 1952, however, Vincent Massey was ready.

Massey has been described as an Anglophile who enjoyed the English aristocracy; a royalist who strongly defended Canadian rights and Canadian achievements; and a man who was not an intellectual, scholar, or artist, but who cultivated those who were to foster a Canadian cultural identity. His distinguished career in education, diplomacy, government, and the private sector, his love of Great Britain but his passion for everything Canadian, and Canada's increasing nationalism made Massey the Crown's best choice for governor general in that transitional era after World War II. Massey's appointment reflected London's willingness to accept a changing relationship between Great Britain and the Dominions. Massey's biographers and Massey himself wrote about his belief that the Crown was the most important reconciling force to enable Canada to maintain national unity and a pluralistic democracy. Massey thought that national unity needed to be seen in the human face of a governor general who would function as the head of the Canadian family and connect the nation's past with its present and its future.

Governor General Massey later remarked that his appointment disturbed those Canadians who preferred a member of the British nobility or royal family to serve as governor general, continuing the traditional linkages between Great Britain and Canada. Massey correctly believed, however, that if Canadians were excluded from the office of governor general, the monarchy eventually would be regarded as an appendage to Canada and not a part of the political system. By appointing a Canadian as governor general, the Crown became Canadian and the sovereign truly king or queen, that is, regent, of Canada. To the United States and other nations not a part of the British Commonwealth, British governor generals continued the belief that Canada was really run by London, not Ottawa. Although some Canadians objected to Massey's appointment, hostility was not directed toward him personally.

As governor general from 1952 to 1959, Massey was the symbol of unity in multicultural Canada when governments rose and fell during national crises. Although Canadians might be suspicious of class distinctions and pageantry, Massey believed that royalism had deep roots in all parts of Canada. Governor General Massey not only continued existing ceremonial traditions in Canada but also restored those previously neglected, including the governor general's wearing a military uniform, the use of a coronation coach to open Parliament with a mounted escort, the changing of the guard at the governor general's residence, and the use of the curtsy by women at official functions. Vincent Massey always believed that the French population of Canada respected and admired the Crown as much as the English in Canada did. The Crown, in his view, kept a multicultural Canada unified.

Massey's appointment as governor general of Canada, finally, signaled a peaceful transformation in British-Canadian relationships. Massey's credentials as both royalist and nationalist, diplomat, educator, and politician enabled him to steer Canada toward a stronger national identity while preserving Canada's British heritage.   —William A. Paquette

ADDITIONAL READING:

Bissell, Claude. *The Imperial Canadian, Vincent Massey in Office.* Toronto: University of Toronto Press, 1986. Bissell's second volume on Massey carefully chronicles Massey's career from 1935 until his death in 1967.

_____. *The Young Vincent Massey.* Toronto: University of Toronto Press, 1981. Bissell's first volume on Massey chronicles Massey's early years and education as a member of one of Canada's most prominent industrial families.

Massey, Vincent. *On Being Canadian.* Toronto: J. M. Dent and Sons, Canada, 1948. Massey's autobiography carefully traces his Canadian upbringing, early service to the Crown, and his promotion of a Canadian national identity.

_____. *Speaking of Canada.* Toronto: Macmillan Company of Canada, 1959. A collection of addresses given by Massey as governor general of Canada from 1952 to 1959.

_____. *What's Past Is Prologue*. Toronto: Macmillan Company of Canada, 1963. Massey's memoir provides a detailed account of his service to both Great Britain and Canada.

SEE ALSO: 1921, King Era in Canada; 1930, Bennett Era in Canada; 1948, St. Laurent Succeeds King; 1957, Diefenbaker Era in Canada.

1952 ■ McCARRAN-WALTER ACT: *the first major U.S. immigration law in thirty years removes a ban against Asian immigration*

DATE: June 30, 1952
LOCALE: United States
CATEGORIES: Immigration; Laws and acts
KEY FIGURES:

Richard Arens (born 1913), staff director of the Senate Subcommittee to Investigate Immigration and Naturalization

Patrick Anthony McCarran (1876-1954), U.S. senator from Nevada

Francis Eugene Walter (1894-1963), Democratic congressman from Pennsylvania

SUMMARY OF EVENT. The United States' response to immigration of foreign nationals has undergone many changes during the twentieth century. In 1903, the Commissioner of Immigration asserted the need to assign officers to patrol the border with Mexico to prevent the illegal entry of Asians, mainly Chinese and Japanese. The Immigration Act of 1917, which virtually barred any immigration from Asian countries, required a literacy test for entry into the United States (although one could prove literacy in one's native language). The literacy test and the eight-dollar "head tax" per entrant, however, were waived for Mexican laborers during World War I at the request of U.S. business interests. The Emergency Immigration Act of 1921 limited immigration from Europe to 350,000 per year, with a limit on the number of persons who could enter from each nation. The National Origins Act of 1924, more popularly known as the Quota Law, further reduced the number of immigrants from European countries to 150,000, and further complicated the formula by which persons from different countries could qualify for entry. Much of the focus of the acts of 1921 and 1924 was on preserving the character of the United States as it was and ensuring that the ethnic balance would remain tilted toward Northern Europeans; however, the number of immigrants who could enter from countries in the Western Hemisphere was not limited by either act.

The Great Depression and World War II caused government and the public to put immigration issues aside for a generation. It was not until the early 1950's, at the height of the Cold War, that immigration again became the subject of intense national debate, and a movement arose to reform immigration law. At the time, there were more than two hundred federal laws dealing with immigration, with little coordination among them.

The movement toward immigration reform actually began in 1947, with a U.S. Senate committee investigation on immigration laws, resulting in a voluminous report in 1950 and a proposed bill. The ensuing debate was divided between a group who wanted to abandon the quota system and increase the numbers of immigrants admitted, and those who hoped to shape immigration law to enforce the status quo. Leaders of the latter camp were the architects of the Immigration and Nationality Act of 1952: Patrick McCarran, senator from Nevada, Francis Walter, congressman from Pennsylvania, and Richard Arens, staff director of the Senate Subcommittee to Investigate Immigration and Naturalization. McCarran was the author of the Internal Security Act of 1951, which provided for registration of communist organizations and the internment of communists during national emergencies; Walter was an immigration specialist who had backed legislation to admit Europeans from camps for displaced persons; Arens had been staff director for the House Committee on Un-American Activities. Each looked upon immigration control as an extension of his work to defend the United States against foreign and domestic enemies.

McCarran was most outspoken in defending the concept of restrictions on the basis of national origin, stating in the Senate that "there are hard-core indigestible blocs who have not become integrated into the American way of life, but who, on the contrary, are its deadly enemy. . . . this Nation is the last hope of western civilization; and if this oasis of the world shall be overrun, perverted, contaminated, or destroyed, then the last flickering light of humanity will be extinguished."

Arens branded critics of the proposed act as either communists, misguided liberals enraptured by communist propaganda, apologists for specific immigrant groups, or "professional vote solicitors who fawn on nationality groups, appealing to them not as Americans but as hyphenated Americans." Among the bill's critics, however, were Harry S Truman, the U.S. president in 1952, and Hubert Humphrey, senator from Minnesota and future Democratic presidential nominee. One liberal senator, Herbert Lehman, attacked the national origins provisions of the existing immigration code as a racist measure that smacked of the ethnic purity policies of the recently defeated German Nazis. Truman vetoed the bill, but his veto was overridden, 278 to 113 in the House, and 57 to 26 in the Senate.

In several areas, the 1952 law made no significant changes: Quotas for European immigrants were little changed, no quotas were instituted for immigrants from North and South American countries, and the issue of illegal immigration was given scant attention. There were significant changes in some areas, however: reversal of the ban on Asian immigration, extension of naturalization to persons regardless of race or sex, and the first provision for refugees as a special class of immigrants.

The Asiatic Barred Zone that had been established in 1917 was eliminated by providing for twenty-five hundred entries from the area—a minuscule number for the region, but the first recognition of Asian immigration rights in decades. This small concession for Asians was offset partially by the fact that anyone whose ancestry was at least half Asian would be counted under the quota for the Asian country of ancestry, even if the person was a resident of another country. This provision, which was unlike the system of counting quotas for European countries, was specifically and openly designed to prevent Asians living in North and South American countries, which had no quota restrictions, from flooding into the United States.

The McCarran-Walter Act also ensured for the first time that the "right of a person to become a naturalized citizen of the United States shall not be denied or abridged because of race or sex." The provision of not denying citizenship based on sex addressed the issue of women who had lost their U.S. citizenship by marrying foreign men of certain categories; men who had married women from those categories had never lost their citizenship.

The issue of refugees was a new concern resulting from World War II. More than seven million persons had lost their homelands in the aftermath of the war, as a result of the conquering and reorganization of countries, primarily in Eastern Europe. The 1952 act did not present a comprehensive solution to the problem of refugees, but did give the attorney general special power, subject to congressional overview, to admit refugees into the United States under a special status. Although this was expected to be a seldom-used provision of the law, regular upheavals throughout the world later made it an important avenue of immigration into the United States.

Finally, the Immigration and Nationality Act also included stringent security procedures designed to prevent communist subversives from infiltrating the United States through immigration. Some of these harsh measures were specifically mentioned by Truman in his veto message, but the anticommunist Cold War climate made such measures hard to defeat.

Over the objections of Congress, President Truman appointed a special commission to examine immigration in September, 1952. After hearings in several cities, it issued the report *Whom Shall We Welcome?*, which was critical of the McCarran-Walter Act. Some liberal Democrats attempted to make the 1952 presidential election a forum on immigration policy, but without success. Dwight D. Eisenhower, the victorious Republican nominee for president, made few specific statements on immigration policy during the campaign. After his election, however, he proposed a special provision for allowing almost a quarter of a million refugees from communism to immigrate to the United States over a two-year period, couching his proposal in terms of humanitarianism and foreign policy. The resulting Refugee Relief Act of 1953 allowed the admission of 214,000 refugees, but only if they had assurance of jobs and housing or were close relatives of U.S. citizens and could pass extensive screening procedures designed to deter subversives. Several similar exceptions in the following years managed to undercut the McCarran-Walter Act, which its many critics had been unable to overturn outright.

—*Irene Struthers*

ADDITIONAL READING:

Dimmitt, Marius A. *The Enactment of the McCarran-Walter Act of 1952.* Lawrence: University Press of Kansas,

1971. A Ph.D. dissertation giving a complete discussion of the 1952 immigration bill.

LeMay, Michael C. *From Open Door to Dutch Door: An Analysis of U.S. Immigration Policy Since 1820.* New York: Praeger, 1987. A comprehensive overview of the forces behind and results of changing U.S. immigration policy. Chapter 5 opens with a discussion of the Immigration Act of 1952. Bibliography and index.

_____, ed. *The Gatekeepers: Comparative Immigration Policy.* New York: Praeger, 1989. Compares immigration policy and politics in the United States, Australia, Great Britain, Germany, Israel, and Venezuela. Helpful in understanding overall immigration issues. Bibliography and index.

Reimers, David M. "Recent Immigration Policy: An Analysis." In *The Gateway: U.S. Immigration Issues and Policies,* edited by Barry R. Chiswick. Washington, D.C.: American Enterprise Institute for Public Policy Research, 1982. Discusses immigration policies and laws from the 1920's through the 1970's. Includes information on Senator Patrick McCarran's role in immigration law.

SEE ALSO: 1849, Chinese Immigration; 1882, Chinese Exclusion Act; 1895, Chinese American Citizens Alliance Is Founded; 1917, Immigration Act of 1917; 1924, Immigration Act of 1924; 1943, Magnuson Act; 1953, Refugee Relief Act.

1952 ■ PUERTO RICO BECOMES A COMMONWEALTH: *a unique relationship between the Caribbean island and the United States is formally constituted*

DATE: July 25, 1952

LOCALE: Puerto Rico

CATEGORIES: Latino American history; Government and politics

KEY FIGURES:

Pedro Albizú Campos (1891-1965), nationalist leader

Luís Muñoz Marín (1898-1980), first governor of the Commonwealth of Puerto Rico

Jesús T. Piñero (1897-1952), first native Puerto Rican governor of Puerto Rico

Harry S Truman (1884-1972), thirty-third president of the United States, 1945-1953

Rexford G. Tugwell (1891-1979), adviser to President Franklin D. Roosevelt and governor of Puerto Rico, 1941-1946

Millard Tydings (1890-1961), Democratic senator from Maryland

SUMMARY OF EVENT. On July 25, 1952, the flag of Puerto Rico was raised in ceremonies marking the creation of the Associated Free State, or Commonwealth, of Puerto Rico. This was the culmination of more than fifty years of efforts to define the relationship between the island and the United States. Luís Muñoz Marín, soon to become the first governor of Puerto Rico, had led efforts to establish the commonwealth. However, there was, and remains, opposition by Puerto Ricans who favor full independence and from others who wish Puerto Rico to become the fifty-first state in the Union. The plebiscite in 1952 and subsequent votes have continued to produce a majority that favors commonwealth status.

The United States obtained Puerto Rico from Spain as a result of the Spanish-American War of 1898. Previously, Puerto Ricans had urged Spain to reform its colonial administration, and some had sought independence from Spain. With U.S. troops occupying the island after the war, responsibility for administering the island was placed in the hands of the War Department until 1900. In that year, Congress passed the Foraker Act, which established an island government headed by a governor appointed by the president. A legislature was established: Puerto Ricans could elect representatives to a Council of Delegates; the upper chamber was appointed by the United States president. This local body had advisory powers only, and most decisions regarding the island were made in Washington, D.C. There, an elected representative from Puerto Rico could sit in the House of Representatives but could not vote on legislation in the full House. Puerto Ricans finally obtained U.S. citizenship in 1917, when the Jones Act was passed by Congress. It also allowed Puerto Ricans to elect representatives to both houses of their island legislature. Not until 1947 could they elect their own governor.

The two most influential individuals in Puerto Rico's search for political identity were Pedro Albizú Campos and Luís Muñoz Marín. Albizú Campos was educated in the United States and joined Puerto Rico's Nationalist Party in 1927. Becoming president of the party in 1930, he led it into opposition against U.S. control and sought alliances with other Latin Americans. Lacking support at the polls, however, Albizú Campos became more radical. In 1936, he was accused of plotting to overthrow the federal government in Puerto Rico and was sent to a federal prison in Atlanta.

Luís Muñoz Marín also was determined to bring self-government to Puerto Rico, but became convinced that this goal would be best achieved through continued association with the United States. Muñoz and his Popular Democratic Party won the first election for governor in 1947 and began negotiations with the United States to recognize the islanders' desires for their own constitution. The Nationalist Party opposed Muñoz and favored complete independence. Pro-independence supporters were angered by the Truman Administration's collaboration with Muñoz and the passage of Public Law 600, authorizing a constitutional convention. In the fall of 1950, they attacked a prison in Rio Piedras, stormed the governor's mansion, and tried to assassinate President Harry Truman in Washington, D.C. The attacks were unsuccessful but highlighted divisions among Puerto Ricans over the island's future. The violence led to a state of emergency and the mobilization of the National Guard, which took over the University of Puerto Rico and stormed the home of the Nationalist Party leader. Dozens of people were killed in the fighting. Albizú, having served his sentence and returned to Puerto Rico, was again arrested.

In June, 1951, Puerto Ricans went to the polls to elect members of a constitutional convention. Seventy delegates from Muñoz's Popular Democratic Party, fifteen supporters of statehood, and seven who favored independence were elected.

The constitutional convention met in 1951-1952 and produced a document that identified Puerto Rico as an Associated Free State, a unique relationship that allowed Puerto Ricans to benefit from U.S. citizenship but gave them the opportunity to elect their own island government. Falling somewhere between a state and a colony, Puerto Rico can elect its own governor, a twenty-seven member senate, and a fifty-one member house of representatives. Puerto Ricans may not vote in U.S. presidential elections, and their representative in Congress may not vote on legislation on the floor. This places restrictions on Puerto Rico, because any changes to the island's status may be approved only by Congress.

When the constitution was sent to the United States Congress for approval in 1952, there was much debate and changes were proposed to provisions that differed from the U.S. constitution. Eventually, Congress passed the legislation, and President Truman signed it into law, establishing Puerto Rico as a Commonwealth in Association with the United States.

The question of the island's status was complicated by the continued migration of islanders to the United States. Approximately seventy thousand Puerto Ricans lived in the United States, mostly in New York, before World War II. Continued population growth on the island and cheaper transportation by airplane brought more Puerto Ricans to the United States in the years after the war. By 1987, there were more than two million Puerto Ricans in the United States, with more than half of that number in New York City and environs. By the 1990's, there were more Puerto Ricans in New York City than in the island's capital city of San Juan.

As United States citizens, Puerto Ricans may move freely anywhere within the United States mainland, as well as back and forth to the island. More and more Puerto Ricans have chosen to migrate to the mainland, but many, whose native language is Spanish, find that adaptation to the new language and culture is not easy. Many Puerto Ricans study English and speak it well, but those who first come to the United States often encounter a period of adjustment. In addition to language difficulties, Puerto Ricans often encounter racial discrimination in the United States. Although the Puerto Rican community has transformed parts of New York City and many other cities of the Northeast, many Puerto Ricans maintain strong ties to their island. Their participation in both lands is part of the unique identity the island and its people feel, and is reflected by the reluctance of many Puerto Ricans to sever the bonds created by commonwealth status.

—James A. Baer

ADDITIONAL READING:

Carr, Raymond. *Puerto Rico: A Colonial Experiment.* New York: Vintage Books, 1984. Part 2 deals with the status of

Puerto Rico, focusing on the policies and platforms of major Puerto Rican political parties.

Carrion, Arturo Morales. *Puerto Rico: A Political and Cultural History*. New York: W. W. Norton, 1983. A thorough evaluation of Puerto Rico's history and a detailed account of Puerto Rico's emergence in the mid-twentieth century as a commonwealth.

Daniels, Roger. *Coming to America: A History of Immigration and Ethnicity in American Life*. New York: HarperCollins, 1990. Chapter 12 compares the experiences of Mexicans and Puerto Ricans in the United States. Contains many statistics regarding income; discusses questions of race and religion.

Fernandez, Ronald. *The Disenchanted Island: Puerto Rico and the United States in the Twentieth Century*. New York: Praeger, 1992. Heavily footnoted, detailed account of political ties between Puerto Rico and the United States. Provides much information regarding the internal politics of Washington, D.C., and San Juan.

Langley, Lester D. *America and the Americas: The United States in the Western Hemisphere*. Athens: University of Georgia Press, 1989. Contains a critical analysis of United States policy in Puerto Rico, especially pages 184-188, with a perspective of cultural imperialism. Discusses the relationship between Puerto Rico and the United States through the Cold War.

Meléndez, Edwin, and Edgardo Meléndez, eds. *Colonial Dilemma: Critical Perspectives on Contemporary Puerto Rico*. Boston: South End Press, 1993. Claims Puerto Rico is a colony of the United States. Includes chapters on contemporary politics, the economy, and feminism.

Wagenheim, Karl. *Puerto Rico: A Profile*. New York: Praeger, 1970. Provides an overview of Puerto Rico's history and economy; good chapters on the diaspora, society, and culture. Includes chronology, many useful statistics, and a sympathetic understanding of the island and its people.

SEE ALSO: 1898, Spanish-American War; 1901, Insular Cases; 1909, Dollar Diplomacy; 1917, Jones Act.

1952 ■ HYDROGEN BOMB IS DETONATED:
the arsenal of nuclear arms gains a new technology with virtually unlimited destructive capacity

DATE: November 1, 1952
LOCALE: Elugelab Island, Eniwetok Atoll
CATEGORY: Science and technology
KEY FIGURES:

Luis Walter Alvarez (1911-1988), U.S.-born atomic physicist who lobbied for the production of the hydrogen bomb

Ernest Orlando Lawrence (1901-1958), U.S.-born atomic physicist and Nobel Prize winner for the invention of the cyclotron

Brien McMahon (1903-1952), U.S. senator and chairman of the Joint Congressional Committee on Atomic Energy

Julius Robert Oppenheimer (1904-1967), theoretical physicist and director of the Los Alamos Laboratories

Lewis L. Strauss (1896-1974), member of the Atomic Energy Commission

Edward Teller (born 1908), Hungarian-born atomic physicist and father of the hydrogen bomb

Harry S Truman (1884-1972), thirty-third president of the United States, 1945-1953

Stanislaw Marcin Ulam (1909-1984), mathematician who developed the idea of the lithium hydride bomb

Hoyt Vandenberg (1899-1954), U.S. Air Force chief of staff

John von Neumann (1903-1957), Hungarian-born mathematician and physicist who invented the MANIAC computer

SUMMARY OF EVENT. In the summer of 1942, J. Robert Oppenheimer, a theoretical physicist, invited several other leading U.S. physicists to Berkeley, California, to decide how to develop atomic weapons for the war against Germany. At this meeting, Edward Teller, a Hungarian-born physicist, suggested development of a fusion, or hydrogen, bomb. The idea for the fusion bomb came from the type of thermonuclear reactions thought to exist in the interior of stars: Two ions of deuterium (heavy hydrogen) fused to make one atom of helium, releasing about four million volts of energy. Most of the scientists had been thinking in terms of a fission bomb, using the enormous energies set free when heavy atoms are split in a nuclear reaction. Although the fusion, or hydrogen, bomb was potentially more powerful, there were many more theoretical and practical problems involved in its development. One of these problems was the fear that the hydrogen bomb might be capable of igniting the oceans in one vast chain reaction, thus demolishing the earth.

The assembled scientists decided to begin work on the fission bomb and to shelve temporarily the problem of fusion. Oppenheimer became the director of the Los Alamos Laboratories, where the first operable atomic bomb was designed and built. Teller also went to work at Los Alamos, but never accepted the decision to concentrate on the fission bomb; he continued to nurse his fusion idea. The other Los Alamos scientists worked hard and successfully on fission: In July, 1945, the first atomic bomb was exploded in Alamogordo, New Mexico. By this time, the Germans had surrendered and the Japanese were reported to be seeking peace, but President Harry S Truman still made the decision to drop the bomb; it has been argued, perhaps unfairly, that he may have done so to impress the Soviets. The explosions were indeed impressive: The cities of Hiroshima and Nagasaki were destroyed and a hundred thousand people were killed.

After the war, many of the scientists began an intensive lobbying effort against the use of nuclear weapons. Teller, now virtually alone in his desire to create the hydrogen, or Super, bomb, was opposed by Albert Einstein and the Emergency Committee of Atomic Scientists. In August, 1949, however, the United States learned that the Soviet Union had exploded its first atomic weapon, Joe 1; many military and government officials were shocked to discover that the United States was no longer the only nuclear power.

Teller and his colleagues, Ernest O. Lawrence, inventor of the cyclotron, and Luis Alvarez, began an intensive lobbying effort to develop the Super, and they gained many influential friends, including Senator Brien McMahon, chairman of the Joint Congressional Committee on Atomic Energy; General Hoyt Vandenberg, Air Force chief of staff; Omar Bradley, chairman of the Joint Chiefs of Staff; and Lewis L. Strauss, the most conservative and powerful member of the Atomic Energy Commission. The nine leading scientists who were members of the General Advisory Committee of the Atomic Energy Commission, under the chairmanship of Oppenheimer, all advised against production of the Super. The five members of the Atomic Energy Commission concurred with this decision by a vote of four to one, but this entire system for decision making on the use of atomic power was negated. On January 31, 1950, a committee of three met at the White House. Louis A. Johnson, secretary of defense, Dean Acheson, secretary of state, and David Lilienthal, chairman of the Atomic Energy Commission, voted two to one in favor of the Super, with Lilienthal opposed. That afternoon, Truman announced his decision to proceed with the rapid development of the hydrogen bomb.

In 1950, it was not yet clear whether the hydrogen bomb would work. In principle, heavy hydrogen would fuse when ignited by the heat of an atomic blast. A mixture of deuterium and tritium (both being forms of heavy hydrogen) would ignite more readily than deuterium alone. The heavy hydrogen had to be kept in liquid form and thus required refrigeration. The first model of the Super was a fission bomb coated with layers of deuterium and tritium and enclosed in a huge refrigeration unit, weighing sixty-five tons. Since this thermonuclear icebox was not a practical weapon, it was called a thermonuclear device, and was named by some scientists "the Superfluous." This device was exploded on the island of Elugelab in the South Pacific on November 1, 1952, sinking the entire island and carving a mile-long crater in the ocean floor. The U.S. scientists did not know that the Soviet Union already had exploded a similar thermonuclear device in 1951; this fact, known only to President Truman and a few of his top advisers, was kept a well-guarded secret, even from Teller.

By 1951, however, Teller and Stanislaw Ulam, a mathematician, already had developed a new idea for a workable bomb that would be made with lithium deuteride instead of the tritium-deuterium mixture and would need no refrigeration. Neutrons produced by the first fission explosion would turn lithium into tritium, resulting in a practical dry bomb. The idea was, in Oppenheimer's words, "technically sweet," but required enormously complicated mathematical calculations. The scientists agreed to work six days a week and to take night shifts in the computer section, but John von Neumann made the most important contribution: a new and much more advanced computer, which he named the MANIAC.

On August 8, 1953, Georgi Malenkov, the Soviet premier, announced that the United States no longer had a monopoly on the hydrogen bomb; several days later, radiation traces showed that the Soviet Union had exploded a dry lithium hydride bomb. On March 1, 1954, the United States responded with a new twist: the three-stage fission-fusion-fission bomb, coated with uranium isotopes for maximum destructive power. This bomb, Shoot 1, was exploded in the Bikini Atoll with the power of about twenty million tons of trinitrotoluene (TNT). The uranium coating guaranteed a widely distributed radioactive fallout; a crew of Japanese fisherman on the *Lucky Dragon*, 120 miles away, became sick and were hospitalized; one of them died.

The idea that the Soviets had exploded a hydrogen bomb before the United States added fuel to the fires of Senator Joseph McCarthy's communist witchhunts. Looking for a scapegoat, security officials accused Oppenheimer of having opposed the development of the hydrogen bomb. A three-person personnel security board judged his case: Thomas A. Morgan, an industrialist, and Gordon Grey, a newspaper and broadcasting executive, voted against him, while Ward Evans, a professor of chemistry, voted in his favor. In 1954, Oppenheimer was denied security clearance and his power was broken; Teller, Lawrence, and Strauss became the new scientific advisers for the Cold War. Forty years later, a highly placed director of Soviet espionage, Pavel Sudoplatov, would confirm that Oppenheimer had provided Moscow with information useful for the development of a Soviet hydrogen bomb.

—Elizabeth Fee, updated by Steve D. Boilard

ADDITIONAL READING:

Jungk, Robert. *Brighter than a Thousand Suns: A Personal History of the Atomic Scientists*. New York: Harcourt Brace, 1958. A straightforward history of nuclear weapons development, which concentrates especially on the moral issues involved.

Laurence, William L. *The Hell Bomb*. New York: Alfred A. Knopf, 1951. Clearly and openly discusses the controversies and questions surrounding the development of the hydrogen bomb at the beginning of the project.

Moss, Norman. *Men Who Played God: The Story of the H-Bomb and How the World Came to Live with It*. New York: Harper & Row, 1968. A British journalist's report on the thermonuclear age. Includes vivid portraits of Edward Teller, strategic analyst Herman Kahn, and conscientious protester Pat O'Connell.

Rhodes, Richard. *Dark Sun: The Making of the Hydrogen Bomb*. New York: Simon & Schuster, 1995. The best of the many books released to coincide with the fiftieth anniversary of the first atomic explosion. Authoritative, extensively documented, and highly readable. Rhodes earlier won a Pulitzer Prize for *The Making of the Atomic Bomb*.

Sudoplatov, Pavel. *Special Tasks: The Memoirs of an Unwanted Witness, a Soviet Spymaster*. Boston: Little, Brown, 1994. Offers some new insights, and confirms some old ones, about nuclear weapons research and development. Claims that Oppenheimer and Niels Bohr provided the Soviet Union with information useful for constructing atomic weapons.

Teller, Edward, and Allen Brown. *The Legacy of Hiroshima*. Garden City, N.Y.: Doubleday, 1962. Teller's account of the development of the hydrogen bomb. Argues that the United States should be prepared to use nuclear weapons.

York, Herbert F. *The Advisors: Oppenheimer, Teller, and the Superbomb*. Stanford, Calif.: Stanford University Press, 1989. York is a former director of the Lawrence Livermore National Laboratory, a primary nuclear weapons research center. He offers normative reflections as well as a concise historical record.

SEE ALSO: 1942, Manhattan Project; 1945, Atomic Bombing of Japan; 1963, Nuclear Test Ban Treaty; 1979, SALT II Is Signed; 1991, Bush Announces Nuclear Arms Reductions; 1993, START II Is Signed.

1952 ■ EISENHOWER IS ELECTED PRESIDENT: *election of a Republican war hero ends two decades of Democratic domination of the White House*

DATE: November 4, 1952
LOCALE: United States
CATEGORY: Government and politics
KEY FIGURES:
Dwight David Eisenhower (1890-1969), Republican presidential candidate
Joseph Raymond McCarthy (1908-1957), U.S. senator from Wisconsin
Richard Milhous Nixon (1913-1994), Republican vice presidential candidate
Adlai Ewing Stevenson (1900-1965), Democratic presidential candidate
Robert Alphonso Taft (1889-1953), contender for the Republican nomination
Harry S Truman (1884-1972), thirty-third president of the United States, 1945-1953

SUMMARY OF EVENT. As the United States moved into a new decade in 1950, the Democrats had been in power in Washington for eighteen years, Cold War tensions seemed to be melting into a hot war in Korea, and apprehensive citizens suspected that communists and corruption were lurking behind the scenes in the Truman Administration. With the approach of the 1952 election, the Democratic Party found itself facing several serious liabilities. The public tended to blame the incumbent party for many of the problems that had beset the postwar United States, a tendency that was exacerbated by the long tenure of the Democrats and by the sweeping changes instituted by the Roosevelt and Truman administrations.

Adding to the Democratic Party's problems was the disclosure, prior to the election, of several instances of Democratic corruption. Democrats were charged not only with plundering at home, but also with blundering abroad. China had fallen to the communists, allegedly because of the administration's mishandling of foreign affairs in Asia. The situation in Korea

was tense and uncertain. The peace talks had bogged down, and Truman's dismissal of General Douglas MacArthur indicated to many that the Democrats had no will to win the war. The Republican Party seized on this issue: Something decisive needed to be done in Korea.

To escalate the United States' concern about the communists, Senator Joseph R. McCarthy had been painting vivid pictures of communist infiltration of the U.S. government, especially in the Department of State. The overall impact of communist infiltration may have been greater than even McCarthy suspected, based on later research. Newer biographies of Kim Philby, Alger Hiss, Julius and Ethel Rosenberg, and others have argued that expansive Soviet spy networks existed in the United States and England. Despite his excesses and outright falsifications, McCarthy's charges hurt the Democrats, who had held power when these networks reached their apex: Because the Democrats had been in office for almost twenty years, many people held them responsible for this supposed communist subversion of the government.

Other problems plagued the Democrats, including the high cost of living. The Korean War had produced a need for heavy spending, adding inflationary pressure to the postwar financial boom and the record expenditures of World War II. Fear of inflation was widespread. Many people in the United States, especially Republicans, believed that it was time to balance the budget and reduce government spending.

The Republicans had problems too, however. As the Republican National Convention drew near, a split within the party seemed imminent. Senator Robert A. Taft and his followers advocated an isolationist, anti-New Deal platform. The senator's foreign policy appealed to many Republicans and gained widespread support in the traditionally isolationist Midwest. However, many powerful Republican leaders feared that Taft had made too many enemies within the party to gain unanimous support. Because he had attached his name to the Taft-Hartley labor law and was bitterly despised by the labor establishment and millions of rank-and-file union members, the Ohio senator had lost much support from certain segments of the voter population.

Many Republicans thus favored a less controversial figure for the nomination. Dwight D. Eisenhower—supreme commander of Allied forces in Europe during World War II, president of Columbia University, and temporary head of North Atlantic Treaty Organization (NATO) forces in Europe— seemed to fill the prescription perfectly. After the general at last declared that he was a Republican, Senator Henry Cabot Lodge II of Massachusetts encouraged his nomination. Following primary victories in New Hampshire and Minnesota, Eisenhower defeated Taft on the first ballot, 595 to 500. To appease the Taft wing of the party and to give the ticket youth and Western representation, Senator Richard M. Nixon of California was chosen as the vice presidential candidate. Eisenhower, however, did not back Nixon fully until after a dramatic television appearance by the Californian, when, challenged to explain aspects of his financial background, Nixon made the famous televised "Checkers" speech, in which he listed his earnings and debts and noted that the only gift he ever had accepted was a cocker spaniel named Checkers. Eisenhower astutely observed that the response to the speech— more than three hundred thousand letters and telegrams to the Republican National Committee positive to Nixon, as well as thousands of pro-Nixon phone calls—made Nixon a political asset.

The leading candidates for the Democratic nomination included Vice President Alben W. Barkley and Senator Estes Kefauver of Tennessee. Governor Adlai E. Stevenson of Illinois declared that he would not run but would accept a party draft. After a struggle on the convention floor, Stevenson was nominated on the first ballot. Senator John J. Sparkman of Alabama was given the vice presidential slot to appease the South. Although the Democratic platform was soft on civil rights and included support of state control of tidelands oil, two prominent Democratic governors, James F. Byrnes of South Carolina and Allen Shivers of Texas, declared for Eisenhower. It thus became respectable to be a Southern Republican, and the Solid South was cracked at last.

During the campaign, several Republican policies became evident. The Tennessee Valley Authority, Social Security, and certain other New Deal changes would stay. Eisenhower announced that his party had no basic quarrel with established Democratic economic dogma. He did promise to balance the budget, reduce federal outlays, lower taxes, safeguard free enterprise, lessen government interference in business, and place fewer curbs on industry.

However, the issues of the Korean War and communists in the federal government overshadowed domestic economic policy. On the subject of the war, Eisenhower declared that he would go to Korea, although he did not specify what he expected to accomplish by going. Americans, tired of the Korean quagmire, found hope in the Republican candidate's pledge; the hero of World War II could certainly solve the sideshow events of Korea. On the communist issue, Eisenhower did not make the McCarthy smear tactics a part of his personal campaign. Nevertheless, he did not disavow McCarthy's aims and in symbolic ways accommodated the emotional thrust of the Red hunt. "Ike," as the public called Eisenhower, also had a strong historical trend in his favor: In the nineteenth century, whenever a party needed to break the opposing party's momentum, it had nominated a general, usually with success in November. William Henry Harrison, Zachary Taylor, and Ulysses S. Grant were not career politicians, but they had parlayed their military success and image as strong leaders into peacetime political victory.

Stevenson, with his urbane and lofty rhetoric, proved no match for the genial and likable general as a vote-getter. The commonly held assumption that Stevenson had elevated U.S. political thinking and therefore appealed to educated and intellectual voters, whereas Eisenhower, often portrayed as dull and lacking in sophistication, appealed only to less-educated voters, has been disputed: Analysis of polling behavior has suggested that the less educated the voter, the more likely he or she was to vote for Stevenson, and the more educated the voter, the more likely he or she was to vote for Eisenhower. College-educated voters preferred Eisenhower by a margin of two to one.

Even Democratic suggestions that a new depression would follow Republican victory were not enough to stem the tide. Eisenhower won thirty-nine states, including four in the Solid South, and 442 electoral votes, to Stevenson's nine states and 89 electoral votes. The Republican Party narrowly gained control of Congress, but retained it for only the first two years of Eisenhower's tenure. In the Senate, the Republicans had a four-seat majority in 1954, losing two seats since 1952. The Democrats retained their hold on the governorships and of state and local government in the Southern states that went for Eisenhower.

—Fredrick J. Dobney, updated by Larry Schweikart

ADDITIONAL READING:

Ambrose, Stephen E. *Eisenhower: Soldier, General of the Army, President-Elect, 1890-1952.* New York: Simon & Schuster, 1983. A classic biography of Eisenhower by an illustrious biographer who is sympathetic to the general.

Childs, Marquis. *Eisenhower: Captive Hero.* New York: Harcourt, Brace and World, 1958. An unfavorable treatment of Eisenhower and his administration.

Dwight D. Eisenhower, thirty-fourth president of the United States, oversaw the beginning of one of the most prosperous periods of U.S. history during the post-World War II years. (Library of Congress)

Eisenhower, Dwight D. *The White House Years: Mandate for Change, 1953-1956*. Garden City, N.Y.: Doubleday, 1963. The first volume of Eisenhower's memoirs, which covers his first term and the campaign of 1952.

Johnson, Walter. *How We Drafted Adlai Stevenson*. New York: Alfred A. Knopf, 1955. One of the leaders of the draft movement describes in detail the preconvention and convention activities of his committee and argues that the draft was genuine.

Klehr, Harvey, et al. *The Secret World of American Communism*. Translated by Timothy Sergay. New Haven, Conn.: Yale University Press, 1995. This translation of Russian documents provides a revealing look at Communist Party operations in the United States from the Soviet perspective.

McKeever, Porter. *Adlai Stevenson: His Life and Legacy*. New York: Morrow, 1989. The best biography to date of Stevenson.

Parmet, Herbert S. *Eisenhower and the American Crusades*. New York: Macmillan, 1972. A renowned presidential scholar examines the campaign and the reasons Eisenhower chose to run. A large portion of the book is devoted to the 1952 election.

Schweikart, Larry, and Dennis Lynch. "Government and Politics." In *American Decades, 1950-1959*, edited by Richard Layman. Detroit: Gale, 1994. A detailed look at the 1952 and 1954 elections, including analyses of voting data.

SEE ALSO: 1947, Truman Doctrine; 1948, Truman Is Elected President; 1951, McCarthy Hearings; 1957, Eisenhower Doctrine; 1960, Kennedy Is Elected President.

1953 ■ TERMINATION RESOLUTION: *Congress ends its policy of special treatment of American Indians*

DATE: Beginning August 1, 1953
LOCALE: United States
CATEGORIES: Laws and acts; Native American history
KEY FIGURES:
Oliver La Farge (1891-1982), president of the Association on American Indian Affairs and a vocal opponent of termination
Dillon L. Seymour Myer (1891-1982), commissioner of Indian Affairs who zealously advanced federal policy toward termination
Arthur Vivant Wakens (1886-1973), Utah senator and the leading congressional advocate of termination
William Zimmerman (1890-1982), acting commissioner of Indian Affairs
SUMMARY OF EVENT. Termination was viewed by its advocates as freeing American Indians from special laws and regulations, making them equal to other citizens, and by opponents as precipitously withdrawing federal responsibility and programs. The term used for the federal policy came to be applied to the people themselves: terminated tribes. Termination actions included repealing laws setting American Indians apart, ending Bureau of Indian Affairs (BIA) services by transferring them to other federal agencies or to the states, and terminating recognition of the sovereign status of specific tribes.

Termination, many have observed, did not deviate from the norm of federal policy. Its emphasis on breaking up American Indian land holdings is often compared to the General Allotment Act of 1887 (the Dawes Act). The latter required the allocation of a certain number of acres to each person and, during its forty-seven years in force, reduced tribal lands by nearly ninety-one million acres.

In public debate, opponents of termination argued that the United States had a special obligation to American Indians because they had been conquered and deprived of their accustomed way of life. All people in the United States, opponents said, have the right to be different and to live in the groupings they prefer. Any changes in federal supervision of American Indians should be implemented slowly and with the involvement of the affected tribes; rather than dissolving tribal communities, federal policy should continue meeting tribes' special needs until those needs no longer exist. Opponents also pointed to American Indian culture, tribal lands, and tribal government—their form of community—as their source of strength.

Advocates of termination asserted that all U.S. citizens should be similar, and there should be no communities with special legal rights. Dissolving separate American Indian communities would expedite the integration of these people into the mainstream. American Indians, according to Senator Arthur V. Wakens, would be freed from wardship or federal restrictions and would become self-reliant, with no diminution of their tribal culture. Wakens saw termination as liberation of American Indians and compared it to the Emancipation Proclamation. Non-natives objected to the Indian Reorganization Act (IRA) of 1934, the prior federal policy, and were swayed toward termination by several arguments: American Indian communal property ownership and their form of government resembled communism; the IRA's promotion of American Indian traditions amounted to condoning heathenism; developers wanted tribal lands made available; and Congress perceived that the resignation of Indian Commissioner John Collier (the IRA's chief advocate) and severe BIA budget cuts had diminished its effectiveness, necessitating a stepped-up program of assimilation.

After Collier's resignation, Senator William Langer asked Acting Commissioner William Zimmerman for a formula for evaluating tribal readiness for termination. On February 8, 1947, Zimmerman presented, in a congressional hearing, three categories of tribes—those who could be terminated immediately, those who could function with little federal supervision within ten years, and those who needed more than ten years to prepare. He discussed the four criteria used in his lists and presented three specimen termination bills. This testimony was embraced by termination supporters and, Zimmerman believed, frequently misquoted.

In 1950, Dillon Myer, a staunch advocate of immediate termination, became Commissioner of Indian Affairs. Although he claimed to be streamlining the BIA, it seemed to some that he was moving to dissolve both the bureau and all IRA programs. Myer was asked to write a legislative proposal for expeditious termination of federal supervision of American Indians. The result was House Concurrent Resolution 108 (August 1, 1953), which passed with little debate. The resolution directed Congress to make American Indians subject to the same laws, privileges, and responsibilities as other citizens; to end their wardship status; and to free specific tribes from federal control as soon as possible. Once the named tribes were terminated, the BIA offices serving them would be abolished.

PL 83-280 (August 15, 1953) also advanced termination. It transferred to the states, without tribal consent, jurisdiction over civil and criminal offenses on reservations in California, Minnesota, Nebraska, Oregon, and Wisconsin. It provided that, by legislative action, any other state could assume similar jurisdiction.

A rush of termination bills was introduced in 1954. As problems with the termination process became known and the membership of congressional committees changed (after 1956), legislation slowed. These acts caused several changes: Tribal lands were either appraised or put under a corporation's management; the federal government no longer protected the land for the tribe; state legislative and judicial authority replaced tribal government; tribe members no longer received a state tax exemption; and tribes lost the benefits of special federal health, education, and other social programs.

Fifteen termination acts were passed between 1954 and 1962, affecting 110 tribes or bands in eight states: the Menominee, Klamath, Western Oregon (sixty-one tribes and bands), Alabama-Coushatta, Mixed-Blood Ute, Southern Paiute, Lower Lake Rancheria, Wyandotte, Peoria, Ottawa, Coyote Valley Ranch, California Rancheria (37 rancherias), Catawba, and Ponca.

Termination of the Menominee of Wisconsin received the most attention. The tribe was specifically targeted in House Concurrent Resolution 108, and their termination act was passed on June 17, 1954. They appeared to be the healthiest tribe economically, as a result of their lumbering and forestry operations, but were not as ready for termination as they seemed. In 1951, the Menominee won a fifteen-year legal battle against the federal government, awarding them $8.5 million in damages for mismanagement of their tribal forest. They could not obtain the award, however, until Congress passed an act appropriating it. The tribe asked that part of the money be released—amounting to fifteen hundred dollars per capita. Senator Wakens' Subcommittee on Indian Affairs told the tribe that if they could manage fifteen hundred dollars per person, they were ready for freedom from federal wardship. Termination, he suggested, was inevitable, and the tribe would not receive the money unless they moved to accept a termination amendment to the per-capita payment bill. The election was not a true tribal referendum, as only 174 members voted; many of these later said that they had not understood what they were voting for.

Final termination of the Menominee did not go into effect until 1961. The tribe had to decide how to set up municipalities, establish a tax system, provide law and order, and sell their tribal assets. There were complications concerning the payment of estimated taxes on Menominee forests. Federal officials saw the tribe's reluctance as procrastination. State agencies could provide only limited assistance, because the tribe was still under federal control.

As a result of these experiences and others, both American Indians and non-Indians became critical of termination. BIA expenditures spiraled in the late 1950's. Many terminated tribe members felt uncomfortable living in the mainstream and often were not accepted socially by non-Indians. Relocated Indians often suffered poverty in the cities and often became dependent on social programs. Some terminated tribes later applied for federal recognition. During its short span (the last act was passed in 1962), termination affected 13,263 of a total population of 400,000, or 3 percent of the federally recognized American Indians. The acts withdrew 1,365,801 acres of trust land, or 3 percent of the approximately 43,000,000 acres held in 1953. The end of federal endorsement of the termination policy was seen in 1969, when President Richard Nixon, in a message to Congress, called for promotion of self-determination and the strengthening of American Indian autonomy without threatening community.

—*Glenn Ellen Starr*

ADDITIONAL READING:

Fixico, Donald L. *Termination and Relocation: Federal Indian Policy, 1945-1960*. Albuquerque: University of New Mexico Press, 1986. Detailed discussion, from World War II through 1981. Discusses the Menominee and Klamath, as well as smaller tribes. Useful analysis of Dillon Myer and PL 83-280.

La Farge, Oliver. "Termination of Federal Supervision: Disintegration and the American Indians." *Annals of the American Academy of Political and Social Science* 311 (May, 1957): 41-46. Summarizes arguments against termination, except when tribes request it and members are ready to handle their own affairs.

Prucha, Francis Paul. *The Great Father: The United States Government and the American Indian*. Vol. 2. Lincoln: University of Nebraska Press, 1984. Portions of chapters 40 and 41 provide a succinct, balanced account of the aims of termination; its articulation in Congress, the popular press, and American Indian publications; congressional and federal actions to bring it about; and its impact.

Stefon, Frederick J. "The Irony of Termination: 1943-1958." *The Indian Historian* 11, no. 3 (Summer, 1978): 3-14. A thorough chronological review that begins with 1887 and ends in 1968. Copiously documented, with many quotations from congressional documents and policymakers.

Walch, Michael C. "Terminating the Indian Termination Policy." *Stanford Law Review* 35, no. 6 (July, 1983): 1181-1215. Well-documented survey of the rise of termination, its effects, and the impact of the fact that Congress did not repeal the termination acts.

SEE ALSO: 1887, General Allotment Act; 1934, Indian Reorganization Act; 1968, Indian Civil Rights Act; 1969, Alcatraz Occupation; 1971, Alaska Native Claims Settlement Act; 1972, Trail of Broken Treaties; 1973, Wounded Knee Occupation; 1978, American Indian Religious Freedom Act; 1988, Indian Gaming Regulatory Act.

1953 ■ REFUGEE RELIEF ACT: *the U.S. government creates a means of admitting displaced persons outside the national quota system, on an emergency basis*

DATE: August 7, 1953
LOCALE: Washington, D.C.
CATEGORIES: Immigration; Laws and acts
KEY FIGURES:
Dwight David Eisenhower (1890-1969), thirty-fourth president of the United States, 1953-1961
Earl G. Harrison (1899-1955), chairman of the Citizens' Committee on Displaced Persons
Patrick Anthony McCarran (1876-1954), senator from Nevada
Eleanor Roosevelt (1884-1962), member of the board of the Citizens' Committee
Harry S Truman (1884-1972), thirty-third president of the United States, 1945-1953

SUMMARY OF EVENT. The events of World War II and its immediate aftermath left millions of people displaced from their homelands. Included among those who had been made homeless by the destruction were Jewish survivors of the Nazi-perpetrated Holocaust and increasing numbers of political refugees who fled their homelands as communist governments took control in Eastern Europe. In the United States, from the close of World War II well into the 1950's, a debate raged about how restrictive or generous U.S. immigration and asylum law should be in view of the nation's own interests and the larger humanitarian imperatives.

Since 1924, U.S. immigration law had been based on a quota system, which was viewed as highly discriminatory against various countries and peoples. Under the pressures of war, however, Congress had allowed temporary immigration to help labor-starved industry. With China as one of the main U.S. allies in the Pacific war, Congress revoked the ban on Chinese immigration in 1943; in 1945, it approved the War Brides Act, which permitted the entry of the alien spouses and children of members of the U.S. armed forces. President Harry S Truman approved the admission of about forty thousand wartime refugees after the war and urged Congress to adopt less restrictive legislation that would permit the resettlement of larger numbers of displaced persons (DPs).

Congress felt pressure to act, not only from the president but also from private charitable agencies that sought to liberalize admission policies in favor of DPs in Europe and elsewhere. Two Jewish aid agencies, the American Council on Judaism (ACJ) and the American Jewish Committee (AJC), joined forces with numerous Christian and other non-Jewish agencies to form the Citizens' Committee on Displaced Persons. This new group was headed by Earl G. Harrison and included on its board of directors many prominent U.S. citizens, among them Eleanor Roosevelt. The committee heavily lobbied the predominantly restrictionist Congress and supported legislation calling for the admission of 400,000 DPs. A long and rancorous debate followed, which produced a substantially watered-down bill known as the Displaced Persons Act of 1948. This act permitted 202,000 admission slots for DPs in Europe who feared to return to communist-held countries. While retaining the immigration quotas of previous years, the act allowed countries to borrow against future years' quotas to accommodate DPs with immediate needs. It only permitted entry of people displaced prior to April 21, 1947, in the Allied occupied zones of Germany and Austria who were registered with the International Refugee Organization (IRO) and who were not communists. It required that the DPs be guaranteed employment by U.S. charitable agencies or other sponsors, and it gave preference to DPs with professional skills. While criticizing its discriminatory features, Truman signed the legislation, which also established the Displaced Persons Commission.

Efforts by the Citizens' Committee on Displaced Persons and others to liberalize the Displaced Persons Act continued, as events in Europe and the deepening of the Cold War led to a climate more supportive of DP resettlement. Although delayed by Senator Patrick A. McCarran of Nevada, amendments eventually passed by Congress expanded the numbers of admission slots to 341,000 and relaxed the cutoff dates for eligibility and entry into the United States. When the Displaced Persons Act expired on December 31, 1951, President Truman relied on the regular immigration quotas and on the U.S. Escapee Program, established under the authority of the 1951 Mutual Security Act, to provide asylum in the United States to political refugees from communism. Truman also established a Commission on Immigration and Naturalization, which held hearings that demonstrated considerable support for liberalized admission of refugees from communism. Even as the 1952 Immigration and Nationality Act, sponsored by Senator McCarran (and therefore often called the McCarran-Walter Act), reemphasized the restrictive quota system for regular immigration, consensus was building to place emergency refugee admissions outside the regular immigration quota system. The Refugee Relief Act of 1953, also sometimes referred to as the Church bill because of the strong support it received from religious refugee assistance agencies, was the result of this ongoing debate about how to restructure U.S. immigration and refugee policy.

The Refugee Relief Act of 1953 made 209,000 special immigrant visas available to refugees and other special categories of persons. These were not tied in any way to the regular immigration quotas for countries under the 1952 Immigration and Nationality Act. This was seen as a major reform by private humanitarian organizations. In the years that followed, the 1958 act enabled the emergency entry of refugees from communism. President Dwight D. Eisenhower, for example, invoked the act just before it was to expire, to provide emergency resettlement opportunities for Hungarian refugees in the waning months of 1956. Eisenhower also took advantage of his parole power, as acknowledged in the 1952 Immigration and Nationality Act and earlier immigration legislation, to provide asylum opportunities for Hungarian refugees. The United States eventually accepted more than thirty-two thousand Hungarians. Thus, through the provisions of the Refugee Relief Act of 1953, subsequent ad hoc emergency refugee legislation, and the Immigration and Nationality Act of 1952, the U.S. government coped with refugee admissions until 1980, when Congress passed the more comprehensive and progressive Migration and Refugee Act.

The Refugee Relief Act of 1953 was one brief but essential mechanism by which the U.S. government sought to fulfill humanitarian and political objectives relating to refugees. It represented an improvement on the Displaced Persons Act, although that much-maligned piece of legislation eventually led to the resettlement of about four hundred thousand persons to the United States, by far the single largest number of European refugees resettled by any country in the immediate postwar era. The Refugee Relief Act of 1953 also represented a bridge to later legislation, such as the Migration and Refugee Act of 1980, by treating emergency refugee admission outside the context of regular immigration quotas. It also represented the mistaken belief in the early 1950's that refugee situations were temporary and amendable to ad hoc solutions.

Still, the United States and other Western nations during the early 1950's established the groundwork for more stable legal and institutional mechanisms for dealing with refugee situations. The United States supported the creation of the United Nations Relief and Rehabilitation Administration in 1943 and the IRO in 1947 to cope with the needs of displaced persons and refugees in postwar Europe. Both were viewed as temporary agencies, as were the United Nations High Commissioner for Refugees (UNHCR) and the Intergovernmental Committee for European Migration (ICEM), which began operations in 1952. In time, however, these bodies developed into permanent features of the international humanitarian landscape with the support of later U.S. administrations.

The building of both legal and institutional mechanisms for coping with humanitarian problems was often highly controversial, heavily steeped in political motivation, and shortsighted. As measured in the huge numbers of persons assisted and protected over the years, however, the efforts are viewed by many as precious if difficult ones, of which the Displaced Persons Act of 1948 and the Refugee Relief Act of 1953 were imperfect but necessary components.   —*Robert F. Gorman*

ADDITIONAL READING:

Carlin, James L. *The Refugee Connection: A Lifetime of Running a Lifeline*. New York: Macmillan, 1989. A fascinating autobiographical account of the development of post-World War II displaced persons and refugee policy.

Fuchs, Lawrence H. "Immigration, Pluralism, and Public Policy: The Challenge of the Pluribus to the Unum." In *U.S.*

Immigration and Refugee Policy: Global and Domestic Issues, edited by Mary M. Kritz. Lexington, Mass.: D. C. Heath, 1982. Explores the history of U.S. immigration, public attitudes, and governmental policies. Shows how World War II and the displaced persons problem served as a watershed for the emergence of greater tolerance of pluralism and diversity.

Loescher, Gil, and John A. Scanlan. *Calculated Kindness: Refugees and America's Half-Open Door, 1945 to Present*. New York: Free Press, 1986. The first two chapters of this comprehensive analysis of U.S. immigration and refugee policy address the Displaced Persons and Refugee Relief Acts.

Nichols, J. Bruce. *The Uneasy Alliance: Religion, Refugee Work, and U.S. Foreign Policy*. Oxford, England: Oxford University Press, 1989. A detailed account of the relations between private voluntary organizations and the U.S. government in the fields of humanitarian aid, immigration, and refugee policy. See especially chapter 5.

Sanders, Ronald. *Shores of Refuge: A Hundred Years of Jewish Immigration*. New York: Schocken Books, 1988. This detailed historical account briefly examines the impact of U.S. refugee acts on Jewish immigration.

Zucker, Norman L., and Naomi Flink Zucker. *The Guarded Gate: The Reality of American Refugee Policy*. New York: Harcourt Brace Jovanovich, 1987. Focuses mainly on refugee and asylum policy after the passage of the 1980 Migration and Refugee Act, but situates this discussion against developments after World War II.

SEE ALSO: 1945, War Brides Act; 1952, McCarran-Walter Act; 1980, Mariel Boat Lift.

1954 ■ BROWN V. BOARD OF EDUCATION: *a landmark Supreme Court decision reverses the "separate but equal" principle and begins the desegregation of public schools*

DATE: May 17, 1954
LOCALE: Washington, D.C.
CATEGORIES: African American history; Civil rights; Court cases
KEY FIGURES:
John Williams Davis (1873-1955), attorney and former Democratic presidential candidate
Dwight David Eisenhower (1890-1969), thirty-fourth president of the United States, 1953-1961
Thurgood Marshall (1908-1993), leading attorney for the Legal Defense Fund of the National Association for the Advancement of Colored People
Earl Warren (1891-1974), chief justice of the United States Supreme Court
SUMMARY OF EVENT. On May 17, 1954, Chief Justice Earl Warren announced an epochal opinion of the United States Supreme Court: "We conclude that in the field of public edu-

cation the doctrine of 'separate but equal' has no place. Separate educational facilities are inherently unequal." Warren did not base this decision solely on the history of the Fourteenth Amendment, because he believed that the amendment was inconclusive regarding public education. Public education, he observed, was only beginning in the 1860's, and "We cannot turn the clock back to 1868 when the amendment was adopted. . . . We must consider public education in the light of its full development and its present place in American life." He continued: "Today, education is perhaps the most important function of state and local governments. . . . In these days, it is doubtful that any child may reasonably be expected to succeed in life if he is denied the opportunity of an education. Such an opportunity . . . is a right which must be available to all on equal terms. We come then to the question presented: Does segregation of children in public schools solely on the basis of race . . . deprive the children of the minority group of equal educational opportunities? We believe that it does."

This decision was a long time in coming, having begun its arduous journey in the years immediately following the Civil War. In 1865, the country had adopted the Thirteenth Amendment, outlawing slavery. In 1866, Congress passed the first Civil Rights Act, providing that African Americans should be accorded equal treatment under the law. Two years later, the states ratified the Fourteenth Amendment. "No State," it declared, "shall make or enforce any law which shall abridge the privileges or immunities of citizens of the United States; nor shall any State deprive any person of life, liberty, or property without due process of the law; nor deny to any person within its jurisdiction the equal protections of the laws." With the ratification of the Fifteenth Amendment in 1870, African American men were guaranteed the right to vote.

As federal troops were withdrawn from the South in the 1870's, there seemed to be a shift in political attitudes toward African Americans. Northern concern diminished, even as the Southern states began to enact laws segregating railroads and streetcars and establishing poll taxes to prevent African Americans from voting. There seemed also to be a shift in the Supreme Court's interpretation of the Fourteenth Amendment as the guarantee of equal rights. This new meaning of the amendment was defined in *Plessy v. Ferguson* in 1896. Ruling that a Louisiana statute segregating transportation was constitutional, the majority of the Court declared that "the enforced segregation of the two races" did not stamp "the colored race with a badge of inferiority." Separate but equal facilities were constitutional. Dissenting from this opinion, Justice John Marshall Harlan asked: "What can more certainly arouse hate . . . than state enactments which in fact proceed on the ground that colored citizens are so inferior and degraded that they cannot be allowed to sit in public coaches occupied by white citizens?"

Segregation proliferated throughout the country in the next few decades. However, several cases brought before the Court by the National Association for the Advancement of Colored People (NAACP) resulted in a gradual weakening of the edifice of segregation. In 1917, the Court declared unconstitu-

tional a Louisville housing statute that perpetuated segregation. In 1927, it held that laws barring African Americans from voting in primaries were contrary to the Fourteenth Amendment. Beginning in 1938, it began to make rulings about segregation in public higher education, declaring that the separation of the races prevented African American students from developing the necessary contacts to make their education complete and useful.

In light of the decisions in *Sweatt v. Painter* (1950) and *McLaurin v. Oklahoma State Regents* (1950), the NAACP began a coordinated push on several fronts. In Virginia and South Carolina, the NAACP argued that the physical facilities afforded to African American schools were inadequate and, using the controversial "doll tests" of social psychologist Kenneth Clark, insisted that these inadequate facilities reinforced lower self-esteem among black children. The lower courts ordered the school boards to comply with the ruling in the *Plessy* case by bringing those schools up to the level of the white schools, but they reaffirmed the principle of segregation itself. In Kansas, the NAACP argued on more theoretical grounds, resulting in a ruling that segregation was harmful to African American students, but the court ruled that it did not have the authority to overrule the Supreme Court precedent in *Plessy v. Ferguson*.

Two Delaware cases also saw lower courts order ameliorative changes while sidestepping the issue of whether segregation itself was unconstitutional. In the District of Columbia, the NAACP brought suit on the sole grounds that separate schools were by definition unequal and therefore unconstitutional. Thus, by the fall of 1952, there were six cases before the Court involving the constitutionality of segregated schools. The court chose to hear the cases argued together. The Kansas case was listed first in order to avoid the impression that segregation was exclusively a Southern problem. Because of this, that case became famous as the school desegregation case: *Oliver Brown et al. v. Board of Education of Topeka, Kansas.*

On behalf of the plaintiffs, the federal government filed a brief as a friend of the court. It declared that "compulsory racial segregation is itself an unconstitutional discrimination." The Court, it argued, should not only overrule the separate-but-equal doctrine but also order that segregation be ended immediately. The Court hesitated, however; some of the justices apparently believed that Congress, rather than the Court, should deal with the issue of enforcing desegregation. South Carolina and Virginia defended segregation vigorously, the former employing John W. Davis as its lead attorney. In contrast, Kansas put forth only a nominal defense, and the Delaware and District of Columbia cases that had been added at the last minute received scant argument.

The Court put the segregation cases over for reargument in the term beginning the following October. They were reargued in December, 1953. By that time, Earl Warren had replaced Fred Vinson as chief justice, and it was Warren who delivered the momentous decision six months later. On May 31, 1955, Warren announced further that the process of desegregation of public schools must proceed "with all deliberate speed."

The movement toward desegregating public schools was a slow one. White Southerners formed citizens' councils and other organizations to resist desegregation at every possible opportunity. In Virginia and Arkansas, local school boards closed public schools and other facilities completely, with state approval, rather than integrate them. Several state legislatures passed resolutions of interposition or nullification, allowing state officials to resist federal enforcement attempts.

As white families fled inner city neighborhoods for the suburbs, many came to see the concept of "neighborhood schooling" as tacit acceptance of de facto segregation. The Court's 1971 decision in *Swann v. Charlotte-Mecklenberg County Board of Education* legalized forced busing of students in order to achieve desegregation.

Court oversight of desegregation plans continued into the 1990's. In several cases from the 1970's forward, the Court declared that de facto segregation of schools arising from "neighborhood schooling" was legal, provided that attendance lines were not drawn primarily on the basis of race.

—*Fredrick J. Dobney, updated by Stephen Wallace Taylor*

ADDITIONAL READING:

Atkinson, Pansye S. *Brown vs. Topeka: An African American's View: Desegregation and Miseducation.* Chicago: African American Images, 1993. Includes bibliographical references.

Bartley, Numan V. *The Rise of Massive Resistance: Race and Politics in the South During the 1950's.* Baton Rouge: Louisiana State University Press, 1969. A scholarly work documenting the measures white Southerners undertook in order to prevent the integration of the public schools and other public facilities. Places these efforts in the broader context of Southern politics.

Kluger, Richard. *Simple Justice: The History of "Brown v. Board of Education" and Black America's Struggle for Equality.* New York: Vintage Books, 1977. A vivid, readable, thorough account of the background of the six cases. Includes an excellent summary of the history of U.S. race relations as a whole. Aimed at the general reader.

Reams, Bernard D., Jr., and Paul E. Wilson, eds. *Segregation and the Fourteenth Amendment in the States: A Survey of State Segregation Laws, 1865-1953, Prepared for United States Supreme Court in re "Brown vs. Board of Education of Topeka."* Buffalo, N.Y.: W. S. Hein, 1975. Includes indexes and bibliography.

Schwartz, Bernard. *Swann's Way: The School Busing Case and the Supreme Court.* New York: Oxford University Press, 1986. A clear, concise treatment of Charlotte, North Carolina's, attempts to comply with the *Brown* decision, and court challenges to those attempts, culminating in the Supreme Court's ruling in *Swann v. Charlotte-Mecklenburg County Board of Education.*

SEE ALSO: 1866, Civil Rights Act of 1866; 1868, Fourteenth Amendment; 1896, *Plessy v. Ferguson*; 1955, Montgomery Bus Boycott; 1957, Little Rock School Desegregation Crisis; 1962, Meredith Registers at "Ole Miss"; 1971, *Swann v. Charlotte-Mecklenburg Board of Education.*

1954 ■ OPERATION WETBACK: *deportation of thousands of Mexican citizens has little long-range impact on the number of illegal immigrants living in the United States*

DATE: June 10-July 15, 1954
LOCALE: California, Arizona, and Texas
CATEGORIES: Immigration; Latino American history
KEY FIGURES:
Herbert Brownell (born 1904), U.S. attorney general
Dwight David Eisenhower (1890-1969), thirty-fourth president of the United States, 1953-1961
Joseph Swing (1894-1984), commissioner of immigration and naturalization

SUMMARY OF EVENT. A fact of life for the nation of Mexico is the existence of a highly prosperous colossus to the north, the United States. While there has long been a tendency for Mexican workers to seek to enter the more-prosperous United States to work, the government of Mexico took a number of steps in the 1940's and 1950's to provide good jobs to keep workers at home. These steps included the building of irrigation projects and factories. Most of these projects were located in northern Mexico and had the effect of drawing a large number of workers to the border area. Jobs were not available for all who came, and many chose to make the short trip across the border into the United States to find work. The average annual income of workers in the United States was more than ten times that of Mexican workers—a strong enticement for Mexican laborers to emigrate to the United States, legally or illegally, temporarily or on a permanent basis.

Mexican laborers who crossed the border into the United States in the early twentieth century most often found seasonal agricultural jobs. Starting about 1930, however, the Great Depression meant that many now-unemployed U.S. workers were willing to do back-breaking work in the fields for low pay. Accordingly, job opportunities for Mexicans evaporated, and those who did not leave voluntarily often were deported. Then, in 1941, war had brought new levels of employment in the United States, and as U.S. farmworkers departed to enter the military or to work in war factories, Mexican workers again began to enter the U.S. to do agricultural work. Most of the jobs they found were in California, Arizona, and Texas.

The U.S. and Mexican governments worked together to start a formal system called the bracero program. The program involved recruitment of Mexican laborers, the signing of contracts, and the temporary entry of Mexicans into the United States to do farm work or other labor. The Mexican government favored the bracero program primarily because the use of contracts was expected to guarantee that Mexican citizens would be fairly treated and would receive certain minimum levels of pay and benefits. The U.S. government favored this formal system because it wanted to control the numbers of Mexicans coming into the United States and hoped the use of contracts would make it easier to ensure that the workers left when the seasonal work was completed. Labor unions in the United States supported the program because bracero workers could be recruited only after certification that no U.S. citizens were available to do the work.

The bracero program worked with some success from 1942 until its discontinuation in 1964. In some years, however, and in certain localities, the use of illegal, non-bracero workers from Mexico continued. Some U.S. employers found too much red tape in the process of securing bracero laborers, and they also noted that bracero wage levels were much higher than the wages that could be paid to illegal immigrants. Many Mexicans crossed the border illegally, because not nearly enough jobs were available through the bracero program. When the U.S. economy stumbled in 1953 and 1954, many U.S. citizens began to speak out against the presence of illegal aliens. They complained that illegal immigrants were a drain on U.S. charities and government programs. They also claimed that the immigrants took jobs at substandard wages that should go to U.S. citizens at higher wages.

When reporters first asked President Dwight Eisenhower and Attorney General Herbert Brownell if they intended to enforce vigorously the immigration laws, both men seemed uninterested in the issue. As popular agitation increased, however, the Eisenhower Administration began to develop plans for Operation Wetback. The operation was designed to round up illegal aliens and deport them, while forcing large farming operations to use the limited and controlled bracero labor instead of uncontrolled and illegal alien labor. Operation Wetback was under the overall control of the Immigration and Naturalization Service (INS), directed by Joseph Swing, while day-to-day operations were supervised by an official of the Border Patrol, Harlon B. Carter.

Operation Wetback took its name from a slang term first used in the southwestern United States to refer to Mexican immigrants who swam the Rio Grande or otherwise crossed into the U.S. illegally, seeking economic opportunities. The INS and its Border Patrol launched the operation in California on June 10, 1954, relying heavily on favorable press coverage to secure the support and cooperation of the general public. INS officials greatly exaggerated the number of agents they had in the field and the number of illegal aliens who had left or had been deported. Press coverage in California was generally quite favorable to Operation Wetback, praising the professional attitude of Border Patrol and INS agents. On the first day, more than a thousand persons were sent out of California on buses chartered by the INS. For several weeks, the number of daily deportations hovered around two thousand. The deportees were handed over to Mexican authorities at border towns like Nogales in Sonora, and the Mexican government sent them farther south by rail, hoping to prevent any quick reentry into the United States.

By July 15, the main phase of Operation Wetback in California was complete. On that day, Border Patrol agents began their work in Texas. There, they met stiff local opposition from powerful farm interests, who were quite content to hire illegal aliens and pay them only half the prevalent wage earned by U.S. or bracero workers. Agents met a hostile press as well, and in some cases had trouble securing a meal or lodging. Still, the operation resulted in the deportation by bus of tens of thousands of illegal workers from Texas. The INS conducted smaller phases of Operation Wetback in Arizona, Illinois, Missouri, Arkansas, Tennessee, and other states. Most of the illegals picked up nationwide were farmworkers, but some industrial workers were apprehended in cities from San Francisco to Chicago.

During the operation, some complaints were registered about the conduct of Border Patrol officers. The officers sometimes were characterized as harsh and hateful in their actions, and they were regularly accused of harassing U.S. citizens of Mexican ancestry. Some of these complaints seem to have been without foundation, particularly in Texas, where the powerful farm interests opposed the entire operation. On the other hand, there were a number of documented cases of U.S. citizens who had darker skin or Hispanic surnames being apprehended and deported to Mexico. Many of the aliens who were detained were kept in camps behind barbed wire pending their deportation. Some Mexicans and Mexican Americans spent several months hiding in terror, having quit their jobs to prevent their being apprehended at work. Deportees had to pay for their bus passage back to Mexico, to the dismay of human rights activists, who pointed out the unfairness of making someone pay for a trip he was being forced to take. The INS responded that the deportees should agree that paying for a bus trip back to Mexico was preferable to prosecution under the immigration laws and a possible jail sentence.

Operation Wetback opened the door to stereotypes of Mexicans in the non-Hispanic community: Some press reports implied that the aliens were ignorant, disease-ridden union busters. As for the effectiveness of the operation in meeting its goals, nearly one hundred thousand illegal immigrants were returned to Mexico in the space of about three months. On the other hand, INS claims that more than one million illegal immigrants fled to Mexico on their own rather than face arrest were grossly exaggerated. Moreover, the boost to the bracero program given by Operation Wetback was only temporary; many employers returned to the use of illegal workers before the end of the 1950's. Operation Wetback, while effective in the short term, provided no long-term solutions to the needs of Mexican workers, U.S. employers, or those who clamored for a more restricted U.S. border.   —*Stephen Cresswell*

ADDITIONAL READING:

García, Juan Ramon. *Operation Wetback: The Mass Deportation of Mexican Undocumented Workers in 1954*. Westport, Conn.: Greenwood Press, 1978. The only book on this subject, García's work thoroughly reviews the background, the deportation program, and the aftermath.

Jenkins, J. Craig. "Push/Pull in Recent Mexican Migration to the U.S." *International Migration Review* 2 (1977): 178-189. A thoughtful discussion of factors contributing to legal and illegal immigration from Mexico to the United States.

Norquest, Carrol. *Rio Grande Wetbacks: Migrant Mexican Workers*. Albuquerque: University of New Mexico Press, 1971. Discusses Operation Wetback in the larger context of Mexico-United States immigration issues.

United States. Immigration and Naturalization Service. *Annual Report of the Immigration and Naturalization Service*. Washington, D.C.: Government Printing Office, 1954 and 1955. These annual reports give the U.S. government's official explanation of the events known as Operation Wetback.

United States. Immigration and Naturalization Service. *Mexican Agricultural Laborers Admitted and Mexican Aliens Located in Illegal Status, Years Ended June 30, 1949-1967*. Washington, D.C.: Government Printing Office, 1968. Shows changes in numbers of bracero workers and apprehensions of illegal Mexican immigrants.

SEE ALSO: 1930's, Mass Deportations of Mexicans; 1942, Bracero Program; 1986, Immigration Reform and Control Act.

1955 ■ FORMOSA RESOLUTION: *passage of a joint resolution affirms presidential power to defend Taiwan and demonstrates the willingness of the United States to wage an active Cold War*

DATE: January 29, 1955
LOCALE: Washington, D.C., Taiwan, Quemoy, and Matsu
CATEGORY: Diplomacy and international relations
KEY FIGURES:

Chiang Kai-shek (1887-1975), president of the Republic of China

John Foster Dulles (1888-1959), U.S. secretary of state

Dwight David Eisenhower (1890-1969), thirty-fourth president of the United States, 1953-1961

Walter F. George (1878-1957), senator from Georgia

William F. Knowland (1908-1974), senator from California

James P. Richards (1894-1979), representative from South Carolina

Zhou Enlai (1898-1976), premier of the People's Republic of China

SUMMARY OF EVENT. In 1949, as the communists took over mainland China at the end of the Chinese civil war, Chiang Kai-shek, president of the Republic of China, or Nationalist China, withdrew with part of his government and army to the island of Formosa and the nearby Pescadores Islands. Formosa, a Portuguese name meaning "beautiful," was still used in the 1950's to describe the island in the West; as Asian nomenclature began to replace colonial-era names, the island's Chinese name, Taiwan, was used exclusively and the name Formosa passed into history. Formosa and the Pescadores had been held by the Japanese from 1895 until their return to China in 1945, at the end of World War II. Chiang claimed that his was still the legitimate government of China and announced his intention to return to the mainland and to power. His troops also held other

islands off the China coast, notably Quemoy, a short distance from the port of Amoy; Matsu, off Foochow; and the Tachens, located about two hundred miles to the north of Matsu.

Both Chiang and the Chinese communists held that Formosa was a province of China, and Quemoy and Matsu were part of the mainland province of Fukien. Though Quemoy and Matsu were small, both sides saw them as stepping-stones. In Chiang's view, they were strategic for a return to the mainland; to the communists, they were a step toward the inclusion of Formosa in their regime. The islands were staging points for occasional raids on the mainland and came under air attack from the communists.

The United States had supported Chiang in the civil war and recognized his regime as the legitimate government for all China. The Korean War (1950-1953), and the Chinese communist role in it, strengthened U.S. antipathy toward the communists. Military and economic aid went to Formosa, and the Seventh Fleet patrolled the Formosa Strait to prevent invasion. Chiang increased the armament and garrisons on Quemoy and Matsu against the advice of many individuals in the U.S. military establishment. The mainland regime placed even larger forces on the shore facing the islands. In August and September, 1954, the communists began a bombardment of the islands, killing two United States military advisers.

Throughout the autumn, debate over policy continued, both within the United States and between the United States and its allies. Some of the Joint Chiefs of Staff and some members of Congress (such as Senator William F. Knowland of California) were willing to encourage Chiang in a return to the mainland and to give U.S. support to his forces on Quemoy and Matsu. This policy was popularly known as "unleashing Chiang Kai-shek." Others saw in such steps either continued defeat for Chiang or involvement in a major Asian war (World War III in some predictions), or both. Secretary of State John Foster Dulles viewed the question of Formosa and the offshore islands within the context of the Cold War, then at its height. To him, the maintenance of a strong Nationalist presence off the coast of mainland China would keep the Chinese communist regime off balance, while offering some hope to those who wanted it overthrown.

As a result of these debates within the government, a somewhat more definite policy toward Nationalist China began to emerge. On December 2, 1954, the United States and Nationalist China concluded a mutual defense treaty. No specific mention was made in the treaty about offshore islands, however. Consequently, a month later, the Chinese communists launched bombardment and air attacks on these islands. On January 24, 1955, as the attacks continued, President Dwight D. Eisenhower sent a special message to Congress in which he asked for authority to use the armed forces of the United States to protect Formosa, the Pescadores, and what he vaguely referred to as certain "closely related localities." This authority, like the mutual defense treaty, would not commit the United States in advance to the defense of the offshore islands, nor would it limit United States action in advance.

President Eisenhower pointed out that the measure was not a constitutional necessity; he already had the requisite authority both as commander in chief and under the terms of the mutual security treaty already signed but not as yet ratified by the Senate. He wanted a demonstration of the unity of the United States and its resolve, while making thoroughly clear the authority of the president. In communist China, Premier Zhou Enlai called the message a war message.

The message went to the new Eighty-fourth Congress, which had Democratic majority in both houses. In response, the chairmen of the respective committees, Democrats Walter George in the Senate and James P. Richards in the House, introduced the joint resolution that became known as the Formosa Resolution. The resolution took as its premise the vital interest of the United States in peace in the western Pacific and the danger to peace from communist attacks in the area. It took note of the statement of mutual interest in the treaty submitted to the Senate. It therefore resolved:

> That the President of the United States . . . is authorized to employ the Armed Forces of the United States as he deems necessary for the specific purpose of securing and protecting Formosa and the Pescadores against armed attack, this authority to include the securing and protection of such related positions and territories of that area now in friendly hands and the taking of such other measures as he judges to be required or appropriate in assuring the defense of Formosa and the Pescadores.

There was strong bipartisan support among U.S. politicians for aggressive anticommunist positions. The House passed the resolution on January 25, 1955, by a vote of 410 to 3. In the Senate committee, an amendment to turn Formosa and the Pescadores over to the authority of the United Nations, and giving authorization to the president only until the United Nations acted, was defeated. Another amendment to limit the authority to Formosa and the Pescadores also lost. A similar amendment to draw a line back of Quemoy and Matsu, limiting the president's authority to Formosa and the Pescadores, was introduced on the Senate floor by Senator Herbert Lehman of New York. It was defeated 74 to 13. The Senate passed the resolution 85 to 3, on January 28, 1955, and President Eisenhower signed it the next day.

The mutual security treaty with Nationalist China was ratified in February. Efforts to persuade Chiang Kai-shek to reduce his forces on Quemoy and Matsu and make them mere outposts failed. That same month, however, Chiang did evacuate the Tachen Islands, which the communists promptly occupied. Communist Premier Zhou Enlai, in an attempt to strike a conciliatory note, told the Afro-Asian Conference meeting in Bandung, Indonesia, in April, that his country did not want war with the United States. He further expressed his willingness to negotiate on Far Eastern issues, including that of Formosa. As a result, by May, without formal statement or agreement, there was an effective cease-fire in the Formosa Straits.

In the wake of the passage of the Formosa Resolution and the ratification of the mutual defense treaty with Nationalist China, President Eisenhower addressed a letter to British prime minister Winston Churchill on February 9, 1955, in which he set forth his ideas on the importance of defending Formosa and the offshore islands. The United States depended on an island (Formosa) and a peninsula (Korea) as its defense line in Southeast Asia. The loss of Formosa would be a serious break in that line. The weakening of Chiang Kai-shek's forces could mean the loss of Formosa. The denial of their expectation to return to mainland China would be destructive of their morale. Therefore, it was important to the United States not only to aid in the defense of Formosa but also not to accept, or seem to accept, the loss of the offshore islands, which were of strategic importance in launching a return to the mainland. These ideas helped set the posture of U.S. policy in the Far East for some time to come.

Judgments of the Formosa Resolution at the time of its passage and in historical perspective must depend greatly on attitudes toward the larger question of policy toward China. The overwhelming vote in Congress in favor of the Formosa Resolution may be taken as clear evidence of opinion there, and presumably of opinion throughout the country, that communist expansion must be resisted, but the United States ought not be involved in further war. From another, but related, perspective, the Formosa Resolution was a reflection of the Cold War mentality that saw no possibility for diplomatic recognition of the communist regime on the Chinese mainland.

Even after this Cold War mentality had waned, the legacy of the Formosa Resolution ensured that the United States maintained residual ties with the nationalist regime in Taiwan even after it afforded diplomatic recognition to mainland China in 1979. As U.S.-China tensions began to increase in the mid-1990's, the consensus among U.S. policymakers was that something should be done if China were to invade Taiwan. Thus, the impact of the Formosa Resolution was not confined to its immediate aftermath.

—George J. Fleming, updated by Nicholas Birns

ADDITIONAL READING:

Bueler, William M. *U.S. China Policy and the Problem of Taiwan*. Boulder: Colorado Associated University Press, 1971. Covers the resolution and its aftermath in detail.

Copper, John Franklin. *China Diplomacy: The Washington-Taipei-Beijing Triangle*. Boulder, Colo.: Westview Press, 1992. Examines how much actual communist threat there was to Taiwan in the 1950's.

Eisenhower, Dwight D. *Mandate for Change, 1953-1956*. Garden City, N.Y.: Doubleday, 1963. This memoir by the U.S. president at the time the resolution was enacted is still a valuable source for the U.S. view of the Formosa situation.

Hickey, Dennis Van Vranken. *United States-Taiwan Security Ties: From Cold War to Beyond Containment*. Westport, Conn.: Praeger, 1994. Examines the complicated network of U.S. military guarantees to Taiwan through the years.

Hsieh, Chiao Chiao. *Strategy for Survival: The Foreign Policy and External Relations of the Republic of China on Taiwan, 1949-1979*. London: Sherwood Press, 1985. Illuminates the Taiwanese perspective.

SEE ALSO: 1950, Korean War; 1972, Rapprochement with China; 1979, United States and China Establish Full Diplomatic Relations.

1955 ■ AFL AND CIO MERGE: *inauguration of the foremost labor organization of the twentieth century*

DATE: December 5, 1955
LOCALE: New York City
CATEGORIES: Business and labor; Economics; Organizations and institutions
KEY FIGURES:
James Barron Carey (1911-1973), secretary-treasurer of the CIO
Arthur Joseph Goldberg (1908-1990), general counsel of the CIO and the United Steelworkers
William Green (1873-1952), president of the AFL, 1924-1952
David John McDonald (1902-1979), president of the United Steelworkers
George Meany (1894-1980), president of the AFL
Walter Philip Reuther (1907-1970), president of the CIO
William F. Schnitzler (1904-1983), secretary-treasurer of the AFL
Joseph Albert Woll (1904-1984), counsel of the AFL
SUMMARY OF EVENT. From late in the nineteenth century until the 1930's, the American Federation of Labor (AFL) was the principal, although never the only, body of organized U.S. labor. In structure, it was a federation of national and international unions, with individual unions maintaining a great deal of autonomy. Most of the affiliated unions were composed of skilled laborers organized by their crafts or skills. AFL membership and prestige was weakened in the 1920's, and even more so in the early Depression years (1929-1932). This downward trend, however, was halted abruptly in 1933 with the inauguration of President Franklin D. Roosevelt and his New Deal program. New Deal legislation, such as Section 7A of the National Industrial Recovery Act (1933) and the later National Labor Relations Act, or Wagner Act (1935), encouraged the formation of unions by the legal guarantee of free collective bargaining.

This encouragement, along with other events and conditions, led to new organizing drives. Several groups within the AFL—in particular, the United Mine Workers, led by John L. Lewis—argued that the drives could not be successful unless they followed the principle of industrial unionism, organizing workers by the industry in which they worked rather than by craft—for example, auto workers, not machinists. This principle was opposed by many of the leaders of the older craft unions. Personal allegiances and antagonism, ideology and partisanship, all embittered the argument.

In 1935, insisting that the AFL was not reaching the mass-production industries, John L. Lewis of the United Mine Work-

ers, together with the leaders of other unions, formed the Committee on Industrial Organization, still within the AFL. After violent debate, the AFL revoked the charters of ten unions representing the Committee on Industrial Organization, which in 1938 expanded and was organized as an independent federation and renamed the Congress of Industrial Organizations (CIO).

In the succeeding years, the CIO built a number of industrial unions, notably in automobile manufacturing and steel, and took a more active part in general politics and social change than had been the AFL tradition. Antagonism between the movements continued, but circumstances frequently led to parallel, if not common, action, and sometimes to cooperation. This was especially the case during World War II, when both organizations were presented as being the voice of labor. After the war, their common opposition to what they regarded as hostile legislation led to common positions on a number of issues of mutual interest.

The division remained, however, for even Roosevelt's effort to bring about unity had been of no avail. By 1952, time and personnel changes seemed to alter the situation. William Green, longtime president of the AFL, and Philip Murray, president of the CIO, died within twelve days of each other, and if John L. Lewis, who had withdrawn the United Mine Workers from the CIO, was still a presence, he was not a necessary part of the negotiations.

The new leaders, George Meany of the AFL and Walter Reuther of the CIO, began talks in April, 1953. Later that year, committees formally instituted by the boards of the two organizations met and appointed a subcommittee of three members from each group to frame a plan of unity. The subcommittees included, respectively, the two chief officers of each—Meany and Secretary-Treasurer William F. Schnitzler for the AFL, Reuther and Secretary-Treasurer James B. Carey for the CIO—with, first, Matthew Woll of the Photo-Engravers, and then Harry Bates of the Bricklayers for the AFL, and David McDonald of the United Steelworkers for the CIO. As a necessary preliminary, the subcommittees worked out and won approval for a no-raiding agreement, by which unions of the two organizations agreed not to recruit members from the other's unions. This new pact was ratified by a majority of the individual unions of both the AFL and CIO, and the agreement was signed on June 9, 1954. A two-year study revealed that the raiding back and forth between the two organizations had resulted in a shift of about eight thousand members, while involving nearly fifty thousand members moving from one union to the other. Both organizations felt that the costs of this raiding could have yielded greater returns in other ways.

Although it did not please all the union leaders, the agreement went into effect. The next step, in February, 1955, was the drafting of a merger agreement by the subcommittees, with the assistance of their lawyers, Arthur Goldberg for the CIO and Joseph Albert Woll (son of Matthew Woll) for the AFL. The rapidly drawn draft went to the full committees, which also approved it.

The proposed agreement took what George Meany called "the short route"—admission of all affiliated unions of both federations. The independence of the constituent unions was to be respected; jurisdictional disputes—a major practical worry—were to be settled by negotiation. Craft and industrial unions were to have equal status. The agreement was approved by the governing boards, and the two counsels were instructed to draft a constitution for the new body. This was revised and approved in May, 1955, by subcommittees, committees, and the two boards. Arrangements were made for separate, simultaneous conventions in New York City, on December 1. These groups met and adjourned, and the convention of the united body met at the Seventy-first Regiment Armory, on Park Avenue and 34th Street, on December 5, 1955, under the combined name of AFL-CIO. The question of a name, which might have provoked recriminations, was settled by the combination of the two preexisting names.

The two conventions had adopted the constitution beforehand; the new body met without serious complications. On Reuther's nomination, Meany was unanimously elected president of the AFL-CIO, and on Carey's nomination Schnitzler became secretary-treasurer. By arrangement, vice presidencies and seats on the executive council and smaller executive committees were apportioned among the leaders of the AFL and CIO.

The constitution made the convention, regularly meeting every two years, the governing body, with interim powers assigned to bodies with progressively smaller numbers, more frequent meetings, and more day-to-day power: the general board, the executive council, and the executive committee. The constitution denounced communism and other totalitarian systems, and provided for the expulsion of unions dominated by communists. It also condemned corrupt and racketeering influence in the affiliated unions and gave the council power to investigate and recommend action. The united federation had, in some constitutional terms, powers that the old federations had not had.

On December 5, 1955, the convention ended nearly twenty years of division; while some unions remained out of the AFL-CIO, notably the United Mine Workers, the new federation represented most of organized U.S. labor. Union membership statistics are, for various reasons, imprecise, but the usual figure of fifteen million members in the new federation made it the largest single body in U.S. labor history, and, quite probably, in the free world.

During the ensuing years, the labor force in the United States changed, and the AFL-CIO changed with it. As automation eliminated jobs from the manufacturing area, white-collar workers increased. The percentage of private-sector jobs decreased, while that of jobs in public and governmental agencies increased. The makeup of the workforce changed also, with more and more two-wage-earner families. Civil rights legislation, more equal treatment of minority groups, and an increase in women in the workforce added more changes to union memberships. These new workers demanded different accommodations from their employers. Health, dental, and life insurance, child care, and other benefits became new needs bargained for by trade unions. Whereas strikes, lock-ins, and sit-ins were an important part of union activities in early years, the AFL-CIO moved more into political circles to assure that labor's views were heard.

The total number of persons employed in the United States has increased nearly every year since the AFL-CIO merger. Total membership has fluctuated, with highs and lows, but the overall numbers have remained nearly consistent, with 16.4 million members in 1995.

—George J. Fleming,
updated by Russell Hively

AFL president George Meany, left, shakes hands with CIO leader Walter Reuther as the labor leaders share a gavel symbolizing the birth of the new AFL-CIO. (AP/Wide World Photos)

ADDITIONAL READING:

Cormier, Frank, and William J. Eaton. *Reuther.* Englewood Cliffs, N.J.: Prentice-Hall, 1970. A biography of the CIO leader who brought his organization into the merger.

Goldberg, Arthur J. *AFL-CIO: Labor United.* New York: McGraw-Hill, 1956. A lawyer's insider account of the merger of the two unions.

Goulden, Joseph C. *Meany: A Biography of the Unchallenged Strong Man of American Labor.* New York: Atheneum, 1972. An account of one of the leaders who put together the merger of the AFL-CIO.

Kofas, John Y. *The Struggle for Legitimacy: Latin American Labor and the United States 1930-1960.* Tempe: Center for Latin American Studies, Arizona State University, 1992. Traces the movement of Latin American labor during the merger of the AFL-CIO.

Phelan, Craig. *William Green—Biography of a Labor Leader.* Albany: State University of New York Press, 1989. A biography of the longtime head of the AFL, up to the time of the merger.

Taft, Philip A. *Organized Labor in American History.* New York: Harper & Row, 1964. A leading study by a respected labor historian.

SEE ALSO: 1886, American Federation of Labor Is Founded; 1905, Industrial Workers of the World Is Founded; 1911, Triangle Shirtwaist Company Fire; 1929, Great Depression; 1933, National Industrial Recovery Act; 1935, National Labor Relations Act; 1935, Congress of Industrial Organizations Is Founded; 1938, Fair Labor Standards Act; 1941, 6.6 Million Women Enter the U.S. Labor Force; 1942, Bracero Program; 1943, Inflation and Labor Unrest; 1946, Employment Act; 1963, Equal Pay Act; 1965, Expansion of Affirmative Action; 1972, United Farm Workers Joins with AFL-CIO; 1972, Equal Employment Opportunity Act; 1992, Asian Pacific American Labor Alliance Is Founded; 1993, North American Free Trade Agreement; 1994, General Agreement on Tariffs and Trade.

1955 ■ MONTGOMERY BUS BOYCOTT:
African Americans fight entrenched discrimination through economic sanctions

DATE: December 5, 1955-December 21, 1956
LOCALE: Montgomery, Alabama
CATEGORIES: African American history; Civil rights; Social reform
KEY FIGURES:

Ralph David Abernathy (1926-1990), pastor of the First Baptist Church of Montgomery
Clifford Durr (1899-1975), liberal white attorney
Fred Gray (born 1930), one of only four black lawyers in Alabama
Martin Luther King, Jr. (1929-1968), pastor of Dexter Avenue Baptist Church

E. D. Nixon (1899-1987), head of the sleeping-car porters' union and president of Alabama's National Association for the Advancement of Colored People
Rosa Parks (born 1913), seamstress whose arrest launched the boycott
Jo Ann Robinson (born 1912), assisted in planning the boycott

SUMMARY OF EVENT. When the Supreme Court issued its decision in *Brown v. Board of Education of Topeka, Kansas* in May, 1954, ruling that racial segregation in public schools was unconstitutional, it marked the beginning of a period of dramatic change in the relationships between African Americans and whites. Until the mid-1960's, that change was hastened by the organized nonviolent resistance by many African Americans to laws and conditions that they regarded as discriminatory. The first occasion in which such tactics proved successful was a boycott of public buses in Montgomery, Alabama.

Although African Americans had achieved some hard-fought successes before 1954—most notably the desegregation of the armed forces—in many respects they remained a separate community, enjoying fewer rights and opportunities and less legal protection than whites. This was especially true in the Deep South, where the doctrine of "separate but equal" was held to apply to most areas of daily life and was used to justify a decidedly unequal segregation. Hundreds of laws, many of them passed in the late nineteenth century, restricted the rights of black Southerners to eat, travel, study, or worship with whites.

The school desegregation ruling brought no immediate change to race relations in Montgomery. Once the capital of the Confederacy, this city of about 130,000 people—50,000 of whom were African American—continued resolutely in the old pattern of racial separation. The African American community of Montgomery had undertaken initial steps to challenge certain local segregation practices that were particularly offensive. E. D. Nixon of Montgomery headed the National Association for the Advancement of Colored People (NAACP) in Alabama. Because he worked as a sleeping-car porter, he was less susceptible to attempts by the white establishment to control his behavior by threatening his job. Jo Ann Robinson helped lead the African American clubwomen in Montgomery, who provided a powerful organizational backbone among the small African Americans middle class in Montgomery. This nascent movement still lacked both a unified structure and a single issue to mobilize the African American community to push for civil rights.

The issue came to a head on December 1, 1955, when Rosa Parks, a seamstress at a Montgomery department store and formerly the secretary of the local NAACP chapter, refused to give up her seat to maintain a row of vacant seats between white and black riders on the public bus system in Montgomery, as required by law. She was arrested and charged with violating the segregation ordinance. Parks's action was in part spontaneous—she had not boarded the bus with the intent to violate any segregation ordinance. Yet she had attended the Highlander Folk School in Tennessee, where members of the community learned to become more effective, and a lifetime of enduring racial indignities had made her acutely aware of the evil nature of segregation.

Immediately, Montgomery's African American community sprang into action. Fred Gray, one of but four black lawyers in Alabama, contacted Clifford Durr, a liberal white attorney, to post bail for Parks. Nixon brought together two ministers, Ralph David Abernathy and Martin Luther King, Jr., with Jo Ann Robinson to plan for a massive boycott of Montgomery public buses, a majority of whose riders were African Americans. It would be necessary to arrange for transportation for scores of African Americans who did not own cars. To coordinate the massive undertaking, Montgomery's African American leaders created the Montgomery Improvement Association (MIA), presided over by King, the twenty-six-year-old pastor of Dexter Avenue Baptist Church. The boycott began on December 5, 1955.

At first, whites reacted with indifference or amusement, until the bus company's revenues dropped by 75 percent. A series of meetings between the city commissioners, representatives of the bus company, and the MIA failed to produce any agreement on the African American's demands—courteous treatment by bus drivers; a first-come, first-served seating arrangement, with blacks filling the rear and whites the front of the bus; and the employment of African American drivers on routes that served predominantly African American neighborhoods of Montgomery. Instead, the city police department began to harass the carpools that had been set up by the MIA to provide alternative transportation and arrested some of the drivers. Police officers arrested King himself for speeding, and on January 30, persons unknown blasted King's house with dynamite. The houses of two other boycott leaders met a similar fate.

These acts of violence and intimidation affected the course of events in several ways. First, they united the African Americans in Montgomery, inspiring them to continue the boycott for more than a year. The violence also attracted national attention to Montgomery and led to substantial outside support for the boycott, assistance vital to its success. Finally, the violence served as a foil for the rhetoric of nonviolent resistance that King so eloquently articulated. In one mass meeting after another, he urged his followers to ignore hostile provocations, to confront their persecutors passively, and to refuse to fight back, relying on the moral authority of their actions to sway the hearts and minds of their antagonists.

While the boycott continued, the legal issues it raised were argued in federal courts. On February 1, 1956, five Montgomery women filed suit to have the Court strike down the city bus seating ordinance. The case was heard on May 11, by which time eighty-nine MIA members faced local charges for conspiracy to interfere with normal business. In November, city officials obtained an injunction against the MIA officials for running a carpool, which nearly brought the boycott to a halt. Nevertheless, the federal suit received a favorable hearing and was affirmed by the Supreme Court in *Browder v. Gayle* in November, and the court ordered the seating on

Montgomery buses desegregated on December 17, 1956. Four days later, King, Abernathy, and Nixon rode the bus downtown and were able to sit wherever they wanted.

The boycott succeeded for a number of reasons, not the least of which was the timely court ruling. It also benefited from fissures in the white community across gender, age, and economic lines. White middle-class women often transported their black maids to and from work, unwittingly aiding the boycott. Within the Chamber of Commerce, a coalition of young businessmen called the Men of Montgomery demanded that the city fathers end the boycott because the city's tarnished image made it difficult to attract outside businesses.

Successful in its immediate objective, the boycott established a precedent for other economic protests over the next decade. Because of his role in the boycott, Martin Luther King, Jr., emerged as the most important spokesperson for African Americans. His tactics of nonviolent passive resistance remained the major tool of the Civil Rights movement until the mid-1960's. Shortly after the boycott's conclusion, King was instrumental in founding the Southern Christian Leadership Conference, which applied the Montgomery formula to other southern cities. African American leaders tried nonviolent resistance and economic protests in Birmingham, Alabama, and Albany, Georgia. The Montgomery bus boycott was an important harbinger of the most profound social changes in the United States during the 1960's, in that it marked a change in the attitudes and strategies of African Americans to confront racial indignity.

—*Courtney B. Ross, updated by Edward R. Crowther*

ADDITIONAL READING:

Garrow, David J. *Bearing the Cross: Martin Luther King, Jr., and the Southern Christian Leadership Conference.* New York: William Morrow, 1986. A thorough, detailed biography of King, which provides an excellent account of King's Montgomery days.

King, Martin Luther, Jr. *Stride Toward Freedom: The Montgomery Story.* New York: Harper & Row, 1958. King's own account of the boycott.

Lewis, David L. *King: A Critical Biography.* New York: Praeger, 1970. A balanced biography that attempts to show why nonviolent resistance might work in the South but fail as a strategy to deal with racism in the Northern and Western cities.

Robinson, Jo Ann Gibson. *The Montgomery Bus Boycott and the Women Who Started It: The Memoir of Jo Ann Gibson Robinson.* Knoxville: University of Tennessee Press, 1987. Provides a powerful portrait of the world of middle-class women in Montgomery and the essential role they played in the boycott strategy.

Thornton, J. Mills. "Challenge and Response in the Montgomery Bus Boycott of 1955-1956." *Alabama Review* 33 (July, 1980): 163-235. Clearly illustrates the context in which the MIA operated and shows how its strategy exacerbated the fissures among the white leadership in Montgomery.

SEE ALSO: 1954, *Brown v. Board of Education*; 1957, Little Rock School Desegregation Crisis; 1962, Meredith Registers at "Ole Miss."

GREAT EVENTS FROM HISTORY
NORTH AMERICAN SERIES

KEY WORD INDEX

CATEGORY LIST

NOTE: The entries in this publication are listed below under all categories that apply. The chronological order under each category corresponds to the chronological order of the entries in these volumes.

AFRICAN AMERICAN HISTORY

1619, Africans Arrive in Virginia
1641, Massachusetts Recognizes Slavery
1661, Virginia Slave Codes
1712, New York City Slave Revolt
1739, Stono Rebellion
1773, African American Baptist Church Is Founded
1775, Pennsylvania Society for the Abolition of Slavery Is Founded
1777, Northeast States Abolish Slavery
1784, Hall's Masonic Lodge Is Chartered
1787, Free African Society Is Founded
1787, Northwest Ordinance
1791, Haitian Independence
1793, Whitney Invents the Cotton Gin
1793, First Fugitive Slave Law
1804, First Black Codes
1807, Congress Bans Importation of African Slaves
1816, AME Church Is Founded
1820's, Social Reform Movement
1820, Missouri Compromise
1830, Proslavery Argument
1830, Webster-Hayne Debate
1831, *The Liberator* Begins Publication
1831, Nat Turner's Insurrection
1833, American Anti-Slavery Society Is Founded
1839, Amistad Slave Revolt
1847, *The North Star* Begins Publication
1850, Underground Railroad
1850, Compromise of 1850
1850, Second Fugitive Slave Law
1853, National Council of Colored People Is Founded
1854, Kansas-Nebraska Act
1856, Bleeding Kansas
1857, First African American University
1857, *Dred Scott v. Sandford*
1858, Lincoln-Douglas Debates
1859, Last Slave Ship Docks at Mobile
1859, John Brown's Raid on Harpers Ferry
1863, Emancipation Proclamation
1863, Reconstruction
1865, Freedmen's Bureau Is Established

1865, New Black Codes
1865, Thirteenth Amendment
1866, Rise of the Ku Klux Klan
1866, Civil Rights Act of 1866
1866, Race Riots in the South
1868, Fourteenth Amendment
1890, Mississippi Disfranchisement Laws
1895, Booker T. Washington's Atlanta Exposition Address
1896, *Plessy v. Ferguson*
1909, National Association for the Advancement of Colored People Is Founded
1910, Great Northern Migration
1917, Universal Negro Improvement Association Is Established
1930, Nation of Islam Is Founded
1931, Scottsboro Trials
1941, Executive Order 8802
1942, Congress of Racial Equality Is Founded
1944, *Smith v. Allwright*
1954, *Brown v. Board of Education*
1955, Montgomery Bus Boycott
1957, Southern Christian Leadership Conference Is Founded
1957, Little Rock School Desegregation Crisis
1960, Civil Rights Act of 1960
1962, Meredith Registers at "Ole Miss"
1963, King Delivers His "I Have a Dream" Speech
1964, Civil Rights Act of 1964
1965, Assassination of Malcolm X
1965, Voting Rights Act
1965, Watts Riot
1965, Expansion of Affirmative Action
1967, Long, Hot Summer
1968, Assassinations of King and Kennedy
1968, Fair Housing Act
1971, *Swann v. Charlotte-Mecklenberg Board of Education*
1972, Equal Employment Opportunity Act
1980, Miami Riots
1983, Jackson Becomes First Major African American Candidate for President

ASIAN AMERICAN HISTORY

1849, Chinese Immigration
1854, Perry Opens Trade with Japan
1868, Burlingame Treaty
1875, Page Law
1882, Chinese Exclusion Act
1882, Rise of the Chinese Six Companies
1892, Yellow Peril Campaign
1895, Chinese American Citizens Alliance Is Founded
1898, *United States v. Wong Kim Ark*
1899, Philippine Insurrection
1899, Hay's "Open Door Notes"
1901, Insular Cases
1907, Gentlemen's Agreement
1913, Alien Land Laws
1917, Immigration Act of 1917
1922, *Ozawa v. United States*
1930, Japanese American Citizens League Is Founded
1934, Tydings-McDuffie Act
1942, Censorship and Japanese Internment
1943, Magnuson Act
1959, Alaska and Hawaii Gain Statehood
1968, Bilingual Education Act
1974, *Lau v. Nichols*
1992, Asian Pacific American Labor Alliance

BUSINESS AND LABOR

1790, Slater's Spinning Mill
1793, Whitney Invents the Cotton Gin
1808, American Fur Company Is Chartered
1810, *Fletcher v. Peck*
1825, Erie Canal Opens
1833, Rise of the Penny Press
1842, *Commonwealth v. Hunt*
1842, Dorr Rebellion
1846, Howe's Sewing Machine
1859, First Commercial Oil Well
1882, Standard Oil Trust Is Organized
1886, American Federation of Labor Is Founded
1887, Interstate Commerce Act
1890, Sherman Antitrust Act
1894, Pullman Strike

1869, Rise of Woman Suffrage
     Associations
1869, Western States Grant Woman
     Suffrage
1872, Susan B. Anthony Is Arrested
1874, *Minor v. Happersett*
1876, Declaration of the Rights of
     Women
1883, Civil Rights Cases
1890, Mississippi Disfranchisement Laws
1895, Booker T. Washington's Atlanta
     Exposition Address
1896, *Plessy v. Ferguson*
1898, *United States v. Wong Kim Ark*
1902, Expansion of Direct Democracy
1909, National Association for the
     Advancement of Colored People
     Is Founded
1913, Alien Land Laws
1917, Propaganda and Civil Liberties in
     World War I
1917, Espionage and Sedition Acts
1917, Canadian Women Gain the Vote
1919, Red Scare
1920, U.S. Women Gain the Vote
1922, Cable Act
1923, Proposal of the Equal Rights
     Amendment
1929, League of United Latin American
     Citizens Is Founded
1941, Executive Order 8802
1942, Censorship and Japanese
     Internment
1942, Congress of Racial Equality Is
     Founded
1944, *Smith v. Allwright*
1951, McCarthy Hearings
1954, *Brown v. Board of Education*
1955, Montgomery Bus Boycott
1957, Southern Christian Leadership
     Conference Is Founded
1957, Little Rock School
     Desegregation Crisis
1960, Civil Rights Act of 1960
1962, Meredith Registers at "Ole Miss"
1963, *Gideon v. Wainwright*
1963, Equal Pay Act
1963, King Delivers His "I Have a
     Dream" Speech
1964, Twenty-fourth Amendment
1964, Civil Rights Act of 1964
1964, Berkeley Free Speech Movement
1965, Assassination of Malcolm X
1965, *Griswold v. Connecticut*
1965, Voting Rights Act

1965, Expansion of Affirmative Action
1967, Long, Hot Summer
1967, Freedom of Information Act
1968, Assassinations of King and
     Kennedy
1968, Indian Civil Rights Act
1968, Fair Housing Act
1969, Stonewall Inn Riots
1970, Kent State Massacre
1970, October Crisis
1971, *Swann v. Charlotte-Mecklenberg
     Board of Education*
1971, U.S. Voting Age Is Lowered to
     Eighteen
1971, Attica State Prison Riots
1972, Equal Employment Opportunity
     Act
1973, *Roe v. Wade*
1975, Equal Credit Opportunity Act
1976, *Gregg v. Georgia*
1977, Canada's Human Rights Act
1978, Pregnancy Discrimination Act
1978, *Regents of the University of
     California v. Bakke*
1978, American Indian Religious
     Freedom Act
1982, *Plyler v. Doe*
1988, Civil Rights Restoration Act
1990, Americans with Disabilities Act
1991, Civil Rights Act of 1991
1993, Family and Medical Leave Act
1993, Branch Davidians' Compound
     Burns

COMMUNICATIONS
1828, *Cherokee Phoenix* Begins
     Publication
1831, *The Liberator* Begins Publication
1833, Rise of the Penny Press
1844, First Telegraph Message
1847, *The North Star* Begins
     Publication
1858, First Transatlantic Cable
1860, Pony Express
1861, Transcontinental Telegraph Is
     Completed
1866, Suffragists Protest the Fourteenth
     Amendment
1876, Bell Demonstrates the Telephone
1900, Teletype Is Developed
1939, Debut of Commercial Television
1947, Invention of the Transistor
1981, IBM Markets the Personal
     Computer
1990's, Rise of the Internet

COURT CASES
1734, Trial of John Peter Zenger
1803, *Marbury v. Madison*
1810, *Fletcher v. Peck*
1819, *McCulloch v. Maryland*
1824, *Gibbons v. Ogden*
1831, Cherokee Cases
1842, *Commonwealth v. Hunt*
1857, *Dred Scott v. Sandford*
1874, *Minor v. Happersett*
1883, Civil Rights Cases
1896, *Plessy v. Ferguson*
1898, *United States v. Wong Kim Ark*
1901, Insular Cases
1903, *Lone Wolf v. Hitchcock*
1908, *Muller v. Oregon*
1922, *Ozawa v. United States*
1925, Scopes Trial
1927, Sacco and Vanzetti Are Executed
1931, Scottsboro Trials
1935, Black Monday
1954, *Brown v. Board of Education*
1962, Reapportionment Cases
1963, *Gideon v. Wainwright*
1963, *Abington School District v.
     Schempp*
1965, *Griswold v. Connecticut*
1971, *Swann v. Charlotte-Mecklenberg
     Board of Education*
1973, *Roe v. Wade*
1974, *Lau v. Nichols*
1976, *Gregg v. Georgia*
1978, *Regents of the University of
     California v. Bakke*
1982, *Plyler v. Doe*

**CULTURAL AND INTELLECTUAL
HISTORY**
1776, Declaration of Independence
1787, *Federalist* Papers Are Published
1820's, Free Public School Movement
1828, *Cherokee Phoenix* Begins
     Publication
1828, Webster's *American Dictionary
     of the English Language*
1831, *The Liberator* Begins Publication
1831, Tocqueville Visits America
1833, Rise of the Penny Press
1836, Rise of Transcendentalism
1846, Smithsonian Institution Is
     Founded
1847, *The North Star* Begins
     Publication
1871, Barnum's Circus Forms
1893, World's Columbian Exposition

1918, Demobilization After World War I
1924, Dawes Plan
1929, Stock Market Crash
1929, Great Depression
1930's, Mass Deportations of Mexicans
1930, Baltimore and Ohio Railroad Begins Operation
1931, Empire State Building Opens
1932, Reconstruction Finance Corporation Is Created
1932, Ottawa Agreements
1932, Bonus March
1933, The Hundred Days
1933, Tennessee Valley Authority Is Established
1933, National Industrial Recovery Act
1934, Tydings-McDuffie Act
1934, The Dust Bowl
1935, Works Progress Administration Is Established
1935, Black Monday
1935, National Labor Relations Act
1935, Social Security Act
1936, Reciprocity Treaty
1939, Mobilization for World War II
1941, 6.6 Million Women Enter the U.S. Labor Force
1942, Bracero Program
1943, Inflation and Labor Unrest
1943, Urban Race Riots
1946, Employment Act
1955, AFL and CIO Merge
1959, St. Lawrence Seaway Opens
1961, Peace Corps Is Established
1967, Long, Hot Summer
1971, Devaluation of the Dollar
1973, Arab Oil Embargo and Energy Crisis
1974, Construction of the Alaska Pipeline
1981, Reagan's Budget and Tax Reform
1988, Indian Gaming Regulatory Act
1989, Lincoln Savings and Loan Declares Bankruptcy
1993, North American Free Trade Agreement
1994, General Agreement on Tariffs and Trade

EDUCATION

1650, Harvard College Is Established
1785, Beginnings of State Universities
1802, U.S. Military Academy Is Established
1820's, Free Public School Movement
1820's, Social Reform Movement

1823, Hartford Female Seminary Is Founded
1833, Oberlin College Is Established
1837, Mt. Holyoke Seminary Is Founded
1857, First African American University
1862, Morrill Land Grant Act
1865, Vassar College Is Founded
1867, Office of Education Is Created
1912, U.S. Public Health Service Is Established
1925, Scopes Trial
1929, League of United Latin American Citizens Is Founded
1944, G.I. Bill
1954, *Brown v. Board of Education*
1957, Little Rock School Desegregation Crisis
1962, Meredith Registers at "Ole Miss"
1963, *Abington School District v. Schempp*
1964, Berkeley Free Speech Movement
1965, Expansion of Affirmative Action
1968, Bilingual Education Act
1971, *Swann v. Charlotte-Mecklenberg Board of Education*
1974, *Lau v. Nichols*
1978, *Regents of the University of California v. Bakke*
1982, *Plyler v. Doe*

ENVIRONMENT

1872, Great American Bison Slaughter
1908, White House Conservation Conference
1916, National Park Service Is Created
1924, Halibut Treaty
1934, The Dust Bowl
1978, Toxic Waste at Love Canal
1979, Three Mile Island Accident
1981, Ozone Hole Is Discovered
1989, *Exxon Valdez* Oil Spill

EXPANSION AND LAND ACQUISITION

1626, Algonquians "Sell" Manhattan Island
1670, Hudson's Bay Company Is Chartered
1673, French Explore the Mississippi Valley
1702, Queen Anne's War
1711, Tuscarora War
1728, Russian Voyages to Alaska
1737, Walking Purchase

1754, French and Indian War
1763, Proclamation of 1763
1763, Paxton Boys' Massacres
1769, Rise of the California Missions
1774, Lord Dunmore's War
1774, Quebec Act
1784, Fort Stanwix Treaty
1785, Ordinance of 1785
1787, Northwest Ordinance
1790, Nootka Sound Convention
1790, Little Turtle's War
1793, Mackenzie Reaches the Arctic Ocean
1794, Battle of Fallen Timbers
1794, Jay's Treaty
1795, Pinckney's Treaty
1803, Louisiana Purchase
1804, Lewis and Clark Expedition
1806, Pike's Southwest Explorations
1808, American Fur Company Is Chartered
1810, *Fletcher v. Peck*
1810, Astorian Expeditions
1811, Construction of the National Road
1813, Creek War
1815, Westward Migration
1819, Adams-Onís Treaty
1820, Land Act of 1820
1821, Santa Fe Trail Opens
1823, Jedediah Smith Explores the Far West
1830, Webster-Hayne Debate
1830, Indian Removal Act
1830, Trail of Tears
1835, Texas Revolution
1840's, "Old" Immigration
1841, Preemption Act
1842, Frémont's Expeditions
1842, Webster-Ashburton Treaty
1846, Mormon Migration to Utah
1846, Mexican War
1846, Oregon Settlement
1846, Occupation of California and the Southwest
1848, California Gold Rush
1850, Compromise of 1850
1853, Pacific Railroad Surveys
1853, Gadsden Purchase
1858, Fraser River Gold Rush
1862, Homestead Act
1864, Sand Creek Massacre
1866, Chisholm Trail Opens
1867, Purchase of Alaska
1872, Great American Bison Slaughter

1790, Little Turtle's War
1793, Mackenzie Reaches the Arctic Ocean
1794, Battle of Fallen Timbers
1799, Code of Handsome Lake
1808, Prophetstown Is Founded
1810, *Fletcher v. Peck*
1812, War of 1812
1813, Creek War
1813, Battle of the Thames
1815, Westward Migration
1815, Treaty of Ghent
1815, Red River Raids
1817, Seminole Wars
1821, Santa Fe Trail Opens
1828, *Cherokee Phoenix* Begins Publication
1830, Indian Removal Act
1830, Trail of Tears
1831, Cherokee Cases
1837, Rebellions in Canada
1847, Taos Rebellion
1861, Stand Watie Fights for the South
1861, Apache Wars
1862, Great Sioux War
1863, Long Walk of the Navajos
1864, Sand Creek Massacre
1866, Bozeman Trail War
1867, Medicine Lodge Creek Treaty
1868, Washita River Massacre
1869, First Riel Rebellion
1871, Indian Appropriation Act
1872, Great American Bison Slaughter
1874, Red River War
1876, Canada's Indian Act
1876, Battle of the Little Bighorn
1877, Nez Perce Exile
1885, Second Riel Rebellion
1887, General Allotment Act
1890, Closing of the Frontier
1890, Battle of Wounded Knee
1903, *Lone Wolf v. Hitchcock*
1924, Indian Citizenship Act
1934, Indian Reorganization Act
1953, Termination Resolution
1959, Alaska and Hawaii Gain Statehood
1965, Voting Rights Act
1968, Indian Civil Rights Act
1969, Alcatraz Occupation
1971, Alaska Native Claims Settlement Act
1972, Trail of Broken Treaties
1973, Wounded Knee Occupation

1978, American Indian Religious Freedom Act
1988, Indian Gaming Regulatory Act

ORGANIZATIONS AND INSTITUTIONS
1627, Company of New France Is Chartered
1650, Harvard College Is Established
1670, Hudson's Bay Company Is Chartered
1768, Methodist Church Is Established
1775, Pennsylvania Society for the Abolition of Slavery Is Founded
1784, Hall's Masonic Lodge Is Chartered
1785, Beginnings of State Universities
1787, Free African Society Is Founded
1789, Episcopal Church Is Established
1790's, First U.S. Political Parties
1802, U.S. Military Academy Is Established
1816, Second Bank of the United States Is Chartered
1816, AME Church Is Founded
1819, Unitarian Church Is Founded
1823, Hartford Female Seminary Is Founded
1833, American Anti-Slavery Society Is Founded
1833, Oberlin College Is Established
1834, Birth of the Whig Party
1837, Mt. Holyoke Seminary Is Founded
1846, Independent Treasury Is Established
1846, Smithsonian Institution Is Founded
1853, National Council of Colored People Is Founded
1854, Birth of the Republican Party
1857, New York Infirmary for Indigent Women and Children Opens
1865, Freedmen's Bureau Is Established
1866, Rise of the Ku Klux Klan
1867, Office of Education Is Created
1867, National Grange of the Patrons of Husbandry Forms
1869, Rise of Woman Suffrage Associations
1871, Barnum's Circus Forms
1875, Supreme Court of Canada Is Established
1886, American Federation of Labor Is Founded

1889, Hull House Opens
1890, Women's Rights Associations Unite
1895, Chinese American Citizens Alliance Is Founded
1905, Industrial Workers of the World Is Founded
1905, Niagara Movement
1913, Anti-Defamation League Is Founded
1916, National Woman's Party Is Founded
1916, National Park Service Is Created
1917, Universal Negro Improvement Association Is Established
1918, Republican Resurgence
1919, Black Sox Scandal
1920, League of Women Voters Is Founded
1929, League of United Latin American Citizens Is Founded
1930, Nation of Islam Is Founded
1930, Japanese American Citizens League Is Founded
1935, Works Progress Administration Is Established
1935, Congress of Industrial Organizations Is Founded
1942, Congress of Racial Equality Is Founded
1955, AFL and CIO Merge
1957, Southern Christian Leadership Conference Is Founded
1960, Quebec Sovereignist Movement
1966, National Organization for Women Is Founded
1968, Chicago Riots

PREHISTORY AND ANCIENT CULTURES
15,000 B.C., Bering Strait Migrations
1500 B.C., Olmec Civilization
700 B.C., Ohio Mound Builders
300 B.C., Hohokam Culture
A.D. 200, Mayan Civilization
A.D. 200, Anasazi Civilization
A.D. 700, Zapotec Civilization
A.D. 750, Mogollon Culture
A.D. 750, Mississippian Culture
1428, Aztec Empire

RELIGION
1620, Pilgrims Land at Plymouth
1630, Great Puritan Migration
1632, Settlement of Connecticut

1636, Rhode Island Is Founded
1649, Maryland Act of Toleration
1654, First Jewish Settlers
1662, Half-Way Covenant
1681, Pennsylvania Is Founded
1692, Salem Witchcraft Trials
1730's, First Great Awakening
1768, Methodist Church Is Established
1769, Rise of the California Missions
1773, African American Baptist Church Is Founded
1774, Quebec Act
1786, Virginia Statute of Religious Liberty
1789, Episcopal Church Is Established
1790's, Second Great Awakening
1799, Code of Handsome Lake
1816, AME Church Is Founded
1819, Unitarian Church Is Founded
1820's, Social Reform Movement
1836, Rise of Transcendentalism
1844, Anti-Irish Riots
1846, Mormon Migration to Utah
1930, Nation of Islam Is Founded
1963, *Abington School District v. Schempp*
1978, American Indian Religious Freedom Act
1993, Branch Davidians' Compound Burns

SCIENCE AND TECHNOLOGY

1776, First Test of a Submarine in Warfare
1790, Slater's Spinning Mill
1793, Whitney Invents the Cotton Gin
1807, Voyage of the *Clermont*
1825, Erie Canal Opens
1831, McCormick Invents the Reaper
1836, Rise of Transcendentalism
1844, First Telegraph Message
1845, Era of the Clipper Ships
1846, Howe's Sewing Machine
1846, Smithsonian Institution Is Founded
1846, Surgical Anesthesia Is Safely Demonstrated
1858, First Transatlantic Cable
1859, First Commercial Oil Well
1861, Transcontinental Telegraph Is Completed
1862, *Monitor* vs. *Virginia*
1869, Transcontinental Railroad Is Completed
1876, Bell Demonstrates the Telephone

1879, Edison Demonstrates the Incandescent Lamp
1883, Brooklyn Bridge Opens
1893, World's Columbian Exposition
1900, Teletype Is Developed
1903, Acquisition of the Panama Canal Zone
1903, Wright Brothers' First Flight
1913, Ford Assembly Line Begins Operation
1920, Commercial Radio Broadcasting Begins
1926, Launching of the First Liquid-Fueled Rocket
1927, Lindbergh's Transatlantic Flight
1930, Baltimore and Ohio Railroad Begins Operation
1931, Empire State Building Opens
1934, Development of Radar
1938, First Xerographic Photocopy
1939, Debut of Commercial Television
1942, Manhattan Project
1945, Atomic Bombing of Japan
1947, Invention of the Transistor
1952, Development of a Polio Vaccine
1952, Hydrogen Bomb Is Detonated
1959, St. Lawrence Seaway Opens
1960, FDA Approves the Birth Control Pill
1961, First American in Space
1969, Apollo 11 Lands on the Moon
1974, Construction of the Alaska Pipeline
1977, Spaceflights of Voyagers 1 and 2
1978, Toxic Waste at Love Canal
1981, IBM Markets the Personal Computer
1981, Ozone Hole Is Discovered
1986, *Challenger* Accident
1989, Human Genome Project
1990's, Rise of the Internet
1993, Astronauts Repair the Hubble Space Telescope

SETTLEMENTS

1565, St. Augustine Is Founded
1584, Lost Colony of Roanoke
1603, Champlain's Voyages
1607, Jamestown Is Founded
1620, Pilgrims Land at Plymouth
1626, Algonquians "Sell" Manhattan Island
1630, Great Puritan Migration
1632, Settlement of Connecticut

1636, Rhode Island Is Founded
1663, Settlement of the Carolinas
1670, Charles Town Is Founded
1681, Pennsylvania Is Founded
1732, Settlement of Georgia
1808, Prophetstown Is Founded
1814, New Harmony and the Communitarian Movement
1846, Mormon Migration to Utah
1846, Oregon Settlement
1848, California Gold Rush
1858, Fraser River Gold Rush

SOCIAL REFORM

1730's, First Great Awakening
1775, Pennsylvania Society for the Abolition of Slavery Is Founded
1777, Northeast States Abolish Slavery
1787, Free African Society Is Founded
1790's, Second Great Awakening
1808, Prophetstown Is Founded
1814, New Harmony and the Communitarian Movement
1819, Unitarian Church Is Founded
1820's, Social Reform Movement
1828, *Cherokee Phoenix* Begins Publication
1831, *The Liberator* Begins Publication
1833, American Anti-Slavery Society Is Founded
1850, Underground Railroad
1851, Akron Woman's Rights Convention
1857, New York Infirmary for Indigent Women and Children Opens
1867, National Grange of the Patrons of Husbandry Forms
1889, Hull House Opens
1920, Prohibition
1921, Sheppard-Towner Act
1935, Social Security Act
1935, Congress of Industrial Organizations Is Founded
1938, Fair Labor Standards Act
1941, 6.6 Million Women Enter the U.S. Labor Force
1955, Montgomery Bus Boycott
1960, FDA Approves the Birth Control Pill
1963, King Delivers His "I Have a Dream" Speech
1965, Expansion of Affirmative Action
1988, Family Support Act
1993, Family and Medical Leave Act

TRANSPORTATION

1807, Voyage of the *Clermont*
1811, Construction of the National Road
1815, Westward Migration
1821, Santa Fe Trail Opens
1823, Jedediah Smith Explores the Far West
1825, Erie Canal Opens
1845, Era of the Clipper Ships
1853, Pacific Railroad Surveys
1860, Pony Express
1866, Chisholm Trail Opens
1869, Transcontinental Railroad Is Completed
1887, Interstate Commerce Act
1903, Acquisition of the Panama Canal Zone
1903, Wright Brothers' First Flight
1913, Ford Assembly Line Begins Operation
1927, Lindbergh's Transatlantic Flight
1930, Baltimore and Ohio Railroad Begins Operation
1959, St. Lawrence Seaway Opens
1973, Arab Oil Embargo and Energy Crisis
1978, Panama Canal Treaties

TREATIES AND AGREEMENTS

1778, Franco-American Treaties
1783, Treaty of Paris
1784, Fort Stanwix Treaty
1790, Nootka Sound Convention
1794, Jay's Treaty
1795, Pinckney's Treaty
1803, Louisiana Purchase
1815, Treaty of Ghent
1819, Adams-Onís Treaty
1842, Webster-Ashburton Treaty
1848, Treaty of Guadalupe Hidalgo
1853, Gadsden Purchase
1867, Purchase of Alaska
1867, Medicine Lodge Creek Treaty
1868, Burlingame Treaty
1871, Treaty of Washington
1907, Gentlemen's Agreement
1919, Treaty of Versailles
1921, Washington Disarmament Conference
1924, Halibut Treaty
1928, Kellogg-Briand Pact
1932, Ottawa Agreements
1936, Reciprocity Treaty
1940, Ogdensburg Agreement
1942, Bracero Program

1948, Organization of American States Is Founded
1949, North Atlantic Treaty
1978, Panama Canal Treaties
1979, SALT II Is Signed
1987, INF Treaty Is Signed
1993, START II Is Signed
1993, North American Free Trade Agreement
1994, U.S.-North Korea Pact
1994, General Agreement on Tariffs and Trade

WARS, UPRISINGS, AND CIVIL UNREST

1495, West Indian Uprisings
1598, Oñate's New Mexico Expedition
1622, Powhatan Wars
1632, Zuñi Rebellion
1636, Pequot War
1642, Beaver Wars
1664, British Conquest of New Netherland
1675, Metacom's War
1676, Bacon's Rebellion
1680, Pueblo Revolt
1702, Queen Anne's War
1711, Tuscarora War
1712, New York City Slave Revolt
1714, Fox Wars
1739, Stono Rebellion
1739, King George's War
1754, French and Indian War
1759, Cherokee War
1763, Pontiac's Resistance
1763, Paxton Boys' Massacres
1765, Stamp Act Crisis
1767, Townshend Crisis
1768, Carolina Regulator Movements
1770, Boston Massacre
1773, Boston Tea Party
1774, Lord Dunmore's War
1775, Battle of Lexington and Concord
1775, Second Continental Congress
1776, Indian Delegation Meets with Congress
1776, First Test of a Submarine in Warfare
1777, Battle of Oriskany Creek
1777, Battle of Saratoga
1781, Cornwallis Surrenders at Yorktown
1790, Little Turtle's War
1791, Haitian Independence
1793, Whiskey Rebellion

1794, Battle of Fallen Timbers
1797, XYZ Affair
1804, Burr's Conspiracy
1810, El Grito de Dolores
1811, Battle of Tippecanoe
1812, War of 1812
1813, Creek War
1813, Battle of the Thames
1815, Battle of New Orleans
1815, Red River Raids
1817, Seminole Wars
1821, Mexican War of Independence
1831, Nat Turner's Insurrection
1835, Texas Revolution
1837, Rebellions in Canada
1839, Amistad Slave Revolt
1842, Dorr Rebellion
1844, Anti-Irish Riots
1846, Mexican War
1846, Occupation of California and the Southwest
1847, Taos Rebellion
1850, Bloody Island Massacre
1857, Cart War
1859, John Brown's Raid on Harpers Ferry
1860, Confederate States Secede from the Union
1861, Stand Watie Fights for the South
1861, Apache Wars
1861, First Battle of Bull Run
1862, *Monitor* vs. *Virginia*
1862, Great Sioux War
1863, First National Draft Law
1863, Battles of Gettysburg, Vicksburg, and Chattanooga
1864, Sherman's March to the Sea
1864, Sand Creek Massacre
1865, Surrender at Appomattox and Assassination of Lincoln
1866, Race Riots in the South
1866, Bozeman Trail War
1868, Washita River Massacre
1869, First Riel Rebellion
1874, Red River War
1876, Battle of the Little Bighorn
1877, Nez Perce Exile
1877, Salt Wars
1885, Second Riel Rebellion
1890, Battle of Wounded Knee
1898, Spanish-American War
1899, Philippine Insurrection
1910, Mexican Revolution
1912, Intervention in Nicaragua
1916, Pershing Expedition